SUZE ORMAN IS EVERYWHERE

"People just can't get enough of financial expert Suze Orman."

—*The Dallas Morning News*

A *Time* Magazine TIME 100 of the World's Most Influential People

A *Forbes* top twenty "Most Influential Women in Media"

A *Smart Money* magazine's Top 30 Power Brokers

Two-time Emmy Award Winner

Six-time Gracie Award Winner

Recipient of the National Equality Award by the Human Rights Campaign

Inductee into the Books for a Better Life Award Hall of Fame

Recipient of an honorary degree Doctor of Humane Letters from
the University of Illinois

"Suze has managed to do for money what *Trading Spaces* did for design and *Top Chef* did for food—make it accessible and entertaining. She's . . . intelligent, articulate, sassy . . . a blast to be around."
—*Entertainment Weekly*

"THE REIGNING SHAMAN AND HIGH PRIESTESS OF PERSONAL FINANCE."
—*The San Francisco Examiner*

SUZE ORMAN IS THERE FOR <u>YOU</u>

"Mrs. Orman's books contain a wealth of practical information. . . . Extremely effective."
—*The New York Times*

"Suze Orman gets down to business . . . *her message is straightforward . . . a winner.*"
—*USA Today*

"Dedicated to guiding regular folks through the natural cycles of their financial life—from buying a first house to writing a will."
—*More*

"The queen of money advice tells you how to get out of debt, plan your retirement, buy stocks, and much, much more."
—*Library Journal*

THE ROAD TO WEALTH

A COMPREHENSIVE GUIDE TO YOUR MONEY

*Everything You Need to Know
in Good and Bad Times*

INCLUDES UPDATED MATERIALS FROM
SUZE'S POPULAR FINANCIAL LIBRARY SERIES

.REVISED AND UPDATED

SUZE ORMAN

RIVERHEAD BOOKS
NEW YORK

RIVERHEAD BOOKS
Published by the Penguin Group
Penguin Group (USA) Inc., 375 Hudson Street, New York, New York 10014, USA • Penguin Group (Canada), 90 Eglinton Avenue East, Suite 700, Toronto, Ontario M4P 2Y3, Canada (a division of Pearson Penguin Canada Inc.) • Penguin Books Ltd., 80 Strand, London WC2R 0RL, England • Penguin Group Ireland, 25 St. Stephen's Green, Dublin 2, Ireland (a division of Penguin Books Ltd) • Penguin Group (Australia), 250 Camberwell Road, Camberwell, Victoria 3124, Australia (a division of Pearson Australia Group Pty. Ltd) • Penguin Books India Pvt. Ltd., 11 Community Centre, Panchsheel Park, New Delhi—110 017, India • Penguin Group (NZ), 67 Apollo Drive, Rosedale, North Shore 0632, New Zealand (a division of Pearson New Zealand Ltd.) • Penguin Books (South Africa) (Pty.) Ltd., 24 Sturdee Avenue, Rosebank, Johannesburg 2196, South Africa

Penguin Books Ltd., Registered Offices: 80 Strand, London WC2R 0RL, England

This publication is designed to provide accurate and authoritative information in regard to the subject matter covered. It is published with the understanding that the publishers and author are not engaged in rendering legal, accounting, or other professional services. If legal advice or other professional advice, including financial, is required, the services of a competent professional person should be sought.

Penguin Group (USA) Inc. and Riverhead Books are not affiliated or connected in any way with *The Suze Orman E-Newsletter* or any of the information contained therein.

A Certified Financial Planner® is a federally registered mark owned by the Certified Financial Planner Board of Standards, Inc.

The term Realtor® is a collective membership mark owned by the National Association of Realtors and refers to a real estate agent who is a member thereof.

While the author has made every effort to provide accurate telephone numbers and Internet addresses at the time of publication, neither the publisher nor the author assumes any responsibility for errors, or for changes that occur after publication. Further, the publisher does not have any control over and does not assume any responsibility for author or third-party websites or their content.

First Riverhead hardcover edition: March 2008
Revised Riverhead trade paperback edition: April 2010
Riverhead trade paperback ISBN: 978-1-59448-458-2

The Library of Congress has catalogued the Riverhead hardcover edition as follows:

The road to wealth: a comprehensive guide to your money/Suze Orman.—Rev. and updated.
p.   cm.
"Everything you need to know in good times and bad times."
ISBN 978-1-59448-982-2
1. Finance, Personal.   2. Investments.   I. Title.
HG179.O758   2008   2007044928
332.024—dc22

PRINTED IN THE UNITED STATES OF AMERICA

10 9 8 7 6 5 4 3 2 1

This book is dedicated to all those
who have the desire to learn more,
to be more, to create more,
and to leave more.

Contents

INTRODUCTION

When it comes to money, I deeply believe that the obstacles that keep us from being more and having more are rooted in the emotional, psychological, and spiritual conditions that have shaped our thoughts: In other words, what we have begins with what we think. This is the cornerstone of my approach to personal finance, and it was with this understanding that I wrote *The 9 Steps to Financial Freedom; The Courage to Be Rich; The Laws of Money, The Lessons of Life; The Money Book for the Young, Fabulous & Broke;* and *Women & Money.* I deeply believe that with self-knowledge and emotional clarity, a life of abundance is within reach for all of us.

But once we have looked within and changed our way of thinking about money, another obstacle emerges—one that can keep us from taking the steps we know we should take. That obstacle is confusion. Many of us are confused about where to turn for information we can really rely on. We are confused about whom to ask for financial advice, and maybe even about what questions to ask. When we do get answers to our questions, we are confused because we can't be sure those answers are correct. In the face of all this, it may seem safer not to do anything with our money than to do something we do not entirely understand. But when we postpone necessary financial decisions, we are relinquishing opportunities to protect what we've earned and to enrich our future choices.

Good financial information gives us the power to act in our own best interests. That's why I have written *The Road to Wealth.*

I've spent much of the past few years traveling around the world, answering questions on my TV show on CNBC, holding seminars on financial topics, and listening as many, many people talked to me about their financial hopes and fears. "Tell me what I need to know," people often say to me. "Here is what you need to know," I answer. This phrase, *here is what you need to know,* captures the very spirit of *The Road to Wealth.* Here you will find answers to the questions you have been asking, as well as the questions you *should* be asking, delivered in the most complete, straightforward way I know. The questions and answers are intended to remove obstacles on your road to wealth. In a world of competing financial interests and sources of information, it's important for you to feel as if you have a guide whom you can truly trust. I am honored that you have chosen me to be your guide.

With this in mind, I have tried to provide sound, clear, comprehensive advice on a wide range of issues, which will take you through the course of your financial life. There is a logical sequence of information here, from creating a strong financial foundation to amassing assets and protecting them from common mistakes and periods of economic downturn. The chapters will see you through various life situations, beginning with freeing yourself from debt, for I believe that you cannot build a strong financial future on a base that is undermined by debt. The next chapters guide you through living together, marriage or life partnership, and the complicated process of buying a home for yourself and your family. Other chapters will help you to prepare for the future by choosing the right kind of insurance, saving for your children's education, investing knowledgeably both inside and outside retirement accounts, making savvy decisions about retirement income, and providing for the loved ones you will one day leave behind. I have chosen topics that, in my opinion, most affect your life, in both good and bad times. In doing so, I have written the practical counterpart to all my other books so that, with your head and your heart in agreement, you can take the necessary steps today so you arrive at your tomorrows happily and with all the wealth that is meant to be yours.

The Road to Wealth is a book designed to help you take action—wherever you are in your life, whatever your needs, and whatever the economic climate.

Money is not stagnant; it is ever-changing. It means different things to each of us at different points in our lives. I encourage you to skip around in this book—go directly to the topics that concern you most right now; later, you can move on to matters that are relevant to that moment. Keep this book close and consult it often. Browse through the Table of Contents and the Index. Use it as a second opinion, to make sure you are getting advice that is right for you. And always, always trust that, with the faith and confidence that knowledge brings, step by step you will get to where you want to go on your own road to wealth.

Suze Orman
New York, 2010

1

Managing Debt

TAKING CONTROL OF YOUR MONEY

If you are not in debt of some kind, you're unusual. For most Americans today, debt is a part of daily life. Using a credit card, borrowing for college, applying for a mortgage to buy a house—taking on debts such as these may well be the first experience many of us have with a financial institution. All the more reason to understand and master the dos and don'ts of debt. Until you know how to manage debt, it's almost impossible to save, invest, or build an intimate financial relationship with a life partner based on anything resembling a strong foundation. Until your debt is in control and part of your life plan, you will not achieve financial freedom.

For many of us, credit card debt is a special trouble spot. To put it bluntly, credit card companies are in the business of separating us from our money. Run up a balance that you do not pay off at the end of the month and you will pay 10 percent, 15 percent, 20 percent interest. Miss a payment, by just a day and you may be docked a $39 late fee. Much of that is pure profit for the company.

In my opinion, credit card debt—in fact, any debt based on overspending—is bondage. It weighs on your spirits, occupies your mind, and backs you into a corner. At worst, it can bankrupt you.

The following questions and answers are intended to help you get and remain free of debt. What I've attempted to do, in part, is to strip debt of its mystique and rob it of its power to inspire fear. No matter the size or the variety of debt, it is always ultimately manageable.

As you'll see below, there are many, many resources for you to draw upon as you work yourself free of debt: agencies to help you break troublesome spending patterns, overcome your debt, and regain control of your finances and your life; counselors and loved ones to support you emotionally; and information, in books and online, to empower you with knowledge. There is much you can do before you reach the "last resort" of declaring bankruptcy, but even if you find yourself in that unenviable position, it is possible—it is always possible—to begin again, to remake your life *your* way.

THE EMOTIONS OF DEBT

Is it ever OK to have debt?

Yes. Debt has a time and a place in all our lives. But the debt you take on must be in alignment with the goals you've set for yourself. Do you want to pursue a dream of attending college, for example? Then a student loan that will help finance your college tuition is "good debt." What about the mortgage you're carrying on the house you live in, assuming that the house is not beyond your means? That's good debt, too, because it enables you to share in the benefits of home ownership and to maintain a safe haven for yourself and your family. What about the loan you took two years ago to help your parents through a rough financial patch or a health scare? Or the car loan you've applied for, assuming you need a car and can afford the payments? In my opinion, all these loan situations are good, worthy, and in alignment with sound goals.

On the other hand, overspending with credit cards to accumulate new clothes or furniture, or to keep pace with your friends' spending, is negative debt. It sacrifices tomorrow's needs to today's desires.

How do I know if I'm in trouble with debt?

With the exception of your mortgage and a few other kinds of "good" debt mentioned above, if you can't pay off everything you owe right this minute—whether it's a personal loan or a $3,000 credit card balance—you're most likely in trouble with debt. I know this sounds radical, but it is a very good rule of thumb. Everyone who has massive debt today started with a small balance and monthly payments he or she believed were manageable. But debt is cumulative and habit-forming: Before you know it, you owe more than you can comfortably handle. I have learned that if you cannot pay your credit card bills in full at the end of every month, you may be heading for trouble.

Why is it that so many people get into "bad" debt?

People go into debt for many reasons, but I have often noticed a correlation—an inverse relationship—between self-esteem and bad debt. I call the result your "debt set point." The lower your self-esteem, the higher your debt set point. If you generally feel good about yourself and are living in a responsible way, chances are you don't have a lot of debt on your balance sheet. If you are spending more money than you have, you are probably spending money not only to obtain more goods and services but also to acquire more self-esteem. The less self-esteem you have, the more debt you create.

What exactly do you mean by my "debt set point"?

Think of your debt set point as your own personal credit limit. It's the point at which you are finally willing—perhaps driven—to put a stop to unmanageable credit card spending. Each of us has our own set point. Yours might be $2,000 or $25,000, but the odds are good that you'll know it when you reach it. It's the point at which you decide to stop the downward plunge. It can be a terrifying point to reach, but in the end it is a blessed relief, because it forces you to take decisive, positive action.

Remember, however, that working on eliminating bad debt involves working on the reasons you got into debt in the first place. This usually means bolstering your self-esteem. Remind yourself that you are not a bad person because you have credit card debt. You are simply a person who has managed your money poorly—big difference! Let me urge you to tell someone—someone you trust—about your credit card debt. It is an important step in beginning to deal honestly with your financial situation and reverse the set point phenomenon.

What qualities put a person at risk for trouble with debt?

I have found that people with large amounts of debt often avoid looking at themselves—and their debt—honestly. Sometimes they are people who have problems with impulse control. When they see an item they want, they just have to have it, without regard to whether they need it or can afford it. People who grew up without much money and later earn a comfortable living sometimes spend too much to make up for what they didn't get as children—without realizing what their motive is. People who feel entitled to the good life, or are unconsciously copying a mother or father who lived beyond her or his means, can be prone to credit card trouble, too. If you feel the need to impress people with what you have rather than with who you are, you are at high risk for credit card abuse. It's worth noting that debt doesn't discriminate; it affects those with money and those without.

The holidays are fast approaching, and I'm starting to feel that typical end-of-the-year anxiety, mostly about the bills that will come swarming in after the new year. Any suggestions on how to rein in my spending?

The holidays can be one of the most tempting times of the year to overindulge—in food, drink, and credit card use. The holidays are also a time when your generosity can overwhelm your common sense. My advice is to be very, very conscious of what you spend money on. Try to plan ahead and get your shopping done early, during the pre-holiday months and especially during sales. Also figure out, before you hit the stores, how much you want to spend on each person to whom you intend to give a gift; then make it a point not to exceed that amount. If you are shopping in a department store, try to use cash. If you do charge some purchases and are tempted to "spread the wealth" (or debt) among your various credit cards, remember that the interest on department store cards is usually sky-high. Finally, I urge you to think of gifts that aren't expensive, but that still have lasting meaning. The truth is that most of us cannot remember the gifts we received last year—no matter how much they cost. Thoughtful, memorable gifts are not necessarily expensive ones.

CARD BASICS

Credit cards are a staple of modern life, and rightly so. They allow you a flexible, convenient way to purchase things you need and want. They also let you make purchases with money you don't yet have, and that's where things can get tricky. If you are careful about which cards you carry, their rates and terms, and how you use them, credit cards can be very useful.

There are three kinds of cards that consumers generally use to make purchases: charge cards, debit cards, and credit cards. The following is a brief primer.

Is there a difference between a charge card and a credit card?

Yes. Charge cards don't provide a line of credit the way that credit cards do; they require you to pay off the entire balance every month. For this reason, on applications and in the monthly statements you receive, you will find neither an interest rate charged nor a minimum balance due. In general, you pay a higher annual fee for the privilege of using charge cards. Unlike credit cards, they tend to carry no spending limit. A typical charge card is the American Express card.

Does the lack of a spending limit on charge cards mean that I can go out and buy a $50,000 sports car?

No, it simply means that the charge card company hasn't told you how much you can spend. If your spending habits appear unusual, you can count on getting a call from one of the company's service representatives, or possibly finding that your card has been frozen until the company figures out what's going on. .

What exactly is a debit card?

Debit cards are not charge cards or credit cards. Like charge cards, they don't offer you a line of credit. Unlike charge cards, they deduct your purchases directly from your checking account. They function very much like ATM cards or personal checks. You can spend only what you've got in your account.

What are the advantages of a debit card?

Debit cards are very convenient. If you have one, you don't have to carry checks or a large amount of cash. Also, merchants who will not accept a personal check may accept them.

Do debit cards have any disadvantages?

Yes. Unlike credit cards, debit cards are not covered by federal regulations that protect consumers in disputes with merchants. Also, many banks charge fees for the use of a debit card, though others don't. Shop around among banks and other financial institutions for the best deal. Be sure to ask whether there's a monthly, annual, or per-use charge for the card, and whether there's any additional penalty for using the card at another institution's ATM. Another drawback: With a debit card, you can't stop payment on a purchase you are disputing the way you can with a check or a credit card payment. A debit card does not help you establish a credit rating. Finally, depending on the state you live in and how quickly you report the loss, a lost or stolen debit card can result in your checking account balance being used up, plus your overdraft protection amount, too.

Will I be charged a fee for using my debit card?

It depends on your bank. Some charge fees on each debit card transaction when you use a PIN. Other banks charge debit card customers monthly fees and/or require you to keep a minimum balance in your account. Before using your debit card, check with your bank as to the charges you may incur for using it.

Do you mean that there's no legal protection for me if someone steals my debit card and empties my bank account?

Well, there is limited protection. According to the Electronic Fund Transfer Act, you have no liability at all once you have reported your card missing. But timing is everything. If you fail to report the missing card immediately—before someone else uses it—but do so within two business days of having lost it, your liability is limited to $50.

(The exception to the two-day rule is if you were on extended travel or in the hospital; in that case, you have no liability.) This $50 limit rises to $500 if you do not notify the bank of your missing card within the two business days, but do notify the bank within 60 days of the time your bank statement is mailed to you. The clincher is that, if you fail to report your card missing within those 60 days, your liability is unlimited.

Please be advised that different issuers and different states offer different additional protection. Some banks won't charge you anything in the case of a lost or stolen card and some states cap liability at $50.

CREDIT CARDS

Most credit card companies make money in three ways: from the interest you pay on balances due; from fees, when applicable; and from fees charged to merchants who accept the card. The first two components, along with a few other privileges and restrictions, have to be looked at very carefully before you decide which card to carry.

All credit cards look the same to me—are they the same?

No. Many credit cards are store- or service-specific cards. Visa cards and MasterCards are what are known as bank credit cards. This means that they are issued by banks or credit unions. Neither Visa nor MasterCard actually supplies the cards you carry in your wallet—banks do—but they do provide support, staff, and infrastructure to the thousands of credit unions and banks that issue the cards. Each bank can set its own credit standards and limits, and offer whatever other advantages it wants to its customers. What's the difference between the two of them? Not a whole lot. Both offer a lot of buying power, and most merchants accept both.

DECIPHERING CREDIT CARD OFFERS

I get many credit card solicitations in the mail offering a "low introductory interest rate." Is this on the level?

Yes and no. Scrutinize these offers very carefully—sometimes when introductory rates are lower, the rates for balance transfers and cash advances are higher; or the low introductory rate may jump by 10 percent or more after a few months. Obviously, you want to choose the card with the lowest introductory rate, and the longer the low rate lasts, the better. If and when the rate goes up, it may be a good strategy to get another card with a low introductory rate. In any case, if you have good credit, you never want a card for which the normal rate is above 11 percent.

Should I pay an annual fee?

No. In my opinion, no credit card should carry an annual fee. If the card you are considering has one, take your business elsewhere.

Several times a month a credit card offer arrives in my mail stating that I am preapproved. Can you explain preapproval?
"Congratulations, Suze Orman! You're preapproved!" All of us receive such promotions, but they don't mean much. All "preapproved" really signifies is that you have passed an initial screening. What it doesn't mean is that you are suddenly eligible for a $10,000, $15,000, or $25,000 line of credit. You must apply and be accepted first.

Why can't credit card companies commit to their "preapproved" offer?
They're being cautious. A lot of bad things could happen to you between the time you fill out the application and send it back to the credit card company and the time when the company processes your application. For example, you could declare bankruptcy. You could apply for five new credit cards at the same time (this is a red flag for the credit bureaus, which take it to mean you're about to go on a spending spree). Or you could lose your job or your house. The credit card companies know this, which is why they slip in a provision that allows them to deny your application. (Of course, it's in much smaller print than "Congratulations, you're preapproved!")

Are there any advantages to carrying a silver, gold, platinum, or black card?
One advantage (which I don't really think of as an advantage) is that the credit lines on Visa or MasterCard gold cards usually start at about $5,000 and can reach as high as tens of thousands of dollars. Also, these cards tend to offer a lot of customer perks, such as frequent-flyer

miles or collision-damage insurance if you use the card to pay for a rental car.

With American Express gold and platinum cards, you'll be sent a complete itemized annual statement at the end of the year, which can be helpful when you're putting your tax information together.

If I need a higher credit limit, is a gold, platinum, or black card the only way to go?
Actually, if you are a big spender and you pay your bills on time, you can maintain a balance on your regular credit card that approaches and sometimes equals the lines of credit that gold or platinum cards offer—and you can avoid paying the high annual fee that some gold or platinum cards charge. If you spend heavily but pay off your balance every month, call your credit card company and ask whether your limit can be increased. If you're a responsible customer, chances are good the answer will be yes.

FIGURING OUT THE ANNUAL PERCENTAGE RATE (APR)

On my credit card statement, what does APR stand for?
APR stands for annual percentage rate and is the fixed interest rate that you will be paying to the credit card company each year for the use of its money. Prorated on a monthly basis, it will be charged to your account whenever you fail to pay off the balance you owe at the end of the month. (The monthly rate is called a monthly periodic rate; to find out your monthly periodic

rate, divide your APR by 12.) Sometimes companies quote and charge a monthly rate; if this is the case, multiply that monthly rate by 12 to figure out your APR. Please note that, depending on how the credit card company calculates its interest charges, the amount you pay could be higher than you expect. Please also note that some companies charge a variable interest rate, tied to general market interest rates.

How do credit card companies calculate interest charges?

Beginning in 2010 there is just one way a credit card company can compute your interest rate charges: based on your average daily balance, including new purchases. Let's say you charge $1,000 on your credit card for a stereo system. When your credit card statement comes in, you're short of cash, so you pay $500 against your $1,000 balance. When you get your next statement, you will owe interest only on the remaining $500.

What is the Schumer Box?

When Congress passed the Fair Credit and Charge Card Disclosure Act (which is a part of the Truth-in-Lending Act), one of its requirements was that all costs associated with a credit card be featured prominently on the application or on the offer itself. These costs must also be easy to read—and without a magnifying glass. The box in which these charges are displayed is known informally as the Schumer Box, after Democratic Senator Charles Schumer of New York, who helped push the Fair Credit and Charge Card Disclosure Act through Congress.

The Schumer Box contains information that you should consider carefully before deciding to apply for any credit card, including information about late fees and cash advances.

GRACE PERIODS AND LATE FEES

My credit card application mentions a "grace period." What is this?

The grace period is the time between the closing date of your billing cycle and the date you have to pay your balance in full. No interest is charged during this period. Beginning in August 2009 federal regulations mandate a minimum three-week grace period for all credit cards. However, with a few exceptions, this grace period applies only if you are not already carrying an account balance. If you are carrying a balance at the end of the month, the grace period does not apply to you. You will owe interest—starting immediately—on any new purchase you make, as well as on your outstanding balance.

What are late fees?

Late fees are charged if you fail to make at least the minimum required payment before the grace period ends. These can add up, though each company's policy is different. Some companies start the clock ticking if your payment is only one day late; others give you a week or two, sometimes more, before imposing a fee. (Interest charges begin immediately.) Remember, the companies require that your payment be received—not postmarked—by a certain date. You have to take into account the time the mail takes to be delivered, so send in your payment early.

How much are late fees, generally?

In general, late fees range from $35 to $39, and in some cases kick in the day after payment is due. This can add a hefty premium to your account.

Will my credit card payment be credited to my account on the day the credit card company receives it?

Federal credit card reform legislation that went into effect in February 2010 mandates that payments received by 5 p.m. be credited as paid on that day. Also, payments made at a local bank branch must be credited the same day. If a due date falls on a holiday or weekend when there is no mail delivery, the payment cannot be deemed late if it is received by the next business day.

MINIMUM PAYMENTS

How is the minimum payment I have to make on my balance every month calculated?

The minimum must be enough to pay all the fees and interest charges for that month, and at least 1 percent of the principal amount. Depending on your agreement with your credit card company, your minimum monthly payment will range from 1 percent to 5 percent of your balance, plus those fees and finance charges. Actually, you want the figure to be higher rather than lower, because if you tend to pay only the minimum each month, the lower your required payment, the longer it will take

you to pay off your debt and, as credit card companies well know, the more expensive that debt will be over the long run. I'll say it now and I'll say it later: It's absolutely essential that you pay more than the minimum amount required each month if you want to get out of debt in a timely and cost-effective manner.

CASH ADVANCES

Is there any difference between charging an item on a credit card and taking a cash advance?

There can be a big difference. The fees and interest rate charged for cash advances can be much higher than those charged for making purchases, so be very careful with cash advances. Even if your basic introductory interest rate is 5.9 percent, and you don't owe a balance, many credit card companies charge an additional flat percentage (for example, 3 percent) on each cash advance, with a maximum fee of up to $50, and some companies may charge you an interest rate of 22 percent or more on your cash advance. The interest charge is levied from the day you take the advance; there is no grace period.

CONVENIENCE CHECKS

Last year, around the holidays, my credit card company sent me a pack of "convenience checks." Should I use them?

You should use so-called convenience checks only

if you are prepared to pay exorbitant interest rates. Call your card company, ask what the interest rate is, and if you don't like it, tear up the checks. These checks are usually "convenient" only for the card companies.

EXCEEDING YOUR CREDIT LIMIT

What if one month I go over my credit limit by accident?

New federal legislation that went into effect in February 2010 mandates that a credit card issuer cannot levy an over-limit charge unless you have already given permission to allow over-limit charges on your card. If you do authorize over-limit charges, you can be charged from $35 to $39 for exceeding your credit limit. I recommend you turn down the over-limit authorization; this will keep you out of trouble and help you avoid unnecessary fees.

ANNUAL FEES AND INTEREST RATES

I don't carry a balance, but all of a sudden my credit card company has begun charging me an annual fee. Why?

Being a "good" customer—paying your bills on time and in full—is not what credit card companies want of you. As far as they're concerned, a "good" customer carries the maximum permissible debt and makes interest payments over a number of months, preferably years. Some credit card companies are beginning to charge an extra fee to those responsible customers who don't carry a balance from one month to the next.

This is perfectly legal, so it's your responsibility to keep on top of any changes your credit card company makes in its rules and regulations.

I just got an offer in the mail for a credit card with "zero percent financing for one year." Should I go for it?

First, be sure you understand what the zero percent financing applies to: balance transfers, new purchases, cash advances, or all of the above? Once you understand this, and if you can really pay off all you owe on this credit card in one year, then the card will cost you nothing. What the credit card company is banking on, however, is that in one year you won't be able to pay your balance—at which time you will probably get socked with an interest rate in the upper teens or low 20s. Before you accept such an offer, be honest with yourself about when you'll be able to pay off your debt, and be sure you know what your interest rate will be after the "zero percent financing" period is up.

My credit card company just raised my interest rate for no apparent reason. Is this allowed?

Believe it or not, the answer is yes. The expression "fixed rate" means very little to a credit card company. Beginning in 2010 the company merely has to notify you in writing of a hike in the interest rate 45 days before the increase takes effect. But another new regulation that went into effect in 2010 prevents the credit card company from raising the interest rate on any existing balances, assuming you are making timely payments. The rate hike can only be applied to new charges. As a consumer dealing with credit card companies, you're usually in the position of "take it or leave it." I would leave it, if I could, and switch to a better credit card.

SWITCHING CREDIT CARDS

If I carry a balance, under what circumstances should I consider switching credit cards?
Consider switching if your interest rate has been raised, or you're being asked to pay an annual fee. If you're a heavy user with a good credit history, credit card companies will want your business. But watch your step: Too-good-to-be-true offers usually are. Do your homework to make sure you really are getting the best deal out there.

A very good way to identify the best credit card offers is by comparing current offers at *www.bankrate.com* or *credit.com*. Credit unions often offer the best card deals. You can learn more at creditcardconnection.org. If you do not have a computer, then look in this month's issue of *SmartMoney* magazine. I also recommend that you research credit card offers made by credit unions. The fees and rates charged on credit union credit cards are often much more consumer-friendly than the rates charged by commercial banks.

Please note: To keep getting the best deal available, you may have to transfer your card balances two or three times a year. Too much trouble? Hardly. It's only a few calls and 15 minutes of pa-

perwork a year, and it might save you hundreds of dollars. When can you stop being so vigilant? When your debt is gone and you've taken the steps to guarantee that it won't mount up again.

CREDIT INSURANCE

I got an offer from a credit card company for credit insurance. Does this offer me protection from a credit disaster?
Typically, credit card companies like to offer four kinds of credit insurance. Credit property insurance protects you against damage to any property that is securing your loan; credit life insurance promises that if you die, your outstanding balance will be paid; credit disability insurance buffers you against a disabling illness or accident that would keep you from working (the companies usually provide a complete list of disabilities covered); and involuntary loss of income insurance protects against your losing your job or getting fired.

In my opinion, credit insurance isn't worth it, particularly because it is very expensive. If you want insurance, take out a general plan from a regular insurance company that covers some, if not all, of the above.

CREDIT CARD ERRORS

Errors are more common than you might imagine. I'd say that roughly 75 percent of all the people I know have stories to tell about erroneous charges on their monthly statements.

You should review your monthly statements carefully. Here are some of the things you may find:

- Your statement lists a charge you don't recognize and certainly didn't make.
- Your statement shows a charge for theater tickets or airplane tickets that you didn't receive.
- You returned an item to a store but it's not reflected on the statement.

If one of these errors, or any other, appears on your credit card statement, by law you are permitted to withhold payment on that particular charge.

If I find an error on my card, what should I do first?

Call the number listed on your statement, report the error, and then immediately put your complaint in writing. The Fair Credit Billing Act (FCBA) says that all inquiries about billing errors must be made in writing and no later than 60 days from the date of the mistaken or disputed charge, or from the date your faulty credit card statement was mailed to you—not from the date you received it. (The 60-day rule covers, among other things, erroneous charges for items you refuse because you did not order them, deliveries to the wrong address, and late deliveries.) Your letter to the credit card company should contain all pertinent identifying information, including your name, address, and account number, as well as a full description of the error in question, including the date of the erroneous charge and the reason you believe it is incorrect.

By the way, always, *always* keep a copy of any correspondence you send to a financial institution, whether it's a bank, a credit union, or a credit card company. Your letter should be typed or word processed, not written by hand. Send it by certified mail, return receipt requested, and make sure you send it to the proper address, which is usually different from the address to which you send payments. (Remember that this is a billing inquiry, not a payment, and you don't want your letter to get lost in the shuffle.) You will often see a phone number and address specifically for billing inquiries on your statement.

Once you've written your letter, you can sit back and allow the credit card company, with its enormous resources, to conduct a proper and thorough investigation. Most cases of mistaken charges are handled quickly and painlessly.

If I'm disputing a charge, can I wait until it's settled to pay my bill in full?

No. Although FCBA rules and regulations state that you are not obliged to pay any charge you are questioning—or, for that matter, any interest on that charge—you cannot withhold payment on the rest of your bill. Be sure to pay the other charges. Otherwise, you'll be accruing penalties and interest charges, and will have no recourse but to pay them.

Please be aware, however, that even though you don't have to pay a disputed charge or interest on that charge while you're still disputing it, the credit card company can continue to charge interest against the amount you are disputing. If and when the dispute is settled in your favor, of course, the company must wipe out the interest along with the disputed charge. But if you lose the dispute, you will have to pay the disputed amount plus the interest accumulated during an investigation. So don't argue with a charge simply to postpone a payment that you really owe.

My credit card company says that I have to prove that the charge I'm disputing is wrong, but I have no way to do this. What should I do?

Your credit card company is in error. It is not the consumer's responsibility to prove there was a billing error. By law, the credit card company is allowed two billing cycles or 90 days, whichever comes first, to resolve your problem. Resolution usually happens in one of two ways: Either the company agrees that the charge was incorrect and credits your account accordingly, or you receive a letter telling you that the charge was correct, along with an explanation.

If I don't pay the charge that I am questioning, will this show up on my credit report as a late payment?

Not if this is the first time you are disputing that particular charge and the dispute has not yet reached a stage where the credit bureaus, which may eventually be contacted by the card issuer, have rendered an opinion on whether or not you owe the money. In general, disputed charges do not count as late payments and are not reported to credit bureaus.

What if, after an investigation, the credit card company insists that the charge I'm dis-

puting is correct, but I still disagree? Do I have any way to appeal the decision?

If you still believe that the credit card company is in the wrong and that the charge is unfair or mistaken, you can take the following step. Send another letter—again, by certified mail, return receipt requested, making sure to keep a copy for your files—explaining why you continue to refuse to pay. Typically, you must do this within ten days of the date on the credit card company's explanation of its position on the matter. If you do this, the card company may now choose to report you to the credit bureaus. But if the company reports you, it must inform you of this, telling you which bureaus it has contacted, and must include a notation to the bureaus that you dispute the charge. Alternatively, you can pay the disputed charge (plus all interest charges).

I've heard that if I find unauthorized charges on my credit card statement, I am only responsible for paying $50 per card. Is this true?

In most cases, it is true that the Truth in Lending Act limits your liability for unauthorized credit card charges to $50 per card. To take advantage of the law's consumer protections, call the credit card issuer at the phone number listed on your card, or if you access your account online, you can often file a dispute online.

The creditor must acknowledge your complaint in writing within 30 days after receiving it, unless the problem has been resolved. If you have not received an acknowledgment after 30 days, stay on top of them and remind them that they are required to respond within 30 days. The creditor must resolve the dispute within two billing cycles (but not more than 90 days) after receiving your letter.

What about ATM cards? Am I only responsible for $50 if my ATM card was used without my knowledge?

It depends on when you reported your ATM card missing or stolen. Your liability will be limited to $50 if you report your ATM card lost or stolen within two business days after the card is lost or stolen. You can be liable for up to $500 of what the thief withdraws, if you report your ATM card lost or stolen after the two business days, but within 60 days after a statement showing an unauthorized electronic fund transfer. If you wait more than 60 days, you could lose *all* the money that was taken from your account after the end of the 60 days and before you reported your card missing. Visa and MasterCard have voluntarily agreed to limit consumers' liability for unauthorized use of their debit cards in most instances to $50 per card, no matter how much time has elapsed since the discovery of the loss or theft of the card.

What if I discover a mistake on my credit card statement two months or more after my statement was issued?

This shouldn't happen to you if you review your statement thoroughly every month. If it does happen, go ahead and dispute the charge in writing, but be prepared to pay some money. Call your credit card issuer and find out what its regulations are. If the cost of investigation exceeds the amount of the charge, you may want to think twice about fighting it.

STOPPING PAYMENT

How do I go about stopping payment on an item that was defective?

The right to stop payment is one of the best protections credit cards offer. There are, however, some important rules and guidelines that have to be followed. You can use your stop-payment privilege only if the defective item cost more than $50. Before you seek to stop payment, you have to have made a genuine effort to resolve the problem with the company that provided the item or service. And you can only stop payment on purchases for which you have not yet paid the credit card company.

What happens when I do stop payment?

The charge will be removed from your bill.

CORPORATE CARDS

I was given a corporate American Express card for business purposes. I left my job before my employer reimbursed me for some of my expenses. Am I liable for these charges, or is my old employer liable?

You may be liable for these charges, particularly if your former employer is disputing any of them. It depends on the agreement you made with your company when it opened the corporate account for you. To find out who is responsible for your charges, call AmEx and ask for a customer service representative, and/or check with your former employer's human resources department.

CREDIT CARDS AND SECURITY

What if I lose my credit card or it gets stolen?

Report any lost or stolen credit cards to your credit card company immediately, and follow up with a written notice, as previously described. In general, it's a good idea to write down the account numbers of all your cards and put your list in a secret spot in your house and/or in a safe-deposit box. Also, be sure to check your cards every now and then to make sure they are all in place.

A friend told me it's not safe to sign my name on the back of my credit card. Do you agree?

I disagree. You should sign the back of your credit card to protect yourself from unauthorized use of your card. This way, a merchant can compare the signature on the card with your signature on the receipt. And what if your wallet is lost or stolen and the cards inside are unsigned? Whoever has stolen or finds the wallet could sign his name on your cards and use them to rack up hundreds or thousands of dollars in purchases. A signed card is not

foolproof, but a signature does make it that much more difficult for someone to take advantage of you.

How can I prevent somebody from using my card?

Keep your cards physically secure in a wallet kept well out of sight. And never, under any circumstances, give your account number or any other financial information over the phone unless you are very sure that the caller represents a legitimate business. If you are in any doubt about this, ask for the phone number of the business and call back. Better yet, ask the business to mail that information to you. As a general rule, I would not reveal my credit card number to anyone whom I had not called.

What about entering my credit card number online?

It is not all that difficult to break into a database and steal records. So if you buy online, be sure the Website you're using is a secured Website (its web address will start with "http" in the url) and that you double-check your statements each and every month, looking for unfamiliar or unauthorized charges.

Are there any specific credit card scams that I should be aware of on the Web?

I would be very suspicious of e-mail claiming to come from your online service provider that ask you to resubmit your credit card number. If this ever happens, call your service provider at once. Consumers have also been ripped off by Websites claiming to be the official homepages of well-known companies. In this scam, a consumer reveals her credit card number in exchange for merchandise. The merchandise never arrives, but the con artist behind the fake Web page now has the consumer's credit card number!

IDENTITY THEFT

What exactly is identity theft?

Identity theft, also known as identity fraud, is when an individual's personal identification information (such as name, address, telephone number, driver's license number, Social Security number, place of employment, employee identification number, mother's maiden name, savings account number, or credit card number) is used without the authorization of that person, to assume their identity for the purpose of obtaining credit, getting credit cards from banks and retailers, withdrawing money from existing accounts, applying for loans, establishing accounts with utility companies, renting an apartment, filing bankruptcy, obtaining a job, or committing crimes ranging from traffic infractions to felonies. Identity theft is a widespread crime in this country, with an estimated 8.9 million victims a year.

How does the identity thief take my identity?

Unfortunately, it is easier than you might think. Once they have some of your personal identifying information, such as your Social Security number, birth date, address, or phone number, they can call your credit card issuer and ask to change the mailing address on your credit card account. The impostor then runs up charges on your account. Since the bill is being sent to the new address, you may not realize for several months that your credit card is close to being maxed out. Or they apply for new credit with your Social Security number, birth date, and mother's maiden name. They give the creditor a new address, claiming you have just moved. The new cards are maxed out and you don't even know they exist until you review your credit report or you are denied credit due to the unpaid balance on these new accounts. Once the new accounts are maxed out, they move on to a new victim.

Where can an identity thief get personal information about me?

The question should be, Where *can't* they get personal information about you? The identity thief does not need to steal your wallet or purse to take your personal identification and credit cards. If you do not shred your mail, bills, credit card slips, and other personal documents, it is easy to "Dumpster dive" in your garbage. Believe it or not, "Dumpster diving" is one of the more common ways that identity theft occurs. This is why I strongly suggest that you invest in a shredder to destroy any paper that includes any personal information before it is thrown away. Another common method is stealing your personal mail (including bank and credit card statements, preapproved credit and mortgage offers, and telephone bills) by completing a change of address form at a post office to divert your mail temporarily to another location, or by stealing it directly from your mailbox. Additionally, they can fraudulently obtain your credit report by posing as someone who has a legitimate legal right to the information, such as a landlord or potential employer. Once they have your credit report, they have all the personal information they need to assume your identity. Please be especially careful when you receive an e-mail from one of your service providers stating that your "account information needs to be updated" or "the credit card you signed up with is invalid or expired and the information needs to be re-entered to keep your account active." Do not respond without first checking with the customer service department of the company to ensure these e-mails are legitimate. Many times the identity thief has stolen the company's logos and incorporated them into the fraudulent e-mail to fool you into thinking the e-mails are official correspondence. So please be very diligent about contacting customer service departments to confirm that the e-mails you have received are authentic before providing any personal information or credit card account information.

I think I may be the victim of identity theft. What do I do now?

As soon as you suspect that you are the victim of identity theft, you must immediately contact the three major credit bureaus—Equifax, Experian, and TransUnion—to advise them that you are a victim of identity theft and to put a fraud alert on your credit profile. When you contact one bureau, it is required to pass along the request to the two other bureaus, but if you want to be extra safe, it

doesn't hurt to file the request directly with each credit bureau. Request that a statement be added to your file asking that creditors call you before opening any new accounts or changing your existing accounts, to help prevent additional accounts fraudulently being opened in your name. Fraud alerts expire every 90 days. To keep the alert active, you must contact the bureaus every 90 days to renew your alert request. Only victims of identity theft who have a police report documenting the crime are able to request an extended fraud alert that is good for seven years. Members of the military are eligible for an Active Duty Fraud Alert that is effective for one year. Please be aware fraud alerts and victim statements are voluntary services provided by the credit bureaus. Creditors do not have to consider them when granting credit.

To place a fraud alert on your credit reports, contact one of the bureaus at:
  Equifax: 800-525-6285; *www.equifax.com*
  Experian: 888-397-3742; *www.experian.com*
  TransUnion: 800-680-7289; *www.transunion* *.com*

Next get copies of your credit reports so that you will know the extent of the unauthorized charges. At *annualcreditreport.com* you can get all three credit reports from the three credit bureaus for no charge. Please understand by law you are entitled to a free credit report from each credit bureau once a year; there is no need to pay for your report. Check the section of your report that lists "inquiries." Where "inquiries" appear from the company(ies) that opened the fraudulent account(s), request that these "inquiries" be removed from your report. To remove the fraudulent charges and the inquiries from your credit report, you will need to fill in a reinvestigation form. Credit bureaus must investigate the items in question within 30 days. In a few months, order new copies of your reports to verify your corrections and changes, and to make sure no new fraudulent activity has occurred.

Once you know which accounts have been tampered with or opened fraudulently, they need to be closed. When you reopen the accounts, use new Personal Identification Numbers (PINs) and passwords. Avoid using easily available information like your mother's maiden name, your birth date, the last four digits of your Social Security number or your phone number, or a series of consecutive numbers. If the identity thief has made unauthorized charges or debits, ask the company to send you the company's fraud dispute forms.

If your checks have been stolen, stop payment immediately and ask your bank to notify the check verification service with which it does business. Although no federal law limits your losses if someone steals your checks and forges your signature, state laws may protect you. Contact your state banking or consumer protection agency for more information.

Finally, file a report with your local police or the police in the community where the identity theft took place. Furnish as much documentation as you can to help the police file a complete report. Be persistent with the police department about getting the report in a timely manner. You will need the police report to correct your credit report and to dispute the fraudulent charges with your creditors.

What if the police won't take a report?

Many police departments are reluctant to write a report for identity theft. But this is a circumstance where you cannot accept no as an answer— you *must* insist that the police file a report. If you get resistance to your request, speak to the head of the fraud unit (or white-collar crime unit) of the police department in the county(ies) or city(ies) where the fraud accounts were opened. If you still have trouble, call and write to the chief of police.

Is a credit freeze a better way to protect myself?

There is no magic bullet that guarantees 100 percent protection from identity thieves, but the ability to slap what is known as a credit freeze on your accounts at the three credit bureaus is the best line of defense available against one of the worst types of identity theft: having someone pose as you to open new lines of credit, or get new loans.

When you put a freeze on your credit reports, it shuts out new lenders and creditors from checking into your personal financial history. (The companies you already do business with retain their ability to monitor your accounts.) A freeze gives you more protection than a fraud alert. An alert is merely a yellow light for creditors and lenders that requires them to verify your information personally with you before granting new credit or loans. A freeze goes a step beyond an alert by not allowing them to look at your record, period.

A freeze makes it extremely difficult, if not

impossible, for you—or anyone masquerading as you—to get a new credit card or loan, because lenders aren't apt to grant new accounts if they can't size up your creditworthiness.

Not surprisingly, lenders jump on the fact that it freezes you out as much as potential thieves, as a reason to hate freezes. Lenders want you to believe that it is a disservice to you if you don't have immediate access to new credit or loans. One of the most common anti-freeze arguments you hear is that people who have a freeze on their accounts and walk into a car dealership on Sunday are not going to be able to get approved for a loan or lease, because the car financing folks can't run an immediate credit check on them.

This is ridiculous reasoning. Anyone who chooses to freeze an account can also unfreeze it when it's needed to let a lender take a look. This can happen in a matter of minutes once you contact the credit bureau—though the rules state that it could take up to a few days. Even if it does take a couple of days, I have to tell you, anyone who needs to buy a car on a whim, or wakes up one morning and must have a new credit card approved that very moment, is financially screwed up. There is no reason rational people can't unfreeze their accounts the week before they plan to start car shopping, mortgage shopping, or credit-card shopping.

Forty-seven states and the District of Columbia have laws that require the credit bureaus to let residents place a security freeze on their credit report; in the other states the credit bureaus have voluntarily extended freeze rights to those residents as well.

If you do live in a state where you can freeze, I

recommend you do it. But it's going to take some patience. Let's just say the three credit bureaus, Equifax, Experian, and TransUnion, aren't exactly rolling out the red carpet to help you put on a freeze. You will need to contact each bureau separately and must make a written request.

To place a freeze, go to the main homepage of each credit bureau and type "freeze" in the search box:

Equifax: *www.equifax.com*; click on the Customer Service link at the top of the page.

Experian: *http://www.experian.com*.

TransUnion.com: *www.transunion.com*.

If you have been a victim of identity theft—and have the police record to prove it—your freeze is free of charge. The rules for non-victims vary by state; some offer free freezes, and others levy a charge of $10 or so. Once your freeze is in place, you will receive a personal identification number (PIN) that allows you to lift (thaw) the freeze with a phone call or by going online—the rules vary among the three credit bureaus. Once again, you may be hit with a small fee to temporarily lift your freeze. (But if you want to permanently remove your freeze, the credit bureaus are all too happy to make that change free of charge.)

What can I do to minimize my risk of identity theft?

It's virtually impossible to prevent identity theft, but you can minimize your risk by cautiously managing your personal information. As a first step, several times a year order a copy of your credit report from the three major credit bureaus to ensure your credit report is accurate and does not include any unauthorized activities. You are entitled to have one annual free credit report from each of the three credit bureaus. The best way to get your free report is at *www.annualcreditreport .com* or by calling 1-877-322-8228. You can create a year-round monitoring system by obtaining one report every four months. For example, get your Experian report in January. A few months later get the Equifax report, and a few months after that, your Transunion report. Remember, this is absolutely free. If anyone ever asks you for your credit card information in return for your credit report, do not give it out. Just use *www.annual creditreport.com* for your free report.

Protect pass codes on your credit cards, bank, and phone accounts. Don't use the same code for all of your accounts. Don't use your personal information, such as your mother's maiden name, your birth date, or the last four digits of your Social Security number or your phone number, as a code. You will find that many companies still use your mother's maiden name or your Social Security number for identification purposes on their applications. Request that they use a password instead.

Never give out personal information unless you've initiated the contact or are certain you are communicating with a legitimate organization. Identity thieves may pose as representatives of creditors, financial institutions, and even government agencies to get you to reveal your Social Security number, mother's maiden name, account numbers, and other personal information.

Outgoing mail should be deposited in post office collection boxes or at your local post office rather than in an unsecured mailbox. Retrieve delivered mail from your mailbox as soon as possible. If you're traveling away from home and can't pick up your mail, put a hold on your mail by calling the U.S. Postal Service at 1-800-275-8777.

Safeguard your trash by shredding your credit card receipts, copies of credit applications, insurance forms, physician statements, checks and bank statements, and any documents that list personal information.

Keep your Social Security card in a secure place. Only give out your Social Security number when absolutely necessary. Request to use other types of identification whenever possible. If your state's driver's license uses your Social Security number, request to substitute another number.

Contact your creditors and ask if you have a choice about how they use your personal information in their account file. If you have a choice, request that your personal information be kept confidential.

Always make sure you know that your wallet or purse is in a secure place, especially at work, and only carry the personal identification cards and credit or debit cards that you absolutely need. Leave your other cards in a safe place at home.

Know the billing cycles of your bills. If your bills don't arrive on time, follow up with your creditors. If a credit card bill is not delivered, this could mean an identity thief has changed your billing address to cover up unauthorized charges on your account.

Beware of promotional offers that ask for your personal information—they may be scams run by identity thieves.

I've heard that I should be especially careful of identity theft on my home computer. How can I protect the personal information I may have stored on my computer?

Home computers can be a gold mine for an identity thief. To keep your computer and your personal information safe, follow the tips below.

- Make sure your virus protection software is updated regularly. Computer viruses can cause your computer to send out files or other stored information that may contain your personal information.

- Only download files or click on hyperlinks sent by individuals that you know. Opening a file from an unknown recipient could expose your home computer to a computer virus or to a program that could hijack your modem.

- Use a firewall program as added protection to prevent an identity thief from accessing personal information stored on your computer.

- For online transactions, only use a secure browser—software that encrypts or scrambles information you send over the Internet. Use only the latest version available from the manufacturer to ensure that it has the most up-to-date encryption capabilities. When submitting information, look for the "lock" icon on the browser's status bar to be sure the information you are sending is secure.

- Try to avoid storing any financial information on your laptop. If you have financial account information on your computer, don't access your account with an automatic log-in feature that saves your user name and password. And always log off when you're finished.

- Before you dispose of a computer, delete all personal information. Deleting files using the keyboard or mouse commands is not

adequate, since files stay on the computer's hard drive, where they can be retrieved. To make the files unrecoverable, use a "wipe" utility program to overwrite the entire hard drive.

Since identity thieves can get some of my personal information from pre-screened credit offers, is there anything I can do to stop having them sent to me?

You can opt out of receiving pre-screened credit card offers by calling: (888) 5-OPTOUT (888-567-8688).

I've heard that the three major credit bureaus share my personal information for promotional purposes. Is there anything I can do to stop this?

You can opt out at *www.optoutprescreen.com*.

I'm constantly throwing away direct marketing mail that contains some of my personal information. I know I should shred this mail, but is there anything I can do to stop receiving these mailings as well?

The Direct Marketing Association's (DMA) Mail Preference Services allow you to opt out of receiving direct mail marketing from many national companies. Go to *DMAchoice.org* to opt out.

What about the Do Not Call registry? Can it really stop telemarketers from calling?

The National Do Not Call Registry allows you the opportunity to limit the telemarketing calls you receive. Telemarketers covered by the Do Not Call Registry will have up to 31 days from the date you register to stop calling you. You may register up to three telephone numbers at one time on the National Do Not Call Registry Website, *www.donotcall.gov*. If you have more than three personal telephone numbers, you will have to go through the registration process more than once to register all of your numbers. There is a limit on the number of phone numbers you can register in this manner.

You can also register by phone at (888) 382-1222, but you can only register one phone number each time, and you must call from the phone number you wish to register.

My identity was stolen, and I'm afraid the thief may have gotten a fake driver's license or a nondriver's ID card using my identity. How can I find out?

Contact your local department of motor vehicles (*www.dmv.org*). If your state uses your Social Security number as your driver's license number, ask to substitute another number.

An identity thief has falsified a change of address form and stolen my mail. Is there anything I can do?

The U.S. Postal Inspection Service (*https://www .usps.com/postalinspectors/mailthft/idtheft.htm*) is the law enforcement arm of the U.S. Postal Service responsible for investigating cases of identity theft. If an identity thief has stolen your mail to get new credit cards, bank or credit card statements, pre-screened credit offers, or tax information; has falsified change-of-address forms; or obtained your personal information through a fraud conducted by mail, report it to your local postal inspector. You can locate the USPIS district office nearest you by calling your local post

office or checking the list at the Website listed above.

An identity thief has withdrawn funds from my brokerage account. What should I do?

If you believe that an identity thief has tampered with your securities investments or a brokerage account, immediately report it to your broker or account manager and to the SEC. You can file a complaint with the SEC online at *www.sec.gov/complaints.html*. Or you can write to the SEC at SEC, Complaint Center, 450 Fifth Street NW, Washington, DC 20549-0213. For general questions, call (202) 942-7040.

I believe my passport was stolen. What should I do?

Contact the United States Department of State through their Website, *www.travel.state.gov/ passport_services.html,* or call a local USDS field office. Local field offices are listed in the Blue Pages or your telephone directory.

If an identity thief has established phone service in my name and is making unauthorized calls, how do I stop it?

Contact your service provider immediately to cancel the account. Open new accounts and choose new PINs.

My wallet was stolen, and I'm afraid an identity thief may have my Social Security number. What should I do?

If your card has been stolen or misused, contact the SSA Fraud Hotline at (800) 269-0271; fax (410) 597-0118; write SSA Fraud Hotline, P.O.

Box 17768, Baltimore, MD 21235; or e-mail *oig.hotline@ssa.gov.*

My identity was stolen, and I'm afraid someone has falsified a tax return using my identity. Any suggestions?

If someone has stolen your identity and you suspect tax fraud, call toll-free: (800) 829-0433. Victims of identity theft who are having trouble filing their returns should call the IRS Taxpayer Advocate Office, toll-free: (877) 777-4778.

CREDIT CARD DEBT AND RELATIONSHIPS

I carry a large credit card balance, and I also owe my sister $5,000. Since the card companies are charging interest, is it okay to pay my sister after my credit card debt is paid? My sister never mentions the loan, but every time I see her I think about it.

No, I don't think it is okay. I've seen money damage personal relationships more times than I can count and, although there are occasions when asking for help from a family member or friend is the right thing to do, the debt should always be taken very seriously—for it is a serious matter. Whether a debt is personal or institutional, it is a debt. Even if your sister has loaned you money on indefinite terms, this doesn't mean that you should not be paying her something on the loan. If you pay her just $25 a month, you will feel better about yourself—and

she will feel better, too. Remember that self-esteem is a key factor in dealing with debt. The fact that you think about the money you owe every time you see your sister indicates that this debt is affecting your relationship with her.

My wife has admitted to me that she has been hiding $3,000 worth of credit card debt. I'm shocked. What should I do?

Your initial reaction to your wife's disclosure may be surprise, anger, and disappointment, but please realize that, by talking about it, she has taken the first difficult, important step in freeing herself—and you—from debt. And please take comfort in the fact that you and she are not alone. Secret debt is surprisingly common.

To your wife and others in her position, I would say: If you are hiding debt of any kind, please do tell your spouse. Debt can't be kept secret forever, and your integrity, self-respect, and relationships with others are at stake. Legally, your spouse shares financial responsibility for your debt. Don't keep him or her in the dark. Together, you can work yourselves free from debt.

If I'm married, am I responsible for money my husband owes on credit cards that are in his name alone, and vice versa?

Personally, I believe that if you are married, you have pledged your support—emotional and financial—to your spouse. Legally, the answer to this question depends on the state in which you live. In many states, you are responsible for your spouse's debt, whether your name is on the account or not. In community-property states such as California, for instance, if the day after your wedding your husband rings up $5,000 in charges on a new Visa card and then cannot pay the bill, guess who is also liable? You are. Be aware that having separate credit cards does not necessarily mean that you and your spouse are not responsible for each other's debt. Check your state's laws. (For more on marital financial obligations, please see Chapter 2, Financial Intimacy.)

In terms of being responsible for a spouse's separate credit card debts during marriage, are the rules different in community-property states and in states without community-property laws?

Yes, they are, and here is what you need to know. If you live in a community-property state (Arizona, California, Idaho, Louisiana, Nevada, New Mexico, Texas, Washington, or Wisconsin), you will most likely be responsible for all the debts incurred during your marriage. There are exceptions, but not many.

I do not live in a community-property state. Am I still responsible for my spouse's separate credit card debts?

Probably not, unless the fine print on the credit card application your spouse signed stated that both of you would be responsible for the repayment of the debt, or unless the debt went to pay for family necessities such as food, shelter, and medical care or for your children's education.

My wife and I separated recently. Can I legally keep her from using our joint credit cards?

If either you or your wife informs the credit card company that you want to close your joint account, the creditor should close the account. (In that event, neither of you can use the account, but both of you are responsible for the full balance accumulated before you closed it.) First, call the credit card company and ask to have the account closed. Then follow up with a letter. As always, send your letter via certified mail, return receipt requested, and keep a copy for your records. If for some reason the credit card company is not cooperative when you call, go ahead and send the letter anyway, and send a copy to the bank's compliance officer. He or she is responsible for making sure the bank complies with federal credit laws. This will get your message across. If the matter ever goes to court, you will have a paper trail that will serve as evidence that you're not responsible for any credit card debt incurred by your separated (or ex-) spouse subsequent to your request that the account be closed.

I am married but about to get separated. Will I be responsible for any debts that my soon-to-be ex-husband accumulates after we are separated?

In most cases, you will not be responsible for the debt that a spouse incurs after the legal separation date, unless it is determined that the debt was incurred to pay for the necessities of life for the family or for the children's education.

How about the debts that my soon-to-be ex-husband incurred before we got married? Am I responsible for those?

No, not usually.

My wife and I recently got a divorce, but she continues to use our joint credit card to make purchases. Am I responsible for paying those bills?

Unfortunately, yes—unless you have notified the credit card company that you want to close the account.

My aunt has offered to help me get out of credit card debt by lending me $15,000 at a very low rate. What do you think?

Borrowing money from your aunt, or from any relative or friend, may seem like a good idea, but be prepared for the possibility that the arrangement may backfire. First, ask yourself whether the loan will really help you resolve to avoid the pitfalls of overspending—that is, to get and *stay* out of debt. In my experience, emergency bailouts often just reset the clock for people who are prone to debt.

If you do decide to borrow this money, keep things businesslike. It's only fair that you pay an interest rate above what your aunt could earn in a savings account or a money-market fund. Make the total amount of debt that you are carrying very clear to her and, if possible, sign a promissory note that spells out the terms of the loan. Otherwise, it can be too tempting not to take your aunt's loan seriously, and too easy to take on new debt. And that could mean putting your relationship with your aunt at risk.

When my parents die and their estate is settled, will I be responsible for any credit card debt they have?

You won't be personally responsible unless your name is on the account. If there is enough money in your parents' estate to pay the debt, the estate will be responsible for payment; if there is no money, most credit card companies will write off the debt owed by the deceased. (For more on estate planning and debt, please see Chapter 11, Wills and Trusts.)

My husband died recently, and I am wondering how his death will affect my credit card accounts.

This is one reason I advise couples to have both joint and individual credit card accounts. If only one partner works and that partner dies, the stay-at-home partner can have trouble obtaining a card in his or her own name without a steady source of income to support the credit card application. Please do not wait until you find yourself in this situation. As for the recent widow above, I would say that if your accounts were held jointly and you are sure you can maintain them on your own, then go ahead and tell the issuers that the accounts will now be in your name only. Also, inform the three credit bureaus that your husband has died. Otherwise you may find that other credit card companies continue to solicit him by mail.

CREDIT CARDS AND CHILDREN

I have two children, ages 10 and 13. What's the best way for me to start educating them about credit cards and debt in general?

It's never too soon to begin your children's financial education. First, be conscious of the messages you send them as you pull out your Visa card to pay for gas or meals at a favorite restaurant. Because no money changes hands, they may assume the gas or the meal is free! Explain how credit works—that the credit card company is temporarily allowing you to use its money, which is normally paid back at the end of the month. Also explain that after the end of the month the company starts charging interest, and will keep charging interest until the bill is paid in full. This is how people get into trouble.

My son, a college sophomore, has gotten himself into a fix with credit cards and owes money to the tune of nearly $3,000. I'm floored, especially since he's on financial aid! How can credit card companies let a 20-year-old spend money he doesn't have?

Your son may not be an entirely innocent victim, but the truth is, credit card companies make it fairly easy for college students to get in over their heads. Why do they target young adults? The companies know that if they can get a customer early, the customer is likely to remain loyal to—or dependent on—their product for a very long time. Often, college students don't need to show an income, or even have their application cosigned by a parent or other responsible adult, to get a credit card sent to them. Card companies assume that if college students get into trouble, their parents will bail them out—even if, legally, they don't have to. A federal law that went into effect in 2010 now prohibits credit card issuers from offering cards to anyone under twenty-one unless the person has verifiable income to cover payments, or has secured a parent or guardian as a cosigner for the account.

Is it a good or a bad idea for a college student to have a credit card?

Despite the potential pitfalls, I think it's a good idea for a college student to have one credit card. The reason: As students get older, it may become harder for them to qualify for a card and to establish credit, particularly if they take their time finding a job after college. I think it is a smart strategy for parents to cosign on a card for a college-age child, but with plenty of safeguards in place:

The credit limit should be set at $500 or $1,000 at most. A duplicate statement should be sent directly to the parents. And I'd stay away from American Express cards—the annual fee is relatively high and there are no spending limits.

My daughter is going to college next month, and she's taking her first credit card with her. What should I tell her?

Set limits on your daughter's use of the card and on her spending. For example, tell her that the card can be used only for certain kinds of purchases (e.g., airplane tickets to travel home) or in emergencies; and make sure to define an emergency! Be clear about your position on bailing her out if she runs up a debt she cannot pay—and don't budge from that position. Explain credit ratings, and tell her that wise use of this card is the way to establish a good credit rating for herself. If she skips payments or pays bills late, her credit rating will suffer, possibly affecting her purchasing power later in life, as well as her ability to get a job or to qualify for insurance.

My daughter is in college. Am I legally responsible for her credit card bills if she can't pay them?

If your name does not appear on the credit card application, then no, you are not responsible for your daughter's bills. If you cosigned the application, then you are.

CREDIT BUREAUS/CREDIT REPORTS

What exactly is a credit score?

Your credit score tells lenders and issuers of credit—including mortgage companies, credit card companies, retail stores, utility companies, etc.—how prompt and responsible you have been in paying your bills and debts. Since the rating system is pretty much universal, it is easy for potential lenders, landlords, and even employers to evaluate your creditworthiness and assess whether you are a good or a bad risk when they are considering entering into a financial arrangement with you. The document that contains the financial information that determines your credit rating is called your credit report.

Can I get a copy of my credit report?

You have the right to receive, at your request, a free copy of your credit report once every 12 months, from each of the nationwide credit bureaus—Experian, TransUnion, and Equifax. The easiest way to get your credit reports from all three bureaus is by going to *www.annualcreditreport.com* or by calling 1-877-322-8228.

Under other circumstances, a credit bureau may charge you up to $10.50 for a copy of your report.

What is a credit bureau?

A credit bureau is a company that keeps a large database of detailed financial information from which your credit report is generated and from whom credit card companies, banks, mortgage lenders, insurers, credit unions, and others purchase that information. Credit bureaus make a terrific living by amassing and selling data about your financial habits, history, and current spending and borrowing practices. This information, in the form of a credit report, is available to those with a legally permissible purpose to see it. Basically, it's the credit bureaus' business to find out as much as they can about your financial history.

There are three major credit bureau companies: Experian, TransUnion, and Equifax.

Their addresses, phone numbers, and Websites are as follows:

Equifax
P.O. Box 740241
Atlanta, GA 30374-0241
(800) 685-1111
www.equifax.com

Experian
P.O. Box 105281
Allen, TX 75013
(888) 397-3742
www.experian.com

TransUnion Corporation
Consumer Disclosure Center
P.O. Box 1000
Chester, PA 19022
(800) 888-4213
www.transunion.com

What's in my credit report?

A standard credit report includes your name, address, date of birth, past addresses (home and work), Social Security number, phone numbers, and the names of your spouse and/or ex-spouses, if applicable. It contains a reasonably complete and up-to-date outline of your financial history, including employment history, marriages and divorces, any liens, any bankruptcy information, and, most important, a credit history. It lists the names of your creditors—including retailers, card issuers, and other lenders. In what's known as a "tradeline," it shows when you opened each of your credit accounts, whether an account is in your name only or is a joint account, how much outstanding debt you have in each account, your credit limits and current balances, and any negative information connected with your accounts, such as a history of late payments during the previous 24 to 60 months. Did someone sue you in court and win? It'll be in your credit file. Do you owe child support? It will be in your credit file. Some people may find it frightening to know that credit bureaus are keeping such detailed information about them, but not much borrowing or lending would take place without credit reports.

How often is my credit report updated?

It is updated whenever someone requests a copy of it. When a bank or an insurance or credit card company calls the credit bureau and asks for information pertaining to your credit history, the bureau puts together all the latest information in its databases. It presents this material to the lender, via computer, as your "report."

What criteria do creditors use in deciding whether or not to extend me credit?

A lot of creditors use three guidelines when deciding whether or not to extend you credit: character, capacity, and collateral. These are sometimes known as the Three C's of good credit.

What do they mean by "character"?

From the point of view of someone who is considering hiring you, lending money to you, or doing business with you, character means that you are trustworthy as far as advancing credit is concerned—i.e., that you pay your bills on time.

What does "capacity" mean?

Capacity refers to your financial status and stability. For example: Do you earn enough to be able to pay interest charges consistently? Do you have an alternate source of income, such as money left to you by your family or an investment portfolio, that could be drawn on in an emergency?

What does "collateral" mean?

Collateral is the material security that a lender may need in order to advance you credit or a loan. It can be a house, a car, or stock certificates. If you default on certain kinds of loans or credit lines, your lender may take possession of your collateral.

After taking these three things into consideration, how does a credit card company decide whether to accept me or turn me down?

After evaluating the Three C's, lenders turn to credit scoring to decide whether your application—for a credit card, a home equity loan, or a mortgage—should be approved or turned down.

FICO SCORE

What exactly is a FICO score?

A FICO score is a numeric value assigned to your credit habits and history by a company called FICO. Every American who has ever used credit now has a FICO score, and all creditors now use them. In the last few years, this score has become one of the most important criteria for evaluating you when you apply for credit. The higher your score, the lower the interest rates you may pay on credit cards, mortgages, and car loans. Conversely, the lower your score, the higher the rates you most likely will pay. To find out what your FICO score is, log on to *www.myFICO.com*. It will cost you $15.95 to get your score. Your FICO score may also be used by a potential employer who is vetting your application, by a landlord, or by any business that will rely on your timely payments, such as your cell phone provider and utility companies.

What are the different ranges of a FICO score?

FICO scores range from 300 to 850; the higher the better. A FICO score above 700 means you are a solid credit risk, a score of 740 or higher is excellent. Here are the six ranges as of December 2009:

Score
760–850
700–759
680–699
660–679
640–659
620–639

To be eligible for the lowest interest rate on your credit cards as well as other loans, you need to have a FICO score that is in the top range (740–850). If you are below 680, you are (in your lender's mind) a greater financial risk.

For a mortgage, can you tell me how much of a difference it makes to be ranked one range vs. another?

Well, to give you an example, as of December 2009, below are the interest rates that you might qualify for on a 30-year fixed mortgage depending on your FICO score. Notice that there is more than a 3 percent difference from the lowest range on the chart to the highest. On a $300,000 mortgage, that could be close to $650 a month savings.

Score	Interest rate on 30-year fixed mortgage
760–850	4.7%
700–759	4.9%
680–699	5.0%

660–679	5.3%
640–659	5.7%
620–639	6.2%

I applied for a mortgage via lendingtree.com, and they put offers out to multiple banks at once to get the best rate. I was told by my friend that this will hurt my FICO score. Is he right?

Your friend is wrong. The FICO people are smart; when they sense you are shopping around for the best deal on a major purchase, such as a home or a car, they will count all lender inquiries in a 14-day period as if they were just one inquiry. LendingTree knows this as well, and it will make all its inquiries within a day or two, to avoid multiple inquiries on your credit report. So the bottom line is that if you are using a company such as LendingTree or are rate shopping on your own, just keep the search less than 14 days and you won't have any problems.

I've heard that if I pay off any balance in full, I will still need to stop using my credit cards two months before I apply for a mortgage. Is this true?

The credit scoring people can't read your mind; they have no way of knowing that your intention is to pay off the balance in full. You want to avoid a situation in which your mortgage lender happens to check your credit score just before you pay off your bill; if it's a hefty balance—even if you intend to pay it off—it's going to affect your FICO score, and that in turn can affect whether you get a mortgage, or the rate that you will be offered.

If I have a good FICO score, how do I get the interest rates on my credit card lowered?

If your FICO score is really good (740 or above) then you should be aware that technically you qualify to get the best (that is, the lowest) interest rates available on the money you borrow. If this is the case and you are paying a high interest rate on your credit cards, call your credit card company and say that if they do not lower your interest rate, you will be switching your account. You might want to actually try to get a card with a better rate first and, when you do, make your current card company beat that rate; if it does not, transfer your credit balance to the new account. But before you close down that first account altogether, read about how closing an account could hurt a FICO score in the question below. To find the best interest rate on credit cards, log on to *www.bankrate.com* or *cardratings .com*. I also recommend you research credit card offers from credit unions. Many credit unions offer the best deals for consumers. You can search for credit unions at *www.creditcardconnection .org*.

I currently have a zero percent rate on my credit cards, and I keep switching to new ones. I was told that this will hurt my FICO score. Is this true?

Yes, it's true that constantly opening new credit card accounts can hurt your credit score. Creditors will think that you are gearing up for a big spending spree, and that will cause problems with your FICO score. To avoid needlessly alarming the credit folks, don't shop for new cards more than once every six months.

Will closing an account hurt my FICO score?
It depends.

When you close down an account it can have a negative impact on your debt-to-credit-limit ratio (also called your utilization rate), which accounts for 30 percent of your FICO score. Imagine that you have four cards, each with a credit limit of $2,000, for a total combined credit limit of $8,000. In your wisdom, you have only ever used one of those cards, which currently has a balance on it of about $1,500. Your debt-to-credit-limit ratio (how much you owe vs. how much credit you have) is about 19 percent ($1,500 divided by $8,000). If you think, "Well, I am not using my other cards, so I should just close them," be careful. If you close an account you are not using, your FICO score may be affected negatively. In the above example, if you have only one card open, which has a credit limit of $2,000, and you have a balance of $1,500, that makes your debt-to-credit-limit ratio 75 percent—bad news for your FICO score. Believe it or not, you just might be better off leaving the extra cards open and unused.

You also need to be careful if one of your credit card issuers decides to cancel your card, or reduce your credit limit; that too can cause your debt-to-credit ratio to rise, because you have less available credit. If you are hit with a credit limit cut, or a card is suddenly cancelled, you might want to open a new credit card—and use it responsibly!—to help maintain a low debt-to-credit ratio.

If I have a high debt-to-credit-limit ratio, is there anything I can do to improve my FICO score?

Yes. You could call and ask your credit card holders to raise your credit limits, and that would bring down your ratio. So, for instance, let's say you have five credit cards with a limit of $2,000 on each, for $10,000 of credit total. But you have used $8,000 of that credit. That gives you an 80 percent debt-to-credit-limit ratio—and that is high. Let's say you call all five credit card companies and get them to raise your credit limits on each card to $4,000. Now your credit limit is $20,000, but you still only owe $8,000, so your debt-to-credit-limit ratio is now only 40 percent. Big difference.

Are there any dangers to calling a credit card company and asking them to raise your limits?
Yes. The first is they may not want to do it. The second is that before you know it, you may have charged even more. So, in the question before, where you only owed $8,000, you now may owe $15,000 or even more. So you must be careful, for, regardless of your FICO score, you do owe the money back that you charge, so you best have the money to pay it back.

Will my score drop if I apply for new credit?
If it does, it probably won't drop much. If you apply for several credit cards within a short period of time, multiple requests for your credit report information (called "inquiries") will appear on your report. Looking for new credit can be equated with higher risk, but most credit scores are not affected by multiple inquiries from auto or mortgage lenders within a short period of time—usually two weeks. Typically, these are treated as a single inquiry and will have little impact on your credit score.

Will reducing my debt help my FICO score?

Reducing your debt figures largely in your FICO score. You do yourself a huge favor by eliminating all credit card debt, or at least by not using your cards as often. The goal here is to improve your credit score, and one way of doing that is to widen the gap between what you owe and what your credit limit is. The less you owe, the better your FICO score becomes.

Will paying cash for purchases help my FICO score?

Your FICO score goes up when the credit bureaus see your balances going down. Especially in the months before you apply for a loan, be very careful how much money you are putting on your cards. If you need to buy something, buy it in cash, if possible. Pay cash when you eat out, go to the movies, shop for groceries, or buy clothes. If you do not have the money to pay cash for something at this point, just don't buy it! Charging all those things could hurt your FICO score.

Will paying my bills late affect my FICO score?

Paying your bills by the due date accounts for 35 percent of your FICO score, so this is extremely important for your current payment history. Do everything you can to get your payments in on time, no matter what, especially in the months prior to applying for a loan. A late or missed payment close to the time that you apply for a loan will lower your score far more than an isolated late payment some years in the past. It can seriously hurt your score, sometimes to the tune of about 75 points. That one skipped payment could take you from a good rating to a horrible one.

Will using a credit counseling service hurt my FICO score?

In years past, using a credit counseling service actually hurt your FICO score, but this is not as true today. The wise people at FICO have realized that people who use a credit counselor want to help themselves and are not trying to avoid paying their bills, so they do not mark down your score as they used to. If you doubt that you can tackle your credit card debt on your own, and you feel that you need help, contact a credit counseling service, such as the National Foundation for Credit Counseling (*www.nfcc.org* or 800-388-2227). These people are experienced, helpful, and relatively inexpensive to use (you should expect to pay about $25 for a budget counseling session, and $50 to be enrolled in a Debt Management Plan [DMP]). They may even be able to negotiate a lower rate or a repayment schedule for you.

What will declaring bankruptcy do to my FICO score?

If you declare bankruptcy, you won't be able to do much to get your score up for a number of years. Bankruptcies stay on your credit report for ten years, and they are an immediate markdown of at least 200 points, even if you had a good credit score prior to the bankruptcy. Just because you have claimed bankruptcy, however, does not mean that you cannot get credit. In many cases, there are lenders who will be all over you like a cheap suit. They know that, legally, you cannot claim bankruptcy again for at least six years. So during those years, they just love to sock it to you with interest rates that are sky-high. Be careful. A number of people who claim bankruptcy have to claim it twice. Your FICO score aside, in my opinion, bankruptcy is a very serious action to take; you need to seek the best advice and think about it carefully. It may or may not make sense for you in your particular situation.

How can I improve my FICO score?

It's important to note that raising your score is a bit like losing weight: It takes time and there is no quick fix. In fact, quick-fix efforts can backfire. The best advice is to manage your credit responsibly over time. Generally, people with high FICO scores consistently pay bills on time, keep balances low on credit cards and other revolving credit products, and apply for and open new credit accounts only as needed. Below are tips on how to improve your FICO score. You can also go to *www.myFICO.com* to use a simulator that will show you how to improve your score in your particular situation.

- *Pay your bills on time*. Delinquent payments and collections can have a major negative impact on your score. If you have missed payments, get current and stay current. The longer you pay your bills on time, the better your score will be.
- *If you are having trouble making ends meet, contact your creditors or see a legitimate credit counselor*. This won't improve your score immediately, but if you can begin to manage your credit and pay bills on time, your score will get better in time.
- *Keep balances low*. High outstanding debt— on credit cards, lines of credit, and other "revolving credit"—can adversely affect a score.
- *Pay off debt rather than moving it around*.

The most effective way to improve your score in this area is by paying down your revolving credit. In fact, owing the same amount but having fewer open accounts may lower your score.

- *Don't close unused credit cards as a short-term strategy to raise your score*. When you close unused credit cards, it lowers the amount of credit available to you without changing the amount of your debt. On paper, you appear to be closer to maxing out your credit cards, so closing unused credit cards could backfire and actually lower your score.
- *If you have been managing credit for a short time, don't open a lot of new accounts too rapidly*. New accounts will lower your average account age, which will have a larger effect on your score if you don't have a lot of other credit information. Also, rapid account buildup can look risky if you are a new credit user.
- *Do your rate shopping for a given loan within a focused period of time*. FICO scores distinguish between a search for a single loan and a search for many new credit lines, in part by the length of time over which inquiries occur. So don't window-shop for a loan over time; focus on what you need, get the best deal you can, and make a decision.
- *Reestablish your credit history if you have had problems*. Opening new accounts responsibly and paying them off on time will raise your score in the long term.
- *Have credit cards—but manage them responsibly.* In general, having credit cards and installment loans (and paying timely payments) will raise your score. Someone with no

credit cards, for example, tends to be a higher risk than someone who has managed credit cards responsibly.

- **Note that it's okay to request and check your own credit report.** This won't affect your score, as long as you order your credit report directly from the credit reporting agency or through an organization authorized to provide credit reports to consumers.
- **Note that closing an account doesn't make it go away.** A closed account will still show up on your credit report, and it may affect your score.

How often does my score change?

Because your FICO score is calculated anew every time a lender or potential lender asks to see it, your score today is likely different from your score of just a few weeks ago. The score is calculated based on the latest snapshot of information contained in your credit report at the time the score is requested. In general, your score changes when the underlying information on your credit report changes. Fluctuations of a few points from month to month are common.

I have become obsessed with checking my FICO score. Does that count against me if I check it all the time?

There's no problem if *you* are checking your score, other than the cost. The only problems arise when potential lenders are constantly checking your score; that's a sign that you may be trying to take on too much credit or debt. But even though you can check to your heart's delight without triggering any red flags, I don't think that's a particularly good use of your time. It's important to realize that it can take months for your credit information to be updated and to be reflected in your FICO score, so constant monitoring isn't going to get you anywhere.

How much will my score change over time?

How much your score changes depends on how you are managing your credit. If you manage your credit consistently over time, your score should remain quite stable. You'll see bigger changes in your score if you significantly change your credit behavior by opening new credit accounts, for example, or if you change account balances in a big way, or don't pay your bills on time. In general, it is a good idea to check your score at least once a year. If you are working to improve your score, you may want to check it every quarter or even every month.

If I've been denied credit, will the credit bureau tell me why?

You are entitled to receive a free copy of your credit report from the bureau that supplied the information to your prospective lender, and it will tell you exactly why you were denied. You must ask for a copy within 60 days of being denied credit. In general, I recommend that you check your credit status from time to time, in order to make sure that it is completely accurate.

What should I look for when I receive my credit report?

You should check everything for accuracy. Make a list of items that are incorrect, out-of-date, or misleading. In particular, look for mistakes in your name, address, phone number, or Social Security number, and for missing or outdated employment information. Your credit report also will list the names of people or companies that have requested your file within the last six months (or two years, if the information was requested by an employer or a potential employer), which will give you useful information.

What shouldn't be in my credit report?

Be on the lookout for bankruptcies that are more than ten years old, any negative information about you that is more than seven years old, credit inquiries older than two years, credit accounts that are not yours, incorrect account histories (especially late payments when you've paid on time), a missing notation when you've disputed a charge on a credit card bill, closed accounts incorrectly listed as open, and any account that is not listed as "closed by consumer," because if your report doesn't note this, the account will appear to have been closed by the creditor in question.

What rights do I have with credit bureaus?

Recent laws oblige credit bureaus to establish toll-free numbers so that if you have a question or a problem, you can contact them without charge. The law also specifies that the bureaus provide a human service representative rather than a computer voice on the other end of the line.

What should I do if I find something listed incorrectly on my credit report?

If you find mistakes on your credit report, fill out the "Request for Reinvestigation" form that accompanies the report. If you did not receive this form, write to the credit bureau and ask for one. List on the form each incorrect item and explain exactly what is wrong. Be sure to make a copy of the form before sending it back. The reinvestigation is free.

Does the credit bureau have to remove inaccurate information from my credit report?

Yes. If something in your credit report is incorrect, or if the creditor who provided the information can no longer verify it, the credit bureau must remove the information from your file. Often, credit bureaus will remove information without reinvestigating it if reinvestigation is more bother than it is worth.

If the bureau reinvestigates, how long will that take?

Once the credit bureau receives your reinvestigation request, it must get back to you within a "reasonable" time. By law, that usually means 30 days, although many bureaus will respond within ten days. Reinvestigation is an easy process for the bureaus, since computers link them all.

If you have found errors in a report issued by one bureau—and don't be surprised if you do—you might want to play it safe and obtain copies of your report from the two other major bureaus, check them thoroughly, and ask that any errors appearing in them be corrected.

What happens if the credit bureau doesn't respond?

If you don't hear from the credit bureau within 30 days, send a follow-up letter. Make it clear that you are sending a copy of your second letter to the Federal Trade Commission at 600 Pennsylvania Avenue NW, Washington, DC 20580. That will really grab the bureau's attention.

My credit bureau seems to be stonewalling me. Do I have any recourse?

If you feel the credit bureau is not abiding by the law or has treated you unfairly, you can send a complaint directly to the Federal Trade Commission. Be sure to send along a copy of all your correspondence with the credit bureau. You can learn more about your credit report dispute rights at *www.ftc.gov*; click on the Credit and Loans link.

Can I add things to my report that I feel are worth mentioning?

Absolutely. If you feel the need to explain a particular entry, you are entitled to add a 100-word statement to your file. Because the credit bureau is required to set down only a summary of what you write, be extremely concise and clear. You can also add positive items to your file—for example, accounts that you've paid on time. Just ask in writing that the information be added to your report.

DENIED CREDIT

I have good credit, but while searching for a better interest rate I applied for five low-interest-rate credit cards. I was turned down by all of them. Why?

Probably because the flurry of activity showed up on your credit report. Such activity makes lenders wary. They assume you are about to go on a spending spree and possibly put yourself into big-time debt. Did it ever occur to them that you might be comparison shopping for a credit card? Of course not. My advice to you now is to wait at least six months before applying for a new credit card. While you wait, check the rates on several cards and select one—and only one—to apply for. (Log on to *www.bankrate.com* for current cards and rates.) And take advantage of the fact that getting turned down means you can request another free copy of your credit report, in addition to the one free report you're entitled to yearly from the national credit bureaus.

My aunt, who is 75, recently applied for her first credit card and had a lot of trouble getting one. I would think that elderly people would be the best credit risks of all!

Not as far as the credit card companies are concerned. Companies are required, however, not to discriminate against older people solely on the basis of age, so if your aunt has a good financial record, she should get the credit she needs. In a landmark 1988 case, the Federal Trade Commission charged in court that a certain finance company was breaking credit protection laws by extending loans to older applicants on far less favorable terms than to younger applicants. It won the case, citing the 1975 Equal Credit Opportunity Act (ECOA), which made it illegal for a creditor to turn down an applicant just because he or she is 62 years old or older. The ECOA requires creditors to figure in income other than wages, such as pensions and annuities, when estimating the financial resources of older citizens—very important, since many older people are retired and no longer earn a salary. It also prevents creditors from changing the terms of a loan or adding interest simply because a person is approaching retirement age. Your aunt should register a complaint with the FTC against the companies that gave her a hard time.

BAD CREDIT RATINGS

Millions of Americans have bad credit ratings, often signaled by FICO scores below about 640–660. (For more about FICO scores and how to improve them, see page 31.) A bad rating doesn't necessarily mean that you're a deadbeat or a slacker. In today's economic turmoil it may mean that you have run into financial difficulties due to a loss of job, divorce, or illness—situations that set many people back temporarily. Millions of Americans have managed to repair their credit ratings, and chances are that you can, too.

I've been told I have a bad credit rating. How did that come about?

A lot of factors—or maybe just one—can contribute to a bad credit rating. Yours could have been caused by a history of late payments on your mortgage, utilities, car, or credit cards. Or perhaps a credit card company forgave your having been a few days late in paying a large balance you owed, but got annoyed when your balance of $13 took you nearly four months to repay and reported you to the credit bureau. There may be a notation in your credit file to the effect that you have not honored certain debts to the IRS, or that you have not paid out a lawsuit you lost, or that you've fallen behind on child-support payments. Or your bad credit rating could have been caused by something much larger and more serious, like a bankruptcy, which is considered the worst indicator of creditworthiness on a credit report.

What are the warning signs of a so-so or a bad credit report?

Most people who have a bad credit report are well aware of the fact—that is, if they are being honest with themselves. They start to notice a pattern. Creditors begin calling to find out what happened to the payment that was due three months ago. They have a history of getting notices from collection services. When they apply for a new credit card, they get turned down. But there's only one sure way to find out if you have a bad credit report—and that is by requesting a copy from one of the big three credit bureaus, along with a copy of your current FICO score. (For information on how to contact the credit bureaus, see page 30.)

How long will negative information stay on my credit report?

Negative information typically remains on your credit report for seven years. This includes late payments, paid and unpaid lawsuits and judgments, paid and unpaid tax liens, collection-agency or profit-and-loss accounts (an account that a lender has written off as not worth pursuing but that nevertheless goes on your credit report), and records of arrest, indictment, or conviction of a crime. If you declare Chapter 7 bankruptcy, this information will appear on your credit reports for 10 years—but no longer. All three of the major credit bureaus will remove successfully completed Chapter 13 bankruptcies (this is the kind where you have paid back a portion of your debts) seven years from the filing date.

How does a bad credit rating affect a person's day-to-day financial life?

A bad credit rating can make getting a credit card difficult—and if you can't get a credit card, there are a lot of other things you can't do. You will run into trouble renting a car or making an airplane reservation. If you don't have a credit card, you may be asked to put down a sizable amount of money as a deposit for everything from a special-order book to such essentials as heat and electricity.

I know I have a problem with my credit score. What can I do to fix it?

Along with taking steps to improve your FICO score (see page 34), here are some tips to begin to generate a good new credit history for yourself:

- Apply for credit with a local retailer, such as a department store.
- Make a large down payment on a purchase and negotiate credit payments for the balance.
- Apply for a small loan at a bank or credit union where you have checking and savings accounts.

If you are rejected for credit in any of these venues, find out why. You may have been denied credit for not meeting the creditor's minimum income requirement or not having been at your address or job for the required length of time. You can overcome these obstacles with time.

I was recently laid off from work and was late on a credit card payment. A friend told me I should request a goodwill adjustment. Can you tell me more about this?

If you have run into a situation, such as an illness or a job loss, that causes you to be late making a payment, a goodwill adjustment is an option you can consider to avoid having the late payment appear on your credit report and hurt your FICO score. You need to contact the creditor, explain your situation, and request that your account be "re-aged." If your account is re-aged, it will be reported as current rather than late. This procedure is called goodwill adjustment because the creditor does it to help the customer get back on their feet. Please be aware that requesting a goodwill adjustment can be time-consuming, since you may need to make several calls and in most cases will need to speak to a manager or supervisor in order to get the adjustment. Now, just because you request an adjustment does not mean it is automatic; it's at your creditor's discretion whether they choose to honor your request. Some creditors choose not to offer goodwill adjustments, in part because late fees generate a significant amount of revenue. Also, federal guidelines only permit creditors or banks to re-age an account once every 12 months and twice every five years. Creditors may also require two or more consecutive monthly payments to be on time before they will make a goodwill adjustment. But it is definitely worth it to ask that your account be re-aged, since a late payment on your credit report can hurt your FICO score. Make sure you also request a copy of all paperwork that the creditor sends to the credit bureaus, just in case the good-will adjustment is not properly reported and you need to correct your credit report at a later date.

TAKING CONTROL OF YOUR CREDIT CARD DEBT

If I realize that my debt is spiraling out of control, should I cut up my credit cards?
Absolutely. Take a pair of scissors and cut up each and every credit card in your wallet, but do not cancel your credit cards—it can hurt your new FICO score (see page 32). Remember to follow up with a letter, keeping a copy for your records, as well. Putting a stop to the vicious cycle of using credit cards to cover cash shortfalls caused by previous debt or continuing to spend more than you have in the bank is a first, crucial step in taking control of your debt.

I'm scared not to have at least one credit card to carry with me. What about emergencies?
If you feel this way, cut up all your credit cards but one, and carry this card in case of emergencies. You can safeguard against overspending with this card by calling the credit card company and asking to have your credit limit lowered to an amount you might need in an emergency—say, $500 or $1,000.

Okay, I've cut up my credit cards. How do I begin to deal with what I owe?
Good! Now, this step may seem difficult, because it asks you to sit down, study your statements, face what you owe, and see what the credit card companies are charging you to owe it. It's the "honesty" step. Here's what to do. Make a list of all the amounts of money you owe, starting not with the largest amount but with the balance on which you pay the highest interest rate. Then list your balances in descending order, by interest rate. Include all your creditors—and I mean *everybody,* from Visa to your sister. Don't forget to include student loans, any money you owe the IRS, and personal debts. About the last item, remember: Debt is debt, and just because most personal debt doesn't in-

CREDIT CARD BALANCES, HIGHEST INTEREST RATE FIRST				
Creditor	Balance Owed	Interest Rate	Payment	Phone Number
Department store	$4,320	21%	$180	
Visa	$6,300	18.9%	$200	
Department store	$3,100	16.9%	$100	
Optima	$4,000	7.9%	$120	
Mom	$5,000	0%	$0	

spire the fear of credit card debt doesn't mean it isn't weighing, pound for pound, on your self-respect. List the amount you owe, the interest rate, and the minimum monthly payment. Also list your creditors' phone numbers. For an example, see the table on page 40.

I owe late payments to some of my creditors. What should I do?

This is where the phone numbers come in. If you're late in making a payment on any of your debts, personal or institutional, call up the person or institution you've borrowed money from right now. Explain why your payment is late. Your creditors already know you don't have the money to pay the bill or else you would have, so don't be embarrassed. If the person on the other end of the line is rude to you, be gracious. If you will have the money in two weeks, or can send only $25, say so. In any case, it's important that you call your creditors before they call you.

Until I made my list, I wasn't fully aware of the astronomical interest rates I'm paying. Can I have them lowered?

Maybe. The likelihood of getting a rate reduction is greater the higher your FICO score. If you have a regular, punctual payment history, it's a very good idea to call and ask to have your interest rates lowered on outstanding debt. First, take a look at what some lower-interest-rate cards are charging. Then call your highest-interest-rate credit card companies, tell them you're considering switching to a better value card, and see if they'll match a lower rate. You can negotiate with

them, and often they will reduce your interest rate right on the spot. If they won't, simply move your balance to a card that offers a lower rate, but only if the fee on the balance transfer is not steep. Some card companies now charge a fee equal to 3 percent or so of the balance transfer.

If you have a low FICO score or history of late payments or other problems with your credit report, you may not be able to negotiate a better rate or switch to a lower-rate card.

I'm looking at the list of what I owe, and it makes me sick. How will I ever get out of this mess?

You can and will get out of debt, a step—and a month—at a time. After you've negotiated the lowest interest rates you can, the single most effective action you can take is to begin paying more than the minimum amounts due each month. Below is a plan to follow.

- First step: Figure out the largest possible amount you can afford to pay each month toward all your credit card balances together. Let's say that amount is $300 a month. You may think this is a lot, but when you carry a lot of debt on at least several different cards, this amount is probably close to what you already pay when the payments are added together.
- Second step: Add $10 to each minimum payment that your credit card company is asking you to pay.
- Third step: Add up all your minimum payments. Let's say the minimum payment for all

your cards together is $200. You've decided that you can pay a total of $300 a month toward eradicating your debt. Subtract the $200 you must pay from the $300 you can pay, and this leaves you with an additional $100 to pay on your credit card debt.

- Making payments: Now you are going to take the "extra" $100 a month and put it toward the credit card that is charging you the highest interest rate. When that card is paid off, you are to call the company and close the account for good.
- Ongoing plan: Now start all over. Let's say you were paying $130 a month on the high-interest credit card account that has now been paid off and closed. Stick with paying a total of $300 a month—unless you can raise it! Factor in all the minimum payments on your remaining cards. Let's say that the total monthly tab now equals $170. Apply the $130 you were paying on the closed account to the card that is *now* charging you the highest interest rate. When this card is paid off, call the company and cancel that card. Then start all over again with the third highest-rate card.

This process may take months or even years to complete, but if you keep paying more than the minimum amount you owe each month, the strategy will work every time. Keep transferring accounts for the best interest rate deals whenever you can, and be sure to track your payments and your monthly statements carefully. Take pleasure and pride in watching the amount you owe become smaller. With each payment, you will be closer to being debt-free.

Why is paying more than the minimum monthly balance so important?

The answer is in the numbers. Let's say you owe $1,100 on a credit card that charges you 18.5 percent interest. If you pay the minimum (let's say it's 1.7 percent) of your balance every month and you never charge another item, it will take you 12 years and six months to pay off your debt. That's a very long time! And your $1,100 balance will have cost you about $1,400 in interest. If, however, you had paid $10 more than the minimum each month, you would have reduced your payment period to six years and cut your total interest payments to $676.37. Ten dollars a month is only 35 cents a day, but it adds up to a savings of about $700 in interest.

Which is more important, increasing my monthly payment or getting a lower interest rate on my balance?

Both are extremely important. With most credit cards, the more you owe and the higher the interest rate, the longer it takes you to pay everything off. This is compounded interest working against you. In some cases, if you owed $4,000 or more, had an 18 percent interest rate, and you paid just the minimum every month, it would take you 40 years to pay off the debt, to say nothing of the thousands and thousands in interest it would cost you.

On the next page is a chart that will show you, pretty conclusively, what a difference a little more money each month *and* a lower interest rate can really make.

Where do I find the money to pay more than the minimum required?

THE IMPORTANCE OF GETTING A LOWER INTEREST RATE

Annual Percentage Rate	Monthly Payment	Amount of Time Required to Pay Off Debt	Total Interest Paid
5.9	$100	45 months	$465
5.9	$110	40 months	$417
5.9	$150	29 months	$298
5.9	$200	22 months	$221
7.9	$100	47 months	$658
7.9	$110	42 months	$587
7.9	$150	30 months	$413
7.9	$200	22 months	$303
9.9	$100	49 months	$874
9.9	$110	44 months	$775
9.9	$150	31 months	$536
9.9	$200	21 months	$389
12.9	$100	53 months	$1,257
12.9	$110	47 months	$1,101
12.9	$150	32 months	$739
12.9	$200	23 months	$528
15.9	$100	58 months	$1,736
15.9	$110	50 months	$1,494
15.9	$150	34 months	$968
15.9	$200	24 months	$678
18.9	$100	63 months	$2,362
18.9	$110	54 months	$1,986
18.9	$150	35 months	$1,229
18.9	$200	25 months	$842

Here's how you do it. From this point on, I want you to spend only paper money. If you go into a store and buy something for $4.25, and give the cashier a $5 bill, take the $0.75 change and put it into your pocket. If you go into another store and buy a pack of gum, do not take the $0.75 out of your pocket. Use a dollar bill to pay for the gum. Take that change and put it into your pocket. At the end of the day, put your accumulated change into a special jar or cup. If you spend only paper money from this point on and save your change, you will have about $30 to $60 worth of change at the end of every month to put toward your credit card debt.

I owe $8,000 in credit card debt, and I have $8,000 in my money-market fund. Should I take the money out of my money-market fund to pay off my credit card?

In truth, if you have $8,000 of credit card debt at a 14 percent annual interest rate (which is the current national average) and you are keeping $8,000 in a money-market fund on which you are earning 5 percent a year (5 percent that is *taxable* to you), you are losing more than 9 percent a year on your money for that false sense of security. You are saving money, but it may be costing you your financial future. So it makes sense to use the savings to pay off your credit card bill, but only if you will still have enough left in your savings (money market account) to cover eight months of living expenses. Every one of us needs an emergency savings account to handle any of life's "what ifs"—the unexpected expenses that can wreak financial havoc if we don't have money set aside.

If you have excess savings you can use to pay off your credit cards, here's what I want you to do. Pay off the cards. Once you've done that, take the entire payment you had been making on your cards each month (that is, when you were paying the minimum amount due, or slightly more) and put that exact amount back into your money-market fund each month. Within a relatively short period of time, you'll have your savings back—and more. At the same time, you must stop charging things you don't need. Try to pay cash for any purchases you make so you don't add to your debt.

My credit card company tells me that I can eliminate my entire debt by paying 50 percent of what I owe. I owe $3,000. Is this a good idea?

The credit card company is trying to cut its losses by offering you a settlement. This may seem like an easy way out, but if you accept the settlement offer, it could affect your ability to get credit in the future.

Why? If you pay 50 percent of your outstanding balance, or $1,500, your credit report will note that the account is now "settled in full." But the credit report also will show a balance remaining on the account—the $1,500 you did not pay—as well as a note explaining this settlement. This flag will remain on your credit report for seven years. Is it worth it? Only you can decide. You may also owe income tax on the amount of the "forgiven" debt.

Can I negotiate with credit card companies?

Yes. If you have any accounts that are currently in trouble because your payments have been late or incomplete, you are, strangely enough, in a fairly good bargaining position. Offer the credit company, or even the collection agency, full or partial payment in exchange for its agreement to remove any negative information about your account from your credit report. Some creditors and collection agencies may be willing to do this, though others may not like this idea in the slightest—you'll never know until you try.

CREDIT COUNSELING

What is a credit counseling service?

Reputable and consumer-oriented credit counseling services are typically nonprofit agencies that help consumers who are having trouble with debt. For a fee, a counselor will sit down with you and discuss all the elements of your debt, review all of your options, and help you figure out the best way to get out of debt. Sometimes he or she will even negotiate on your behalf, establish a debt management plan, and advise you of the possible consequences of declaring bankruptcy.

Are all credit counseling services the same?

Please be very careful selecting a counseling service, because all credit counselors are not the same. The credit counseling industry today has become increasingly competitive due to credit card debt now topping $800 billion in the United States, with nearly nine million people contacting a consumer credit counseling agency each year. A report released by the National Consumer Law Center and the Consumer Federation of America, titled *Credit Counseling in Crisis,* found the honest, reputable agencies are losing out to companies that are in the nonprofit credit counseling business to make quick money. Instead of offering a range of diagnostic and counseling services, these companies sell debt consolidation as a solution for nearly every person with debt problems. Some of the less reputable credit counseling agencies often harm rather than help, with improper advice, deceptive practices, excessive fees, and abuse of their nonprofit status. That being said, if you find you need help, one of the best credit counseling services, in my opinion, is the National Foundation for Credit Counseling (*www.nfcc.org*), at (800) 388–2227. These people are experienced, helpful, and relatively inexpensive to use (a budget counseling session typically costs $25; the cost of enrolling in a Debt Management Plan [DMP] is $50, and then $25 per month). They may even be able to negotiate a lower rate or a repayment schedule for you.

What is a debt management plan?

A debt management plan, or DMP, is a voluntary arrangement between you, your creditors, and the Consumer Credit Counseling Service. A DMP does two things at once: It helps you get out of debt in an honorable, organized way, and it helps your creditors get back the money you owe them. Here's how it works: A consumer agrees to deposit a certain amount of money each month in an account and distributes this money among the consumer's creditors. Incidentally, if you enter into a DMP, many creditors will agree to lower their interest rates and fees or, in some cases, eliminate them altogether. Your credit counselor can fill you in on the details of your credit card companies' policies.

What is the impact of a debt management plan on a FICO score?

Using a credit counseling service does not hurt your FICO score.

As to consumers' ability to obtain credit, it is at the discretion of individual creditors as to how they interpret a consumer's credit report history and whether or not they will extend credit. Many creditors see a debt management plan as a positive step and will recognize that consumers are making an effort to regain control of their finances, reverse negative payment history, and to avoid writing off an account or bankruptcy. While the initial impact of a debt management plan may be minimal, there is direct positive impact over time that helps a consumer's credit standing. After a client has made numerous timely payments through a debt management plan, some creditors will remove any references of a debt management plan arrangement from a client's credit report. The client's credit report will reflect that they are meeting their debt obligations, which improves a client's score over time.

What questions should I ask a credit counseling service?

It is important to first learn about what credit counselors can and cannot do for you. The best way to do this is to list all your debts and categorize them as secured or unsecured. Credit counselors cannot help you with secured debt, such as your home or car loan. If you decide you want to get help from a credit counselor:

1. Ask for information about the agency before signing up. You do not need to provide personal information in order to find out the basics of what an agency can do for you.

2. Ask about counselor qualifications. How are the counselors trained?

3. Ask about privacy. Does the agency protect consumer information? Do they sell consumer information to others?

4. Ask about both DMP and non-DMP services. A DMP is not likely to work for you if you are most concerned about secured

debts, such as home or car loans. But you may benefit from non-DMP counseling and/or diagnostic services.

5. If a DMP is not right for you, ask about the other services the agency provides. Be very cautious if the agency says that they only do debt consolidation or debt management plans.

6. If you are interested in a DMP, ask how the plans work. What sorts of concessions are likely? Will the agency help with all your unsecured debts? Can you get regular account information? How often are payments made? How long is it likely to take to complete the plan?

7. Ask about any educational courses or seminars the agency provides.

8. Be sure to ask about fees. If the agency tells you a fee is voluntary, get specifics on what that means. Find out how much you will be paying an agency. If the agency is reluctant to talk about fees, you should look elsewhere.

9. Ask how working with a credit counselor will affect your credit rating.

10. Be sure credit counseling is the right solution for you before you sign up. You should also understand the alternatives to counseling, such as negotiating on your own and/or declaring bankruptcy.

I went to a credit counseling company, and they said they would charge me $800 up front and that I should stop paying my credit card bills altogether. They told me that with their help, this would lead to a deduction in what I owe. Is this true?

Please steer clear of this company. This is how

unscrupulous services typically work—they ask for money up front, plus a percentage of what they claim to save you. And they really make a mess of things; in negotiating a lower payment with your creditors, they typically ruin your credit record. Here's how: They tell the creditors you do not have a penny to your name. They offer your creditor two options: accept a super-low payment or accept zippo. The creditor might accept the lower payment—rather than get nothing—but they are not going to be happy about this. So they will report to the credit bureaus that you are a terrible credit risk. That's going to make it difficult for you to ever get a decent deal on a loan or credit card in the future. It's better to work with a reputable nonprofit credit counseling company such as NFCC or to contact the creditor directly and try and work out a plan in which you agree to pay a certain amount each month. The creditor wants to get their money back, so they are going to try to work out a deal with you.

CREDIT REPAIR CLINICS

What about the credit repair clinics, or "credit doctors," that are advertised in newspapers and the mail, and on radio, television, and the Internet, that promise that negative information can be removed from your credit file for a fee?
Credit repair clinics should be avoided at all costs. They can't do anything for you that you can't do for yourself. No one can instantly repair credit. Only time, deliberate effort, and a personal debt repayment plan will improve your credit. Credit protection and credit repair scams are one of the top consumer complaints reported to the FTC;

the FTC estimates the loss to consumers is easily in the millions. Please be very careful if they ask you to make false statements on a loan or credit application, misrepresent your Social Security number, or advise you to get an Employer Identification Number from the Internal Revenue Service under false pretenses—you will be committing fraud. The truth is that you can help *yourself* rebuild a better credit record. Start by contacting your creditors when you realize that you are unable to make payments. If you need help working out a payment plan and a budget, contact your local credit counseling services, such as NFCC. NFCC services are available at little cost. Also, check with your employer, credit union, or housing authority for no-cost credit counseling programs.

What do credit repair clinics do that is so bad?
One thing credit repair clinics do is appeal to your paranoid side. The world of finance and of big government is not on your side, they claim, and with their enormous knowledge of various "loopholes," they can help get you out of debt. What they are usually doing is paraphrasing the portion of the Fair Credit Reporting Act that requires a credit bureau to reinvestigate any information in your file that is misleading, incorrect, or incomplete. Credit repair clinics want you to ask for reinvestigation again and again.

What would be the point of reinvestigating again and again?
The only point is to clog up the system so that, in the end, the credit bureaus will simply shrug their shoulders and give in. Is that a loophole? I don't think so. Not to mention that this approach

seldom meets with success. Plus, credit bureaus are very suspicious of reinvestigation requests that look as if they are sent from a credit repair clinic.

What else do credit repair clinics do?

They advise you to dispute practically everything in your credit file. That includes your Social Security number, your address, and even your name! Some clinics will go so far as to suggest that their customers take on a new identity, and become entirely new people. This is certainly one way to get a clean slate, but one I hardly recommend. (In case you were wondering, under the new credit repair statutes, changing your identity to avoid debt is strictly against the law.)

PAYDAY LOAN COMPANIES

What are payday loans?

Payday loans (also called cash advance loans, check-advance loans, postdated check loans, or deferred-deposit check loans) are cash-advance loans secured by a personal check minus a fee charged by the payday loan company. Fees charged for payday loans are usually a percentage of the face value of the check, or a fee charged per amount borrowed. The average fee for a payday loan is $20 to $25 per $100 borrowed, and is due in full on your next payday. Most lenders allow for the original loan to be rolled over to the next payday for an additional fee of $20 to $25 per $100 borrowed. Under the Truth in Lending Act, the cost of payday loans—like other types of credit—must be disclosed. Among other information, you must receive, in writing, the finance charge (a dollar amount) and the annual percentage rate, or APR (the cost of credit on a yearly basis).

How do payday loans work?

Let's say you write a postdated personal check for $120 (which includes a $20 finance fee) to borrow $100 for up to 14 days. The check-casher or payday lender agrees to hold the check until your next payday. At that time, depending on the particular plan, the lender deposits the check, or you redeem the check by paying the $120 in cash, or you roll over the check by paying a fee to extend the loan for another two weeks. In this example, the cost of the initial loan is a $20 finance charge. If you roll over the loan three times, the finance charge would climb to $80 to borrow $100. A payday loan can start a vicious cycle of borrowing from future earnings to pay today's bills.

REESTABLISHING CREDIT

I got into trouble with debt and am trying to fix my bad credit rating. How do I start over again?

It's human nature to want to wipe the slate clean. Unfortunately, this is not always possible. The most important thing is that you are facing your credit history—and that you clearly want to take steps to improve the situation.

If you haven't done so already, start at the very beginning. Get a copy of your credit report and study it carefully. Make sure that all the information contained in it is accurate and up to date.

The second step is to do whatever you can to try to pay some portion, if not all, of your delinquent accounts. This sends your creditors a clear message: You are not dodging your debts. You have a sincere desire to pay what you owe.

How about trying to establish credit again? Is this impossible?

No, it's not impossible, but it may take some time. Some good sources of information and advice are two excellent books about credit rebuilding published by Nolo Press (*nolo.com*), *Money Troubles* and *Credit Repair*.

What do creditors like to see as evidence that I'm able to handle money responsibly?

You need a record of stable employment and should have lived in your current house or apartment for at least six months. And though there are disadvantages, I would apply for a gas card, a department store card, or both. Because of their high interest rates, you won't want to make any major charges on these, but gas and department store cards are often considered good stepping-stones to establishing credit. And make sure you make timely payments every month! Remember, you are being given a second chance, and you don't want to slip up.

Do references from a bank help?

Yes. If I were starting to rebuild my credit after a period of not paying my bills on time, one of the first things I would do is open a checking or a savings account, or both. Creditors look at these accounts as solid evidence that you are able to handle money in a responsible way.

Can I try to take out a loan from a bank to reestablish my credit?

Sometimes this can be a very good idea, but make sure that the loan is a small one. Remember, you are trying to show your creditors that you are an honorable and consistent person who can pay your bills regularly over a long period of time. Credit is not a right. It is a privilege.

What about applying for a new credit card?

Ironically, you may find it's easier to get a credit card following a bankruptcy than with a simple history of late payments or arrears. Start with a gas, store, or secured credit card. If you have declared bankruptcy, be careful: You may be playing with fire if you apply for a credit card. You could find yourself in trouble once again.

My credit is bad, and as a result all the credit companies have turned me down. In the mail recently I got a solicitation from a company who offered me a "check guarantee" card for a small fee. Should I get it?

Probably not. A check guarantee card is issued by a bank or lending company and guarantees to a merchant checks that you write, up to a specific amount. I would advise you to stay away from these cards, since you will likely only be covered for the amount of money you have in your account anyway, and you could simply pay with cash and avoid the fee charged for use of the card. Better to look into a secured credit card.

What is a secured credit card, and where can I find one?

A secured credit card is just what it sounds like: a

credit card secured by a cash deposit, usually of $300 or more. The bank issuing the card will generally extend a credit limit of 100 percent to 120 percent of your initial deposit. If for some reason you fail to pay your credit card bill, the savings institution will simply take the money you owe from your deposit. In the meantime, your security deposit earns interest. Make sure you use a secured card that reports your payments to the credit bureaus; the idea is to use the secured card to reestablish your credit, so you need to confirm your payments will be reported. If you pay your bills in a timely fashion you will begin to build a good credit history. No one will know the account is secured—not even the credit bureaus.

Do you recommend secured credit cards?

Yes, I do. In fact, I recommend them even for people who are not in credit card trouble, since they are so safe. Of course, they are especially useful if you are trying to reestablish good credit after a period of delinquency.

Are the fees and interest rates for secured credit cards the same as for credit cards that are not secured?

Consumers who have had trouble with their credit in the past may find that the price of obtaining a secured credit card is somewhat higher than it would be for other people. Many secured cards charge an annual fee of $50 or so. The annual percentage rate for balances on purchases and for cash advances can often be more than 20 percent. Additional deposits will increase your credit limit with a good payment record, but your credit line may increase after 12 months even if you don't make additional deposits.

All in all, a secured credit card may be less convenient and a little more costly than other cards, because the amount of your credit line will be limited by how much you have deposited, but these two factors may help to keep your spending—and debt—under control. If you've had trouble with credit card debt in the past, a secured credit card may be just what you need.

Following a period of bad credit, I have recently repaired my problems with credit card companies. Am I now going to run into trouble if I apply for a mortgage?

The answer is probably not. However, with mortgage lenders, as with credit card companies, your case will be helped considerably if you can prove that your past troubled credit history was directly caused by circumstances either beyond your control or unlikely to happen again—illness, a messy divorce, a lost job. If you have declared bankruptcy, your chances to get approved for a mortgage increase significantly if the bankruptcy was resolved at least two years earlier and you've established good credit since then.

BORROWING TO REPAY DEBT

Many of us are tempted to borrow from our future to get what we want today. This can be dangerous, especially if you do not understand the financial ramifications of your actions. The following questions and answers will help you to make informed decisions about the potentially risky practice of borrowing to pay off credit card debt.

401(K) OR RETIREMENT PLAN

Can I borrow from my 401(k) to pay off back taxes, a student loan, or my credit card debts?
Probably. Many employers will allow you to borrow up to 50 percent of the money in your 401(k) or retirement plan, up to $50,000, to pay for things that qualify, including a house, a college education, and sometimes debt repayment. This loan, you should know, does not come interest-free; interest rates are set by your company. They are generally reasonable. Typically, they are about 2 percent above the prime rate, the basic interest rate set by the government.

What are the advantages of borrowing from my 401(k)?
One of the biggest supposed advantages of borrowing money from your 401(k) is that since you are effectively borrowing your *own* money, from yourself, the interest you pay, as well as the principal, goes right back into your account. You have five years to pay back the money you borrow. Please read on to see why I don't want you to do this.

If I borrow money from my 401(k), won't this prevent my 401(k) from increasing in value?
Possibly, depending on what the markets are

doing you could be losing out on some of the growth potential of your money. But if you are paying 18.5 or 21 percent interest on your credit cards, for example, and can't transfer your balance to a lower-rate card, you might actually save money by borrowing from yourself at 8 or 9 percent.

Are there other disadvantages to borrowing money from my 401(k)?
Yes, there are several. One major disadvantage: If you happen to leave your job or get fired, the money you borrowed will be due in one lump sum within a few months of your departure. If you do not have the money to repay the loan at that time, your remaining loan amount will be taxable to you as ordinary income. If you are younger than 59½ at that time, you will also pay a 10 percent federal penalty.

A more universal and less well-known disadvantage is this: If you borrow money from your 401(k) to pay off your credit card debt, you will be taxed twice on the loan amount. Here's how this works. The money you borrow is money you contributed to your retirement plan before taxes; the money you use to pay off the loan is after-tax money. Later, when you withdraw your 401(k) money for retirement, it will be taxed again. If at all possible, if you borrow from your 401(k), please try your best to make your normal contributions as well as your loan payments, or your long-term loss may be too great.

But let's look at what a 401(k) loan can do to your retirement savings. Say you are 35 years old, make $40,000 a year, and have a 401(k) balance of $20,000. You contribute $2,400, or 6 percent of your salary, per year, and your employer match is $1,200. Assume that you get an annual return of 8 percent on your account. If you continue saving at this rate until age 65, your retirement nest egg will be about $624,000.

You decide to take a loan from your 401(k) to pay off your credit card debt. You take out a $10,000 loan on your 401(k) with five years to repay it. But you can't afford to continue making contributions while you repay it. What happens? When you reach age 65, your account will be worth $458,673. That difference of roughly $127,000 in savings translates into a loss of $7,620 a year in retirement income, assuming returns of 6 percent. That's about $630 a month, which is quite a chunk of cash. Are you convinced?

Are there preliminary charges for a 401(k) loan?

Sometimes. With a 401(k) loan, fees are variable. Some employers will charge you for taking out the loan and some won't. Some make you pay a fee of up to $100 just to fill out the paperwork, and some charge a yearly fee while the loan is outstanding.

Is taking out a 401(k) loan easy?

Yes, fairly easy. You may have to fill out a form with your human resources department, or you may be able to apply over the phone with the financial company that manages your 401(k). Loans from either source take time to process, however, so if you're desperate, comparison shop. Ask your employer and a lender how long a 401(k) loan and a home equity loan will take

to process, respectively, and when you will have the money in hand.

If I take out a 401(k) loan, who decides which of my investments within the 401(k) are sold off?

Who decides which of your investments are cashed in depends on your company's internal policies. Some companies will let you decide; others will make a decision for you. If you have any doubts about how this works in your company, ask the benefits adviser in your human resources department. If you do have a choice of which investments to liquidate, I would start liquidating money that is parked in either money-market funds or bond funds and then move on to your worst-performing equity funds. If you're unsure of how your equity funds have been performing, request a summary of the latest returns of your investments in the 401(k) plan from your human resources department. Check your funds' overall returns for one year, three years, five years, and, if available, ten years. See which funds have had the highest and most consistent returns overall, and which have had the lowest returns. Start liquidating the ones with the lowest returns and move up the list from there.

What happens if I cannot pay back the loan to my 401(k)?

If you can't pay back the amount that you borrowed in five years' time, your loan is considered to be in default. At that point, your employer and the IRS consider the outstanding balance as a taxable withdrawal, and you will pay taxes on the money as if it were ordinary income. If you're under age 59½, you may also have to pay a 10 percent early withdrawal penalty. This is a potentially vicious circle, since it often obliges individual consumers to cash in even more of their 401(k) plan assets—which are also taxable and subject to the same possible early withdrawal penalty—to pay the loan.

HOME EQUITY LOAN

What about taking out a home equity loan to pay off my credit card debt?
A home equity loan is another option, with its own advantages and disadvantages, but I believe that the disadvantages are far fewer than with borrowing from a 401(k). Like a loan from a 401(k), a home equity loan may well carry a lower interest rate than your credit card does; unlike a 401(k) loan, often that interest is tax-deductible, so you can convert a high-interest, non–tax-deductible debt to a lower-interest, tax-deductible debt. The problem is this: If you do not have your credit card spending under control, before you know it you can easily find that you have charged your cards to the max again *and* have a home equity loan to repay. If you do this, you will effectively have doubled your debt load and put your home at risk of foreclosure.

If I have $80,000 equity in my home, can I take out a $80,000 home equity loan?
No. You can't automatically get a home equity loan equal to the amount of equity you have in your home. Most banks will allow you to borrow only up to 80 percent of the value of your house, less all current mortgage balances. If your house is worth $200,000, for example, 80 percent of its value is $160,000. Subtract the balance you owe on your mortgage—let's say that's $120,000—and this gives you the amount you can get as a home equity loan (if you qualify): in this case, $40,000. You qualify for a home equity loan depending on the amount of equity you have in your home *and* on your ability to meet your other debts and financial obligations.

I have a friend whose bank let him borrow more than 80 percent of the value of his home.
When real estate values are rising, banks may allow you to borrow 80 percent or more of the value of your home, but it can turn out to be quite costly for you. Most mortgage companies that lend more than 80 percent will make you pay what is called private mortgage insurance, or PMI, which will add quite a bit to the loan. (Please see page 174.) So it's best if you can stick to home equity loans that are 80 percent or less of your home's value.

Are there fees to take out a home equity loan?
Again, sometimes. Some can carry no fees except for an appraisal on your home (at a cost of $200 to $300), and some lenders will charge fees up front to take out the loan or for the paperwork, which can add another $100 or $200 to the bill. But if you look carefully, you should be able to find a home equity loan with no fees, no points, and a very small appraisal fee, if any.

What happens if I cannot pay back my home equity loan?

It is quite possible that the bank will foreclose on your home, which means that it can be sold to repay the loan.

What is an equity line of credit?

An equity line of credit will not give you a lump sum but will enable you to borrow money as you need it against the value of your house. One of the big risks with a Home Equity Line of Credit (HELOC) is that the interest rate is often variable; if the general trend of interest rates is higher, then your borrowing costs for the HELOC will increase. And remember, your home is the collateral. Be very careful using a Home Equity Loan (HEL) or HELOC; borrow against your home for only important and necessary costs; a vacation or hot tub is not a good use of either a HEL or HELOC.

BORROWING FROM A 401(K) VERSUS TAKING A HOME EQUITY LOAN: A COMPARISON

How is an equity line of credit different from a home equity loan?

A home equity line of credit usually has a rate that varies according to what market interest rates

BORROWING FROM YOUR 401(K) VS. A HOME EQUITY LOAN: WHICH IS BETTER?		
	401(k) Loan	**Home Equity Loan**
Tax-deductible	No	Probably
Payback period	5 years	5 to 15 years
Subject to income tax if not paid back	Yes	Possibly
Due/Payable if you leave current employer	Yes	No
Giving up potential growth	Yes	No
Double taxation	Yes	No

	401(k) Loan	**Home Equity Loan**
Monthly payment	$208	$208
Number of payments	60	60
Total paid	$12,455	$12,455
Total interest paid	$2,455	$2,455
Tax savings (at 28%)	0	$687

are doing, while a home equity loan has a fixed interest rate. Also, with an equity line of credit, you do not have to pay back principal each month if you don't want to; you can pay just the interest. So the payback period for an equity line of credit is not set. A home equity loan, on the other hand, works pretty much like a regular mortgage. You get a fixed interest rate and pay back the loan over a set period of time, usually five to fifteen years. So make sure you're extremely disciplined if you consider an equity line of credit.

Which makes more financial sense: taking out a home equity loan or borrowing from my 401(k)?

In my opinion, taking out a home equity loan is, hands down, the better choice, but I want to stress that you should only consider a HEL for truly necessary expenditures. Needs, not mere "wants." Take a look at the chart on page 54, and see how the two choices measure up.

Now consider the actual numbers. Let's examine what it means to borrow $10,000 at 9 percent interest (assuming a 28 percent tax bracket). In both scenarios, the payback period is five years.

Please note: This does not take into consideration the double taxation of a 401(k) loan when repaid. If you can avoid a loan from your 401(k) plan, please do.

COLLECTION AGENCIES

I am in deep trouble with debt. I can't pay my credit card bills or my car loan. Is somebody going to put me in jail?

No. A creditor can't put you in jail because of debt. But it can turn your account over to a collection agency, take you to court to sue for the amount that is due, garnish your wages, or foreclose on your house. Credit card companies can be really tough when it comes to collecting money.

Aren't credit card companies regulated as to how they collect a debt?

No. It's only when a credit card company, or primary creditor, turns a debt over to an outside collection agency that debt collection is regulated.

Collection agencies *are* federally regulated, but there are few laws that govern how a primary creditor, such as a bank or a credit card company, gets its money back.

How long do I have before a credit card company turns my account over to a collection agency?

Typically, three to six months. Here's how it works. When your credit card account is two weeks late, you will usually receive a friendly reminder in the mail or sometimes even a phone call from the credit card company. If you haven't paid the minimum due on your account after two months, it's very likely you'll get another letter, this time less friendly, and perhaps several more phone calls. At this point, your card might be frozen—which means you can't make any more purchases until the matter has been resolved to the credit card company's satisfaction. After three or four months of delinquency—meaning that you haven't responded satisfactorily to letters and phone calls or that you promised to pay and you didn't—a lot of creditors will consider your account a "bad debt." This is when the collection agencies come in.

What do the collection agencies want from me?

Collection agencies have one purpose: Getting you to pay back the money you owe. Usually they work on commission, receiving between 10 percent and 60 percent of what they manage to collect. Sometimes they will turn their cases over to a lawyer, who will draft a letter warning you that if you do not pay off your delinquent balance at once, you will be sued and taken to court. Once your account has gone to a collection agency, you have lost the opportunity to negotiate with the credit card company. If you call the card company, they will simply refer you to the collection agency.

What if I don't hear from the collection agency for a while? Does this mean I'm off the hook?

Probably not. Some collections begin years after the inception of a debt.

A collection agency contacted me, demanding immediate payment of a debt I know I do not owe. What should I do?

Be on the lookout for dishonest bill collectors, and never make a payment on a debt that you feel is not valid. Instead, within 30 days of receiving such a call or letter, make a request in writing that the collection agency verify the validity of the debt. Further, ask that the collection agency send written verification that this debt was incurred by you. Recently, the courts have upheld rulings that demands for immediate

payment in an initial contact by a collection agency are in violation of the Fair Debt Collection Practices Act (see the following question).

I am being pursued by a collection agency. Are there any laws governing how a collection agency can behave?

Yes. The Fair Debt Collection Practices Act (FDCPA) was passed to protect customers from being shaken down by collection companies. This act restricts the tactics they may use. Please note: The FDCPA applies to outside collection agencies, the ones that most credit card companies hire after their own attempts have failed, and not to the collection department within the card company or other lender.

What are collection agencies not allowed to do?

As a result of the FDCPA, collectors cannot phone your home so often as to harrass you. They cannot call before 8 A.M. or after 9 P.M. They cannot threaten you or use obscene language. They cannot call you directly if they know you are being represented by an attorney, and they cannot call you at work if they know your employer prohibits such calls. They cannot call your friends, your neighbors, or the people you work with and reveal your financial situation.

Can a collection agency obtain information on my whereabouts from government records, such as Social Security records or my tax returns?

No, a collection agency cannot make use of government records. But an original creditor can gather information from a state motor vehicle department about reregistration of a car, from your voter registration records, from the post office, or from a utility company or a bank, in order to locate you.

My collection agency does everything it is not supposed to do. Can I sue?

Yes, you can sue a collection agency, but a better first step might be to use the provisions of the FDCPA to warn your collection agency that it is acting in defiance of the law. What you should do is to write a letter telling the collection agency to stay away from you, to leave you alone, and to cease all communications with you. In this letter, inform the collection agency that under provision 15 of the U.S. Code, section 1692c, this letter constitutes your formal notice to stop all future communications with you except for the reasons specifically set forth in the federal law.

I have written a letter like the one above, but I'm still being harassed. What can I do?

Contact the Federal Trade Commission and register a formal complaint. (Go to *www.ftc.gov*)

If you can prove continued harassment, the collection agency is open to a lawsuit—one you could win if you have the proper documentation or proof. There have been several successful suits against collectors where the consumer won in court.

Do I have any other legal recourse against a collection agency?

If you think that the collection agency may be behaving in a way that you suspect is illegal, file a complaint with the Federal Trade Commission. The FTC does not settle individual disputes, but your complaint can be used to monitor and investigate collection agencies. You should also contact your state's consumer protection agency; start with your state attorney general's office and ask for the department that handles consumer complaints (go to *naag.org*).

STATUTES OF LIMITATIONS

If I choose not to pay my debt for whatever reason, how long do I have to run and hide from the credit card companies in case they sue me?

I just want to make it clear that running away from any financial obligation is never the right response. But to answer your question: It depends on the state in which you live and what kind of debt you have. In every state, the statute of limitations for credit card debt begins to tick from the date you fail to make a payment that was due, as long as you never make another payment on that credit card account. If your state's statute of limitations on credit card debt is seven years and your last payment was due on January 10, then the statute of limitations on your debt will run out seven years from that January 10, assuming you haven't made another payment.

Say I charge $5,000 on my credit card, and the due date is January 10. I don't pay in January but I pay the minimum amount in

February. Then, in March, I get a statement saying the next payment is due March 10, but I don't make that payment. I never make a payment again. Does the statute run from January 10 or from March 10?

The statute will start to run as of March 10. Be careful in making additional payments, because they start the legal clock ticking all over again. In some states, simply making an oral promise to pay resets the clock. In other states, the promise to repay must be in writing, and signed by you.

How long does the statute of limitations for credit card debt last in the various states?

Here's the list, as of the year 2009:

Alabama	3 years
Alaska	3 years
Arizona	3 years
Arkansas	5 years
California	4 years
Colorado	6 years
Connecticut	6 years
Delaware	6 years
District of Columbia	3 years
Florida	4 years
Georgia	5 years
Hawaii	6 years
Idaho	5 years
Illinois	5 years
Indiana	6 years
Iowa	5 years
Kansas	3 years
Kentucky	5 years
Louisiana	3 years
Maine	6 years
Maryland	3 years
Massachusetts	6 years
Michigan	6 years
Minnesota	6 years
Mississippi	3 years
Missouri	5 years
Montana	5 years
Nebraska	4 years
Nevada	4 years
New Hampshire	3 years
New Jersey	6 years
New Mexico	4 years
New York	6 years
North Carolina	3 years
North Dakota	6 years
Ohio	6 years
Oklahoma	3 years
Oregon	6 years
Pennsylvania	4 years
Rhode Island	10 years
South Carolina	3 years
South Dakota	6 years
Tennessee	6 years
Texas	4 years
Utah	4 years
Vermont	3 years
Virginia	3 years
Washington	3 years
West Virginia	5 years
Wisconsin	6 years
Wyoming	8 years

I am pretty sure the statute of limitations on my debt has run out. Why do I keep getting calls from a collection agency?

If an original creditor or bank becomes aware that the statute of limitations on a debt is about to run out, it will sometimes sell the debt to a collection agency. The collection agency will take a chance that you do not know that the statute of limitations is running—or has run—out, and will try to collect anyway. It's a good idea always to be aware of statutes of limitations on your debt.

Under what circumstances can a state's statute of limitations be extended?

A statute of limitations will be extended for the length of time you are out of state, in prison, or, if you are a minor and somehow get yourself into debt, by the length of time it will take you to reach age 18.

STUDENT LOANS

What do you think about student loans?

If you have no other way of paying for college or graduate school, I think taking out a student loan is one of the best and most honorable investments you can make for your future. In my opinion, student loans fall in the category of "good debt." Why? Because you are borrowing money to invest in yourself and your future.

If I take out a student loan, will I get a tax deduction?

Yes, if it is a federal loan and you meet certain income eligibility limits. As of 2009, you can deduct up to $2,500 of student loan interest.

Is there just one kind of student loan, or are there many different kinds?

There are several kinds of student loans, which

are described at *http://studentaid.ed.gov/*. I also recommend the *finaid.org* website to learn about your college financing options. Probably the oldest and best known is a Perkins loan. With Perkins loans, the U.S. government lends a certain amount of money to a college, which in turn lends it to students who need it. (For more on borrowing to pay for college, please see Chapter 5.) The Perkins loan carries a very low interest rate—5 percent. Then again, it is one of the smallest loans out there: It has a ceiling of $5,500 per year, and no more than $27,500 over the course of your undergraduate study. If you are a graduate or a postgraduate student, you can borrow up to $8,000 per year, with a cap of $60,000.

How long do I have to pay off my Perkins loan?

You may have to begin repaying your Perkins loan nine months after you leave college, and you may have up to ten years after that to pay off the full amount. Colleges often sell these loans, with their outstanding balances, to banks. This doesn't mean much to you, except that you will now be making payments to the bank rather than the college.

I need more money than a Perkins loan can give me. What are my options?

You might consider a Stafford loan. A Stafford—sometimes known as a Federal Family Education Loan (FFEL), a Ford loan, or a direct loan, depending on whether the lender is the college, a bank, or the federal government—exists to make up the difference between the cost of college tuition and the expected family contribution, or

EFC. The EFC is the amount the college believes a family should be able to pay after it has crunched the family's financials. Each dependent student—either at a two-year or a four-year institution—can borrow between $5,500 and $7,500, depending on your year of study, at a fixed interest rate. If you qualify for a subsidized Stafford loan (based on financial need) the fixed interest rate is 5.6 percent for the 2009–2010 school year, 4.5 percent the following school year, and 3.4 percent in 2011–2012. The subsidized rate is scheduled to rise to 6.8 percent for loans taken out in the 2012–2013 school year. The "subsidized" means that the federal government pays the loan's interest while the student is in school. An unsubsidized Stafford has a fixed interest rate of 6.8 percent in 2010 and beyond; everyone is eligible for an unsubsidized Stafford regardless of financial need, but the student is responsible for the interest payments during school, or the student can choose to have the payments added to the loan balance that will then be repaid once he or she leaves school. The maximum total a dependent student (one who has access to parental support) can borrow for undergraduate studies is $31,000 ($23,000 subsidized). You begin repaying the loan six months after you leave college, and you typically have ten years to pay back the entire amount, though often there is room for negotiation.

To apply for a Stafford loan, you must fill out the Free Application for Federal Student Aid (FAFSA form).

What is the difference between a subsidized and an unsubsidized Stafford loan?
If you receive a subsidized Stafford loan, you will not be charged any interest until you begin to repay the loan (six months after you leave college). Until then, the government assumes responsibility for your interest payments. With an unsubsidized Stafford, you (not the government) are responsible for the interest payments while you are at college and for the first six months after you leave. This doesn't mean that you have to pay interest every month; you can defer the interest payments and add them to the principal to be repaid after you have graduated.

My folks have talked to me about taking out a PLUS loan. What is this?
The PLUS loan is a federal loan that parents or legal guardians can take out to help pay for a student's college costs. The PLUS can cover the difference between the cost of attendance (COA), and the amount of financial aid that you will be receiving. The cost of attendance is the total amount it costs a student to go to school. For full-time students this includes tuition, fees, room and board, allowances for books, supplies, transportation, costs related to dependent care of disability, and miscellaneous expenses. The yearly limit on a PLUS loan is equal to the cost of attendance minus any other financial aid you receive. For example, if your COA is $10,000 and you receive $4,000 in financial aid, your parents could borrow up to but no more than $6,000.

I want to apply for a student loan, but my credit rating isn't great. Will I have problems?
Oddly enough, you probably won't, if you apply for a federal student loan. (Credit does affect your ability to obtain a private student loan from a bank.)

Please note: If you are a veteran, the child of a veteran who died or was permanently disabled in battle, or a nursing student, a pharmacy student, or a Native American, special grants and dispensations are available to you. Check with your college or university.

Who exactly grants and manages my loan—the Department of Education or a bank?

Who your loan holder will be depends on the type of loan you take out. If you take out a Perkins loan, your loan will be managed by the school that lends you the money or by an institution that the school assigns to service the loan. If you take out a direct loan, the funds for your loan are lent to you directly by the U.S. government and it will be managed by the Direct Loan Servicing Center at the U.S. Department of Education. If you borrow an FFEL, the funds for your loan are lent to you from a bank, credit union, or other lender that participates in the FFEL program and will be managed by your lender or its servicing agent. Your lender or the Direct Loan Servicing Center (*www.dlservicer.ed.gov*) will provide you with additional information about your loan.

If I really cannot make my payments, is there anything I can do?

Yes. Options range from having your loan canceled, which means you will not ever have to pay it back (this is almost impossible), to getting either a deferment or a forbearance. What you can or cannot do depends on what kind of loan you have and the reason you cannot pay. Beginning in 2009 there are now additional repayment plans based on your income, and you may qualify for loan forgiveness if you opt to work in cer-

tain public-sector jobs. You can learn more at the *finaid.org* website.

Under what circumstance can a student loan be canceled?

A student loan can be canceled if you are permanently disabled or die, or under certain other circumstances that also apply to deferment. Please read on.

STUDENT LOAN CONSOLIDATION

What does it mean to consolidate my student loans?

In effect, consolidating means taking all your loans, bundling them into one loan, and getting a new fixed rate. You can also get a longer repayment schedule—although, of course, I would advise you against doing this; in fact, I would recommend that you take any monthly savings you reap from the lower interest rate and pay off your student loans or (even better) your credit card debt more quickly. To consolidate your student loans, apply online at *www.loanconsolidation.ed.gov* or call (800) 557-7392.

Should I consolidate my student loans?

Though the interest rates on Stafford and PLUS loans became fixed in 2006, interest rates on those loans taken out before 2006 remain variable, and will continue to change annually. Depending on the current interest rate environment, you may want to consider consolidating your student loans, if you have never consolidated them before. New annual interest rates on variable rate student loans are set once a year, on July 1. If you are thinking about consolidating at a time when interest rates in general have been falling, depending on your situation and where you are in the calendar year, you might want to wait to see whether the new rates on July 1 will be lower than the current ones. Here's what to do. If you are just a short period of time away—let's say it is February or March—instead of consolidating now, hold off until May 1 and check out the interest rate the government is paying on the 91-day Treasury bill. That's right—the rate on the 91-day Treasury bill is the rate to which student loan rates are tied. (You can check T-bill rates by logging on to *www.publicdebt.treas.gov/servlet/OFBills.*) There are formulas that govern how loan rates work. In the case of Stafford Loans, for example, the new loan rate, announced on July 1, will be equal to the May T-bill rate plus 2.3 percent. The new PLUS loan rate will be equal to the May T-bill rate plus 3.1 percent. If doing the math leads you to conclude that the July rates will be lower than the current rates, wait until the new rates are announced, then consolidate. If you think they will stay the same or go higher, don't wait; check the current rate and consider consolidating now.

What should I do if I am still within the grace period?

If you have just graduated and you are still within the grace period—the period during which you do not yet have to pay back the loan—wait until about five weeks *before* your grace period is up to apply for a loan consolidation. That way, you take full advantage of your

grace period but still consolidate your payments as soon as possible once it has ended.

POSTPONING OR CANCELING STUDENT LOAN PAYMENTS

How do I cancel my loan?

If you have called the loan holder and you feel you qualify for a cancellation, you must apply for it. Call the Department of Education's Debt Collection Service Information Center at (800) 621-3115 and request an application. Fill it out and return it with all the paperwork the department will request.

What is a deferment?

A deferment simply means that you defer the loan repayment—wait until a later date to make it. During that time, in most cases, no interest accrues.

Under what conditions can a loan be deferred?

Conditions will vary with the kind of loan you have and when you obtained it, but in general your loan can be deferred if you, your spouse, or one of your dependents becomes disabled; if you go back to school part-time; if, for whatever reason, you are currently unemployed; or if you have young children. If you have a federal loan and are suffering an economic hardship, you can probably get a deferment of up to three years. You are automatically eligible if you are on Supplemental Security Income or are getting any kind of public assistance. If you join the U.S. military you may qualify for a deferment or even, under certain circumstances, a cancellation. You may also qualify to have your loan deferred or canceled if you get a job in law enforcement, become a teacher working with the underprivileged or needy, or get a job in a health-care profession in a part of the country where there is a shortage of health-care workers. You can also get a deferment or a cancellation if you decide to perform community service, such as serving in the Peace Corps. Finally, you can get a deferment if you enroll in a rehabilitation program for the disabled. Again, please note that each situation is different. Call the holder of your loan and ask under what circumstances you would qualify for a deferment of your loan.

If I have been in default on my loan, can I still apply for a deferment?

No. If you are in default, you will not be able to get a deferment. If you have merely been late in making payments a few times and are not in default, you may be eligible for what is called a retroactive deferment.

How do I defer my loan?

You have to apply for a deferment. Call the holder of your loan and explain why you think you qualify for a deferment. The loan holder will send you the appropriate paperwork.

If I get a deferment, how long will I be allowed to defer my payments?

Usually for about six months to one year. The economic hardship deferment is for three years but, as always, each case will be different depending on the kind of deferment, what kind of loan you have, and when you got it.

If I get a deferment and I need to apply for another one, can I?

Yes. Each time you are granted a deferment, the holder of the loan will let you know how long that deferment will last and when you should reapply, if necessary.

In a deferment, does the interest on my loan keep accumulating?

On a subsidized loan, no. On an unsubsidized, yes.

If I do not qualify for a deferment or a cancellation, is there anything else I can do?

Yes. You can apply for a forbearance. A forbearance is very much like a deferment in that you are allowed to put off making payments for a certain length of time. But with a forbearance interest *always* continues to accrue during the time you are not making payments. Also, with a forbearance, it does not matter when you obtained the loan or what kind of loan it is, which makes a forbearance far easier to get than a deferment.

I have been in default and I know I cannot get a deferment. Can I get a forbearance?

No. You cannot get a forbearance if you have been in default.

If I have a number of loans, do I have to get a forbearance on each of them?

No. The number of loans on which you apply for forbearance will depend on how much money you are short. Since the interest continues to accumulate while you are not making payments on these loans, you have to be very careful. If you have many loans, apply for forbearance on the lowest-interest-rate loans first. It may seem better to postpone the higher-interest-rate loans, but in the long run it is not. Remember that the interest is still adding up.

My loan payments are currently more than 20 percent of my gross income. Can I get a forbearance?
Yes. When your loan payments total 20 percent or more of your gross income, your loan holder is actually required to give you a forbearance if you want one.

How long will a forbearance last?
The length of time varies according to the loan holder, but it is usually up to three years.

If I apply for a deferment, forbearance, or a cancellation of my loan, can I stop making payments at that time?
No. When you are applying for a deferment, cancellation, or forbearance, you must continue to make payments until you are notified that the request has been granted. If you don't, you may end up in default. Keep a copy of any request form you submit, and document all contacts with the organization that holds or manages your loan.

DEFAULTING ON A STUDENT LOAN

More than 20 years ago, I took out a student loan. I've never repaid it and I've never heard from anyone. Will the same be true for my children if they do not pay back their student loans?
I'm afraid not. It used to be the case that if you took out a student loan and did not pay it back, you might not ever hear from anyone. But that is no longer true. If your children do not pay back the money they borrow, they will hear about it immediately and will suffer financial consequences in a big way.

When exactly am I considered to be in default?
You are not usually considered to be in default until you have not made student loan payments or had any contact with the loan holder to apply for a deferment, forbearance, or cancellation for at least six months.

If I have not repaid my student loans for years and the interest and penalties have mounted up, can I negotiate to get those penalties dropped or reduced?
You can try, but your chances are not good. To my knowledge, student loan holders seldom successfully negotiate or make a deal.

I am about to default on my student loans. What will happen to me if I do?
If you do default on your student loans, your lender or the agency that holds your loan, by the authority of the state and of the federal government, may take action to recover the money, including suing you and/or notifying national credit bureaus of your default. This may affect your credit rating for up to seven years, making it very difficult to borrow from a bank to buy a car or a house, or rent an apartment, among other things. If you are working or ever do work, up to

10 percent of your wages may be garnished, and if you are due to receive a tax refund, it can be taken to pay your student loans. If you decide to return to school, you will not be entitled to receive any more federal student aid.

Is there a way for me to get out of default?

Yes—by making 9 out of 10 consecutive monthly payments on your loan. Not only will you then be able to apply for a deferment, you can also request that your default be cleared from your credit report.

I am in default. I want to pay off my student loan, but I cannot afford the current monthly amount that is due. Will my lender adjust the amount for me?

By law, you are not required to pay more on your student loans than you can reasonably afford. Gather all your financial paperwork, call your lender, and ask about what is called a reasonable and affordable repayment plan.

What happens if I am granted this reasonable and affordable plan?

If you stay on schedule and make at least six monthly payments in a row, you will be eligible for new federal student loans. After 9 out of 10 monthly payments, you will no longer be in default. Then you are eligible to apply for a deferral.

I am currently in default on two student loans but not on a third. Can I consolidate my loans?

Yes, you can. In fact, if you were to refinance or consolidate your loans, you would no longer be in default on those two loans.

WAGE GARNISHMENT

If I default on a student loan and I am working, does the Department of Education have legal authority to garnish my wages?

Yes. And not only the Department of Education but also the agencies that guarantee your loans. They have the right to take up to 10 to 15 percent of your wages.

I thought I had to be sued and get a court judgment in order for my wages to be garnished.

That is true of all loans except student loans. If you default on any other kind of loan, your creditors must get a court judgment against you, after which they can garnish up to 25 percent of your wages.

Will I know in advance if my wages are going to be garnished?

You will be notified beforehand. The Department of Education is obliged to let you know in writing 30 days before the garnishment date. It must tell you how much you owe, how you may enter into a repayment schedule so your wages are not garnished, and how you can obtain a hearing on this garnishment process to try to stop it.

How long do I have to respond to this letter?

You have approximately 15 days to respond, and your response must be in writing.

If the Department of Education is going to garnish my wages, at what point will it let my employer know?

The Department of Education will let your employer know it is going to garnish your wages

about 20 business days after you receive its notice. It assumes you will receive the notice by five
business days after the date they mailed it.

***If I have just started a new job after not
working for the past year, can my wages be
garnished?***
Yes. However, if you were fired or laid off and
did not return to work for a full year, you can
object to this garnishment and you may win.

***I barely make enough to live on now. How can
my wages be garnished?***
If you do not earn at least 30 times the federal
minimum wage per week, your wages cannot be
garnished.

***I have been in default for some time, and I
seem to have slipped through the cracks. When
is the statute of limitations up?***
Never. If you haven't paid your student loan,
you remain responsible for it and for any interest
on it, too.

***If I default and the Department of Education
comes after me, what can they get?***
Almost everything: your bank account, your car,
and any other property and/or assets you own—
as well as garnishing your wages.

STUDENT LOANS AND BANKRUPTCY

***I have been told that if I claim bankruptcy I
will not be able to get rid of my student loan.
Is that true?***

That is true. No student loan can be dismissed
because of bankruptcy, no matter when it was
taken out or when it comes due. The *only* exception to this rule is if paying back a student loan
will cause you what is considered undue hardship. But bankruptcy courts have very strict definitions of undue hardship. In many cases, if
you meet those definitions, you would also qualify to have your loan canceled—a far better
choice.

***If I file for Chapter 13 bankruptcy, can I in-
clude my student loan payments in my repayment plan?***
Yes, but be careful. Chapter 13 bankruptcy allows an individual who has consumer (household) debts to make a plan to pay creditors, but
there are limits to the amount of debt you can
include, and other restrictions. Also, under
Chapter 13 some of your creditors will get back
only part of the amount you owe them and, essentially, the debts will be discharged—but this
is not true of student loans. If you file for
Chapter 13 and choose to pay back only a small
amount per month on your student loans, you
will still owe the balance at the end of Chapter
13 bankruptcy.

AUTOMOBILE DEBT

Why are you not a fan of car leasing?
When you lease a car, you take on a monthly expense that, in most circumstances, you will continue to have to pay for the rest of your life.

Here is why: With leasing, you do not own the car you are driving; you are paying a monthly fee merely to use that automobile for a few years. At the end of the leasing period, you either have to give back the car or purchase it for a predetermined price—a price that is usually set in such a way that it makes no sense for you to go ahead and purchase it. That's because these days, the leasing companies entice you with a lower monthly fee to draw you in and then they make up their profits with an inflated *residual price*—the price you would have to pay to buy the car outright—at the end of the lease. So what you normally do after the lease period is up is turn in your leased auto to the dealer and lease another. And then what do you do? You do it again and again—for the rest of your life.

If I have lost my job and cannot make my lease payments on my car, is there any way to get out of the lease?

To get out of your lease, here are your options. You can:

- Buy the car outright or finance it.
- Sell it for as much as possible and pay that amount plus any additional amount you may still owe to the lease company.
- Try to find someone to assume the lease obligations.

If you cannot sell your car outright, you may want to try to find someone who will assume your lease payments. However, keep in mind that when a person assumes a lease from you, it

still does not mean that *you* are off the hook! If the new leaser does not make the payments, the lending company will come after *you*. So be careful with whom you make your agreement to assume the lease.

If you decide to sell the car on your own, you still have to come up with the difference between what you owe the lease company and what you sold the car for. And what happens if you do not have that money? You're in trouble again. Therefore, to make sure you don't find yourself short, you need to prepare for this unknown *when you first consider leasing* if money is tight for you at that time. When you have leased your car, see if you can also get approved for what's called a *signature loan*, for about $10,000. If you have been approved for a car lease, you can usually qualify for this other loan. This loan will give you the backup to help you get through an unforeseen crisis. Here's how.

Let's say, again, you have leased a car and an unforeseen problem happens and you can no longer make the car payments. Before you turn back the car to the dealer or lender, see if you can sell it on your own. The way you can do this is to run an ad to sell your car for the payoff *only*—do not try to escalate the price to make money, for it will not happen. (You want to attract buyers who can solve your problem, not scare them away.) When a potential buyer makes an offer on your car, negotiate the best price you can in a nice manner. Hopefully, you will arrive at a sum that will help you pay off the lender with what you've negotiated plus your signature loan. If you have any portion of the signature loan left over, pay it back to the bank immediately. You have now eliminated a large car payment for forty-eight to sixty months, and the lease is closed or, more important, paid as agreed upon according to the lease's terms.

If you decide just to return the leased car to the leasing company without trying to repay the balance on your lease, be aware that there is a big downside. After you return the car, the company may try to sell the car at an auction. Even if the car sells at auction, however, you will still owe the difference between the balance on your lease at that time and the auction proceeds for the car. Sometimes the company even charges you more for penalties and recapture of depreciation. It is probable that your lease company has a used-car lot. The person who runs that used-car lot can go to that auction and buy your car for, say, $4,000. The problem is that you owed $12,000 on the car at the time you had to give it back. So even with the $4,000 from the sale of the car at auction, you still owe $8,000 to the lease company, and now you have no wheels to get around.

In the meantime, the lease company has your car back on its used-car lot, and the car is up for sale. The company can probably sell it quickly for $10,000. Between the $8,000 you still owe and the profit the company is collecting on the sale of the car, someone is making out like a bandit, and it is not you. You are still paying for a car that *you* do not even have. This is what is known as a bummer.

I've heard that leasing is better than buying a car because of the tax write-offs.

I know that some financial experts want you to ignore all the dangers of leasing. They will show you the tax advantages of leasing over buying and why, in your case, you should lease rather than buy. I do not care about the tax advantages for most people. They are not significant compared to your overriding need to know how you are going to handle any unforeseen financial crisis in your life.

Say you are in a car accident or the car happens to get stolen. As we said earlier, the deal you made with your leasing company most likely means you will owe more than the car's current market value, which is all your insurance company may reimburse you for. You can buy extra insurance, called *gap insurance*, to protect you against this, and maybe your lease deal included it. But do you know for sure?

Many people who lease just love getting those great tax write-offs for the first year and also love how they look driving a fancy car. However, I have watched as some have become absolutely clinically depressed after they saw their car being carted away because they could no longer make their lease payment and yet were still responsible for those payments.

CHILD SUPPORT DEBT

My ex-husband has not paid child support in three years, and I need the money. How do I find him and collect?

The federal government and each of the 50 states maintain what is known as a parent locator service that can tap into Social Security numbers, Department of Motor Vehicles records, unemployment rosters, and other databases to find missing child-support delinquents. Check with your state office of child support collection, and you may just find him.

When I got divorced, the judge issued a court order for my spouse to pay child support. He hasn't paid. What's next?

Since the child support was ordered by the court, your spouse is in arrears. You can go back to court and request that a judgment be issued against your spouse for the amount owed.

My ex-spouse is officially in arrears and is threatening to claim bankruptcy so he won't have to pay. Can he do that?

He can try, but he almost certainly won't succeed. Delinquent child support—along with back taxes and outstanding student loans—is a kind of debt that cannot be eliminated in a bankruptcy proceeding. All that filing bankruptcy can do for your spouse is to delay the day of reckoning. While it is true that in the midst of a bankruptcy hearing all active attempts to collect a petitioner's debts must cease, when the proceeding is finished he will still owe back child support, and he will still have to pay.

MEDICAL DEBT

Medical bills can be some of the hardest bills to face. Not only can they be large, they can also represent a physical or emotional crisis for the patient or for a loved one. Here are

a few guidelines for dealing with large medical debts.

I have recently undergone surgery. When I got the bills I was shocked. I found many charges that had broad categories but no itemization. How do I know what I am paying for?

Often, you don't know what you're paying for with a medical bill, and sometimes the hospital is hoping that you won't find out. Ask the hospital to itemize all charges, and it will comply.

My hospital bill is filled with codes, and I have no idea what they mean.

Call your hospital administrator and ask to review your bill with her. Ask her to translate every code on the bill for you. Then look it over again to be sure that you received the coded medications or services.

What is the likelihood that there are mistakes on my hospital bill?

An estimated 8 out of 10 hospital bills contain errors that on average can add an extra 25 percent to the tab. That is a lot of money. When you examine your bill, look for double charges, exorbitant charges for inexpensive items such as aspirin, and for items or services that you didn't receive. If possible, while in the hospital, jot down medications you receive and services rendered, so that you have a record to compare with the bill, when it comes.

I have gotten a huge medical bill, and I do not have the money to pay it. What can I do?

Depending on who sent the bill, call your hospital or your doctor. Explain the situation. In general, medical institutions tend to be less demanding and more lenient than a typical bank or credit card company, and many will accept a partial payment and/or suspend late fees and interest charges. If you stay in touch, chances are good your practitioner or hospital won't send the bill to a collection agency.

I am covered by insurance, but my insurance company will not pay my hospital bill, and the hospital is hounding me. Do I have to pay?
No, but you have to do some legwork. Make an appointment with the hospital administrator, show her copies of the claim forms you have submitted to the insurance company, and tell her that you cannot and will not pay the bill with your own resources. Many hospitals retain an ombudsman to help patients with insurers, so ask if one is available to help you.

Credit card companies have turned me down because of late payments reflected on my credit report. Most of these charges are related to an illness I had last year, and my HMO was supposed to pay them. The credit bureaus refuse to remove them. Help!
Unfortunately, this is a problem that's becoming commonplace. If I were you, I would contact the Federal Trade Commission (*www.ftc.gov*) to complain. If more and more people do this, maybe the FTC will act. But don't blame the credit bureau entirely—often, it is hard to tell if a collection account springs from unpaid medical bills or from a delinquent health insurance payment.

After you write to the FTC, assemble all the information you can about your insurance benefits and submit this material to the collection agency. It might also be worthwhile to contact the doctor or the hospital in question and explain that your credit is in jeopardy. And it is always worthwhile to provide documentation and an explanation—brief and concise—to your credit bureau. This will help to provide assurance that this is a one-time-only problem.

If my medical debt is so large that I feel I will never be able to pay it, can I get rid of it if I claim bankruptcy?
Probably, but you should consult a lawyer and get advice about your specific case.

IRS DEBT

I owe the IRS $5,000 in back taxes. What are my options if I do not have the money to pay?
You have only one option, other than to pay in full, and your eligibility for it depends on your never before having been delinquent with tax payments. If this is true, and if you owe the IRS $25,000 or less, you automatically qualify for what is called an installment plan. With an installment plan, you pay back taxes in installments over a period of months or years. If you owe more than $25,000, you may still qualify but you must fill out additional forms and may be assigned a revenue officer to oversee your account. If you have been in trouble with the IRS in the past, this is probably not an option. Otherwise, call your local IRS office.

I have been told that the IRS will sometimes

take less than the full amount if you offer to pay in full. Is this true?

Yes, in some cases the IRS will settle for less than the full amount owed. The official term for this kind of settlement is "offer in compromise." With an offer in compromise, you make one lump-sum payment and your debt is forgiven. There's a minimum you must offer, so please check with the IRS about this and other restrictions. Bottom line: It's a possibility.

If I file for bankruptcy, will my IRS debt be eliminated?

In most cases, the answer is no. But filing a Chapter 13 bankruptcy can help you to spread out your IRS payments over time, halt the accrual of interest charges and penalties, and suspend collection efforts, the garnishment of your wages, and the enforcement of any liens. So although filing for bankruptcy usually won't wipe the slate clean, it can provide some breathing room.

The only time an IRS debt can be considered for elimination is when every single one of the following conditions has been met. Even then, there's no guarantee, so please check with your tax adviser.

1. The taxes that you currently owe were assessed at least 240 days before you filed for bankruptcy.
2. The taxes you currently owe are based on a tax return that was filed at least two years before you filed for bankruptcy.
3. The taxes you currently owe are based on a tax return that should have been filed at least three years before you filed for bankruptcy.

4. The taxes you currently owe are not the result of a fraudulent return or an effort on your part to evade tax collection.

PREVENTING DEBT FROM JOB LOSS

How do I prepare for a job layoff or other income loss?

To make sure you are always prepared for the unknown, the first thing you need to do *after* paying off your credit card debt is establish an emergency fund to pay your monthly living expenses while you're not working. I want you to have enough cash saved for at least eight months. Yes, that's right: eight whole months of expenses in savings. I no longer believe that the three- to six-month time frame that has traditionally been recommended for a reserve fund is enough. For one thing, because the economy has changed and job layoffs have become more prevalent, the time it takes to find another job is getting longer and longer.

How much do I need to have saved for an emergency fund?

In setting up an emergency fund, the first problem you may encounter is not knowing how much it actually costs you per month to live. Suppose you bring home a monthly paycheck of $3,000. By the end of the month, it's all gone. You may think that is how much you need to live each month, but the truth is that you may be spending far more than that. This is why your credit card debt keeps rising. To find out how much you really do spend each month, please do the exercise below. I don't want you to guess or estimate, but to work from the real figures over the past year.

1. Go through your records and receipts for the last complete calendar year. This includes all checks, all credit card charges, and all ATM withdrawals and cash advances.
2. Make categories for each month, such as telephone, gasoline, food, utilities, vet bills, recreation fees, and babysitting. You will have to record *every* expenditure you made in those twelve months—if you no longer recall what it was for, put it under "miscellaneous."
3. After you've filled in all the categories for the entire 12 months, add up the total for each category.
4. For each category, divide by 12. This will give you the *average* amount you spend on each category per month.
5. Now add together the averages for every category. This will tell you what it costs you to live each month.

Keep in mind that you're doing this exercise to get an *average* amount you spend per month. There will be months when you spend less and months when you spend more. I want you to work from the average figure. Doing this exercise completely is one of the only ways you can really get a grip on the knowns of your life.

I find it impossible to save. How am I ever going to be able to set up an emergency fund for eight months' worth of expenses?

Well, my friend, if this is the case, the way for you to create an emergency fund is simply to take every extra penny you have, put it into a money-market account, and *save it there*. You have to make a decision here. Which means more to you: having a Starbucks coffee this afternoon and going to the movies tonight, or knowing that you and your loved ones will be protected even if you lose your job or get sick? Doing what is right for you—including making sure you'll have what you need in any situation—may mean giving up what you *want* right now to pay for what you *need* later on. I hope you decide to do this, for you'll be amazed at how much control over your life you will feel with your emergency fund standing behind you.

While you are figuring out how to save for an emergency fund, here are some actions you can take. If you own a home with equity in it, you might want to establish an equity line of credit with the amount that you need to get you through those eight months of expenses—just in case.

Equity is the value of your home above and beyond what you owe to the mortgage company. If your house has appreciated in value since you purchased it, your equity, or cash value, in that home has increased as well. You might be able to use that cash as an emergency fund through an equity line of credit that you arrange for with a bank or mortgage company. If you are eligible, the lender of this equity line of credit will provide you with a checkbook that will let you write checks against the equity in your home. You will pay interest on only the portion of the funds that you actually use. I want to be clear: tapping home equity is not ideal—you put your home at risk since it is the collateral for the loan. Please push yourself to build a bona fide emergency savings account so you do not need to tap your home equity.

If you do not own a home or if your home currently has no equity in it—or even if it does—I want you to take another step toward having the money you will need in case of an emergency. Here's what to do. Apply for and take out one or more credit cards with available credit limits that cover the amount that you will need for your eight months of living expenses. If you cannot get credit limits that cover the entire amount, come as close as you can. If the unforeseen happens—if you become ill or lose your job—you can use this credit by taking cash advances. That said, again, *please* do not use this money to incur debts if you are currently employed. That would be plunging yourself back into the unknown, big time. And understand that you will pay a very steep price for your cash advance; interest rates of 22 percent or more are common. Once again I need to stress this strategy is truly a last-resort suggestion. To repeat myself: doing everything you can today to start to build a real savings account at a federally insured bank or credit union is the best way to prepare for any of life's "what ifs."

I have been offered a voluntary severance. Should I take it?

This is what you need to consider: When you're offered a severance package, it normally gives you one to two weeks of pay for every year you have worked for a company. When you hear this, you may think, "Well, all right, they're going to give me $30,000 without my having to work for it; that sounds like a good deal. I'll take it." The question is: Will you get the whole $30,000 to put in your pocket? The answer is

no. For tax purposes, severance is considered income, just like your paycheck—and in addition to federal, state, and local income taxes, you'll have to pay Social Security and Medicare taxes on that money. By the time you get your check, you'll be lucky to get $20,000.

Still, if you think you can quickly find another job, this might look like found money to you. Be careful here. You have to understand that, if the economy is in a recession or there is a tight job market in your field, finding another job might not be as easy as you think. You have to run through these possibilities in your mind, along with your financial calculations. What would happen if you could not find another job—an equally good job—for eight months, a year, or a year and a half? What would you do for income once the severance runs out? Are you willing to spend your emergency fund, if you have it in place?

If you're considering taking a voluntary severance package offered by your company, please ask for a complete rundown of everything that's included in the package, especially company-paid health insurance and the right to keep your health insurance at your own expense under COBRA laws. (COBRA, short for the Consolidated Omnibus Budget Reconciliation Act of 1985, guarantees you the right to continue in your former employer's group health plan for up to eighteen months, at your own expense, even if you voluntarily leave a job.) Also ask whether you'll be eligible for unemployment insurance, should you need it. And please test the employment waters before your accept a severance offer, so you will have a good sense of whether you will in fact be able to land a new job quickly.

BANKRUPTCY

Who is bankruptcy for, exactly?

Bankruptcy is for anyone who can't pay back all his or her debts. There are different forms of bankruptcy for different circumstances. Two of the most common are Chapter 7, in which all your debts (except student loans and taxes) are excused, and Chapter 13, in which filing for bankruptcy gives you the opportunity to work out repayment schedules that are fair to you and your creditors, while protecting your assets from being seized by your creditors. In 2005, Congress passed a bankruptcy reform law that makes it much more difficult to file for Chapter 7 bankruptcy, the kind that allows you to entirely eliminate most debts; many more debtors would now have to file for Chapter 13 bankruptcy, where most debts—including credit card debts—must be repaid on a schedule worked out by a court. Still, bankruptcy can offer some debtors breathing room and a chance at reestablishing a responsible and less stressful financial life.

What is involuntary bankruptcy?

Involuntary bankruptcy is a situation in which your creditors, rather than you, file the petition for bankruptcy.

I feel terrible about considering bankruptcy, but years of unplanned medical bills have forced me to this point!

Terrible things—illness, death, natural disaster, or an unforeseen financial blow—can happen to anyone. Bankruptcy laws take this into consideration—in fact, they exist to help people in situations like these. If you've faced great adversity, you should be permitted to start over again, and declaring bankruptcy can help.

I'm deeply in debt, and I'm thinking of filing for bankruptcy. If I do, will the consequences be significant?

Filing for bankruptcy has serious, long-term emotional as well as financial consequences. It is not referred to as the "ten-year mistake" for nothing! I want to emphasize that bankruptcy is not to be taken lightly. I consider it an option to be acted upon reluctantly, after much thought, when—and only when—there is no other way out.

What kinds of questions should I ask myself before filing for bankruptcy?

Filing for bankruptcy may help you to resolve your debt problem, but it won't help those to whom you owe money. Imagine how you'd feel if someone who owed you a lot of money sent a letter saying, "Sorry, I'm bankrupt, I won't be paying you back." Ask yourself these questions: To whom do you owe money? Credit card companies? Friends? Businesses? Will you have to see or deal with any of these people or institutions after you file for bankruptcy and, if so, how will that make you feel? What financial hardship, if any, will you cause for others if you take such a step? Is there absolutely no other way for you to climb out of debt, little by little, with work and determination?

I'm in debt because of overspending on my credit cards. I really don't owe a lot, but I'm

thinking of filing for bankruptcy so I can start over. Is this a good idea?

Not under the new laws. Chances are, if your income is high enough, you will be obliged to pay back your credit card debts. Even if the debts will be forgiven, however, you must consider issues that go beyond your immediate financial difficulties. Please remember this: If you do not pay your debts, someone else will have to. In the case of debt to a bank or a credit card company, the institution in question will have to absorb the loss you incur and will probably, in one form or another, pass that loss along to the rest of us. For example, your bankruptcy could affect the scoring system that credit bureaus use, which might mean that someone you don't know will be turned down for credit.

Declaring bankruptcy is one of the most important financial steps you will ever consider taking. It will bring a whole new set of complications and difficulties into your already complicated and difficult life.

First, think about what declaring bankruptcy will do to your credit report. If you declare bankruptcy, you will find it hard to get credit, and any offers will come with extremeley high interest rates and fees. It will be difficult to rent an apartment, buy a house, or rent a car without a credit card. It is very likely that you will lose property you had counted on keeping for a long time. Future job opportunities may be affected too, which could lead to future financial problems. And in many cases, someone else— perhaps a friend, a spouse, or a cosigner—will be saddled with your debts.

Before filing for bankruptcy please under-stand the magnitude of what you are about to do. Please understand the sacrifice you are making, as well as what you will gain. Please understand what you are asking of others. Finally, if you decide that this is the only way out, I hope you will start over from a place of pride and courage, not one of shame.

Is there a minimum amount of debt you can be in before filing?

No, there is not. An attorney I know sees people who file for Chapter 7 and Chapter 13 bankruptcy with debts of as little as $5,000. I wouldn't recommend this, since your debts should be large enough to justify the legal expenses you will incur as well as the long-term consequences of bankruptcy.

Should I contact a lawyer before I consider filing for bankruptcy?

Definitely. Before you do anything, check with an attorney who can explain the current state of the law, the pros and cons of filing for bankruptcy, and the differences between the kinds of bankruptcy.

TYPES OF BANKRUPTCY

There are several kinds of personal bankruptcy, but Chapter 7 and Chapter 13 are by far the most common. Chapter 12 bankruptcy applies to farmers, and Chapter 11 bankruptcy is often used by major corporations that cannot repay their debts.

CHAPTER 7 BANKRUPTCY

What is Chapter 7 bankruptcy?

Until now, Chapter 7 bankruptcy has been the most common type of bankruptcy. Under Chapter 7, a court-appointed trustee assembles all your assets, sells them for cash, and then allocates and distributes the money to your creditors. You can hold on to any assets that are exempt under federal law and/or the laws of the state you live in. Basically, Chapter 7 is a way for you to erase most of your debts—but not without giving up some of your property.

What qualifications must I meet to file for Chapter 7 bankruptcy?

You must meet an income qualification. According to the new federal law, if over the course of the next five years you are expected to have enough income to repay 25 percent or more of your unsecured debts, including credit card debt, child support debt, medical debt, and IRS debt, you would be *unable* to file for Chapter 7 bankruptcy and would be steered to Chapter 13 instead. You will also have to get credit counseling with an agency approved by the United States Trustee's office before filing, and additional counseling once your bankruptcy case is over.

How do I go about filing for Chapter 7?

First, you must fill out a number of forms and applications listing your income, the amounts and kinds of your debts, and what assets you possess—house, land, car—above and beyond your debts. (You can find these forms in books about bankruptcy published by Nolo Press, *www.nolo.com.*) You must divulge complete financial information in a petition for Chapter 7 bankruptcy. If you forget a debt, or leave one out, it may not be erased. Even worse, if you fail to list all your assets you could later be liable for fraud.

After I finish filling out the forms and applications, what happens?

After completing the paperwork, you file a petition for bankruptcy with the court (for a fee), and a court date will be set. Your creditors will be informed that you have filed for Chapter 7. You will then be appointed an impartial trustee, a person charged by the court to oversee your bankruptcy plan.

How much will filing for Chapter 7 bankruptcy cost?

The court fee is about $300 and additional fees can cost another $1,000 or more. If you can't pay this amount all at once, you can pay it in installments. In addition, you should hire an attorney. If you cannot afford the services of an attorney, look in your phone book under free or discount legal services. Legally you can always represent yourself at your hearing, but it is never a good idea to act as your own lawyer.

Once I have filed for bankruptcy, will creditors and collection agencies stop breathing down my neck?

In most cases, yes. The filing of your petition automatically stays, or stops, your creditors from garnishing your wages, emptying your checking or savings account, pursuing you, or attempting to sue you for nonpayment. But this should not be the main reason you file for bankruptcy.

What are the responsibilities of the court-appointed trustee?

The trustee is responsible for overseeing all your financial affairs after you have petitioned for Chapter 7. A month or so after you have filed, you will attend a short hearing attended by your creditors and your trustee. This hearing is a question-and-answer period in which the creditors are given a good look at what you own and at the extent of your debts. After the hearing, the trustee will arrange to sell off your nonexempt property. This could include some equity in your home and your car, a portion of your property, and a certain amount of cash. Your trustee will then divide the proceeds among your lenders and creditors.

Are all debts considered the same in bankruptcy court?

No. By law, debts are divided into two categories: dischargeable and non-dischargeable. A court will determine how the law applies to your debts.

What kinds of debts can I get rid of during a Chapter 7 bankruptcy hearing?

After the bankruptcy proceeding, you will not have to pay what is known as dischargeable debt. The most common kinds of dischargeable debt in a Chapter 7 hearing include back rent you owe a landlord; outstanding utility bills, including gas, electricity, and phone; some court judgments against you (but not child and/or spousal support, which cannot be discharged); credit card, charge card, department store card, and gasoline card bills; documented loans from your friends or family; any outstanding legal or medical bills; and most, if not all, unsecured loans ("unsecured" here means debts that have no collateral attached to them).

What debts cannot be charged off in bankruptcy?

You are responsible for what's called non-dischargeable debt, including any loan that was issued, funded, guaranteed, or insured by a government entity or a nonprofit corporation (such as taxes, government fines, and student loans). You are also liable for any debt that the court determines you incurred due to irresponsible behavior or that was incurred long before you got into general financial trouble. Also, if you bought expensive items or took out a cash advance right before filing for bankruptcy, these debts will be considered non-dischargeable. You may be responsible for any secured debts—i.e., debts with collateral—and any debts arising out of trouble with the law. If you were sued for personal injury while you were driving drunk, or if you owe any debts because of traffic violations, fraud, larceny, embezzlement, assault, or libel, you will still be responsible for these debts after a bankruptcy proceeding. You will also be liable for any alimony or child-support debt. Your non-dischargeable debts will be treated as if no bankruptcy had been filed, so a creditor can seek payment by any legal means.

What property will I lose if I file for Chapter 7?

The types of property you stand to lose (called "nonexempt" property) depend on the laws of your state. Among other things, however, you could very well lose (if applicable) your second home, your second car, any stock or bond certificates, CDs, money-market funds, and any valuable collections (stamps, coins) or heirlooms, as well as part of your marital estate.

What is "exempt" property?

Exempt property is property that you get to keep after you file for a Chapter 7 bankruptcy. There are state exemptions and federal exemptions, and you can choose under which auspices you want to file after considering which offers you a higher allowance. Typically, you can keep your home up to a certain dollar value (in California, for example, the state exemption for a homestead allowance can range from $50,000 to $150,000): your clothes, your furniture and appliances, your personal effects, your jewelry, your retirement plans and life insurance, and your income from Social Security, disability, unemployment, welfare, and/or alimony. If you bought your car with an auto loan, then it is considered a secured debt that cannot be discharged unless you give the car back; in other words, if you want to keep your car, you'll have to keep paying your car loan. There are cases in which you may wish to "reaffirm" that debt.

Are my IRA and 401(k) protected during a Chapter 7 filing?

Yes. 401(k) plans, company pension plans, and other ERISA-qualified plans are generally exempted from the bankruptcy estate, and a 2005 Supreme Court ruling also protects IRA assets from bankruptcy.

What is a reaffirmation?

Depending on your financial and personal circumstances, you may want to keep possession of a piece of property you feel you cannot do without. If so, you may want to look into the possibility of reaffirming the debt. This means that, in spite of the bankruptcy proceedings, you agree to pay all or a portion of the money to the creditor in question. In return, the creditor promises that he will not repossess your car, or whatever else it is that you are anxious to hold on to. Before you take this step, however, I would strongly advise that you contact an attorney to make sure you know all your rights.

I don't have any assets to hand over to the trustee. Can I still file for Chapter 7?

Yes. In fact, most Chapter 7 cases involve persons who have few, if any, assets to liquidate to satisfy their creditors' claims.

What is an insolvency period?

The insolvency period is the three-month period before you filed for bankruptcy. This is also known as a look-back period. A trustee or a judge will examine your payments during this period to see whether you showed preference to some creditors. For example, did you repay your aunt Milly the $500 you owed her but claim poverty when Visa and American Express asked for what you owed them? If it is found that you engaged in avoidable preference, the money will be returned to the court and distributed proportionally among your creditors.

My property has been liquidated and the proceeds distributed. Now what?

Now the court will arrange for a final hearing. At that point, it will usually discharge your remaining debts.

What does "discharge my debts" mean?

Discharging your debts is another way of saying your dischargeable debts are over and done with—history. You no longer owe your creditors anything, and they are forbidden by law from trying to collect any unpaid percentage of the original debt. You are legally off the hook. Usually, under Chapter 7, debt is discharged within six months, often within half that time. You'll probably be informed by mail of this discharge.

Can a discharge ever be revoked?

In certain circumstances, yes, but it's rare. A discharge can be revoked if for some reason the discharge was obtained fraudulently, or if the debtor failed to disclose any property during his financial disclosure.

Are there any grounds for denying a discharge?

Again, it's rare, but the court can deny a discharge if the debtor has not kept adequate financial records, if he has perjured himself before the court, or if he has concealed, destroyed, or failed to note any property that because of the bankruptcy petition is now in the court's jurisdiction.

A creditor of mine is trying to collect a debt that the court has discharged. What should I do?

In some cases, this is considered civil contempt.

Discharge is permanent. File a motion with the court that handled your bankruptcy filing, reporting the creditor's action and requesting that your case be reopened to look into this matter.

Can I be fired for filing bankruptcy?

Legally, no.

A friend of mine who once declared bankruptcy recently applied for a job. When her prospective employer looked at her credit report, he turned her down on the basis of the bankruptcy, even though that was 13 years ago. Is this legal?

It may not be legal, but it's a fact of life. Think about it: 1.4 million people claim bankruptcy every year. It's virtually impossible for credit bureaus to keep up with the record-keeping required to make sure all the negative information is removed when the time's up in each and every case. So it's up to you to see that your information is up-to-date and accurately reflects your credit standing.

Can filing a Chapter 7 bankruptcy stop a bank from foreclosing on my house?

It depends on your state's laws. Please check. Filing a Chapter 13 bankruptcy *will* postpone foreclosure indefinitely, as long as you resume making monthly payments on your mortgage. Check your state's laws to find out if personal residences are exempted from liquidation during bankruptcy.

After many years of struggle, my husband is declaring bankruptcy. Should he file alone, or should we file together?

The answer to your question depends on many

factors, including whether or not you own your property together and, if so, what type of property it is. If you file together, you will erase your own debts, your husband's debts, and all your jointly held marital debts. If your husband files by himself, his individual debts will be wiped out, and so will his share of your joint debts. But that still leaves you liable for your share of your joint debts. Further, in community-property states, where husbands and wives equally own all property earned or received during the marriage, your share in the property is considered part of the bankruptcy estate even if you don't file jointly with your husband during his bankruptcy.

What about property I owned alone, before my marriage?

Property you own separately is not affected by your husband's bankruptcy, unless you've put him on the title or commingled those assets with him.

CHAPTER 13 BANKRUPTCY

What is Chapter 13 bankruptcy?

Chapter 13 bankruptcy is for people who are employed or are earning a regular income from a pension, an annuity, or some other source but who are unable to pay the full extent of their debts. Chapter 13 is a repayment plan executed under the supervision of a court, and it involves an agreement on your part to pay back a portion of the money you owe, based on the amount of your income and the size of your

debts. Because of the new bankruptcy law, more people who once would have filed Chapter 7 bankruptcy are being directed into Chapter 13 bankruptcy.

Do I file for Chapter 13 in the same way I would file for Chapter 7?

Yes. You fill out the same papers, pay a filing fee—usually about $274—and get a court-appointed trustee. You will also need to attend credit counseling with an agency approved by the United States Trustee's office. But, in addition, you have to submit to the court a plan for the repayment of your unsecured debts, including credit card debt. The court will either accept or reject this plan. In the case of secured debts, you agree to pay back, at the minimum, the amount of the claim that the creditor is willing to accept, or else you agree to surrender the collateral.

Do I pay the money directly to the trustee?

Yes. After you have filled out a form listing your assets and income and set up a confirmation hearing, your court-appointed trustee will begin making payments to all your creditors according to the terms of the court-approved repayment schedule.

Do all my debts count here, or are there exceptions, as was the case with Chapter 7?

Certain debts cannot be renegotiated in a Chapter 13 bankruptcy, including child support, alimony, and local, state, and federal taxes. You also continue to be responsible for any and all regular mortgage payments. If you miss a payment, the lender can have your home removed from under the bankruptcy and foreclose on it.

How long does Chapter 13 last?

It can take three, sometimes four, years before your debts are discharged. As with Chapter 7, you will need to attend credit counseling after your case, as well.

Can anybody file for Chapter 13?

If your secured debt is less than $1,010,650 and your unsecured debt is less than $336,900 (whether you are single or married), you may be eligible to file for Chapter 13 (these figures are accurate as of the year 2009). Stockbrokers and commodity brokers are legally prohibited from filing for Chapter 13.

What if I can't keep up with my Chapter 13 repayment plan? Does this mean I have to file for Chapter 7?

If you find that you cannot honor your repayment schedule under Chapter 13—if you lost your job, fell ill, or got a divorce, for example—you should contact your court-appointed trustee immediately. Depending on your situation, the trustee may be able to get the court to cut you some slack, particularly if your inability to repay your debts is only temporary. If it looks like it could be long-term, the court has several options: It could alter your repayment schedule to reflect your new circumstances, it could discharge your remaining debts on the basis of hardship, or it could convert your Chapter 13 bankruptcy to a Chapter 7 bankruptcy.

A COMPARISON OF CHAPTER 7 AND CHAPTER 13

Which is better, Chapter 7 or Chapter 13 bankruptcy?

I think you mean, "Which is less bad?" The answer to this depends on your financial situation. Each form of bankruptcy, Chapter 7 and Chapter 13, has its pros and cons. If you have really serious financial problems, no doubt you will prefer a straight Chapter 7 proceeding, if you can get one.

What are the relative advantages of Chapter 7 bankruptcy?

From start to finish, from the date you file to the date your debts are discharged, Chapter 7 is faster to complete than Chapter 13. And it gives people a "fresh start" (though not without a lot of drawbacks, as I've mentioned). In a Chapter 7 bankruptcy, the amount of dischargeable, unsecured debt, such as credit card debt, you can erase from your life is unlimited, provided all assets and debts were declared and there is no suspicion of fraud in your filing.

What are the relative disadvantages of Chapter 7 bankruptcy?

The disadvantages of Chapter 7 bankruptcy are numerous. First of all, you have to give up your nonexempt property—including, say, a second home or second car—hand it over to the court, and allow it to be sold. Even after you file under Chapter 7, some of your debts may survive (those deemed secured and non-dischargeable, such as a car loan, and those that a creditor feels were incurred with the intention to defraud the creditor), and with respect to those debts you can still be approached by collection agencies. If a friend or a family member cosigned any of your loans, he or she will now be stuck with your debt—which is not at all nice. Once you have filed for Chapter 7, it is very difficult to reverse the process. And, of course, like any bankruptcy, a Chapter 7 bankruptcy will not look good on your credit history.

What are the relative advantages of Chapter 13 bankruptcy?

The main advantage of Chapter 13 is that you get to keep all your property, whether it is exempt or nonexempt. Your creditors can't garnish your wages or send collectors after you, and you are protected against foreclosure. In Chapter 13, you are allowed to separate your debts by class. Different classes of creditors are due different percentages of payment. You also have a lot longer to pay back your debts than you do under a Chapter 7 (remember, not all of your debts may be dischargeable under Chapter 7). And if you arrange to pay back your debts in full, your creditors can't go after anyone who has cosigned a loan.

What are the relative disadvantages of filing Chapter 13?

Your total debt, secured and unsecured, has to be under $1,347,550, as noted earlier (less than $1,010,650 of secured debt and $336,900 of unsecured debt). You pay back your debts out of your own income, which can tie up your income for a long time. If debts survive after your bankruptcy is closed, you have to keep on paying back those debts. You could find yourself in this situation for many years, which could have a serious effect on your future income.

What are the tax obligations of a person who files for bankruptcy?

Your tax obligations will depend on whether you have filed under Chapter 7 or Chapter 13. If you file under Chapter 7, this petition creates a separate, taxable bankruptcy estate consisting of all assets that belonged to you before the filing date. Your trustee is responsible for preparing and filing any taxes attached to this estate. You, the individual debtor, are responsible for any taxes that are not connected to the estate (i.e., your income taxes). If you file under Chapter 13, this petition does not create a separate taxable estate, and you continue to pay taxes as you did before you filed for bankruptcy.

How will my bankruptcy affect my credit report? Am I wiping the slate clean?

"Wiping the slate clean" is a misleading phrase because your credit report will show that you filed for bankruptcy for seven to ten years after the fact. This puts all lenders on notice that you are a risky person to lend money to.

If I claim bankruptcy, does that mean I will not be able to get another credit card?

Years ago, that is exactly what it would have meant. Nowadays, however, some credit card companies actually seek out people who have claimed bankruptcy and offer them credit cards. "What's wrong with that?" you may ask. Well, once you have claimed bankruptcy, you cannot do so again for a period of years. Within that time, if you get into trouble with your credit cards, there is no way you can get out of paying your debts.

How often can I file for bankruptcy?

I wouldn't make a habit out of it! Legally, however, you can file for Chapter 7 bankruptcy once every six years. Most Chapter 13 plans have three- to five-year payouts, so while technically you can file Chapter 13 as often as needed, it is unlikely you'll be filing more often than the term of your payment schedule.

2
Financial
Intimacy

PEOPLE FIRST, THEN MONEY

Falling in love is simple—or so it often seems in retrospect. Sooner or later, however, disagreements crop up, and love becomes a much more complicated business. Can you guess one of the most common subjects of disagreement between couples, married and unmarried? No surprise here—it's money. Everywhere I go, I hear the same complaint: "We're fighting about money." Arguments about money are the catalyst for more separations and divorces than you can imagine. Why? Because people's attitudes and fears about their money give it power—and the ability to wreak havoc on the most important relationships in their lives.

Yet there's a simple answer. I have said it before and I'll say it again: Place people first, money second. Whether you are falling in love, living with someone, getting married, getting divorced, or starting your life over again following the death of someone you love, the people in your life come first. This doesn't mean that money has no relevance to love, however.

Of all the kinds and degrees of intimacy that exist in the world—physical, emotional, social, professional, or domestic—financial intimacy is one of the most satisfying and perhaps the hardest to achieve. If you and your partner or spouse haven't walked carefully through all the money matters that might come up in time, I promise you that money will one day become an obstacle in your relationship. When financial change comes to you—and, for better or worse, it will come—it will have the potential to become a minefield of undisclosed expectations or fears.

The following questions and answers aren't meant to scare you away from making a commitment to the person you love. They are meant to demonstrate just how important—and how sacred—a lifetime commitment is and to explain the role that money plays in making it work.

EMOTIONS AND MONEY

Are people really so different from one another when it comes to money?

Yes, they are. How they are different can be very hard to see when you're in love and love is new, and can be very painful to discover after you've made a commitment. But to get an idea of some potential sore points, consider how you've handled your own money as a single person. Have you sometimes spent money that you needed for other expenses and obligations? Put off saving for the future? Occasionally let your bills pile up? These things may not strike you as significant, but when a second person, a fiancé or a spouse, has a stake in your finances and you have a stake in his or hers, undisciplined habits, thoughtless spending, or even incompatible views on how to manage money can strike at the core of the safety and security you want to feel in a relationship.

How can my girlfriend's and my different attitudes toward money potentially be damaging to our relationship?

Start to pay attention and you'll see. Every day, probably without realizing it, you observe how your girlfriend behaves with and reacts to money. You witness the big things, like how she handles her debts, and the little things, like whether she is generous or cautious when leaving a tip. Believe me, if some of the things you've noticed irk you now, they will irk you more over time. In the early stages of love, people tend to overlook what they don't like about each other's management of money; the subject seems at once both too petty and too important for discussion. So most people don't mention it at all. If you find yourself in this situation, you are giving money the ultimate power: the power of silence.

What are the most common problems couples face concerning money?

Most couples *think* they have problems with money for one or more of the following reasons: one partner spends too much while the other spends too little; one partner doesn't care enough about money while the other cares too much; or one partner has too much money, and therefore too much power, while the other has too little. Sound familiar?

In my experience, however, the problems couples face have little to do with money itself. They have more to do with how partners feel about money. Since most of us have been taught to view money as a kind of report card, signaling

how well we're doing relative to others, we tend to measure our self-worth by our earning potential, the size and location of our houses, the clothes we wear, the cars we drive, the schools we send our children to, our bank balances, and so on—and not by our thoughts, feelings, and deeds. We value the financial results of our actions more highly than we value the actions themselves or their effect on other people. This is especially true if we have come to believe, as so many of us have, that money is synonymous with security—that money and money alone will provide for us and keep us safe. When our perceptions and priorities are thus skewed and we put money before people, *that* is when we encounter problems in relationships. Talking about money is an antidote. It lays bare some of these underlying issues, and that's how problems can be prevented or solved.

What kinds of financial issues should my fiancé and I discuss before we get married?

You should talk openly about your respective attitudes toward spending, debt, and saving. Be sure not to simply ask (or think), "Who's going to pay for what?" although that's an important question we'll get to later. You and your fiancé should ask each other—and frankly answer—questions about how well you share, how much you tend to spend and on what, how much you save, how you invest, and what your long-term financial goals are.

Start by discussing how each of you feels about basic issues of financial responsibility. Will you support each other in adversity? Do you both view any obligations you may have to your respective families in the same way? How do you feel about respective responsibilities to ex-spouses or children from a former relationship, if any? On a more mundane level, who will manage the household bill-paying and bookkeeping?

Be candid about your past and present. Is one of you in debt—carrying a large credit card balance, perhaps, or a student loan that hasn't been paid off? As a couple, what will you do about that? Does one of you have a bad credit rating, and if so, how will you work together to repair it?

Discuss the future. Do you plan to pool your money or wish to keep part, or all, of it separate? What will happen if one of you gets a job offer that requires the household to move—how will you decide whose job takes precedence? If you plan to have children, what will you do if one of you wants to stay home with them? Do you see eye to eye about the financial decisions involved in child-rearing, such as the costs of private versus public schools? And even though retirement may seem a long way off, do you agree about the importance of investing for the future? Do you have similar goals and dreams for your later years? Are your investment styles in sync?

If you don't start thinking and talking about these issues now, they are likely to become more complicated and difficult to discuss as time goes on. Though you may not be in full agreement on every issue before your marriage, your relationship will be stronger for having talked through some of your similarities, differences, and concerns.

You say our investment styles should be in sync. Why?

People have different tolerance levels for risk. Some are very conservative when it comes to in-

vesting. They want steady growth and a consistent income over the years. Others are willing to accept potential short-term losses on investments that promise greater returns in the long run. Still others are willing to invest in something that carries significant risk if there's potential for a very large gain. But far too many people haven't discussed how much risk they and their partners are willing to take with their shared wealth.

What if my future partner's attitude toward money is very different from mine? Do you believe that people can change their financial attitudes and habits simply by talking about them?

Yes, I do. For one thing, if you can state clearly and frankly what you find admirable, on the one hand, or problematic and troubling, on the other, about the way your loved one deals with money, then your point of view is known to both of you. Second, once you start talking honestly about money, you will be better able to understand the basis of each other's attitudes and behavior. This will help you both to compromise on issues of money management. For example, if you know that a partner who seems to be unreasonably reluctant to spend money is probably simply afraid of losing what he or she has—believing that there isn't enough wealth in the world to go around—you may be more patient in your approach to him or her. If you're aware that a fast-spending partner is attempting to use money to compensate for a lack of self-esteem, you and your partner can work together to resolve this deeper issue. The goal in every case is to gradually build a financial relationship that satisfies both of you. Remember, though, that worthwhile changes often come slowly. Promise each other you will keep your dialogue about money going.

My fiancé always ends up getting angry when we talk about money. How come?

The *way* people talk about money—their expressions, their tones of voice, their timing—can be as revealing as what is actually said. Remember, for most people, talking about money is an intimate and unfamiliar act. If your fiancé gets angry when talking about money, that in itself is a very important key to his feelings about money and may be, at least partly, a result of the way he was raised.

How does a person's family background affect his or her feelings about money?

How people have been raised has a huge effect on how they view and manage money. The odds that you and your fiancé come from identical financial family backgrounds are pretty slim. I'm not talking about how much money your family or your partner's family had when you were growing up; I'm talking about how the subject of money was handled. Was money a source of anxiety, embarrassment, or conflict? Was it discussed openly? In urgent whispers? Not at all? Did one parent overspend, while the other watched every penny? Did the family pretend it had more money than it did? Do you or does your partner feel embarrassed about your economic background? Any number of childhood experiences can create fear, shame, or anger about money, any of which can inhibit open discussion and wise management. My advice, once again: Keep talking, calmly and compassionately, until you get all this stuff out in the open. Get to know the person you're going to marry in a financial way, and you will know him or her better than you ever imagined. The same, of course, applies to you.

LIVING TOGETHER

I am about to move in with my boyfriend of five years. Do I need to prepare myself financially for this?

Absolutely. Today, many couples—young couples just starting out, older couples who prefer not to marry, and same-sex couples—are living together, accumulating wealth together, and buying property together, and they require many of the same financial and legal protections that married couples have. In some instances, they require added protection, since—if they eventually split up and divide their assets—they have few of the automatic legal protections that married couples have.

A note: Some unmarried couples choose not to marry because they dislike the prospect of being bound by a legal contract. Some think marriage is just a formality; others have been married and burned, and don't want to make the same mistake again. Whatever your reasons for not marrying, you should be aware that without a written agreement, you may be legally vulnerable in a number of ways.

How am I vulnerable if I live with someone without an agreement?

To take a typical case, consider what might happen if you and your live-in partner decide to buy a home together. If your partner is making a larger contribution to the down payment than you are, it may seem to make sense to hold the property solely in your partner's name. But if you split up, guess who gets the house? Your partner does. Or say that both names are on the title, although you contributed a larger amount for the down payment. What happens if you split up? You could lose your larger share and only get half. Or perhaps you assume you have the rights of joint tenancy with your partner—meaning that, if your partner dies, 100 percent of the house will go to you. But when he dies, you discover that you misread the title and that instead of being a joint tenant, you are a tenant-in-common. This means that your partner's share of the house goes directly to his estate, which he may have left to his younger brother. By law, the brother can move in with you. Property can become a troublesome issue without a contract.

Are there any other problems I can get into without a contract?

Yes, especially if you separate. If you have been financially dependent on your live-in partner, for example, without a contract you will have no legal right to receive ongoing financial support from him or her. Also, you may have no right to share in any of the assets your partner may have accumulated, perhaps with your help, during the years you lived together. This may or may not come as a surprise to you, but it has caused real grief to many longtime partners who assumed they would be provided for, but weren't.

Other issues can arise. What if your partner becomes sick, so sick that he or she can't make medical decisions? He or she may have expressed to you a firm wish not to have any extraordinary medical measures taken. Well, guess what? If your partner's closest blood relative wants to have him or her hooked up to a ventilator, you have no legal right to stop it. And what if you and your partner have agreed that you will inherit each other's estates in the event either of you dies? Without a will, in the eyes of the court, you are not your partner's legal heir, as you would have been if you were married.

Is there any way I can protect myself financially while my partner and I are living together?

Yes. But before we get into cohabitation agreements, there are a few basic things that you should do. First, make all your financial expectations and intentions very clear to your partner. If you give him or her $500 as a birthday gift, write the word "gift" on the check so that, in the worst-case scenario, a court will not view this check as evidence of a promise to support your partner. If you make a loan that you expect to be repaid, write "loan" on the check. Never put money in a joint account just because you think it will add trust or convenience to your relationship, and don't put both names on a title unless you truly want to be *joint* owners, by which I mean fifty-fifty.

Why do you advise against putting my partner's name on my accounts?

If your partner ever filed a palimony lawsuit against you, a joint account or joint ownership of property could be viewed by the court as powerful evidence of an understanding between the two of you to share everything. In some states, including California, the courts make decisions on the validity of cohabitation agreements if there seems to be an "implied" agreement between the two partners. (I'll say more about this later.) In other states, a written agreement is required.

My boyfriend and I are about to move in together and probably will get married. Should we merge our expense money or keep it in separate accounts?

You may want to merge the money you earmark for common expenses that you fund on a monthly basis. Otherwise, I'd advise you to keep separate accounts for your individual personal expenses, savings, and investments. I recommend this for legal reasons, but I also suggest that married couples keep personal discretionary money in individual accounts. The reason: You two are individuals with separate identities. Your money is an integral part of who you are. When you marry or live together, you're creating a new, third entity—a partnership—that deserves a bank account of its own. Apart from the financial obligations you assume together, you each have a right to decide how and when to spend the money you've earned.

Should we have joint credit cards?

No. Keep separate credit cards, so as to establish your own credit record, now and for the future.

What sort of account do you suggest my fiancé and I open jointly?

You and your fiancé can open a money market account with a good mutual fund company and tap into it every month for your joint expenses, or you can do the same by opening a checking account linked to a savings account at a federally insured bank or credit union. The savings account will earn a higher rate of interest; when you need money to pay the bills you can easily transfer money from the savings account to the checking account at an ATM or using online banking.

How should we determine who contributes what to cover our monthly expenses?

I always recommend making your respective contributions in proportion to your current wages, salary, and other income. Here's how to do this: Let's say that your joint expenses, including rent, utilities, food and other household goods, entertainment, and maintenance will come to about $3,500 a month. (When estimating your monthly costs, always add an extra 10 percent for unexpected expenses, now and down the line.) Add together the monthly income that you and your partner each bring home, after taxes and retirement savings. Let's say that figure is $7,000. Now divide the total of your joint expenses, $3,500, by the total of your joint take-home pay ($7,000). This gives you the percentage (50 percent) of your take-home pay that each of you should contribute to your joint account—that might be $3,000 for you, and $500 for your partner. Of that $3,500, you'll use $3,000 to pay your bills and $500 for emergencies.

COHABITATION AGREEMENTS

How can I avoid legal and financial complications if I am planning to live with someone?

There is a very good answer to that question. I

suggest that you and your partner ask your lawyers to draw up a cohabitation agreement. This is simply a written document that states your mutual rights and obligations with respect to joint and separate property, as well as any other financial obligations or expectations you wish to agree upon in advance of moving in together. If you discover that you and your partner have different ideas about the financial aspects of living together, it's better that you find out now rather than later.

Can't we just draft this agreement on my computer? Does it have to be prepared by an attorney?

You can draft a cohabitation agreement yourselves, but please have your attorneys review it. Attorneys can identify any loopholes or mistakes of law. Plus, if one partner alone creates the agreement and it's not reviewed by legal counsel, the terms of the agreement could later be construed by a court against the partner who drew it up.

Should we each have our own attorney?

Yes—for the same reason people should have separate attorneys when drawing up a prenuptial agreement (more about these later). If your cohabitation agreement comes before a court, the court might question its validity if it appears that either one of you has not been fairly represented by counsel. This is especially true if a lot of money is at stake.

Do courts really honor cohabitation agreements?

Almost every state in the union honors *written* co-

habitation agreements. Many states will consider oral or implied agreements, but since memories often differ during the dissolution of a relationship, it can be very hard to prove a point made by an oral agreement.

What is an implied agreement?

The court defines an implied agreement as a pattern of actions or conduct suggesting an unspoken understanding between the two parties in question. Such actions or conduct may include owning joint property, maintaining a shared checking or savings account, or a history of one partner working and the other staying at home. If you have been financially supporting the woman you live with for some time and the two of you break up, a court could find that the two of you had an "understanding" that this state of affairs would continue—even if no such understanding was put into words.

How about an oral versus a written agreement?

An oral agreement is exactly that—an actual exchange of spoken words with a clear agreement reached. It's better to have it on paper—that's my advice. Written agreements are superior to oral and implied agreements. They are more specific about date and content, and they provide more peace of mind. In the worst case, they will clarify for a court the nature of your intentions when you drew up the agreement. Even better, they offer you and the person you love a chance to go over your finances with a fine-tooth comb, eliminating possible future areas of disagreement or misunderstanding.

SAME-SEX COHABITATION

What's the legal difference between same-sex cohabitation and heterosexual cohabitation?
Legally, there's no difference. As unmarried partners, you, like unmarried heterosexual couples, lack the legal protections that marriage automatically confers, so you have to create these legal safeguards for yourselves.

Remember, you cannot rely on a family court to protect you or assist in dividing up your property if you separate; there is no jurisdiction in this country that will automatically recognize your inheritance rights. Further, if you have children, you cannot collect child support and you cannot appeal to the judicial system for custody or visitation (except in those few places where a same-sex partner can adopt his or her partner's children). Even more than heterosexual couples—who can, after all, get married in a pinch—gay couples in serious relationships should have some or all of the following: wills, living trusts, health-care proxies, durable powers of attorney, and written agreements about the disposal of jointly owned property. Though some of these agreements may not be fully enforceable in many jurisdictions, they do provide a framework to guide your actions at times when you may be emotionally overwrought and unable to make sound, fair decisions.

In 2004, Massachusetts became the first state to grant same-sex couples the right to marry, which entitles the couple to all rights under state law. Marriage is the only category that offers full recognition of spousal rights for same-sex couples and heterosexual couples equally. As of December 2009 other states that recognize same-sex marriage include Connecticut, Iowa, New Hampshire (effective January 2010), and Vermont. Other states may adopt similar laws in the future.

It's especially important for you to put everything in writing. In just about every state, written *and* oral contracts between unmarried couples—including same-sex couples—are, hypothetically anyway, legally binding. But oral contracts are hard to prove, and in some parts of the country, a gay or lesbian partner may find it exceedingly difficult to enforce the terms of an oral or an implied agreement in court.

How should we draft a cohabitation agreement?
There are several excellent books to help you get started, including *The Living Together Kit* by attorneys Ralph Warner, Toni Ihara, and Frederick Hertz; *Legal Affairs: Essential Advice for Same-Sex Couples,* by Frederick Hertz; and *A Legal Guide for Lesbian and Gay Couples* by attorneys Hayden Curry, Denis Clifford, Robin Leonard, and Frederick Hertz. Further, if you have significant assets, you should consult a qualified attorney. I know a gay couple who went so far as to make a videotape of themselves stating their intentions in front of a lawyer, to be sure that no one in either of their families could challenge the rights they had granted to each other.

I am in a same-sex relationship, and my partner and I own property together. What happens in the event we break up?

If the property is held jointly, either party can petition the court to sell the property and divide the proceeds of the sale according to the terms of an agreement, or fifty-fifty in the absence of an agreement. The partners can also try to reach an amicable agreement between themselves by putting the property on the market and dividing the proceeds of the sale, or one partner can buy out the other's share.

My partner's name is on the title of the house we are living in together, but I have been paying the mortgage. Now we are breaking up. Do I have any rights to the property?

The property will go to the partner who holds title, unless the unnamed party can claim that he or she had an agreement with the partner to share the asset. (In some states, only written agreements can supersede the title.) The dispute will be resolved in the ordinary "business" division of the local court, rather than the family law division, and contract law rather than family law will apply.

If my partner and I haven't bought property together, are we financially obligated toward each other in any way?

It depends on whether you've signed an agreement specifying obligations to each other. If you wish to formalize a set of financial obligations, it's better to have a written contract.

Can my same-sex partner and I enter into a common-law marriage?

No. As of this writing, common-law marriages don't extend to same-sex couples. And so far, only Massachusetts, Connecticut, Iowa, New Hampshire, and Vermont offer formal recognition of same-sex marriages.

COMMON-LAW MARRIAGES

What exactly is a common-law marriage?

Some states—currently there are 15 states and the District of Columbia—legally recognize that a man and a woman who have lived together for a sustained period of time, and who think of themselves and present themselves to the public as man and wife, are joined in "common-law" marriage within that state and are entitled to the protections of marriage. Since the marriage is not formally recorded, however, the burden of proof is with the couple—or one partner.

What kind of proof do you need to show that you are in a common-law marriage?

The laws differ from state to state. In general, partners must prove that they have the mental capacity to marry, and they must have lived together under one roof for a significant period of time (this period is not defined in any state). They must share the same last name, refer to each other as "my wife" and "my husband," and file joint tax returns. Their friends and acquaintances also must consider them to be "married."

If you are in a common-law marriage and it breaks up, do you file for divorce the same way you would if you were formally married?

Yes.

Do marital rights automatically accrue to a person who lives with you as a spouse over a long period of time?

Only if you live in one of the states that honor common-law marriages. In many other states, you can consider yourself to be husband and wife, file joint tax returns, and so on, but if you're not legally married you have no rights if your partner dies or leaves. It's even possible that if your partner were in an intensive care unit, you wouldn't be allowed to visit in a non–common-law state—because you would not be considered "next of kin." Establishing a durable power of attorney for health care ("durable" because it remains in effect even if you become incapacitated) is the only way to protect yourself against this possibility.

I am 58 years old and I have lived in a common-law marriage with my partner for many years. Does Social Security make any allowances for us?

In general, no, though there are a couple of ways in which you and your partner could achieve dependent status under Social Security Administration rules. The first is if one of you adopts the (age 18 or younger) child of the other one. The second is if you and your partner live in a state that honors common-law marriages.

Which states currently recognize common-law marriages?

Alabama, Colorado, District of Columbia, Georgia (if created before 1/1/97), Idaho (if created before 1/1/96), Iowa, Kansas, Montana, New Hampshire (for inheritance purposes only), Ohio (if created before 10/10/91), Oklahoma, Pennsylvania (if created before 1/1/05), Rhode Island, South Carolina, Texas, Utah.

PRENUPTIAL AGREEMENTS

What exactly is a prenuptial agreement?

A prenuptial—or premarital or antemarital—agreement is a legal contract entered into before marriage that specifies how a couple's assets and debts are to be divided in case of a divorce. A pre-nup can also delineate certain expectations partners bring to the marriage, i.e., which partner will work, which partner will stay at home with the children, and various inheritance rights. Think of it as the best way to ensure your financial security in the future.

I thought pre-nups were just for rich people.

You are not alone. Years ago, pre-nups were primarily used by people who had considerable wealth that they wanted to protect. Even now, the pre-nups we tend to hear or read about are those signed by movie stars or others with many assets. Yet these days, pre-nups are very common among people of ordinary means. Most women and men have assets they wish to protect—or the prospect of future assets they want to make secure plans for. In fact, people with very few current assets may enter into a pre-nup in order to protect future earnings or inheritances, or shield against future debts incurred by a spouse who may prove to be financially irresponsible. Ultimately, a well-written pre-nup can protect you no matter what financial circumstances arise.

I'm still not convinced I need a pre-nup. Can you give me some examples of situations in which someone would want to have one?

Yes. Here are some scenarios in which pre-nups would be useful. You and your spouse-to-be both work, and you decide you want to keep future earnings or stock options separate. You put that in the pre-nup. One of you has previously been through a bitter divorce, and you know how painful, divisive, and expensive wrangling over marital property can be, so you determine any divisions beforehand and record them in a pre-nup. You've inherited an extensive portfolio from your parents, a portfolio that may take you—and possibly your spouse—a lot of time and effort to manage. You will both reap the rewards during your marriage. Even so, you want to make sure that this portfolio and its growth remain in your name alone should the marriage dissolve. That, too, goes in a pre-nup.

I know that one day I'm going to inherit my parents' vacation home. Since my folks no longer use it very much, my fiancé and I have begun spending weekends there and are full of plans to fix it up together. Still, this house has been in my family for several generations, and I want to make sure it remains in my family. Is this something a pre-nup can cover?

It certainly is, and it's a perfect example of the protection a pre-nup can provide. A pre-nup is a good idea whenever you want to ensure that an asset—whether property, an equity stake in property, securities, valuables, or a retirement plan—is protected.

Isn't it kind of insulting to tell the guy I'm going to marry that I want a pre-nup? Won't he think that I don't have much confidence in our future together?

That's a common worry, but if the safety, happiness, and general welfare of both partners is a clear priority for each partner, negotiating a pre-nup will be seen as a mark of respect for yourself, your partner, and the financial future you will have together. Moreover, it's an opportunity to express your most intimate concerns about money, security, child-rearing, and other issues—and to do so before marriage's normal challenges and problems cause emotions to run high. In my experience, talking honestly about money and the future brings partners closer together. If this is important to you, my advice is to let your beloved know how you feel. Chances are that he will want you to be protected and to feel safe, just as you want him to be.

Okay, you've convinced me. How do I go about getting a prenuptial agreement drawn up?

One thing *not* to do is rely on one of the many "how-to" CD-ROMs for creating your own prenuptial agreement. Computer programs and resource books are a good starting point for a discussion with your partner, but after you've both jotted down some notes, ask a good attorney to draft your agreement according to the laws of your state. Pre-nups made with a CD-ROM are too easily contested—do-it-yourselfers beware!

Before signing a pre-nup, each of you should consult a separate attorney to make sure that the final agreement works for each of you. This may seem awkward, but it allows you to express any remaining concerns privately, acts as a final protection against oversights, and can prevent confusion later on.

Are we required by law to have separate lawyers?

Yes, in some states separate legal representation is required for the agreement to be valid. Even where separate representation isn't required, it can smooth a separation settlement by weakening any claim by either of you that you did not know what you were signing, did not understand the agreement, or were unfairly represented by counsel. Your lawyers should sign the agreement as well, to show that they have reviewed it carefully.

How should I prepare for this meeting? What will the lawyers who are drawing up my pre-nup want to know?

Several things. First, it is very important that you and your partner disclose to each other all of your assets and liabilities. Full disclosure is essential, and will include all respective property, income, debts, obligations and expenses, and anything else that will affect the value of your estate, now or in the future. Second, you and your partner must agree that you are entering into the pre-nup freely and without undue coercion. Courts can be very sensitive to the issue of coercion. If one partner is deemed to have exerted undue pressure on the other to sign, a pre-nup can be overturned. Also, the terms of the pre-nup must be fair.

What does "fair" mean in this context?

In this context, "fair" means that the agreement takes into account your age, your partner's age, your state of health, your job, your income, your standard of living, your family responsibilities if applicable, and your preexisting assets, whether these include real property, an investment portfolio, an insurance policy, or anything else of value. You and your partner must show evidence that you understand all of each other's assets and income. Sometimes, your lawyers will suggest that you or your partner bring copies of recent tax returns, monthly statements from a brokerage firm, or other financial documents that could affect the pre-nup. Also, you must both show that you fully understand the legal and financial consequences of the agreement. If a court later deems the agreement unfair or incomplete, it can be thrown out.

What, exactly, is the definition of property?

In most courts of law, property includes everything from your old coin collection to your retirement funds. It also includes your car, your boat, your furniture, your jewelry, your house, any debts, patents, book or music royalties, intellectual property (such as novels and screenplays), artwork—you name it. Property basically includes everything you can think of, other than human beings.

What else does a pre-nup include?

It can include almost anything that does not violate public policy. Future debt, future stock options, future retirement benefits—all can be designated. There have been pre-nups that cover who will get the baseball season tickets and who will feed the dog.

Is there anything that can't be put in a pre-nup?

Issues that touch on child custody and child support in a pre-nup will not be binding in court. Anything that appears to anticipate illegal actions (such as illegal gambling or even murder) are not enforceable, and the same goes for anything that binds one or the other partner to obligatory sexual duties. (Courts don't want to enforce sexual duties, for obvious reasons.) Any agreement that would leave a spouse totally destitute or a ward of the state is also unenforceable.

Can a pre-nup replace our wills and living trusts?

No. The chief intent of a pre-nup is to cover what happens in the event of a dissolution, not a death.

Do all 50 states recognize pre-nups?

Yes. There is a nationwide Uniform Prenuptial Agreement Act (UPAA). The particular laws of each state may differ as to the conditions for enforcing a pre-nup, but even community-property states—which mandate dividing marital assets and debts fifty-fifty at divorce—recognize the primacy of a pre-nup that specifies the division of property or debt in another way.

Do judges pay attention to pre-nups? If they don't, is it worth asking my fiancé to sign one?

Until recently, judges were not all that favorably inclined toward pre-nups. Years ago, many states did practically everything they could to discourage divorce. Courts in those states tended not to honor pre-nups, because pre-nups, they believed, planted the idea of divorce in partners'

minds. Well, times have changed. Most judges now have come to recognize that some couples may be better off divorced—and if they do divorce, they are much better off for having signed a pre-nup. Generally speaking, courts now enforce these agreements. Exceptions include contracts the court views as giving one spouse a powerful incentive to end the marriage, for example, if a spouse is entitled to more money if the marriage lasts a certain number of years (they see this as promoting divorce, which they still look unfavorably upon). Agreements that are viewed as a contract to evade creditors illegally, or, again, that the court believes one party intimidated the other into signing, are viewed unfavorably.

Where and when will we sign our agreement?

You'll probably sign your pre-nup in a lawyer's office and, in the best case, you'll sign at least six to twelve months before your wedding date. I will tell you this much: Don't sign on the way to the wedding! Courts will invalidate a pre-nup if they find that both parties did not have ample time to think about what they were signing.

Do pre-nups have to be witnessed and/or notarized in order to be valid?

Rules vary from state to state. In New York a pre-nup must be notarized to be valid. In other states neither witnesses nor notaries are necessary. Your attorney(s) will be aware of the requirements in your state.

How much does it cost to draft a pre-nup?

The cost varies from a couple hundred dollars to several thousand dollars for financially complicated agreements—still not much when you consider that a bitter divorce can cost tens of thousands of dollars and take years to resolve.

What if we want to make some changes after the contract is drawn up and signed?

This isn't a problem. You will follow the same procedure you used when you had the contract drawn up in the first place. Have the agreement witnessed and notarized, if necessary, and state expressly whether you're replacing the earlier document with this one or simply amending certain terms listed in the previous agreement. If you draft an agreement *after* you are married, it is technically known as a postnuptial agreement. The enforceability of postnuptial agreements varies from state to state.

If we draw up a pre-nup in one state and then move to another state, is the pre-nup still valid?

Not always, and possibly not in every detail. Have your original contract reviewed by a good attorney in the new state. If anything needs to be changed, he or she can make those changes. Be aware, however, that enforceability of postnuptial changes, like postnuptial agreements, varies from state to state.

If we have a pre-nup that divides our property differently from what is dictated by the laws of our state, will our pre-nup stand?

In most cases, yes. If the contract is drawn up correctly, your agreement will allow you to modify or even wriggle out of the state property system, even if you live in a community-property state. Then you can implement an agreement that better suits your needs.

We've been married for more than 20 years and so much about our financial situation has changed since we first drew up our prenuptial agreement. Should we change the pre-nup or should we just dissolve it? It seems like there's no reason to have one anymore.

I don't think you should ever dissolve your pre-nup. Changes in your financial status, which may strike you as a reason to abandon your pre-nup, can easily be accounted for in an amended agreement. (In the best case, such changes will have been anticipated in the original document, *if* it was drawn up correctly.) The primary reason you have a pre-nup is so that you and your spouse will have assurance that both of you will be protected, whatever may come. "Whatever may come" is a key phrase here— you never know what the future holds, so why risk exposing yourselves to the unknown by dissolving a protective agreement? Have it amended instead.

I'm a widow with three children from a previous marriage, and I am getting married again next spring. Should I get a pre-nup?

Certainly, if only to protect your children. Without a pre-nup, your new husband will acquire a legal right to inherit at least a portion of the assets you may intend your children to inherit. A pre-nup is especially important for widows (or widowers) who want to protect a deceased spouse's money for the children. It's also a useful instrument to soothe grown children's suspicions or ease resentments about a new stepparent; it demonstrates that any assets due to go to them will be protected for their use.

PRE-NUPS AND DEBT PROTECTION

Without a pre-nup, am I responsible for debts my spouse incurred before we were married?
In most cases, you are not responsible for such debts. You may, however, be responsible for debts incurred during marriage. If you and your spouse have a joint credit card issued in both your names, for example, you are each responsible for all debt on that card.

What happens to me if the credit card my spouse uses is issued only in my spouse's name?
That's trickier. Let's consider credit cards that your spouse has in his or her name alone, for his or her own purposes. If your spouse creates a large debt and cannot pay, the creditor has a legal right to come after you—unless you have filed a pre-nup with the credit card company stating that you are not responsible for your spouse's separate debts. Why? Because your partner probably checked "married" in the marital status box on the application, and thus triggered a clause, in very fine print, stating that the cardholder's spouse will also be responsible for the debt, unless otherwise noted.

Can a pre-nup give me protection against most of my partner's debts?
In some states, you can protect yourself by having a pre-nup that specifies which debts you will not be responsible for. For example, you could state that any credit cards in your spouse's name alone will not be your responsibility. This option may or may not be available in your state. Check

with a lawyer to see whether sending a copy of your prenuptial agreement to all pertinent credit card companies, including those with which you set up new accounts, will afford protection.

MARRIAGE AND MONEY

My husband and I have been married only six months, and already we're squabbling about finances. He spends money on computer equipment. I spend money on household goods. He insists on paying the bills and then forgets to do it. I feel as if a gap has opened up between us.
You're in good company. Building a shared financial life is a challenge. Most single adults have clear, even entrenched, financial housekeeping preferences—some balance the bank statement every month, others balance it once a year or not at all. Some pay the bills as soon as they come in, others don't mind being late. The challenge is in devising a plan that will work for both you and your partner.

First things first. No matter who pays the bills, it's important that you both be familiar with everything about your finances. You should know the monthly costs of food, clothing, shelter, insurance, car loans, and more. If you have children together, you should have calculated how much their education is going to cost. You should each be aware of how much the other partner is spending each month on items in your joint budget, how much each of you are saving for retirement and what securities the other holds in investment accounts. This is the only way for you to be respectful of the money you have in common—and respectful and protective of each other in your essential role as partners.

To answer your question, why not consider paying the bills together every month? If that doesn't work for you or makes you crazy, one of you might do it one month and the other the next, or switch every six months. Ideally, you should both think about, touch, and manage your money.

What about spending money? That's where my wife and I have the biggest arguments.

Spending and bookkeeping go hand in hand. The best strategy is to sit down together and draft a spending plan, or budget. Together, decide how much of your joint income you will devote to discretionary spending after necessities have been paid for. Make policy decisions. How often will you get a new car? How many vacations will you take this year, and what will they cost? How much will you spend during the holiday season? What percentage of your income will you save for retirement or give to charity? Agree on or compromise over what you need, want, and can afford. Develop a shared vision for the future, and a means of getting there. Remember—both of you, working with small sums of money over time, can create a great deal more wealth and security than either of you could alone. The key is to work together.

Is there any advantage to trying to keep our money separate by filing separate tax returns?

In most cases, no. One exception involves child and spousal support from a previous marriage. In some states, including California, an ex-spouse's tax return can be subpoenaed by the other party and used to request adjustments in the amount of child or spousal support. A new spouse might want to keep his or her tax information out of the picture, and filing separately would achieve that end. Another involves IRS liens on a partner's refund. In general, however, as of this writing, filing separately costs more in taxes because it removes certain tax advantages gained by filing jointly. The rules in this arena are subject to change, so if the amounts involved are significant, check with your accountant.

In general, what are my legal obligations to my spouse?

Your legal and financial obligations to your spouse are exactly the same as your spouse's obligations to you—the law is egalitarian with respect to the marriage contract. According to the statutes in most states, this contract obliges each of you to provide basic financial support to the other. Husband and wife take on what are known as "obligations of mutual respect, fidelity, and support." These include payment for shelter, food, and medical care, and become applicable if a spouse becomes ill or loses—or quits—a job.

What are my legal rights with respect to my spouse?

Again, your legal rights in marriage are exactly the same as your spouse's rights. They include the right to file joint income-tax returns with the IRS and state taxing agencies; to create a "family partnership" under federal tax laws, which allows you to divide business income among family members (often lowering the total tax); to create a marital life estate trust; to receive spouse's and dependents' Social Security, disability, unemployment, veterans', pension, and public-assistance benefits; to receive a share of your deceased spouse's estate; to claim an estate-tax marital deduction; to receive family rates for insurance; to avoid the deportation of a noncitizen spouse; to enter hospital intensive-care units and other places where visitors are restricted to immediate family; to make medical decisions about your spouse in the event of disability; and to claim the marital communications privilege, which means a court can't force you to disclose the content of conversations between you and your spouse during your marriage.

You mentioned debts earlier. Am I liable for debts my spouse incurred before we got married?

No. You don't marry debt. But as soon as you commingle your assets with your spouse's, any *joint* account you set up becomes fair game for prior creditors. You can get around this law in certain states by keeping or opening a bank account in your own name, which creditors theoretically can't touch. Even so, the IRS has the power to put a lien on a refund due when you file a joint tax return. So your spouse's prior tax liens are the scariest debts to marry.

What happens if my spouse files for bankruptcy?

If you were legally married when your spouse's debts were incurred, creditors may be able to come after you even after bankruptcy has been filed—even if you two are now divorced. Moreover, if you are both deemed liable for the debt, your spouse's discharge of the debt in bankruptcy court will not relieve you of the debt, which, believe it or not, can show up as a flag on your credit report. The obligation to share in a spouse's debt is a major risk of marriage.

What does the marital contract say about the illness or death of a spouse, and about divorce?

It says a lot. In case of serious illness, the marriage contract gives you the right to make decisions about your spouse's medical care if he or she is not competent to make those decisions. In the case of a spouse's death, the marriage contract may include a legal obligation by your spouse to share his or her estate with you (and vice versa). Many states allow a spouse to take "a forced share," meaning a set amount every spouse is entitled to by law, regardless of a deceased spouse's wishes. The amount varies, but it can be up to one-half of the estate. You have the right to retirement and government benefits based on your spouse's contributions—including disability payments, income from various pensions, and Social Security. In the event of a divorce, you have the right to claim a share of the property and income you and your spouse accumulated during marriage, and in some cases, you may be entitled to half of all combined joint assets.

What about property that I acquired before the marriage? How is this regarded by the courts?

Property acquired before marriage is generally known as separate property. It remains separate for as long as you keep it in your name alone, your spouse doesn't have access to it, and your spouse doesn't contribute to its maintenance. (To be safe, specify your intention to keep your property separate in a pre-nup.) Problems can arise if your partner contributes time and/or money to help maintain a premarital property, thus increasing its value. In some states, whether or not your partner makes a contribution of time or money, the appreciation of the property—that is, any increase in value—may be considered a joint asset, unless the pre-nup states otherwise.

What if I owned rental property before I was married and continue to earn money from it during the marriage—is the rental income still considered my separate property?
Good question. In some states, if you and your partner both invest time and effort in the management of the property, the current income may be considered a joint asset. If you use a management company, the rent is more likely to be considered a separate asset. Laws about this vary widely, so check the laws in your state.

What if I'm left an inheritance or given a gift of money by my parents after I'm married? Is that considered joint property?
In most states, the answer is no—*if* the money was given specifically to you and you keep it in your name only, or if you buy something with it in your name only. Please note, however, that the longer a marriage goes on, the more the lines blur between partners' separate property. Keeping clear title is crucial.

What about marriage and Social Security? I am a married woman who works and pays Social Security taxes, but a friend of mine told me she'll be eligible for Social Security benefits based on her husband's work record, even though she's never worked or paid Social Security taxes. Does this mean that the Social Security taxes I'm paying are wasted, since I could get benefits on my husband's record without ever working?
Your friend is correct. However, the Social Security taxes you are paying are not wasted—not by a long shot. As a married woman who works and pays Social Security taxes, you are eligible for your own retirement benefits. You may get a higher benefit when you retire than you would if your benefit were based solely on your husband's earnings. You may be able to retire before your husband does and receive benefits based on your own earnings. Also, as a working woman, you are eligible to earn disability protection for yourself and your dependent children and, in the event of your death, your survivors may be eligible for benefits based on your earnings.

Both my husband and I work and pay Social Security taxes. On which record will my benefit be based?
You will choose, based on which amount is higher. You are entitled to receive benefits based on your own work record if you have worked long enough to become eligible—usually ten years. However, if the benefits you could receive as a spouse are higher than your own Social Security retirement benefits, you and your spouse will receive a combined benefit based on the higher spouse's benefit.

JOINT ACCOUNTS

Should my wife and I open a joint bank account?

In my opinion, a joint checking account or a money-market fund with both of your names on it is essential. You have decided to join your lives and share your financial resources, and this account is symbolic of that union. Unless you plan to start calculating who drinks more orange juice or uses more toothpaste, you must have a place to house the money you use to pay for your shared bills and expenses. You must also start saving together for the future.

OK, I've done the monthly income-and-expense calculations you suggested earlier. Our expenses, including the additional 10 percent, come to about $4,000 a month. Now what?

Now you and your spouse should prepare to contribute exactly the same *percentage* of your salaries toward the expenses that you share, just as I advise couples who are living together to do. But remember: The amounts you contribute do not have to be the same to make your contributions equal, only the percentages.

It doesn't seem fair that I have to contribute more just because I make more. Does this mean I have a bigger say in how we spend the money?

On a percentage basis, you are not contributing more; you and your husband are contributing the same *proportion* of your salaries to the joint account. Also, in most states, both parties' income is legally considered joint property, since

the marriage is a financial as well as an emotional partnership, remember? Third, even though you may be paid more than your spouse, this does not mean you work harder. Nor should you have more power over your resources or be entitled to a larger voice in decision making. The world, as most of us discovered when we were children, is seldom a fair place—if it were, women wouldn't make an average 74 cents to every dollar a man makes. The measure of a committed relationship is this and only this: Is each partner bringing all possible resources to the relationship?

If we have a joint checking account, do we need individual checking accounts as well?

Yes. Grown-ups need discretionary income. Sharing is important in a marriage or other committed relationship, but so is autonomy. Consider how you would feel if you had to ask permission to buy a new tie or pair of shoes every time you needed one. That would be stultifying, wouldn't it? Remember that there are three entities here—yours, mine, and the big one, ours. Ours is most important, but yours and mine still count.

My husband has been responsible for making a monthly deposit to our joint checking account for the car payment. Now that the car is paid off, he says he shouldn't have to put that money into the joint account. Do you agree?

No. You and your husband now have a chance to increase your future nest egg—so please don't blow it! When a loan has been paid off or a former expense (day care, for instance) disappears, the amount of money you were paying toward it should continue to be paid at the same interval—into an investment vehicle you choose together, toward a goal you both share.

Once our individual and joint accounts are set up, how do we save for our future together?
The first step is to contribute as much as you can to your employers' 401(k) plans or other work-related retirement plans and/or to an IRA. (If you are self-employed, fund a SEP-IRA or a KEOGH plan.) As your circumstances improve, regularly contribute to a non–retirement plan investment vehicle as well. Once again, use a proportional-contribution approach to creating this nest egg, which you should plan to share equally in the future. If one of you makes considerably more money than the other and wants to invest more than the proportional amount, it is up to both of you to decide—preferably in a pre-nup—to whom that money will go in the event of a divorce.

NET WORTH AND SELF-WORTH

Although my spouse and I contribute proportional amounts of our salaries, my share is smaller, so I feel as if I'm not pulling my weight. What can I do?
In spite of how you may feel at times, the smaller amount you earn does not make you more or less important, deserving, or entitled to participate in decisions. Many people who do meaningful work, *vital* work, are underpaid—teachers, social workers, stay-at-home moms—while others are paid handsomely for work that in the long run may not make a difference to anyone. Do not—I repeat, do not—value yourself or your partner by income. Begin, and continue, as equals. People first, then money. If this is a problem for either of you, there is emotional work that you need to tackle now!

My partner and I have lived together for about three years, and I have supported her financially during that time. My income is large in comparison to hers, and it seems that this discrepancy has created a chasm between us. She feels she will never be able to match my contributions to the relationship, so what's the point? How can I level the playing field?
Different income levels can become a sticking point in a relationship, but they don't have to be. Money can be one of the most creative forces in the world, as well as one of the most destructive. What's certain is that money is a force we have to reckon with. Those with less money or with simpler possessions than others around them—especially when the others are their partners or spouses—are likely to feel inadequate or intimidated. Finding a solution begins with acknowledging the problem, as you have done.

Then how do we bridge the gap created by our different incomes?
First of all, be extremely careful not to create an environment in which your partner feels that her lack of financial resources is holding you back or keeping you from doing the things you love; that can only add to any feeling she may

have that she's less than a full partner, and may also make her feel that she will never have—or be—enough. Keep this in mind before blurting out, "Hey, let's go to Paris for the weekend!" Tailor some of your activities to her resources. Try eating at home or in restaurants that she can afford, too. It is very important that she be able to carry her own weight when it comes to money. Otherwise, before you know it, she'll feel powerless, which leads to feeling resentful.

Second, I want you to examine your own heart. Deep down, do you feel your partner is worth less because she makes less? If so, is there anything that you can do to help her make more? Ask yourself what you believe makes for true equality and where equality lies. In a bankbook? In your bedroom? In your heart? Once you've examined yourself, talk with your partner about her perceptions of your different financial capabilities. Be as honest, supportive, and reassuring as you can be.

If your partner were to ask me for advice, I would say this: Recognize that gifts of the heart are priceless. Your boyfriend may be able to buy anything he wants for himself, but he can't buy you and he can't buy love. What you bring to this relationship has great value that has nothing to do with money. You do, however, have to be strong and not overextend yourself financially just to keep up with him. You have to pay your own way when you can, and know when to draw the line when it comes to matching your partner's spending.

I make very little money, but my spouse makes a lot—and says it's OK if I use my money for my own needs and don't contribute to the joint household bills. Will this work?

In my opinion, this won't work—in fact, chances are that as the years go by, it will backfire. When one person pays for everything, what usually happens is that he or she slowly begins to feel a sense of ownership toward everything, as well as a creeping resentment toward the person who is not paying his or her way. What's more, the person who is not making a financial contribution gradually feels less powerful, more dependent, and less entitled to participate in joint financial decisions, which is each partner's right in a committed relationship. If you are working, it would be best for you to contribute an equal percentage, even if that means you pay just a few dollars a month. In a shared life, you *both* have to pay.

What if I would like to stop working for money and stay home to take care of the children?

The first thing to ask yourself is this: Is staying at home financially feasible? To answer this question, I recommend that you and your spouse add up all your expenses—everything from the mortgage to food, clothes, and schooling for your children. (If you are paying for day care, you can reclaim those costs.) Now, how much of your spouse's income would be left over each month if you stopped working? If there would be little or nothing left, and you both decide that this is the right course to follow, then you must share equally in the responsibility of caring for your money. If there is some discretionary money, it should be split fifty-fifty, regardless of who's bringing it in. Remember, in most states, all married couples' income is considered to be jointly owned, and that should be the guiding principle of your partnership.

If I do decide to stay home with the children, how do we live on one income?

There is no simple formula for "finding" the money in this situation. You and your spouse must work together to adjust the variables, whether it means seeking a higher-paying job for the partner who earns more money, moving to a more affordable house or apartment, or learning to make do without certain luxuries.

Once we've figured out the financial side of my staying home with the children, what else should my spouse and I think about?

After you've worked out the finances, the most important thing is that you and your spouse agree that it's desirable for you to stay home with the children. Resentment on either side is a pretty clear indicator that the arrangement won't work. You must agree, too, that any assets accumulated belong to both of you, not solely to the partner earning money. And you must find a way to ensure that you both keep in mind that the partner who is staying home is a full, equal partner with equal rights and isn't subtly belittled. After all, the stay-home partner will be doing work equal to, if not more important than, that of the partner who marches off in a gray suit to the office every morning.

Both my husband and I go to an office every day. What if one of us loses our job?

If your relationship is strong and you've talked about this contingency beforehand, you'll get through the crisis. Remember the extra 10 percent I asked you to put into your joint fund every month? This is one of the things it's designed for; it's there to help you both in times of trouble. Handling setbacks together is part of the challenge and joy of marriage.

DEALING WITH PREVIOUS MARRIAGES

The man I'm about to marry has an ex-wife and two children whom he still supports. Will my income be considered by the court when it is deciding how much his alimony and child support payments will be?

Technically, no, it will not. However, if the ex-wife petitions the court for increased payments, the court will look at your joint household income and expenses. If your spouse has more disposable income because you and he have combined incomes, then your non-parental income has essentially entered the picture. Your income may be exempt from consideration if you and your husband keep your money separate, although in some states your income tax returns can be subpoenaed to find out your combined household income before setting (or changing) the amount of your husband's payments.

Are these payments tax deductible?

Typically, alimony payments are tax-deductible to the person who makes the payments but taxable to the recipient; child support payments are generally tax-free, but not tax-deductible.

If my ex-spouse doesn't pay child support, can the court still enforce her visitation rights?

Yes. Financial and custodial arrangements are considered by courts to be distinct and separate issues.

How can I keep from feeling resentful of the time and money my spouse spends on his previous family? What's legitimate, and what's too much?

How much time your spouse spends with his or her ex-wife and children is a matter that must, in the end, be decided by him or her. No formula applies. That "blood is thicker than water"—or time, or money—is a principle that operates when considering past obligations as well as current ones. Try to look at your spouse's emotional and financial commitment to a former family as a mark of personal honor that promises security to you as well as to them. Still, if you feel left out or overlooked, calmly talk to your spouse about your feelings—taking care to talk *to,* not *at,* your spouse. Make an effort to view this former family as an extension of your new family; otherwise, you risk losing access to the part of your spouse that cares for them. Don't cut off a part of him or her from you.

SEPARATION

How is separation different from divorce?

Separation gives both partners the opportunity to find out what it would be like to live apart from each other—in separate residences and often with separate finances. In some states, you can file for legal separation only as a prelude to divorce. In other states, you can be separated indefinitely, without ever getting a divorce. Basically, legal separation is defined as no longer living together and not having the intention to reconcile. It is a kind of limbo, since one of you has probably moved out, but you are still legally married and cannot marry another person.

What is an informal separation?

An informal separation is simply a way of saying that one of you has moved out, often to give one or both of you time to think things over. Though you may eventually get a divorce, this is not necessarily the intention of either of you when you informally separate. In some cases, you may not *want* a divorce, perhaps for religious, financial, or practical reasons, such as the maintenance of your health insurance coverage. Note that in an informal separation, you may both have the same legal responsibilities and duties to each other as you did when you were living together.

Then what is a legal separation?

In some states, moving out with no intention of returning *constitutes* a legal separation, which can fix the date for certain financial matters. (Before separating, check with an attorney or your state attorney general's office to see whether this applies in your state.) When your separation is a conscious first step toward filing for divorce, you and/or your spouse can apply for a formal legal separation. Before filing a petition for separation with the county court, ask your attorney to prepare a legal separation agreement or to look over an agreement that you and your spouse have drafted together.

Is one type of separation better than the other?
A lot depends on the intentions of the parties involved. A formal separation agreement obviously spells out legal and financial matters much more clearly than an informal separation does. Therefore, a formal separation guarantees greater certainty. For example, it can state whether your spouse will support you financially during the period when you are living apart. If you have children together, it can detail visitation and support arrangements. It can specify how you will divide the property that you share. This diminishes the potential for misunderstandings and strife, and if you do end up getting a divorce, a lot of things will have already been set down on paper.

Why is the date that you agree to separate important?
Depending on the state in which you live, the date of separation can matter a great deal in determining the financial outcome in a divorce or legal separation. Among other issues, it can affect how much alimony may be at stake, your responsibility for any debt incurred by your spouse before and after the date of separation, and how you'll divide retirement assets (though not your right to a share of your spouse's Social Security benefits, which is based on the date of divorce).

If you know or sense that you may be headed for divorce, try to plan your separation date with all these factors in mind. To take just one example, I learned firsthand how important setting the separation date can be when the husband of a very good friend of mine came home and announced, apparently out of the clear blue sky, that he wanted a divorce. He asked my friend to move out as soon as possible. I couldn't figure out what had happened and why it was so sudden and urgent. A few days later, as my friend was preparing to move, I happened to read that the company her husband was working for had just been bought out and that in two months' time all employees were going to receive generous stock options and a pension plan. My friend's husband knew that if this took place after he and his wife were officially separated, there was a good chance that he wouldn't have to share this windfall with her. It was a tense two months, but she waited them out before taking any action to separate, which was a very smart move on her part.

Why do people separate in the first place? Shouldn't they just make up their minds to get a divorce or not get a divorce?
Couples have many reasons for agreeing to separate. Some want to find out what living apart feels like. Others need time and solitude to analyze the relationship—what is right about it as well as what is wrong. If you are married to someone who has shown problematic behavior (for example, excessive drinking, infidelity, or verbal or physical abuse), separating shows that you are deadly serious about asking that person to change or else. Or you may know that you want a divorce and can't bear the thought of living with your spouse until the divorce is official. Or you may have religious or financial reasons for staying married for a little while longer. Finally, you may live in a state where you have to be legally separated before you can file for divorce.

Can I throw my spouse out of the house, espe-

cially if I owned the house before we got married?

It is a staple of state law that neither spouse can be excluded from the other's dwelling. If a domestic situation becomes violent, barring the violent partner from the house requires a court-issued restraining order.

Can I "date" my husband while the two of us are separated?

My advice would be to consult your attorney before you consider dating your spouse during a separation. A lot depends on whether you have filed (or are planning to file) for a divorce in which one of you is at fault. Imagine, for example, that you separate from your husband and file for a divorce from him on the grounds of mental cruelty, then date him again to see if your relationship can be rekindled. If the reconciliation doesn't work out, the court isn't likely to take your complaint of mental cruelty very seriously. (Some states, however, are "no fault" and no evidence of mental cruelty or infidelity needs to be shown—only that "irreconcilable differences" arose.)

But what if my spouse and I intend to reconcile somewhere along the line?

Again, I would consult your attorney. In general, if you and your spouse are planning to reconcile, I don't see a problem in your sharing a pizza.

What is the downside of separating from my spouse?

In many cases, the downside is financial. You may have come to rely on your spouse's income,

and without it your expenses will seem outsized. In the worst-case scenario, you may be cut off from the prospective income of your spouse and may not have enough money to rent or buy a new residence and support yourself. Finally, remember that even though you are living apart, you and your spouse are still married and therefore still responsible for each other's debts.

How do things stand legally if I tell my spouse I want to separate? And what if I move out?

It depends. In some states, if you want to separate but your husband doesn't, moving out may unwittingly give your husband grounds for a fault divorce. In some states you can be charged with desertion if you separate informally.

Is there any way I can protect myself legally?

Yes. Make sure that all these issues are covered and very carefully worded in a separation agreement that you work out with your spouse and your respective attorneys.

My husband and I have just agreed to a separation. Where should I concentrate my efforts, money-wise?

Once a separation seems inevitable, you must turn your attention to financial matters as quickly as you can. If you procrastinate, you may one day find that you are responsible for credit card debt that was incurred right after you moved out, or that one of your joint accounts has been wiped clean of its assets, or that the home equity line of credit that was there in case of emergencies now has a loan against it for $20,000, for which you are responsible. Do not be afraid to separate your accounts immediately. If you end up getting back together, you can always reopen those accounts.

In specific financial terms, what exactly should I do?

What follows is an overview of everything that should be done immediately after it becomes clear that a separation is imminent:

- Consult an attorney regarding the divorce laws in your particular state, and their applicability to your particular situation.
- If you don't already have a checking account in your name only, open one.
- Close all joint accounts, including credit card accounts. Don't freeze money accounts, because one or both of you may need access to the funds. With your attorneys' approval, split the money from joint accounts equally.
- Make copies of all financial documents that show your true debts, assets, and expenses, including tax returns, bank records, household and credit card bills, records of expenses for the children, and any records of every penny you spend to live from month to month.
- Start keeping track of all debts incurred and money paid to each other after the date of separation. This includes money spent on joint bills, improvements to the home, moving expenses, children, insurance premiums—everything that pertains to the two of you. If you decide to pay support to your spouse while you are working things out, make sure that all these sums are documented and that you have an agreement in writing as to what these funds are to go for. If you have such

an agreement, these payments may be tax-deductible, although they will be considered taxable income to your spouse.
- See a tax specialist to decide whether you are going to file your tax return jointly or separately.
- Sit down and figure out what you are worth as a couple. First determine the value of everything you own jointly. Gather documentation of all your joint assets—your home or homes, real estate, jewelry, art, furnishings, automobiles, investments, retirement plans, bonds, mutual funds, savings or money-market accounts, etc. In addition, consider a tricky and relatively new area, stock options, which give an employee the right to buy a company's stock at a great discount but often may not be exercised for years after they are issued. If your spouse has stock options, see an attorney at once, as most states are still sorting out whether, in a divorce, a stock option that may not be exercised until years after the divorce should be considered a joint asset at the time of divorce.
- After you determine what you have in assets, as well as your expenses and income, try to work out an equitable division. Don't do this before you have all the relevant information and documentation, however, because you can't negotiate without the facts. Finally, don't agree to anything without consulting an attorney and a tax specialist.
- Reduce your spending wherever possible to generate some savings for the rocky road ahead.

What about debt? Once we are separated, am I still responsible for any and all debts that my spouse incurs?

In most scenarios, the official date of separation in a final judgment or decree officially determines when you are no longer responsible for any new debts that your spouse incurs in his or her name alone. That's one reason to make sure all joint credit card accounts are closed when you separate. Make sure, too, that you divide all debts and know who is responsible for each one. Before doing so, set up a credit card account in your name to make sure that you qualify for credit, since sometimes your individual credit rating can be affected when you close out a credit card account. Also, contact all professionals and service providers (doctors, lawyers, dentists, etc.) and inform them in writing that if any work is being done for your spouse, you will not be responsible for the bills. The IRS has recently loosened its rules regarding "innocent spouses," making it easier to disavow the income tax obligations of an ex-spouse, so be sure to check with your accountant about any potential tax liabilities. Even if all these precautions are taken, it's still possible that creditors might come after you seeking payment for bills your spouse incurred. Thus the more accounts you can close, the better off you are. Note, too, that under the "obligations of mutual respect, fidelity, and support" clause of the marital contract, you may still be held responsible for debts your spouse runs up for the necessities of life during the separation period and before any divorce is final. Necessities of life include housing, food, clothes, children's expenses, and medical expenses.

Please note that, for many people, the hardest part of separation or divorce is money. People can move away from each other and start new lives, either temporarily or permanently, but they often seem unable to cut financial ties as cleanly—this is particularly true when minor children are involved. Sometimes letting go of jointly managed money seems like the ultimate move, and they're not ready to do that yet. For other couples, living in two places increases their costs of living and may force them to sell their house and other assets. In other cases, guilt keeps the money together. Or the person who has always handled the money keeps handling it because it's familiar and easy, or because both parties are simply too lazy to separate the funds. But whatever the reason, it is a mistake to remain financially intimate after you have severed domestic and emotional ties.

Why is financial intimacy bad if my spouse and I are separated?

I have seen it time and time again: When a spouse continues to foot the bills after a separation, resentment builds up on one side and an unhealthy dependence is created on the other. Having one spouse continue to make a house payment for a brief period so that you can avoid having to sell your house suddenly and ill-advisedly, for example, is certainly worth considering, but don't wait too long to separate your financial lives. Otherwise, mutual respect and individual financial power will go out the window.

If you decide to pay for items for your spouse after you have separated, it is very important to set a time limit. Establish a start and a stop date. Put this in writing, so that there is no misunderstanding. Remember, when one person is in shock—usually the person who is being left— he or she is not going to hear things accurately or remember them clearly. Do not set yourself or your spouse up for additional misunderstandings or disappointments. With your attorneys' help, put *all* your temporary arrangements in writing. Both of you should sign this and keep a copy.

If my spouse and I have been separated for a long time and I haven't been working, can I collect any of his Social Security benefits?

Not according to the rules of the Social Security Administration, which pays benefits only to the main beneficiary—in this case, your spouse— once he or she reaches retirement age and applies to collect them, *unless* you are divorced from your spouse. As far as the SSA is concerned, a marriage is a marriage until it is legally dissolved. If you live in Kansas and your spouse lives in Texas, and you haven't spoken for five years, but neither of you has gotten around to dissolving your marriage, then in the eyes of the SSA you are still legally married and therefore you are not eligible for your own benefits based on your spouse's work record. However, if you've been married for at least ten years, you may be eligible for dependent's benefits. The bottom line is, if you are close to the ten-year mark, wait until you have passed it to get a legal divorce so that you can qualify for Social Security on your spouse's record. However, in order to collect, you must be divorced.

What are the presumptions of the court with respect to custody of children?

Courts in most states believe that joint legal custody is best for children and encourage joint physical custody as well. They will not award sole custody to a parent unless there's a strong showing of proof of the unfitness of the other parent. But courts in some states will not award joint custody unless both parties agree to it. Incidentally, this is one issue that can't be predisposed of in a prenuptial agreement.

Who is responsible for an incapacitated child?

The father and mother share equal responsibility for an incapacitated or disabled child. In most states, when the child turns 18, he or she is considered a conservatee (the age may vary from state to state); the parents become the child's conservators and manage any state or federal money for which the child is eligible. In turn, the state may access money that you or your spouse have put aside to be held for the benefit of the child. If you have a child (or, for that matter, a parent) who will need long-term assistance, please see a good trust lawyer who deals with asset protection.

THE EMOTIONS OF DIVORCE

To my great disappointment, my marriage hasn't worked out, and my husband and I have decided to split up. I never thought this would happen, and I alternate between fear and outright panic. What should I be thinking about?

First, be assured that you will get through this, just as you have gotten through other difficulties in your life. How well you get through it will largely be determined by whether you reach for your courage or turn away from it into feelings of pain and helplessness. During this transition period, you are going to have to make quite a few decisions, and it is vital that, when you do so, your mind and body be as strong as possible. Act with strength, which will create more strength. Eat well, exercise, and allow yourself plenty of sleep. Consider counseling or a support group for you and your children. Even if the motions feel hollow at first, the actions are powerful and will nourish your courage.

It is also important for you to remember that when you got married, you and your mate gave your word that you would honor each other for better or for worse, forever. Now that you are facing a divorce, you are breaking that vow in the practical realm, but you must still honor the "for worse" part of that promise on an emotional level—if only for your own sake. Your thoughts, your words, and every single action you take at this time will govern your future and give you control over it.

How can my thoughts and words give me control over my future?

I'm a firm believer that your thoughts and your words create your destiny. One of my favorite books is a tenth-century Hindu text called *The Outlook of Shiva*, written by a scholar named Somananda. In it, Somananda instructs us to act as if we already embody our goal, no matter how large the disparity between what we are and how we feel now, and what we wish to become or achieve. It is important for us not to allow doubt, sadness, anger, or confusion to cause us to abandon our intention. Instead, we must be-

gin by clarifying our highest and noblest goals, and then we should try to maintain "an unwavering awareness" by affirming these goals with confidence and conviction. In this way, Somananda explains, our being aligns itself with our intention, and our goal becomes manifest. In short, become it by thinking it. Be it by saying it.

Sometimes I feel as if going through the death of somebody I love would be less difficult than a divorce.

You're not alone. Over the years, I have come to believe that a death—whether foreseeable or unexpected—is in some ways easier to cope with than a divorce. With death there usually is no blame. Everybody suffers loss—the person who's died and the loved ones left behind. A life is gone. The community gathers around you in mourning. Friends and relatives, some of whom you may not have seen in years, check in to see how you are doing. If you have children, they draw closer to you. There is usually not much ambiguity, emotional or financial. The house is yours to sell or keep as you see fit, the car is yours, the retirement account, the life insurance policy, the possessions—everything that was "ours" is now yours. When someone you love dies, the loss is enormous, to be sure. But you don't lose the love, which remains pure.

So in emotional as well as financial terms, divorce is actually very different from experiencing the death of a loved one?

Yes. If you are the bereaved party in the event of a divorce, you may be faced with an ex-partner who is living a perfectly happy life, perhaps with somebody else. You may feel that for all you gave to the relationship, you got little back in return. You may also be filled with regrets about how you behaved, fearing that you may have forced your partner to leave you. Perhaps you are making do with less while your former partner is living on more. If you have children, your former partner may take them away from you one or two nights a week and every other weekend and show them a great time. The children themselves are likely to be as confused and angry as you are. As for the community, not everyone is rallying around you unconditionally, the way they probably would have if your spouse had died; no one's dropping off supper for you, and the phone is hardly ringing off the hook. Instead, some of your friends may feel uncomfortable around you. In fact, some of them may be taking your ex-spouse's side, compounding your loss. To rebuild your life from this point of disequilibrium will take enormous courage.

I am so full of hatred toward the person who came between my husband and me that I don't know what to do!

Of course you feel this way, especially if you're being left for someone else—even if you recognize that the person who takes this role rarely comes uninvited. Nevertheless, if all your energies are devoted to hatred or revenge, you won't have a whole lot left for more constructive pursuits. If you think about this hatred all the time, then you'll talk about it and act on it, and you will be building a hateful, vengeful foundation on which to live the rest of your life. Try to

pull away from the hatred as much as you can and instead expend your energies on caring for yourself. If you're really having difficulty, check out anger-management classes offered in your area.

How can I even begin to cope with the emotions of separation and divorce?

As I said, a good place to start is by remembering that every action you take today will have an effect tomorrow. Are you saying to yourself, "I've never been so angry in my life"? If you are, you should keep in mind that acting from anger not only threatens to impair your good judgment when it comes to making vital decisions, it can also increase your attorneys' fees. You're better off paying a therapist, who charges a lot less, than paying an attorney to listen to your emotional issues. What usually happens to people who angrily refuse to settle with their partners is that they end up spending a lot more time in conflict—and paying more money as a result.

So anger has a financial as well as an emotional cost. Just how much more does it cost not to settle or compromise?

On average, a divorce trial in court can cost up to three times as much as an out-of-court settlement, and that's just money. The emotional costs also can be huge.

Are you saying that I shouldn't take my divorce to trial even if my ex-spouse is being completely unreasonable?

No. If your estranged spouse is being unreasonable and there seems to be no amicable way to resolve your differences, do not be afraid to go to court to have the judge determine the final accounting, assign responsibility for any debts, divide any remaining assets, and settle issues of child and spousal support, attorneys' fees, and so on. Sometimes it is better to have a rational judge decide your fate than to let your angry spouse (or your angry self!) call the shots. You must do this, however, with eyes that are open, unclouded by any toxic emotions that can prevent you from seeing plain facts or probable outcomes.

In addition to anger, what are some other reactions people have when they are facing a divorce?

One common reaction is to insist that you don't care about the outcome of the divorce or about what happens to your ex-spouse or to yourself. "I just want to get all this behind me and get on with my life," people say. There are other destructive phrases that I hear, too. "I don't want anything. He [or she] can have it all." Or "I'm not worried about the money. I know he [or she] will be fair." None of the above is an advisable attitude or belief. Anger and revenge will get you nowhere fast, but so will the martyr approach, in which you throw up your hands and let your spouse have everything. This makes little emotional or financial sense. You were half of your marriage, after all. As for believing that your estranged spouse will continue to be fair to you because he or she has been fair up to this point, well, when it comes to dividing assets—which means giving up money—people can behave very strangely, and someone you once thought

of as the most generous person in the world may surprise, appall, and disappoint you.

If you find yourself thinking or saying any of the phrases above, I want to ask you: Are you still being mindful of the awesome power of words? Do you know that when you say you don't care what happens, you are in effect creating a situation that almost surely will prevent you from getting on with your life in a conscious, rich, and productive way? Remember, you may spend many more years divorced from your spouse than you spent married to him or her; therefore, the decisions you make during this crucial time will affect you (and perhaps your children) for many years to come. Do not take casually what is happening to you right now. Divorce is as serious a commitment to the future as marriage was. Now is the time I want you to summon words of wealth.

What do you mean by "words of wealth"?

Words of wealth are words like these: "I want to get on with my life, but I care deeply about what happens now, because what happens now will affect me and possibly my children forever." You must be mindful of the present tense, and also keep in mind how swiftly the future becomes the present. And the future may not involve just you, but also your children and their children. Say the words of wealth to your attorney and to your ex, and say them with grace until they become true.

I don't really care about the money—I just want my wife back!

So often when divorce is imminent, the person who is being left finds it very hard to face what is happening. He or she starts thinking or saying things like, "I can get her back if I do whatever she wants." But you are not one iota likelier to save your marriage by downplaying the importance of money or giving up your rights to it. All you are likely to do with this kind of thinking is impoverish your future, financially *and* emotionally. With thoughts and words like the ones above, you are about to serve yourself a double whammy. Not only will you repel money, money that is rightfully yours, but the person you are trying to bring closer will be repelled, too—by your lack of self-respect and your powerlessness. No one is attracted to weakness. Maybe you can put your marriage back together, maybe not. But please don't base your financial actions (or, for that matter, your emotional actions) on an unproved possibility. Protecting yourself will have absolutely no effect on a possible reconciliation, I can promise you that. If anything, your actions now—strong, powerful, clear, graceful, and rich—will better the chances for a reconciliation.

And in the meantime, you're telling me to be very watchful of my feelings, day in and day out.

Yes. Count on feeling fine one day, and the next day feeling wretched. On the days when the blues hit you big time, give yourself permission to take a break. Try not to make any decisions if you don't have to. For the first six months after your breakup, rate yourself on a scale of one to ten twice a day—when you get up and about eight hours later—a one rating being extremely happy and ten being miserable. If ever you feel you are a five or more, please do not make any

decisions regarding your money or your divorce on that day. If you are asked to, simply say, "Not today, thank you," let it go at that, and address the matter when you feel better. Remember, check yourself *twice* a day, because sometimes a phone call, a song on the radio, a comment from a friend, or even two people walking down the street holding hands can set off a chain of emotions that transform a one into an eight before you know what hit you. "Not today, thank you," is an expression of self-respect, coming from a position of power.

I am the person who was left. What angers me most is that my ex-husband seems to be doing so much better than I am. How can I get myself to start doing as well as he seems to be?

Please realize that you are not in a contest to see who can get through this divorce with the fewest breakdowns or, for that matter, the fewest feelings. If you are the one who was left, do not be surprised if your spouse seems to be doing better than you are. Try to be glad your spouse is thriving, as this will certainly make your life easier! Remember that the chances are pretty good that he or she has been thinking about this divorce for a long time, long enough to get used to the idea, whereas for you it is brand new and devastating. Your job now is to rebuild your life by identifying and then acting in your own best interests.

Do not get pushed into doing anything during this difficult time. Start using your daily ratings immediately and take action only when you feel ready. You have the power to set the pace of the divorce. You have the power, too, to drag it out, but that won't help you. Use your power wisely, and proceed when you are ready. I urge you also to seek therapy or counseling if you can possibly afford it and/or to consult a member of the clergy. Though it's very helpful to receive sympathy and emotional support from family and friends, if you let them see you at your lowest point too often, it may be hard to restore equilibrium to your relationships later, when you feel stronger. You don't want friends to treat you like a victim for the rest of your life, do you? Plus, you may need assistance beyond sympathy. A professional counselor's impartiality may help make you stronger, both in the short and long term. (Take care in choosing one: As in every profession, there are good practitioners, and less good ones. Ask around.) If there are children involved, a counselor may also help you in dealing with their pain and confusion and in deciding whether they, too, need professional help.

I left my wife and now I am overcome by all sorts of emotions that I find it hard to live with. Any advice?

For the person who leaves, the responsibilities are immense. Regardless of your feelings today, you have just delivered a terrible blow to the person who was once the love of your life. For your own benefit as well as your ex-spouse's, I want you to proceed slowly and with compassion. Your marriage didn't work out. Now it is your responsibility to conclude it as successfully as possible. How you end something as profound and important as a marriage is a reflection of how you live your life—financially, emotionally, and spiritually.

ANNULMENTS

I am a practicing Roman Catholic, and I am wondering if instead of a separation and a divorce I can get my five-year marriage annulled.

There are two different kinds of annulments, a legal annulment and a religious annulment. The latter is associated with the Catholic Church and doesn't eliminate the need for a divorce. If you are Catholic and you do divorce and wish to marry someone else, the church will not formally recognize your new marriage until your old marriage is annulled.

How do I go about getting a religious annulment?

If you are a divorced Roman Catholic and you want to remarry under the auspices of that church, you should first make an appointment to see your parish priest. Next, a church court, known as a marriage tribunal, meets to discuss all the elements of your previous marriage, including the reasons leading to the divorce. During this meeting, the tribunal may ask you to provide a list of friends and family members who were "witnesses" to your marriage, as well as certain legal documents pertaining to your marriage, such as your marriage license.

Will the church contact my ex-husband?

Yes, it will. He will be notified by the marriage tribunal that you want your marriage to be annulled. He then has the right to show the tribunal proof that your marriage was valid. Next the tribunal will review all the evidence, written and oral, and decide whether or not, according to the policies of the Catholic Church, you have grounds for an annulment. If they say no, you have the right to appeal. If you lose your appeal, you can take your request for annulment all the way to Rome!

How long does a church annulment take?
Anywhere from several months to several years.

You mentioned a legal annulment. How does this work?
A legal annulment is a court order that basically announces to the world that your marriage was never legally valid to begin with—it's as though your marriage never took place.

But my marriage did take place! Why would a court declare it invalid?
The most common reason that a court is willing to declare an annulment is that one spouse lied to, defrauded, or misled the other. The assumption is that if the spouse who was lied to had known the truth, he or she would not have gotten married. Other reasons include a bigamous marriage (one in which your partner was already married), a marriage in which one of the parties wasn't of legal age, a marriage in which one of you was forced into wedlock, or a marriage that took place while one or both of you was intoxicated or under the influence of drugs.

Are legal annulments available in all states, or just a few?
Legal annulments are available in most states. Remember, though, that if you and your partner have children, an annulment will not have any effect—nor should it—on your responsibilities as a parent.

DIVORCE

Why are so many people getting divorced these days? It wasn't always that way, was it?
No, it wasn't. For whatever reason—changing values, sexual and women's liberation, or a generation that has different expectations of what a marriage should be and is less willing to "stick it out"—the fact is that these days, one in two marriages ends in divorce. Of the 50 states, Nevada ranks first with the highest divorce rate, and Massachusetts, Georgia, and the District of Columbia bring up the rear.

How much does it cost to get a divorce?
That depends on a lot of factors, the most important being whether your divorce is amicable, or whether you and your spouse are willing to fight it out to the bitter end. You can get divorced for a few hundred dollars or a few thousand dollars, or you can go all out and spend a small fortune litigating a long divorce trial in court. No matter what state you live in, a pretty good rule of thumb is that the more issues you and your spouse can agree on, the less you will spend on attorneys' fees. Also, obviously, the more experienced or well-known the attorney you retain, the greater his or her hourly rate will be. An experienced lawyer, however, may be able to accomplish more in less time.

Can I shop around for an attorney on the basis of cost?
Yes. Many divorce lawyers offer a free brief con-

sultation. Request estimates based on several possible divorce scenarios, including an amicable divorce and a hostile divorce. These will only be approximations, of course, but they will still give you a pretty good idea of how much a divorce will cost you in the end. Interviewing a cross section of lawyers is a good idea for another reason, too: One attorney may tell you that the things you want from your divorce are impossible to get; another attorney may promise you the moon but disappoint you in the end. Consulting with several can help give you a good grounding in what is possible, as well as which attorney you will feel most comfortable with.

So how do I find a really good divorce attorney?

Don't just let your fingers do the walking through the Yellow Pages. Get referrals from friends who have been in the same boat. A shrewd, experienced attorney is essential, particularly if your divorce proceedings promise to be bitter or drawn out. If this is the case, you should try to find someone who has had extensive courtroom experience. In general, you should be conscious of whether you want a conciliator or a gladiator, and, in either case, make it a priority to find an attorney who is experienced in family law. He or she should be someone with whom you feel very comfortable, though it is also important to remember that your attorney is not your best friend or your confidant, but your lawyer and advocate.

Are there any resources other than referrals for finding a good divorce lawyer?

Yes. Martindale-Hubbell has a directory of lawyers by specialty. Go to *martindale.com*. Or call the American Academy of Matrimonial Lawyers at (312) 263-6477, or go to its Website at *www.aaml.org*. Your local bar association may also be a good resource.

I am about to meet with my divorce attorney. What should I bring with me?

Bring the complete list of joint assets that you prepared at the time of separation. You should also bring an inventory of your outstanding debt, whether it's credit card debt, a mortgage, or a student loan. And if you are looking for spousal or child support, you need to know your typical monthly budget and both of your incomes.

My husband and I have been separated for a year. I've retained an attorney and have made a list of all my assets and liabilities. How do I go about filing for divorce?

During the separation, one of you will file a petition for divorce or a complaint in the appropriate court in your or your spouse's county of residence (the name of the court varies from state to state), and this will start the formal divorce proceedings. If you do the filing, you are considered the plaintiff, or the petitioner. Your spouse is considered the defendant, or the respondent. There is no legal preference given to the party that files first.

What goes into a petition for divorce?

Your petition simply puts forth the facts of when you were married, when you separated, your key financial assets and debts, and the number of children who will be affected by the divorce. It also indicates what you want from your spouse, whether it's spousal support, child support, custody of the children, etc.

Does my spouse get a copy of this petition?

After you file your petition, your spouse must be notified and acknowledge formally that you have filed. He may sign what is called a waiver of service, which basically means that he will not be served formally by a process server. This usually happens if a couple has agreed to divorce amicably. If the opposite is true, then your spouse will be served by a process server.

What if for some reason my spouse can't be served—if I don't know where he is, for example? Does this mean we have to stay married forever?

Don't worry, the answer is no. In most states, you can publish a legal notice in your local paper informing your spouse that you have filed a petition for divorce. If after a certain amount of time your spouse fails to come forth, you can obtain a divorce even if your ex doesn't file court papers.

We have two children together. What about them?

If there are children involved, this is the time when one of you may need to file a request for temporary child and spousal support, and for custody, visitation rights, or alimony—or anything else that may apply to your situation—with the local court handling your divorce. You will receive from the court a temporary order soon after this filing, and a permanent order once the divorce is final. Even after that, the court has the right to alter child support provisions until the children are emancipated, i.e., until they turn 18 or graduate from high school; thus either ex-spouse can petition the court for a change in support payments or custody arrangements until the children become

legal adults. The court also retains jurisdiction over spousal support until that is terminated.

Can child support obligations stop before my child turns 18?

Yes, if your child goes into the military, if he or she takes on a full-time permanent job, if he or she gets married, if he or she becomes legally emancipated, or if he or she dies.

I am paying my wife child support for our three children. Are these payments considered tax-deductible by the IRS?

No. Similarly, if you are a child receiving child support, it is not considered taxable income by the IRS. (Alimony is indeed tax-deductible to the payer, and must be reported by the recipient as income.)

What comes after the temporary order?

Next comes the process known as legal discovery—informal or formal—which determines exactly what assets must be divided. If you have children, this information will be used to calculate the amount of child support or alimony that you will have to pay or that you will receive.

What's the difference between informal and formal discovery?

Informal discovery is when your attorney asks your spouse's attorney for information, whether financial, legal, or medical, and your spouse is willing to answer each question honestly and to the best of his ability. Basically, he voluntarily discloses the information that your attorney requires. Formal discovery becomes necessary if your spouse will not provide information needed by your attorney. It involves subpoenas for documents, written interrogatories, and oral depositions under oath.

How long does the discovery process take?

It can take anywhere from a week or two up to several months, depending on whether or not you and your spouse agree on things.

My attorney told me that I am going to be deposed. What should I keep in mind during the deposition process?

A deposition can be nerve-wracking, so try to keep calm. Answer all questions truthfully, no matter how painful that may be, but at the same time be very careful about what you say. Try to keep your answers brief and factual, and do not stray from the question that's being asked. If you give more information than is asked for, you may inadvertently harm your case.

What if my spouse refuses to be deposed?

You can request a court order requiring him to appear at a deposition. If your spouse violates the court order, he will risk being held in contempt of court, which might lead to the judge's immediately ruling in your favor.

DIVIDING ASSETS IN DIVORCE

I dread dividing up the assets from our 14-year marriage. How do courts and attorneys go about deciding who gets what?

It is common for a divorcing couple to make de-

cisions about dividing their property and debts themselves rather than leave it to a judge. But if a couple cannot agree, they can submit their property dispute to the court, which will use state law to divide the property.

If this is your case, let me start by saying that an attorney who deals with family issues offers this rule-of-thumb advice: Choose your battles carefully. If there is a lot of property to be divided, I advise you to concede gracefully on the smaller stuff and you'll be on higher ground when it comes to the items that really matter. In short, it's not worth fighting over who gets the orange towels.

In general, the court system is in place to see to the division of property and debts and to settle issues of spousal support, child support, custody, and visitation. In community-property states, everything is divided fifty-fifty, but in other states, the judge has wide discretion to divide assets and debts and to fix spousal support based on equitable principles of need.

How, exactly, do the states differ when dividing property at divorce? Are there major differences between community-property and equitable-distribution states?

Yes, there are important differences. But nowhere does division of property necessarily mean a physical division. Rather, in every state the court awards each spouse a percentage of the total value of the property. (It is illegal for either spouse to hide assets in order to shield them from property division.) Each spouse gets items whose worth adds up to his or her percentage.

States divide property under one of the two

schemes you mentioned: equitable distribution or community property.

- Equitable distribution: Assets and earnings accumulated during marriage are divided equitably (fairly), which allows a judge enormous discretion in the event that the parties don't settle. Equitable distribution principles are followed everywhere except in the community-property states listed just below.
- Community property: In Arizona, California, Idaho, Louisiana, Nevada, New Mexico, Texas, Washington, and Wisconsin, all property of married people is classified as either community property, owned equally by both spouses, or the separate property of one spouse. At divorce, community property is generally divided equally between the spouses, while each spouse keeps his or her separate property.

How do we distinguish between community and separate property?

Very generally, here are the rules for determining what's community property and what isn't:

- Community property includes all earnings during marriage and everything acquired with those earnings. All debts incurred during marriage, unless the creditor was specifically looking to the separate property of one spouse for payment, are community-property debts.
- Separate property of one spouse includes assets and debts acquired before marriage or after separation, as well as gifts and inheritances given just to that spouse, and the proceeds of

a pension that vested (that is, the pensioner became legally entitled to receive it) before marriage. Property purchased with the separate funds of a spouse remain that spouse's separate property. A business owned by one spouse before the marriage remains his or her separate property during the marriage, although a portion of it may be considered community property if the business has increased in value during the marriage or if both spouses worked at it.

- Property purchased with a combination of separate and community funds is part community and part separate property, so long as a spouse is able to trace how separate funds were used. Separate property mixed together with community property generally becomes community property.

What are some of the points that a typical court considers when dividing assets and determining support?

Courts most commonly consider the following issues: the duration of the marriage; the earning power of each party, i.e., how well each of you is equipped to maintain your present standard of living; the marketable skills of the party seeking support; how long the party who has been supported until now has stayed at home; whether children will make it harder for the party seeking support to find work; and what would be involved, i.e., time and expense, to educate or retrain the stay-at-home partner for the current job market. The court's goal is that the party seeking support will eventually be able to support him- or herself. The trend in many states is to award spousal support in longer marriages (i.e., more than seven to ten years), for a period of time equal in length to half the duration of the marriage. The court also considers the means of the partner who is being asked for support, and child support and custody arrangements, when applicable. In determining child support, the court often looks to the percentage of time the child or children spend with each parent and the respective incomes of each parent. The court will also consider age, health, and extenuating circumstances, such as whether you're caring for an invalid child or parent. Some courts have schedules that use a percentage of income or an income amount as the basis to set support levels.

My spouse and I have lived in the same house for 12 years. Now that we're getting divorced, how will the court decide who gets to stay and who has to go?

The hardest decision most divorcing couples face is who gets to keep or stay in the home that the two of you lived in together. Who keeps the house and who moves out can be a murky legal area because the law does not mandate who must move out. Of course, if your name is not on the title, you will have to go.

When there are children involved, it's another story. The primary caretaker usually is allowed to stay in the house with the children until the children reach 18 years of age. If you are the primary caretaker, please see an attorney before you separate from your spouse, because if you have moved out and there's a subsequent legal battle for the house, many judges will lean toward keeping the situation as it is rather than

disrupting the children's lives yet again. If there is any physical threat to the children, then you must seek a restraining order that would prevent your spouse from staying in the house. Usually, though, the decision will be made between the two of you, alone or with the aid of legal counsel or a mediator (more about mediators later).

My husband and I have agreed to sell our house rather than haggle over it. How do we figure out how much it is worth?

Many people decide to take this route. Use local resources. Contact a real estate agent and see if he or she can provide some recent sale prices of homes in your neighborhood that are comparable to yours. If you aren't satisfied with the answers you get, you can hire a real estate appraiser. The important thing is not to value your house based on its tax appraisal, because tax appraisals are typically considerably lower than the price your house might actually fetch. If you really have agreed to sell, then the market itself will determine the value. That is, a willing buyer and a willing seller agreeing on a sale price establish the fair market value of a home.

What are the capital gains rules these days about selling a house?

If you are single, you get a capital gains exclusion of $250,000. This means you won't be taxed on the first $250,000 of profit from the sale of your house. Married couples may receive an exclusion of $500,000. The only glitch is that you have to have lived in your house for at least two of the five years prior to selling it to be eligible for the exclusion. Keep this time limit in mind if you are thinking of moving out but putting off the sale of the house for a few years. A partial exclusion is available under certain circumstances if you have lived there for less than two years. Consult with your tax adviser. Special rules also apply if you rented the property or used part or all of it for business.

Is this a one-time-only exclusion?
You can use this exclusion every two years and as many times as you like.

Do I have to "roll over" the proceeds of my sale into a new property?
No.

What happens if my husband and I make more than $500,000 profit from the sale of our house?
You will owe capital gains tax on any gain above $500,000. In 2010 the tax rate is 15 percent (0 percent if you are in the 10 percent or 15 percent federal income tax bracket.) The rate rises to 20 percent in 2011.

How do you divide up the value of your house?
The value of the house is set on the date of divorce, not on the separation date. In other words, let's say you decide that the marriage is over, and you and your spouse separate and you move out. Two years later, the divorce is final. If the value of the house has increased over those two years, you will get to participate in that increase in value.

Can your spouse leave you, move to another

state, and sue for divorce there to get a better deal for him- or herself?
Yes. This is why many high-profile figures who divorce try to get the proceedings switched to a community-property state, where the split is fifty-fifty. Bear in mind, though, that laws regarding residency requirements before filing for and being granted a divorce vary widely from state to state.

If I move from one state to another, can my marital property rights change?
Yes, and sometimes drastically. For example, if you move to California and you own marital property in another state, this property may be considered "quasi-community property." Accordingly, you may have to split it equally in the event of a divorce. Quasi-community property is an asset that would be considered community property if it was acquired or located in the state you live in when you divorce, but may not be considered as such in the state where it is located.

In a divorce, can a spouse take back a gift given specifically to you—or at least claim his or her "half" of such a gift?
Not if it really was a gift. But transfers often can be ambiguous, and thus the gift-giver may be able to claim that whatever changed hands wasn't really a gift at all.

I suspect my soon-to-be ex-spouse is hiding assets. Is there anything I can do to force him to disclose everything he owns?
In many states there are particular requirements

of disclosure for a divorce. If you later discover that there were hidden assets, the court can award all of them to you—not just the 50 percent you might otherwise have expected to be granted. You can always reopen a divorce action if you believe your ex-spouse defrauded you in the settlement. This holds true in every state.

My husband and I were divorced shortly after he declared bankruptcy. Am I protected from his creditors, or can they come after me?

If you live in a community-property state and your husband incurred his debts during your marriage, you are responsible for those debts after divorce—unless the marital settlement agreement states otherwise and the creditor knows of that agreement. Remember, though, there is a statute of limitations on debt, so if his creditors do not sue you within the prescribed time—a period that varies from state to state—they will lose their right to do so. If you do not live in a community-property state and your husband has filed for bankruptcy by himself, you are not liable for his debts.

DIVORCE, RETIREMENT BENEFITS, AND SOCIAL SECURITY

My spouse and I both count our retirement plans among our assets. At what point does the court begin to assess the value of our retirement plans?

Many states value retirement plans and/or bene-

fits from the date of separation, not from the date of divorce, because this date marks the point at which a couple's common interest and mutual support ended. Keep this in mind because it may affect what you and your spouse are entitled to. For instance, many employers make their contributions to their employees' pension plans at the end of the calendar year. If you separated from your spouse and moved out on December 24, and on December 25 your spouse's employer made the annual retirement plan contribution, you might very well have missed out on your right to claim any portion of that year's contribution. (Many self-employed people put the year's retirement money into their Keoghs or SEP-IRAs at the very last minute of the tax year, so also take that into consideration.)

Make sure, then, that you know how your and/or your spouse's retirement plan works. When are the valuations of it made? Where a retirement plan is involved, consult an attorney before making any move and obtain a copy of the benefit schedule for both your and your spouse's retirement plan.

My husband and I are divorced, and I don't have a substantial work record of my own. Is it possible for me to claim Social Security based on his record?

You are eligible to receive dependents' benefits if you and your spouse are 62 years of age or older, your marriage lasted for at least ten years, and the marriage was dissolved at least two years before you make a claim (this refers to the actual date that your divorce became final). Please note, however, that this two-year waiting period does not apply if your ex-spouse was already receiving retirement benefits prior to your divorce. When your ex-spouse becomes eligible for retirement benefits at age 62, you can begin collecting dependents' benefits.

Timing is everything here. Again, let me share a recent memory. A woman I know decided that she wanted to divorce her husband, and she wanted to do it immediately. Luckily, the divorce promised to be very amicable. They had seen an attorney and had papers drawn up, which she was about to sign when she called to ask me a question about their investments. I asked her how long they had been married, and she told me nearly ten years. I suggested she wait, because if she went ahead and signed those papers right away, she would not, when the time came, be entitled to Social Security benefits based on her spouse's earnings. Social Security benefits are based on the date of divorce, not the date of separation. Since my client had never worked outside the home and hadn't built up Social Security of her own, signing the divorce papers before their tenth anniversary would have turned out to be a big mistake. If she wanted to, I told her, she could move out, they could separate, and for all intents and purposes they could go on with their lives as if they were divorced. Then, after their tenth anniversary, they could sign all the necessary papers to make the divorce legal.

Waiting to pass the ten-year mark affected not only my client's Social Security but also her alimony. The seven-to-ten-year mark is important because many states use these anniversaries as benchmarks for what constitutes a long-term marriage. In the case of a spouse who has not worked outside the home or who was earning very little during the marriage, a long-term marriage judgment may be very favorable for purposes of spousal support.

What if my former spouse decides to wait until age 65 to claim his Social Security benefits? Does this mean that I have to wait, too?
No. Your former spouse must merely become *eligible* for his or her retirement benefits for you to begin collecting dependents' benefits.

What percentage of my ex-husband's Social Security benefits will I get?
If you were married for 10 years or longer you are eligible for the greater of your own benefit amount, or half of your ex-husband's benefit. The benefit you receive as an ex-spouse in no way impacts the benefit your husband will receive, or if he remarries, the benefit for his new spouse. Please note, if you remarry you are not allowed to collect Social Security based on your ex's benefit.

Does the amount that I get in Social Security dependents' benefits have any effect on the amount that my former spouse will be receiving in retirement benefits?
No. It is important to understand that by claiming these benefits, you are not in any way "punishing" your former spouse. Your dependents' benefits will not take away from any of the money he or she will collect. You are simply getting what you are entitled to by law.

What if I remarry and lose my Social Security dependents' benefits, but my second marriage

doesn't last? Can I reclaim those original dependents' benefits?

Yes. And if your second marriage lasted for more than ten years, too, then you could very possibly be eligible to claim dependents' benefits based on your second husband's work record. You can choose the benefits of either husband as long as you did not marry a third time before the age of 60.

If my former spouse dies, will my Social Security dependents' benefits continue?

Yes, though they will automatically become survivors' benefits.

If my former spouse remarries, will this have any effect on my Social Security dependents' benefits?

No.

What criteria do I have to meet in order to be eligible for my former husband's Social Security benefits?

Curiously enough, this is a matter that you have to work out with the Social Security Administration, not with your former spouse. You may very well be entitled to retirement benefits if you are at least 62 years old, are not married when you apply for benefits, are not already receiving Social Security spousal or survivors' benefits, and were married for at least ten years.

How do I establish my eligibility for Social Security benefits?

You should visit the Social Security office nearest where you live at least three months before you turn 62. You should bring along with you proof of your identity, your age (as well as the age of your former spouse), your marriage, and your divorce. Or you can learn more online at *ssa.gov.* Type "divorce" in the search box.

COLLABORATIVE LAW

I have heard the term "collaborative law." What does it mean?

Collaborative law is a fairly new option for working out all the issues involved in your divorce. It involves you, your spouse, and your attorneys sitting down together to hammer out a divorce settlement that is fair to you and your spouse. (The attorneys must have training in the collaborative law process.) Collaborative law is now available in all but a few states—Montana, Wyoming, and South Dakota—and it is rapidly catching on worldwide.

What are the benefits of collaborative law?

For one thing, it can be cheaper and less anxiety-provoking than using either a mediator or an arbitrator. It's also an amicable way for you and your spouse to settle your differences, and it can pave the way toward a much more cooperative relationship in the future, which is particularly important when there are children involved. You can learn more at *collaborativepractice.com.*

What are the disadvantages of collaborative law?

One of the biggest drawbacks of collaborative law is that if it doesn't work and you end up needing the court to step in and intervene, both your attorney and your husband's attorney must agree to recuse themselves from your case. Basically, you'll each have to hire a new attorney and start all over again. Another risk is that the dynamics of your relationship with your ex—for example, his tendency to bully you—may be replicated in the collaborative-law situation.

What is the difference between this method and using a mediator?

The difference is that a mediator is a neutral third party, whereas in collaborative law, there is no neutral third party present.

MEDIATION

My attorney has suggested that my husband and I explore the possibility of using a mediator. Do you advise this?

I usually recommend trying mediation for at least one session. A mediator can help you decide how your property is going to be divided and can also be very helpful in resolving custody arrangements. A mediator is a kind of counselor or referee and, just like a ref, he or she is impartial, with no allegiance to either you or your husband, and works to help you both reach a fair, consensual resolution. Please realize that if you are able to reach an agreement with the help of a mediator, it will probably be necessary for you to have your attorneys finalize the agreement and submit it to the court to ensure that it will be legally binding.

Are mediators lawyers?

Many mediators are attorneys, but others come from a variety of backgrounds. They can be psychologists, social workers, marriage counselors, clergymen, or financial experts. They do not need to be licensed, but in some states they do need to have received specialized training in mediation. To locate a mediator in your state, contact the Association for Conflict Resolution at *www.acrnet .org*.

In what circumstances would a mediator not be helpful?

I would not recommend a mediator in cases where custody arrangements or the division of property are unusually complicated, or in cases where emotions are running so high that you and your spouse can't work together. If you are afraid of your spouse for any reason, I would stay away from mediation. I would also keep away from a mediator if you do not feel sure of what your priorities and goals are with respect to negotiation. You should use a mediator only if you and your spouse are able to engage in rational discussion and if you believe you can reach a general agreement about how you want to split things up.

How much do mediators charge?

Depending on what part of the country you live in and the experience and reputation of the mediator in question, he or she will charge anywhere from $60 to $300 an hour. Mediation can work in as few as two hours, or it can last several months, with several sessions scheduled each week.

What happens if mediation works out?

If things work out, then your mediator will usually formalize your agreement in writing. He or she will give each of your attorneys a copy of the agreement to review, and if they give their go-ahead, both of you will sign it. The mediation agreement will be incorporated into your divorce agreement. In some instances, the agreement is signed right after the mediation is concluded, especially if your attorneys have been present during the negotiations.

ARBITRATION

What is the difference between a mediator and an arbitrator? In what situation would it be wise to use an arbitrator?

If you are in a situation where you don't want your divorce to go to trial in a formal courtroom but are concerned that your spouse may manage to get the mediator to see things his way, you might want to seek out an arbitrator. An arbitrator is frequently an attorney, but can also be a retired judge or therapist. Like mediation, arbitration is a private matter. Only the fact of a resolution becomes part of the public record. In both mediation and arbitration, you avoid going to court, but that's where the similarity ends. Mediation is usually a conciliatory process: You and your spouse agree on who gets what, and in the end, despite the unavoidable pain of divorce, you both leave satisfied. Most important, the mediator has no power to grant a decision. Arbitration is different because, by definition, the arbitrator can impose a decision on the division of property, just as a judge does. The only differences between an arbitrator and a judge are that

you and your spouse select the arbitrator and pay his or her fees rather than using a government-appointed judge, and usually you cannot appeal an arbitrator's decision. To locate an arbitrator in your area, you can get in touch with the American Arbitration Association at *www.adr .org*.

That doesn't sound so bad. What are the drawbacks of hiring an arbitrator?

Mediation is typically much faster than arbitration, in large part because both parties have agreed to conduct themselves in an amicable way. In effect, you and your spouse are in charge of the outcome. Arbitration, like a court trial, takes that power out of your hands. Remember, the arbitrator is legally allowed to make far-reaching decisions about the allocation of your assets, based on evidence, the facts presented to him or her, and the laws in your particular state. With arbitration, the process is less formal than it would be in court, and usually you pay less in attorneys' fees, but you each have to pay half the arbitrator's fee. Also, you will have to live with whatever decisions the arbitrator makes. Finally, some people fear that since arbitrators are not really judges, they aren't as qualified to render fair decisions.

Are mediation and arbitration the only two options for us unless my husband and I agree to go to court?

Well, there's also a "marriage" of mediation and arbitration techniques. It's called "med/arb," and it's a little of both. The "med" part assumes that you and your husband will try to work things out in as amicable a way as possible. If this fails, the mediator becomes an "arb," and can make decisions on your and your husband's behalf.

THE REALITIES OF DIVORCE

Both my husband and I want to get our divorce over with as quickly and painlessly as possible. What happens after we've met with our attorneys and discussed all our assets and liabilities?
Once you've met with your attorneys and discussed your assets and liabilities, it's time to negotiate the settlement. If the marriage has been very short, no real property is involved, there are no children, and there aren't a lot of assets (or debts) to divide, you may be able to divorce through a summary disposition, which is basically the quickest, most efficient way to file for divorce. In a summary disposition, you and your spouse agree on the basic terms of the dissolution and jointly file simple paperwork with the local court setting forth your plans. Usually, the actual filing is done without an attorney (self-representation in legal terms is known as "in pro per"), though in some cases even a summary disposition is done with attorneys or with a joint attorney overseeing the paperwork. In most states, the judge or a research assistant will review the documents and attempt to verify that the agreement is a fair one. (Remember, you can't get a summary dissolution if there are children involved!) In some states you may not even have to show up for a court hearing; in other states a brief hearing may be held, so that the judge can ensure that both sides are getting a fair deal.

What about those cases when a divorce is not friendly?
In these cases, it is not just a good idea for each of you to have an attorney—it is a must. In some cases, even attorneys will not be able to hammer out an agreement, and the two of you will have to go before a judge. The attorney's role, as always, is to represent your interests, suggest appropriate settlement terms, convey settlement offers, advise you as to what the court is likely to do in your situation, and help with the division of property and debts. The attorney does everything he or she would do in an amicable situation and also fights your battles for you and insulates you from your estranged spouse. Once the terms have been decided—who gets what and when—either by the two of you or with a court order, a marital settlement agreement, stipulated judgment, or court's final judgment of divorce is drafted, signed by the parties and lawyers, and finally signed by a judge, which makes it a legally binding order. If you cannot come to an agreement, you will end up settling your dispute in court.

It looks like my spouse and I are headed toward court. What should I keep in mind?
You should know that when it comes to divorce, the court system is set up to make sure that the division of property is handled fairly and to ensure the welfare of any children involved. When you go to court, the outcome is solely in the hands of the judge. This means that you are putting the fate of your future, your home, your children, and your pension and retirement plans in the hands of a total stranger. You should also know that the court usually doesn't care whose "fault" the divorce is!

Are you saying that my husband and I should really try our best to work out the terms of our divorce instead of going to court?

Yes. It won't be easy—in fact, it will be emotional and probably very difficult—but, in my opinion, if you and your spouse can agree on terms between yourselves and reach a clear resolution, you may very well be better off than you would be entrusting your fate and your future to an unknown judge. But if you simply cannot resolve your differences, you shouldn't be afraid to put the matter in the hands of a court.

If my wife and I are already in court, heading toward trial, is there any way to reach a settlement of some kind at this point, or is there no turning back?

There is always room to "turn back" and reach a settlement. Turning back isn't a failure, it's a solution—and, in a lot of cases, a wise one. Even if you are committed to taking your spouse to court, an out-of-court settlement may be reached days or perhaps minutes before the case is to begin. In fact, 90 percent of divorces are settled before trial, no matter how hell-bent both parties are on having a judge hear their case. However, I ask you to be very careful, because this is the time when big mistakes are often made. Imagine this scenario: You are about to go into the courtroom, nervous as can be. Your lawyer, who has been talking in hushed tones to the lawyer representing your ex, approaches you and says your ex is willing to settle the case right now if you give in on a few points. The decision has to be made right away, because once the trial begins it is too late. So you give in on the points and instantly feel a wave of relief. Two months down the road, how-

ever, you realize that you may have made a mistake solely to avoid a courtroom confrontation. Do not make decisions that will affect the rest of your life when you feel pressured. If you have gone all the way to trial, do not—unless you know the precise ramifications of everything you are agreeing to—accept a last-minute settlement.

With our court date just a few weeks away, my estranged husband has offered me a certain amount of money in a one-time payoff. This seems to me more attractive than receiving money from him every month because I can put him and our marriage behind me. Any advice?

In some instances, a spouse may offer a one-time, lump-sum offer of settlement, which in effect is a "buy-out" of any future obligations, excluding child support. A once-and-for-all settlement needs to be looked at with caution, because the spouse required to pay is using today's dollars to settle what might be a significantly greater amount tomorrow. If you are considering a settlement, consider all the factors and make sure you get professional advice. You also need to check out all the tax implications of such an arrangement.

Six months after I filed for divorce, my day in court is finally here. I am extremely nervous. What happens during a trial?

Courtroom trials are fairly predictable and never particularly fluid—that is, they stop and start and stop again. After opening statements, the court hears the case of the plaintiff (that's you, the person who filed for divorce). This is followed by a cross-examination by the attorney for the defendant (your spouse), which is followed by redirect (your attorney's chance to cross-examine the cross-examination). Next the defendant's case is presented, followed by a rebuttal by the plaintiff's attorney, and then, typically, there are closing arguments. Depending on how complex your case is, the judge may issue his or her decision immediately or choose to deliberate for a while and then issue a written decision.

What happens after the judge issues his or her decision?

Usually the attorney for the person who prevailed in court drafts a divorce decree. A divorce decree is basically a summary of the judge's decision, which also includes whatever matters you and your spouse decided between yourselves. After the decree is sent to the opposing counsel for approval, it is submitted to the court for its approval.

Can my ex-husband or I appeal the judge's decision?

If you have a legal basis for appeal, of course you can. You cannot mount an appeal simply because you don't happen to like his or her decision. Remember, an appeal takes time and money, and the trial court's decision is rarely overturned. For people who have just spent a lot of money on attorneys' fees, the notion of spending even more money—and prolonging the agony of divorce—often doesn't seem very appealing. A much more efficient way to deal with the aspects of the judge's decision regarding alimony or child custody and support issues that rub you the wrong way is to file a petition for modification based on changed circumstances. This basically leaves the

judge's decision in place, but requests that the court modify one or more provisions that you do not like. Also, in some states, within a short period of time after the court judgment, a motion for reconsideration based on new evidence may be made.

Does the divorce decree affect any pretrial court orders?

Yes. Typically, it replaces them.

Assuming that neither of us appeals the judge's decision, now what?

Now a record of your divorce decree is filed at the county courthouse and you are officially divorced. For better or for worse. This is the time to make sure that all your documents—the deed to your house, the title to your car or boat, your will or trust, your insurance policies, retirement plans, IRAs, and every investment or asset that was previously held jointly—reflect your new status. Please don't let this paperwork slide, for decisiveness will help the healing and make you feel stronger for having put your past behind you. With the clutter gone, you'll be freer to put your energies into starting over again.

LIFE AFTER SEPARATION AND DIVORCE

For years my husband and I filed joint tax returns. Now that we're no longer separated, do I simply go back to filing singly? If so, at what point do I start doing this?

Any and all income you earn from the date of

separation may, if you choose, be filed on a separate tax return. There may be tax ramifications, possibly negative, when you decide to do this, so make sure you consult an accountant. If you still have any doubt as to what you should do, or if you and your spouse cannot decide how you should file your taxes, file separately. The law allows people who file separately to amend their taxes within a three-year period and to file again jointly, but the law does not let people who file jointly amend their taxes later to file separately. You can't file a joint return in the year your divorce decree or legal separation agreement is final.

If you file taxes separately, you and your spouse must decide together how you will divide deductions—the home mortgage interest, charitable deductions that you made together, property taxes, day-care expenses, etc. You will also need to allocate income from joint accounts to one or both spouses for next year's tax returns.

When filing jointly, each of you is liable for what the other puts on your tax return. Be particularly wary if you distrust your spouse when it comes to money. If your spouse overstates deductions or understates income and the IRS catches it, you as well as your spouse may be held responsible for all back taxes and penalties, plus interest. If your now ex-spouse cannot pay these back taxes and penalties, the IRS may, with certain exceptions, come after you. So if money has been a problem between the two of you, you might want to protect yourself and file separately for peace of mind, even if it will cost you more.

My ex-wife is getting in the way of my visitation rights with my children. What should I do?
I will tell you what you should not do, and that

is withhold money that the court ordered you to send her for child support. That is not only breaking the law, it could also threaten your children's well-being. If you and your ex-wife aren't speaking to each other and can't work this out in a civil way, then you must bring a contempt of court action against her. Unless your ex can prove that she has very good reasons for keeping you away from your kids, she will be ordered by the court to do what is legal and may have to pay your legal costs and a fine, and possibly face going to jail for a short period.

My husband is continually late with his child support payments. Is there anything I can do?
Unfortunately, you are not alone. The legal term for past-due child support is arrearage, and it is a national shame. If I were you, I would hire an attorney to go after your husband, assuming he has some money to chase after. A less expensive method is to contact your state's Child Support Enforcement (CSE) program. The federal Website, *www.acf.dhhs.gov/programs/cse,* has links to state agencies.

If your spouse is behind in child support payments, you may be able to engage the help of a government official, either someone from the IRS or a child support–enforcement advocate, to seize the assets of your errant spouse. Whether to hire your own attorney or rely on the government depends on the laws of your particular state.

What about these private child support collection agencies I keep reading about in the newspaper?
Working with one of these agencies is a

possibility, but I would check out the fees very carefully first. Some take a huge chunk of any money they recover on behalf of your children.

THE DEATH OF A LOVED ONE

For those of you who are in a position to learn about your finances from your loved ones, I beg you not to put this topic off one minute longer. Discuss with your spouse or partner everything you need to know about your estate—including insurance, the children's best interests, the location of all documents, and a list of whom to notify—before one of you dies. I urge you both to make your preferences clear—whether you wish to be buried or cremated, where you would like your remains to rest, and what kind of service or ceremony you would like to have. A loved one's death is overwhelming, but having some of the details worked out and a sense of purpose in those first painful days will provide some relief to whichever one of you survives.

When you have just suffered a loss, it's not the time to start learning about money. When you are in a marriage or other close relationship, it is vital—and I cannot stress this enough—that both of you know everything there is to know about your money. Not only how to spend it, but how to invest it and why. Both of you should know where all your important documents are and should know the answer to this question: If one of you were to die tomorrow, would there be enough income for the other person to be finan-

cially secure? Please ask this question while your partner is still around to answer it. Little by little, step by step, you can and must learn to handle your money and make decisions that will be right for you in the long run.

My husband of six years recently died after a short, unexpected illness. I feel utterly wiped out emotionally. How can I start to put my life in order?

To have someone you love taken from you forever creates a pain so deep that there is often little anyone can say or do to help. Having faced the emotional and financial aftermath of death many times with former clients, I have come to believe that we never quite know the meaning of life until we draw close to death. Everything is put into perspective and yet, in our grief, most of us put thoughts of money out of our minds, which can be a terrible mistake. The death of a partner forces us not only to deal with a new emotional reality, but also to accept a new financial reality.

I am totally unprepared to deal with financial matters in the midst of all this emotion! Do you have any suggestions?

Allow yourself time to grieve and to heal—but be mindful that the longer you neglect the financial consequences of a spouse's death, the harder it will be to pick up the pieces once you feel ready to take charge. Over the years, I have been called upon many times to reassemble a client's financial life after a spouse's death. Some people who came to me were lucky; when their spouses or life partners died, they had a friend or someone they could trust to help them along on their new financial course. But many bereaved men and women had sought the advice of a so-called professional when they were most vulnerable and ended up losing everything, or nearly so. By the time they found their way to me, these people had handed over their life insurance proceeds, their portfolios—their futures—to con artists posing as concerned advisers or to commission-hungry salespeople. It is hard enough to find the courage to go on after you have lost your emotional equilibrium, but it is almost impossible when you have lost your financial stability, too. Difficult as it may seem to you now, in the early stages of your grief, I ask you please to keep your financial realities in mind as you come to terms with the death of your spouse or life partner. The actions you take at this time will have important effects later, when the death and your grief are not so new and raw.

My mother, who is 70, lives in Florida and has a burial plot in New York. She recently called and asked me if I thought it was wise for her to prepay her funeral expenses. She has been quoted a package which would send her body back to New York and pay for the chapel, the rabbi, and the cemetery fees, all for under $4,000. What should I tell her?

Well, my first words of advice would be for you to look at some basic numbers. Actuarially speaking, your mother is likely to live another 17 years. If she takes that $4,000 today and invests it in a good no-load mutual fund that averages a 10 percent return, in 17 years that $4,000 will be worth $20,218. If you adjust for inflation at, say, 3 percent, that $20,218 would still be worth $12,232 in today's dollars. And not only does she lose the

investment potential of her $4,000, but buying this package leaves her no room to change her mind about her funeral arrangements. What if she meets a wonderful man in Florida, marries him, and decides she would like to be buried with him? The short answer to your question is, I think prepaid funerals are a waste of money.

My wife just died very suddenly, and my children and I are devastated. It's hard to think about funeral arrangements at this time, but I have no choice. Where should I start?

Losing someone you love can be paralyzing—but you must take care of the business of death, which can seem as complicated as the business of life. Here is a checklist of matters that will require your immediate attention, whether you feel like attending to them or not. If you have a friend or a relative who can assist you, please ask for help. Even though you may think you are capable and thinking clearly, you are probably in shock.

• The first job that you will be faced with will be making proper arrangements for the burial or cremation of the person you loved. (If you are not certain of the deceased's wishes, before you do anything else, please check to see if there is an organ donor card on the back of his or her driver's license. If there is, please contact the nearest hospital so that these wishes can be carried out.) You must contend with the remains, surely one of the most painful tasks you'll have to perform, but I want you to take care and pay attention, for these first moves can become emotionally and financially costly if you or someone close to you is not vigilant and well informed.

- If the death took place in a hospital, you will be asked the name of the funeral home that you would like to use. The hospital staff will call the funeral home and take care of transporting the remains to the home.
- If the death took place at your home or anywhere other than a hospital, you will have to contact the funeral home or cremation society of your choice, which will then make arrangements to transport the remains.
- If you want the burial or cremation to take place in a state different from the one in which your loved one has died, again, either you or the hospital will place the call to the out-of-state funeral home or cremation society you want to use, and they will take care of the transportation arrangements for you.
- If you don't know which funeral home you want to use, ask your friends, your clergyman, or an administrator at your local place of worship for a recommendation. Most churches or synagogues have a list of funeral homes for you to call. If you do not have this resource and none of your friends can make a recommendation, call your local hospital for assistance.

I've heard horror stories about funeral homes ripping off grieving survivors. When I go in, what should I be aware of?

Many years ago the government passed a law called the Funeral Rule, which states that a funeral home must provide you with a full disclosure of its practices, services, and fees. This includes the cost of caskets, obituary notices placed in newspapers, and embalming; any payments made on your behalf for flowers, funeral escorts, honorarium to clergy, limousines, copies of the death certificate, memorial cards, and musicians' fees; and any additional service fee that the funeral home may charge. If you wish, you can obtain this list from a number of funeral homes so that you can compare costs. If you choose a funeral home and are not happy with the available funeral arrangements, please talk to the funeral director first, and if the problem is not resolved to your satisfaction, contact your state licensing board.

The service can be held at the funeral home or in a place of worship. If you know what kind of service your partner wanted, so much the better. One often hears of people who choose the music they'd like to have played at their funeral services, and the survivors cherish that music forever. The burial can be public or private, and you can hold a private burial right away and a memorial service later on.

Unless you or someone else planned for the final disposition of the remains ahead of time, the funeral home or cremation society will discuss with you whether you need a burial plot and also can assist you in making arrangements to purchase one.

How much should I spend on a funeral?

That's up to you, of course, but when it comes to planning the service, carefully consider your options. You shouldn't try to prove your love by choosing the most expensive options available; in fact, you should take into consideration your available resources and immediate future expenses before you make any choices regarding funeral or burial services. For instance, let's say you have $8,000 in a savings account and your expenses for the next month will total $3,000. If you spend $8,000 on the funeral, you'll be unable to pay your bills. Dignity, remember, costs not a penny. Public and private good-byes can be dignified, holy, and simple at the same time.

My husband is a veteran of two wars, and I'd like to know beforehand how I can arrange a proper veteran's burial when the time comes.
If your partner or loved one was a veteran, he or she may be eligible to be buried in any of the 115 national cemeteries, free of charge. If so, veterans' assistance may provide transportation of the remains to the nearest veterans' cemetery and a marker or a headstone. In a veteran's burial, a U.S. flag will be used to cover the casket and then will be presented to you. If you choose a veteran's burial, you will have to document the fact that the deceased was a veteran. You will need to have proof of his or her:

Rank
Branch of service
Separation papers (Form DD-214)
Date of entry into the service and date of departure
Date of birth and date of death
Social Security number (as well as your own)
Name and address of the executor or trustee of the estate

Can I choose to have my husband buried in a private cemetery as opposed to a national one and still have a military funeral?
Yes. If you use a private cemetery, you still can apply for a burial allowance, a flag, and a government headstone or marker from the Veterans Administration. If you did not know of such an

allowance at the time of burial, you have two years from the date of death to apply for a reimbursement. To apply, just look in your phone book to find the number of the VA office nearest you. For more information, log on to *www.cem.va.gov*.

My husband was buried only last month. Now comes the hard part—settling back into my life. Any ideas on where to start?
When you are trying to live through a loss of great magnitude, it is all too easy to lose touch with practical matters—especially those touching on money. Yet money continues to be important. After the funeral and during your period of mourning, how are you going to pay for the everyday expenses? Often people find that nearly every penny they have is in a retirement account, in a life insurance policy, or locked up in equity in a home, where they can't readily get to it. They can be left with very little cash to draw upon. If you haven't done so before, you will now have to try to estimate your monthly expenses and be sure that you can pay them while matters concerning your husband's estate are settled.

My husband left me a life insurance policy. Won't this take care of things for the short term?
Even if the deceased had a life insurance policy, the insurance company might not release the funds for many months. This is particularly the case if the cause of death is unclear or if the death appears to have been a suicide. I have a friend whose brother died in a car-racing accident. It just so happened that he had raised his life insurance policy from $50,000 to $250,000 the month before his accident. Because of the

timing, the insurance company did not release the insurance proceeds until it had thoroughly investigated the possibility of a suicide. In the intervening months, his widow was left in terrible financial straits.

So I should be very careful before I start spending what I think I have?

Yes. Before you do anything, it is essential that you have a clear picture of what you are going to need to get by for the next few months and where that money is going to come from. My advice, as always, is to have an understanding of your finances long before you find yourself in a tragic situation.

All my friends are offering to pitch in and help me. Should I take them up on their offers?

Most definitely. That's what friends are for. Following a death, I would suggest you ask whomever you have chosen to help you with the funeral arrangements to collect your mail for the next few weeks. It would also be helpful if he or she could see if there are any bills that need to be paid immediately and keep track of when the rest of the bills will come due. If you are corresponding through the mail about financial matters related to the estate, please ask your friend to make sure that copies are made of letters and documents being sent by you. It is always important to be able to document anything that you have said or that has been said on your behalf during a time of sorrow. Later you may remember these early days only as a blur of pain and confusion.

Do I need to contact an attorney or can I do everything myself?

The way your spouse has set up his or her estate will determine the extent to which you will need the help of an attorney. If everything the two of you owned was in joint tenancy with right of survivorship (JTWROS) and you are the sole beneficiary of the life insurance proceeds, IRA, or retirement accounts, everything will automatically pass directly to you upon your spouse's death. Similarly, if all your joint assets were held for your benefit in a revocable living trust (a legal entity that holds your assets while you are alive), then settling the estate will be easy. Once the appropriate institutions are presented with a certified copy of the death certificate and whatever other papers they may want to see, everything will simply and automatically be switched over to your name. However, there may be decisions to be made about taxes that will require the immediate assistance of an attorney.

My husband had lots of different accounts. He didn't have a living trust. Will settling his estate take longer?

Unfortunately, yes. If your partner kept a variety of separate accounts, had only a will, and held the house title in his or her name only (even if the intent was that it should pass on to you), then the process will be a longer one. You should contact an attorney within the first few days after your spouse's death. If you do not have an attorney, please find one who specializes in probate administration to make sure that everything is in order and to help you organize what must be done.

So I will need an attorney. Is there anything I can do to save time and money?

Yes—particularly to save money. There are certain tasks that you can complete on your own or with the help of a friend. For example, a friend could call the insurance companies and the bank or brokerage firms to find out what paperwork needs to be completed to report the death. The most important part of your immediate job will be helping to locate and describe all of your loved one's assets and liabilities—debts, outstanding loans, everything your loved one owned and owed to the world.

Now that my husband has died, I'm hearing many new words whose meanings I'm not sure of. Could you translate a few of them for me?
The legalese of death can sometimes seem like a foreign language. Below are brief definitions of some of the terms you will probably come across:

Decedent: The person who is deceased.

Executor/Executrix: The man or woman the decedent designated to carry out the terms of the will.

Co-executors/Co-executrixes: The people (sometimes more than one) the decedent designated to carry out the terms of the will.

Administrator/Administratrix: The person the court assigns to oversee your estate or your spouse's estate if there is no will.

Personal Representative: In some states this is the title of the court appointee, whether a man or a woman.

Trustee: When the estate is held in trust, this is the person who is responsible for carrying out the terms of the trust.

What precisely are my duties and responsibilities as the survivor, both to my late spouse and to myself?

The duties that a spouse or life partner must carry out vary from those of the executor or executrix. Here is an overview of what you, the survivor, should be attending to immediately:

- Order at least 15 certified copies of the death certificate. You will need these in order to collect insurance proceeds and to change names on bank accounts, deeds, and other assets. Please do this right away. The funeral home usually will be able to obtain the number of certified death certificates you request. Otherwise, your county has an office of vital statistics at the county courthouse, where death, birth, and marriage certificates are kept and can be obtained upon request for a fee.

- If you do not already have one, please open a bank account in your own name.

- If you do not have a credit card in your own name, you may want to wait to notify the credit card companies where you have cards listed in both of your names. While it is illegal for a company to cancel your credit card because your spouse has died, it is not unheard of for a company to lower your credit limit if the limit was based on the deceased's income. (It's always a good idea to have a credit card in your name alone so that, over the years, you will build up a credit history.)

- Do not pay off any credit card debts that were not yours alone before you check with your attorney or executor. Some attorneys or advisers might counsel you not to pay off the deceased's debts because it's unlikely that creditors will spend the money to come after the estate to recoup small amounts of debt. I disagree with this advice because I believe that honoring a debt, when possible, is honoring both the dead and the living. If there isn't enough money in the estate to pay off all debts, the probate court has a "schedule" specifying which debts are given priority and the order in which the debts are to be paid—which is why I want you to check with your attorney before you begin paying any debts.

- Review any insurance coverage that the deceased may have had with banks or credit card companies. You may have more than you know. For instance, offers for life insurance at just a small cost every month often come in the mail via a bank statement or credit card bill. Your spouse may have impulsively signed up for such coverage. This kind of thing happens more often than you might think. Call every credit card company and bank that the deceased had accounts with and ask whether they also have an insurance policy in the name of the deceased.

- Consider whether you will have enough money to live on in the coming months or will need money from the estate before it is settled. Go through six months of your and your late spouse's records and estimate your monthly expenses. If there is not enough money in your existing accounts to cover your projected expenses, the amount you need will be requested from a judge in probate court. The judge will decide on a family allowance while the estate is being settled.

- Contact your local Social Security office—or call the national office at (800) 772-1213 or log on to the Web at *www.ssa.gov*—to see if you qualify for any benefits. You will qualify for benefits if:

You are 60 years of age or older.
You are 50 years of age or older and disabled.
You care for a child who is under age 16 or disabled.

If your surviving parent is 62 years of age or older, and you are your parent's primary means of support (you provide at least half of their support), they will qualify through Social Security for survivor's benefits when you die.

In addition, Social Security allots a small amount of money—$255—to surviving spouses or minors if they meet certain requirements. Do not overlook that, for sometimes every little bit can help.

If you and your spouse both were collecting Social Security, you might want to stop collecting yours and collect your late spouse's if that amount is higher. In any case, you have to choose whose you will receive.

Your children will get Social Security if:
They are unmarried and under age 18.
They are under age 19 and still in school full-time.
They are disabled, no matter how old they are.

- Please make a note: Do not forget that your own will or trust should be changed now, for most likely you have left everything to the person who has just died. Make sure that you change the beneficiary designation on your IRA, life insurance policies, pension plans,

401(k) plans, and any other investment or retirement plans.

I am both the surviving spouse of my late husband and also one of the executors of his estate. Do I have duties in addition to the ones you just named above?

If you are an executor or executrix as well as the surviving spouse, then the following obligations also pertain. Please note that an executor is held personally and legally responsible for all of the actions associated with these duties. This is not a job that should be taken lightly or treated as honorary. The duties of the executor primarily fall into the following categories:

- Paying all outstanding bills, including taxes to the IRS
- Tallying and securing all assets in the estate until they are ready to be distributed among the rightful heirs
- Supervising the settlement procedures and managing the estate during this process
- Distributing all the assets to the designated beneficiaries at the appropriate time.

The following is a legal checklist for the executor.

- Your first job as executor is to locate the will or trust and all assets, including life insurance policies, retirement, bank, and brokerage accounts, and stocks and bonds. If no will or trust can be found, then call the deceased's attorney, if there is one, to see if he or she has a copy of a will or trust. If nothing else, an attorney may know if one was ever written. If no will can be found, the estate passes by what is known as intestate succession, which means that the assets in the estate that would otherwise be subject to a will will be distributed by a formula determined by law. In this case, there will be a court-appointed administrator.

- If the will is located, it must be submitted to the probate court, where it must be validated by a judge. When the will is proved and admitted to probate, then the executor is officially appointed by a document known as letters testamentary. This is the official document that legally empowers the executor to take action on behalf of the estate.

- The executor must protect the estate. This means that heirs are not allowed to remove any of the assets that have been left to them until the probate court grants final approval for distribution, unless an earlier distribution is allowed by the judge or by law.

- During the probate procedure, the executor must keep careful track of all expenses as well as income (receipts, statements, etc.) that the estate pays out and receives.

- If the surviving spouse has not already obtained certified copies of the death certificate, you should obtain at least 15 copies.

- Notify all the insurance companies of the death, including life, disability, auto, and homeowner's insurance companies. Notify all the banks, brokerage firms, mutual fund companies, retirement plans and plan administrators, and any other institution where the decedent had accounts or deeds, or even accounts that were in both spouses' names. This includes the Veterans Administration if the decedent was a veteran.

- Often individual bank accounts in the decedent's name will be changed first to the name of the executor, even if the executor is not the spouse, so that the executor can access funds if needed. However, if a joint tenancy with right of survivorship is involved, the money and title of the account will go directly to the surviving spouse or partner. For example, Jane and John have a bank account held in JTWROS. If John were to die, Jane would get the account immediately. However, if John had an account in his name alone, and John's brother were executor of John's will, the account would first be transferred to his brother's name as executor while the estate was being settled, even if John left everything to Jane. The account would be transferred to Jane's name upon settlement as the sole beneficiary.

- Before any accounts are closed, please make sure that the financial needs of the surviving spouse are going to be met. It is best to clear it with the attorney before closing existing accounts.

- Make a complete inventory of the decedent's safe-deposit box. As part of the probate process, the executor will distribute the contents according to the will. If the key cannot be located and the surviving spouse's name is not on the box, you won't be able to open it without a court order, although some states permit access to look for such estate-planning documents as wills and trusts. Most states don't seal the boxes anymore, but the bank can make access difficult. If the box is held in the trust, the trustee will have access. Without the key, you will always end up paying the bank $150 or more to "drill" the box open. (Please don't make those you leave behind go through this. Leave the key and instructions with your other easy-to-find documents for your family members or whoever is going to be the executor or trustee of your estate.)

Remember, if the estate is to be distributed through a living trust and the deceased's assets were transferred to the trust during his or her lifetime, it does not have to go through probate court, and the trustee named in the trust will carry out the actions designated in the trust.

STARTING OVER AFTER A DIVORCE OR THE DEATH OF A LOVED ONE

My husband died several months ago. What should I be keeping in mind during this period?
Take good care of yourself. Starting over from a place of loss can be even harder than starting out for the first time. When you were first entering your adult life, you were equipped with hope, ideals, expectations, and strength. These are undependable commodities when you're starting over with feelings of loss and emptiness. Will any of us be spared the painful test of starting over, one way or another, one day or

another? I don't think so. This test seems universal to me.

If you are starting over, you already know that you must replenish your strength. It is a treacherous time financially as well as emotionally, and you must be very, very careful with your money. Facing the "whats" and "what ifs" of starting over requires immense courage. Questions such as these come up:

- What if I can't make it? I've never really handled money before.
- I've never had to work. What if I can't pay my bills?
- My husband left me with just a small settlement, and it's all I have.
- What should I do with the money?
- What if the insurance money doesn't last?
- What do I do now?

All these questions seem to come down to one thing: I'm scared!

There is nothing wrong with being scared. Though the questions you have may differ from those above, the common denominator is fear—fear of not making it, fear of loneliness, fear of tomorrow—and this fear comes at a time of life when you are at your most vulnerable. That's the bad news. The good news is that, even though you may not believe it right now, I have seen men and women in this situation, and who were ready to give up, go on and create for themselves a new life they cherish. A life they call their own.

How did these men and women get from a place of loss and fear to a new life?

By drawing on the faith and courage that reside in each of us. Remember, after a loss we must rejoin the world of the living. We don't have a choice! Bear in mind that your thoughts, words, and actions during this time have the power to make your life easier.

Despite my loss, I feel pretty clearheaded these days. Am I kidding myself?

To some degree, probably yes. I can't tell you how many times I have sat across from people who had just suffered losses and were starting over. I would review their situations and say, "OK, we have to do thus and such, and then we will do this and that, and finally this." They would agree with me, behaving as if they understood what I was saying, and I would take the necessary actions based on our conversation. Inevitably, six months to a year later, they would come back and say, "Can you tell me why we did what we did with the money?" It became obvious to me that they had not heard a word I had said during the early days of their grief. It was as if they had been present in body but not in mind. I would explain the reasons for the actions we took again, and this time they would finally get it.

What would you suggest doing financially after the basic issues have been taken care of?

Many of us emerge from a divorce or the death of a loved one with assets we must manage and protect, perhaps for the first time in our lives. After seeing the ways in which people tend to jeopardize these assets in their grief, their anger, their exhaustion, or their confusion, I have come up with a rule that has never once failed: Take no action with your money other than keeping it safe and sound for at least six months to a year after a loss.

Why do I need to wait six months to a year? I'm not that much of a basket case, am I?

One way or another, you have just been through a hard time, dealing with the legalities and expenses of divorce or the difficult tasks you've had to take on after a death. I am simply telling you that you are not equipped now—emotionally or financially—to make the big decisions that will have to be made. These include decisions about investing your money on your own or entrusting it to an adviser. If your money is in a secure place, a place that has allowed you to feel safe and comfortable about it until now, I want you to leave it there and to wait until your emotional equilibrium is restored before you take any action with your money. If you feel your money is *not* currently safe, make the financial changes that will get your money to a safe place, and then do nothing else for the time being.

How can I make sure that my money is being invested safely during this period?

My advice would be to seek out a financial adviser who comes highly recommended by a friend who has money under management with that adviser. If you have no friend who can recommend someone, what you want for now is a fee-based financial planner—one who does not sell products of any kind. When you go to see this adviser or planner, you may want to take a friend or relative with you for support. The first thing you should say is, "I am not going to buy anything for at least one year. I just want to

make sure that the money I have is safe and sound. I want to put any money that is not safe now into a money-market fund or Treasuries, and that is all. No new purchases of any kind are to be made on my behalf."

What if I get a call from my late or ex-spouse's financial adviser?

I wouldn't be surprised if you did. Once a financial adviser has built a relationship with one partner, a separation or death gives him or her the opportunity to establish a rapport with the spouse who previously was merely a name on joint documents. Believe me, this opportunity is not lost on the adviser. Remember, this person has been aware of what went on not only with your money but also in your personal life. If there is to be a divorce, and therefore a dividing of the assets, the adviser is going to be one of the first to know what you each will be left with. If there is a death, the total picture of your finances is right at his or her disposal. So do not be surprised if you get a cozy call from an adviser with whom you have never really had a relationship to ask you to come in and see him or her to go over what to do with the money in your portfolio. But ask yourself this: How many times did the adviser or broker your spouse was using to manage your joint money talk to you before your world fell apart?

Should I talk to this financial adviser, or use the six-month plan that you suggested earlier?

You should wait. You're not ready. Just because your late spouse or ex-spouse was using a certain adviser does not mean that he or she will be the right adviser for you. I'm not suggesting that this adviser is necessarily wrong for you, only that this is your life, and everyone in it from this point on must be someone with whom you feel safe and comfortable. Ask yourself the following questions:

- Why was it that you never had a relationship with this particular person to begin with?
- If you did have a relationship with him/her, did you like and trust the relationship?
- Did you feel as if he/she had your best interests and concerns at heart, or just those of your spouse/partner?

Bide your time. These questions will answer themselves in due course.

So you're saying I should be careful with all people who will potentially have anything to do with my money?

Absolutely. Cold callers, hungry brokers, and needy financial-planning types all read the obituaries to see if they can somehow expand their businesses. A sympathetic call when you are feeling vulnerable is often a self-interested call—and you're not the "self" in question here. Please say that you are grieving now and ask that solicitors who appear out of the blue call back in a year. They won't.

What about life insurance? Is there an optimal way to deal with my insurance company?

Yes. If you are entitled to any life insurance proceeds, regardless of the amount, take the payment in full, even if the insurance company tries to persuade you to take it in installments or offers to invest it or hold on to it for safekeeping. Most insurance proceeds are income tax–free, so you will not incur any penalties by taking them in a lump-sum payment. You may need to deposit some cash into a checking account right away to cover immediate expenses. Then put the rest into a money-market account or anywhere you know it will be safe but also accessible, in case you need funds for your living expenses. Leave the money there until you are more emotionally stable, so that you can intelligently decide what to do with it—again, six months to one year later.

What about making other big changes in my life? Should I put these off, too?

Yes, if you can. Over the next few months, I would like you to try to make as few changes in your life as possible. At the same time, I would also like you to begin asking yourself some essential questions. How do you feel about where you are living? Are you frightened by the amount of money it takes to live? Are there areas in which you could easily cut back your spending? In time, clarity will set in, and you will know what you must do, however painful, whether it's selling the house, taking a job or a second job, or cutting back on what you can do for your children. In time you will be able to do what you decide you need to do.

3

Home Ownership

The Door to More

Ahome is one of life's most significant resources. A home is the place where you live, of course, but it's also an investment that can bring you satisfaction and security for years to come.

If you've been thinking about buying a first home, are actively hunting for a new home, or simply want to understand more about the opportunities and pitfalls involved in becoming a homeowner, read this chapter carefully. Millions of homes are bought and sold each year, but too many buyers and sellers are unaware of the important variables to look for—and look out for—in the process. They let banks, realtors, and mortgage brokers make decisions for them, often to their detriment. Don't let this happen to you.

The questions and answers below will help you think through the issues involved in buying or selling a home. These include figuring out what kind of house you can truly afford, which type of mortgage will serve you best in different economic environments, the factors that may affect the value of your investment in your home, how to hold your title, and how to measure tax benefits. I hope you will also get a sense of the tremendous security and freedom that come with owning a home free and clear.

To Rent or Buy?

I pay a very low rent, but everyone tells me that I should buy a home. What do you think?
Once upon a time, your decision would have been simple. For our parents and their parents, owning a home almost always made better sense than renting, in large part because mortgage payments were often equal to or smaller than the rents they paid. People tended to live in the same house for 30 years, so the immediate, large expenses associated with buying a home could be amortized over a long period of time. Today, our culture has become far more mobile; in order to be sure that ownership makes sense for you, you must think about how long you will live in a home and have a clear sense of whether property values are moving up or down in the area where you'd like to live.

If you're young, have no idea where you will be living three years from now, and pay less in rent than you would pay for a mortgage, property taxes, and insurance on a similar house or apartment, renting may be preferable for now.

If, on the other hand, you know you will live in the same house for five to seven years, believe that real estate prices are on the rise, have money available for a down payment, and have found a home you like with a mortgage, property taxes, and insurance you can afford, then owning is the way to go.

I really don't have the desire to own a home, but I do have the money. Should I continue to rent or buy?

If you can afford a down payment and monthly mortgage payments and expenses, you probably would benefit financially if you bought a home. But you've already answered the first question every potential home buyer should ask himself or herself, which is: *Do I want to own a home?* If not, don't buy, because home ownership is a big responsibility. Many longtime renters are surprised by how much time and money is required to keep a house and property running smoothly and looking good. If you decide to keep renting, however, invest your savings so that you can easily purchase a home should your feelings change.

A friend told me the tax break for owning a home always makes renting a bad deal, tax-wise. Is that true?

The federal tax break your friend is talking about allows homeowners to deduct the annual amount of the interest they pay on their mortgage loans from their income for tax purposes. This can indeed be a great savings, if your mortgage-interest payments are greater than the standard deduction allowed by the federal government. Before you decide to buy, calculate the tax break you'll receive on your yearly mortgage interest payments, and be sure that the deduction will exceed the current standard deduction. Chances are good that it will, since real estate prices, and therefore the amounts of

mortgage loans, have risen so much in recent years.

As a homeowner, you may be able to take advantage of other tax benefits, such as a deduction for your property taxes, but the mortgage interest deduction is what most people have in mind when they say that owning makes for a better tax deal than renting.

What is the current standard federal deduction?

The standard deduction varies according to your filing status, your age, whether you are blind, and whether you can be claimed as a dependent on another taxpayer's return. The basic standard deductions for the 2010 tax year are as follows:

- Single: $5,700
- Head of Household: $8,400
- Married, filing a joint return: $11,400
- Married, filing a separate return: $5,700

(Please note: These amounts are adjusted annually. You can find the most recent standard deduction information at *irs.gov*.)

You said that renting may be wiser if I don't know where I'll be living during the next few years. What difference does it make how long I plan to live in a home?

When you buy or sell a piece of real estate, you pay a number of fees up front that are collectively known as closing costs—so called because they are due from both the buyer and the seller at the time the title to the property is transferred and the deal is closed. These fees can easily cost both buyer and seller several thousand dollars, and that's in addition to the possible costs of paying a realtor to help you buy or sell, plus moving and renovating costs, etc. If you are going to be in your home for fewer than three years, your home may not increase enough in value to cover all these expenses, and you could actually lose money if and when you have to sell. In an ordinary market, you should plan to live in your home for five to seven years or longer.

I've been thinking about buying, but I feel that my romantic status might be changing over the next year or two. Should I buy now, or continue to rent until I know for sure?

The question of whether you will require the same amount of living space and the same kinds of amenities in the next few years is an important one. If you are a single person, a one-bedroom condo may seem ideal now, but if you hope to get married and start a family in the next few years, you'll need more space pretty quickly. Life changes make for subtle differences. For a couple that is newly married and without any children, buying a great house in a not-so-great school district might seem sensible; but if the couple has children later or tries to sell the house to people with children, they may discover that the house they bought was not the best buy overall. The goal is to think long-term and to try to evaluate what your requirements will be three, five, or ten years from now. Until you're able to do this, you should probably continue to rent or stay in the home you currently own.

I'm afraid that I will have trouble maintaining a home. Does that come into play when I'm debating buying versus renting?

Being physically able to maintain your home, regardless of your age, is an important consideration. Owning a home is a lot of work. Senior citizens thinking about purchasing a home should consider whether they would be most comfortable with the amenities that a full-service apartment complex or condominium community can offer. Younger men and women who do a lot of business traveling might also find apartment living more convenient. If you cannot maintain a house yourself, you must include home maintenance costs in your financial estimates when deciding if you can afford to own a home. Plan ahead. I suggest putting at least $75 a month into a maintenance fund.

FIRST STEPS TOWARD BUYING A HOME

Once you start thinking about owning a piece of real estate, it can become an all-consuming passion. It's during the initial excitement about buying a home that most people make their first mistake. Before figuring out what they can afford, they drive through the areas in which they want to live, looking for houses with FOR SALE signs. They jot down the phone numbers of real estate agents selling those houses. They place a few calls, just out of curiosity, and before they know it—and before they've worked out their own budget—they've made dates to take a look at what's on the market. This is the usual sequence—and, if you allow yourself to follow it, you can find yourself in over your head. Here are the questions you need to ask and answer before you begin shopping for a home.

CALCULATING THE SIZE OF THE MORTGAGE PAYMENT YOU CAN AFFORD

I saved eight months' worth of expenses for an emergency fund. I would like to use this money for a down payment on a home. Is this a wise thing to do?

Unless you are convinced that you are immune from emergencies, I don't think this is a very good idea. Emergency funds should be a permanent part of your financial picture; that's how you will always have the ability to weather any unforeseen problem.

Let's say you use the money for a down payment. Next you'll tell me that you need to furnish your great new home. So you are going to run up some hefty credit card balances. Everything seems great until that unforeseen disaster occurs: You get laid off. You now have no job, and no emergency fund, and no ability to tap your credit card for a cash advance, because you are currently at your maximum balances. Tell me, how will you pay your mortgage now? I fear that you could lose your house. And I am not being overly cautious; during the real estate downturn that began in 2007 millions of homeowners have lost their homes to foreclosure. So that's why I want you to always have an eight-month emergency fund.

What are the most important things to consider before I buy a home?

Perhaps the most important consideration is what your financial limits are. The following is a list of financial realities to think about.

How much cash will you be able to come up with for a down payment?

Will you have the additional cash necessary to pay the closing costs?

What is your monthly income, before and after taxes?

Apart from the money for a down payment, how much money have you saved? (Include everything—savings accounts, retirement accounts, and any other key assets.)

How much debt do you have? (Again, include everything—credit cards, student loans, and/or car loans.)

How much do you spend each month paying off your debts?

How long have you been in your current job?

What does your credit history look like?

What are the costs of houses in the area(s) that you are thinking about living in?

How much are average property taxes in the area(s) you are thinking about living in?

What are current interest rates, and are they projected to get lower or higher in the near future?

How much does homeowner's insurance cost for houses of the general size and location that interest you?

What is the very first step I should take before I go and look at houses?

Before you do anything, you must know how much you can afford to spend. As a homeowner, you will have many more expenses than you had as a renter. Before you fall in love with a house and talk yourself into buying something that you may not be able to comfortably afford, I want you to start out knowing exactly how much you can pay and why.

Figuring out what you can afford is simple, as long as you are honest with yourself about your income and financial obligations. Just follow the steps below.

1. Calculate your current net monthly income after subtracting taxes, Social Security contributions, retirement contributions, and all other automatic withdrawals from your paycheck. Write that figure here:
Figure 1: _____.

2. Total the monthly payments on all your debts—include car payments, credit card payments, personal loans, and student loans. (Don't include mortgage payments or rent.) Be honest! Write the total here:
Figure 2: _____

If Figure 2 equals more than 30 percent of Figure 1, stop right here. (Multiply Figure 1 by 0.3 to get 30 percent.) You are not currently in a financial position to own a home comfortably. You must first reduce your debt.

3. Find the sum that represents your monthly living expenses. Include food, transportation, gasoline, haircuts, dental, education, utilities, insurance—in other words, any regular bills that you pay, *excluding* the amount of your current rent or mortgage payments but *including* your debt payments (Figure 2). Write that figure here:
Figure 3: _____

4. Subtract Figure 3 from Figure 1. Write the result here:
Figure 4: _____

Figure 4 is the maximum monthly amount you currently can afford to spend on a mortgage payment plus property taxes, homeowner's insurance, maintenance, possible PMI costs, and the other hidden costs of home ownership.

Keep in mind that this formula does not account for the tax savings that owning a home will confer. You will want to figure those savings into your monthly calculations before you shop for a home. Since you will likely save on both your federal and state taxes, be sure to consult a tax adviser.

5. Subtract 35 percent from Figure 4 (multiply Figure 4 by 0.65). Write the result here:
Figure 5: _____

Figure 5 is the highest comfortable monthly amount you can currently afford for a mortgage payment alone.

I've heard people say that after calculating the size of the mortgage payments that I can afford, I still need to "play house." What does that mean?

Playing house is a way of trying new financial situations on for size. This is how it works: Open up a brand-new savings account. Remember, this is something you want to do well *before* you are really serious about buying a home. Set a date once a month—for instance, the 15th. For the next six months, on that date, I want you to deposit into your new account the exact difference between what your current housing costs (rent, or the total payments you are making on the home you currently own) and the amount you project you will have to pay on your new home.

For example, let's say that you are renting, and it costs you $1,500 a month to rent. The house you want to buy will cost you $3,500 a month (including mortgage payment, PMI, property insurance, taxes, utilities, and maintenance). You must deposit the difference between the two ($3,500–$1,500, or $2,000 a month) into the new savings account, no later than the date you set.

Or say that you currently own a home and want to buy a bigger home. Your current total monthly payments come to $3,000, and your new home will cost you $6,200 a month. To play house, you must deposit the difference between the two ($6,200–$3,000, or $3,200 a month) into a savings account no later than the date you set.

These examples feature the minimum costs. They don't include all the expenses, such as lawn maintenance and snow removal. So if you really want to do a thorough job, you should also figure out which of those other expenses you will have to pay and how much they will cost you.

After doing this for six months, evaluate how making those higher payments while playing house has affected your lifestyle. If you've made all the payments comfortably and on time, you know that you can truly afford this particular home right now. Better yet, you have already accumulated funds to put toward increasing your down payment, helping you with moving costs or closing costs, or even doing a few small renovations on the new home!

If, on the other hand, you missed payments or were late in making any, you cannot afford the house you were thinking about buying quite yet. Instead, look to see the monthly payment that would have been comfortable for you, and try that. Maybe the solution is to consider a smaller house or a larger down payment. Nevertheless, you may just have to wait until your finances improve. The good news is that you now know how much you realistically can afford at this time *without* having lost any money in finding out. You should also have a nice sum of money in your savings account that will help you achieve your future goals.

I know I will save money on taxes with a mortgage interest deduction. How can I get that tax savings to help me pay my bills month to month?

If you are working for an employer, notify your employer that you have bought a home and request an increase in the number of your exemptions. (As of 2010, each exemption removes $3,650 a year from your taxable income.) If you do this, your employer will withhold less money from your paycheck for taxes, and you will have use of that money every month. Please consult a tax professional first, however, so that you are absolutely sure your employer is withholding the right amount of tax.

How much can I expect to pay in homeowner's insurance?

A quick way to figure out your monthly homeowner's insurance costs is to multiply $35 times per $100,000 of the value of your house. For example, if you have a home valued at $200,000, you would multiply 35×2 to get a monthly homeowner's insurance cost of $70. This is a rough approximation. To get an exact quote, you will need to speak to an insurance agent. The cost of insurance varies according to state, the price of the house, its condition and location, and the amount of coverage you'll need to feel comfortable. Call a local insurance agent and get an estimate on the house you wish to buy.

How do I figure out what my yearly property taxes will be?

When you sign a contract to buy a house, you get a title report that includes the most recent real estate tax information on the property. Though tax rates can go up from year to year, the most recent figures from the title report will be a good indicator, unless the price of the house has risen dramatically since the last annual tax assessment. For advance warning, ask your real estate agent for an estimate or call the local tax assessment office in the area where you want to buy.

My husband says if we are approved for a mortgage, we can afford the house. Is he right?

If your husband thinks the bank will guide you, he's wrong. Every loan that has ever gone into foreclosure or bankruptcy was approved by a bank. A loan officer qualified those borrowers, and then something went wrong. In the wake of the great bursting of the real estate bubble that began in 2007 I think it's clear that bank lenders, mortgage brokers, and real estate agents aren't the best source of information. You need to make up your own mind, based on a clear-eyed assessment of your financial situation. People who are in the job of selling you a product—a

mortgage—or whose compensation is based on the size of your purchase (the real estate agent) may have an incentive to encourage you to buy more than is financially prudent. To avoid having something go wrong with your home purchase, make sure *you* feel comfortable with the monthly mortgage and other payments you'll have to make—in other words, decide for yourself what you can and can't afford.

Please note that a mortgage may seem to be a loan that you use to pay for your home, but technically it is a lien on your home by means of which a lender secures a loan for you. It is what's known as a secured loan. If you fail to pay back the mortgage, the lender has the ability to foreclose on the property.

What is foreclosure?

Foreclosure is the legal process by which a lender assumes a borrower's property rights in lieu of payment of a mortgage—and by which the borrower who has failed to pay loses his or her rights and interest in the property. In other words, in foreclosure the lender takes the home away from you and, typically, sells it at auction in order to recover the loan.

What is a short-sale?

A short-sale is when you sell your home for less than the amount you still owe on the mortgage, and your mortgage lender agrees to "forgive" the difference. For example, if you have $250,000 left on your mortgage and you can no longer keep up with payments on the loan, but you can only sell the home for $225,000 in a down market, the lender may agree to let you sell it for the $225,000 and "forgive" the $25,000 difference. A lender will agree to do that if it thinks that it is financially wiser than pushing you and the house into foreclosure, where the eventual sale price could be even lower. Please know that typically the amount of the mortgage that is forgiven in a short-sale is considered taxable income you must report to the IRS. (In 2007 a special regulation suspended the taxation of the "forgiven" amount through 2012, but only for a principal residence; please check at *irs.gov* for current taxation rules.)

THE DOWN PAYMENT

Once you've arrived at the size of the mortgage you can afford, let's turn to the next item that will influence the price of the home you can buy: how much money you have for a down payment. A down payment is paid up front and is usually expressed as a percentage of the purchase price. Below are the questions you'll need to ask and answer about down payments.

Does it matter how large a down payment I make when purchasing a home?
During the real estate bubble in the early 2000s you could indeed get a mortgage with no down payment, or just 5 percent or less. But as we all learned, there was a downside to not making a down payment: when values fell, homeowners did not have any built-up equity in their homes and were less likely to want to stay in those homes. There is a saying that a down payment means the homeowner has "skin in the game," that is, you have a financial investment in the home.

In the wake of the real estate meltdown that began in 2007, the down payment has come back into vogue. Many lenders once again prefer that borrowers put down 20 percent of the total purchase price of the home. Thus the traditional down payment on a $200,000 home is $40,000. But don't panic if you don't have 20 percent to put down. You can still get a mortgage with a smaller down payment of 10 percent, or perhaps even less. In fact, the popular FHA-insured mortgage program requires a down payment of just 3.5 percent. But understand that when you make a down payment of less than 20 percent you will have to pay for an additional type of insurance, however, which I'll discuss in detail when we talk about mortgages.

I understand the concept of the down payment, but I don't have a lot of cash. Where can I find the money?
Finding cash for the down payment is often the biggest hurdle people face when buying a home. If you've gone through all the obvious possibilities—savings, investment accounts, bonuses at work—and are still short, consider the following options, but know that using them will come at a price.

- A loan against your 401(k)
- A withdrawal of up to $10,000 from your traditional IRA/Roth IRA. (This withdrawal from a traditional IRA is subject to income tax but not a penalty if you meet the specific first-time buyer definition—but be careful, because income tax may eat up a good portion of the withdrawal. Roth IRAs have special rules here as well, so please get tax advice before taking any steps.)

Naturally, you should think long and hard before you use money from your retirement accounts because these represent important components of your long-term savings plan; tapping into them will certainly interfere with their growth and diminish your nest egg. (To learn more about the pros and cons of borrowing from retirement savings, as well as the rules that apply, please turn to the section on borrowing from a 401(k) in Chapter 1.)

Many employers will let you borrow as much as 50 percent of the money you have in your 401(k), up to a ceiling of $50,000. With a traditional IRA, you can *withdraw* up to $10,000, but this is not a loan; you will have to pay income taxes on that money.

With a Roth IRA, you are permitted to withdraw any portion of your original contribution at any time. Your withdrawal of contributions is tax- and penalty-free. If you also withdraw part of your gains, using the first-time homeowner provision, and are under age 59½, you will owe ordinary income taxes on the earnings part of the withdrawal but no penalty.

If I do not have 20 percent to put down (I have about 10 percent), but I can get a mortgage and can easily afford the monthly mortgage payments, should I go ahead and buy the house anyway?

In most cases, yes. You can feel especially confident if a) you believe you will live in the home for at least seven years, and b) the value of the home you want to buy has not been overly inflated by a booming real estate market.

Which is more important—a down payment of 20 percent or the money to make the mortgage payments?

In my opinion, having the money to pay the monthly mortgage bill and meet other ongoing expenses, such as property taxes and insurance, is more important. You may be able to scrape together the money for a down payment, especially if it's less than 20 percent of the price of the house. But if you fall behind on your mortgage payments or other obligations, you will not enjoy, and may even lose, your home. Don't become "house-poor." Make sure you will be able to enjoy your home—and life's other pleasures— *after* you move in.

CREDIT HISTORY

Once you have cleared the two big hurdles of determining the size of the mortgage you can afford and identifying the source of your down payment, there's a final step to take before going out to look for a home in your price range. The last step will be to qualify for a mortgage, which may mean working on your credit.

Please turn now to the sections on credit reports and FICO score in Chapter 1 and thoroughly review the information about obtaining and correcting your credit report and improving your FICO score. Any lender you approach will perform a credit check, and you will want to be sure that you are prepared to pass the test.

Can you give me an example of how a FICO score can reduce my mortgage?

A great credit report can snag a high FICO score. And that can translate into saving thousands of dollars on your loan costs. For example, let's say you are looking for a $250,000 30-year fixed-rate mortgage. If you have a great FICO score (760–850) you could qualify for a 5 percent interest rate that would give you a $1,342 monthly mortgage. (This interest rate is as of December 2009; you can find current illustrative mortgage rates based on your credit score at *myfico.com*.) Over the life of the loan you would pay about $233,139 in interest. Now let's look at the other end of the spectrum: You earn a very low FICO score (620–639 is the low range), which means your mortgage rate is a far costlier 6.5 percent. Your monthly mortgage payment balloons to $1,580 and you'll pay more than $318,861 in interest over the life of the loan. This translates into $85,722 more in interest simply because lenders think you're a credit risk. To see how to improve your FICO credit score so you can quality for a lower-rate loan, please see the information on FICO scores on page 34.

Before I go to a lender to find out if I can qualify for a mortgage, should I find out what my credit report looks like?

You should *always* know what your credit reports and FICO scores look like. That way, you'll have enough time to correct any errors.

Is there a free Website that will give me a rough idea whether my credit and FICO score are good or bad before I pay for a credit report or apply for a mortgage?

Yes. You can get some general information that explains what goes into a credit score at *www .myfico.com*, but the actual score will cost you $15.95 per score. (You have three scores, one each from Equifax, Experian, and TransUnion. As of the summer of 2009 consumers were only able to purchase their Equifax and TransUnion scores. Mortgage lenders, however, will check all three scores.)

If I am using a real estate agent or mortgage broker, can he or she correct my credit report for me?

No, a real estate agent or mortgage broker will not correct your credit report. If there are mistakes on your report, however, many agents and brokers *will* help you draft a letter to your prospective lender explaining why the report is not accurate. But please get to your credit report before your prospective lender does, and clear up or annotate any inaccuracies you find.

If my credit history is less than perfect, is there anything I should do before I apply for a mortgage?

If you think you will be applying for a mortgage in the near future, please do the following:

Keep your credit card balances as low as possible. Do *not* have your cards maxed out when you apply for a mortgage. Be punctual with all your payments. Now is not the time to be even one day late.

Do not apply for a low-interest-rate credit card at this time.

Do not switch multiple small balances from your high-interest-rate cards to one low-interest-rate card. Instead, try to pay down as many card balances as possible.

Why should you take these precautions? When mortgage lenders look at your credit report, one of the things they'll check for is your credit limit—the maximum amount of money you can charge against your credit cards. If you have a Visa card with a $5,000 limit, a Master-Card with a $10,000 limit, and a Discover card with a $3,000 limit, a mortgage lender will view this as the potential to create an additional $18,000 debt. Try not to let your maximum potential debt grow. Also, you don't want to apply for any new cards, to prevent unnecessary credit inquiries on your report. A lender will wonder why you are seeking additional credit.

I checked my FICO score, and it is lower than I thought. If I have a low credit score, can I still shop around for a mortgage?
Yes, you can, but it would be to your advantage to work on improving your FICO score before looking for a mortgage. A higher FICO score could save you thousands on your mortgage. (For more information in how to improve your FICO score, please see p. 34.)

FINDING THE RIGHT HOUSE AND LOCATION

Now that you have been armed with accurate information about what you can afford, it's time to look for a home. When shopping for real estate, the old saying *is* true: The three most important variables are location, location, and location. The ongoing value of your home is very strongly determined by—you guessed it—its location.

Should I get a real estate agent from the start, or should I look around on my own?
If you are knowledgeable about a region, start by driving around. Identify neighborhoods in which you might want to live. Then call a real estate agent who specializes in the neighborhoods you've chosen. However, if you are moving to a new area and don't have a clear sense of where you want to live, you can speed up the house-hunting process by asking an agent (or agents) to take you around. This will clue you in to how well an agent knows the areas she or he represents.

Even at the very beginning of the process, it is important to work with an agent you feel you can communicate with. Choose carefully, for this person can control the properties you see and can influence how effectively you bid on the properties you like. Make sure he or she answers your questions clearly and is available when needed.

Is looking for a house on the Web a good idea?
I think using the Web is an excellent way to *start* looking for a house or apartment. Browse the Web to get an idea of available properties and prices in your region. If you like what you see, then visit in person. A site that I think you will find useful is *www.homeagain.com*.

When is the best time of day to look at a home in person?
Visit a prospective home at as many different times of day as you can, and on weekdays and weekends, too. Here's why. Imagine you find a house that you love. You drive by on a Sunday afternoon and stop in on the following Wednesday

afternoon. During both visits, the neighborhood seems peaceful and quiet. You buy the house, and on your first Monday morning there, at 7 A.M. horns blare and tires screech. It happens that your street is a good rush-hour shortcut around the town's business district. There go your peaceful mornings and dinner hours.

Some reliable sources of information about the character of a neighborhood, including whether or not it's safe, are the seller's neighbors. If you see people gardening, playing with their children, or pulling into or out of their driveways, ask them a few questions about the street and the surrounding dwellers. They'll often be very candid.

We've found the perfect neighborhood. What should we look for in a house?

First, look beyond the apparent charms of a house. Many people, especially first-time home buyers, fall in love with a single quality in a house—a new kitchen, for example, or even a lovely pair of French doors leading into a garden—and neglect to consider the whole package. Bring a notepad, walk through every room, and make a list of problems. If you don't see anything that is damaged, inadequate, or displeasing, you may not be looking hard enough. Return with a friend, tour the house or apartment separately, and compare notes afterward. I guarantee that each of you will have seen a different house.

What are some common problems that buyers tend to overlook?

To be sure you are not buying someone else's problems, make a list of the following things to look for or do.

Turn on all the water faucets and let them run; check the water pressure, and make sure that the hot water is plentiful.

Flush all the toilets.

Make sure that the appliances (refrigerator and freezer, air conditioners, dishwashers, washers, and dryers) are in working order and are not more than ten years old.

Check all outlets, lights, and light switches.

If you're looking at an old house, ask the seller (or the real estate agent, if you don't meet the seller) when the plumbing and electrical systems were last replaced or repaired.

Turn on everything at once and see what happens—if lights dim when the air conditioner and the washing machine are running, you'll probably want an electrical engineer to take a look before you contract to buy the house.

Ask the seller or agent how old the roof is and whether it has ever been replaced.

Return after a heavy rainstorm to look for leaks inside, and test the basement for dampness. If it is damp, and if you're still interested in the house, inform the inspector.

Remember that thoroughness is the byword of a happy purchase.

Does it matter how the neighborhood is zoned?

It certainly does. A friend of mine bought a beautiful home in a resort town with a backyard overlooking unused farmland. A year later, the land was sold to a restaurant developer. She spent thousands of dollars putting up fences and planting mature hedges to block out her new neighbor. The lesson is simple: Ask about the zoning laws in the area surrounding your prospective new home.

We're moving to a town we selected because one of the schools is rated the best in the state. My husband says this is good for resale value. Is this true?

Yes. Most young families want to live in highly rated school districts, and buying in one will help secure the resale value of your home, even during tough times. Be careful, however, that the home you're buying is really *in* a good school district and not merely *near* one. Again, the seller's neighbors can save you some heartache if you take the time to ask them a few questions.

BUYING A CO-OP/CONDOMINIUM

What is the difference between a cooperative apartment and a condominium?

Co-ops and condos are both typically units in apartment buildings or townhouse developments in which the individual dwellings are occupied by separate owners. The primary difference between the two is in how the owners hold their individual apartments.

In co-ops, residents do not own the actual apartments they live in. The cooperative corporation owns the building, and residents own shares of the corporation, which are allocated according to the size and value of their respective apartments. As a tenant/shareholder in a co-op, you hold a proprietary lease that allows you to occupy the apartment. A co-op board approves the purchase or sale of shares and usually exerts control over issues of home renovation

and the operation and maintenance of the building. Cooperatives are common only in big cities.

Buying a condominium is more like buying a house. You are purchasing a piece of real estate—your unit—that is part of a larger building or development, and you are also buying a share of the common areas. Generally, in condominiums you do not need anyone's permission to sell or lease your unit.

In both cases, residents pay monthly fees for the general upkeep of the building and for any staff wages. These fees are called maintenance fees in co-ops and common charges in condos.

I'm a city dweller and most of the homes for sale in my price range are either co-ops or condominiums. Is there anything special to know?

Yes. Before you start looking for a co-op or condo, be aware of two important distinctions between buying a single, detached home on the one hand and a co-op or a condo on the other. The most important difference is that the mortgage interest rate you pay may be higher when you buy a co-op or condo. With these, the theory goes, a lender is taking on a larger risk because the value of your apartment (your "unit") depends partially on the maintenance, condition, and operation of the other units and common areas in the building. When you have your particular unit inspected, ask the engineer to examine the building's common areas and systems. This additional service will probably add to the inspection bill but will be valuable information should you decide to purchase.

Second, and this is a big one, if you buy a co-op you will need to adjust your total monthly payment to include the monthly maintenance charge, which incorporates property taxes as well as fees for general building upkeep and the employment of any staff. With a condominium, you will pay your taxes individually but will owe a monthly common charge for the operation and maintenance of the building's common areas.

BUYER'S AGENTS

Real estate agents are paid on a commission basis. The typical commission on residential real estate is 6 percent of the selling price. The higher the sale price, the more the real estate agent makes. Since the agent's commission is based on the sale price and is paid by the seller, all agents effectively work for the seller.

But a new breed of agent, called a buyer's agent, is entering the marketplace, and he or she works for the buyer. A buyer's agent is paid a percentage of the selling price of the home at the time of the closing and is generally paid by the listing, or selling, agent from that agent's commission.

If I use a buyer's agent, what should he or she do for me?

In general, a buyer's agent should identify and show you a selection of homes that meet your needs and budget. Once you have decided on a home you like, he or she should research the property, help you decide on the price you should pay, and make an offer to the seller or the seller's agent on your behalf. A buyer's agent should also help you to determine how much house you can really afford. All of the above should be written in a contract between you and your agent, which should also include the length

of time the agent will represent you and how the fees will be paid. The terms can be specified to meet your needs, so ask for what you want.

If you want to find a buyer's agent, start by looking at the Website *www.naeba.org*. The initials stand for the National Association of Exclusive Buyer Agents.

If I want to live in a very desirable area, where houses are sold almost before they are listed, will getting a buyer's agent help?

In an area that's highly competitive, using a buyer's agent won't guarantee you a home, but it will help ensure that you will pay a fair market price for the home you get.

How much should I expect to save by using a buyer's agent?

According to the National Association of Realtors, a buyer's agent may save you about 8 to 10 percent of the cost of the home.

COMPARABLE MARKET ANALYSIS (CMA)

How do I know how much I should pay for a home?

Obtain a comparable market analysis (CMA) from your real estate agent. A CMA provides a comparison of the prices of homes currently on the market and homes sold within the last month and within five blocks of the home you want to buy. Information provided in a CMA on comparable properties should include square footage, number of rooms, location, and size of the property.

If I am not working with a real estate agent, can I get a CMA online?

You can, but be sure you know how to interpret it. That said, check out *www.realestate.com* and click on the Home Values link, or you can also check recent sale prices at online sites such as *zillow.com* and *trulia.com*.

PREAPPROVED LOANS

I've been told that before I even go to look at homes, I should either be prequalified or preapproved for a mortgage. What do you think?

A prequalification is just an informal review of your circumstances by a lender. A prequalification letter isn't binding and doesn't mean much. On the other hand, to get a preapproval letter requires an in-depth investigation by a potential lender. In competitive housing markets, you'll probably need to be armed with a preapproval letter from your lender. Such a letter provides the seller and the real estate agent with proof of your eligibility and seriousness as a potential buyer. This can be especially helpful if you are dealing with a seller who needs to move quickly. Also, in a tight market where houses are sold the day they are listed, a preapproval letter might keep you in the game.

What exactly is the difference between being prequalified and preapproved for a mortgage?

Preapproval specifically authorizes you to receive a particular mortgage amount for a specific period of time prior to your finding the property

you want. *Prequalification* is merely an informal, non-binding assessment of your financial status. With a preapproval letter you are a cash buyer. This is very attractive to a seller, who doesn't want to worry about whether your loan application will be rejected after he or she takes the house off the market. While it certainly makes you an appealing buyer in a tight market, don't get a preapproval without thinking the mortgage deal through carefully. You need to do the same kind of research and comparison shopping you would do for any mortgage. Also, a mortgage preapproval can require you to pay a fee up front. It is good only for a specified period of time, for example, 30 days, and if you don't use it, you will lose the money you spent on the fee.

When preapproving people, our lender estimates the borrowers' housing costs at 35 percent of their gross income. My mom says I should never spend a penny more than 25 percent. Who's right?

Your mom and your lender are not the only ones arguing this point. Twenty years ago, 25 percent of gross income was the standard housing-expense figure recommended by most lenders and financial advisers. But as real estate prices rose in many parts of the country until 2006 or so, the recommended percentage edged higher. What does this mean in terms of cold, hard cash? Let's say you and your partner make a combined gross income of $60,000. Using the 25 percent rule, you could afford $15,000 per year, or $1,250 per month, for your housing costs. If you go with your lender's guideline of 35 percent, you could afford $21,000 per year, or $1,750 per month. That's a difference of $500 per month, enough to create a dramatic difference in the home you buy and also in the way you live. If you want to use the gross income formula to decide what you can afford, I suggest you use the percentage used by the FHA: 31 percent of your gross income.

In my view, however, the whole "gross income" debate is antiquated. Today's worker brings home a check that is very different from his or her parents'. I recommend that you calculate your spending limits based on your real, or net, income. Your lender's figure of 35 percent may stretch you to your limit and leave you without a safety net. Your mom's advice, on the other hand, may be too conservative or constraining. Your object is to *keep* the home you buy, and the best way to do that is to make sure your total monthly payments fit into your monthly budget.

How much debt can I have and still be preapproved for a mortgage?

As a general rule, lenders look askance at anyone who must spend more than 36 percent of gross income each month to pay back debt. This includes *all* debt—credit card payments, student loans, car loans, and outstanding bills, in addition to monthly mortgage costs, homeowner's insurance, and property taxes. If you have debt that you cannot pay down because you lack cash to do so, you probably have not only too much debt to get a mortgage but also not enough cash to make a down payment. If this is the case, you may be heading for trouble.

Does the length of time I have worked at my job matter when I am getting preapproved for a mortgage?

Yes. Though your recent job history is not the most important item on your mortgage application, lenders do like to see that you have been either at your current job or in your current line of work for at least two years. This suggests that you are fairly stable. But don't panic if you have recently made a job change—all it means is that, if the lender requests it, you may need to provide additional information about your job.

WHEN TO BUY OR SELL

Is now a good time to buy or to sell?

First, let's all agree that your home is not simply an investment. Your home is a place of security; it is where you live. You don't live in a stock or a mutual fund. So always look at real estate in terms of whether it is the right house for you and your family to live in.

With that bit of perspective, here's a tip for you to use so you can understand what is going on in your real estate market. I want you to check the real estate sales info in your local newspaper; most papers carry a list of recent transactions at least once a week. I want you to track two important trends. First, are homes selling for more than their asking price, or less than their asking price? And are homes selling quickly or slowly? Keep track of this for a few weeks and you are bound to see a pattern.

If the trend in your area is that homes are taking longer and longer to sell and are selling for less than the asking price, then you most likely are in what is known as a *buyer's market*. That's great if you in fact are looking to buy. Since market conditions are in your favor, you can be a serious bargainer. I wouldn't hesitate to go in and make a bid that's 20 percent below the asking price. After some negotiating, I bet you'll come away with a good deal. But, of course, since many of us already own a home, if we go to buy another one it may mean we need to sell our existing home. And if you're a seller in a buyer's market, well, obviously the opposite is true: You're going to need to negotiate and bargain. Or if that doesn't float your boat, then you need to decide if you really want to sell in a buyer's market.

MAKING A BID

My wife and I found a house we want to make a bid on. We have never gotten this far before, and the real estate agent is telling us to bid 25 percent below the asking price. Is she right?

I don't like cut-and-dried rules like this one. The key to making a good bid is to come from a position of strength, and the first step in creating a position of strength is to see as many houses in your purchasing area as you possibly can. Even if you find the house you want on the first try, go out and see more just to establish the basic price range in your area. If you see two or three houses that you believe should be about the same price as the one you like but are $50,000 less, you know the seller's asking price

is well above market. After you've thoroughly assessed the market value of the area, come up with a bid based on the limits you set before you started to look. Depending on the area and the volume of sales, I'd generally come in below the asking price. How much below depends on the market. In very fast-moving markets in the late 90s, a fairly priced home could sell to the first bidder who matched the asking price or could even sell for more than the asking price. In a slower market, where houses take on average two or more months to sell, the seller might accept a bid as low as 25 percent below the asking price. It depends on the markets.

I've made my final bid, and it's $5,000 short of what the sellers are asking. Nobody else seems very interested, but the seller won't budge. What can I do to bridge this gap without going over my limit?

Remain unemotional—if you get the house, great; if you don't, there will be other houses. Don't be afraid to move on. Remember, there are many houses you can buy, but the seller has only one house to sell. That said, it doesn't hurt to ask the real estate agent to take off a percentage point or more on the sale, thus creating a savings to pass on to you. This sometimes works in slower markets, where the seller and the agent are more invested in the sale than you are. Try to cash in on that investment.

We're in the middle of a bidding war over our dream house. We're about to go beyond our predetermined maximum. The real estate agent feels we could carry the extra $50,000 *of debt, but I'm not 100 percent sure. What should we do?*

Sometimes buyers get hit with an irrational sense of urgency—"This is my dream house and I'll do anything to get it!" If you catch yourself thinking this, be aware that you may be getting yourself into financial trouble. You established your limit in a rational frame of mind; that's why figuring out your limit before you look is critical. There are many other good, affordable homes that can make you happy. Keep on looking.

The real estate market in my area is still going crazy. By the time I get to a house it is already sold, and the bids are at least 25 percent above the asking price. What should I do?

If you have done your homework, you know exactly what you can afford. If your limit has been reached, just walk away. Do not get caught up in the frenzy. What goes up always, in time, comes down. In the meantime, there can be temporary price declines that create a buyer's market, as we're seeing in parts of the country as I write this, rather than the kind of seller's market we saw in the last half decade.

In almost every bidding war I've seen, the asking price for the house has been significantly under the market value, but it sells way over the market value. Why?

Listing a house under market value is a popular selling technique, especially in hot real estate markets. The point is to get as many people as possible interested in the house; when people see the house, they feel they've found a bargain. Along with lots of other people, they become hooked on the house. That's how a bidding war begins. Before long, the house is sold for much more than the asking price, which was the real estate agent's objective all along.

CONTRACT OF SALE

The contract of sale is a binding agreement between the seller and the buyer. The seller promises to transfer title to his or her property to the buyer at an agreed-upon price. Because the document is binding, it's important to make sure it has all the necessary contingency clauses so that, in case your stated conditions are not met, you can walk away with no liability. The contract must be written, and it should clearly describe all the provisions and conditions of the sale, such as the purchase price, the amount of the down payment, the closing schedule, and whether or not the deal is contingent upon the buyer's obtaining mortgage financing. Other contingencies may include the loan provisions (such as your qualifying for a 30-year fixed-rate loan at no more than 8 percent a year), an acceptable home inspection (usually conducted within 10 to 14 days after the contract is signed), and a termite inspection. Both buyer and seller will sign this document (probably several copies of it), and you should receive an original to keep. Sometimes the contract is referred to as an agreement of sale, contract of purchase, purchase agreement, deposit receipt, or sales agreement. If something in the contract is confusing, don't be afraid to ask for an explanation from your agent or a real estate lawyer. In some parts of the country (e.g., New York City), even if the contract is standard boilerplate, it is customary for an attorney who specializes in real estate to review and explain it.

In some cases, another set of documents, commonly referred to as escrow instructions, will be signed by the seller and the buyer. This agreement includes where the down payment and the deed will be held, the title insurance company, and more. An escrow company is a neutral party that holds the deed, loan documents, and your money until all terms and conditions of the agreement are satisfied.

HOUSE INSPECTIONS

One of the contingencies in your contract of sale will be that the home passes inspection. Now's the time to complete the inspection process, before you make your final purchase.

Inspections—there are often more than one—by a good engineer and/or inspector ensure that the house is sound and without the kinds of problems you can't easily see—termites, structural flaws, geological or environmental risks, or asbestos, to name just a few. Please don't skimp in this area.

I've called around and priced building inspectors. Getting the house inspected will cost me nearly $400. The house is almost brand new. Do you think it's worth the additional expense?
Absolutely. Have you heard the expression,

"They don't build them like they used to"? New homes are just as susceptible to faulty construction and other problems as old ones are. Whether you are buying a new home or an old one, please always order an inspection, both for your peace of mind and for the safety of your family and your investment.

MORTGAGES, MORTGAGES, MORTGAGES

If you've followed along this far, you've learned how to create a secure position for yourself as a buyer. You've learned how to establish your purchase price and how to face the real estate market with confidence and minimum emotion. We've discussed the contract of sale. In the following section, we will deal with the mortgage itself: how to shop for one, what to look for, and what to avoid.

USING A MORTGAGE BROKER

Can you explain what a mortgage broker does?
A mortgage broker assists a buyer in finding the best mortgage loan to finance a home. The broker can make the process easier because he or she has access to loan packages from many different lending institutions. A broker can advise you on the maximum loan you can really afford and help you compare mortgages. In addition, he or she will put together and present your entire loan package to the seller or seller's agent, helping you to get through all the needed paperwork and documentation as smoothly and easily as possible.

A good mortgage broker can also advise you about how to handle any minor black marks you may have on your credit history, and may be willing to shave up to half a percentage point off your closing costs by taking a smaller fee.

That said, I strongly recommend that you remain in control of selecting and applying for your mortgage—you need to work *with* a broker, not close your eyes and let the broker do it all.

Isn't it expensive to use a mortgage broker?

Mortgage brokers typically charge you a small fee and also receive a commission from the bank that issues your mortgage. Still, using a broker could save you money if he or she gets you a better mortgage interest rate than you could get on your own.

Does the buyer always pay the mortgage broker's fee?

Normally, the buyer pays the fee. Before deciding to go with a broker, ask him or her to state in writing exactly how much his or her services will cost and who will pay for them.

We didn't go through the preapproval process, so we haven't established a relationship with any particular bank. The seller has accepted our bid, and we have signed the contract of sale. Now the real estate agent says we need to get a mortgage broker and has recommended someone she knows. Should I trust her?

The real estate agent's interest is, of course, in seeing the deal completed as quickly as possible. That said, I wouldn't automatically discount her advice. In fact, you can probably assume that the broker she recommends has had success in getting loans for other clients. Nonetheless, it's important for you to do your homework. Ask your friends for suggestions, meet with other brokers as well as this one, and don't let the agent (or anyone else) pressure you into working with a person with whom you're not comfortable.

Is negotiating directly with a bank a complete waste of time?

No. At the very least, you should check current interest rates charged by the banks in your area. To find a list of current rates at local banks, look in the real estate section of your local paper—rates are usually posted in the Sunday edition. Since rates can change quickly, you may also want to check the Web every day or two. Try *www.bankrate.com.*

From beginning to end, how long does it take to be approved for a mortgage?

As a general rule, the process typically takes less than a month. If you find it's taking longer, call your broker or lending institution and ask for an explanation for the delay. Don't be shy—remember that you're in control of your money.

I have a great mortgage broker. Why is it important that I learn about the mortgage process? Isn't it a waste of the broker's expertise?

This is a common and unfortunate misconception. Think of a mortgage broker as a guide through the process, not as someone who makes decisions for you. Just as you need to determine your own spending limits, you need to understand the terms of your mortgage—it's a matter of personal power.

FINDING A MORTGAGE ON THE INTERNET

My friend skipped the banker and the broker and is using an Internet service to get a mortgage. What do you think about Internet mortgage services?

The Internet can be a great source of information about interest rates and available mortgages, and can also provide one of the quickest ways to get a loan. But be warned that it can spread misinformation. Some of the most reliable loan sites are *www.lendingtree.com* and *www.quicken loans.com*.

LOCKING IN YOUR RATE

What does it mean to lock in an interest rate, and is it a good idea to do it early?

Locking in an interest rate simply means that you have a commitment from a lender for a particular interest rate for a specific period of time: say, a 6 percent rate on a 30-year mortgage, assuming that you close within 60 days. You would lock in the number of points, if any, at the same time. Normally, you are applying for a mortgage on a specific property when you lock in the interest rate.

The longer you have a particular interest rate locked in, the higher the interest rate tends to be, because the bank wants to hedge against interest rates increasing during the longer period of time.

If you think interest rates are going to rise before you close on the property you want to buy, then locking in an interest rate early is an important move. On the other hand, if interest rates are high and expected to go down before you close on your house, try to wait until late in the process to lock in your rate. If you are considering locking in an interest rate, carefully evaluate the terms of the loan, including whether you will have to pay an additional fee in order to lock in.

What happens if I don't lock in an interest rate?

Sooner or later you *will* lock in an interest rate, but in the meantime you will have a floating interest rate. This means that between the time you are approved for a mortgage and the time you close on your home (usually a few months), the interest rate on your loan will float up or down, depending on the going rates. This is something of a gamble and may create some additional anxiety for you if you are worried about rates going up. On the other hand, if you think rates are headed down, it may not be a bad choice.

Why is it that when the Fed lowers interest rates, it does not affect the interest rate of my mortgage?

Fed fund rates only deal with interest in short-term loans. Mortgages are long-term loans, and their fate is determined by what happens with ten-year bonds. When people sell bonds, the price of the bond goes down and therefore interest rates attached to that bond go up. That is why when Alan Greenspan lowered interest rates in June 2003, mortgage rates started to go up the following day. There is no direct correlation with the Fed lowering interest rates and the interest rate of your mortgage; they have nothing to do with each other and never will.

I've heard of a traveling rate lock. What is that?

A traveling rate lock is a locked-in rate you have negotiated before you find a particular house you want to purchase. The rate "travels" with you for a certain period of time (usually 30 to 90 days) as you look at homes. If you think interest rates are going to rise between the time you go shopping for a home and the time you find a place to buy and close on it, you may want to look into a traveling interest rate. Some people suggest that a traveling rate lock is also desirable when you are in a very competitive "seller's market," where you are a stronger candidate as a buyer if you have a mortgage commitment in place.

What happens if I find a property I want to buy during the lock-in period but don't close during that time?

If you do not close on a property in the agreed-upon time period, you will lose the lock-in rate. That said, you may be able to pay an additional fee to extend the rate-lock period. Deposits and contracts are not enough to sustain a lock-in—you must close the sale. If you paid a fee for the lock-in rate that you didn't use, not closing in time could cost you money. And if interest rates have risen, you could wind up paying more for your mortgage. You should always know for what period your rate is locked in, and keep track of how long you have left before the lock-in expires. Also remember that if you have to postpone your closing, your loan documents will have to be revised and the lender will charge you a fee for the revision—possibly a couple hundred dollars.

I recently applied for a loan and locked in my

rate; however, the loan did not close on time and now the bank is not honoring the lock, and the new rate is a lot higher, can they do that?

Yes. However, what you need to know is that locks can be extended and it is usually your mortgage broker's responsibility to do this. If you are not working with a mortgage broker, you can do this on your own. Now, this most likely will cost you a small amount of money, but it can be worth it. Also when applying for a loan, it is important to stay on top of things and make sure that your lender closes on time, and good mortgage brokers may even offer to take that extra cost to lock out of their own pocket. So when you lock, you have got to stay on top of it big time to see if rates go up after the point of the lock.

ANNUAL PERCENTAGE RATE (APR)

When I applied for a loan, the mortgage broker quoted two different rates. One is the annual rate and the other is the APR. What is the APR?

APR stands for annual percentage rate. With some mortgages, your lender will include your closing costs in the amount you are borrowing. The APR is the actual annual rate you will end up paying over the life of the loan, including all additional costs. The annual rate is how much you will be paying per year on the mortgage alone.

Should I make my decision about which mortgage is right for me based on APR?

It's best to compare mortgages based on annual interest rates, not APR. In many instances, comparing based on APR can cost you. In fact, it is a very poor way to comparison shop for a mortgage—and it can easily cause you to make costly wrong decisions.

APR was created in order to provide a way for borrowers to account for additional costs—such as points and fees—that are often associated with a mortgage. This sounds good, because sometimes it isn't easy to choose between a loan with a lower rate and higher fees, say, or a loan with a higher rate and lower fees.

The problem is, the APR calculation makes three very bad assumptions. First, it assumes zero inflation over the years—in other words, that the buying power of a dollar 10, 20, even 30 years from now will be exactly the same as the buying power of a dollar today. Second, the APR calculation assumes that your mortgage will never be paid off, and will certainly not be prepaid, which means it doesn't take into account the likelihood that you will refinance or sell your home—a major oversight given that the average life of a home mortgage these days is fewer than four years. Finally, APR does not take tax consequences into consideration. This can be significant, since higher fees on a mortgage may not be deductible, while the higher interest rate typically is.

Here is an example of how making a decision based on APR could hurt you if you were considering two loan packages on a $200,000 fixed-rate 30-year mortgage with zero points. Let's say that Lender A is offering a rate of 5.875 percent, and Lender B is offering a higher rate of 6.125 percent. But a closer look shows that Lender A is also charging $3,000 more in fees than Lender B. How do you compare? If you look at APR, Lender A (the one offering 5.875 percent, with $3,000 higher fees) has an APR of 6.1 percent. Lender B (the one with 6.125 but no fees) has an

APR of 6.2 percent. So, according to the APR, Lender A is a better deal, even though the fees are $3,000 higher.

This is exactly what all high-fee lenders are hoping you look at—and that you then stop looking and sign right up. But let's look at the real story. Based on the interest rate alone, the payment difference between Mortgage A and Mortgage B is $32 per month. Is it worth paying $3,000 in fees to Lender A in order to save $32 a month? Hardly. It will take you about 8 years just to get your investment back, which makes it an especially bad choice if you think you might move or refinance before then, as most people do.

To make the decision to go with Lender A even worse, if that's possible, borrowers rarely take the value of today's dollars into account. Rather than giving Lender A the windfall of your hard-earned $3,000, you should give it to yourself. Reduce the loan balance on your mortgage by the fees you are saving. In the example above, that would reduce the loan from $200,000 to $197,000—which makes the payment difference based on interest rate just $4 per month, instead of $32 per month! The actual break-even point with Lender A is after 155 months (more than 12 years!).

One more thing: You have to calculate your tax savings on the slightly higher interest rate. When you look at this, it makes even more sense to avoid paying higher, nondeductible fees.

The obvious correct choice is to go with Lender B, even though Lender A has the lower APR.

Bottom line: Forget APR and always, always think twice about advertised low rates when they are accompanied by higher fees.

CONFORMING AND NONCONFORMING LOANS

I'm applying for a loan and the lender wants to know if I want a conforming loan or a nonconforming loan. What is the difference?

The amount of the loan determines whether it is a conforming loan or a nonconforming loan. Loans under $417,000 are known as conforming loans. Loans above that amount are called nonconforming loans, or jumbo loans. (A new tier, called jumbo conforming was created in 2009; in certain high-cost areas loans above $417,000 but below $729,750 are considered to be in this new tier. This new tier is based on FHA loan limits; to find the most up-to-date conforming loan limits for your region go to: *https://entp.hud .gov/idapp/html/hicostlook.cfm.* Conforming loans get a better interest rate than nonconforming loans, usually by about one-quarter to one-half of a percentage point better. During the credit crisis that began in 2008, the spread between conforming and non-conforming was closer to one full percentage point.)

Last year, when I got a mortgage, a conforming loan was limited to $359,650. My loan was for $389,650, so it was considered a nonconforming loan and I had to pay a higher interest rate. This year my mortgage amount is considered a conforming loan. What should I do?

In theory, and if the numbers make sense, here's what you should do: If you are planning to stay in this house for as many years as it would take to recoup the costs of refinancing and the conforming-loan interest rate is low enough to make sense, look into refinancing. Be careful, though, for you may have taken out your original loan at a time when overall interest rates were lower than they are now. Just because your loan now qualifies for a conforming-loan status does not mean the current interest rate environment makes it beneficial to refinance.

PRIVATE MORTGAGE INSURANCE (PMI)

I've tapped into all my resources but I'm just not going to clear the 20 percent down payment hurdle. I understand I still might be able to get a mortgage, but I will also have to get PMI. Can you explain PMI?

Private mortgage insurance, or PMI, exists for the benefit of banks and lenders. They require that borrowers take out this insurance if they can't put at least 20 percent down on the purchase of a house. Above and beyond the lender's right to foreclose on a house, PMI gives the lender additional protection in case of default. Paying for PMI means that your up-front and monthly expenses will both be larger, although some lenders may offer alternative payment options. PMI doesn't protect you, the borrower. It's meant to protect the lender.

How long will I have to pay PMI?

You usually are required to pay PMI until you have built up at least 20 percent to 22 percent equity in your house. Your equity is based on the fair market value of the property minus the remaining principal amount of your loan. So if you have a home that is worth $200,000 and you owe $190,000 on your mortgage, you have $10,000, or 5 percent, of equity in your home.

How much does PMI cost?

The cost of PMI varies according to the size of the down payment you make (the smaller the down payment as a percentage of the home price, the higher the cost). But if your down payment is 10 percent, say, then PMI will cost you $43 a month for every $100,000 you borrow. Typically, your PMI premium is paid separately from your mortgage, though also on a monthly basis and sent in with your mortgage payment. It is not tax deductible.

To show you how PMI works, let's say you are buying a $200,000 home and making a 10 percent down payment, so you are taking out a $180,000 mortgage. Let's further say it's a 30-year fixed-rate mortgage with a 6 percent interest rate, giving you a monthly mortgage payment of $1,199. Your PMI premium would be $77 a month, on top of your $1,199 monthly mortgage, for a total monthly payment of $1,276. Now, remember, that $77 a month isn't tax-deductible.

Is there a better way to pay my PMI—one that makes it tax-deductible?

Yes, there is. It is called *upfront single premium mortgage insurance.* Here's how it works.

When applying for a mortgage, you can ask your lender to draw up the mortgage so that it lets you pay all your PMI costs up front, as a one-time fee. If you do this with a $180,000, 30-year mortgage, for example, the PMI will add a total of two points, or 2 percent, to the amount

of your mortgage, for an additional $3,600 up-front. The good news about this is twofold: First, you can add the cost of PMI into your mortgage, so that, rather than forking over the $3,600 in cold, hard cash, you can take out a $183,600 mortgage ($180,000+$3,600=$183,600). In this example, when you add your PMI cost to your mortgage, you increase your monthly mortgage payment to $1,224—$24 a month more than the original mortgage—but you also eliminate the $77 monthly PMI fee. So, all told, you save $53 per month. The second part of the good news is that, since PMI is now included in your mortgage, it is tax-deductible, reducing your net after-tax cost even further. *Voila!*

Not bad, right? But here's an even better idea, if you can afford it: Opt for a 25-year mortgage with the PMI paid up front. Because the mortgage has a shorter term, the PMI insurance is going to cost you less—only three-quarters of 1 percent of your loan amount instead of 2 percent. In the example above, the $3,600 up-front cost will be cut to $1,350. Thus, your total loan amount is now $181,350, and your monthly mortgage cost is $1,211—only $11 more a month than the 30-year loan without any PMI! Remember, that's for a 25-year, not a 30-year, term. You will save thousands of dollars in interest payments as a result of the shorter loan term (see page 187), will build equity faster, and can deduct your PMI from your taxes. Smart move!

If I opt for regular monthly PMI payments, will they stop automatically when I've attained 20 percent equity in my home?

Under federal law, PMI on loans made after

July 29, 1999, will end automatically once the mortgage is paid down to 78 percent. Each year your lender must send you a reminder that you have PMI and that you have the right to request cancellation if you have met certain requirements.

Even though by law the lender must notify you when your equity has reached the necessary level, this does not always happen. Please make sure that at your closing your lender lets you know in writing under what conditions your PMI costs will be cancelled and then keep checking; you would be amazed at how a lender can conveniently forget to check on your behalf. For those of you who purchased a home and have a mortgage with PMI before 1999, check your equity level on your own.

Does this law apply to me if I am paying PMI on an FHA loan or on a piggyback or 80/10/10 loan?

No, it does not.

What do I need to do to cancel my PMI?

First, you will need an up-to-date appraisal of the house, confirming that you have indeed reached the 22-percent-in-equity mark. The lender will probably want further proof, such as a comparable market analysis, that the equity mark is stable (in other words, that the property will hold its value or appreciate). If this is your first home, be aware that the lender may try to reject your claim on the basis of your first-time buyer status. Or the lender may argue that it expects rapid price fluctuations. So make sure that you are coming to this negotiation armed with a clean credit record and with proof that

you have indeed reached the 22-percent-in-equity mark.

I received a big bonus at work and was able to pay ahead enough on my mortgage to reach my 22-percent-in-equity mark in only a year's time. But my bank says I have to pay PMI for at least two years. Is that true?

Some PMI agreements require the borrower to make PMI payments for a predetermined time period. When you are shopping around for your loan, look for an agreement without this clause. If you somehow got stuck with it and find yourself capable of paying ahead more quickly than you thought you could before the required PMI period is up, run the numbers to see whether it makes sense to pay up earlier anyway. You may find that it does, even though you are making some unnecessary PMI payments.

I was told that the best way to get around PMI is to take out what is called an 80/10/10 loan. Can you tell me what that is?

An 80/10/10 loan, also known as a piggyback loan, was a very popular way to get around PMI costs during the real estate bubble from 2003–2007. Remember, any loan for more than 80 percent of the purchase price requires PMI insurance. Let's say you have only 10 percent to put down. Rather than taking out one loan for 90 percent that would require PMI, you take out two loans: one for 80 percent, which does not require PMI, and a second one, often from the same lender, for 10 percent. The 80 percent loan will be at the going interest rate, and the 10 percent loan at a higher rate, in some cases considerably higher. During the real estate bubble the theory was that home values would increase so quickly and so dramatically that you could refinance into a regular mortgage (without the piggyback) in a few years once your equity reached 20 percent. That theory has backfired on millions of homeowners who found themselves unable to refinance once home values began to fall, not rise, and they were (and are) stuck still paying their high-rate on the second loan.

THE MORTGAGE MENU

There are so many different kinds of mortgages available—I find it very confusing. Can you explain the differences?

There are indeed a lot of different kinds of mortgages, but the main ones among which you will probably be choosing are fixed-rate mortgages, adjustable-rate mortgages, fixed and variable combined mortgages, and Federal Housing Administration (FHA) mortgages. In addition, some mortgages have prepayment penalties if you repay the mortgage before a specific date. Some are due in full when you sell, and others may be taken over by buyers.

Can you explain the interest aspect of a mortgage?

As with any loan, interest on a mortgage is a fee the lender charges for the use of its funds. The cost to you of borrowing the money is the interest rate, which is expressed as a percentage paid annually on the loan. To figure out how much interest you will be paying over the life of your fixed-rate mortgage, deduct the principal amount you are borrowing (say, $200,000) from the total amount you will have to pay back over the life of the loan. Assuming a 6 percent interest rate on a 30-year fixed-rate mortgage, for example, the total amount you must pay over the life of the loan is approximately $431,676. Now subtract $200,000 from $431,676 to calculate the interest you will pay over 30 years on such a loan: $231,676.

Why do I need to know the total amount of interest I'll be paying?

There are two reasons it's helpful to know the total amount of interest you'll be paying. First, it gives you the true cost of owning your home. Second, it gives you an idea of how much you'll be able to save in taxes over the years, depending on your income-tax bracket. Knowing the total amount of interest you'll pay is one of the benefits of a fixed-rate mortgage.

Is there a way to lower the mortgage interest rate I'll have to pay?

The key to getting the lowest possible interest rate on your mortgage (as well as on your credit cards, car loans, and other consumer credit, by the way) is to make sure you fall within the highest range of FICO scores. FICO scores are the single most commonly used criteria for evaluating your creditworthiness when you apply for a loan or a line of credit. (For a full explanation of FICO scores, for information on how to get your score, and for tips on how to improve a score, please see page 30.)

FICO scores range from 300 to 850, and they are divided into ranges that correspond with the interest rates major lenders currently charge. In December 2009, the ranges were:

760–850
700–759
680–699
660–679
640–659
620–639

A score between 300 and 620 puts you in the "sub lenders" category, where it is almost impossible to get a mortgage loan.

To be eligible for the lowest mortgage interest rate, you typically need to have a FICO score that is in the top range (760–850). Other factors also come into play in determining your loan terms, such as the size of your down payment, your income, etc, but a FICO score of 740–760 or better greatly increases your odds of qualifying for the best loan terms. If you are below 620, you are (in your lender's mind) in financial trouble and if a lender agrees to offer you a mortgage it will probably be with a seriously high interest rate.

To find the best interest rates available on mortgages, log on to *www.bankrate.com, www.quickenloans.com,* or *www.lendingtree.com.*

FIXED-RATE MORTGAGES

Fixed-rate mortgages are one of the most popular types available. They are very stable, because the interest rate paid on them is fixed. This means that your monthly payments will always be the same. For example, if you borrow $200,000 at a 6 percent fixed rate for 30 years, the monthly payment will be fixed at $1,199 a month for 30 years.

Can you only get a fixed-rate mortgage for 30 years?

No. A 30-year fixed-rate mortgage was the mortgage of choice for many years, but now you can get a fixed-rate mortgage for different lengths of time, including 10, 15, and 20 years.

Is there an advantage to borrowing for one period of time instead of another?

What is advantageous for you depends on your financial situation. I'll say more about the length of your mortgage later but, basically, there are two rules to keep in mind.

The first rule is that the longer your mortgage term, the higher your interest rate will probably be. In other words, the bank will charge you a higher rate for a 30-year mortgage than for a 15-year mortgage, usually about a quarter- to a half-percent.

The second is that the longer your mortgage term, the lower your payments will be each month. In other words, the monthly payments on a $200,000 mortgage at 6 percent will be $1,199 on a 30-year mortgage, $1,433 on a 20-year mortgage, $1,687 on a 15-year mortgage, and $2,220 on a 10-year mortgage.

How do I know if a fixed-rate mortgage is right for me?

The best time to use a fixed-rate mortgage is when interest rates are low and you think they will be going up, *and* you will be living in the house you want to buy for at least five to seven years. Fixed-rate mortgages are also a good bet if interest rates are low and you are retired or about to retire. If you are living on a fixed income, you'll want to be sure that as many of your expenses as possible, including your mortgage payment, are fixed as well.

ADJUSTABLE-RATE MORTGAGE (ARM)

As you might guess from the name, this type of loan is the opposite of a fixed-rate mortgage. It has an interest rate that falls or rises as general market interest rates fall or rise. Normally, an adjustable-rate mortgage starts with a relatively low interest rate, which is fixed for six months to several years, and then the rate adjusts to market rates. Keep in mind that, in most cases, sooner or later the interest rate on an adjustable-rate mortgage will rise. You may see this type of mortgage referred to as an ARM or a variable mortgage.

Is there any protection for me if I have an ARM and interest rates go sky-high?

Protection should be built into your mortgage agreement in the form of a yearly cap and a lifetime ceiling cap. The yearly cap means that no matter how high interest rates rise, the bank/lender will not be allowed to increase your mortgage rate by more than a specified amount each year, usually about 2 percent. The lifetime ceiling cap means that the interest rate on your mortgage can never exceed a particular figure, usually about 6 or 7 percent more than the orig-

inal interest rate. But be careful; not all ARMs offer this protection.

Similarly, if interest rates were to drop significantly, there would be a floor below which the bank wouldn't be obliged to lower your interest rate.

Can you give me an example of how an ARM works?

Say you have a three-year ARM that starts at 4 percent and has a 2 percent yearly cap, a 10 percent lifetime cap, and a minimum interest rate of 3.5 percent. During the first three years of your loan, your interest rate will be fixed at 4 percent. In the fourth year, no matter what interest rates are, the most you will have to pay is 6 percent (4 percent plus the 2 percent annual cap); and the least you will pay is 3.5 percent (because your rate can't drop below that figure). In the following years, the worst that could happen would be that the bank would raise your interest rate by another 2 percent a year, say, from 6 to 8 percent until the interest rate on your loan reaches 10 percent. Even if interest rates go to 15 or 20 percent, your interest rate will remain at 10 percent.

Obviously, if you are going to take out an adjustable-rate mortgage, you should try to get the lowest possible yearly and lifetime cap, which is more important than either the starting interest rate or the frequency with which your rate can be adjusted.

How often can my interest rate be adjusted?

Many people considering an ARM focus on getting a low starting interest rate and overlook the important issue of the frequency with which their rate can be adjusted. I believe caps and frequency are both more important issues than the starter rate. The interval at which your lender can adjust your rate will be stated in the terms of your loan, and it will probably be either once a year or every six months. As you might imagine, there can be a big difference between the two.

If interest rates are going to rise, an ARM with a lower starting interest rate that can be adjusted every six months could end up costing more than an ARM with a higher starting rate that can be adjusted only once a year. So even if you are going to be stretched during the first few years and are concerned about keeping that starting rate down, I ask you to think long term and consider what might happen after the starter period is over.

Is a rate that changes annually always preferable to one that changes every six months?

If interest rates are low and expected to rise, you will want to lock in the longest possible period between rate changes, which is typically a year. If interest rates are high and expected to fall, you might want to opt for more frequent interest rate adjustments; that way, you benefit more quickly from any rate decreases.

How is the annual increase on an ARM calculated?

Here's how it works: Your interest rate is set on a percentage basis, called a margin, above a designated index. Margins are normally 1 to 5 percent over the selected index. After your starter fixed-rate period ends, the amount by which your lender will be able to increase or decrease the interest rate you pay is based on the rise or fall of the index and the margin of your particular loan. Let's say your mortgage interest rate is tied to the six-month U.S. Treasury bill index and your margin is 2 percent above the index. If the Treasury bill index rises to 6 percent, the maximum your bank could charge you next year would be 8 percent (6 percent plus 2 percent), assuming the increase doesn't exceed your yearly cap amount. When getting an ARM, try to get the lowest possible margin over the index.

Besides the six-month Treasury bill index, what other indexes can the annual increase (margin) be tied to?

The margin also can be set in relation to the Federal Cost of Funds index, the 11th District Cost of Funds Index (COFI), the one-year Treasury Constant Maturity Securities, or the London Interbank Offer Rate (the LIBOR index).

Does it matter which index my ARM is tied to?

Yes, it does. Some indexes are more volatile (they move up and/or down more quickly) than others. Your goal is to be tied to the index that will keep you at the lowest average rate over the course of the mortgage. The problem is, you don't know which index will do this. Remember the general rules, though: When interest rates are high and projected to go lower, you want your mortgage to be tied to an index that fluctuates rapidly so you can cash in on those lower interest rates quickly. If interest rates are fairly low at the time that you get your mortgage, you want an index that changes less often so that you can hold on to that low rate as long as possible.

How do I figure out whether an index is volatile?

Look at how the index has performed in the

past. For instance, in the late 1990s, when interest rates were low, the best indexes were the stable ones: the six-month Treasury bill index and the one-year Treasury Constant Maturity Securities. As a general rule, if interest rates rise and the index you are tied to lags, you will save money. Conversely, when interest rates are moving down, you want to be tied to a fast-moving index so that your rate will be lowered more quickly. The COFI (Cost of Funds Index) will probably serve you best in an interest rate environment that is headed down.

Who sets the index rate?

The six-month Treasury bill index is set by the federal government according to the rates it pays on Treasury bills. Your lender does not control the index.

A margin rate can't be too low, right?

Actually, wrong. A rate that's too low can cause what's called a negative amortization. This happens when your monthly payments become so small that they fail to cover the full amount of interest due; then the bank adds that interest to the amount of principal you owe. In this scenario, you could end up owing more than the original mortgage amount! Many adjustable-rate mortgages are susceptible to negative amortization. Ask your lender about your loan.

What should I look at when considering an ARM?

Consider the following issues:

- How long will the starting interest rate be in effect?

- What is the yearly cap on the mortgage?
- What is the lifetime cap on the mortgage?
- What is the lowest interest rate the loan can have?
- Which index is the interest rate going to be tied to?
- What margin can the lender charge you, based on the index?
- Once the initial period has ended, how often can the lender adjust the interest rate?
- Does the mortgage have a negative amortization?
- Is there a penalty if you want to prepay your mortgage?
- Can a new buyer take over your loan?

A number of Internet programs can help you run the numbers using different interest rates and other variables. Make sure to figure out the worst-case scenario. A calculator I like is called "What Will My ARM Loan Payment Be?" at *www.mortgage101.com/arm-loan-calculator.*

FIVE TWENTY-FIVE (5/25) OR SEVEN TWENTY-THREE (7/23) MORTGAGES

What is a fixed and variable combined mortgage?

A fixed and variable combined mortgage (also known as a hybrid mortgage) mixes aspects of a fixed-rate mortgage and an ARM. You will probably see these referred to as five twenty-fives (5/25) or seven twenty-threes (7/23), and you can get them as *convertible* or *nonconvertible* mortgages.

What is the difference between a convertible and a nonconvertible mortgage?

I consider a *convertible* hybrid mortgage to really be a sort of fixed/fixed-rate mortgage. Here, your interest rate is fixed for the first term of the loan; then it's adjusted once, to another fixed rate, for the remaining 25 or 23 years of the loan. For example, a convertible 5/25 mortgage would have a fixed interest rate for the first 5 years and then would convert to another fixed interest rate for the remaining 25 years.

With a nonconvertible hybrid mortgage, your interest rate is fixed for the first term of the loan. After that, the loan converts to an ARM. These types of loans are commonly called Hybrid ARMs.

Five and 25 add up to 30, and so do 7 and 23. Are these essentially 30-year mortgages?

Yes, these mortgages will be amortized over 30 years. You choose whether your initial interest rate is fixed for five or seven years and whether, for the remaining 25 or 23 years, you will convert to a new fixed rate or a variable rate that is determined at the time of signing up for the mortgage.

Do nonconvertible mortgages that convert to a variable rate then work like a regular ARM?

Yes. After the initial five or seven years, your adjustment will be tied to an index, to which the lender will probably add a margin of between 1 and 3 percent.

How do I know if a fixed and variable mortgage is a good choice for me?

If you do not plan to live in the home you are buying for at least five or seven years, and if in-terest rates are going up (making a traditional ARM less attractive), a fixed and variable mortgage might make sense for you. That's because the initial interest rate may be quite a bit lower than the rate on a traditional 30-year fixed-rate mortgage, saving you a lot of money over time. This is something to consider if you are buying a starter home or are pretty sure that you will want to move again soon.

Consider this example. You want a $200,000 mortgage. The interest rate on a 30-year fixed loan will be 6 percent, and the rate on a 5/25 will be 5.5 percent. If you live in the house for the next five years, you will pay $1,199 each month on the fixed loan, for a total of $71,940. With a 5/25 loan, you will pay $1,136 each month, for a total of $68,196. If you sell your house at the end of five years, you will have saved more than $3,744 by having the 5/25.

Is there any difference between the 5/25 and the 7/23, aside from the different periods of time that you keep your initial fixed rate?

Because you are locking in the rate for a longer period with a 7/23, the interest rate may be a quarter or half point higher than on a 5/25.

PORTABLE MORTGAGE

I've heard a lot about a new kind of mortgage that I should check out called a portable mortgage. What exactly is a portable mortgage?

A portable mortgage allows a borrower to keep their mortgage if they move to a different primary residence. Portable mortgages had been creating quite a buzz in a favorable-interest-rate environment, but before jumping into a portable mortgage, please compare your options, because in almost all cases a portable mortgage just does not make sense. Here's how they work. Let's say a 30-year fixed rate with zero points is being offered at a rate of 5.875 percent. The remaining balance can be transferred to a new primary residence when the borrower moves. The rate would remain at 5.875 percent, and the loan would continue to amortize without being reset to 30 years.

Does a portable mortgage cost me more than a fixed mortgage?

You are paying a premium of roughly 25–50 basis points in rate for this type of mortgage, so the longer you remain in the home, the more you stand to lose. If you intend to stay or wind up staying in the home for 10 years or more, this mortgage is a poor choice because you pay a much higher rate for the first 10 years.

If I am only going to be staying in my home for the next five years and not buying another house, should I get a portable mortgage or an ARM?

Here is a rule of thumb: If you intend to move within five years, then you would be much better off selecting a 5/1 ARM, where the interest rate is locked for five years and then changes every year after that.

If I plan to sell my house in a short period of time and buy another home, does it make sense to get a portable mortgage?

That depends on what happens to interest rates and how much of a home you plan to buy. Since you can only take the remaining balance with you when you change residences, you may find yourself requiring additional funds to close. This may cause you to need a second mortgage or home equity line of credit in order to make up for the shortfall in funds required to purchase your new home. The second mortgage will likely be at a higher or variable interest rate, thus negating or minimizing the benefit of the portable mortgage.

When does a portable mortgage make sense?

If you are on a fixed income, expect to move within four to seven years, have very low risk tolerance, expect to downsize during your next move, and think interest rates are going to be higher when you do move, then the portable mortgage may be a good option for you.

FEDERAL HOUSING ADMINISTRATION (FHA) MORTGAGE

As of 2009, the Federal Housing Administration (FHA) mortgage program insures loans ranging from about $271,050 to $729,750 for a single-family home (depending on the region of the country), with as little as 3.5 percent down. The FHA, a division of the federal government controlled by the Department of Housing and Urban Development (HUD), may be willing to give you a mortgage even if you have had bad credit in the past.

What are the differences between qualifying for an FHA mortgage and for a conventional mortgage?

The FHA program insures mortgages that are

issued by FHA-approved lenders. If you are interested in an FHA-insured loan, first inquire with a lender you are interested in working with if they are authorized to originate FHA-insured loans. Often the qualifying standards for an FHA-insured loan can be more relaxed than the standards for a conventional mortgage. The FHA specifies 31 percent of your gross monthly income. Even so, it is ultimately your responsibility to calculate what you will be able to pay.

What counts as part of my monthly housing costs?

Your monthly housing costs are made up of your mortgage principal, interest, taxes, and insurance—often abbreviated as PITI.

Does the FHA program let me have a higher PITI than a conventional lender?

Yes. If your gross monthly income is $3,000 and you are allowed by a conventional lender to have a PITI payment equal to 28 percent, then you know that you cannot spend more than $840 each month on housing costs ($3,000 multiplied by 0.28 equals $840). A conventional lender will also limit your total debt, including credit cards, to between 33 and 36 percent of your gross monthly income.

The FHA will allow you to have higher debt-to-income ratios. If your PITI can be 31 percent of your gross monthly income, as the FHA allows it to be, multiply $3,000 (your gross monthly income) by .31. You can spend up to $930 each month on your PITI. Further, the FHA allows you to have a total long-term debt ratio of up to 43 percent of your gross monthly income.

Are the interest rates offered by the FHA comparable to a conventional loan?

Yes, they are essentially the same.

If I get a mortgage from a regular bank and put less than 20 percent down, I have to pay for PMI. If I get a mortgage from the FHA and put less than 20 percent down, do I still have to get insurance?

Yes. The FHA will issue the insurance, charging you about 1.5 percent (as of 2009) of the loan amount up front, which may be included in closing costs, and about 0.5 percent of the loan amount divided by 12 to be paid monthly.

Is there a maximum FHA loan amount I can apply for?

Yes, though the amount varies by county and can change from year to year. The size of the loan you may be eligible for will depend on the county that you live in and the median price of real estate in your area. Contact your local FHA office, which you can find on the Web at *www.hud.gov/local.html.* You can also look up your region's current FHA limits at *https://entp.hud.gov/idapp/html/hicostlook.cfm.*

Who is best served by an FHA mortgage?

Before the credit crisis that began in 2008, FHA-insured loans were most often used by borrowers who had tarnished credit histories, and who were borrowing relatively modest sums. But in 2009 the FHA-loan limits were raised to as much as $729,750 in high-cost areas, making this loan program a viable option for many more prospective borrowers. The combination of a more lenient credit check and a low down payment has boosted the popularity of FHA-insured mortgages in recent years.

When you say that I can have "problems" with my credit history and still get an FHA mortgage, does that include bankruptcy?

Yes. If your bankruptcy was discharged at least two years before you apply for a loan, the FHA will consider your application. No lender, however, including the FHA, will give you a mortgage if you are currently considered a bad credit risk and/or do not have sufficient income to carry a mortgage obligation.

ASSUMABLE MORTGAGES

What is an assumable mortgage?

An assumable mortgage allows the buyer to "assume" the seller's current mortgage. If the seller's current mortgage is a lower rate than current mortgage rates, then this sort of mortgage makes sense. Most mortgage loans have a due-on-sale clause preventing the loan from being assumed by the new owner, although the Federal Housing Administration mortgages and mortgages supplied by the Department of Veterans Affairs can be assumed. It's important to note that assumable loans are rare and only available for the principal balance.

INTEREST-ONLY MORTGAGES

What is an interest-only mortgage?

Interest-only mortgages require the borrower to pay interest only for the first few years, and interest and principal in the later years of the loan. This type of loan is popular with individuals who are self-employed with inconsistent incomes or professionals who are just beginning their careers such as lawyers or doctors who know that their incomes will significantly increase in a few years.

BALLOON LOAN

What is a balloon loan?

In a fixed loan, the principal and interest have been amortized over the life of the loan. In a balloon loan, only the interest, or some combination of interest and principal, have been paid when the loan term expires. The balance is due in full, which is called a balloon payment. The balloon payment is more common to second mortgages. For example, if you borrow $10,000 for ten years and your monthly payments have included only interest, you must pay the $10,000 in principal at the end of the term. Similar to ARM loans, balloon loans are another option to get a lower interest rate in the first few years of the mortgage. These mortgages charge less interest for a set time frame, but require the borrower to either refinance at the end of that period, pay off the loan, or convert it to a fixed payment schedule. Please be very careful with balloon loans. Since no one can predict how interest rates will increase, you can find yourself in a situation where you have to refinance at a high interest rate, or you may be forced to sell your home to pay the balloon loan. Or as so many homeowners experienced during the financial crisis that began in 2008, there is no guarantee that when it comes time to refinance that you will have enough equity in your home to qualify for the refinance. As a general rule of thumb, I think it is wise to stop before you use a balloon mortgage and ask yourself: Should I really be buying this home if the balloon is the only way I can qualify for a mortgage right now? It is so important to understand the potential risks of any mortgage that is not a plain-vanilla fixed-rate mortgage.

LOANS FOR VETERANS

What is a VA Loan?

VA stands for Veterans Administration and it is a loan or a mortgage that the Department of Veterans Affairs makes available for all those considered to be veterans.

Who is eligible for a VA Loan?

Veterans who served on active duty during wartime for 90 days or more; veterans with active service only during peacetime who have served more than 180 days; veterans of enlisted service that began after September 7, 1980, or officers with service beginning after October 16, 1981, who in most cases have served at least two years, are all eligible for a VA Loan.

If you are full-time active duty military personnel who has served for at least 60 days, you are also eligible for a VA Loan, as well as Reservists and National Guard members who served in support of operations in Kosovo, Afghanistan, or Iraq for at least 90 days. Reservists and National Guard members who have com-

pleted six years of service and have been honorably discharged or who are still serving may also be eligible. You can learn more about eligibility at *http://www.homeloans.va.gov/elig2.htm.*

I am eligible for a VA mortgage, what are the advantages of going this way, or should I just get a conventional mortgage?

VA loans, I think, are really quite attractive, especially when interest rates are low. The reason is that if you sell your house, the VA loan is assumable by the next buyer even if they are not a veteran. The new buyer would have the same terms as your loan.

Another advantage of a VA loan is that given today's high prices of homes in some areas you might not have saved enough money to put down the required 20 percent to avoid PMI (Private Mortgage Insurance) costs. With a VA loan, even if you do not have 20 percent to put down, in fact even if you have 0 percent to put down, you can still get a loan without having to pay that extra PMI cost.

I heard VA loans are not worth the trouble because the application process takes forever to complete. Is that true?

It used to be true years ago, but that is no longer true today. The Department of Veterans Affairs has made the application process far simpler and now applying for a VA loan is very similar to applying for a conventional mortgage. The one extra bit of documentation is a VA certificate of eligibility. Your lender can obtain this paperwork for you. Or you can track it down at the VA Website *www.homeloans.va.gov* or by calling (800) 827-1000 for more information.

With a VA loan how much can I borrow to buy a home if I have no money to put down?
The VA does not set loan limits, but typically lenders who issue VA-backed mortgages will follow the general loan limits for a specific region, as determined by the FHA. In 2009 those loan limits ranged from $271,050 to as much as $729,750 in high-cost regions. Your lender can tell you the current limit for your area, or you can find it at *https://entp.hud.gov/idapp/html/hicostlook.cfm.* You will have to pay a funding fee, which can range from .5 percent to 3.35 percent, depending on the loan type. If you have more than 5 percent to put down, you could get a reduced funding fee.

If I already have a VA loan, can I refinance?
You absolutely can.

THE LENGTH OF THE MORTGAGE

Which is better, a 15-year or a 30-year mortgage?
I will say more about this later, but as a general rule I recommend the 15-year mortgage to those who can afford the higher monthly payments associated with the shorter payment period. Here's why. (Please note that these figures do not take into account any interest tax deduction.) If you borrow $200,000 at 6 percent for 15 years, every month you will pay the lender $1,688. At the end of your mortgage term, you will have paid a total of $303,840. If you borrow $200,000 at 6 percent for 30 years, your monthly payments will be lower—about $1,199—but you'll be

COMPARING MONTHLY PAYMENTS ON MORTGAGES OF DIFFERENT TERMS				
Mortgage Amount	Monthly Payments		Per-Month Difference	Total Interest Savings with 15-year vs. 30-year Loan
	15 Years 5.5%	30 Years 6%		
$50,000	$409	$300	$109	$34,400
$100,000	$817	$600	$217	$68,700
$150,000	$1,226	$899	$327	$103,000
$200,000	$1,634	$1,119	$435	$137,500
$250,000	$2,043	$1,499	$544	$171,900
$300,000	$2,451	$1,799	$652	$206,300
$400,000	$3,268	$2,398	$870	$275,100
$500,000	$4,085	$2,998	$1,087	$343,800

making those payments for twice as long. After 30 years, you will have paid a grand total of $431,640. Once you do the math, it becomes clear that a 15-year mortgage can save you money—in this example, $127,800.

Can you explain in more detail the difference between a 15-year and a 30-year mortgage?
Before I explain this, I want to remind you that there are also 10-year, 20-year, and even 40-year mortgages. But 15- and 30-year mortgages are the most popular ones by far.

The basic difference between a 15- and a 30-year mortgage is obviously the length of the loan. Beyond that, the interest rate on a 15-year mortgage is typically half a percent lower than on a 30-year mortgage; as a tradeoff, you will pay a larger sum each month. For a long time, 30-year mortgages were the standard (and sometimes the only) choice for most people, which is why many of us still think of them as the way to go. But it pays to do the math.

I bought my own first house by taking out a 30-year mortgage. I didn't know I had a choice, and I was told, "Oh, everyone gets a 30-year mortgage," so that's what I did. Almost ten years later, I realized that the difference per month would have been only about $115. If I had realized that I could own my home in 15 years instead of 30 for an extra $115 each month, you can bet I would have figured out a way to come up with the extra money. In many places, the difference between the payment on a 15-year mortgage and on a 30-year mortgage will usually not be more than $400 a month.

Another benefit of a shorter term: If you are not inclined to put your monthly savings from the smaller payments on a 30-year mortgage into an investment account for your future, the higher payments on a 15-year mortgage will effectively do your saving for you.

How large are the savings on a 15-year mortgage, compared with a 30-year mortgage?
The table on page 187 demonstrates the differences between the shorter and longer mortgage terms, both in monthly payments and in overall costs, based on common loan amounts. This table assumes that you'll keep the house for the full life of the loan and does not take into account your tax deductions for interest payments.

Note: Please keep in mind that if you borrow more than a specific sum your mortgage will be considered a jumbo loan (rather than a conforming loan), which usually means you will be charged an interest rate half a percent higher than a smaller loan amount would. Thus, interest rates for a jumbo loan in the example above will be 6 percent on a 15-year mortgage and 6.5 percent on a 30-year mortgage. In 2009 the upper limit for a conforming loan was $729,750 in some high-cost areas. Your lender can advise you on the conforming limit for your region.

Why don't more people get 15-year mortgages?
I think that when we consider what we can afford at the time that we buy our homes, we try to stay safe. We figure that as we earn more money, we can pay off our mortgage faster. But few of us are disciplined enough to pay more money than is required, even as our incomes rise.

I like the idea of paying off my mortgage faster with a 15-year loan to save on interest

costs, but I worry if I can afford the higher payments?

A great option is to take out a conventional 30-year mortgage and then make extra payments whenever you can. That can mean sending in more than the required payment every month, or simply making one extra payment a year (13 payments rather than 12). For example, if you were to make 13 payments a year you would reduce the payback time on a 30-year mortgage to 25 years and save yourself thousands of dollars in interest payments. If you want to send in extra payments you need to be aware of two important issues: First, check that there is no prepayment penalty on your mortgage. A prepayment penalty means you will pay an extra fee if you pay off the mortgage ahead of schedule. Some loans just charge the fee in the early years of the mortgage, so find out the rules. If you do decide to pay extra on your mortgage make sure you clearly note—and the lender honors—that 100 percent of the extra payment is to be applied to your principal balance. You do not want to let the lender apply it to interest.

Why is the tax deduction on a mortgage so much larger at the beginning of the loan?

Because loans are structured so that you are paying mostly interest for the first few years. And the interest payments are the part that is tax-deductible.

Here's how a typical loan is structured:

During the first year of a 30-year loan, only 13 percent of your monthly payments goes toward paying off the principal amount you borrowed, and 87 percent goes toward paying off the interest.

By the 10th year of the loan, 25 percent of your payment goes to paying off the principal and 75 percent goes to paying interest.

By the 20th year, 50 percent of your payment is applied to the principal and 50 percent goes to paying interest.

By the 25th year, 70 percent of your payment will go to principal and 30 percent will go to interest.

By the 30th and final year, 99.5 percent of your payment will be applied to principal and only 0.5 percent will go to interest. That's not much of a tax deduction for you—but you'll still be paying the same monthly sum.

POINTS

What are points?

A point is the equivalent of 1 percent of the total amount of the mortgage. A lender generally charges points up front for lending you money. The lender usually also dictates the number of points you pay, but this is typically a negotiable issue. Expect to pay fewer, or no, points with a higher-interest-rate loan and more points with a lower-interest-rate loan.

Do I have to pay the points before I start to make payments on my mortgage?

Typically, yes. Points are due in cash at the time of the closing (when the seller transfers the house to you). Sometimes the lender will let you add the cost of the points to the amount of your mortgage, in which case you will pay them off over time. Please be careful here; in essence, you'll be paying interest on the points.

My lender is offering me a lower interest rate if I pay a certain number of points up front. How does this work, and is it a good idea?

It's very common for a lender to offer you a range of combinations of points and interest rates. For example, a bank might offer you an interest rate of 7 percent and no points, or an interest rate of 6.8 percent and one point, or an interest rate of 6.5 percent and two points, and so on. Different lenders will offer different combinations. You also can "buy down" your mortgage by paying more up front in points to get an even lower interest rate.

Lenders have a lot of flexibility in setting points, so feel free to negotiate. But watch out when your mortgage is an ARM; since the initial rate may be in effect for only a year or two, paying a big chunk of money to buy down the initial rate could harm rather than help you. And in every case, take into consideration how long you plan to stay in the house; the shorter your stay, the less sense paying points up front may make.

My real estate agent says that paying points is a good idea because they are tax-deductible. Is that true?

Points paid as prepaid interest that meet IRS tests are tax-deductible in the year that you close. Whether paying them is a good idea really depends on the answers to two questions: Again, how long are you planning to live in the house? And what will the difference in your monthly payments be? Once you've answered these questions, it's time to crunch some numbers.

Say you want to borrow $200,000 for 15 years, and a bank is willing to lend it to you at an interest rate of 6.8 percent and no points, or at 6.5 percent and one point, or at 6.25 percent

and two points. First, figure out how much each option will cost you up front, at the closing. Of course, you'd owe nothing if you have no points to pay. You'd owe $2,000 if you have to pay one point ($200,000 multiplied by 0.01), and $4,000 if you have to pay two points.

Next, compare your monthly payments. If you borrow $200,000 for 15 years at 6.8 percent, you will have to pay $1,775 each month, or $319,500 over the life of the loan. If you borrow $200,000 for 15 years at 6.5 percent, you will pay $1,743 each month, or $313,740 over the life of the loan. If you borrow $200,000 for 15 years at 6.25 percent, you will pay $1,715 each month, or $308,700 over the life of the loan.

Finally, add the cost of the points to your total payment in each scenario. In the first situation, you pay no points, so $319,500 is the total amount this mortgage would cost you. In the second situation, add $313,740 to the $2,000 you will pay in points: This mortgage would cost a total of $315,740. In the last situation, you would pay $4,000 in points, so add $4,000 to $308,700. This mortgage would cost you $312,700.

This is just a simple calculation to give you a sense of what to look for. But think about this: If you paid just one point on this loan, or $2,000, versus two points, or $4,000, what would that $2,000 be worth if you invested it over the life of the loan? If you consider the question this way, you will really know if it is worth paying those points. Just so you know, after 15 years at an 8 percent annual rate of return, $2,000 would be worth $6,344 before taxes. After taxes you would probably come out almost even. In real life, the chances of your investing that money over that period of time are almost nil. But as you can see, there are many ways to look at this and what you choose to do will depend on your particular situation. Get professional help to make sure you have taken everything into consideration.

What else should I take into consideration before deciding to pay points up front?

Before you decide that the two-point, 6.25 percent interest rate combination is the way to go, remember the two questions I told you to ask yourself. You've answered the question about monthly payments: With this option, they will be reduced. As to the second question: If you think that you will really stay in the house you are purchasing for the full 15-year term of the mortgage, then, yes, it is probably worth paying the extra money in points in order to get the lower interest rate. (Studies show, however, that the average family buys and sells (or refinances) every five to seven years.) We didn't even calculate the tax savings you would get in the year that you paid the points in cash, which, assuming you are in the 28 percent tax bracket and you paid $4,000, would be $1,120. But, as you can see, the tax savings alone should not be the determining factor when deciding how many points to pay on your mortgage.

What if I have to finance the points?

That complicates the question, because the objective of paying the points is to lower your interest rate and save money over the life of the loan. If you finance the points, you'll be *increasing* the size of your debt by the value of the points and, of course, you will be paying interest on the additional money you borrowed, too. Try not to do it.

ESCROW ACCOUNTS

My lender wants me to add my property taxes and home insurance to my mortgage payments every month, for deposit in an escrow account. Is this a good idea?

No. In fact, if you have a choice in the matter, I would run in the opposite direction. Many lenders require these payments to be made with your mortgage, but many others do not, though by law they have the right to do so. Here's how they work. You pay the lender monthly, and the lender holds the money in an escrow account or in trust on your behalf, and then pays the taxes and insurance for you. At least, that's the way it is supposed to work. The kicker is that sometimes the lenders themselves do not make the payments. I have known quite a few people who have received notice from their insurance companies that their policies have lapsed. Another kicker is that in the majority of states, lenders do not have to pay you interest on the money they are holding for you.

In which states do lenders have to pay interest on escrow accounts?

Fifteen states require the payment of interest on escrow accounts: California, Connecticut, Iowa, Maine, Maryland, Massachusetts, Minnesota, New Hampshire, New York, Oregon, Rhode Island, Utah, Vermont, and Wisconsin.

If I have a mortgage that requires an escrow account, do I have to pay into it forever?

Generally, escrow payments are required for the entire term of the loan. However, some lenders might consider a reduction or waiver of the escrow requirement once a certain amount of the loan is paid back. Since this varies from lender to lender, I recommend that you discuss this with your prospective lender and/or mortgage broker.

I am about to get an FHA loan and I have been told that an escrow account is mandatory. Is that true?

No. Escrow accounts are not mandatory on FHA loans, no matter what a lender may say. The issue is at the discretion of the lender. If you are applying for an FHA loan, try to find a lender who will waive the escrow arrangement. If the lender says no, offer instead to set up a savings account with that lender, keeping your tax and insurance money in your own name, earning interest. In fact, in many states if you offer to do this, the lender by state law must waive the escrow requirement. Ask your real estate agent if this is true in your particular state. But please be careful: Many lenders who agree to waive your escrow accounts will then try to charge you a one-time waiving fee of about 1 percent of the loan amount. Ouch.

TITLE INSURANCE

If you're buying a home, you can be sure that the bank that's providing your mortgage will ask you to buy title insurance. Here's what you need to know.

What is title insurance?

Title insurance is insurance coverage that protects your mortgage lender against a mistaken or incomplete title search by a title company—for example, a search that fails to turn up a lien against the title, such as for back property taxes or a disputed title claim—and promises to pay the costs of settling such claims.

How much will title insurance cost?

It's important for you to know that title insurance protects the bank that approves your mortgage loan, not you, against any title claims. So typically, it covers the amount of a mortgage, and the policy's value declines as the mortgage is paid off. You pay the premium just once—when the loan is taken out. Typical rates are several tenths of a percent of the mortgage amount—often between 0.4 and 0.7 percent. This adds up to between $800 and $1,400 for a $200,000 loan.

Since traditional title insurance only protects the bank, should I buy title insurance that protects me as well?

Yes, probably. It's not a bad idea for you to have this kind of insurance, because the cost is just several hundred dollars more. Without it, you wouldn't be protected at all from a title problem. But if you do buy your own policy, check for exceptions that may leave you with less protection than you want. If any exceptions are a concern, ask the title insurer if they can be taken off the policy.

If I am about to get a second mortgage, do I have to get title insurance for my lender?

Not all lenders require title insurance on a second

mortgage, but many who focus on a higher-risk market—large second-mortgage loans or loans turned down by banks but accepted at higher rates by finance companies—do require title insurance. It should cost slightly less than the title coverage on a large first mortgage—perhaps 0.3 or 0.4 percent.

What should I ask for when shopping for title insurance? Is there any way to lower the premium I am about to be charged?

It's possible to lower the cost of title insurance. Try taking the following steps.

- Ask the seller to pay for your coverage. In some states, the seller must pay. In others, it's something that can be negotiated.
- Ask the title insurer or the lawyer doing the new title search whether you can have the seller's title policy reissued to you. If the policy isn't too old and the insurer agrees, you may be able to save hundreds of dollars.
- Shop around. In some states, there have been charges that real estate agents are getting kickbacks from title insurers to send business their way. Honest insurers don't pay kickbacks, of course, and prices vary. Don't be afraid to ask for the best deal.

TAKING TITLE TO YOUR HOME

When you buy a piece of property, the way you take title—that is, the way ownership is recorded on the deed—becomes very important. There are five main variations on how people take title to a house: as an individual, joint tenancy with right of survivorship, tenants in common, tenancy by the entirety, and community property. These options are discussed in detail in Chapter 11.

It's worth repeating here, however: In almost *all* cases—whether you are an individual, a married couple, or two individuals, and no matter how you choose to hold the property—title to your home should be held in a living trust.

How should married couples take title to a home in states that aren't community-property states?

In states that aren't community-property states, married couples are usually (but not always) best off when they take title to a home by what's known as joint tenancy with right of survivorship (JTWROS). Joint tenancy with right of survivorship means that two or more owners each have equal ownership in the whole property. It is a very efficient way to own property together and be sure that it will change hands after death with minimum complications and expenses. When you hold something in JTWROS and one joint tenant dies, his or her ownership is automatically passed to the remaining joint tenant or tenants without having to go through probate court. In fact, you cannot will or otherwise leave your interest in a property held in joint tenancy to anyone other than your joint tenant or tenants. (JTWROS is not limited to married couples; life partners and others can use it, too.)

An important benefit of taking title this way is that when one joint tenant dies, his or her portion of the property receives what's known as a step up (or down) in cost basis, which is used to calculate taxes owed on any gain in the value of the home. This can represent a tremendous tax savings if the surviving spouse, tenant, or tenants has to sell the house.

Here's what that means: If you and your spouse or life partner buy your house for $300,000, that $300,000 is considered the cost basis of the property for tax purposes. Since you both own the property equally, the cost basis is shared equally between you, which means that, in essence, you each have a $150,000 cost basis in the house. Let's say that many years later, when your partner dies, your house is worth $650,000. The new tax basis for this property will now be half the value of the house at the time that your partner dies, in this example, $325,000, plus your original cost basis of $150,000, or $475,000. The step up in tax basis on your deceased spouse's or partner's half of the property represents a tremendous tax savings to you because it reduces the amount of money you could be liable to pay in capital gains tax if you sold the house.

If you want to leave your share of your home to someone other than your spouse, however, joint tenancy with right of survivorship is *not* the way to go.

What's the best way for married couples to take title in a community-property state?

The best way to take title is by community property. Community property is defined as any property and income accumulated by and belonging jointly to a married couple. Taking title this way is similar to taking title by joint tenancy with right of survivorship, except that community property is available only to married couples and it carries an additional benefit: When one spouse dies, the other spouse gets a step up (or down) in tax basis on the *whole* property, not just half of it. In many cases, this step up confers a huge tax advantage. The only problem is that in most cases transfer is not automatic, so it's advisable for married couples to hold homes held by community property in a revocable living trust or, if your state allows, to hold title in community property with right of survivorship. This means that when one spouse dies, the other spouse automatically owns the property and does not have to go through probate court. This is the best possible way for married couples to take title.

Which states allow property to be held as community property?

Community-property states include Arizona, California, Idaho, Louisiana, Nevada, New Mexico, Texas, Washington, and Wisconsin.

Which states allow title to be taken by community property with right of survivorship?

Arizona, California, Nevada, Texas, and Wisconsin let married couples add the right of survivorship to community property. Alaska also has a provision that allows property to be classified as community property with a right of survivorship.

I am in my second marriage. Both my new husband and I have children from our previ-

ous marriages. We are about to buy a home together, using money we accumulated before we met each other and, although we plan to live in the house for the rest of our lives, we would like our respective children to inherit the money each of us has invested in it if something happens to us. What is the best way to take title?

The best way for you to take title is under a format known as tenants in common, or TIC—*not* by joint tenancy with right of survivorship. Here is the difference. When you take title in JTWROS, when the first spouse dies the house automatically passes to the remaining spouse or joint tenant. This kind of ownership overides the wishes contained in a will or living trust. In other words, no matter what your will says, if you die, the house will pass directly to your husband. If your husband's will or living trust leaves everything *he* owns to his own children, then when he dies his children will inherit your share of the house as well as his. Your children will receive nothing.

When you take title by TIC, this problem disappears. Your will or trust will be the document that dictates who will inherit your portion of the home when you die.

There's a problem with this, too, of course: Your children (or his, if he dies first) may want to sell their interest in the home, meaning that the remaining spouse might have to buy them out or move. That puts a serious burden on the remaining spouse. To solve that problem, what you could do is to set up a trust, known as a QTIP trust, with the title of the house held in TIC. Upon your death, your half of the house would pass into the QTIP trust, which would allow

your husband to keep the house as long as he lives or wants to remain there. When he dies, that half of the house would pass directly to your children.

My husband has severe credit card debt, and I am afraid his creditors will come after our home. I live in a state that allows residents to hold title in tenants by the entirety, and I have been told that this would protect the house from creditors. Is that correct?

Yes, it is. Tenants by the entirety can be a very good way for married couples—but only married couples—to take title to a property, though only about 30 states permit it. In general, it operates much as JTWROS does; each spouse owns the property equally, and when one spouse dies the property passes automatically to the surviving spouse without going through probate. But here is the additional benefit: As long as you own your home by tenancy in the entirety, no creditor can come after the home (or any other asset that you hold this way). The reason: Each tenant is considered separate, so tenants are not liable for each other's debts, and the home is completely protected against creditors. Please know, however, that once you sell the home, you are fair game for creditors who go after the sale money, since that money is no longer protected by tenancy in the entirety. As long as you own your home under this kind of title, however, creditors cannot touch it at all.

I have just received a large inheritance from my father, and I want to use some of the money to buy a home for my wife and me. The problem is that I promised my father I would protect his legacy—that I wouldn't let any-thing happen to it in case of a divorce. How should I take title to the house?

Keeping a home as a separate asset within a mar-riage can be tricky. Typically, when a person in-herits property or cash and wants to keep it safe from the possibility that a spouse will make a fi-nancial claim against it during a messy separa-tion or divorce, the first spouse simply takes care not to commingle this asset or cash with any property belonging to the other spouse or with any property or money held jointly by the cou-ple. You would keep your inherited property in your name only, without allowing your spouse access to it, and that would be that. With a house, however, the question of who makes the mortgage payments, pays the taxes, and pays for home improvements arises; if your wife con-tributes time or money to any of these, you may find that she has a claim to part of the apprecia-tion in the value of the property in the event of a separation and divorce. Please make sure that you consult a good real estate lawyer or trust attorney to protect the wishes of your father.

CLOSING THE DEAL

Simply put, this is the moment when you are "closing," or completing, the deal. People wonder why there needs to be a formal closing and why they have to pay so many fees for what should be a simple process. There are a lot of reasons for the rules surrounding a closing; most of these rules are meant to protect everyone involved. What would you do if it turned out

that the title the seller transferred you was a fake and the money you gave him or her had disap-peared?

When you buy or sell a home, everybody wants guarantees—the seller wants a guarantee that the buyer's check is worth more than the paper on which it is written; the buyer wants a guarantee that the title being exchanged for the check is legitimate; the real estate agent wants a guarantee that she will be paid the agreed-upon commission for the sale. The closing protects the bank, the buyer, the seller, the agent, and any-one else involved from fraud. The following sec-tion is meant to help you close the deal safely, without jeopardizing your investment.

PRECLOSING INSPECTION

We had the house we're buying inspected by a professional right after our bid was accepted. It's been only a month since then, and we're ready to close. Do we still need to perform a preclosing inspection?

Yes. For one thing, you'll want to make sure that everything you contracted to buy is still in the house at closing time. Let me tell you the story of my friend Ann, who skipped the preclosing inspection. Buying the house had been easy be-cause during the negotiations, the woman Ann was buying from became a friend. As contracts were being signed, Ann and the seller spoke can-didly and came to a verbal agreement about what was and wasn't going to be left behind. Most of that conversation was easy and pleasant, but when Ann brought up the antique sconces in the dining room, there was a long pause before the seller told Ann that the sconces were part of the house and would be left behind.

A month later, Ann called this woman to make her preclosing appointment for the day before they were scheduled to sign everything. The seller told Ann that she was swamped with her own move. She asked if Ann could just skip it, saying, "Everything is exactly as you remember it." Ann, who was busy, too, agreed. Sure enough, when Ann walked into the dining room on the day after the closing, everything was exactly as she remembered it—minus the sconces!

Okay, so this wasn't the end of the world. But what if the seller had taken more than just a few light fixtures? What if Ann walked in and found the light fixtures, the refrigerator, and the air conditioners missing?

This happens more often than you might think, so please make the time for a preclosing inspection.

When should I schedule a preclosing inspection?

Try to schedule the inspection for the day before the closing, and make sure to schedule it no earlier than two days beforehand. As soon as you have a closing date, call the real estate agent or the seller to set a date. From this point in the process, you are in the driver's seat. If the seller cannot be present for the inspection, then it's easy enough to get the keys from the agent.

I've scheduled my preclosing inspection. What should my wife and I look for as we walk through the house?

Make sure the home has not sustained any unexpected damage since you signed the contract of sale. Remember, as a buyer, you probably haven't seen the inside of your future home since your bid was accepted, 30 to 60 days ago or more. Things can change in that time. Here's a four-point plan for a successful walk-through:

1. Checklist: List all the items the seller has agreed to leave behind, bring the list with you, and use it. Never rely on a verbal agreement.

2. On and Off: Test everything that can be turned on and off, including the lights, the refrigerator, the water (hot and cold) in the kitchen and bathrooms, the dishwasher, and the washer and dryer. Let the water run for a few minutes so you can make sure that it flows where it is supposed to flow, and keep all the appliances running from the time you enter the house until the time you leave (at least 45 minutes).

3. Open and Close: Quickly open and close all windows and doors, and don't overlook the oven doors, washer and dryer doors, closet doors, and pantry doors. Make sure you can open and close everything without a problem. The other reason to do this is that you never know what surprises you might find in a cellar or a remote closet—this check can reveal holes in the walls, droppings, or other signs of infestation. Obviously, your inspector should have checked for these back when you were signing the contract of sale, but anything can develop, particularly if there has been a lengthy delay before the closing.

4. Broken or Damaged: Ideally, the house should be completely empty when you do the walk-through, so that you can make sure nothing was damaged when the seller moved out.

Make sure there is no visible damage to the ceilings, floors, or walls—look for large cracks or water damage; you may be shocked to discover what the seller's furniture or Oriental rugs were hiding. If you are buying a home in a condominium building or a cooperative, it is probably worthwhile to knock on the downstairs neighbor's door and ask if there has been any water damage or leaks recently from your future home. If the house is not yet empty, it may be difficult for you to confirm these things, so take your time and consider taking photographs of the condition of the house if you are nervous about the seller's movers inflicting damage.

Can I bring somebody to help with the preclosing inspection?

Yes. You can bring anyone you choose to the preclosing inspection. But you should bring only people who can help you evaluate the state of the house you're about to purchase. Unlike your initial inspection, the preclosing inspection is strictly for determining that your house is in the condition you expect. You should have your real estate agent there, and if you're purchasing the house with a partner, both of you should be present. A professional engineer is probably unnecessary.

The sellers are insisting that they need to be present during the inspection and my realtor says they have a right to be there. What should I do if I find something wrong?

Do absolutely nothing until you've left the house. Do not raise an issue with the sellers directly or, for that matter, with the seller's real estate agent. If you find something damaged, just make a note

of it. Let's say you notice a broken windowpane. After you and your own real estate agent have left the premises, tell him or her what the problem is and let the agent address the issue with the seller's agent. If you are not working with your own agent, you will probably want to present the issue to your attorney, who can also deal with either the seller's agent or his or her attorney.

If your seller insists on being present during this inspection, try to avoid answering any questions he or she may have for you. Sometimes a seller will make informal requests, such as asking to keep this or take that sentimental object. You may feel uncomfortable, but if the seller is determined to put you in this awkward spot, always say that the seller will have to have his or her attorney put that question in writing. Otherwise you could end up listening to a pleading seller who might distract you from your primary purpose, which is to inspect the house.

We're buying a brand-new house. Do we need a preclosing inspection?

Yes. New doesn't always mean perfect. Have an inspector look for cracking in the staircases or window frames; such cracking can occur as a new foundation settles. Also, you and the developer should have come to an agreement on what will be included in your new home. Have the developer put everything in writing, and bring that list with you when you go to your preclosing inspection.

Our closing is a week away and the developer still hasn't treated the wood floors. I don't want to delay the closing, but I really need the developer to finish up this job. What should I do?

I'm sorry to say that this situation is fairly common with new houses. Developers often work right up until the last minute to complete a job, and certain tasks may actually be completed on the day of the closing. During your preclosing inspection make a list of all unfinished work, and give this list to your real estate agent or lawyer. He or she will present this list to the developer and ask that these tasks be completed before the closing. This way the onus falls on the developer to complete the job he agreed to under contract and, assuming that he needs more time, you are not the party asking for an extension on the closing date.

The seller had a brass mirror hanging on one of the walls. I didn't want it, but now that it has been taken down, there is a rectangular stain outlining where the mirror hung. Can I make the seller repaint the wall?

Making the seller pay for damages and/or missing items of this nature is tricky. The best way to deal with a situation like the one you've described is to present your real estate agent and your attorney with the problem. They will present the problem(s) to the seller's attorney and real estate agent and ask that the issue be resolved before the closing.

Just because you include a problem on your list doesn't mean the seller will pay for or remedy it, but your requests, if they are legitimate, may put some pressure on the seller. Remember, as eager as you may be to close on and own the house, a seller who has come this far with you (and who may be purchasing another home dependent upon the sale of this one) is just as anxious to close the deal.

CLOSING COSTS

What are closing costs?

Closing costs may include the following: loan application fees (if not already paid), lender's points, prepaid homeowner's insurance, an appraisal fee, escrow fees, lawyer's fees, recording fees, title search and insurance, tax adjustments, agent commissions, and PMI (if necessary). On average, these costs range from 2 to 4 percent of your total purchase cost, depending on where in the country you live.

How can I get an estimate of what my closing costs will be?

By law, your lender must give you a "good faith" estimate of your closing costs within three days of receiving your application for a loan.

These fees are a little confusing. Could you give me an approximate breakdown of what to expect for each of the major categories?

Yes. Here's a list of costs. Please note: They represent the high end of the spectrum, so your costs may be smaller.

- Credit Report: Most credit reports cost about $25, which includes the bank's markup. All lenders run credit checks on their applicants.
- Loan Application Fee: Unbelievable as it may seem, many lenders charge you to apply for a loan. The going rate is between a few dollars and a few hundred dollars—make sure you ask.
- Independent Appraisal Fee: The lender wants to make sure its loan is in keeping with the value of the purchase. Therefore, an independent appraiser must estimate the value of

your home. Appraisals can run from $300 to $500.

- Lender's Points: This is the charge that the lender imposes in connection with the loan. A point is equal to 1 percent of the loan amount. On a mortgage of $200,000 with 1 point, the figure would be $2,000.
- Title Search and Insurance: You and the lender want to be sure the title to your future home is free of any liens and that the seller can give you a clear title. Title insurance costs from $500 to much more.
- Processing fee: This one is a little hard to swallow. The lender charges you to process the paperwork for your loan. This is different from the application fee, and will run about $380 on average.
- Preparation fee: Yes, the lender may charge you to prepare all the paperwork as well. This will cost another $200 to $300.
- Prepayment of Interest: Depending on the time of the month you buy the house, you will have to come up with an amount of money to prepay the interest on your mortgage until the loan closes. Assuming a $200,000 mortgage at 6.5 percent and 15 days of prepaid interest, that will come to about $534.

With those costs alone, you're nearing $4,000, and there will probably be others. Normally, there are transfer taxes, mortgage taxes, recording fees, real estate tax escrow, escrow fees, insurance escrow, inspection fees, attorney's fees, agent's fees, and others that are labeled junk fees. On average, the closing costs for a $200,000 mortgage are about $5,000.

My uncle told me to fold some of my closing costs into the mortgage itself. Is this financially wise?

No. I will give you one fundamental piece of advice that applies to most financial decisions such as this: Never pay tomorrow what you can afford to pay today. Why? In the case of a 30-year, $200,000 mortgage at a 6.5 percent interest rate, $5,000 in closing costs will end up costing more than $11,378 over the life of the mortgage. Every month, you'll be paying out about $32 extra to carry that $5,000 over 30 years. If you invested that $32 a month at 8 percent for 30 years, you would have $47,692. That's a lot of money. Think long and hard about giving it up.

That said, if you plan to live in your new home for five years or less, folding in the closing costs may make sense for you.

RENTING TO THE SELLER

We are buying a house, and the sellers need to stay a month after the closing. What should we do?

When sellers need to stay beyond the closing date, draw up a rental agreement that establishes the date the sellers will move out. Add a substantial financial penalty for every day they remain in your house beyond that date (say, $1,000 per day). During the period of overlap, you'll be forced to carry two separate mortgages and/or rents: one for the new house you've bought from the seller, and another for the house you're still living in while they stay the extra month. There-fore, the sellers must be responsible for their share.

Your lawyer or real estate agent should know how to handle this situation.

REFINANCING

All my neighbors have been refinancing their mortgages. What exactly is refinancing, and why do people do it?
Refinancing just means that you are replacing the current mortgage on your house with an-other mortgage of a different rate and/or size and duration. People who originally mortgaged their houses when interest rates were high often refinance to take advantage of lower rates. Basi-cally, people refinance in order to decrease their mortgage payments or to pay off other current debts with the proceeds of the new mortgage. People who have an adjustable rate, or variable, mortgage (on which the mortgage payments change as interest rates change) that they want to convert to a fixed-rate mortgage (on which the payments are the same over the life of the loan) may also want to refinance when interest rates get low.

Is refinancing my mortgage to help me pay down my other debt a bad idea?
Needing to refinance to pay other debts isn't the ideal position to be in, but there are times when it may be appropriate. If, for example, you plan to keep your home for at least the next few years

and new interest rates are lower than the current interest rate on your mortgage or the interest rate on the debt that you owe, *and* the closing costs are minimal, refinancing may make sense for you.

What may *not* make sense is refinancing only to lower the balance on your credit card debt or other debt when you are increasing the interest rate on your mortgage. I also do not think it is wise to swap credit card debt for home debt, whether it be a refinanced mortgage or a home equity line of credit. The reason is that credit card debt is "unsecured," that is, you do not have any collateral that the credit card company can seize if you become delinquent in your pay-ments. All home loans and HELOCS are what is called "secured" debt; your home is the collat-eral. Fail to keep up with the payments and you could face losing your home as the lender has the right to foreclose to recoup its "secured" debt. So it makes little sense to me to take on more se-cured debt to pay off unsecured (credit card) debt. Also, take into account any closing costs you may have to pay when you refinance—they can be several thousand dollars. If you are think-ing about refinancing in order to lower the pay-ments on your current debts other than your mortgage, you might consider an equity line of credit instead, because you could avoid the higher closing costs.

I'm about to refinance, and I'm thinking about taking equity out of my home to pay off my credit card debt. Is this a good thing to do?
On the surface this looks like a terrific move because you are getting rid of credit card debt,

where the interest payments aren't tax-deductible, and trading it for home equity debt, in which the interest payments are tax-deductible. But here's where you need to be careful and responsible. If you were to mess up and not pay your credit card bills, the worst that could happen is that your credit score would become mud and you would probably find it very difficult to get a credit card or a loan. But if you roll the debt into a home equity line of credit or loan, you now have a much bigger problem: If you miss your payments, you could lose your house. That's because your house is your collateral for the loan. If you can't pay the loan, the lender is going to want the collateral. Another problem is that by getting rid of your old credit card debt, you could tempt yourself to run up a lot of new debt. If you lack the self-control to manage your spending, be very careful about making this move, or at least ask the credit card company to lower your credit limit so there won't be any new problems.

Over the past few years, interest rates have gone up, but seem to be holding steady now. How do I know when it makes sense to refinance?

First, you need to take the amount of your current monthly mortgage payment and subtract it from the amount of your new monthly mortgage payment if you refinance. (There are tons of free online calculators that can help you with this comparison; *bankrate.com* has a good one.) This will give you your monthly savings if you refinance. The next step is to see how long it will take you to recoup the cost of the refinancing. To do this, simply divide your monthly savings into your closing costs; that will show you how many months it will take to break even. For example, let's say you currently have a $2,000 monthly mortgage that you can refinance to $1,900. So we're talking about a $100 monthly savings. Now let's say your closing costs on the refinance are $2,000. If we divide $100 into $2000 we're looking at a 20-month period until you break even. If you expect to stay in the house at least that long, then it's smart to refinance. But if you think you might be moving, then I would recommend sticking with your existing mortgage.

I'm 50 years old, I just refinanced my house, and I'll be retiring in twelve years. Should I pay off my mortgage or contribute everything I can to my 401(k) plan? My 401(k) plan does not match.

Given the high price of real estate, it is most likely that your biggest monthly expense is your mortgage payment. And in today's market environment, I think it will be very difficult for you to achieve a spectacular rate of growth on your 401(k) plan, generating enough income to pay your mortgage payment in retirement. So I am leaning toward paying off the mortgage. Let me explain why. Let's say you have a $130,000 mortgage at 5 percent for 15 years and your mortgage payment is $1,000 a month. For your 401(k) to generate $1,000 a month after taxes, you will need to accumulate approximately $450,000 in your 401(k) by the time you retire. If you had that much, and we assumed a 3.5 percent to 4 percent return, your 401(k) would generate about $16,000 before taxes and $12,000 after taxes. If you ask me, it is a lot easier to pay off the $130,000 mortgage over the next 12 years than to require your 401(k) to generate $12,000 in after-tax income when you are retired. So please pay off your mortgage first.

Do you suggest everyone pay off their mortgage early and not contribute to their 401(k) plans?

No, but when you're approximately 45 to 50 years of age, you finally know you are in a home you are going to stay in. And at that point, why not eliminate what is probably your biggest monthly expense? Your retirement will be all the more secure knowing you can stay in your house without any mortgage worries.

If I refinance, can I take any points I pay off my taxes?

Yes, but the tax situation is different with refinancing than with taking out an original mortgage because the points you pay when you refinance can't be deducted from your taxes immediately in a lump sum; you spread the deduction out over the whole length of the mortgage. Say you refinance your home with a 15-year mortgage and pay $3,600 in points. The deduction on these points must be spread out evenly over the life of the loan. That means you can deduct $240 each year for 15 years. There's one exception. Let's say that two years into your mortgage, interest rates drop further and you refinance again. Now the balance of the points that you paid on the last mortgage is completely deductible. If you paid $3,600 in points two years ago and have deducted $480 of that off your taxes so far ($240 a year), you can deduct $3,120 this year. And, of course, you can also

deduct the appropriate portion of your new points.

Is there anything else to keep in mind when I am thinking about refinancing?

It's very important to understand that when you refinance you are not only changing the rate of your loan but also could be adding years to your loan. For example, say you originally borrowed $150,000 for 15 years at 8.85 percent with monthly payments of $1,508. You have been making those payments for six years, so your remaining principal balance is $110,000. If you refinance only that $110,000 by getting another 15-year loan at 7 percent, your monthly payments will drop to $989, but you will also be adding six years to the life of the loan. You can figure out the total cost of your new mortgage over the next 15 years by multiplying $989 by 180 (the number of months in 15 years): You will be paying $178,020. To figure out the total remaining cost of your old loan, multiply your current monthly payment of $1,508 by 108 (the number of months in nine years) and compare: If you don't refinance, you're going to pay $162,864. As you can see, even though your monthly payments will be lower with the new mortgage, over time it will cost you $15,156 more—not including closing costs on the new mortgage.

So if I can afford my monthly payments, I really shouldn't refinance, since I'll actually be losing money by doing so?

Not necessarily. You still might want to refinance in order to take advantage of a lower interest rate, but if you do, consider increasing your monthly payments to at least the amount that will enable you to pay off your mortgage in the period of time remaining on your *original* loan. Using the figures in the example above, you would have to pay $1,376 every month to pay the loan off in nine years. You would be paying $132 less each month than you would have with your original mortgage, which over the next nine years ($132 multiplied by 108 months), adds up to savings of $14,256. Even if your closing costs cost a few thousand dollars, in this case refinancing would be worth it.

I'm about to refinance a 30-year mortgage I've had for four years. I don't really want to shorten the length of my mortgage to 15 years, but I don't want to go backward either. How can I avoid starting over at a full 30 years?

Here's an easy way. To use your example, let's say that four years ago you took out a 30-year mortgage for $200,000. Now, four years later, your balance is probably roughly $192,000. When looking to refinance, using the technique above, you'd probably refinance your existing balance of $192,000 at the lower rate, and you'd then have 30 years remaining on your new loan. But here's a neat trick. Instead of refinancing $192,000, you could refinance the original principal balance of $200,000. Then, when you go to the closing table, you'd pay the old mortgage company the $192,000 you owe them, leaving you with $8,000. If you take that $8,000 and prepay principal on the *new* mortgage, interestingly, that puts you in precisely the same spot on the mortgage amortization schedule that you were in before you refinanced. You'd only have 26 years left to pay.

This strategy works with any loan amount and any payment period. One caveat: If your new mortgage has a prepayment penalty—which is rare, but they do exist—then it may not work for you.

What are the advantages and disadvantages of refinancing my 30-year mortgage as a 15-year mortgage?

The benefits are huge. The only real disadvantage is that your monthly payment will go up, relative to the payment on a 30-year loan—though probably not by as much as you think.

Here are a couple of things to keep in mind about a 15-year mortgage. First, just because you are paying off the loan in half the time of a 30-year mortgage doesn't mean that your payments will be twice as high. As a rule of thumb, payments on a 15-year mortgage are typically only about 25 percent higher than on a 30-year mortgage.

One reason for this "discount" is that the interest rate you pay with a 15-year loan is usually about .5 percent lower than with a 30-year loan. So if you take out a 30-year, $200,000 mortgage, for example, you might pay 6 percent, resulting in a monthly payment of $1,199; if you took out a 15-year, $200,000 mortgage, you'd probably get a rate closer to 5.5 percent, for a monthly payment of $1,634—only about 25 percent higher. And because you'll be paying off the 15-year loan faster, a greater portion of every payment you make will go toward your principal, so you'll be building equity more quickly. At the end of 15 years, you will own your home outright.

Yet you don't have to wait the full 15 years to

see a big benefit. Five years down the road you will have built up a lot more equity in your home than you would with a 30-year option. In fact, the benefits of the shorter term start accruing instantly, though you may not realize this until you go to refinance again or decide to take some equity out of your home—either to buy a new home or for an important expense, like your child's college education.

If I can't afford a 15-year mortgage, is there another good option?

Yes. If the monthly payments on a 15-year loan are too high, look into a 20-year loan. Surprisingly, the payment differential between a 20-year and a 30-year loan is only about $100 a month for every $100,000 you borrow.

Here's where this tactic can come in handy. Oftentimes, when I arrange refinancing for a client, the amount the client is going to save because of a lower rate is just about the same amount as that monthly differential—say, $200 a month on a $200,000 mortgage. Now, the client can either take that extra money and, quite frankly, spend it on incidentals—which many people do—or consider refinancing at a 20-year term and keeping the monthly payment pretty much the same. You won't miss the extra monthly cash you never pocketed, and there's a tremendous benefit in terms of building equity and owning your home more quickly.

What are the other advantages of choosing a 15- or 20-year mortgage?

There are two big potential advantages that people may not know about.

One is that a shorter amortization term creates a potential savings on private mortgage insurance, or PMI—which you typically have to pay when you take out a loan with a down payment of less than 20 percent. If you choose a 15- or 20-year loan, the amount of PMI you have to pay is dramatically reduced, because the loan is considered less risky; plus, you reach your equity threshold more quickly, so you eliminate the PMI at an earlier stage.

The second benefit occurs if you take out a 15-year or 20-year adjustable-rate mortgage (ARM). Now, I know that people typically choose an adjustable-rate mortgage because they want a smaller initial monthly payment. But sometimes people truly have an option—they can afford a larger payment, but the ARM appeals to them because they're planning a move in, say, five to seven years and want to pay the smallest amount of interest possible in the meantime. If you go for a 15- or 20-year ARM, as opposed to a 30-year ARM, the chances are that your initial guaranteed interest rate would be lower—that's number one. Number two is that your equity buildup will accelerate. And here's where it gets interesting: Because you will have paid off more principal, when your ARM does come due for an adjustment, even if your rate rises, the difference in your monthly payments will be less because your loan balance will be lower.

I have a little vacation home that I am still financing. Do you recommend refinancing a second home?

Actually, I recommend refinancing your main home because the mortgage rates—including refinanced rates—on second homes or rental properties tend to be higher than on a primary home. If you have enough equity in your primary residence, investigate refinancing it for the purpose of paying off the other property. You may be able effectively to consolidate your debt at the lower interest rate.

EQUITY LINES OF CREDIT

If I don't want to refinance because interest rates have risen, is there any other way to gain access to the equity I've built up in my home?
Yes. You can either take a home equity line of credit or a home equity loan. Because most people take such a loan or line of credit to pay back past debt or prevent future debt on such things as renovations, more information appears in Chapter 1, Managing Debt.

What is an equity line of credit, and who should consider using one?
An equity line of credit is a preset maximum amount of money that a lender is willing to allow you to borrow, based on the current available equity in your home. You may tap this line of credit any time and in any way you like, usually by simply writing a check. You do not pay interest until you use the money, and you will pay interest only on the amount that you actually use. Please note that you may choose *never* to use the line of credit. In many cases the interest rate fluctuates. Typically, it is not fixed, and neither is the payback period.

A home equity loan, on the other hand, is a lump-sum loan that comes with a fixed interest rate and, in most cases, a fixed payback period.

Before you apply for an equity line of credit against your home, you have to have an adequate amount of income and a certain level of equity already paid in to your house, as determined by your lender's standards. Assuming you meet the basic qualifications, a home equity loan *may* make sense for you if you need money for only a short period of time (a few years, maximum), if you are planning to sell your home within two years but you need some extra cash now, if interest rates are projected to fall, if you need to secure a source of funds in case of an emergency, or if you want to lower the interest rates on your other debts but not on your mortgage.

Do you recommend an equity line of credit or a refinancing strategy when interest rates are low?
As a general rule, you don't want to take out an equity line of credit if you need to use the money over a long period of time, because the interest rates on equity lines fluctuate. Therefore, if you are going to need the money for a long time, the bank is offering you low closing costs, and interest rates are low, refinancing at a fixed rate makes more sense, but be careful of prepayment penalties.

Refinancing is a good plan only if you are going to be staying in the house for at least as long as it takes to recoup the costs of refinancing. If you are planning to sell the house within two years, an equity line of credit is the better choice.

Is the reverse true in a high-interest-rate environment?
A home equity line of credit is the smarter move if interest rates are high and expected to fall.

Since, again, the interest rates on most equity lines are variable, you will benefit when rates fall.

There is no way I'm going to qualify for another mortgage or an equity line of credit, because we ran into some bad times recently and our credit is terrible, not to mention the fact that our house is actually declining in value. But we really can't make our payments. Is there anything we can do?

If you are at the end of your financial rope and there is no one in your life who could loan you the money to straighten things out, I would suggest calling your mortgage company and asking if it would consider offering you a hardship case reduction of interest. It is in the lender's interest to do this because the lender would find it as difficult as you would to sell a property that is decreasing in value. Of course, this will work only if the interest rate you are paying is higher than current interest rates.

PAYING OFF YOUR MORTGAGE

I'm planning to retire in five or six years and don't have much money. My sister says I should not pay off my mortgage early because it is a good tax deduction and because I could be making more by investing the extra money for growth in the stock market. Do you agree?

Your sister's points would be valid if you had plenty of money to meet your monthly expenses and invest. But if you are making up for lost time in your retirement planning, tax deductions may not save you over the long run. Also, don't forget that as time passes, the portion of your monthly mortgage payment that goes to pay off interest—the part that gives you the deduction—gets progressively smaller. Finally, if money is tight because you don't have much income, taxes are not your biggest problem.

About investing the money more productively somewhere else, it is true that you might make a better return in stocks, and if you can, you should. But you might also do worse. If you remember that your retirement income will largely be fixed and that you may have difficulty meeting high monthly expenses, paying off your mortgage could be a smart move to provide security.

If your current investments are not consistently earning as high a return as the interest rate you are paying on your mortgage, paying off the mortgage could be an excellent move.

Why is paying off the mortgage quickly a good move if I'm worried about my income when I retire?

Paying off your mortgage eliminates one of your biggest monthly expenses and allows you to make the most of the income you have. Imagine that you have just retired and are having a little trouble living on the fixed income available to you. For about ten years, you have been living comfortably in a house that you financed with a 30-year mortgage of $150,000 at a fixed rate of 7 percent. Your monthly payment is $998, and you have 20 years to go. What can you do to be more financially secure in this situation? You can go back to work, you can make sure that whatever money you have is earning the highest rate of return safely possible, you can reduce your expenses, or you can combine these strategies.

Returning to work could be highly impractical for you, even if you are still healthy and strong. Plus, there is a huge difference between wanting to work and having to work, and I'm sure you don't want to spend your retirement years forced to work. In terms of investing, if you are at or near retirement age, your best bet is going to be something that yields a nice safe dividend or interest income, which could give you a few hundred dollars each month but probably not enough to pay the mortgage, unless you have saved a hefty amount of money. Finally, trimming your expenses during your retirement years can be difficult—there are only so many things you can reduce or cut out.

If you are concerned about money after you retire, if you want to keep living in your home, and if you don't have current credit card debt, you might well want to pay off that mortgage as soon as possible, with the goal of having it paid by the time you retire. Ask your lender to estimate the additional amount of money necessary to pay off your mortgage in the number of years between now and your retirement.

I am getting ready to retire and have some savings—enough to pay off my mortgage in full. Should I do that, or just keep paying monthly?

Assuming that your savings are not entirely held in retirement accounts and that there will not be a substantial tax burden when you liquidate them, I think that if you have the money available to

pay that mortgage off in full right now, and your income is not high enough to make the mortgage tax deduction worth it, you should consider doing this. You could substantially increase your cash flow. Here's why:

Let's say you have 20 years and $128,718 left to pay on a $150,000 fixed-rate mortgage that you borrowed at 7 percent (a $998 payment each month). We'll also assume that you will get Social Security but not a pension, you have $200,000 in a money-market fund earning 5 percent, and you have a modest retirement account, but not much else. Finally, we'll say that you are single and in the 15 percent tax bracket. We won't take the taxes owed on the money you earn in the money-market fund and the taxes saved on the interest for the mortgage into consideration, because they effectively cancel each other out. (Your tax savings on the mortgage would be $1,366 and the taxes owed on the money market interest would be $1,500, so we'll call that even.)

Now, I understand if your instinct is to hold on to that $200,000 in the money-market fund, because having a nice chunk of money in the bank makes everyone feel safe. But sometimes you can jeopardize your financial safety by letting money sit in the bank instead of using it wisely. If that money-market fund with the 5 percent interest rate is generating about $10,000 each year, or $833 each month, and you add to it $165 each month from your Social Security check, that's enough to make your mortgage payment each month.

But consider this: If you take $128,718 out of the money-market fund and pay your mortgage off completely, you will have $71,282 left in your money-market account, which should generate $297 each month at that 5 percent interest rate. And even though your interest income is reduced from $833 to $297 each month, you have no mortgage payment, so your monthly expenses have dropped by $998. If you think about it, there really is no comparison.

I think your goal should be to have paid off your home by the time you begin to receive Social Security. At that point, your expenses will be reduced by whatever the amount your mortgage payment was, and your income will be increased by your Social Security benefit.

I don't know how secure I would feel not having more cash in the bank. What if something happens and I need the money?

Remember, your money has not disappeared into thin air. It is, effectively, in your home, which, in certain circumstances may be a safer place for it than a stock mutual fund or other kinds of assets. Think about what kind of "somethings" are likely to happen to you. One possibility is that you might have to go into a nursing home. If you don't have long-term care insurance or other nursing home coverage, you would have to spend almost all your cash before you would qualify for Medicaid. But many states view your home as an exempt asset when you are qualifying for Medicaid, no matter how much equity you have in it. In other words, in many states, you can qualify for Medicaid and still own your house. Also, if you ever need extra income, you can get that through a reverse mortgage, which you do not have to qualify for.

My bank wants me to take out a biweekly mortgage, saying that it will reduce my current mortgage by eight years and it will not cost me one extra penny. Should I do this?

The bank is not being truthful. The biweekly mortgage will cost you more, because you are sending in one more payment a year on the biweekly than if you stuck with the monthly. That is why it reduces your mortgage. In addition, most banks will usually charge a $300 setup fee and $5 every time you make a payment. You can accomplish the exact same thing without any of those extra fees by simply sending in one extra payment yourself. If you do, it will reduce a 30-year mortgage to 22 years and a 15-year mortgage to 12 years. If you do want to send in an extra payment, check with your lender to see if your mortgage allows for this "prepayment." If it doesn't, you will be hit with an early prepayment fee. The only time it makes sense to pay the bank to do it for you is if you are not disciplined enough to do it on your own—then it is a wise investment to take out a biweekly mortgage.

REVERSE MORTGAGES

A reverse mortgage is a special kind of mortgage loan sometimes used by older Americans to convert the equity they hold in their homes into cash that they can use to live on. If you have equity in your home and if cash is tight and you need a source of income, this can be a useful tool to help provide financial security in your retirement years.

A reverse mortgage is aptly named. The payment stream is literally "reversed"—instead of you making monthly payments to a lender, as you do with a conventional mortgage or home equity loan, a lender makes payments to you, based on the amount of equity you hold.

How do I qualify for a reverse mortgage?

You must be at least 62 years old and own your home or condominium. You may be eligible even if you still owe money on a first or second mortgage. In fact, many older Americans get a reverse mortgage to help pay off their first mortgages. There are no income or medical requirements.

How much money can I get on a reverse mortgage?

The maximum size of your reverse mortgage will depend on your age at the time you apply, the kind of reverse mortgage you choose (more about this below), the value of your home, how much equity you have in it, current interest rates, and sometimes where you live. In general, the older you are, the more valuable your home, and the less you owe on it, the larger the potential income from the reverse mortgage will be.

Does the income from a reverse mortgage have to be paid back?

Yes, it does, but payments are not due while you are still living in your home. The loan, plus the interest you are paying on the loan, come due only when you no longer occupy your home as a principal residence. This typically occurs when you (or your spouse, in case you are married) pass away, sell your home, or permanently move out. Please know your heirs will never be in the position to owe more to the reverse lender than the value of the home when it is sold.

What if my family does not want to sell the home when I die, but wants to keep it?

They won't be forced to sell the home to pay off the loan. You or your family can pay off the reverse mortgage and keep the home.

What can the money from a reverse mortgage be used for?

It can be used for anything you like: daily living expenses, medical costs, home repairs or improvements, long-term health care, to pay off debts or prevent foreclosure on your home, or even travel.

Are there different ways to take the money from a reverse mortgage?

Yes. The options for taking your money are: all at once (lump sum); fixed monthly payments (for a period up to life); a line of credit; or a combination of a line of credit and monthly payments. The most popular option—chosen by more than 60 percent of borrowers—is the line of credit, which allows you to draw on the loan proceeds at any time.

Are there different kinds of reverse mortgages?

Yes. There are two basic kinds—FHA-insured and loans backed by a private lender, which are sometimes known as "proprietary reverse mortgages." The Federal Trade Commission (FTC) has useful information to know before you opt for a reverse mortgage. Go to *www.ftc.gov* and type "reverse mortgage" into the search box.

What is an FHA-insured reverse mortgage?

FHA stands for Federal Housing Administration, a quasi-government agency that, as an insurer of reverse mortgages, guarantees that you will continue to receive your money even if a lender defaults. This kind of reverse mortgage offers a monthly payment amount plus a line of credit. As with other reverse mortgages, the mortgage amount is not due as long as you live in your home. Closing costs, a mortgage insurance premium, and sometimes a monthly servicing fee are required. Interest is charged at an adjustable rate on your loan balance; any changes in the interest rate charged affect how quickly your loan balance grows over time, not the amount of the monthly payments you receive.

FHA reverse mortgages may provide smaller loan advances than lender-insured plans.

What is a lender reverse mortgage?

A lender's proprietary reverse mortgage typically offers a monthly payment amount or a monthly payment amount plus a line of credit. The interest you pay may be charged at a fixed rate or an adjustable rate, and additional loan costs can include a mortgage insurance premium (which may be fixed or variable) and other fees.

There are advantages to lender-insured plans. The amount you borrow may be larger than the amount you can borrow from an FHA-insured plan, and you may also be allowed to mortgage less than the full value of your home (thus preserving home equity for later use by you or your

heirs). However, these loans may involve greater loan costs.

Does my home have to be in good condition to qualify for a reverse mortgage?

Yes. Your home must be structurally sound, meaning that there are no major defects, such as a bad foundation, a leaky roof, or termite damage. Once you have filled out a loan application, the lender will send an inspector to your home. If defects are found during the inspection, you will be responsible for finding a certified home improvement contractor who will make the necessary repairs.

If you don't have enough money to pay the contractor out of your own bank account, you can use a portion of the reverse mortgage money to pay for the home repairs.

After closing on your reverse mortgage, you have up to one year to complete the repairs. The lender who closed your loan will call you from time to time to check on the progress of the repair job.

Do I have to pay taxes on the money I get from a reverse mortgage?

No. Reverse mortgages are considered loan advances and are not taxable.

Does the money I get from a reverse mortgage affect my Social Security, Medicare, Medicaid, or SSI benefits?

No, the payments you receive from a reverse mortgage will not affect your Social Security or Medicare benefits. If you receive Supplemental Security Income, reverse mortgage advances will not affect your benefits as long as you spend them within the month you receive them. In most states, this is also true for Medicaid benefits. When in doubt, check with a benefits specialist at your local agency on aging.

How much will it cost to take out a reverse mortgage?

The costs of getting a reverse mortgage can include an origination fee (which can usually be financed as part of the mortgage), inspection and appraisal fees, and other charges similar to those for a regular mortgage.

What institutions offer reverse mortgages?

Reverse mortgages are offered by banks, savings and loans, and other financial institutions.

What can I do to protect myself against getting a bad reverse mortgage?

One of the best protections you have with reverse mortgages is the federal Truth in Lending Act, which requires lenders to inform you about the plan's terms and costs. Be sure you understand them before signing. Among other information, lenders must disclose the annual percentage rate (APR) and payment terms. On plans with adjustable rates, lenders must provide specific information about the variable rate feature. On plans with credit lines, lenders also must inform you of any charges to open and use

the account, such as charges for an appraisal, a credit report, or attorneys' fees.

You should know one more thing before applying for a reverse mortgage: You must first meet with a reverse mortgage counselor. A reverse mortgage lender can provide you with the names of approved counseling agencies in your area. A list of approved counseling agencies nationwide is posted on the Web by the U.S. Department of Housing and Urban Development (*www.hud.gov/offices/hsg/sfh/hecm/hecmlist.cfm*). The counselor's job is to educate you about reverse mortgages, to inform you about other options available to you given your situation, and to assist you in determining which reverse mortgage product would best fit your needs.

CAPITAL-GAINS TAX

The capital-gains tax rules on selling a home have improved dramatically in recent years. Here's what you need to know.

What is capital-gains tax and how does it affect the selling of my house?

Capital-gains tax is the tax payable on a gain resulting from the sale of a security or property that you have held longer than 12 months. Say

TAX RATES ON NET CAPITAL GAINS		
Ordinary Tax Bracket	2003–2007	2010*
10% and 15%	5%	0%
All others	15%	15%
*After 2010, tax rates revert to pre-2003 act law.		

you are a single person and bought your house 15 years ago for $100,000. Since then, you have put $20,000 worth of improvements into the house, and now you are about to sell it for $375,000, after fees and commissions. Your cost basis is the original price that you paid for the house plus the amount that you spent to improve it—in this case, $120,000 ($100,000 plus $20,000). You will owe capital-gains tax on the amount for which you sold the house minus all fees ($375,000), less your cost basis ($120,000), which is $255,000. However, every individual taxpayer is now entitled to a federal $250,000 exemption on a principal residence if they qualify, so you may be able to subtract $250,000 from $255,000. The result is that you may owe federal capital-gains tax on only $5,000 of your profit.

The capital gains tax rate in 2010 was 15 percent for most taxpayers. If you were in the 10 or 15 percent ordinary tax bracket there was no capital gains tax levied in 2010. These tax rates are subject to change in subsequent years.

If I'm married, can my spouse and I each take a $250,000 exemption?

Yes, so if you're married and meet the tax requirements you have, in essence, a $500,000 exemption. In the above example, you would not owe any capital-gains tax if you were married.

How do I qualify for this exemption, and can I take it every time I sell a house?

You can take the exemption every two years, but keep in mind that it applies only if you are selling your primary residence. You need to have lived in a home as your primary residence for at least two of the last five years in order to qualify for this exemption.

If I buy a home, how much can I expect that home to increase in value every year?

You can't expect any such thing. I believe owning a home is a great investment, but it is not the same as a stock that you trade. You can't live in a stock, but the main purpose of a home is shelter for you and your loved ones. Over time the value of your home should indeed rise, but that does not mean it will always rise every year. I imagine that is very clear after what happened to real estate values when the housing bubble began to burst in 2007. You need to have realistic expectations; the long-term trend is that homes, on average, rise at a rate that has exceeded the rate of inflation by one percentage point. That works out to an average of 4 percent to 5 percent. Again, that does not mean you are guaranteed 4 percent each and every year. It is just illustrative of the long-term trend.

TRANSFERRING TITLE TO THE CHILDREN

Now that I am getting older, would it be a good idea to transfer the title of my home to my daughter to avoid estate taxes as well as probate fees?

Depending on your financial goals and your estate-planning strategy, there are instances in which transferring the title of your house into your child's name may be a smart move, but it can also easily backfire.

First of all, if you give your house to your daughter, you will need to file a gift tax return to be used against your unified credit, or the amount of money or property you can leave to your beneficiaries without incurring gift or estate taxes. (For more on "gifting," please see page 574.)

That said, with a gift your daughter gets your cost basis on the home. With an inheritance, her tax basis is the fair market value at your death. So, making a gift could save considerable capital-gains taxes if your home has gone up in value. On the other hand, if your daughter were to get into any financial difficulty—if she were sued, for example, and someone won a judgment against her, or if she got involved in a nasty divorce—your house (which is now technically her house) would be vulnerable, which would threaten your own security. Also, if you ever needed the extra income you could get from a reverse mortgage, unless your daughter, who would hold title to the property, is older than 62, you would not be eligible to apply.

If my parents have put my name on their title and I want to take my name off it, how do I do that?

Very, very carefully—for you have to take into consideration the effect this will have on estate taxes, both theirs and yours. While the current estate tax exclusion for 2009 was $3.5 million and the tax disappears completely in 2010, it is scheduled to revert to just $1 million in 2011 unless Congress acts to make it higher. There are also gift-tax issues to consider as well. If your parents' house is worth a lot of money, you should talk to an estate planner before removing

your name from the title; this may help you to minimize the estate-tax consequences to you and your children.

REAL ESTATE AS AN INVESTMENT

Is real estate a wise investment?

If you are talking about simply buying a home to live in, then in my opinion it is probably one of the best investments you will ever make. Let me tell you why. The average rate of appreciation is 4 percent to 5 percent a year. Now that doesn't mean you are guaranteed a positive return every year. I am talking about the long-term average that includes both up and down years. Let's take a home that costs $100,000 (it does not matter how much homes are in your area—just increase or decrease the figure according to your area). With a typical 20 percent down payment, you will invest $20,000 in this house. Now let's assume that the house value appreciates 4 percent to 5 percent a year. That is a $4,000 to $5000 increase on a $20,000 investment or a 20 percent return on your money. Where else are you going to get a 20 percent return on your investment today, have a home to live in, and get a tax write-off on the interest payments on your mortgage?

Friends of mine are encouraging me to invest in a real estate development, but I think the properties are overpriced. Any suggestions?

It was not a normal trend in 1999 when technology stocks and the overall stock market were going up by 25 to 80 percent a year. This kind of overvaluing has occurred in some areas of the country in real estate. This overvaluing of real estate is not normal either. Not many people wanted to admit that we had a real estate bubble forming. But whatever you call it, it's not normal when home prices rise that quickly. And when something is not normal, a correction almost always occurs to bring prices back in line with the normal rate of growth. By "correction," I mean that prices may go down for a while. This is what happened with the stock market after 1999, and this is what happened when the real estate bubble began to burst in 2007. As I write this in late 2009 we are still living through a severe downturn in home values in many parts of the country. Investing in real estate can make sense, but only if you have realistic assumptions about the long-term appreciation potential of a piece of property. Remember, the long-term trend is that home values on average increase at a 4 percent to 5 percent annual rate. If your investment is predicated on 10 percent or 15 percent annual returns you are not being realistic and it could cost you big-time.

You must be very careful to know all that you need to know before you take the plunge.

4

Insurance

Preparing for the Unexpected

Having the right kind of insurance at the right stage of life is an essential part of any good financial plan. Yet, over the years, I've discovered that many people find buying insurance a daunting task. With hundreds of different policy options available for each type of insurance—including health, home, car, and life—figuring out the kind of policy you should have and the amount of coverage you need can be time-consuming and baffling. Sometimes even choosing the *type* of insurance you need may be difficult. And once you've decided on the appropriate kind and amount of insurance, it may not be what the insurance agent wants to sell you, which only adds to the confusion.

Take, for example, the "whole life" life insurance policy your agent may have sold you many years ago. I'll bet you're still hanging on to it. "Well, why not?" you might ask. We all need insurance coverage as we get older, don't we? Yes, we do. But the kind of insurance you need as you age is probably not whole life, which is most useful for young families, as a protection against the death of a breadwinner. You probably *do* need long-term care insurance, which many of us know very little about. Evaluating basic insurance needs at different times in your life is financial self-protection at its most fundamental and involves a primary lesson of planning for financial freedom: respecting your money and being careful about the choices you make with it. You certainly can't count on salespeople to be careful for you.

As you read this chapter, you may come to realize that you have bought a policy that you do not need. Not to worry: This is a problem that can be fixed, and I will show you how to fix it. Before you act, however, I implore you to read the entire chapter and to always secure new insurance coverage before you drop old policies. A new policy won't help you if something happens to you a week before it becomes effective.

Let's begin by addressing the most basic questions about insurance: what type of insurance you need, what kind of policy will work best, and what amount of coverage you should have.

Insurance Basics

What is insurance, anyway?

All insurance policies are like a bet between you and the insurance company. The company agrees to reimburse you for the cost of your losses—for example, the loss of your health, or the loss of your house in a fire, or the premature loss of your life. The insurance provider is betting, however, that over the long run, you will be safe and healthy and pay more in premiums and deductibles than the company will pay you in benefits. Usually the company is right. Your bet—a crucial one—is that maybe it won't be. The premiums you pay and the deductibles that you agree to buy you the peace of mind that comes with knowing that your assets will be protected, whatever happens.

Are there special guidelines to follow when buying all types of insurance?

Yes. Whenever you buy insurance of any kind, make sure you've done the following:

- *Compare policies.* Always shop around to be sure that you're getting the best policy for your money. Remember, however, that the cheapest policy will not always be the best one for you. Don't compare only costs; compare resources and services, too.
- *Ask yourself the following questions:*
  Have you read every word of the insurance policy that you are buying?
  Do you understand the definitions the insurance company uses?
  What will your policy specifically cover?
  What will your policy specifically not cover?
  What will it take to qualify for your benefits?

- *Review your policies each year* and make sure that they are still responsive to your needs. Have you made major improvements to your house? Did your youngest child finish college? Did your spouse become eligible for Social Security? Have you and your spouse divorced? These kinds of life changes may mean that your insurance coverage should change, too.

What is a premium?

A premium is the price you pay for your insurance coverage, whether or not the benefits are paid. Your premiums will vary, depending on, among other things, how much protection you want to buy, how long your policy will last, the size of your deductible, your age, your health, and how often you make payments.

What is a deductible?

If you need to make a claim on your insurance policy, the deductible is the amount of money you will have to pay out of pocket before the insurance company will begin to pay any benefits. Depending on your policy, your deductible can be either a fixed dollar amount or a percentage of the total cost of your claim. In other words, you could be responsible for paying the first $500 of a claim, or you could be responsible for 10 percent of the total amount of a claim. Deductibles often have an annual limit beyond which you are not required to pay anything, even if you have additional claims.

What is coinsurance?

Coinsurance is the fixed percentage of the covered fees that you are required to pay after your deductible has been subtracted from the amount of money owed on a particular claim. Coinsurance requirements are found, mostly, in health insurance policies. So if you have a policy that requires you to pay a $300 deductible and 20 percent coinsurance, and you have medical bills of, say, $1,300, you would be responsible for $300 (your deductible) plus 20 percent of the remaining $1,000, or $200 (coinsurance). In this example, the claim would cost you a total of $500, while the insurance would pay $800.

Insurance premiums are so expensive. Is there any way to reduce them?

It always pays to compare policies from different insurance companies. When you do, you'll find that increasing your deductible generally lowers your regular premiums. But before leaping to that option, be sure that you will be able to afford the higher deductible. There's no point in lowering a high premium by agreeing to pay a $5,000 deductible if, in the event that you need to pay it, you won't have the money! This is a good example of the principle that money attracts money: If you can save enough in an emergency fund to cover a higher deductible, you can afford to take this risk and save money on your premiums. By the same token, if you've got the money to pay your premium once a year, rather than spreading it out, you may find savings of about 8 percent in overall costs. Another possible way to save money is by purchasing multiple insurance policies from the same company. (But be sure to compare the costs of other companies' policies before you commit to a single insurer.)

What does it mean if a policy is guaranteed renewable, and why is this important?

It is extremely important, because it means that the insurance company guarantees that it will renew your policy—usually a health or life policy—every year, regardless of what health problems you may develop over time. In other words, as long as you told the truth on your application—about, for example, any so-called preexisting health conditions—and continue to pay your premiums, your coverage cannot be cut off.

So guaranteed renewable policies are a must, right?

Definitely. You don't want your coverage can-

celed if you've gone to the trouble of finding a good plan.

How do I buy insurance?

Most people use insurance agents, who make their livings by earning commissions on the policies they sell you. A growing number of financial planners, accountants, and attorneys are also selling insurance these days. You can often buy insurance directly from the insurance company, but you will most likely still pay a commission. You can also buy insurance over the Internet, through your place of work, through membership organizations, or through nonprofit groups to which you belong. How to buy insurance and whom to buy it from will never be a problem; there's no end to the number of people who will try to sell you insurance. The key is to buy the best insurance for your needs at the most cost-effective price.

My neighbor says I need to make sure that my insurance agent is independent. Is that true?

Absolutely! Independent agents, who are sometimes called brokers, can sell you insurance from any of many different insurance companies and are supposed to get you the best possible deal. The opposite of an independent agent is a "captive" agent—a person employed by a particular insurance company, who is authorized to sell you only the policies of that company. In most circumstances, you do not want to deal with a captive agent.

So why do people use captive agents?

Because they don't know better. People just walk into an insurance company, or are solicited by one, and assume that because the company is reputable they will get a good deal. You want an independent agent who's free to offer you every policy issued by every insurer. The way to a good deal is comparison shopping. A captive agent can't help you there.

I read a magazine article about low-load insurance companies. Do they offer good deals?
These are companies that sell their policies directly, not through an agent. This is supposed to save them money, which they then can pass on to you. But unless you're willing to do the research to figure out exactly which insurance policies you want, you will be better off with an independent agent, who knows more than you do.

What do the letters CLU and CPCU mean on my insurance agent's card?
CLU stands for Chartered Life Underwriter. CPCU stands for Chartered Property and Casualty Underwriter. Both are designations that must be earned through a combination of accredited courses, rigorous exams, and experience in the field.

Even if your agent or broker hasn't earned a CLU or CPCU designation, they must be licensed by the state they work in. If you want to make sure your agent is licensed, you can call your state's insurance department. At the same time, you can find out whether or not there have been complaints filed against the insurance company or agent you are using or considering using.

How can I tell if an insurance company is reliable and financially viable?
Check its "financial strength rating" as determined by one of the major indepdendent rating

agencies: AM Best (*www.ambest.com*), Moody's (*www.moodys.com*), and Standard and Poor's (*www.standardandpoors.com*). Before you buy an insurance policy from any company, please be sure the company carries all of the following ratings: AM Best, A- or better; Moody's, AA or better; Standard and Poor's, AA or better. Don't settle for just one of these ratings; at a minimum make sure you check at least two. And insist upon seeing the ratings in print; don't take anyone's word for it.

The first insurance agent I ever dealt with had a really high-pressure sales pitch. I'm still not sure if I bought the right coverage. Are they all like that? My policies are up for renewal and I'm thinking about trying someone else.
Try another agent—someone who will be less impatient to make a sale. Remember, though, that you can't expect salespeople to take responsibility for your money; that's your job. I'm guessing, but it sounds as if you signed up the first time you visited the agent's office, no questions asked. Please take the time to read, compare, and question a number of policies. You shouldn't work with an agent who makes you feel bad for taking the time to do those things.

HEALTH INSURANCE

In recent years, private health insurance has become an increasingly complex and expensive item for all of us. At the same time, it is perhaps the most vital kind of insurance we can have. Without the proper health insurance, an illness or accident can wipe you out financially in a New York minute.

What would happen if I really needed medical care and I didn't have health insurance coverage?

Most hospitals (but not all!) would be obligated to care for you in an emergency, such as a car accident or a heart attack. But this care is not free. Ultimately you would be responsible for paying the medical bills, which could be substantial. One trip to the emergency room could put you and your family in debt for years.

But the perils go deeper. Without health insurance, you (and your children, if you have any) are statistically less likely to seek preventative care, such as an annual checkup, because you can't or won't want to pay for it out of your own pocket. As a result, any serious illness you may get is likely to be diagnosed late, which means that your treatment could be far more expensive and less effective.

Not having health insurance means, in short, that you could be deprived of the care you need and deserve—and still find yourself hundreds of thousands of dollars in debt. No matter what your age or state of health, protecting yourself with adequate medical insurance is an act of self-respect.

I just graduated from college and I'm on a tight budget while looking for a job and an apartment. I'm also healthy. Can't I do without health insurance until I can get coverage through my job?

No. In the first place, not all employers offer subsidized health coverage. Second, if they do offer it, you may have to wait three to six months to qualify for coverage. In the meantime, prudence apart, get used to taking responsibility for your health and finances. You'll find it liberating. Young as you are, and meager though your resources may be, health insurance is vitally important. No one can afford to take their health for granted. You might consider a short-term plan, often called a "gap" plan. It is designed to be low cost, can be issued quickly, and provides coverage for up to a year.

There is so much talk in the news about health insurance that I am totally confused. What do I need to know to make a decision as to what type of coverage I should have?

Start by considering the following questions:

- How much can you comfortably pay in premiums and deductibles?
- Do you have a doctor whom you trust and depend on and want to keep seeing? Would he or she be available under the plan you are considering?
- Does anyone in your family have ongoing health-care needs? Does the plan cover the services he or she depends on, including specialists?

What sort of health insurance do most people have?

Sad to say, many Americans—about 46.6 million, including 8.3 million children—don't have any health insurance. (As I write this in late 2009, Congress is debating legislation that will greatly reduce the number of uninsured.) They can't afford it, or believe they can't afford it. But of those Americans who do have health insurance, most are enrolled in the so-called "managed care" plans. What managed care means is that the insurance companies try to control—that is, "manage"—the costs of the medical care they're underwriting. Their most significant control mechanisms, from your point of view, are the following. First, they restrict your access to a list of doctors who accept the insurance companies' schedule of fees for whatever care you may need. (Your favorite doctor may or may not be among those on the list the plan provides.) Second, the companies may require you to get a referral from your doctor—the one you've designated as your "primary care physician"—in order to see any specialist. Third, they require that the specialist also accept the insurance companies' fee schedule. Fourth, the company consults with—"second-guesses" might be the more accurate phrase—your doctor on many procedures and tests that your doctor (or specialist) may consider necessary.

Are all managed care plans equally restrictive of my freedom of choice?

No, but the general rule is: The greater your freedom of choice, the higher the cost. Here are brief descriptions of the three principal types of managed care plans:

HMOs (HEALTH MAINTENANCE ORGANIZATIONS)

In general, HMOs are the least flexible health insurance policies. Premiums for these plans have gone up in recent years, in part because mandated benefits and pressure from consumers have made insurers more "generous" in giving access to the care you need. Despite the rising premiums, HMOs tend to be the least expensive form of health insurance. Copayments, when they are required at all, are usually small, and preventative care services are almost always covered. In exchange, you must see only approved doctors and will need to get permission from your primary care physician before you see specialists or seek alternative care.

PPOs (PREFERRED PROVIDER ORGANIZATIONS)

A PPO gives you an incentive to stay within its network of doctors by covering more of your costs when you use a preferred provider. You may pay a flat co-pay or a percent of the fee for the services you receive. If you see providers who are not in the network it will generally cost you more, but you at least have the flexibility to see any doctor you like out of the network. PPOs usually allow you to see specialists without prior approval, but they do not always cover preventive care services and you will generally pay more out of pocket when you use services. PPO rules can be complex, so be sure to ask questions to learn what is and isn't covered before you buy this type of insurance.

POS (POINT-OF-SERVICE) PLANS

This is a type of flexible plan where you are encouraged to use network providers but are allowed to choose health-care providers outside of your plan, usually at a higher copayment or deductible cost. The major difference between a

POS plan and a regular PPO is that you can decide if you want to follow the HMO type "rules" and get your primary-care doctor to refer you to specialists or you can pay more out of pocket by going to the providers of your choice without going through the referral process. This is called a point-of-service plan because you decide, at the point of service, whether to use it more like an HMO or PPO.

A COMPARISON

Which type of policy is the best?

There really isn't a single "best" policy. You should base your decision on your own needs and preferences, both financial and medical. Clearly, though, if your overriding concern is keeping access to your family doctor, and he or she isn't among the approved medical caregivers in any available HMO, you should go for a PPO or a POS, regardless of the extra cost. If cost is a big concern, then whichever of the managed care plans you choose, be aware that it will be cheaper if you buy it as part of a group—typically, a group of employees.

How do I get on a group health insurance plan?

If you're employed, you're usually eligible through your company, if it's large enough. You may also be eligible through some other membership organization such as a union. The policies offered are almost always of the managed care variety, which have been sold directly to the employer or organization and then made available to you. Group health insurance is what the

majority of Americans have. It's cheaper than an individual policy because employers or organizations can often negotiate a lower rate and may subsidize part of the cost to eligible employees. They may also extend coverage to spouses, partners, and children of employees or members.

But what am I supposed to do if I'm self-employed, or unemployed, or work for a small business that doesn't offer a group plan?

You must buy individual health insurance from an insurance broker or company. Your best buy, if you're like most people and care a lot about costs as well as comprehensive coverage, is one of the managed care options: an HMO, a PPO, or a POS.

What if I'm on a really tight budget? How can I be safe on individual health insurance?

From a strictly financial point of view, you could think about purchasing catastrophic coverage. Catastrophic coverage pays for major medical and hospital expenses if you get seriously ill or injured. Premiums are lower on this type of insurance because you pay out of pocket for your usual expenses, such as checkups and even minor emergencies, and you will have a relatively high deductible if something major happens. Try to find a policy that is guaranteed renewable, has a maximum lifetime benefit of at least $1 million, and covers at least 80 percent of your doctor and hospital bills after you meet the deductible. Be cautious about plans that have caps on major expenses such as hospitalization. You may not realize the cost of care in your area and find yourself underinsured. Basically, with catastrophic insurance, you're betting that you will stay very healthy and that you will be able to pay for your basic preventative services. At the same time, you are protecting yourself from financial ruin if you should need substantial care.

Can't I get better coverage than that, for not too much more money?

That depends on what you mean by "too much." Ask about a base plan. There are many kinds of base plans that all generally cover most of your expenses when you need to stay in a hospital, when you have "medically necessary" surgery, when you visit a doctor, and when your doctor orders lab tests. The broadest—and most costly—of the base plans is indemnity insurance. It gives you the most freedom when picking doctors, treatments, and hospitals. Your insurance provider pays a fixed percentage of your doctors' charges, however large or small those charges are and whatever doctor you choose to see. But, again, you pay for this freedom with higher premiums. For some people the option of choosing any doctor they fancy is worth any expense. But beware: In some plans you will need to make up the difference between what your doctor charges and what the insurance company deems a "reasonable and customary" price for those services, even if you've already paid your (high) deductible.

Are there any ways to save money on an individual policy?

Here are two: First, some insurance companies offer discounts to people who are in good physical shape. Second, if you choose a high-deductible plan that meets IRS guidelines, you can set up your own health savings account (HSA) so that you'll be paying for your health insurance on a tax-deductible basis. HSA accounts can be used for dental, vision, and complementary medicine as well. Make sure the plan you choose is HSA compatible.

I've heard about these health savings accounts (HSAs). How do they work?

HSAs are accounts to which you can contribute money on a tax-deductible basis, then use the money later to pay your medical expenses. Any money that you don't use in a single year can be placed in an interest-bearing account and continue to grow with taxes deferred. These may be especially useful if you have a high deductible or copayment rate on your medical insurance. For more information, go to *www.irs.gov* and search for Publication 969, "Health Savings Accounts."

I just started my own business and, so far, I am the only employee. Am I stuck buying individual health insurance?

It is actually possible to buy group health insurance for groups of one, although not all insurance companies or states allow this option and the specifics of the plans vary widely. One thing to keep in mind when considering this option is your own health. If it's poor, a group plan for one may be for you; such plans can't reject members for health reasons.

Once I have an individual policy, can I keep it forever?

It depends on your policy. Guaranteed renewable policies can be kept forever, as long as you pay your premiums on time (although the insurance company can raise your premiums). Optionally renewable policies usually allow the insurance company to stop your coverage, but only within specific time periods, such as the anniversary date of the policy. Conditionally renewable policies can be terminated by the insurance company for certain specific reasons (such as if you are covered under a group plan at work and you retire), but not if your health becomes poor. If your policy is optionally or conditionally renewable, check to see if your insurer is required to inform you when it is about to expire, and whether you have an option to convert the policy to individual or individual family coverage.

The insurance policy I'm considering has a stop loss provision. What does that mean?

Although most major medical policies require you to make copayments, they typically limit the total amount you would have to pay within a given period of time, usually a year. That limit is the stop loss figure, and it varies by company and policy. If your stop loss is $3,000 per year, you will never have to pay more than $3,000 (in addition to your premiums); after you have paid $3,000, the insurance company will pay 100 percent of your covered expenses. Consider stop loss provisions when you are comparing policies.

What's the difference between health insurance continuations and conversions?

In certain circumstances, your eligibility for your insurance plan may change (for example, if you lose your job or begin working part-time; if you are widowed, divorced, or separated from your insured spouse; or if you are too old to be covered under your parents' insurance, etc.). Both federal and state laws almost always require, in these types of circumstances, that you be given an opportunity to continue or convert your health insurance policy. Continuation means that you can keep the coverage, often at your own expense, for a specific period of time. Conversion means you have the option of converting your group coverage to individual (or individual family) coverage.

COBRA

If I have group insurance through my employer and I lose my job, will I automatically lose my health insurance and have to buy an individual policy?

Not right away. The Consolidated Omnibus Budget Reconciliation Act of 1985 (COBRA) requires most employers with 20 or more employees to give you the opportunity to continue your health insurance for up to 18 months, at your expense. Your employer can charge you up to 102 percent of its cost of your insurance—which sounds like a lot and is almost certainly more than you were paying in premiums before, but still might be cheaper than buying your own individual policy. But please shop around; if you are healthy you often can find less expensive coverage through an individual policy.

How do I know if I'm eligible for COBRA?

You are eligible for COBRA coverage in a number of different circumstances, including: if you lose your job, if you quit your job, if your spouse who was the primary insured member of your family dies, if your child is no longer a minor, if you are getting divorced from a spouse who is the primary insured member, or if you begin working part-time. These are called qualifying events. You are not eligible if you work for the federal government, in the District of Columbia, or for an employer with less than 20 workers. (If you work for a small business, you might be eligible to continue your health insurance anyway, depending on the state in which you live. Check with your state's department of insurance.)

I work full-time and I'm pregnant. After the baby is born I would like to work part-time for a while. As long as I'm still working for the same employer, why would I need COBRA?
Because you usually need to work a minimum number of hours per week, often more than half of a normal workweek, in order to qualify for your employer's medical plan. The extra cost of COBRA, to you, is something to keep in mind if you decide to try to work out a part-time schedule with your employer.

My sister works for a small restaurant in town with only 12 employees, so the owner offers health insurance that isn't subject to COBRA. What are her options if she loses her job?
Many states require all employers to offer you the opportunity to convert to an individual policy, but the coverage may be more limited than what your sister had under the group plan, and the premiums may be higher. Call the department of insurance in your state to see if she will at least have this option.

How long can I keep my health coverage under COBRA?
Usually for no more than 18 months. However, your coverage can be extended for up to 36 months under certain extenuating circumstances, such as if the primary insured person dies. If you become eligible for Medicare (which makes you automatically ineligible for COBRA coverage), but your spouse isn't eligible for Medicare, your spouse can extend his or her COBRA coverage for up to 36 months.

What if I become disabled while I have insurance coverage under COBRA?
You may be able to extend your COBRA coverage for up to 29 months, but your premiums will rise for those additional months, depending on your particular situation.

I'm about to get laid off. I had great coverage with my employer's plan, but it's going to cost a lot to keep it up under COBRA. Can I opt for one of the COBRA versions of the less comprehensive, cheaper plans that my company offers?
No. Your coverage under COBRA must be the same as the coverage you had before you were laid off. Your employer might permit you to drop certain types of coverage, like your vision care. That could save you some money, but your employer is not required to help you.

My husband and I are both self-employed, so we share an individual health insurance policy. Now we're getting divorced. How do we decide who gets to keep it?
Here's one decision you don't have to make.

Neither of you can keep a shared individual policy. Typically, you must each reenroll as individuals, or you can choose to go to different insurance companies.

I don't ever want to worry about my children's health care. Both my husband and I have health insurance. Shouldn't we play it safe and add our children to both plans?

You could, but it really doesn't make sense. If one or both of your plans are individual, it's going to cost a lot of extra money to cover your kids on two plans. Similarly, group plans charge more for family coverage and tend to offer similar preventative care services. If you compare your two plans, you may find that you won't be getting much, if any, additional coverage by signing the kids up for both. It'd be far better to take that extra money and invest it for growth. Alternatively, buy a separate policy for the children, so they'll be covered in the event of your job loss.

COBRA coverage costs so much money! Is it really the right thing for me?

If you're in good health, you may be able to find a better deal than paying COBRA premiums, if you're willing to do the research. But make sure that you compare services, not just prices.

I'm in such poor health that I'm afraid I won't be able to get health insurance. Is there anything I can do?

High-risk health insurance pools guarantee health insurance to all individuals, no matter how sick they may already be. While pools vary from state to state, they are generally operated by an association of all health insurance companies doing business in a state. These companies are not providing coverage out of the goodness of their hearts. They have been required by the government to offer coverage to state residents who have either been rejected by other insurers for similar coverage or are insured at a higher premium or with more severe restrictions than they would be under the pool. These pools are not perfect—premiums are often high and the benefits may not be adequate to meet your needs—but they do offer an insurance alternative for people in poor health. Call your state insurance department.

MEDICARE, MEDICAID, AND MEDIGAP

By the year 2050, 22 percent of Americans will be over age 65. No wonder health care for the elderly is a serious political issue.

And it's serious not only because of the size of the elderly population. For many of us, the crux of the matter is this: Just when we go on fixed incomes and no longer have funds available to pay for private medical insurance, our medical needs and costs are likely to go up—sometimes way up. This is when Medicare and Medicaid will come in to save the day.

That's the idea, anyway. But these are difficult times in which to grow old in America. Our whole scheme of social insurance—the famed "safety net" of Social Security, federal disability insurance, unemployment insurance, Medicare, Medicaid, and other federal programs—is under great stress. The main reason is the ballooning elderly population and the fact that health care costs and expenditures keep rising well above the rate of inflation. The withholding taxes younger Americans pay are used to support the current retired generation, which is still a relatively small group. But as retired Americans become a huge group, and as the working, withholding tax-paying population becomes a relatively small one, the painful question arises: Who is going to make up for the shortfall in support for the safety net? The problem is not just financial; it's also intensely ideological. There are conflicting views as to how much of the support should continue to be shouldered by society as a right and responsibility of membership in that society, and how much should be borne by the individuals who are growing old.

The problem will not be solved easily or quickly. We will have plenty of opportunities to follow proposed solutions as they're being discussed—indeed, to influence them with our votes. But big changes are already upon us. Job security has been a nostalgic dream for some time, as employees who expected to be working at the same job until retirement are now routinely laid off ("reengineered" or "downsized"), their places given to younger workers who may or may not be technologically more clever but are certainly cheaper. For many older Americans, full Social Security still kicks in at 65, with average annual benefits of $13,836 as of 2009, but we are already seeing benefits reduced for younger Americans; anyone born after 1959 only qualifies for full benefits at age 67.

In what follows I'm going to focus on the most insurance-like social programs—Medicare, Medicaid, and Medigap insurance, a private supplement to Medicare.

MEDICARE COVERAGE

What is Medicare?

Medicare is the largest federal health insurance program, and it is the major health insurer for Americans over age 65 and Americans who are disabled. Once you qualify, you can use Original Medicare, which is a traditional fee-for-service health plan, or, in many cases, you can use a managed care organization—an HMO or a PPO that contracts with Medicare.

What does Medicare cover?

There are free services in each state that will help you understand the details of Medicare eligibility and coverage. Very briefly, if you are 65 or older, you can get a certain amount of coverage for hospital and doctor visits from Medicare. The type of coverage Medicare offers depends on whether you are covered by Medicare Part A, Part B, or both.

MEDICARE, PART A

If you qualify for Social Security you are automatically covered by Medicare Part A. In most cases there is no premium charge to you for this coverage because part of the Social Security tax you paid while you were working went toward this coverage.

Part A generally covers inpatient-type benefits such as:

- Hospital care
- Skilled nursing facility

- Home health care
- Hospice care

MEDICARE, PART B

Medicare Part B coverage is automatic, but there is a monthly premium. Individuals with income below $85,000 in 2010 and married couples with joint income below $170,000 paid a per-person monthly premium of about $97. The premium was more at higher income levels. The premium is adjusted annually. It is voluntary coverage, however, from which you can opt out and for which you won't be charged. If you accept it, the monthly premium is commonly deducted from your Social Security check.

Part B provides for:

- Physician's services
- Outpatient hospital care
- Physical therapy and the use of medical equipment
- Ambulance expenses

Note: Neither of these policies provides coverage for dental care or vision care.

So, I don't have to do anything to purchase Part B?

No. When you become eligible for Part A benefits, you will be sent an enrollment form for Part B, but you should fill it out only if you want to *reject* the coverage. If you fail to reject coverage within two months from the date you received the form, you will be automatically enrolled in Part B. If you opt out of Part B you can enroll later at any time, but at a higher cost to you.

What percentage of my medical bills does Part B cover?

It normally covers 80 percent of the approved charges for covered expenses, subject to a calendar year deductible. In 2010 the deductible was $155.

What do you mean by approved charges?

The approved charge is the lesser of the actual charge or the amount indicated in Medicare's annual fee schedule.

Do you have to be over 65 to receive Medicare?

Not necessarily. You are also eligible for Medicare at any age if you have qualified for Social Security Disability Insurance for any reason—such as, for example, if you've developed permanent kidney failure.

How do I get Medicare and when do benefits begin?

Once you apply for and begin receiving your Social Security benefits, you will automatically be eligible for Medicare when you turn 65. Coverage begins on the first day of the month in which you turn 65. When you are covered, a Medicare card will be issued to you.

If I am over 65 and need to go into a nursing home, Medicare will automatically pay for it, right?

No—this is a huge and costly misunderstanding that many people share. Not only does Medicare not automatically pick up your nursing care costs as a senior citizen, it will almost *never* cover them. Medicare has very limited coverage for long-term care. It is usually only available if you are in an acute-care hospital for three days before entering a "skilled nursing facility"—a facility that must be Medicare-certified—and Medicare must define the type of care you need as "skilled" medical care, not custodial care. Custodial care is what 99.5 percent of the people in nursing facilities receive; only about 0.5 percent of the people in nursing homes receive skilled care. Even if your care falls under this 0.5 percent, you are only covered for reasonable and customary expenses for the first 20 days; for the next 80 days you are required to pay about $138 a day and Medicare covers the remaining reasonable and customary expenses. After those first 100 days, you are on your own no matter what. The bottom line is that Medicare rarely pays for nursing home costs.

If Medicare won't pay for me to stay in a nursing home, will it pay for my care at home?
Possibly, in a very limited number of cases. If a doctor certifies that you need to be cared for at home by a part-time or full-time skilled nurse, speech therapist, or physical therapist, and the provider is Medicare-certified, you might receive some coverage. But be aware that very few situations qualify under these conditions.

My father still lives at home but he had a stroke last year and needs a lot of assistance, including physical therapy. What can he expect Medicare to pay for?
Because he needs physical therapy, Medicare will cover some of his expenses. But usually if you are capable of living at home, Medicare will pay only if your doctor certifies that you need

very particular occasional skilled assistance, such as physical therapy or speech therapy, and that you will improve with such treatment.

My father really needs help at home with things like cleaning and cooking, since he can't stand up for long periods of time. Will Medicare cover these services temporarily, as he should be able to do them again once he recovers?
No. Even if your father's nonmedical needs are related to an injury, Medicare will not pay for home health care. He needs long-term care insurance for this. Long-term care insurance covers care he receives in an adult day care center, continuing care retirement communities, and assisted living facilities. It will increase his premiums to have all these types of facilities covered, but if he has the protection, he will have more flexibility in seeking care later.

My mother needs to go into a nursing home. What kind of skilled nursing care will Medicare pay for?
Not very much. If she has been hospitalized for at least three consecutive days within the last 30 days and if she will be receiving skilled nursing care in a certified facility, Medicare will pay for the reasonable and customary costs of the first 20 days and part of the cost (less her copayment) for the following 80 days of her stay.

What if she can't afford those copayments?
If she has Medigap Plan C insurance (discussed later in the chapter), it will pay for the copayments between the 21st and 100th day of her stay, if Medicare approves her stay.

What if she has to stay longer than 100 days?
She will have to pay out of her own pocket. This is when long-term care coverage becomes essential.

Does Medicare pay for any nursing services, ever?
Yes, when you're dying, Medicare will pay for a portion of hospice care. A caregiver is provided to ease the pain and suffering of the patient and his or her family during their last days together, and it will not matter whether you need the services at home or in a facility.

MEDICARE PART D

I keep hearing about Medicare part D. Do I need this?
Medicare D is the prescription drug plan. If you already have a Medigap policy with drug coverage, you may be able to keep that coverage. If not, a Medicare D policy will provide you with prescription drug coverage. For the best rates, enroll in a Medicare Part D plan when you become eligible for Medicare. The Website *www.medicare.gov* has tools to help you figure out the best option for your situation.

MEDIGAP COVERAGE

Can you explain Medigap insurance?
As you can see, Medicare will not cover all your medical costs. Also, like other health insurers, Medicare will require you to pay deductibles in or-

der to receive your benefits. Therefore, you may want to buy additional coverage to protect you from having to spend a lot of money on these fees. Medigap is a type of insurance policy designed by private insurers to supplement Medicare coverage (although it does not cover long-term care). There are many different types of Medigap policies and they vary in quality and cost.

How do I know which Medigap policy to purchase?
The standard policies are referred to as plans A through J. A is the most basic (and least expensive) and generally as you move through the alphabet, the number of benefits expands to J, which is a more comprehensive and more expensive supplement. Just so you know, any insurance company that sells Medigap coverage is required to offer plan A, with the basic benefits.

The most popular plan is C. You will need to decide which policy is right for you, but if you purchase Medigap, look for a policy that covers at least a 20 percent coinsurance cost for doctor bills, hospital and doctor visit deductibles, excess doctor fees, and preventative care. Don't ever buy more than one of these policies, because they expand on one another, so you would be paying twice for some benefits.

Here are the basic features of each plan:

- Plan A pays the coinsurance required by Medicare Part A for the 61st through the 90th day that you are hospitalized in each benefit period and for the 60 nonrenewable lifetime hospitalization inpatient reserve days that you can use to extend your coverage; up to one year (over your lifetime) of your eligible hospital expenses after Medicare benefits have been used; the first three pints of blood you need each year; and the Part B coinsurance after your annual deductible is paid.

- Plan B includes everything in Plan A, plus it picks up the inpatient hospital deductible that Medicare Part A requires.
- Plan C includes everything listed above in plans A and B, and pays for the coinsurance in a skilled nursing care facility during days 21 through 100 in each benefit period; the deductible required by Medicare Part B; and most of your medically necessary emergency care in a foreign country.
- Plan D covers everything listed above for plans A through C, *except* the deductible required by Medicare Part B, and includes a benefit of up to $1,600 per year for services you would need at home on a short-term basis if you were recovering from illness, injury, or surgery.
- Plan E covers everything listed above for plans A through C, *except* the deductible required by Medicare Part B, and includes coverage for up to $120 per year for preventative care, such as flu shots, cholesterol tests, or annual checkups.
- Plan F covers everything listed above for plans A through C, plus 100 percent of any fees you would be required to pay as excess charges under Medicare Part B.
- Plan G covers everything listed above for plans A through C, and pays 80 percent of the excess charge fees described in Plan F. Plan G also includes coverage for "at-home recovery"—that is, authorized care you might receive in your home, such as assistance with bathing, once you've been released from the hospital.

- Plan H covers everything listed above for plans A through C, *except* the deductible required by Medicare Part B.
- Plan I covers everything listed above for plan E, plus the excess charges benefit in plan F and at-home recovery as in Plan G.
- Plan J includes every benefit listed above, *except* that it covers 100 percent of your excess charges (as in plan F, rather than the 80 percent coverage for this fee in plan G).

Will a Medigap policy cover any home or long-term health-care needs?

In certain limited circumstances, Medigap may cover some home health-care services but, as you can see, even the most comprehensive Medigap policy will not cover long-term care costs. Remember, the care must be Medicare-approved in order for the Medigap policy to kick in.

If Medigap policies are standardized, why do different insurance companies charge different amounts of money for the same policies?

There are many different reasons for this, including the laws of the state you are in and the way the company calculates its premiums. It is absolutely worth your while to compare prices, and it is quite easy to do this because you know that the terms of the policies are the same: A plan C from one company should offer the exact same benefits as a plan C from another company, no matter where you live.

Does everyone need Medigap?

Not necessarily. And it may not always be the best buy, even if you decide that you need some supplemental insurance. For example, you may be eligible to participate in some group health coverage through the employer you had before you retired.

Can I be turned down for Medigap coverage if I am in poor health?

This is an important point. When you qualify for Original Medicare Part B, you have a six-month open enrollment period during which you can buy any Medigap policy offered in your state, no matter what your health status is. This is the best time to decide whether you want to make Medigap part of your insurance coverage.

My neighbor has part of her Social Security check paid directly to a company, which she says she uses instead of Medigap. Can you tell me more about this?

She most likely is talking about what is known as a Managed Care Organization.

What is a Medicare Advantage Plan?

Medicare Advantage is a program that you purchase from a private insurer who then provides your Part A and Part B Medicare coverage, and can also include additional coverage as well. If you have a Medicare Advantage plan you cannot have Medigap.

How do I choose a good Medicare Advantage Plan?

Please take the time to investigate as many plans as you can, but no less than two plans offered in your area. When you do, be sure to compare the following features:

- *Cost of care.* Although many Medicare Advantage Plans do not charge premiums beyond the amounts you are currently paying to Medicare, some do. Check what your potential plan covers and how much it will cost you. Is it a bare-bones plan, meaning that it offers the minimum coverage required by Medicare? Are you willing to pay a slightly higher premium for broader coverage? Please pay attention when comparing potential out-of-pocket costs by looking at the deductibles and the copayments each plan offers.

- *Type of coverage and optional benefits.*

- *Choice of providers.* Many of you prefer to choose your own doctors, but you may not be able to do so if you choose a Medicare Advantage Plan that requires you to use its network. Medicare Advantage Plans can be HMOs, where you must use doctors within the plan, PPOs, where you have more choice of in-network doctors, as well as private fee-for-service plans. Be clear on this point ahead of time, so that after you have enrolled you are not surprised to learn that you cannot see your regular doctor.

- *Quality of care.* Find out if your Medicare Advantage Plan encourages preventive care by paying for some of those services. You can learn more about Medicare Advantage Plans, and compare plans offered in your area at the Medicare website: *http://www.medicare.gov/choices/advantage.asp.*

MEDICAID

Medicaid (which is called MediCal in California) is a combined federal and state welfare program that covers medical care for poor Americans (and about 40 percent of all the people who are in nursing homes today). In order to qualify for Medicaid, you must be poor or medically needy, over age 65 or under age 21, blind, disabled, or receiving certain welfare benefits.

I've heard of people trying to "qualify" for Medicaid in a nursing home by putting everything into their children's names. Isn't this financially risky?

It is definitely risky, and not only financially. A major risk is that people on Medicaid have very limited control over their (also limited) medical options. Also, when parents sign over all their resources to their children, they become completely dependent. That can be emotionally and financially unhealthy for everyone involved. Finally, depending on the value of the assets transferred, there can be significant negative tax consequences for your children. Please consult with a qualified elder-law attorney before you transfer any assets or make any decisions. It may not be worth it!

My wife needs to go into a nursing home. How do I know if she will qualify for Medicaid?

It can be frustrating to sort through the rules concerning Medicaid, which change frequently and vary from state to state. Generally, your wife will have to have a doctor certify that she needs the specific kind of care that nursing homes provide. She will also need to be living in a state that provides the relevant Medicaid benefits; be at least 65 years old, disabled, or blind; and have only a limited amount of income and assets. If you find yourself in this situation, seek the assistance of an attorney who specializes in elder-

care law in your state or contact your local office on aging, which may be under the aegis of the state health department.

I would like to move from New York to Virginia, to be in a nursing home near my daughter. How do I establish Virginia's residency qualifications?

Just move to Virginia and plan to stay there indefinitely. As long as you're in the state and have no plans to leave, you are considered a resident and should be immediately eligible for Medicaid. But just to be sure, check out the state's eligibility requirements.

What are the financial requirements for Medicaid? How much income can I have and still qualify for Medicaid coverage in a nursing home?

If you are single, everything counts. That means that all your income (earned or unearned) is taken into consideration in determining whether you qualify. This includes your Social Security, alimony, pension, worker's compensation, annuities, unemployment, interest, gifts, and dividends.

The income limits for Medicaid eligibility are set by each state; some states have no limit, others impose restrictions. You can find your state's rules by going to *govbenefits.gov* and choosing "Medicare/Medicaid" in the search box. You can also learn more at the *elderlawanswers.com* website; choose your state in the drop-down box on the site's homepage.

As an unmarried person, what other assets can I have and still qualify for Medicaid coverage of my nursing home stay?

Most unmarried people must turn over almost all their assets to the nursing home in order to have Medicaid pay their bill. However, most states will allow you to keep your house if you'll most likely be able to return there or if a member of your immediate family or your spouse is living there at the time you apply for coverage. You can often keep your car, no matter what it is worth, if you use it to receive medical care. Otherwise, you can only keep a car that is worth less than $4,500 and investments up to about $2,000.

This is only the most general information. There are a lot of other rules about what you can and cannot keep, but the bottom line is that as an unmarried person you must give up almost everything you have worked so hard to accumulate in order to qualify for Medicaid coverage in a nursing home. Unmarried and married persons should each get legal advice as to the available options regarding assets.

As a married person, how do I determine if I qualify for Medicaid?

Again, rules for married people vary from state to state. In community-property states (Arizona, California, Idaho, Louisiana, Nevada, New Mexico, Texas, Washington, and Wisconsin), all of your income from any source, no matter which spouse the checks are made out to, is considered to be equally divided between both of you. So if you live in one of these states, half of all the income you and your spouse have is considered yours, even if, for example, most of it comes from your spouse's pension.

In any other state, only checks that are made out to you count toward your Medicaid eligibil-ity. In other words, if you get a Social Security check made out only to you, Medicaid considers it to belong only to you, even if you normally deposit it in a joint bank account with your spouse. If you receive dividends or interest on an account with both your names on it, that money is considered to be evenly split between the two of you.

Once I qualify, what happens to my healthy spouse?

He or she will be given a basic living allowance, a generally modest amount of money that doesn't have to go toward the nursing home, to make sure that he or she is not totally impoverished. Your elder-care specialist can help you estimate the amount that your stay-at-home spouse would be able to keep—or even have the amount increased according to his or her needs—because it will be completely different in each state, as are the formulas that determine it.

Do married people also have an asset eligibility test?

Yes, after qualifying on the income test, you also need to pass an asset eligibility test. Your home (up to certain limits), car, and personal property are generally protected for your healthy spouse. Married couples can also keep some money in investments or cash: usually about $80,000, which sounds like a lot, but remember, this is all the stay-at-home spouse will have, aside from his or her income, which has basically just been cut in half. You can see that you have to lose most of your assets in order to qualify.

Studies of individuals entering nursing homes have documented that half of the people in the study on Medicaid were not poor when they entered the facility. They had to "spend down" their assets until nothing was left before Medicaid took over.

Is it true that even if I qualify for Medicaid, the state can put a lien against my property after I die?

Actually, yes. The 1993 OBRA Act requires any state that receives funds for Medicaid to have a recovery plan in place. More and more states, in fact, are actively starting to recoup Medicaid expenses. What's more, your family or other beneficiaries will have to pay despite the fact that there is no way to prove that the amount of money Medicaid is seeking from your estate was actually spent on you. So please be careful here and get advice from an elder-care specialist.

But you said that the house I lived in with my wife is exempt from such recouping efforts! I mean, she's not suddenly going to find herself homeless, is she?

No, she won't. Generally, while your spouse is living in the house they will not try to take it. Once your spouse dies, however, and the estate is left to her beneficiaries, the state could try to make a claim against it. Your wife should consider revising her estate plan so you don't end up owning her share of the house and other assets.

Can I just give my money to my kids and then apply for Medicaid?

Please don't do this! Medicaid is a form of public assistance and all types of public assistance make you liable for prosecution if you lie on your application or knowingly defraud the program. The government can look back in time to see whether you have given away money to anyone, including your children or any other relatives, in the past 60 months. If you give away your assets in order to get Medicaid benefits primarily to pay for your care in a nursing home, you may be making yourself vulnerable to this type of accusation and, if you are found to have knowingly defrauded the program, you may become ineligible for Medicaid benefits for a period of time and possibly be accused of fraud. Further, any professional financial advisers who recommend that you do this could be sent to jail or fined. Beyond the illegalities of such actions lie the more personal issues of the effect asset transfers have on your autonomy and your family.

So if I give my assets to my children and get caught, how long do I have to wait before I can apply for Medicaid again?

The length of time you can be barred from Medicaid depends on how much money you gave away. The state takes an average-per-month cost of what nursing homes charge in your area and divides that monthly figure into the value of the assets you gave away. So let's say you gave $200,000 worth of assets, and the average price of a nursing home near you is $5,000 a month. Dividing the first figure into the second yields 40, which means that you'll be barred from eligibility for 40 months.

What if I give away stocks? Is that the same as giving away money?

Of course. An asset is an asset. It won't work, either, to put the stock in a living revocable trust. That will extend your noneligibility to 60 months—5 years.

If I don't want to apply for Medicaid but I have worked out a good combination of Medicare and Medigap coverage, can I rest easy?

Medicare and Medigap will certainly cover some of your needs, but if you really want to know that you have taken care of potential nursing home costs, you need to purchase long-term care insurance.

LONG-TERM CARE INSURANCE

For a society that's growing older by the minute, we're not providing very well for our old age. We expect individuals and families to do it mostly on their own. But even as individuals and families, we seem to be in denial about what's happening to us. Nowhere is this more obvious than with respect to long-term care insurance—perhaps the most essential kind of insurance—which many of us will need when we are old. Long-term care will be a fact of life for most of us, so let's face it here and now. Having done so, you will, I hope, go on to buy this kind of protection.

What is long-term care?

This is any type of medical, social, or support service you may need over an extended period of time. Elderly or chronically ill people may eventually need help bathing, dressing, taking medicine, shopping, doing laundry, cleaning, or getting around outside. These services can be extremely expensive and, in most circumstances, Medicare, Medicaid, and Medigap will not pay for them.

What are my chances of needing long-term care?

The frightening reality is that after age 65, most people have a 50-50 chance of needing long-term care. The odds of needing such care are higher than the odds of your house burning down or of your getting into a serious car accident. You are covered for those possibilities, aren't you? Well, the average age at which people enter a nursing home is 84 years and the average stay is two years and nine months. As of 2008 the national average cost for nursing care was about $6,400 a month for a private room and $5,800 for a semi-private room. In high cost areas you could pay double that amount. That's a lot of money if you have to pay out of your own pocket.

I took care of my kids when they were young, and I expect them to take care of me when I am older. What's wrong with that?

Nothing. Many adult children do take care of their parents. Younger family members (usually the women) provide 70 to 80 percent of all home health care and long-term care for their elders. However, there are enormous financial, emotional, and psychological costs when families have to maintain an intensive level of care over an extended period of time. Long-term care insurance doesn't mean your children can't, or won't, care for you, but it does ensure that you will not be placing a financial burden on your family at a time when they will already be under considerable stress.

Doesn't standard health insurance offer long-term care benefits?

Typically, no, it doesn't. And when it does, the benefits are limited.

But I've heard long-term care insurance is very expensive.

If you think long-term care insurance is expensive, you should compare it to the cost of a nursing home stay. Let's say you are 55 and will need to be in a nursing home at age 84: The projected yearly cost of a nursing home 30 years from now, if you live in middle America (assuming an annual compound rate of inflation of 5 percent), would be approximately $244,000. Given that the average nursing home stay is two years and nine months, that would mean a total cost to you of about $671,000. The total cost of a top-notch long-term care (LTC) policy, if you started it at the age of 55 and paid each year until you were 84, would be $82,000. Look at the numbers: You will pay more than 8.2 times as much for the total cost of a nursing home stay (that is, if you only stay two years and nine months) as you did for all your LTC premiums. (This assumes that there were no increases in premiums, and that you did not invest the premium money over those years.) Please note: In the year 2008, a stay in a nursing home in the metropolitan New York area was already above $131,000 a year for a private room. For you New Yorkers, think about what that cost will be in 30 years!

But why should I buy it, if I take good care of myself?

Don't we all buy insurance in the hope that we will never need it? As I said, you are more likely to use your long-term care insurance policy than you are to use your fire or car insurance policy. One in 1,200 people will use their fire insurance, one in 248 people will use their car insurance, but one in two people who have long-term care insurance will use it, and it is the one insurance that you most likely do not have.

Should my marital status affect my decision about whether to purchase this insurance?

Everyone has to make the decision that's best for them, but here are some things to keep in mind: When you have to go into an assisted-living center or a nursing home and are leaving a healthy spouse behind, it is critical that he or she still have the means to live. Price a couple of nursing homes in your area and ask yourself what would happen to your partner if she had to pay those bills and support herself at the same time. Most of us would be financially devastated. Now, if you are single and no one will be hurt if you need to use all your income and assets to pay for nursing-home care, that's one thing. But do you have children that you want to provide for after your death? Charities you want to give to? Finally, is spending it all on a nursing home what you want to do with the money you have worked so hard for? That said, be sure that you and your partner will be able to comfortably afford those premiums, even after you are both retired. Otherwise, don't buy the policy.

Is long-term care insurance tax deductible?

As of January 1997, if you purchase a long-term care policy that meets certain definitions established by the Health Insurance Portability and Accountability Act of 1996, your premiums, within certain limits, can be itemized as a tax deduction for medical expenses. These are called tax-qualified policies. Ask your accountant or an attorney or financial planner with an elder-care specialty about whether the policy you are considering would qualify. But remember: Your premiums, along with other out-of-pocket deductible medical expenses, will have to be in excess of 7.5 percent of your adjusted gross income to qualify for a deduction.

What's the difference between a non-tax-qualified policy and a tax-qualified policy?

One big difference is that, with a tax-qualified plan (TQ), your long-term care insurance premiums may be tax deductible, as described above. With a non-tax-qualified plan (NTQ)—which has become less widely available in recent years—you may not get the tax deduction. The other major difference is in what triggers the benefits in a TQ versus an NTQ policy. This is called "making it through the gatekeepers."

If you have a TQ plan—which is fast becoming the most common type of plan—in order to make it through the gatekeepers, you must generally meet one of the two conditions that follow.

The first condition is not to be able to perform certain *activities of daily living (ADLs)*. In order to function normally, most of us need to be able to (1) feed ourselves; (2) clothe ourselves; (3) transfer ourselves (get in and out of bed, chairs, and the like, unattended); (4) be continent; (5) use the toilet; and (6) bathe ourselves. With a good TQ policy, if you got to a point in your life where you could not perform *any two* of the qualifying ADLs without substantial assistance, then you would qualify for benefits.

The second condition is *cognitive impairment,* which simply means that you qualify if you come down with, say, Alzheimer's disease or cannot think or act clearly and therefore become a danger to yourself or others.

In NTQ plans, you can usually claim your benefits with a different condition, which is known as *medical necessity*. This is where a doctor certifies that it is medically necessary for you to have long-term care—for example, if you are unstable and in danger of falling. This is a good gatekeeper to have in your policy, since it is generally easier to satisfy than the two-ADL gatekeeper. But again, it is becoming less widely available.

In the past, I have always preferred NTQ policies. But as said, today many insurance companies are no longer offering NTQ plans. As well, the government has stated that the benefits you receive in an NTQ plan could be taxed as income, so if you ever used the benefits, you might have to pay taxes on them (although most likely you would have at least a partial offset for deductible medical expenses). Also, NTQ premiums tend to be a little higher—about 5 percent. Meanwhile, benefits from a TQ plan can definitely be received income-tax free. Based on all this, a tax-qualified plan is probably the better, safer way to go.

If you do buy an NTQ policy, be sure that the insurance company will allow you to convert your policy to a TQ policy any time you want to, without new underwriting. Check the policy carefully for this, and make sure that if you do convert the policy at some future date, the company will base your new premium on your original age of entry into your former (NTQ) policy.

How do I know if I can afford to buy an LTC policy?

If you are not able to pay your bills or are just making ends meet each month, long-term care insurance is certainly not for you. But if you are able to save some of your income each month after your expenses, and you have liquid assets of at least $50,000 and own your home, then long-term care insurance may be worthwhile for you. The key thing is to be absolutely sure that you will be able to pay your premiums once you are retired.

Ask yourself the following questions:

- Could you keep this policy if your premiums increased by 20 percent?
- Do you expect your income to increase or decrease in the next 10 years? If it decreases, will you be able to keep the policy in effect?
- How will you pay the premiums—from savings, from income, or will your family pay them for you?

Long-term care insurance is meant to help keep you from going into the poorhouse in case of the need for long-term care, not to put you in the poorhouse while you are paying for the insurance. It will do no good to buy a policy at age 55, retire at age 65, and then, at age 75, find that you can no longer afford the premiums. No matter how long you've paid into a policy, in most policies once you stop paying you'll no longer be covered. If you think you may not be able to afford your coverage in later years, you would be better off not to purchase the insurance in the first place, and to invest the money instead.

I'm only in my 50s. If the average age of entry into a nursing home is 84, shouldn't I wait until I am about 80 to buy LTC insurance?

Please don't. By then, the cost may become prohibitive. Not only that, your health may prevent you from being able to qualify for it. As with all insurance policies, you have to meet certain health requirements in order to purchase an LTC policy.

What is the optimal age to buy long-term care insurance?

I would say the optimal age is about 59, as long as you are sure that you're going to be able to make those payments when you're 74 and beyond. Remember, these premiums should not make daily living difficult for you and your spouse, now or after your retirement.

I am currently 50 years old and my agent says it is the perfect time to buy an LTC policy, but I have heard you say one should wait until age 59. Why?

Two reasons. First, by age 59 I believe that most people have a clear outlook on their financial future and know what they will be able to afford when they no longer have a paycheck coming in.

As of the writing of this book, at 50 the cost of a good policy with appropriate benefit levels is about $4,000 a year. Are you sure that you know beyond a shadow of a doubt that you will be able to afford $4,000 a year for the rest of your life? For most people, I don't think so. And nothing would be less useful than for you to have paid $4,000 a year for 20 or 25 years and then have something happen that causes you to drop the policy just when you might need it. At the age of 59 you will have a better sense of your income in retirement. That said, if you do know beyond a shadow of a doubt that you'll always be able to afford the premiums and if you are afraid that if you wait, you may suffer an illness that would make you ineligible for long-term care insurance, then it's fine to go ahead and buy long-term care insurance in your early 50s.

Second, let's look at cost. Let's say that instead of buying a policy now at $4,000 a year, you invested that amount of money for nine years in a tax-free money-market account, and that you averaged just 4 percent a year on those funds. In nine years you would have $44,000. Now let's look at what a premium for the same policy would be at age 59 assuming you were in the same state of health: about $5,200 a year, assuming there are no price increases (a big assumption). That is a difference of about $1,200 a year in what insurance would cost you at age 50. If you took that $44,000 and just left it in that money-market fund, it would generate more than $1,700 a year in interest. Even after paying tax on the income you should have enough to cover the $1,200 more a year you would need. Meanwhile, you haven't had to pay premiums during those nine years.

There are risks to this strategy. One is that something might happen to you during those nine years that would call for long-term care insurance. Only you can determine the size of that risk and your tolerance for it. Another is that premiums will go up for new policy holders but not for those who are currently owners of a policy. Finally, you should take into consideration that you will have lost nine years of the compounding of your daily benefit amount. So if you bought a policy at age 50 for $130 a day benefit with an inflation rider of 5 percent compounding, then when you were 59 your benefit

amount would have grown to be worth $202. To be even, you might want to buy a policy starting at $202 a day benefit when you were 59.

I repeat, however, that my biggest reason for advising you to wait until 59 is to make sure you have a grip on your long-term financial picture so that you know you can truly afford your policy until the day that you use it or die.

I'm 68 years old. Have I missed the boat?

It depends on your financial situation. Your premiums are going to be a lot higher than if you had bought earlier, but the cost could still be well worth it, if you can afford to pay it. The cost of a good policy in 2009 is more than $9,000 for a 68-year-old; that is more than twice as much as if you had purchased it in your 50s. If you enter a nursing home at age 84, you will have paid $9,000 a year for 16 years, or $114,000. That's a lot of money, but what if you are in that nursing home for one year (a year and nine months less than the average stay)? Sixteen years from now it will cost well over $200,000 a year to live in a pleasant nursing home, almost twice what you will have paid in premiums. I realize this example does not take into consideration what would happen if you had invested the premiums instead of buying a policy, but the point is still valid, for most people do not invest their premiums annually. Almost everyone over the age of 49 is a good candidate for long-term care insurance. I don't care how high your premium will be, the total cost of your long-term care policy is most likely going to be less than the cost of one year in a nursing home. So even at age 68, long-term care insurance still makes sense for you, if you can afford it.

How much should long-term care insurance cost me?

You should spend no more than 5 to 7 percent of your monthly income on premiums. This is a type of insurance where it really pays to compare prices because policies vary significantly in terms of the benefits they offer.

That said, you may not have to pay as much as you think you will if you find the right company. Based on your age and assuming that you are in excellent health, below is one example of what an excellent long-term care policy with a $200 daily benefit amount, five-year coverage, 20-day elimination period, a compound 5 percent inflation provision, and full nursing-home and home-care coverage might cost you in 2009. (I'll explain more about the benefits you should look for below.)

Annual Premiums

Age	Cost
54	$4,278
55	$4,347
56	$4,553
57	$4,771
58	$4,998
59	$5,236
60	$5,485
61	$5,747
62	$6,020
63	$6,436
64	$6,881
65	$7,356
66	$7,864
67	$8,406
68	$9,172
69	$10,007
70	$10,918

Please note: The benefit period, the elimination period, the inflation provision, and the home health-care coverage will all need to be identical when comparing prices among different companies. There can be big pricing differences among companies offering long-term care insurance (or any insurance, for that matter). I have seen policies from two or three carriers offering essentially the same benefits with a difference of up to $1,500 a year. When you compare prices, make sure that you are comparing apples with apples—comparing policies with exactly the same benefits across the board. Otherwise your price comparisons won't yield the information you're really looking for.

What should I look for in a long-term care policy?

You should look for an appropriate daily benefit amount that reflects the cost of skilled-facility care in your area, an adequate benefit period, an elimination period that's between zero and 50 days, an inflation provision, and home health-care coverage.

What is the daily benefit amount?

The *daily benefit amount* tells you the maximum amount the policy will pay per day if you use the benefits. Policies generally offer between $50 and $400 a day for nursing care and 50 to 100 percent of nursing-care benefit levels for home health-care. If the policy that you are considering is sold under the original guidelines, as of the year 2009 I would recommend purchasing about a $200-a-day benefit (without considering the inflation provision, which I'll say more about later), which is the average cost of nursing care today. Ultimately, the benefit amount you select will depend on how much of your care you expect the policy to pay for. Calculate the daily benefit amount you need by estimating how much other income you will have and will be willing to apply to a long-term care stay at the time you might need to begin using benefits.

These days policies are being offered based on what is known as a pool-of-money or benefit-account approach. In the pool-of-money or benefit-account design, the policy starts off looking like the traditional policies, in which you purchase a specific benefit amount for a specific period of time. However, in the new policies, the insurer takes the total amount of benefits you have purchased with your premiums and conceptually puts it in a benefit account. At claim time, that account can be accessed for any kind of covered service. Using the example of a four-year plan at $100 a day, this would mean that the insured has $146,000 (without considering inflation benefits) available to fund his or her care needs within the daily or monthly policy limits. This results in a policy that will pay for home health care or a nursing home, in any order, in any combination, for as long as the pool of money or benefit account lasts. So, even though the original policy that was purchased this way had a four-year benefit period, in reality there is no four-year limit on your use of the policy; the only real limit is the $146,000 ceiling that was established when the

policy was purchased. When the pool of funds or benefit account runs out, your coverage ends. This is a good way to use your coverage to best meet your needs.

What is a benefit period?

The *benefit period* is the length of time some of the older policies will pay for your long-term care. For an individual, I recommend choosing a four- to six-year plan; for qualifying couples, I recommend choosing a six- to eight-year shared plan, if your insurance company offers it.

What is an elimination period?

It's like the deductible in your medical insurance. It is the time period during your initial stay in a nursing home, to take one type of long-term care option, when you will not receive benefits. Such periods are typically between zero and 100 days, and you are responsible for paying your costs until the period ends. Compare the premium costs between a shorter elimination period (say, 30 days) and a longer period (60 to 90 days). If the difference in premium cost is not significant (it will usually be just $100 to $200 a year), consider buying the shortest possible elimination period you can afford in order to adequately protect your assets and estate. If it is available and you can afford it, I always recommend a zero-day elimination period, but your elimination period should never be longer than 50 days. Think about it—wouldn't you rather pay an extra $200 a year now versus your expenses of about $300 a day, years from now, for 30 to 90 days? If it pains you to pay less than a dollar a day for that extra coverage today, how are you going to feel about payments of about

$300 a day down the road? Be smart and go for the shorter elimination periods.

What is an inflation option provision?

This provision allows for your daily benefit and your lifetime benefit account maximum to increase by a certain percent each year to help keep pace with rising long-term care costs. Some policies may cap this growth by an amount or by an age limitation. Other policies let you increase your benefit maximum every few years by purchasing additional insurance at your current age rate. This is crucial. The younger you are when you purchase your insurance, the more time you will have for the benefit maximum to grow. If you are between the ages of 40 and 70, the best choice will be the 5 percent compound inflation benefit with no age limit or financial cap, if you can afford it. After age 70, the decision to buy an inflation option depends on your particular situation. The 5 percent simple interest choice is less expensive in the early years, but a larger initial benefit may prove to be short-sighted.

What are non-forfeiture benefits?

If you decide to drop your long-term care coverage, non-forfeiture benefits could give you back some of the premiums you've paid in. Sounds good, but please keep in mind that a non-forfeiture benefit can make your premiums up to 35 percent more expensive. If you can afford this, it's probably better to take the extra money and invest it for growth on your own.

What should I look for in the home health-care provision of a policy?

In general, long-term care means nursing-home care, which means treating a condition from which one is not expected to recover. Home health care (HHC) may include long-term care, but more typically it means care that is provided for shorter periods while one recovers from an accident or illness at home. The home health-care (HHC) clause allows you to receive certain kinds of care at home if this care is administered by professionals, friends, or individuals deemed qualified by the insurance company. Some plans state that if you belong in a nursing home but would rather be at home instead, the policy will pay your long-term care benefits at home, just as if you were at a nursing home. I view HHC as coverage you would need at home for the short term—for a broken hip, for example. With HHC, you are expected to get well. With long-term care, you are not expected to get better.

Many insurance companies include far more than traditional home care in their policies. There are policies that offer benefits for assisted-living centers, adult day-care centers, adult congregate-living facilities, and other community-based care providers. So it is important that you find a policy that has a broad emphasis on home-care benefits. Make sure to find out what is covered.

Why is it important that an HHC policy offer so many different kinds of care alternatives?

It is important that you have a choice of the kind of care you may want instead of having to take the kind of care that your carrier is willing to pay for. Given that most of us would prefer to avoid being put in a home or being institutionalized at all, it is crucial to know that there are policies out there today that contain options that include being able to move into a private residence that has been converted to allow barrier-free access and has some monitoring staff available around the clock, but that offers you a private room, furnished with your own belongings. This kind of benefit is a growth market for the future. Nursing homes are now mostly providing skilled care for patients who used to be in hospitals. More and more custodial patients are finding better care options outside the nursing home.

How much coverage will I need in the home health-care portion of my policy?

In years past, when there were not many options available, I used to recommend 50 percent of the nursing-home long-term care benefit amount for HHC. So if your long-term care daily benefit amount were $100, the HHC daily benefit amount would be $50. I now recommend that your HHC benefit be 100 percent of what the long-term care benefit amount is for three reasons:

1. In major metropolitan areas, HHC services may cost every bit as much as nursing homes do.
2. Although HHC services typically cost less than nursing homes do today, I expect demand will drive up the costs of services in the future.
3. If you purchase the pool-of-funds policy, there is no penalty if the costs of your HHC are much lower, because the money stays in the pool and is available for you to spend on other types of care or on extending the time the current care plan will be active. (To go back to the $146,000 example, it would take eight years to exhaust this benefit if your expenses were only $50 per day, even if you had purchased a four-year plan.)

My husband is in an assisted-living facility. Would LTC insurance have covered this cost?

It depends. Most policies cover care in an assisted-living facility at some level. The definition of a long-term care facility may vary by policy, by insurance company, and by state. Again, you want a policy that is flexible about where you receive care and allows you to have as many options as possible when you need them. But while you want the policy to be flexible, you don't want it to be vague: Ideally, your policy should specify a number of different types of facilities that would be acceptable to you, and it should cover you in all states, in case you move. A good policy will follow you wherever you go in the United States. Make sure it does before you buy it.

What is a waiver of premium?

This means that once you actually begin to receive benefits and continue to receive them, you won't pay premiums. Check to see if there is a stated period of time for you to be receiving benefits before this waiver goes into effect. All good policies should have a waiver. Also, in a good shared policy, once you have been paying premiums for at least 10 years *and* one of you begins to need long-term care, premiums should stop for both of you. At the death of the partner needing long-term care, the surviving partner should have a paid-up policy without needing to pay further premiums.

What does restoration of benefits mean?

Let's say you had a four-year benefit period but were able to leave the LTC facility after three years. If you then stay out of the facility for 180 days or more, this provision compels the company to restore your benefits back to the full four years. This way, if you end up in the nursing home again, you will be covered for another four full years. In an individual policy, I would not pay more for this provision. But in a shared policy, if the increase in cost is 6 percent or less of the annual premium *and* the surviving partner's benefit is restored in full after the death of the partner in the nursing home, I would seriously consider it.

My company offers a group long-term care insurance plan. Should I just sign up for that?

Employer-offered group plans may be cheaper than individual plans, but most have longer elimination periods, limited benefit periods, fairly rigid benefits, poor inflation protection, and no spousal discounts. And, depending on the state, they may not be guaranteed renewable. Indeed, your employer and/or the insurance company can cancel the plan without your consent. So check out the costs and benefits of an individual plan and compare them to the plan your employer is offering. Also, if you purchase a group plan, make sure that you can convert your policy into an individual policy should you leave the group—for example, quit your job.

What conditions must be met before the benefits start coming?

Partly, the answer depends on whether your pol-icy is tax-qualified or non-tax-qualified. (Please see page 241 for a complete description of the differences.) Among other differences, tax-qualified and non-tax-qualified policies have different benefit eligibility triggers and definitions for activities of daily living (ADLs), the six activities you need to be able to do to function normally, including bathing, eating, dressing, transferring, continence, and going to the toilet. Typically, your benefits become available to you when you cannot perform two or more of these ADLs, so it's important to ask how each of these is defined in your policy.

Is there anything else I need to look out for when buying a long-term care policy?

Remember that you must be relatively healthy at the time you purchase long-term care insurance. Most policies no longer require it, but check to make sure that a hospital stay is not required before the insurance company will pay for your long-term care in any facility. Your benefits should be as comprehensive as possible: They should cover custodial (or personal) and intermediate care, at home or in an institution, including adult day care.

What else should I look for?

Your benefits should not exclude preexisting conditions, at least not for more than six months after the policy goes into effect. Once you begin receiving benefits, you should not have to pay premiums after a maximum time period of 90 days, including the elimination period, until you are on your own again. You should have to satisfy the elimination period only once, no matter how many times you need care. There should not be any changes in premium levels unless there is an across-the-board increase for everyone who carries the plan in your state, region, or country. It should be a guaranteed renewable plan and have a grace period, keeping your policy in effect in case you forget to make a payment. If you purchase a benefit period that is less than lifetime, make sure that the policy has the "restoration of benefits" feature.

How can I know whether the company I'm thinking about is a good one?

The most important thing to be sure of is that the company you're considering is a financially strong one that is going to remain in the long-term care business over the long haul. When I first started researching long-term care insurance in 1986, there were only about four companies selling it. Today, there are about 130. That number fluctuates at any given time by 30 or 40, depending on which companies have decided to give it a try and which have decided to check out of the long-term care business. Here are the questions you must ask about each company you are considering in order to find out whether the company will still be supplying long-term care benefits when you may need them.

- How long has the company been selling long-term care insurance? The only acceptable answer is ten years, minimum. If the answer is one year, two years, or three years, the company is still experimenting.
- How much LTC insurance does the company currently have in force? The only acceptable answer is hundreds of millions of annual premium dollars. With that much money in long-term care, the company is already making a handsome profit—and not thinking of getting out of the business.
- How many times has the company had a rate increase for those who already own a policy? The only acceptable answer is two times or fewer.
- In how many states is the company currently selling long-term care insurance? The only acceptable answer is in every state. Because each state regulates its own insurance policies, and because it is tedious and expensive for insurance companies to be licensed to sell every kind of insurance in every state, if the company is selling long-term care insurance in only one state—yours—you can be sure it is still experimenting.
- Is your company on the block to be sold? The answer you want to hear is no. Even if the company has a great long-term care insurance track record now, what would happen if the company that bought it wasn't one you felt safe with?
- What are the company's ratings from the following independent companies, all of which rate the safety and soundness of insurance carriers? Ask your LTC insurance agent to show you the current financial safety ratings issued by these major rating companies. I have included the minimum grade that is acceptable:
AM Best: A+ or better
Moody's: AA or better
Standard & Poor's: AA or better
The only acceptable answer is that at least

two of the major insurance rating companies must have awarded top ratings to the company you're considering.

- Is the company certified by the Insurance Marketplace Standard Association (IMSA)? The only acceptable answer is yes. Good companies regulate themselves and their market practices to be able to display this seal of approval.

LIFE INSURANCE

Originally, life insurance was designed to protect people while they were relatively young, in case the family breadwinner died early. Later, if the breadwinner survived until the children had grown up and he or she had built a retirement nest egg, the insurance would be canceled.

Today, things are different. A huge industry exists to sell you as much life insurance as it can, whether you need it or not. And if you don't watch out you will end up paying huge commissions for unnecessary coverage. There's a good reason why people say that life insurance isn't something you buy; it's something that's sold to you.

Many people think of life insurance as a universal financial-planning tool, as a safe haven for savings and a substantial legacy for the family after they are gone. As we grow older, however, there are often better places to hold—and grow—our money, and there can be serious disadvantages to leaving a large life insurance policy among our assets when we die. In any case, no one should ever use life insurance, or any kind of insurance, as a savings vehicle.

If you're single and have no dependents at all, you can skip this section, because there is no need for you to have life insurance. However, if you have relatives who depend on the money you bring in with every paycheck, the following information is essential for you to understand.

These are the four basic questions to ask yourself about life insurance:

- Do I need it?
- How much do I need?
- How long will I need it?
- What kind of life insurance policy do I need?

How do I know if I need life insurance?
Here's how. Compile a list of all your family's expenses and total them. After you have done this, review your expenses and figure out how dramatically your family's financial situation would change if your children were suddenly without one or both parents. Fixed expenses, such as the mortgage payment, would remain the same. Some expenses, such as the grocery bill, would decrease. What if the remaining partner had to go to work? Would your child-care situation change? Could the remaining partner's income cover the financial goals you've set for the future—paying for your children's education, for example? How much would it take to live? How much do you have saved?

Now compare the reduced income after the death of one or both parents with the expenses of maintaining the household. If the survivors would have enough to live, then you do not need insurance. You may still want some for peace of mind, but you don't *need* it—and there is a big difference between *needing* insurance and *wanting* it.

If your survivors would not have enough, then you need insurance to protect you and your loved ones.

How much life insurance do I need?

Most people think all they'd need is enough to help their family get by until the members come to terms with the loss. As a result, they usually sign up for the $50,000 or so worth of insurance that's part of their benefits package at work. But since an unexpected death affects different people in different ways, how much insurance you buy is a decision that must be discussed with the people who would be affected. All the questions must be asked: Would they feel comfortable knowing that they have enough money to get by for a year, or two, or eight?

My insurance agent says I don't need to go through all this—that I can just buy enough coverage to replace my salary for eight years. Is that wrong?

Many experts will tell you to purchase six to eight times your annual salary, but experts are not the ones who have to live your dependents' lives. You might prefer to know that everyone will be OK no matter what, even if no one is ever able to work again. Perhaps you want to provide for your children for ten years, rather than eight. Each of us has our own financial what-if comfort level.

The final decision should strike a balance between security and affordability.

Is there any kind of financial guideline you can give me?

An ideal death benefit would be equal to 25 times your beneficiaries' income needs. I know that sounds like a lot, but if your policy is that large, your survivors will be able to invest the proceeds in safe bonds (yielding 4 percent) and live off the income, without having to dip into the principal. That's a tremendous amount of security for them. And if you stick with term insurance, I think you will be surprised how affordable a large policy can be.

What's the theory behind that recommendation?

This is the idea: You want your insurance payment to be a sum of money that your beneficiaries can invest to generate enough income to cover their expenses without having to dip into the principal. If they end up having to use up some of the principal each year to meet their living expenses, they will eventually run out of money. You don't want that to happen.

In my case, if I die, I know that my wife would need to have some support, but she makes the same amount of money I do and I know she would continue to work. How do I figure out what she would need?

Assuming you also have monthly expenses of $3,000, in theory, all she would need from the insurance proceeds before taxes is $1,500 a month. (That is, assuming her financial needs will be roughly equal to what they were for both of you when you were still alive.) You have three choices. You can purchase the minimum amount of insurance needed to cover that shortage of $1,500 a month, which is $450,000 worth, plus whatever will be needed for first-year expenses (about $18,000). Or you can purchase $900,000 worth of insurance to cover all your expenses in case, at some later date, your wife won't be able to work. Or you can purchase any amount in between that would make you both feel comfortable.

OK, let's say that my wife needs only $1,500 a month. But I've bought a $900,000 policy, so investing half of that—actually, at 4 percent interest, a little more than half—should cover her needs. What should she do with the remainder of the $900,000?

She will want to invest enough safely for the principal to generate that $1,500 a month every year, without touching the principal. The rest she should invest for growth in case the day comes when she loses her job. If you had decided simply to purchase the minimum amount of insurance needed in this situation, which was $450,000, she would have to invest all of that to generate the $1,500 a month income she needed and hope she was able to keep on working while she built up a nest egg.

I did everything you said and I talked to my insurance agent, and the bottom line is, we just can't afford to buy as much insurance as I would like. Any suggestions?

Make sure your agent is pricing term life insurance for you. Term is far less expensive than other forms of life insurance that go by names such as whole life, universal life, and variable life. I strongly believe that term is the best insurance for the vast majority of people, and it literally costs a fraction of the other forms of life insurance. Insurance agents who rely on commissions are not necessarily going to recommend the least expensive option to you. But I will: Term life insurance is an affordable way to protect your family.

Are there any quote services that you particularly recommend?

Yes. Check with the following services; you would be surprised how much they can differ.

Select Quote: (800) 963-8688; *www.selectquote .com*

Accuquote: (800) 442-9899; *www.accuquote .com*

How long will I need to keep my life insurance policy?

That depends. As the years go by, the money that you're saving in your retirement plans, the money you accumulate on your own, and the mortgage you're paying toward owning your house outright will change how much insurance you need, or whether you need it at all. One of your goals should be to make sure that by the time you are retired, you'll have enough income from your retirement plans to support yourself and, later, your loved ones after you're gone. Once you have enough to live on, there will probably be no need for life insurance. That said, never, *never* cancel or attempt to change a policy without checking with your doctor and having a thorough physical, as you may want to keep insurance you otherwise would not have needed for medical reasons. Bottom-line goal: By the time you are 65, at the latest, your need for life insurance, and your need to pay the premiums on your life insurance, should be gone.

What kind of life insurance do I need?

In my opinion, there is only one kind of life insurance that makes sense for the vast majority of us: term life insurance. When you sign up for term insurance, you're buying a just-in-case policy for a finite length of time. These policies are not very expensive, especially if you're fairly young, because the insurance company knows you have relatively little chance of dying while the policy is in force.

I am 25 years old and single with no dependents. Should I buy life insurance?

In this situation, you probably don't need life insurance as much as you need to be saving for your retirement and possibly increasing your disability coverage. On the other hand, the younger you are, the cheaper your life insurance premiums will be, which is useful if you purchase a 20- or 30-year term policy with your future spouse and children in mind.

What is the difference between term life insurance and a cash value policy, also known as whole life insurance?

Term life insurance protects you for a certain number of years (typically 1 to 20), and once the "term" of the policy is over, you can usually renew the policy and begin another term, though at a higher cost. If you die during the term of the policy, the insurance company pays out a specific amount of money (called the death benefit) to your beneficiaries. Because you do not build any cash value and are paying for protection for a specific length of time, it follows that when you are younger, term life insurance is the least expensive kind of life insurance. However, the older you get, the more expensive term insurance becomes, since it is more likely that the company will have to pay out the death benefit. By the time you are in your 70s, the premiums on term life insurance will be very high but, if you have planned properly, you should no longer need it.

A cash value policy, or what is more commonly known as a whole life policy, is a "permanent" policy, in which you are guaranteed coverage for life. Your premiums are priced accordingly, since the insurance companies know that, unless you let the policy lapse, they will sooner or later have to pay out the death benefit. These policies have a cash value, which means that the insurance company takes your annual premium, deducts some administrative fees and a profit margin plus the cost of death protection, and puts the rest (your "cash value") into a savings account.

Which is better, term or whole life insurance?

Term life insurance is the most cost-effective insurance you can buy. There is really no comparison. Term life insurance policies are cheap. Why? Because people are living longer—beyond the term of coverage—so insurance companies don't have to pay out as many life insurance claims. This is key to understanding life insurance: Insurance companies sell insurance to make money. They will sell you a term policy at a reasonable rate when you are young because they know it is unlikely that you are going to die during the term. You want a flexible policy that offers you security without costing very much, because you probably won't ever need to use it. Whole life insurance is mostly just a costly way to maintain a savings account.

Are there different types of term life insurance policies?

Yes. You can buy what is known as a "level" term policy. With a level term policy, your premiums would be level for the term you have chosen, usually 5, 10, 15, or 20 years. The insurance company takes your current age and the term you choose into consideration and figures out the average stable premium you will have to pay to keep the policy in effect for all those years. Obviously, the older you are and the longer the term you sign up for, the higher the premium will be.

You can also buy annual guaranteed-renewable term insurance, where, at the end of each year if you renew the policy, the premiums increase to reflect your new age.

Another option is decreasing term insurance (which is normally used by people whose main financial obligation also decreases, like a mortgage). This kind of policy starts with a specific death benefit that decreases each year until your policy expires at zero.

If I get term life insurance, what size term should I look for?

The longest period of coverage that you can purchase is usually no more than 30 years. Many people, not only salespeople, may encourage you to get the longest term possible. However, I recommend buying a term that is simply long enough to protect your family until you have been able to accumulate enough money in your savings and investments to take care of your family.

My insurance agent offers policies that have names other than whole and term. Are there different types of cash value accounts?

Yes. The most common types are whole life, universal life, and variable life. Whole life and universal life policies mean that the insurance company will invest your cash value and give you a declared (though variable) interest rate. Variable life policies give you mutual-fund type options for your cash value and you can choose how to invest those funds.

So does my death benefit grow as my cash value accumulates?

In most cases, no. This is a decision you make when you purchase this type of insurance. Your death benefit is constant, which means it is paid out at the same rate at any time for as long as the policy is in effect. Your premiums are also constant in cash value policies, and are designed to remain the same until the policy matures at an age set by your particular policy, usually 95 or 100 (the age when your premium payments would cease and the cash value would equal the face amount). Most people, obviously, do not expect to live to age 100.

My insurance agent told me that cash value life insurance is better because it offers tax-favored growth. Is that true?

Yes and no. Money that you invest in a cash value life insurance policy will grow tax-deferred—if and when it grows. It is not uncommon for a whole life policy to lose money in its first five or six years, in part because of the commissions and administrative fees. Remember, the commissions on most cash value policies are high. This may explain why your insurance agent is so enthusiastic about this type of policy. There are many other ways to invest and reduce taxes without paying a commission or lots of fees: Put your money in an IRA or a 401(k) and you'll find a similar tax benefit and, the odds are, more growth.

What is universal life insurance?

This is a variation of whole life insurance, except that the investment portion of your insurance premiums goes into money-market funds and grows at a variable rate. After your first payment, this type of policy allows you to pay premiums at any time and in any amount within a particular minimum and maximum rate set in the contract. The premiums you pay and the interest that your money earns is the amount of cash value that your policy has at any given time, less the expenses of the insurance company, which can be considerable and can also increase over time. As with whole life insurance, the insurance company makes many of the investment decisions.

Because whole life and universal policies have cash values, if you decide not to keep your policy, or if you suddenly need money while you're alive, you can cash out. But commissions on life insurance policies are some of the most lucrative commissions in any business—and once you've paid them, you can't get them back. If your goal in buying life insurance is to put money aside, there are far, far better ways to save.

What is variable life insurance?

Similar to whole life insurance, this type of policy provides death benefits or cash values that vary according to the investment returns of stock and bond funds managed by your insurance company (although you can choose where to invest your premiums). This can be a very uncertain type of policy because your premiums change and there is no guaranteed cash value, although theoretically it can pay off at higher rates than whole or universal life policies. Remember, though, that the risk is to your money.

Can I borrow money against a whole life insurance policy?

You can take out what is called a policy loan, as long as it doesn't exceed the cash value your policy will have on its next anniversary. In many cases, you don't ever have to repay this loan, since the amount of money left in the policy generates enough interest to pay the loan charges. If you don't repay the loan, however, your death benefit decreases by the amount of your loan plus interest. The interest rate you have to pay for a loan is set in your contract.

I realize that you don't recommend it but, if I wanted to, could I convert a term policy into a whole life policy?

Yes, many term policies are "convertible," which means they can be exchanged for another type of policy, including whole life. Frequently, this involves paying the difference between the premiums for the two policies. But in most cases, I'd advise you not to do this. If you are unhappy with your term insurance for some reason, look for a different term policy that will better meet your needs. Make sure your new policy is in force before you drop your old one.

OK, I made the big mistake and bought a whole life policy. What should I do with it now?

First, you need to go to a doctor and make sure that you have a clean bill of health. Then you can apply for and purchase a term life insurance policy for whatever length of time you think you require in order to save enough money to provide for your family if you die. Once you have been approved for your new term policy, then and only then should you cash out your whole life policy and invest the "cash value" in a good no-load mutual fund. Add to your investment what you're saving on premiums, which will be much lower now.

I told my insurance agent that I want to cash out my whole life policy but he says I'm crazy because it's only over the long run that these policies make money. He says if I take it out now I'll be losing money. Is that true?

You may be losing some of your investment in the short term because the insurance company has deducted so many fees, but you are almost certainly going to make it up and then some over the long run (ten or more years) if you invest that cash value and the excess premium money in a no-load mutual fund or exchange-traded fund (ETF). The insurance company is the party that is really going to lose money, because they won't have the use of yours anymore.

Will I have to pay taxes if I cash my whole life insurance policy out?

If you cancel the policy, you get a lump sum payout and you will pay taxes on it only if the cash value plus your dividends equals more than the total of all the premiums that you paid into

it—frequently, it won't be, which is why you are cashing it out in the first place.

What happens if I stop paying my premiums on a whole life insurance policy?

Usually you have a certain amount of time (often a few years) to reinstate or renew the policy, as long as you can establish your insurability again. If you find yourself in this situation, don't just automatically get your old policy reinstated. Make sure that it is still better than any new policy you could get.

What is double indemnity?

Many life insurance policies pay double the death benefit if the death of the insured is accidental. For instance, if your death happened because of a car accident, and you had this feature on a $200,000 policy, it would pay out at $400,000. Medical emergencies, such as heart attacks, do not count. It should be noted, however, that this benefit is paid very infrequently. For example, if the insured gets into an accident and dies after 90 days, most policies with this feature will not pay the double indemnity benefit. This benefit is largely a scare tactic, and not worth the cost.

Is suicide covered in a life insurance contract?

If the policy doesn't specifically exclude it, suicide often becomes covered two years after you purchase your policy. During those two years, if the insured commits suicide, the insurance company normally returns the premiums but doesn't pay out a death benefit.

My husband of ten years just died. When I notified his life insurance company, I found out

that his first wife is still the beneficiary on his policy! They didn't even speak to one another and I know he must not have realized that he never made the switch. Is there any way to challenge this?

Unfortunately, it will be difficult and expensive to challenge your husband's mistake. You will have to notify the insurance company of your intent to dispute the beneficiary, and it will be up to a court to decide whether your claim is appropriate, which often requires proving that your spouse was incompetent. This is why it is crucial that you review your insurance policies periodically and make sure that everything is up to date.

I've just had a baby. Now my mom is telling me that I will need to buy life insurance in my newborn daughter's name. Is this a good idea?

No, don't do it. Remember, life insurance is meant to replace income that other people are dependent on. Your baby has no income and doesn't need her own life insurance. She needs your life insurance, if something should happen to you.

Is it ever a good idea to take out a life insurance policy on another person?

It can be, if you have a financial interest in that person, usually a spouse or a business partner.

Do you always need to take a medical exam before you can buy life insurance?

Almost always. The major exception is if your employer offers life insurance through a group policy.

If I have a terminal illness, is it too late for me to get life insurance?

In most cases, yes. Major insurers will generally not sell you life insurance under these circumstances, although certain people with HIV may be able to purchase such a policy.

What is a living death benefit?

These are riders on life insurance policies, also known as accelerated death benefits. They pay out your death benefit while you are still alive, usually if a doctor certifies that you are terminally ill with less than a year to live. The idea is that you can use these funds for medical care or comfort. The benefit may increase the price of your premiums and usually doesn't pay as much as your heirs would have received after your death.

What is a viatical settlement?

This is another expensive option used almost exclusively by people who are terminally ill. A viatical company will pay you part of the cash value of your whole life insurance policy while you are still alive in exchange for ownership of your policy. They will continue to pay your premiums and they will collect the full benefit after you die. This is a good option if you really need the cash, but it means that you are selling your policy for less than it is worth. It also means you are not leaving your death benefit to the loved ones whom you purchased the policy to protect.

My brother and his wife got a second-to-die life insurance policy. What is that?

This type of insurance, which is sometimes called a survivorship life policy, insures two people, usually spouses, and doesn't pay until both insured people have died. Such a policy is normally worth considering only if you are going to leave a very large estate that will incur substantial estate taxes.

Federal tax law allows you to leave an unlimited amount of money, tax-free, to your spouse. When your spouse dies, the federal taxes will be due on both your estates, and usually must be paid within nine months of the death of the second spouse. A second-to-die life insurance policy could theoretically be used to cover those taxes.

Keep in mind that, as of 2009, federal estate taxes are due only when your estate is worth more than $3.5 million (anything over the exempt amount will be taxed at a rate starting at 45 percent). Unless Congress votes to change the law, the estate tax is scheduled to be repealed for 2010, and revert to $1 million in 2011. If you don't have this amount of wealth, don't even think about buying such a policy. If you think that your estate will be large enough to be subject to federal estate taxes, see a good estate-planning lawyer before you buy one. You may be able to avoid estate taxes in ways that make more financial sense for you, such as establishing trusts.

Is there anything else I need to consider when purchasing second-to-die life insurance?

Ask the agent what would happen in the event that you and your spouse divorced. Is there any provision that allows you to divide or alter the policy? Also, find out what provisions the policy makes, if any, should the estate-tax laws change in a way that would make the insurance unnecessary.

Can I make a trust the beneficiary of my life insurance policy?

Yes. Once your trust is set up, just ask your insurance company what specific language is required when you designate the trust as your beneficiary. (You might, for example, need to designate the name of your trustee, in his or her capacity as trustee.)

Is there any other way to reduce the amount of life insurance I need?

If you are married, you can consider joint and survivor benefits from your retirement plan to make sure part of your income will continue to be provided to your spouse. When you retire and are entitled to begin receiving your pension, you will have a series of joint and survivor options, which means that you can choose what percentage of your monthly pension you want your spouse to receive after you die. If you take a reduced payment while you are alive, your spouse will receive proportionally more after you die. This can reduce your life insurance needs.

I'm going to go for the 50 percent joint and survivor benefit for my wife because I figure she'll need about half my income since one can live more cheaply than two. Does that sound right?

That's a very common way of thinking about your joint and survivor benefits, but it is often wrong. Even though your wife will only need to support herself after you die, her cost of living may continue to rise. All her bills aren't going to be cut in half when you die. For example, the taxes on your home, if you own one, will only increase, as will the costs of maintaining the property. Find out how much money would be deducted from your pension check if your joint and survivor benefit was as high as it could be (100 percent) and consider whether you'll really miss the extra money.

DISABILITY INSURANCE

We are more likely to consider how to take care of our families after we die than we are to consider how we would take care of ourselves, and them, if we were to become disabled. Just think about it—if you were injured so severely that you could no longer work, how would you pay your bills? In financial terms, disability is potentially more problematic than dying. Dead, you have no further expenses. Disabled, you not only can't work, but your expenses may be higher, depending on what kind of medical care and services you need to accommodate your disability.

What is disability insurance and who needs it?

If you were seriously ill or injured, disability insurance replaces a portion of the salary you were making before you became disabled and unable to work. Single and self-employed people should seriously consider disability policies if there would not be financial support from another source if you became so sick or injured that you were unable to work. Even if you have a partner who could make up some of your income, you need to consider whether you and your family could survive comfortably without your salary.

How is disability defined?

A disability is defined as a limitation of your physical or mental ability to work resulting from sickness or injury. It may be partial, in which case you are unable to perform certain job functions, or total, in which case you are unable to work at all.

Is disability insurance the same thing as workers' compensation?

No. Workers' compensation protects you if you are injured while performing your job. Disability insurance is a form of health insurance that replaces all or part of your income while you are injured or ill for any reason. You may already have disability coverage if you work for a large company. You normally start receiving disability benefits three to six months after you become injured and unable to work.

Doesn't the Social Security Administration (SSA) insure me if I'm disabled?

It surely does, but there are good reasons for going to the private insurance market for disability insurance, if you can afford it.

What sort of coverage is offered by the SSA?

Not a whole lot. The average disability benefit in the United States (paid out, incidentally, to approximately 7.6 million beneficiaries across the country) was $1062 a month for 2009. But this benefit can make a huge difference to a disabled worker and his family.

Who qualifies?

In order to qualify, you typically need to have earned 40 work credits; half of which must have been earned in the 10 years ending with the year you become disabled. (In 2009 you earned one work credit for every $1,090 in wages. You can earn up to four credits a year. For the most recent income/credit rules go to *www.ssa.gov.*)

Younger workers with less than 40 credits (10 years of employment) can still qualify for benefits with fewer credits.

To receive a disability benefit the beneficiary must prove that he or she has a significant physical or mental condition that can be expected to result in death or that has lasted, or can be expected to last, for a continuous period of 12 months or longer (the rules for children are different). The disability must also prevent the beneficiary from engaging in any substantial gainful activity. These qualifications must be "validated" by your doctor. The SSA will not accept the diagnosis of a chiropractor, an acupuncturist, or a physical therapist.

To receive benefits you must not earn more than the SSA's Substantial Gainful Activity (SGA) limit. In 2009 the monthly SGA limit was $980. (For blind persons the 2009 SGA was $1,640.) The SGA limit changes annually; you can find the most recent information at *www .ssa.gov.*

The SSA has compiled a list of conditions that it considers "disabling." You can find the most recent list of impairments that qualify for disability insurance at the *www.ssa.gov* website. Type "disability evaluation" in the homepage search box. Or contact your local Social Security office for assistance.

Qualifying impairments are divided into 15 broad categories:

* Musculoskeletal System
* Special Senses and Speech
* Respiratory System
* Cardiovascular System
* Digestive System
* Genitourinary System
* Hematological Disorders
* Skin Disorders
* Endocrine System
* Impairments that Affect Multiple Body Systems
* Neurological
* Mental Disorders
* Malignant Neoplastic Diseases
* Immune System Disorders

Within each category are dozens of subcategories with specific eligibility test/requirements. To learn the requirements for a specific condition to be deemed eligible, go to the Social Security website, or ask for assistance at your local Social Security office.

Is it possible to be declared disabled by a commercial insurance company and not by the Social Security Administration?

Yes. Each insurance company sets its own eligibility requirements. It is entirely possible to be deemed disabled by a commercial insurance company and not by the Social Security Administration. A key question often is: Disabled for what sort of work? To receive benefits, the SSA requires that you be disabled from doing almost any sort of work, while commercial companies may require only that you be disabled from doing your own particular line of work. Of course, the cost for broad coverage can be high.

So under SSA rules, I mustn't be able to work at all?

Not "gainful" work. The Social Security Administration defines gainful employment as any employment from which you are earning $980 or more per month (in 2009).

Can a person survive solely on Social Security disability benefits?

It's extremely difficult, if not impossible. For that reason and others, it is important that you find out whether there is any job that your limited physical condition will permit you to do. It is also important that you find out exactly what benefits you may have coming to you from any other sources. Remember, the Social Security Administration with all its attendant benefits, whether retirement, disability, survivors, or dependents, was initiated in the 1930s as a kind of rock-bottom safety net, not as a replacement for your entire income.

PRIVATE COMMERCIAL DISABILITY INSURANCE

I hope I've said enough about the SSA's disability insurance program to indicate its weaknesses—that is, your vulnerabilities if you depend on it. The benefits are by no means to be sneezed at. Nor, for that matter, are the disability insurance plans that may be available through your employer, usually in the form of workers' compensation. For many people, however, the coverage provided by social insurance of this nature is simply not enough—for them or their families. To find out if they are enough for you, ask yourself a hard question: If I were to become seriously ill or injured, could I and my

family survive comfortably without my earned income? If the answer is no, then commercial disability insurance is the way to go.

What should I look for in a disability policy?

Ideally you should have coverage that would pay you the typical maximum benefit of 70 percent or so of your income after an accident that leaves you unable to work at your current job. It should cover you in case of an illness or an accident, it should always be noncancelable and guaranteed renewable, and, in the best case, should offer a residual benefit protection.

Beyond that, I would want a policy that covered me for what is known as "owner's occupation," not "any occupation." As I said, this is the option that most sharply differentiates what's available on the market from what social insurance offers. An owner's-occupation policy means that if I become disabled and can no longer perform my current occupation, regardless of what other kinds of work I might be able to do, the insurance company will pay me benefits. An any-occupation policy would pay me only if I could not perform any job at all. Let's say I'm a writer and for some reason become disabled and unable to write. I would want my disability policy to pay me benefits even though I might be able, for example, to sell fruit from a cart. An any-occupation policy, of course, wouldn't pay unless I were unemployable.

Why is it so crucial that my disability insurance be guaranteed, noncancelable and renewable?

Because if it isn't, your insurance company can

cancel your policy. This way, the only reason your policy can be canceled is if you stopped paying your premiums. Also, your insurance company cannot increase the premium (generally until age 65) and change any policy provisions.

My agent suggested a modified-occupation disability policy. What does that mean?

This policy will pay you benefits only if you can't work at a job considered appropriate for someone of your age, education, and experience. Note that this might not mean the same job you had before. Say you play the violin in your city's orchestra but you have an accident, which seriously injures your hands. A modified-occupation disability policy would probably not pay out as long as you were still able to teach violin classes at a local college, for instance. Ask your agent to give you examples of what types of jobs you would be considered "qualified" for in a variety of different disabling circumstances. If the options would be unacceptable to you, you'll want to make sure that you have owner's-occupation coverage.

What if I can work at a new job, but it doesn't pay as well as the one I had when I became disabled?

This is another case in which it is important to know that you have the right kind of disability policy. You want your policy to have something called residual benefits, which means it will guarantee a certain percentage of your old job's income in comparison to your new job's income. For example, if your policy guarantees you a 70 percent residual benefit and you became disabled, you would be guaranteed 70 percent of the income you made in your old job. So if you were making $80,000 before your accident, but your new, post-accident job pays only $50,000, your insurance company will have to pay you $6,000 each year to make up the difference between your new salary ($50,000) and 70 percent of your old salary ($56,000).

What kind of elimination period should disability insurance have?

The elimination period, which is the amount of time after your injury or the onset of your illness when you receive no benefits, varies from policy to policy. Try not to have more than a 60-day elimination period. In the meantime, make sure that you are working toward establishing an emergency fund for yourself, if you have not already done so, so that you could cover the costs of living for a few months without your paycheck.

Would my disability benefits increase over time if I were disabled forever?

This is an important question. You would find it difficult, or impossible, to live on an income that doesn't keep pace with inflation. Cost of living adjustments (COLAs) or riders cover this possibility and they may be included in your policy or they may cost extra. These riders allow you to increase your coverage (and your premiums, usually modestly) periodically without having an additional physical.

CAR INSURANCE

Most of us know a little something about car insurance, probably more than we know about our medical insurance. Why? Because we are required by the state we live in to have certain types of coverage. But the state-mandated amount of coverage may not be enough. On the other hand, agents are only too happy to sell us *more* than enough. In this section, I hope to clarify what's the right amount for you.

What are the different kinds of standard coverage I can get for my car?

Standard car insurance includes four types of protection: auto liability, medical payments, collision, and comprehensive coverage.

Auto liability coverage protects you in case you cause an accident. It has two parts. The first is bodily injury liability, which pays your medical expenses and those of anyone else injured in the accident. There is no deductible for this portion of the coverage. Most states require you to have a minimum amount of liability coverage, but bear in mind that the minimum may not be adequate if, for example, you cause a serious accident and get sued for pain and suffering. You can also buy *medical payments* coverage, which will pay your expenses and those of your passengers if you experience a serious injury in a car crash, whether you caused the accident or not. Note, though, that car insurance medical benefits won't pay all medical expenses. There are limits.

The second part of the standard liability policy pays the repair expenses if you accidentally damage somebody else's property (like another person's car or house) with your car.

Collision insurance is an option. It is typically not required by the state. Among other things, it protects your car in the event of an accident,

whether you caused the accident or not. If your car is valuable, this might make sense. You can choose whether or not to have a deductible.

Comprehensive insurance, which is also optional, pays for the repair or replacement of your car if it is damaged by a fire, a falling object, an earthquake, a flood, theft, vandalism, or another type of non-automotive accident.

I keep seeing all those numbers that look like dates when I hear about auto liability. What does 30/50/20 mean, for example?

These numbers refer to the limits of your liability policy in a particular accident. If you have these particular numbers, it means you have $30,000 in bodily injury coverage per person, $50,000 in bodily injury coverage per accident, and $20,000 in coverage for property damage.

How much liability coverage should I have?

Standard minimum recommendations for homeowners and people with significant assets are at least $100,000 in bodily injury coverage per person, $300,000 in bodily injury coverage per accident, and $50,000 in property damage liability. Those with fewer assets should consider $15,000 in bodily injury coverage per person, $30,000 in bodily injury coverage per accident, and $10,000 in property damage liability.

Can my whole family and all of my cars be covered by one policy?

Yes, usually, although you don't have to set it up that way. Generally, eligible cars are any four-wheel vehicles owned by an individual or married couple, or leased under contract for at least six months. If one of you has a motorcycle or a motor home, for example, you may have to purchase additional coverage.

Apparently I live in a no-fault state. What does this mean, and do I need liability coverage?

Most states use a no-fault auto insurance system. Other states use traditional third-party systems to settle claims. No-fault states require drivers and their insurance companies to pay their own costs after a car accident, whether they were responsible or not. But you still may need liability insurance, because if you cause an accident and the costs to the other injured people are above a certain threshold, they can sue you. If they win a judgment against you and you don't have sufficient liability coverage, the difference may have to come out of your own pocket. In a state with a traditional third-party system, or a "fault" state, your insurance company pays your claim only if you can prove that you did not cause the accident.

Is the medical payments coverage required?

No-fault states typically require you to buy medical payments coverage, while fault states do not. An argument for buying this type of coverage anyway is that it will pay no matter who caused the accident.

Couldn't my medical insurance pay for this?

Good question: It pays to be on the lookout for duplicate coverage! You're quite right, your medical insurance might cover *you* in such a circumstance. But beware: It won't cover any passengers or other injured parties who are not covered by your health-care policy.

How do I know how much collision and comprehensive coverage I need?

This is generally the more expensive part of car insurance. It is optional in all states, although if you leased your car or took out a loan to buy it, the dealer or bank that loaned you the money probably requires you to purchase it. Most companies have vehicle pricing services. Blue-book valuations are not used very much. Most companies will insure for the price you paid for the car, as long as it was a reasonable cost. As usual, if the deductible is higher, you can reduce the price of the premiums.

Should my car insurance reimburse me for my replacement costs or for the actual cash value of my car if it's stolen or damaged?

It will cost you more in premiums to have replacement cost coverage, but it may be worthwhile because such coverage will replace or repair your car without deducting for its depreciation. Actual cash value policies only pay you for the value of the car at the time it is stolen or damaged, which is reduced to account for depreciation.

What if my car is damaged in an accident by a driver with no insurance? Do I have to pay for everything myself?

There is insurance you can purchase, called uninsured-motorists coverage, that would protect you in these circumstances. (There is also uninsured motorist property damage and a collision deductible waiver.) Some states require you to have this coverage; it kicks in if an uninsured driver hits your car and you have medical bills. There is also something called underinsured motorists coverage, which makes up some of the difference if a driver hits you and has some, but not adequate, insurance. In other words, you can make a claim on your own insurance policy if the person who hits you doesn't have any insurance for you to make a claim on. However, note that all of these policies have benefit limits.

How do I know how much car insurance I really need?

The state you live in and, if you borrow money to buy your car, the lending institution, will require you to have certain kinds of coverage. Basic policies usually include some combination of liability, collision, comprehensive, uninsured or underinsured motorist, and medical payments coverage. As for what level of coverage you need, consider your personal situation in order to figure out what will make you feel safe: Is your car brand new or old? How much would it cost you to replace it? Do you have the resources to pay your medical bills and car repairs? Do you have valuable assets you want to protect?

My son just turned 16 and got his driver's license. My car insurance premiums are going to increase like mad if I add him to my policy. Is there anything else I can do?

If your son is going to drive, he's got to have insurance, and insurance companies know that young drivers are risky drivers, so they charge you high rates to protect themselves. If your son isn't going to be taking his car to school every day, you can try to have him classified as an occasional driver, although not all companies will allow you to do this. Many companies do offer modest discounts if he has good grades or has taken a particular type of driver's education course, so ask your agent about these rules. Finally, if you want to save on car insurance costs, not only should you not buy your son a new car, you should have him driving the oldest and cheapest car you own. That is, as long as it's a safe car—saving money on your premiums isn't everything!

Do I have to put my kids on my car insurance policy? Couldn't I make them get their own?

You could, but unless the kids are independently wealthy, you won't save money. In general, it will be more expensive for your teenager to have his own individual car insurance than to increase the premiums on your family policy.

Is there any way to reduce my auto insurance costs?

The premiums on your car insurance are based on, among other things, your age, your sex, where you live, the type of car you drive, and your driving record. In some states a version of your credit score can also impact the premium you are offered. The higher your credit score the lower your premium. However, there are a surprising number of small discounts that it is possible to negotiate. When you price different car insurance policies, make sure the agent knows if you have a clean driving record, because some companies give discounts to drivers who have no points on their licenses. Most insurance companies reduce your premiums based on a combination of your age, sex, and marital status. (Twenty-five is the general rule for single women and married men; 30 is the general rule for single men. Married women are often eligible for the lower rate no matter what their age.) If you are in college or even graduate school and get good grades, some insurance companies will offer you small discounts, even for a few years past graduation. You can check with your company to see how they do it; some demand a GPA of 3.0 or higher, some require you to be on a dean's list, and others want to know that you are in the top 20 percent of your class. Ask your insurance agent for a list of cars that are considered "lower risk" and make sure that your agent knows that your car has air bags and other special safety features, such as an alarm system or antilock brakes, if it does. If there are multiple cars in your house, see if you are entitled to a multiple-car discount.

These discounts might seem arbitrary, but they aren't. All the discount-qualifying characteristics mentioned above are statistically associated with drivers who have fewer accidents. Umbrella insurance may also reduce your insurance costs.

If my friend drives my car and gets into an accident, will my insurance policy still be effective?

If you loan your car every once in a while, your insurance policy should probably still cover an accident. Rates generally do not increase if a friend is involved in an accident while driving your car.

HOMEOWNER'S INSURANCE

If you financed your home when you purchased it, your lending institution required you to get some insurance on the building. But many people don't have enough coverage, and they pay too much for what they have. Your homeowner's insurance needs to cover the cost of rebuilding or repairing your house if it is damaged in a fire, a storm, a robbery, or other type of catastrophe. Below are the questions and answers that will help you decide if you have the right kind and right amount of insurance for your home.

What should a standard policy for my home cover?

Standard policies generally cover the house and its contents, the latter usually for 50 percent to 70 percent of the amount for which you insured the structure. In other words, if you insured your house for $200,000, your policy probably covers the contents of your home up to $100,000 to $140,000. Homeowner's policies also normally include liability coverage for damage or injury incurred inside or outside your house.

What if the contents of my house are worth more than 50 percent of what my home is insured for?

You can increase your content coverage; your premium will increase to cover the additional coverage. Make sure that personal property insurance covers you for the replacement cost of your possessions, not their actual cash value.

Figure out how much you need by making a list of everything you own and estimate what it would cost you to replace it all.

What is the difference between an actual cash value policy and a replacement-cost policy?

An actual cash value policy will reimburse you for the cost of your belongings less their depreciation, while a replacement-cost policy means that the insurance company must reimburse you for the actual cost of replacing the lost or damaged item. If you have a couch that you purchased for $1,000 a few years ago, a cash value policy might reimburse you only $800 for that couch, assuming a depreciation of 20 percent, while a replacement-cost policy would pay you enough to get the same couch. You can see why replacement-cost policies are better.

What are the basic types of homeowner's insurance I can buy?

There are seven basic types of homeowner's insurance, including renter's and condo owner's coverage.

- HO-1: A basic policy not available in all states. It is rarely purchased by consumers because of its limited coverage. It covers damage due to falling objects; the weight of ice, snow, or sleet; accidental discharge of water or steam from household appliances; freezing; volcanic eruption; and other perils.
- HO-2: Protects against 17 perils, including all those included in HO-1, plus the additional perils of fire, lightning, windstorm, hail, riot, and vandalism. People who have mobile homes are normally eligible for a variation of this type of policy.
- HO-3: This is the most common homeowner's policy. It protects your home against all perils except for those that are explicitly excluded by the policy. Some of the excluded perils include earthquakes, floods, termites, landslides, war, tidal waves, and nuclear accidents. Normal wear and tear, mechanical breakdown, vandalism if the home is unoccupied for more than 30 days, and continuous water seepage over a specified period of time are also typical policy exclusions.
- An HO-5 is most often added to HO-3, to expand the coverage to include additional perils.
- HO-4: This is renter's insurance. It does not cover the dwelling or detached structures, which are the landlord's responsibility to insure. It protects the possessions of tenants in a house, apartment, condo, or duplex against the same perils specified in HO-3. It also provides additional living expense, personal liability, and medical payments coverage. Make sure that your policy includes coverage for the replacement cost of your possessions, not their actual cash value.
- HO-6: This is a policy for co-op and condominium owners. Condominium insurance is like HO-4 (renter's) except that it takes into account the fact that you own the inner walls of your condo or town house. It can also fill in any gaps in your condo association's coverage. It is important to note that HO-6 policies include loss assessment coverage; however, the coverage limit included may be inadequate. If your co-op board or condo association needs

to assess charges because of some uninsured loss to the building or liability situation, having substantial loss assessment coverage is important.

- HO-8: This is a type of policy that covers perils like those listed in HO-1 but is meant for people who own older homes. It insures the house only for repair costs or its actual cash value as opposed to its replacement cost in cases where rebuilding the home with the materials and details of the original would be prohibitively expensive. Basically, this policy will pay to restore the damaged property but not at the level of quality or authenticity of the original. This policy is rarely offered.

Each homeowner's policy is divided into two sections. The first part covers your dwelling, other structures on the property, your personal property, and certain types of loss of use, such as rental or additional living expenses. The other part should provide personal liability coverage, medical payments coverage, and additional coverage for claims expenses, first aid, and damage to other people's property.

Why would I need liability coverage in my homeowner's insurance?

This type of coverage is designed to protect your assets if you are sued by someone who is hurt or whose property is damaged due to your negligence. This could be damage you or a member of your family causes or even your pet (although certain types of attack dogs, such as pit bulls and the like, may be excluded from your policy). An example would be if you lived in a two-family house, and you turned the water on to run yourself a bath but then took a phone call. You forgot about your tub, and it overflowed and damaged the ceiling of the unit below you. Liability coverage should pay to repair that damage. You may need special coverage for a home office.

If I already have comprehensive medical coverage, what does the medical payments section cover?

Again, your comprehensive health insurance should pay for you no matter what. This coverage is for protection in the event that *someone else* injures himself or herself on your property or because of your negligence and needs medical care. The classic example might be your mail carrier falling and injuring his back because your walkway was covered with ice and snow that you failed to remove.

Will homeowner's insurance cover all my personal property?

Regardless of the personal property limit you see on any policy, it is important to know that within this limit for personal property your policy also contains what are known as "special limits of liability." These are sublimits for special classes of property defined in the policy, such as jewelry, money, silverware, watercraft, and business personal property, for which the policy will not pay more than a smaller, set amount. Some of these special class sublimits can be eliminated by adding a personal article floater, sometimes known as a rider, to your home, condo, or renter's policy.

I rent one of my extra bedrooms to a college student. Would my homeowner's policy cover her property if my home were broken into?

Usually not, because most policies only cover your property (as the policyholder) and the property of people related to you who live in your house.

So if I have $200,000 in homeowner's insurance and my house is destroyed, do I get $200,000?

Not necessarily. In many policies you actually have to rebuild the structure to get this money, and limits often apply to the cost of rebuilding.

My agent says I can get extended replacement cost coverage or replacement cost coverage. Which is better?

If you have a total loss, say a fire destroys your home, you need to rebuild your home. If building costs have been rising faster than current home values you could find that the cost to rebuild exceeds the value of your policy. For example, you may have a $300,000 policy, but when you go to rebuild you find out the cost is going to be $360,000. That's where extended replacement coverage can save the day for you. This type of policy will pay out up to 125 percent or so of your policy's value. So in the above example, if you had a $300,000 policy with extended replacement cost coverage, your maximum payout could actually be as much as $375,000. If, however, your policy was for "replacement" cost your maximum payout would be limited to 100 percent of the policy's limit; in this example you would be eligible to receive no more than $300,000. I always recommend you consider getting "extended replacement cost" coverage. It buys you extra protection from rising building costs.

What should I do if something terrible happens and I need to make a claim?

Your insurance company will either send you a "proof of loss" form to complete or will arrange for an adjuster to visit your house. Either way, you need to document your loss as best you can to make sure that you get the full value that you are entitled to under the policy.

Is it true that if I make two homeowner's insurance claims, they can cancel my policy?

It depends on your insurance carrier but, yes, it can indeed happen. So if you can afford it, I always suggest you get a higher deductible and pay for the minor home-related losses out of pocket. Home insurance is for major disasters, not for filing small claims so you can get back the money you contributed to premiums. Filing one claim in most cases will do nothing to raise your rates or cancel your policy. But multiple claims, as few as two with certain policies, may cause your insurance company to raise your premiums or even cancel your homeowner's insurance policy. So it is best to get a policy with a high deductible, so that you've got no reason to file lower-cost claims. Another advantage to a higher deductible is that many insurance providers also offer a discount for such a policy.

What is the best way to document my losses?

Make a list of everything that was stolen or damaged, and provide a description of each item, the date you bought it, and, if you have replacement-cost coverage, what it would cost to replace it. If you have receipts, bills, photographs, or serial numbers, these things will generally help your case. Hold on to your damaged items until the adjuster has a chance to look at them. Take photographs or videos of any damage to your house, noting everything you want the adjuster to see, from cracks in the walls to missing tiles. Generally, you have one year to amend your claim if you find additional damage. It can be helpful, if tedious, to prepare for this possibility ahead of time by videotaping the contents and condition of your home and keeping records on the details of your major purchases. A safe-deposit box is a good place to keep these items.

You said jewelry might be restricted, and I found out that in fact it is restricted in my policy. My insurance company will only pay up to $1,000 for all jewelry, and I know my engagement ring alone is worth more than that. How can I increase this protection?

All policies limit the amount of money your insurance company would pay for specific items, such as jewelry or computer equipment. If the standard coverage is too low for your comfort, you can buy additional protection by adding an amendment called an endorsement to protect a particular item (for example, your engagement ring). But please make sure that it's really worth paying the extra premiums to extend your coverage on the items.

What is off-premise protection?

This facet of your homeowner's policy covers your possessions outside your house. For example, if you are mugged on the street or your luggage is stolen on vacation, off-premise protection should reimburse you for the items you lose. If you need to pay extra for this coverage,

think carefully about the size of the deductible and the likelihood that you would be carrying around items that are worth more. If the deductible is pretty high, and you don't normally run around wearing or carrying a lot of expensive stuff, it might not be worth it. And be careful if the big-ticket items you do tend to travel with include your engagement ring or your laptop computer. If they are only covered up to a certain level and you haven't extended their protection, a high deductible on top of the reimbursement restriction could make this coverage a waste of time.

What is additional living-expense protection?

In the event your home is damaged, your insurer will reimburse you for the costs associated with maintaining a temporary residence elsewhere while repairs are made on your home. Some policies offer unlimited coverage, in which you are reimbursed for the total cost of necessary expenses, without a time limitation. The most common loss of use coverage seen on homeowner's policies is coverage for a dollar amount equal to 20 percent or 30 percent of the dwelling limit listed on the policy.

When I purchased my home, my bank required me to get a certain level of homeowner's insurance, so that's what I got. If it weren't enough, wouldn't they have made me purchase more?

If your coverage isn't enough to cover the bank's potential loss, yes, they probably would require you to buy more coverage. But don't rely on the bank to tell you what amount of insurance you need. The bank only cares about covering the loan amount. You have additional needs: protecting your personal property, having solid additional expense coverage, and making sure your policy keeps up with rising building costs.

Bottom line, financially, what should I look for in homeowner's insurance?

You want to be able to replace your home and its contents if something should happen to your house. The cost of doing that after a catastrophic loss will probably be greater than the depreciated cash value of your property. This means that, as usual, you want replacement-cost coverage. You also want to have automatic inflation adjustments built into your policy.

UMBRELLA POLICIES

Umbrella insurance acts as a shield for your assets if you are sued. It is an extra layer of liability protection that kicks in when your other insurance policies, such as homeowners or auto, have reached their limits.

What does an umbrella policy cover?

An umbrella policy can offer coverage into the millions of dollars in case you are sued under either your homeowner's or auto insurance policy as the result of an accident or injury—including one involving a natural disaster, such as a storm that blows a tree, for example, onto a neighbor's house. The amount of coverage offered by umbrella policies varies, and the types of accidents a policy covers also vary.

I thought I was covered by my homeowners or auto policy for liability. Why do I need an umbrella policy?

Most homeowner's and auto insurance policies do offer some liability protection, but the coverage may not be enough to protect your assets in case of a suit. An umbrella policy provides protection that is over and above that of your normal auto and home insurance coverage, and that kicks in after your homeowner's or auto insurance policy has paid its maximum amount.

Let's say, for example, that you are a homeowner and your homeowner's policy insures you for liability up to a maximum amount of $500,000. If a person injures herself on your property, sues you for $1 million, and wins the lawsuit, without an umbrella policy it might be up to you to come up with the additional $500,000. If you have assets—such as a vacation home, investments, or a 401(k)—you could risk losing them to pay the uncovered portion of the judgment. If you own enough umbrella insurance, however, you will be covered for the difference. That's why, if you're considering an umbrella policy, I recommend buying a policy that fully protects you. Your combined insurance policies—homeowner's, auto, and umbrella insurance—should cover a maximum amount equal to at least the amount of your net worth.

How much will an umbrella policy pay?

Umbrella coverage ranges from $1 million to $5 million or more. And there may be additional costs; most insurance companies require you to have a certain amount of regular insurance coverage before you purchase an umbrella policy, so you may need to upgrade to the maximum coverage for both your home and your car, which can be costly.

How much does it cost?

You can expect to pay between $150 and $300 a year for $1 million in coverage, about $225 to $375 a year for $2 million in coverage, and about $50 more a year for every additional $1 million in coverage after that.

Do umbrella policies carry high deductibles?

There isn't a deductible per se. The idea is that your liability coverage on your home and auto policies is used first to settle a judgment. Only after you have used up the coverage from those policies does your umbrella coverage kick in. Essentially the amount of liability coverage stated on your primary auto and home policies is the umbrella deductible.

How do I decide whether I need umbrella insurance?

One issue to consider is whether you're susceptible to being sued for a large amount of money. Do you have a significant estate or substantial future earning power? If so, you might want to consider protecting it. Certain activities also put you at increased risk for a suit. Do you have clients, employees, or even friends with young children who visit your home often? Do you have neighbors, and would any damage to their homes be expensive to repair? Do you drive a car every day? Do you have a child who will soon be driving?

If you answer yes to one or all of these questions, you may want to think seriously about an umbrella policy. Given the potential catastrophes an extra policy can help you to avoid, the added

expense may be well worth the cost. If you answered no to all of the questions, it may be wisest to stick with the coverage you already have.

How much umbrella liability coverage should I buy?

Remember that you're covering damages to others. Do you live in a wealthy town, where you could be an easy target for a big settlement? Do you travel a lot? Do you entertain a lot? Do you operate a home-based business and have employees or clients coming to your home on a regular basis? (Many self-employed people wrongly assume that this is covered in their homeowner's policy.) If you answered yes to any of these questions, it is particularly important for you to have umbrella liability insurance.

But how much to buy is a decision that you should make with a financial professional, for there is no set formula.

MORTGAGE PROTECTION INSURANCE

What is the difference between private mortgage insurance and mortgage protection insurance?

If you bought your home without putting down at least 20 percent of its cost, you probably had to buy private mortgage insurance (PMI) to get your mortgage and you probably had to pay it until you had at least 20 percent equity in your home (and you had to initiate the cancellation process). Such insurance protects the lender in case you stop making your mortgage payments and the house goes into foreclosure. Some insurance agencies will offer to sell you after-death mortgage protection insurance, which is basically an arrangement where you pay your premiums and, should you die before your mortgage is paid and while your policy is still in effect, the insurance company pays off whatever is left on your mortgage.

Do the premiums on mortgage protection insurance go down as the balance on my mortgage goes down?
No. Your premiums will stay the same, because they are calculated with that decrease in mind.

How do I know if I need after-death mortgage protection insurance?
Most likely you do not, although you need to consider your individual situation. Do you have beneficiaries who will need a place to live without worrying about making mortgage payments? Still, in that case, I think it makes more sense to buy a good term life insurance policy that includes enough money to pay off your mortgage as well as provide for your family's other needs after you are gone.

We just refinanced our mortgage. What happens to our old mortgage protection insurance?
If you still want to keep it, call your insurance company. You will probably be able to get a new policy with a lower premium.

Is there any way to reduce my premiums on mortgage protection insurance?
Some companies do offer a modest reduction if you and your spouse both have this type of cov-

erage. But if you have made the decision to protect your home this way instead of just covering this cost on your term life insurance policy, consider whether you both really need it. If you both contribute equally to paying your mortgage, then maybe it makes sense, but if one of you does not work outside the home, for example, it doesn't make sense for you to both have this coverage because, presumably, your working spouse will be able to continue working and making these payments after you are gone.

You keep mentioning that increasing my deductible will reduce my premium costs. Can you be more specific about what that means in terms of homeowner's insurance?
If you raise your deductible from $250 to $500, you can reduce your premium by about 10 percent. Raise the deductible to $1,000 and you may be able to reduce your premium by 20 percent. A $2,500 deductible could cut your premium by 30 percent. Remember, you are taking a gamble that you will save more on your premiums than you will ultimately wind up paying in deductibles. Just be sure that you will actually be able to pay the deductible if you need to. That's another important reason to make it a priority to have money set aside in an emergency savings account at a federally insured bank or credit union.

How can I save on homeowner's insurance?
If you can afford it, raise your deductible. You may be able to get a discount if you buy your homeowner's and car insurance from the same company—but make sure both policies compare favorably to others you're considering. Take steps

to make your home safe: Buy fire extinguishers, and install smoke detectors, security systems, and deadbolt locks. And this is yet another good reason not to smoke. Ask your insurance agent about these measures; you may find that they all translate into cost reductions. Ask about senior citizen reductions and loyal customer reductions if you have been with your insurance company for at least five years, and investigate whether any associations you belong to offer discounted group coverage. Finally, here's a common mistake: Don't include the value of your land when you are figuring out how much insurance to purchase. Your lot isn't included in the coverage, so it doesn't make sense to pay as though it were.

RENTER'S INSURANCE

I don't own a home—I rent. Do I need renter's insurance?

If you had personal property that was damaged by a fire or you were robbed, how much would it cost you to replace what you own? It doesn't matter whether the home your possessions are in belongs to you or someone else, right? Many renter's insurance policies also contain some liability protection for you as well, in case you damage your apartment or in case someone else is hurt in your apartment. If you have anything of value that you want to protect then, in my opinion, renter's insurance is a good thing.

Does renter's insurance just cover my personal property?

Actually, no. Usually there is liability and medical payments coverage, in case someone injures himself in your apartment and sues you along with the landlord. Also, renter's insurance can cover your loss of use if something catastrophic should happen to the building and you were forced to live somewhere else while the owners repair or rebuild it. This can be key protection for renters, since you often don't have as much control over the maintenance of your property and its systems as owners do.

FLOOD INSURANCE

I am about to buy a home in what they call a low-to medium-risk area for floods. Do I need flood insurance?

I think you do. Between 20 and 25 percent of the flood insurance claims come from low- to medium-risk areas.

If I do not have flood insurance, is there a national program that will help me in case of a natural disaster?

Yes, if your area is declared a federal disaster area, then you can get help through the Federal Emergency Management Agency (FEMA), *www.fema.gov,* from the crippling financial losses often caused by flooding.

If FEMA will give me money to replace my home, why should I pay for private flood insurance?

Because floods are often too small or too localized to qualify for federal assistance. More to the point, even if a flood does qualify, the assistance from FEMA comes in the form of a loan or small grant. In fact, grants are usually given in amounts that barely cover losses, much less enable you to rebuild. FEMA disaster loans charge an interest rate of about 3 percent (in 2009) and can have a 30-year repayment period. The current loan limit for homeowners to rebuild a primary residence was $200,000 in 2009; homeowners and renters are also eligible for loans of up to $40,000 to replace or repair personal possessions such as clothing and automobiles.

The bottom line is that there is a big difference between paying back a loan, even if it is at a low interest rate, and having an insurance plan that will pay for everything.

How much does a flood insurance policy cost?

The average cost of a policy in 2009 was $540 a year.

Does FEMA offer flood insurance?

Yes. Under FEMA's National Flood Insurance Program (NFIP), federally backed flood insurance is available in communities that adopt and enforce regulations to reduce flood losses. The good news is that more than 20,000 communities in the United States and its territories that are faced with potential flooding participate in the NFIP, so the chances are excellent that NFIP insurance is available to you.

For more information about NFIP flood insurance and to find out if it is available in your particular area, call the NFIP at (888) 379-9531 or visit the *floodsmart.gov* website.

I am about to buy a home in a high-risk flood area and my mortgage broker is telling me that I have to buy flood insurance. Is this correct?

Yes, if you are buying a house in a designated high-risk area and receive a mortgage loan from a federally regulated lender, your lender must, by law, require that you buy flood insurance.

What is the maximum flood insurance I can buy?

- Up to $250,000 for single-family, two-to-four family, and other residential buildings
- Up to $500,000 for nonresidential buildings, including small businesses
- Up to $100,000 for contents coverage for residences for owners and/or renters
- Up to $500,000 for contents for businesses, including small businesses

If I am a renter in a high-risk flood area, can I buy flood insurance?

Yes.

If I hear on the news that a flooding is expected in my area, can I get a policy right away?

No. Policies go into effect 30 days after the policy is purchased. So please do not wait until you are faced with an emergency to get yourself covered.

If I own my home outright and I live in a high-risk flood area, am I still required to buy flood insurance?

If you own your house outright, no federal agency will force you to buy flood insurance or keep the flood insurance you had to have when you still had a mortgage. Property owners who do not have a mortgage insured by a federal agency are free to buy the insurance or not buy the insurance—it all depends on your assessment of the risk that you will be taking.

EARTHQUAKE INSURANCE

Many of us trust that after a natural disaster, the government will step in with aid so that any financial losses we suffer will eventually be recouped. That is not generally true. The government is likely to provide disaster assistance, but it does not protect the individual homeowner from loss. The most common federal aid after a disaster comes in the form of low-interest loans, which must be paid back over time.

In the last decade, the insurance industry has paid out record amounts of money for insured losses caused by earthquakes and hurricanes. With respect to earthquakes, the industry has come up with two main ways to deal with the possibilities of large losses. Some insurers simply won't accept new policies or renewals in areas of high seismic risk. Others have been working with Congress to establish a federal natural disaster insurance program to augment the capacity of private industry to provide disaster insurance. If you live in an area that is prone to earthquakes, you should be aware of the following information about earthquake insurance. Please note: While the principles of earthquake insurance are the same in every state, the specifics about coverage, availability, and affordability vary from company to company and state to state.

Who sells earthquake insurance?

In general, only large multiline, multistate companies insure catastrophes.

In the future, Congress may pass legislation creating a federally backed insurance program but, as of the writing of this book, that has not yet happened, though a new state-managed program has just been initiated in California.

I have been offered earthquake insurance from a small insurance company and the rates are far better than those I've been offered by a large company. Which way should I go?

Watch out. Small insurance companies usually lack the financial resources to pay for a large catastrophic event. It's better to stay away from small insurers offering earthquake coverage.

What does a typical earthquake insurance policy cover?

A typical earthquake policy insures for loss against structural damage, damage to contents, and loss of use (residential) or business income (commercial).

What does loss of use or business income coverage mean?

Loss of use covers the costs of a hotel or other rental and meals until the structure is repaired.

Business income covers the income and rental losses arising from the shutdown of the business (sometimes called business interruption).

Everyone tells me that earthquake insurance is not worth it because of the high deductible. Do you agree?

It is true that earthquake insurance policies have high deductibles. A typical deductible is 10 to 15 percent of the value of your property. So if your home is worth $200,000 and your deductible is 10 percent, then you would be responsible for the first 10 percent (or $20,000) worth of damage to that home before your policy would kick in. The same would be true for the contents of your home. The reason that many people say it is not worth it is that for a well-built wood-frame house, this deductible generally exceeds the structural loss for most moderate earthquakes. Due to improvements in structural soundness and design, recent earthquakes have caused less damage to structures than to the contents within those structures.

I live in California and was just offered a policy by the CEA. What is the CEA?

Pressure put on state officials by insurance carriers to carry earthquake insurance has resulted in the creation of the California Earthquake Authority (CEA). This new agency provides "mini" earthquake insurance policies, not covering pools, patios, fences, driveways, or detached garages. These policies have a 10 percent or 15 percent deductible, and coverage of a home's contents can range from $5,000 to $100,000 and provide a maximum of $15,000 in living expenses.

As of 2009 the average annual premium for $400,000 of dwelling coverage, $50,000 of contents coverage, with a 15 percent deductible was $924.

If an earthquake produces more claims than available resources can handle and you have a CEA policy, you may be required to pay an assessment, which could add up to as much as 20 percent of future earthquake premiums. The cost of these new policies varies throughout the state, depending on the earthquake risk and the age and construction of the home.

What questions should I ask an agent when buying an earthquake policy?

- Why should I buy earthquake insurance?
- Is there another way for me to replace my property if I don't have earthquake insurance?
- Is the earthquake insurance coverage included in my existing homeowner's policy or do I have to buy a separate policy?
- What will earthquake insurance cover?
- How much earthquake insurance coverage should I buy?
- How much will it cost me annually?
- Will the coverage I buy apply to the combined value of my house (the structure itself) and the contents of my home (furniture, clothing, electronic equipment, collections, etc.), or should I evaluate my potential losses separately?
- How much is the deductible?
- Is the deductible for my earthquake insurance coverage different from the deductible for my basic homeowner's coverage?
- How is the deductible on my earthquake

insurance coverage going to be calculated in the event of a loss? Will a separate deductible apply to the structure, contents, and detached structures, or does one deductible apply to the entire loss?

- Does the policy have a guaranteed replacement cost coverage? If so, how would this coverage apply if I suffered a loss?

- If you own a condominium, ask how earthquake insurance would benefit you. (Ask specifically what insurance would cover if you were forced to vacate the premises for safety reasons.)

- If you're a renter, ask how earthquake insurance would benefit you. (Ask specifically if additional living expenses would be covered if you were forced to vacate the premises for safety reasons.)

- Will my car be covered by earthquake insurance?

- What about other structures—the garage, for instance? Would it be covered by the same policy or will I need to get a separate policy or add a rider to my primary policy?

- If I have to vacate my home, will earthquake insurance cover the hotel expenses? If so, for how long?

- Is breakage of fragile articles covered if I purchase earthquake insurance? Is there a better way to cover these items?

- Does the type of home I live in (brick, veneer, masonry) or whether my home is bolted to the foundation affect the premiums or benefits of earthquake coverage?

- Does the earthquake policy exclude certain repairs?

- How long do I have to wait after an earthquake before I can file a claim?

- What about aftershocks that can be attributed to the original quake? Would I be covered for resulting damages without another deductible?

- Are there additional "endorsements" to the earthquake coverage that I should also consider, such as building code upgrades, structural report coverage, demolition, etc.?

MISCELLANEOUS PRIVATE INSURANCE

My company has just developed something called a "cafeteria plan" that gives employees the option to choose our benefits now, including some insurance options. How will this work?

Each plan is different, but generally, these plans offer a menu of flexible benefit options for employees. You may be able to choose within a particular type of insurance, such as a standard health insurance plan, an HMO, and a PPO, or you may be able to choose among different types of insurance benefits, like life or disability. You generally get a specific number of points or credits that you can use to customize your benefits. You'll need to consider the needs of your family carefully when choosing the form your benefits will take, but you're lucky to have the flexibility. Make the most of it.

My company offers flexible spending accounts, but they seem like a lot of trouble. Are they worth it?

Flexible spending accounts are funds in which you can have your employer deduct money from your paycheck on a before-tax basis for you to use to pay for your out-of-pocket medical expenses, your copayments, or other related health-care expenses such as eyeglasses, or for child-care or other dependent-care expenses. This is your money and you can choose how much to withhold from your paycheck. The savings come because you aren't paying taxes on this money, which can save you hundreds of dollars over the course of the year. The catch is that you must submit paperwork to be reimbursed and you must use all the money you set aside in 12 to 15 months; otherwise you lose it, so be careful in estimating your expenses. If your company offers this benefit, try it out the first year with a relatively small contribution to your fund and see how it feels. You may find that the bit of extra trouble is worth the savings and, as a bonus, it may help you realistically identify how much your medical or dependent-care expenses actually cost you each year, since you're keeping track.

When my daughter got engaged, a friend told us about wedding insurance. It sounds silly, but we are spending an awful lot of money on this celebration. Should I investigate further?

This is something to consider. The principal idea of wedding insurance is that it will protect you if a wedding guest is injured and sues you or will reimburse your unrefundable deposits if you have to cancel the plans (though not if the bride and/or groom change their minds and decide not to marry). Some homeowner's insurance policies will cover the liability of the reception, should a guest injure himself, but filing a liability claim will likely result in either a significantly higher renewal premium or the actual cancellation of the homeowner's policy. Wedding insurance policies typically range anywhere from $185 to about $500.

My daughter is going to be a college freshman in the fall. We got some information in the mail about tuition insurance. What do you think about it?

Not much. Tuition insurance would reimburse you for the money you've spent on tuition (and usually room, board, and fees) if your daughter were to drop out of school before a given semester ends due to illness or injury, in exchange for a premium of about 1 percent of the semester's costs. It's your decision, but I think this insurance is basically unnecessary. Keep in mind that a semester is only three or four months long and that most universities will refund tuition, at least partially, if a student withdraws within the first four to six weeks. Also, if your daughter becomes sick or injured during the last few weeks of a semester, it is often possible to arrange for her to complete her course work and exams during the following semester at no extra cost (just extra work for her!). If you compare this policy to, say, term life insurance, you'll see that you would be paying a relatively high premium for pretty modest coverage over a short period of time.

You probably think that cancer insurance is a bad investment, too. But there is a history of cancer in my family, and I have seen how some of my relatives suffered financially after an illness. This might not be for everyone, but shouldn't I consider this protection?

Of course the last thing you want to worry about when you are really sick is money. But that is why you have comprehensive health coverage! Cancer insurance preys on your fear of cancer, but if you have good general health insurance you should already be protected in case you develop cancer or any other debilitating illness. Why should you pay twice for the same coverage? And if you don't have coverage, why buy narrow protection from only one disease when you can buy expansive protection?

What is a rated policy?

This is a type of policy that may be offered to you if you have some type of unusual risk factor, like a dangerous job or poor health, and usually comes with relatively high premiums.

My travel agent always encourages me to buy flight insurance. Do I really need it?

No way. Flight insurance exploits your fear of flying. As you have probably heard before, your chances of dying in a car are much greater than your chances of being in a plane crash. In any case, a good term life insurance policy will cover you in the air and on the ground. Check to see if your life insurance policy has an aviation clause. The credit card you use to pay for your airline ticket may also provide this type of coverage for no fee, so check your membership agreement.

When I rent cars, I'm never sure if I should pay for the rental car liability or collision insurance. What do you think?

I think you absolutely need liability coverage on a rental car, but you often don't need to buy it from the rental company. Many comprehensive auto liability policies cover you when you rent a car. Check to make sure that yours does and then don't duplicate this coverage at the rental counter. Your car insurance may also cover comprehensive collision in a rental car, so check that out, too.

Does my credit card cover the insurance that I need for a rental car?

Your credit card may provide such coverage as long as you use it to pay for the car rental. If you pay for a rental car with an American Express green card, for example, and you are not a student, you will be covered for collision and damage but not liability. Do some research with your credit card company; the chances are that you've got this covered.

5

Paying for College

Ahead of the Curve

In recent years a few welcome developments have made it easier to pay for college. One is a federal push to make college more affordable, which includes new educational tax credits, federally sponsored savings accounts that promote saving for college, and new deductions for interest paid on student loans. (For more about student loan interest deductions, please see page 61.) Second, new state-sponsored college savings plans have proliferated, and many of these now work in your favor, from both an investment and a tax-savings standpoint. Third, college officials are acknowledging that higher education has become wildly expensive and, without help, increasingly unaffordable to all but a few. According to the College Board, in the 2008–2009 school year, the average cost of tuition, room and board, books and supplies, transportation, and other expenses at a public four-year college was $6,585, while the average cost at a private four-year college was almost $25,143. Colleges and universities help defray costs for many students. According to the 2007–08 National Postsecondary Student Aid Study, 66 percent of undergraduate students were awarded some form of financial aid.

Still, parents have to be careful when choosing from the menu of available options, since how you put together your college savings package can affect your eligibility for financial aid. The details—whether you're married or divorced, live in Montana or New York, have a child who's gifted, or invest in an UGMA account—matter in determining how much you will have to spend, and how much you can save, when you want to provide for your child's higher education.

Even if you're starting late, don't worry. The important point is to start. Read the following questions and answers, and begin with a few simple actions. Open a Roth or an Education IRA. Sign up for a 529 plan. Check out websites devoted to financial aid, and gather further information about everything on the website *www.savingforcollege .com*. There is more support and there are more options out there than you may be aware of.

Investing for Education

What do you think is the best way to invest money to finance a child's education?
Your investment strategy will depend on how many years you have ahead of you before your child or children enter college. Whenever you're considering how to invest, the period of time in which you can allow your money to remain invested for growth is a critical factor. If you have a minimum of ten years before your first child enters college, I suggest investing in growth stocks, growth mutual funds, or exchange-traded funds (ETFs). In the shorter term, however, the ups and downs of stocks can be a problem. During a

sudden downturn in the market, if you had to cash in your stocks for a tuition payment you could lose not only your gains but also some of your principal. If you know you'll need to begin spending your savings within four or five years, be conservative. Keep your money in money-market funds, Treasury notes, and certificates of deposit. Depending on your income level, series EE bonds, which have a tax exclusion on interest when used to pay for qualified higher education expenses, may be a smart investment if you have more than five years left to save. If you have a little more time than this—say, six to seven years—and feel you can tolerate a moderate amount of risk, consider using not all but a portion of your money to invest for growth.

In what kind of plan or account should I be keeping my investments for a child's education? Where you hold your investments is just as important as the kind of investments you decide to make. Should you keep them in your name or in your child's name? Should they be held in a UGMA account, an Education IRA, a prepaid tuition plan, a 529 savings plan, or a Roth IRA? Since there are many choices, let's go through them one at a time.

UNIFORM GIFTS TO MINORS ACT/UNIFORM TRANSFERS TO MINORS ACT (UGMA/UTMA)

UGMA, or the Uniform Gifts to Minors Act, and UTMA, or the Uniform Transfers to Minors Act, were created to make tax-free gifting of money or assets to children easier and more efficient. As a parent, you can open either an UGMA or an UTMA account in your child's name. (Grandparents and friends of the family can open accounts as well.) You fund it with gifts of money, and then, if you wish, you can purchase stocks, bonds, annuities, or other investment vehicles with the balance. UTMAs allow more flexibility than UGMAs in the types of investments that can be held. UGMA and UTMA accounts are governed under the laws of the state where the account is set up, but generally, you or an adult delegate serves as the account custodian until your child reaches the age of majority (depending on the state, this age is generally 18 for UGMAs, and 21 for UTMAs but some UTMAs may be as late as 25), at which point he or she controls the money.

With either account, annual taxes on the gains, or unearned income (such as dividends, interest, and short-term capital gains), are negligible until total gains in the account reach $1,900. After that, the gains are taxed at the parents' highest marginal income-tax rate—that is, until the child reaches age 19. Children who are dependent, full-time students will pay the kiddie tax until they reach age 24.

Given the greater tax advantages of the Coverdell Education Savings Accounts (see page 287) and of Section 529 college-savings plans (see page 295), both of which let parents or guardians hold the money saved for college in the parents' or guardians' name, UGMA and UTMA accounts are much less attractive than they used to be as a method of saving for children's college education. That said, virtually every bank and stock brokerage firm (full-service, discount, and online) manages these accounts on a daily basis. You should be able to set up an account with any major institution.

Are there any differences between UGMA and UTMA?

Yes, one significant difference. Though in most ways UTMA and UGMA accounts are alike, UTMA has this benefit: It may allow you, the parent, to maintain control over the account for a slightly longer period of time—until, for example, your child finishes college. Unlike the regulations governing UGMA, those governing UTMA permit the custodian to postpone final distribution of the account funds until the child reaches age 25, depending upon the state in which the account is set up. This is important, especially if you think your child may put off attending college, may wish to attend graduate school after college, or may not wish to attend college or graduate school at all. In some states, the child can do whatever he or she wishes with the money in an UGMA account once he or she reaches age 18—go skiing, form a rap group, or support an unappealing significant other. In all states, the money is irrevocably the child's once he or she reaches 21. Over the years, I have seen many UGMA accounts that were supposed to fund a college education go instead to buying a new car or supporting a drug or alcohol habit, while the parents had to watch, brokenhearted and powerless to intervene. This is one major potential drawback of saving in either an UGMA or an UTMA account, but at least an UTMA delays the risk.

Can you elaborate on the tax benefits of saving in an UGMA/UTMA account rather than in an account held in my own name?

Yes. The potential tax savings can be significant, thanks to the difference between income-tax brackets for adults and those for children.

Here are some examples, based on tax laws as of the year 2009:

- The first $950 of unearned income in a minor's UGMA/UTMA account is exempt from tax—regardless of the child's age.
- The second $950 of unearned income from securities given to a child is taxed according to the minor's tax bracket—again, regardless of the minor's age.
- The child's age becomes a factor only when unearned income exceeds $1,900. If the child is younger than age 19 (or a full-time student between ages 19 and 23) at the close of the tax year in which gains have exceeded that limit, investment income over $1,900 is taxed at the parents' highest marginal tax rate. Such income must be included on either the parents' tax return or a separate return. Since certain deductions may be available only to the child, filing a separate return for this income may result in lower taxes. If the minor reaches the age of 19 at any time during the year when gains on the account exceed $1,900, all income in excess of $950 is taxed at the child's rate.

Children who are full-time students and between the ages of 19 and 24 will also be hit by the kiddie tax. Only full-time students who provide more than half their support from earned income will be exempt from the kiddie tax.

Will an UGMA account make it harder for my child to qualify for financial aid?

Yes, and this is the second potential drawback of using UGMA/UTMA to save for college. Because an UGMA/UTMA account is held in your child's name, funding it can seriously reduce your child's chances of qualifying for aid or the amount of aid he or she receives. Let's say, for example, that the annual tuition of the school that your dependent daughter wants to attend is $8,000, and that, apart from your home and retirement savings, you and your spouse have assets of $30,000 in your name. Under these circumstances, the college would expect you to contribute 6 percent of that $30,000, or $1,800, per year for your daughter's college expenses. The remainder might possibly be paid with the help of some form of financial aid. If the same $30,000 were held in an UGMA account in your daughter's name, however, the college would expect you to use these funds at the rate of 35 percent, or $10,500, per year for colleges expenses. That's a big difference! When you consider paying $10,500 from an UGMA rather than $1,800 from your own account, it's easy to grasp one of the fundamental weaknesses of a savings strategy based on UGMA/UTMA.

Are there other ways to put money aside for college and also get the child's-rate tax advantage of an UGMA/UTMA?

Yes, so read on. However, if you plan to put money aside for your children's education, please consider keeping it in a separate account in your own name. The advantages of doing so include ongoing control of the money and a better chance of qualifying for financial aid.

EDUCATION TAX BENEFITS/CREDITS

The government provides a tax deduction and two federal tax credits to help you finance your children's educations. The tax credits are called the Hope Scholarship and the Lifetime Learning Credit.

Who qualifies for the new tax deduction?

Many people can deduct either $2,000 or up to $4,000 of higher-education expenses from their income each year for tax purposes. To be eligible for the maximum $4,000 deduction, adjusted gross income for a single filer must be $65,000 or less, and for joint filers must be $130,000 or less. For the reduced deduction of $2,000, the AGI limits are $80,000 for single filers and $160,000 for married filing jointly taxpayers. Before choosing to claim the deduction, you should see if you are eligible to claim one of the following two credits, as the credits may have a larger impact on reducing your tax bill.

What is the Hope Scholarship Credit/American Opportunity Tax Credit?

The Hope Scholarship Credit was renamed the American Opportunity Credit by the American Recovery and Reinvestment Act of 2009. The credit now allows you to deduct as much as $2,500 a year directly from your income-tax bill for each student and can be claimed for the first four years of postsecondary education. Remember, a credit is not deducted from your income for tax purposes; it is deducted directly from the amount of the tax you pay, and therefore is far more valuable. Forty percent of the credit is a re-fundable credit that can be claimed even if you do not owe any taxes, with some exceptions. One hundred percent of the first $2,000 in qualified tuition, fees, and course materials (books, supplies, and equipment needed for a course of study) are covered by the credit. Twenty-five percent of the next $2,000 of qualified tuition fees and course materials is also covered. The American Opportunity credit is claimed on a per student basis, so if you are the parents of twins you can claim up to $2,500 a year for each of them. The modified AGI phase-out levels for married filing jointly in 2009 is $160,000 to $180,000 and $80,000 to $90,000 for single filers.

What is the Lifetime Learning Credit?
The Lifetime Learning Credit equals up to $2,000 of tax savings for qualified education expenses, which can include vocational school, professional-level programs, graduate school; as well as college. Taking even a single course may qualify you for the credit. You can deduct 20 percent of the first $10,000 of out-of-pocket costs for qualified expenses (tuition and fees for enrollment) for all the students in the family, up to a maximum of $2,000 per family per year. It is important to be aware that this is different from the American Opportunity credit, which is a per-student credit rather than a per-family credit.

In 2009, the income ranges for the modified adjusted gross income phase-out are $100,000 to $120,000 for married couples filing jointly and $50,000 to $60,000 for single parents. Married taxpayers filing separately are not eligible for the credits.

EDUCATION SAVINGS ACCOUNTS

What is a Coverdell Education Savings Account?
A Coverdell, once commonly called an Education IRA, is another way for families to save for college. Withdrawals made from Coverdells that are used for qualified education expenses are free of tax.

The maximum contribution to the Education Savings Account in 2010 was $2,000 per child. Coverdells are not just for college; they can also be used to fund elementary- and secondary-school expenses, such as private-school tuition. The child must be under the age of 18 when contributions are made. The contribution is not tax-deductible and does not have any effect on the amount you can contribute to traditional IRAs, Roth IRAs, or combinations of the two.

Who can set up an Education Savings Account?
Anyone who meets the AGI requirements can set up and fund an Education Savings Account for a specific child. The contributor does not have to be a parent or relative, only someone who wants to provide for a child's education. To contribute the maximum each year, the contributor's AGI—as of 2010—cannot be more than $95,000 a year if they file taxes singly, or $190,000 if he or she is married and file jointly. The maximum amount of the contribution is reduced as income rises above those levels and is phased out completely once an AGI reaches $110,000 for single filers and $220,000 for couples.

I am a grandparent who wants to set up an Education Savings Account for my grandchild, but my income comes from my pension and interest on investments. Even though I am not employed and do not draw a salary, can I still set up an account?

Yes, you can. Unlike a Roth IRA or a traditional IRA, the Education Savings Account doesn't place restrictions on the source of money used to fund it. In this way, the law makes it possible for grandparents—and possibly even the children themselves—to make contributions.

How are distributions from an Education Savings Account taxed?

Distributions from an Education Savings Account are not subject to tax if used for "qualified higher-education expenses," and as long as the Hope and Lifetime Learning credits are not used in the same year for the same educational expenses for which the distributions are used. This means that the earnings, or gains, on your contributions will never be taxed if the funds are properly used. However, ordinary income taxes and a 10 percent penalty can be slapped on earnings if distributions are used for anything other than qualified education expenses.

When must all the money in an Education Savings Account be distributed?

All funds in an Education Savings Account must be distributed before the beneficiary reaches age 30. However, if the primary beneficiary reaches that age and hasn't used the funds in the account to pay for college or advanced education, the account can be transferred to another beneficiary without tax or penalty if that person and the first beneficiary are members of the same family.

If I am already making a contribution to a state tuition program, can I also set up an Education Savings Account?

Yes. You can fund both a qualified state tuition program, such as Section 529 plan, and an Education Savings Account in the same year for the same child. When it comes to taking *distributions*, however, be aware that combined distributions from an Education Savings Account and a qualified state tuition program cannot exceed a child's qualified educational expenses for any one year.

Should the Education Savings Account be my first choice to fund my child's education?

These are a terrific way to save for college, but given the annual limit of $2,000 you should also look into 529 College Savings plans. Many 529 Plans allow total contributions of more than $300,000 for a single beneficiary, and there is no income cutoff to be eligible to contribute to a 529. Since you can contribute up to $2,000 a year to the Education Savings Account, you'll only be able to amass about $91,000 over an 18-year period, assuming an average annual 10 percent return on your money. This amounts to 50 percent of projected four-year private-college tuition costs in the year 2010.

Note: There are other ways to save for a child's education, and one of them is a Roth IRA. (See page 328 for a full definition.)

USING A ROTH IRA TO FUND A COLLEGE EDUCATION

You say you like the Roth IRA as a saving vehicle for college. Why is that?
The Roth IRA, normally used as a vehicle for retirement saving, also can be a terrific way to save for college, although, like the Education Savings Account, your contributions are made with money on which you've already paid taxes. The Roth lets you save more money than an Education Savings Account does. In 2010, you could save $5,000 in a Roth IRA ($6,000 if you are at least 50 years old). Second, you can withdraw your original contributions (though not your earnings) at any time for any purpose, without owing taxes or penalties. Finally, not only can you qualify for a Hope Scholarship or Lifetime Learning Credit while your child is receiving Roth IRA distributions, your child may have a better chance of qualifying for financial aid than with an Education Savings Account.

Can you give me an example of how a Roth IRA would work to help fund a child's education?
Yes. Say you are 30 years old and have a child. As part of a plan to save for the education of this child, you put the maximum amount allowed each year into a Roth IRA in your name. For the next 18 years, you continue to add the yearly maximum allowed to the Roth IRA, and you get an average annual return of 10 percent on your contributions. When your child is 18, you will have approximately $228,000 in your Roth

IRA. You will be 48 years old—not so far from your own retirement. You will be able to take out your original contributions of $90,000 to help pay for your child's education (or, for that matter, for any other purpose) without penalties or taxes. That's only $10,000 less than you would have amassed in an Education IRA at $2,000 a year for 18 years at 10 percent. And remember, the laws governing a Roth IRA allow you to withdraw your original contributions at any time, for any reason, whether or not your child ever goes to college. Finally, after you take out your original $90,000, you will still have about $130,000 in earnings remaining in the account, and that money will continue to grow income tax–free. It will never be taxed at all if you leave it in the Roth IRA until you turn age 59½ and have waited at least five years from the time you first began funding the account.

Who is eligible to fund a Roth?
As with the Education Savings Account, eligibility for a Roth has an income cap. In 2009 to contribute the maximum allowed per year, the contributor's MAGI cannot be more than $105,000 for those filing singly and $167,000 for those filing jointly. The contribution is phased out for those earning more than these amounts and is eliminated altogether when MAGI reaches $120,000 for single filers and $177,000 for joint filers.

I want to use additional savings vehicles while my child is young. If I open a Roth IRA, will I be able to fund a 529 plan in that same year?
Yes. You can fund both a Roth IRA in your

name and a Section 529 plan for your child in the same year.

Will a Roth reduce my child's chances of qualifying for financial aid, as an UGMA account can?

No. Because a Roth is primarily a retirement savings vehicle, the money in your Roth will not make it harder for your child to qualify for financial aid.

PREPAID TUITION PLANS

What is a prepaid tuition plan?

Prepaid tuition plans are just what they sound like. You invest in the plan, and your investment buys a certain number of tuition credits at your state's college or university system at today's prices. Thus, no matter what increases take place in state tuition rates in future years, the number of semesters or years you have purchased for your child today is guaranteed. You select the number of years of college you want to purchase, the type of college (2- or 4-year college), and a payment plan to fit your family's budget. The size of your payments will be determined by your child's age or grade—in other words, by how many years there are left before he or she is ready for college. When your child goes to college in the future, the plan will pay the full instate tuition and mandatory fees at any public college in your state.

Who is eligible to invest in a prepaid plan?

The rules vary from state to state, but typically anyone with an interest in the educational future of a child—including a parent, grandparent, aunt, uncle, friend, or employer—can enroll and invest. An adult enrolls by buying a contract. To be eligible to buy a contract, you *or* the child on whose behalf you're investing must be a resident of the state at the time of enrollment. A parent or grandparent can purchase a contract in the state of Maryland for a child who lives in Maryland, for example, even if the parent or grandparent is a resident of Florida.

Is there an age limit for the beneficiary?

Again, this depends on the state. Many states, in an effort to make sure that the child in question is not too close to college age when the plan is purchased, impose an age limit.

I live in Maryland. Can you give me an example of how my state plan might work?

Yes. If you had enrolled in the Maryland Prepaid College Trust in the year 2010, you would have signed a contract stating that your payments would be based on the cost of tuition and mandatory fees for the 2010–2011 academic year. Later, when your child goes off to college, the plan would pay benefits based on the cost of the selected college at the time you signed your contract. Each year, the cost of college continues to rise. For example, in 1996 the tuition and mandatory fees at the University of Maryland's College Park campus were $4,169 for an instate, full-time student. By 2001, these costs had increased to $5,341 and for the 2008–2009 academic year, tuition and mandatory fees increased to $8,053—a 93 percent increase in just

12 years. The plan invests your payments based on its projections that tuition will increase by an average of 7 percent each year, and that mandatory fees will increase at a rate of 10 percent a year.

In general, when you apply for a prepaid plan you are told how much your total payments will be to purchase one semester to five years of college, based on the age or grade of the child now. For example, if your child were in the fourth grade and you paid for four years of university tuition in Maryland using the five-year monthly payment option, your total payments to the plan would be $45,480. This is slightly more than half of the projected tuition cost beginning in 2014, your fourth grader's freshman year in college, which is $65,587.

Can my payments qualify as a gift under federal law?

Yes. The Internal Revenue Code provides that payments to a prepaid tuition plan are a "completed gift" for federal gift-tax purposes. The code also provides for a five-year averaging provision for individuals who contribute amounts greater than $13,000 ($26,000 for married couples) in a given taxable year. So total gifts of $65,000 per individual ($130,000 for married couples) are allowed in one tax year without federal gift-tax consequences.

When I use the money in my prepaid tuition plan for my child to go to college, can I also use the Hope Scholarship and/or Lifetime Learning Credits that same year?

Yes. The Hope Scholarship and the Lifetime Learning Credit can be used at the time that the tuition benefit is being paid to a college or university as long as the credits are not used for the same expenses. However, the parents' income level determines whether or not the credit can be taken.

Are there tax incentives to invest in a prepaid tuition plan?

Yes. The earnings portion of these plans are entirely exempt from federal taxes, as they are in 529 plans (please see page 297). Earnings here are defined as the difference between the benefit paid to the college and your original contributions. Typically, you owe no state tax on the earnings when benefits are paid to a college. In most cases, all state taxes on the earnings in the plan are deferred while the money remains in the plan. Also, depending on your state, you may be able to deduct payments from your annual income for each contract you have purchased up to that state's limit. Payments in excess of the state limits per contract can be deducted from your income in future years, until the full amount of your payments has been deducted. Changes in your state or federal tax laws could alter the tax treatment of state prepaid tuition programs, so stay tuned.

What happens if I put money into a prepaid tuition plan and my child does not go to college, or she receives a scholarship? Can I get my money back? Will I owe taxes on the money I get back?

In general, you can get your money back if your child receives a grant or scholarship for benefits that would otherwise have been paid to a college by your plan. If your child were to suffer a death or disability prior to enrollment in college, you would receive your payments plus the investment return for the period of time the money was in the plan.

If your child does not attend college for reasons other than death or disability, you will receive a reduced refund plus half of the investment return for the period the money was in the plan. (If there's a loss, it would be minus that amount.) If your child has enrolled in college but does not finish all the years paid for, you will receive a refund equal to the benefits that would have been paid to the college.

If the contract is less than three years old and you cancel, you will receive the payments you have made up until that point.

If the contract has been in existence for three years or more, you will receive your payments plus (or minus) half of the investment return for the time the money was in the fund.

All refunds are subject to taxes. Any portion of a refund in excess of contract payments (in other words, the earnings on the investment) is subject to state and federal taxation at your tax rate.

Any state deduction previously taken on your contributions would have to be added back into your income.

What are the limitations of prepaid plans?
In my estimation, there are three important limitations:

- The first is that you are paying for your child to go to a state school. What if he or she doesn't want to attend a state school? This is a possibility you have to consider. Some plans allow you to transfer your funds to an out-of-state college or university but at a much reduced benefit.
- Second, these are prepaid *tuition* plans, which means that you prepay only tuition—not room and board or the cost of books and computers, which can make up a significant part of an education bill.
- Finally, your investment grows merely at the rate at which your school's tuition costs increase. If you invest in a prepaid plan, you win only when the tuition costs of the college you choose rise more quickly than the annual rate of return you might be earning in other investment vehicles.

PREPAID TUITION PLANS FOR PRIVATE COLLEGES

I've heard about a new prepaid 529 plan for private colleges and universities. What can you tell me about them?
The 529 plan you are referring to is called the Independent 529 plan. The Independent 529 plan is sponsored by a group of currently about 270-plus private colleges and universities across the country known as the consortium. The program manager is TIAA-CREF Tuition Financing Inc. (TFI). The way it works is very simple: You deposit a sum of money, which buys you what is known as a tuition certificate. This certificate is redeemable toward tuition at the colleges that are members of the consortium. So in essence you are purchasing a percentage of future tuition for each program year. For instance, lets say you make a

$5,000 up-front contribution. This $5,000 may buy 30 percent of future tuition and mandatory fees at College A and 50 percent of future tuition and mandatory fees at College B. Certificates may be redeemed for college anytime between 36 months and 30 years after purchase. The percentages are set by the participating colleges at the time the tuition certificates are issued, and may not be adjusted later on. Each college is required to "discount" its tuition by at least one-half percent in setting its percentages. This contrasts with many state prepaid programs that are now charging premiums over current tuition levels.

How would I know what school my child is going to attend when my child is just a few years old?

When you first purchase a certificate of deposit, you will be asked to identify five "favorite" colleges to use as a gauge to illustrate how your account is performing. You can alter your selection of the five "favorite" colleges at any time. Quarterly you will receive statements that will show how much tuition you have purchased for each favorite, based on the college's tuition and certificate discount rate.

Will more private college or private university options be available by the time my child goes to college?

The Independent 529 plan expects more private colleges and private universities will join in the future. When your beneficiary redeems their certificates they can use it at any participating college, including colleges that join after the certificate of deposit has been purchased.

Is there a minimum contribution requirement or maximum contribution limit for the Independent 529 plan?

The minimum contribution for each certificate owner is $500 in total purchases within the first two years after the initial purchase. The maximum contribution is $183,000 per beneficiary. This, by the way, is an amount equal to 5 years tuition and mandatory student fees at the most expensive member college for a newborn. The Independent 529 plans also have an automatic purchase plan, where you can purchase a certificate for as little as $25 per month.

Do these Independent 529 plans offer the same federal tax benefits as the state-sponsored 529 plans or other 529 prepaid tuition plans?

Yes they essentially work the same in every way except how they go about funding the tuition. Independent 529 plans offer the same federal tax benefits as state-sponsored 529 plans or other 529 prepaid tuition plans.

Are there any fees associated with the Independent 529 plan?

One of the reasons I really like the Independent 529 plan is there are absolutely no sales, application, or maintenance fees.

Can I get a refund if a beneficiary does not attend a member college?

Yes. You can request a refund if your beneficiary does not attend a participating college. In addition, if your beneficiary attends a member college you can also request a refund to pay for other educational expenses besides tuition and mandatory fees.

How does a refund work?

A purchaser may request a refund at any time after the one-year anniversary date of purchase. The certificate's refund value is adjusted by the actual investment return it has earned with a maximum annualized growth rate of 2 percent and a maximum annualized loss of 2 percent.

Are there any penalties if a beneficiary attends a public college?

No. There are no penalties as long as the beneficiary uses the funds for qualified higher education expenses at an accredited college or university, public or private. If funds are not used for qualified higher education expenses, they are subject to income tax and a 10 percent federal penalty.

Does the Independent 529 plan affect eligibility for financial aid?

The Independent 529 is no different from a regular 529 College Savings Plan: Money invested in a 529 is treated as a parental asset. No more than 5.6 percent of your 529 assets are factored into your financial aid calculation. That's far better than an UTMA/UGMA where 20 percent of assets are counted.

What if my child gets a full or partial scholarship?

It depends on what the scholarship covers. If the scholarship covers the cost of qualified expenses, you can withdraw the funds up to the amount of the scholarship without incurring the 10 percent federal tax penalty but earnings are still subject to income tax.

What if the beneficiary or certificate owner dies before a certificate is redeemed?

If the designated beneficiary dies before the certificate is redeemed, the owner may change the beneficiary to a family member of the deceased beneficiary, or may request a refund. The 12-month holding period for refunds is waived if the beneficiary dies. A contingent certificate owner is named when an account is opened. The contingent certificate owner assumes ownership of the account upon death of the original certificate owner.

What if I do not have the full tuition amount saved in my Independent 529 account?

If the value of your certificate is less than the full amount of tuition and mandatory fees, you will be responsible for the difference at the current rate.

What if I have purchased more than the full tuition amount? What do I do?

If the value of your certificate is more than the full amount of tuition and mandatory fees, you have several options. You can: (1) save the excess for a subsequent year, (2) transfer the benefits to another family member, (3) request a refund. Keep in mind if the refund is not used for other qualified educational expenses it is subject to 10 percent federal penalty in addition to regular income tax.

What happens if the private college I'm interested in attending ends its Independent 529 plan membership?

The college will be obligated to honor all certificates that were purchased prior to its withdrawal.

Where can I find more information about this program?

Please go to *www.independent529plan.org*. The site offers detailed information on the plan, and lists all the participating colleges.

SECTION 529 SAVINGS PLAN

What is a Section 529 savings plan?

A Section 529 savings plan is a state-run, tax-deferred savings plan that allows you to set money aside for your child's education. Basically, a Section 529 plan is an investment program. Unlike prepaid tuition programs (see page 292), these plans do not lock in future tuition costs at today's prices. Instead, they let you invest in a tax-advantaged way against the rising costs of education. Section 529 plans carry fewer restrictions than prepaid tuition plans do, especially as to your choice of college or university.

Should I choose a 529 prepaid plan or a 529 savings plan to fund my child's education?

It depends on what type of risks you are willing to take with your money. With a prepaid plan, it is just that—prepaid—you do not have to worry about the ups and downs of the market. That said, fewer than half the states currently offer a prepaid plan while regular 529 Savings Plans are available in nearly every state, and you are not limited to investing in your own state's plan. You can choose any 529 savings plan regardless of where you live or where your child ultimately attends school. With a savings plan you would have more money for college, but you could also have less than you put in; it all depends on which investment choices you make for your money within the savings plan and how they perform.

What are the main differences between a prepaid plan and a savings plan?

Many prepaid programs have a specific enrollment period each year. Prepayment contracts must be purchased during the enrollment period, and the price of the contract is adjusted each year when the new enrollment period begins. Savings programs do not have restricted enrollment periods and accept new accounts and contributions at any time.

Almost all state-sponsored prepaid programs require that either the account owner or the beneficiary meet state residency requirements. The vast majority of savings programs, however, are open to residents of any state.

Most prepayment contracts are of limited duration. For example, the program may specify that the contract will be terminated, and a refund made, if the benefits are not used within 10 years after the beneficiary's normal college matriculation date. Most savings programs, however, have no program-imposed limit on account duration, and can remain open indefinitely as long as there is a designated beneficiary on the account.

Most contract-type and voucher-type prepaid programs provide only for undergraduate tuition and fees, while savings programs can generally be used for any costs that meet the definition of "qualified higher education expense," including graduate school.

Do all 50 states have 529 plans?

All 50 states, and the District of Columbia, now operate 529 plans. Some states have more than one. Most of these programs are open for you to participate in even if you live in another state. A great summary of the different plans offered in each state is available through Joseph Hurley's website *www.savingforcollege.com* and in his invaluable book, *The Best Way to Save for College— Complete Guide to 529 Plans.*

How much can I contribute to and/or accumulate in a 529 plan?

This is set by each state; but it is typically a very substantial sum. Some plans allow maximum contributions of more than $300,000 for a single beneficiary. A 529 plan imposes no income limitations. Your contributions to a 529 account come out of your taxable estate. To avoid a gift tax, the best plan may be to fund your 529 at just $13,000 per year per donor, or use the IRS-approved five-year election. This election allows you to contribute $65,000 in a lump sum for single individuals or $130,000 for married couples and use the gift tax exclusions for five years for that particular beneficiary (assuming you make no other gifts to that beneficiary during that five-year period).

Can a person other than a parent put money into a 529 plan?

Yes. Anyone can put money into a 529 plan, regardless of his or her relationship to the child. And, by the way, if you're thinking about going back to college, you can contribute to a 529 plan for yourself and reap the tax benefits.

What are the tax benefits of 529 plans?

They are considerable. All money taken out of a 529 plan is exempt from federal taxes if used to pay higher education expenses. The 2006 Pension Protection Act made this federal tax-free treatment permanent for 529 withdrawals used for college. There may also be state tax advantages. Many states follow federal income tax treatment in excluding the earnings in your 529 accounts from state and local income taxes, and several offer a deduction for all or part of your contributions into their programs. A few states also provide other financial benefits to program participants, such as scholarships, matching contributions, or favorable state-aid treatment.

With the current capital gains tax and dividend tax being so low, does it make more sense to invest in stocks that pay dividends or a 529 plan?

Zero tax is better than some tax. Qualified distributions from 529 plans remain tax-free, while long-term capital gains and dividend tax rates in 2009 are a maximum of 15 percent. Also, interest income and short-term capital gains coming from taxable investments are still treated as ordinary income and taxed at rates as high as 35 percent. In many 529 plans you can find investments offering the protection of principal and competitive interest rates, without incurring any tax.

Why should I invest in a 529 plan when I can't be sure that my child will attend a public university in my state?

There's a misconception that 529 plans are only geared to families that send their children to a state school. That's just not true. The states offering prepaid tuition contracts covering in-state tuition will allow you to transfer the value of your contract to private and out-of-state schools (although you may not get full value, depending on the particular state). If you decide to use a 529 savings program, the full value of your account can be used at any accredited college or university in the country (along with some foreign institutions).

How do I transfer my account from one state's 529 plan to another state's 529 plan?

A transfer of assets from one state's plan to another for the same beneficiary is a qualifying rollover, but this type of rollover can be done only once every 12 months. However, there is no limit on the frequency of rollovers where the beneficiary is replaced with a qualifying member of the family. A rollover can be transacted either through a direct "trustee-to-trustee" transfer (program permitting), or by a withdrawal of funds followed by the contribution of equivalent funds within 60 days to a different 529 plan.

A qualifying rollover will not be treated as a distribution for federal income tax. Be sure to find out how the 529 plan you are investigating handles rollover requests, as there may be restrictions imposed by the program.

Is it wise to invest in a 529 plan out of state

that's been getting better returns than my state's 529 plan?

It depends on your goals, your tax bracket, and how much better the out-of-state fund is doing. Also take into account how much you benefit from the state deductions, if any, on your contributions. Compare those bottom-line numbers with the return on the out-of-state Section 529 plan you are considering. The numbers will tell you which way to go.

My child is a senior in high school. Is it too late for me to start using a 529 plan?

Not necessarily. Assess your potential for tax savings by looking at your most recently filed tax return. Did you pay any tax on interest, dividends, or capital gains distributions? If you did, a 529 plan represents an opportunity to convert taxable investment income into tax-free investment income. Even if an account has a life of only a few years—remember that it will usually take two to five years to earn a degree—you will be saving taxes. In fact, many parents facing college bills in the near future want to have their money in safe, interest-paying investments. This is where the tax protection of a 529 plan provides the greatest advantage.

It gets even better if you live in a state that offers a tax deduction for contributions to the home-state 529 plan. Instead of paying college bills out-of-pocket, you can reap the benefit of a state income tax deduction by first making a contribution to the 529 plan, and then using your account to pay the bills. Bottom line: College expenses become a write-off for state income tax purposes.

If I have a 529 savings plan for my child, will it affect his or her financial aid eligibility?

Generally speaking, the money you put *into* your 529 plan should not hurt your kid's chances for federal financial aid. According to the U.S. Department of Education (DOE), the balance in a 529 savings plan is an asset belonging to the parent or other account owner. This is the good news, because a parent's assets are "assessed" in the aid eligibility formula at no more than 5.6 percent. The formula is much higher for assets held in a child's name. And 529 plans owned by grandparents are not factored into the equation at all.

That being said, please keep in mind that schools don't necessarily follow the federal aid formula when doling out their own scholarship funds. I am hearing that many families feel that financial aid offices are punishing them if they have assets in 529 plans, by reducing or denying their own aid awards. The most frustrating part of all of this is that there are no regulations or guidelines that all schools must follow in regards to 529 plans.

In the meantime, if you have a 529 savings plan and are concerned about its future impact on your kid's aid eligibility, consider spending the 529 assets on college expenses as quickly as possible so the account does not impact next year's award. It might also help to switch the beneficiary designation away from the college student, either to a younger child or to you. You could also think about revoking the 529 funds, as long as the resulting tax and penalties are not too severe.

Can I change the beneficiary of my 529 account?

Yes, as long as the new beneficiary is a family member who has one of the following relationships to the current beneficiary: a son or daughter (natural or legally adopted); a stepson or stepdaughter; a brother, sister, stepbrother, or stepsister; a father or mother; a stepfather or stepmother; a niece or nephew; an aunt or uncle; a son-in-law, daughter-in-law, father-in-law, mother-in-law, brother-in-law, or sister-in-law; the spouse of the designated beneficiary (who must have the same principal place of abode) or the spouse of any of the relatives listed above (who must have the same principal place of abode); or a first cousin. All 529 plans accommodate a change in the beneficiary without imposing a penalty, although some may have age or residency restrictions, and some may charge a fee. There are no federal income tax consequences of a beneficiary change; however, there can be gift tax consequences when the new beneficiary is at least one generation below the old beneficiary.

Can I claim the American Opportunity Tax Credit/Hope Scholarship credit or Lifetime Learning credit in the same year that I withdraw from my 529 account to pay for college?

Yes. The Hope or Lifetime Learning credit can be claimed regardless of whether funds used for qualified tuition and related expenses come from a 529 account. However, in order to prevent "double dipping," Section 529 requires that qualified higher educational expenses be reduced by any expenses used to determine the American Opportunity/Hope or Lifetime Learning credit.

Can I transfer my child's existing UGMA/UTMA assets into a 529 plan?

Yes. If you are custodian, you can liquidate the current investments and reinvest the proceeds in a 529 plan. The sale of investments may generate a tax on capital gains. It is your responsibility as a custodian to comply with state law in handling UGMA/UTMA funds. Some parents will be disappointed to learn that a transfer of assets to a 529 plan will not result in a transfer of ownership rights from minor to the parent. The minor will assume direct ownership of the 529 account at the age of 18 or 21 as determined by state law. For this reason, consider spending down current UGMA/UTMA assets for the benefit of the minor, and replacing those funds by contributing your own money into a 529 plan.

How do I sign up for a 529 plan?

Most 529 plans require you to complete a simple enrollment form. After that, you can make your contributions by check or credit card, or sign up for regular automatic withdrawals from a bank account.

Who decides how the money in a 529 plan is invested?

With a prepaid plan the administrator of the plan is responsible for the investment decisions, but for a 529 savings plan, you are responsible for choosing among the investments offered by the plan. A 529 savings plan operates much like a 401(k) in this regard.

How do I tell which plans currently are rated best overall?

The *www.savingforcollege.com* website is a terrific resource for 529 plans. The site includes a 5-Cap rating system of 529 Plans; one-cap is least attractive, and five caps is most attractive. You can learn more at *http://www.savingforcollege.com/5_cap_ratings*.

What happens if my child decides not to go to college?

If your child decides not to go to college, you can use the money in the Section 529 plan to pay for another "member of the family's" education by rolling over your balance to the new family member 529 account. Or you may request a refund. This refund is known as a nonqualified distribution and will be taxed to the owner of the account. The money you contributed will be refunded to you without taxes, but your earnings will be taxed as ordinary income. You will also pay a 10 percent penalty on the earnings, but not the original contributions, which are returned. Additionally, if you took a state tax deduction on your state income taxes, you will have to repay that to the state.

What happens to the money in the plan if my child dies or becomes disabled?

The penalty is usually waived.

I received a number of offers from different companies stating that if I use their credit card or register the credit cards I currently use with their program, they will contribute a percentage of the money I spend in the 529 plan of my choice. There are so many offers to choose from; do you have any recommendations?

Customer loyalty programs are a great way to get free money for college—companies give you money back for college as a way to earn your loyalty. Some of the popular college savings "accelerators" that I like are:

Upromise (*www.upromise.com*). Offers variable rebates from thousands of participating merchants; simply register your credit cards to get a percentage of your spending back into your Upromise Account.

BabyMint (*www.babymint.com*). Offers variable rebates from participating merchants when you simply register your credit cards to get a percentage of your spending. If you get the BabyMint College Savings Credit Card, you earn an additional 1 percent rebate on every purchase. BabyMint also has a Tuition Rewards program where the shopping rebates you earn are matched by tuition credits when your child chooses to attend any of the 175 participating colleges or universities. If your child chooses to attend a school that is not in the network, you can still use your BabyMint merchant rebate, but you won't qualify for any Tuition Rewards.

Fidelity Investments 529 College Rewards® American Express® Card (*www. fidelity.com*). Earn 2 points for each $1 you spend. Once you reach 5,000 points, or $2,500 in purchases, points can be automatically converted into a deposit in your eligible designated Fidelity 529 account (5,000 points = $50 deposit). To apply, call (866) 598-4971, or apply online at *www.fidelity.com*.

FINANCIAL AID: THE BASICS

Who awards financial aid and what forms does it take?

Most financial aid comes from the federal Department of Education (*www.ed.gov*). Federal student aid can take many forms. Those forms include grants, work-study programs, and loans. Grants are outright gifts for educational purposes; you don't have to pay them back. Work-study programs allow you to earn money for your education while attending school. Loans let you borrow money, often at a favorable rate, to pay educational expenses. In addition to aid that is provided by the federal government, you can also learn about state programs by contacting your state department of education.

How do college grants differ from scholarships? Are they better in the long run?

Grants are the best kind of aid there is. Unlike scholarships, grants can't be rescinded if a child fails to maintain his grade point average or athletic commitments. Like scholarships, grants do not have to be repaid.

What are some of the best undergraduate grants to pursue, and how much help will I get if I qualify?

The Pell Grant is the best-known federal grant for undergraduate students, and in 2009–2010 the maximum amount awarded is $5,350 for the year. Another federal grant, the Supplemental Educational Opportunity Grant (SEOG), is available to undergraduates with "exceptional" financial need—those whose families can contribute very little to the cost of college. Even so, the largest SEOG grant you can receive is $4,000 per year. By all means, try to get one or both of these, but don't count on grants to get you through four years of college.

How does a scholarship differ from a grant?

Hundreds of thousands of scholarships and fellowships from several thousand institutional and private sponsors are awarded each year. Generally, scholarships and fellowships are reserved for students with special talents, whether those talents are academic, athletic, or artistic. Associations organized by ethnicity, sex, and religion, promoting certain fields of study, or even geographic regions of the country also offer scholarships to students. Basically, if you look hard enough, you can find at least several scholarships for which you qualify to apply. Unlike loans, scholarships do not have to be repaid, but they may be rescinded.

Where can I get information about private grants and scholarships?

There are some excellent sources of information on the Internet. Check out *www.fastweb.com,* a scholarship search engine that lets Internet users search, without cost, a database of more than 180,000 scholarships. Also see the U.S. Department of Education's Website, *www.ed.gov.*

As a parent, can I take out a federal loan?

It's the student who typically applies for and receives a federally guaranteed loan. Loans have become a major part of many students' financial aid packages. They often come at very low interest rates—as low as 5.6 percent in 2009.

One loan that students are likely to be eligible for is a federally granted student loan known as a Stafford loan. In addition to carrying a low interest rate, this loan does not require credit checks or collateral. The repayment terms are liberal, and deferment options are numerous and flexible. I always recommend that a student borrow before a parent, because Stafford loans offer the lowest interest rates. But there are annual loan limits for Staffords based on the student's year of school. In 2009–2010 the maximum total that could be borrowed via a Stafford ranged from $5,500 for freshmen to $7,500 for seniors. If you need to borrow more, the next best option is for the parent to apply for a Federal PLUS loan. The fixed interest rate on PLUS loans is either 7.9 percent or 8.5 percent. Both Staffords and PLUS loans are preferable over private student loans. The federal loans offer fixed rates and flexible repayment terms. Most private student loans work like credit cards: the interest rate is variable and can be higher than 15 percent; private loans also tend to have fewer repayment options. You can learn more about Stafford and PLUS loans at *www.finaid.org.*

What are the advantages of taking out a PLUS loan over a private student loan?

A federal PLUS loan is in my opinion a great option for families that will need to borrow to pay for school. Up until 2008 one drawback of a PLUS loan was that the parent had to start repaying the loan within six months of the loan being disbursed. A new law now allows parents who take out a PLUS to defer making payments until their child is out of school. That's a big help. First off, it means you won't be forced to start payments during the years your child is in school and you are no doubt using some current income to pay for various school costs. The other nice advantage of not having to start repayment immediately is that your child will be able to help you with the payments as she or he will be out of school by the time you start making payments.

Now, that said, if you can afford to make the interest payments while your child is in school that is preferable to letting the interest accrue and be added to your original principal loan amount. By paying the interest during the school years you will have a smaller balance to pay off.

The interest rate you pay on a PLUS loan is a fixed rate of either 7.9 percent or 8.5 percent. The difference is whether your child's school has you borrow directly from the federal government, or if you will get your PLUS through a third-party lender. With a private student loan the interest rate is typically variable. Your credit rating will determine the interest rate on a private student loan, and if anything happens to your credit rating your interest rate can rise on the private student loan. You don't have that concern with a federal PLUS loan. Fixed is fixed. The interest rate will not change. The credit check for a PLUS loan is also more lenient than with a private student loan. The credit check for a PLUS looks only for "adverse" actions; such as a bankruptcy in the past five years, or if you are behind in your mortgage and other bill payments.

I also prefer PLUS loans because the repayment terms can be more lenient than those of a private student loan. You can learn more about PLUS loans at *www.finaid.org*.

What other kinds of aid are available?
The Federal Work-Study Program is one common form of supplemental financial aid that many students qualify for. Those who qualify

work part-time in a university department or office that is, whenever possible, related to the student's field of study.

When looking for a school that will give me financial aid, I was told to look for one with a large endowment fund. Why?
Schools with large endowment funds can afford to be more generous with financial aid. Such schools tend to define "need" liberally, particularly when the student is talented. For you, this means a better chance of receiving a scholarship or an aid package.

Can I apply for financial aid before my child is even accepted at a college?
In the case of federal financial aid, the answer is yes, and the sooner you apply the better, because the money is awarded to applicants on a first-come, first-served basis. Starting in January of the year in which your child will enter college, you should fill out a Free Application for Federal Student Aid (FAFSA), the form the government uses to determine how much federal aid you qualify for based on your income and that of the child attending college. You can find the form on the Internet site *www.ed.gov*, or you can request an FAFSA from your child's high school, any college, or the Federal Student Aid Information Center; (800) 433-3243.

Do college financial aid applications require both parents to list income and assets? I am divorced and solely responsible for my children's education, but I'm afraid my children won't qualify for financial aid if their father's income is considered.

This is a common problem. Financial aid is complicated enough, and divorce makes it more so. Colleges want to know about the finances of both parents, and remarried parents must also provide financial information about their new spouses. Most colleges consider each student's individual situation and make case-by-case decisions.

Should I use a financial adviser to plan for my children's college education?

You can and should do a lot of research and thinking about your family's needs on your own, but you can also benefit greatly from talking to a financial adviser who is familiar with recent developments in this area of financial planning. *SavingForCollege.com* posts a directory of advisers who know the ins and outs of 529 plans. The National Institute of Certified College Planners (*www.nicap.com*) trains financial professionals in the art of college financial planning and can refer you to capable advisers nationwide.

6

Retirement Planning

Putting Your Money to Work

As Americans live longer, we will spend an increasing number of years living on our retirement incomes. We know we can't count primarily on Social Security to provide this income and that, if we wish to maintain a comfortable standard of living during a long retirement, many of us will have to rely primarily on our retirement savings.

This chapter is intended to guide you to a safe and comfortable retirement. The questions and answers will help you to plan well for the years ahead. They include crucial information about funding and withdrawing funds from 401(k)s, IRAs, stock option plans, and many of the other retirement programs that may be available to you.

The tax advantages of today's retirement plans allow your savings to grow far more quickly and effectively than ordinary, taxed savings vehicles can. Please invest in as many of them as you are eligible for. If you have doubts about the best investment choices for your retirement plan, seek guidance from a good professional adviser who can help you construct a sensible financial profile (you'll find some tips on hiring a professional in Chapter 7). But whether you're investing with the help of an adviser or alone, don't forget that it's your money that's at stake. Watch your investments carefully. It's a matter of securing your dreams.

For more information about investing techniques, please see the chapters on stocks, bonds, mutual funds, and annuities.

Retirement Plans

How many different kinds of retirement plans are available?

The answer depends on whether you are an employee or are self-employed. Below is a list of the most popular retirement plans. Most are for use by employees of companies; the plans with an asterisk are typically limited to those with self-employment income. Entries marked with a Q are qualified plans, which means that employers can receive a tax break for their contributions to these plans.

Defined Benefit Plan—Q
Target Benefit Plan—Q
Defined Contribution Plan—Q
Profit-Sharing Plan—Q
Money-Purchase Pension Plan—Q
Stock Bonus Plan—Q
457 Plan
401(k)—Q
Roth 401(k)—Q
403(b)

TSA
Traditional IRA
Roth IRA
Converted Roth IRA
Rollover IRA
*Simple IRA
*Sep-IRA
*Keogh Plan—Q

What is a qualified retirement plan?

A qualified retirement plan is what large companies usually offer to their employees. As defined by section 401 of the U.S. Tax Code, qualified plans were created as a tax incentive for employers to contribute to employee retirement plans. Every year, your employer is allowed to deduct from company taxes certain contributions it makes to the plan on your behalf.

What are the benefits of qualified retirement plans?

The advantage to you as an employee is that your contributions in a qualified plan are made with pretax dollars from your paycheck. This means that you are not only investing your money for the future, but you are also using a percentage of money that otherwise would have gone to Uncle Sam. Better still, your pretax dollars grow tax-deferred—that is, you don't have to pay any income taxes on your contributions or your investment gains until funds are withdrawn from the plan at retirement. This is also true of certain other retirement-savings vehicles, such as a traditional IRA.

Another advantage is that many employers match part or all of employee contributions.

Qualified plans also qualify for special taxation rules such as ten-year averaging and capital-gains tax and ten-year averaging. (Note: The ten year averaging rule is only available to people born before 1936.)

But the most comforting feature of a qualified plan is that it is protected against claims by your employer's creditors. Your money is held in trust for you and should be relatively safe.

Is a qualified retirement plan tied to my employer? What if I change jobs?

You can take the vested account balance in a qualified retirement plan with you, so to speak, when you change employers. By transferring your retirement account to another retirement vehicle, even one held at a private bank or brokerage company (this is known as an IRA rollover), you can avoid tax consequences. In some cases you may be able to transfer your old retirement plan directly to your new employer's plan.

If my company has a qualified retirement plan, who can participate?

A qualified plan cannot discriminate; all eligible employees can participate. (Some companies may have a waiting period before new employees can participate in their retirement plan.)

Is there such a thing as a nonqualified plan? What is it?

A nonqualified plan does not meet certain IRS or Employee Retirement Income Security Act (ERISA) requirements, so that, among other things, it can be used to disproportionately reward employees at higher income levels in a company. (This is something that, by law, qualified plans can't do.) Employees who participate in nonqualified plans have a lot more flexibility and freedom in organizing their investments while still participating in tax-deferred growth. There are few vesting requirements, if any, in a nonqualified plan—in other words, contributions basically belong to the employee as soon as they are made. But there *are* restrictions. Participants in a nonqualified plan may not be able to transfer their money into another retirement account. If they leave the company where their plan is managed, or if they retire, they may have to withdraw all the money in the plan as a lump sum payment and pay ordinary income tax on it. Also, the assets of the employees are not held in trust, so they are not protected against the claims of the employer's creditors.

Are most retirement plans governed by the same rules in regard to how long money has to stay in the plan and what happens when it is withdrawn?

Yes. Almost all retirement plans, except Roth IRAs, Roth 401(k)s, and 457 plans, are governed by very similar withdrawal and taxation rules. In most cases you cannot take money out of your retirement plans prior to the age of 59½. If you do make a withdrawal before you turn 59½, the money you take will be taxed as ordinary income and you will have to pay a 10 percent early-withdrawal penalty to the IRS, as well as a possible state penalty and taxes on that level. You also *must* start taking money out by April 1 after the year you turn 70½. At this age, there is a minimum you must withdraw from your re-

tirement account, a figure based on a formula devised by the plan. If you fail to withdraw the minimum, the IRS will assess a 50 percent penalty on that amount. Of course, after the age of 59½, you can take out any amount of money you want—there is no maximum. Just remember that whatever you take out will be taxed as ordinary income.

THE HOWS AND WHYS OF RETIREMENT PLANNING

I know that planning for retirement is important, but I'm always trying to catch up with my bills. When do I really have to start?

I don't even need to know how old you are to answer this question: The time is *right now*. Here's why: Time is the most important factor in the growth of your money. The more time your money is given to grow, the more money you will have when you retire, and the earliest money you contribute grows the most. Planning and investing for your future are signs of self-respect. Start now.

My goal is to save and invest $100 a month for my retirement, but first I want to make a couple of substantial purchases. I'm only 25 years old. How much difference will a few years make?

A few years will make a big, big difference! Let's say you decide to start putting $100 a month in a good no-load mutual fund now, at age 25. Over the years, the fund does very well, averaging a

10 percent return per year. How much will you have when you turn 65? More than $630,000. Now, let's examine what will happen if you make those large purchases instead. Say you wait 10 years to start investing $100 a month. You may think, no big deal, in 10 years I'll be only 35, and how much difference can $1,200 a year, or $12,000 over ten years, really make? It's going to cost you big time: about $400,000. That's right—if you wait until you are 35 to start investing that $100 a month, you will have only about $230,000 at age 65. Wait until you are 45 to start, and you will have only $76,000. If you think time doesn't matter, you are wrong!

Why does time have such a dramatic effect on the growth of money?

The answer involves one of the all-time winning financial concepts: compound returns, sometimes known as compound interest. Compounding creates advantages beyond the obvious benefits of saving and accumulating money. The longer you continue to save, of course, the more you will amass in your retirement account(s). But it's also true that the longer your money is invested, the more money your original contributions can earn—all by themselves—for you.

Here's how it works: Let's say you invest $6,000 a year in your 401(k) account, which earns an average annual return of 8 percent. Let's say you do this for 20 years. The first year, your money will earn $480 in interest, or increased equity value. The next year, as you make your second $6,000 contribution, the account will automatically be returning 8 percent not only on your contributions but also on the first year's $480 gains. The gains on $12,480 (your

two original $6,000 contributions, plus the $480 return) is about $998. If you continue to contribute $6,000 every year, and the account continues to earn an 8 percent average annual return, within a decade the annual gain your account earns will be greater than your annual $6,000 contribution. Eventually, the annual gain will be many times greater than your annual contribution to your account.

To see how time makes a difference, look at the chart on page 311 and watch the return column. You'll quickly see that it doesn't take very long for your average earnings to outpace your yearly contribution.

See what's happening? Even though it took nine years for your annual returns to equal your yearly contribution of $6,000, it took only six years more for your returns to add up to double your yearly contribution, more than $12,000 a year. After that, it took only three years for your gain to be $18,000 a year, triple your yearly contribution. Keep in mind that the chart illustrates the magic of compounding in an account earning only an 8 percent average annual return. If you are able to get a higher rate of return, compounding will produce even more dramatic results. If you do not have $6,000 a year to put away, don't be discouraged. It is all the more important for you to start saving now so that time can do as much as possible for you. With as little as $100 a month, you stand a chance of becoming a millionaire. Time is on your side.

Is money always worth so much more if it's left alone for a long time?

Compounding will make your money grow over time. That is why you need to think of

THE BIG BENEFITS OF COMPOUND RETURNS OVER TIME

Years in 401(k) plan	Annual contribution	Average Annual Gain at 8% per year
1	$6,000	$480
2	$6,000	$998
3	$6,000	$1,558
4	$6,000	$2,163
5	$6,000	$2,816
6	$6,000	$3,521
7	$6,000	$4,283
8	$6,000	$5,106
9	$6,000	$5,994* (your gain equals your contribution)
10	$6,000	$6,954
11	$6,000	$7,990
12	$6,000	$9,109
13	$6,000	$10,318
14	$6,000	$11,623
15	$6,000	$13,033* (your gain is more than double your contribution)
16	$6,000	$14,556
17	$6,000	$16,200
18	$6,000	$ 17,976* (your gain is about three times your contribution)
19	$6,000	$19,894
20	$6,000	$21,966

your money not only in terms of what it can buy today but also in terms of its potential future value. For example, if you want to spend $20,000 on a trip or a car or some other desirable commodity, try to calculate the cost of that commodity not in today's dollars but by taking into account the potential future earnings of those dollars. If you invest $20,000 in an account with an annual rate of return of 10 percent and never add another penny, in 20 years that money could easily grow to $135,000. So, as you can see, your car or vacation could really cost you $135,000 in future savings! Sure, inflation will erode the value of your money over time, so go ahead and assume a 3 percent inflation rate each year for 20 years—but a $20,000 purchase is still going to cost you $75,000 (adjusted for inflation).

When you start to see what things truly cost and understand your money's potential value over time, you will begin to understand money. Does this mean that most of your desires are more expensive than they appear to be? Yes. Does it mean that you can't ever buy anything expensive again? No. It means that you will be conscious of the true cost of what you buy, and can make appropriate decisions about whether you can afford to buy it.

My retirement accounts may be all I can rely on in my old age. Should I be conservative and choose only safe investments?

A conservative investment strategy may sound like a good idea, but it isn't, especially if you are under age 40. In order to keep up with inflation, you must invest your money for growth. The younger you are, the more aggressive you can afford to be with your investment strategy. As a general rule, if you are going to invest your money for at least 10 years, invest most of it for growth. Also, remember that in a retirement account, any gains, interest, or dividends are, in most cases, tax-deferred. (In a Roth IRA, in most cases, earnings are tax-free.) What this means is that in a retirement account, your deferred tax money as well as the tax-deferred return it earns go to work for you. This can make a tremendous difference in the accumulation of money.

I'm afraid I'll lose my money if I invest for growth. Is this a valid fear?

When you invest in the stock market, you may see your holdings decline in value from time to time, and you need to feel comfortable with that. If you are going to lie awake at night worrying about your money, then stocks may not be the best investment route for you. But if you invest for the long term, at least 10 years or longer, and you put the same amount of money into the same investment vehicles every month over time—an investment method called *dollar cost averaging*—in the long run, you probably will not lose money. The concept of dollar cost averaging is explained in greater depth in Chapter 7, but basically it means that you are averaging out the cost of the shares you are purchasing over time. In other words, if you put the same amount of money into the fund each month and the share price fluctuates, you will be buying more shares when the price is lower and fewer shares when the price is higher—you are effectively paying the *average* price. If you are in a good fund for a long time, it's a great opportunity for you when the value of the shares drops, because you can buy shares at "bargain" prices and average down your cost per share.

So it's OK to keep purchasing stocks that drop in value within my retirement account?

If you have at least 10 years until you need your money, dollar cost averaging into a good mutual fund may be the best thing you can do. You should continue to buy that particular fund if it is not dropping in value at the same time that similar funds are rising in value. If the value of your fund is dropping while similar funds are rising, you need to find out what is going on; this may be a reason to change funds. But if everything similar to your fund is dropping, think of a low share price as a great opportunity to invest for retirement.

Dollar cost averaging makes it sound as though it's better to invest over time rather than all at once. Is that true?

Yes, particularly when you are talking about retirement investing, because you can significantly increase the possibility of future growth. See Chapter 7 for an in-depth explanation.

THE MOST POPULAR RETIREMENT PLANS

The most widely available retirement plans include 401(k)s, 403(b)s, and IRAs.

401(K)S

What is a 401(k) plan?

A 401(k) is a voluntary retirement plan that companies may offer to their workers. Employees set aside a percentage of their wages, up to a certain maximum, and invest those funds within the retirement plan. The percentage you can contribute varies from company to company, and the federally mandated yearly maximum may increase over the years, since it is tied to inflation and the consumer price index (CPI). (In 2010, the yearly federal maximum contribution is $16,500 [or $22,000 if you are age 50 or older]. Maximums for later years will be adjusted for inflation.

With a traditional 401(k) your contributions are made from pretax income; that helps reduce your taxable income for the year you make the contribution. With a newer type of 401(k), called a Roth 401(k), your contributions are made with after-tax income. While you do not receive that "up-front" tax break, your withdrawals in retirement can be 100 percent tax-free. With the traditional 401(k) your withdrawals will be subject to income tax.

An employer often contributes to its employees' 401(k)s by matching the employees' contributions up to a certain percentage. The contributions and the interest or gains that accrue are not taxed until the funds are withdrawn. If you invest in a Roth 401(k) you will not owe any tax on your withdrawals in retirement as your contributions will be made with after-tax dollars. There are restrictions on when and how 401(k) funds can be withdrawn.

How does a 401(k) plan work?

You decide how much of your paycheck (up to the maximum allowed) you will contribute to your 401(k) plan. That amount is deducted from your paycheck. If you invest in a traditional 401(k) your contribution is taken out of your paycheck before taxes are taken out and is deposited automatically into the plan. If your employer offers a Roth 401(k) and you choose the Roth, your contributions are made with after-tax money; that is, you do not receive an initial tax break on the amount you contribute. Normally, you have a choice of several possible mutual funds and other investment vehicles with a variety of levels of potential risk and return. You will be given information about the investment options when you sign up for the 401(k). Many corporations do not allow you to participate in their 401(k) plans until you have worked there for at least one year.

Am I locked in to the investment choices I made when I signed up for my 401(k)?

Not usually, unless you are invested in your company's stock. Typically, if your investment objectives change or you don't like the performance of the funds that you have chosen, it's simple to change your allocations. Most plans allow you to make changes daily, if you want, simply by placing a phone call. Some plans allow changes only once a month, or once a quarter, so be sure to ask. No matter how it is invested, your money, as long as it stays in the plan, will not be taxed. Thus, your investments can grow while you defer taxes, and your total taxable income will be lowered.

If I invest in a traditional 401(k) with pretax dollars, when will I owe taxes on the money in my 401(k)?

Taxes on your 401(k) account are deferred until you withdraw the money at retirement, at which time the money that you withdraw will be taxed as ordinary income. Tax rates on ordinary income currently range from 10 percent to a maximum of 35 percent (please see page 369). Generally, if you withdraw any money before you turn 59½, you will owe a federal tax penalty of 10 percent in addition to the ordinary income tax. Your state may also impose a penalty and state income tax on the withdrawal. Also, when you make withdrawals from a 401(k) plan before age 59½, your company will withhold 20 percent of the amount you have withdrawn for

taxes. If you owe more than 20 percent, you will be required to pay it when you file your taxes. If you owe less than the 20 percent, of course, you will get a tax refund.

If I'm not yet 59½, is there any way to avoid that 10 percent early-withdrawal penalty within my 401(k)?

Possibly. It will depend on how old you are and if you are still working for the company that has your 401(k) plan. If you are 55 or older and you leave your employer (retire, quit, or get fired), you can withdraw whatever you want to without any penalty from your 401(k). You will still have to pay taxes on the money you withdraw, but you will not have to pay the 10 percent penalty. The penalty also does not apply if you take money from your 401(k) and roll it over into a rollover IRA account. You could also avoid the 10 percent penalty by taking a loan against your 401(k) plan rather than making an actual withdrawal.

Another way to access money in a 401(k) without paying a penalty is to use a payment method called Substantially Equal Periodic Payments (SEPP). To use this method, you will have to withdraw a certain amount of money every year until you are 59½ (or for five years, whichever period is longer). If you started to withdraw money from your 401(k) at age 52, you would need to continue withdrawing money until you are 59½ (seven and a half years being longer than five). But no matter what you do to avoid paying a penalty, you cannot get around paying taxes on the money you withdraw, if you invested in a traditional 401(k).

How long can I keep money in my 401(k) plan?

There is no fixed time limit. In most cases, the longer you leave your money in a 401(k), the better off you're going to be. Unfortunately, there is an age limit. The IRS says that you must begin to withdraw money from your retirement plans by April 1 of the year after you turn 70½. There is one important exception to this rule: If you are still working for wages when you turn 70½, and your money is in an employer-sponsored plan, such as a 401(k), and you own less than 5 percent of the company you work for, you can leave your money in the plan until April 1 following the calendar year in which you do finally retire. Bear in mind that this exception applies only to employer-sponsored plans, not to plans such as IRAs, which we will discuss later.

What if my employer does not offer a 401(k) or any retirement plan?

It never hurts to ask for one. Get together with your coworkers and ask your employer to establish a 401(k). If you and your colleagues do some preliminary research, you will find there are many mutual fund companies that will be happy to tailor a 401(k) plan for your company. I would start by calling two large money managers, Fidelity Investments, (800) 835-5091; and Vanguard Group, (800) 523-1188. In the meantime—or if your company absolutely will not offer a retirement plan—you can open an individual retirement account or a Roth IRA. (Even if you participate in a company 401(k), you can still open an IRA, though you may not be able to deduct your contributions.)

I'm in a 401(k) plan at work and make about $200,000 a year, but my employer will not let me contribute as much to my 401(k) as other employees are allowed to. Why?

You are what the government considers a "highly compensated employee"—someone who makes at least $110,000 a year as of the year 2010 or owns 5 percent or more of a company. To meet government rules, your employer may not be able to allow you to contribute the maximum amount allowed. That is because the government doesn't want the amount of money contributed to the plan by highly compensated employees to be much larger than the amount contributed by employees who aren't paid as well. A plan is considered "top heavy" if higher-paid employees contribute substantially more than lower-paid employees. If lower-paid employees are contributing very little to the 401(k), then you, as a highly compensated employee, may not be able to contribute anything at all.

One of the investment options in my 401(k) is my company's stock. Should I invest in that?

Generally, I think it is okay to invest in your employer's stock, as long as you thoroughly diversify your investments—in other words, as long as you don't invest all, or even much, of your 401(k) money in your company's stock. You already have a lot invested in your company—your job and job security—and even very solid companies can experience frightening declines in the value of their stock, for a variety of reasons. Putting aside the disaster for Enron employees who had much of their retirement savings in company stock that plunged in 2001–2002, consider this example: In 2000, Microsoft employees watched *their* stock drop from $120 a share to $45 a share. As bad as that sounds for outside shareholders, try to imagine the horror felt by employees who had invested their retirement savings in their company stock. Not to mention those employees who were retiring that year and were planning to live off their 401(k)s—not a nice situation. So don't put all your eggs in one basket. My recommendation is to have no more than 10 percent of your total assets invested in company stock.

I'm not crazy about the investment options for my 401(k). Can I do anything about it?

Possibly. Many employers allow what is known as a partial rollover. You take a percentage of the money that is in your 401(k) (usually no more than 50 percent is allowed) and you transfer it into another retirement account (held in your name by another custodian, such as a bank or a brokerage firm). Not all companies allow partial rollovers, but some do.

My company says it will match my 401(k) contributions. What does that mean?

It means just what it says—your company will match the contributions you make to your 401(k) plan by putting money into your plan. An employer's contribution is usually set by a formula and has a maximum. For instance, for every dollar you put into your 401(k) plan, your employer might give you 50 cents, up to a certain percentage of what you put in. Some generous employers will match any percentage of your contributions dollar for dollar. If your employer does match any

percentage of your 401(k) contributions, you cannot afford to pass this up—this is free money. Think about it—if your employer matches 50 cents on the dollar, for every dollar it matches you are essentially getting an automatic 50 percent return on that money.

I have credit card debt. Should I continue to participate in a 401(k)?

Regardless of your financial situation, it depends on if your employer provides any matching contributions. That's free money that you don't want to pass up. In many plans, the employer will match your contributions up to a certain dollar limit. In that case, it makes sense for you to contribute up to that limit. Then after you've maxed out on the employer match, you can make a decision about whether to continue with your contributions. You need to decide if the rate of return on your 401(k) and the value of your contribution being tax-free (if you contribute to a traditional 401(k) and not a Roth 401(k)) outweigh the benefit of paying off the credit card debt. If the interest rate on your credit card balance is higher than what you can earn on your 401(k), then you might want to temporarily suspend those extra contributions and pay off the debt. If you have a zero interest rate on your credit card and are doing well in your 401(k) plan, don't stop contributing.

What does it mean to be vested in my 401(k) plan?

Being vested means you have the right to take the amount of money that your employer contributed to your retirement account, as well as your own contributions, with you if you leave. Until you are vested, even though your employer's money is in your retirement account, it is not yours if you leave your job. This way a company protects itself against giving money to employees who may leave right away. (Not only would they lose you, they'd lose their money as well.) Vesting entices workers to stay with a company longer to get access to money the company has put in their retirement accounts. Regardless, some companies allow you to vest in your 401(k) plan right away; others make you wait as long as from three to seven years.

I am not yet vested in my 401(k) account, but I want to leave to work for another company. Does that mean I lose all the money I contributed into my 401(k)?

Absolutely not. When you leave a job, for any reason, you can always take your own 401(k) contributions with you. It is only the matching contribution made by your employer that may not be fully vested, and therefore isn't "yours" when you leave.

My company does a four-year vesting, based on 25 percent a year. What does that mean?

Some companies phase in vesting rights, such as 25 percent the first year, 50 percent the second year, 75 percent the third year, and 100 percent the fourth year. Let's say you have been working for a company with this type of plan for almost two years. Each month, you have been contributing $300 of your salary to your 401(k), and your company has been contributing $100. If you leave one month before your second an-

niversary with the company, then, in addition to your own contributions, you will be entitled to 25 percent of the company's contributions, or about $575, plus gains (or losses) on that money. If you could wait to leave until after your second anniversary, a month later, you would be 50 percent vested, and entitled to half of what your company has contributed over the two years, $1,200, plus gains or losses.

If I leave the company where I currently have my 401(k) plan, do I have to take my money out of that plan?

It depends on the company. Many employers will allow you to leave money in their 401(k) plans. Others will require you to roll it over. Generally as long as you have at least $5,000 invested in the 401(k) you can leave it right where it is. That said, often it is wiser to roll it over into an IRA.

Are there benefits to leaving money in a 401(k) plan after I retire?

If you are 55 or older in the year you retire, the big advantage of leaving some or all of your retirement funds in a company plan is that you can make withdrawals as often and in any amount you want without paying an early withdrawal penalty.

Is there a downside to leaving my retirement money invested in a 401(k) plan when I retire?

It depends on your company plan. Your money might earn more elsewhere. Often there are a limited number of investment options in a 401(k) plan, and some plans limit you to making investment changes once a quarter, although this is not as common a restriction as it used to be.

My company offers a Roth 401(k). How is that different from my traditional 401(k)?

Consider yourself lucky. With a Roth 401(k) you get no up-front tax break on your contributions; just as with a Roth IRA (see page 328) the money you invest is after-tax. But the big payoff is that when you retire, all your withdrawals will be 100 percent tax-free. Remember, with a traditional 401(k) all withdrawals are taxed at your ordinary income tax rate. My general advice is that if you have at least 10 years until retirement, it makes a lot of sense to opt for a Roth 401(k) if your company offers it.

403(B) PLANS

Who can invest in a 403(b) plan?

Employees of nonprofit organizations, for example, some hospitals, universities, and charitable organizations, generally have 403(b) plans available to them.

What's the difference between a 401(k) and a 403(b)?

From your perspective as an investor, they work almost identically, and when I refer to 401(k) plans in this book, you can assume that what I'm saying applies to 403(b) plans as well. The main difference is that in some 403(b)s, you cannot change the amount of money that you put in every month. You must decide once, at the beginning of the year. Many 403(b) plans don't offer as many investment choices as

401(k)s—most 403(b)s offer only mutual funds and annuities—but, again, that depends on where you work. Another difference is that long-term employees using 403(b) plans can often do what's called a "catch-up election," which allows them to contribute more than the yearly maximum allowed if they have more than fifteen years of service (subject to certain requirements). If you have a choice between a 401(k) or a 403(b), check them both out carefully. You will probably find that the 401(k) is a better deal. However, if all you have is a 403(b) at your disposal, use it.

Is a 403(b) a qualified plan?

Not technically, but it functions like one.

What is a TSA?

TSA stands for tax-sheltered annuity; it is a form of 403(b) plan. It invests the retirement contributions in an annuity with an insurance company. A TSA is also sometimes knows as a TDA, or tax-deferred annuity.

What is a 457 plan?

This is a voluntary, nonqualified retirement plan typically offered to employees of state and local government agencies. 457 plans may also be offered to employees of nongovernmental tax-exempt or nonprofit organizations, but provisions may differ from those listed here. A government-sponsored 457 plan usually allows participants to annually defer up to $16,500 in wages, or $22,000 if you are age 50 or older (as of the year 2009); as with 401(k)s and 403(b)s, these amounts are scheduled to increase annually. Please see page 370. Your contributions and earnings will not be taxed until you begin to withdraw the funds. A government-sponsored 457 plan is different from a 401(k) or a 403(b) plan in that there is no minimum retirement age and no 10-percent federal penalty for early withdrawal of funds. These plans also contain a provision allowing, under certain conditions, rollover of assets from government-sponsored 457 plans into other retirement plans, such as IRAs, 401(k)s, 403(b)s, and other 457s. Also, in government-sponsored 457 plans a special catch-up rule applies if you are three or fewer years away from retirement, letting you contribute up to twice the annual maximum otherwise in effect in any given year.

THE NOT-SO-WELL-KNOWN RETIREMENT PLANS

What is a defined-benefit pension plan?

A defined-benefit pension plan is a qualified retirement plan that promises to pay a specific amount to an employee who retires after a certain number of years. The benefit might be an exact dollar amount, for example, $4,000 per month. More common, the benefit might be determined by a formula that takes into account factors such as salary and length of employment with the company. For example, you might receive a monthly payment of 1 percent of your average salary during the last five years of employment for every year of service with your employer.

A defined-benefit pension plan is funded by the employer that creates it, not by the employees. The money that is held within a defined-benefit plan is not allocated to individual accounts; it is kept in one big account with all the money for all the employees. Money from this plan is usually not available for withdrawal until you reach retirement age, at which time you can receive it as a lump-sum payment, if your plan allows it, or as a lifetime annuity. If you take the money as an annuity, you won't be able to roll it over into an IRA and continue to defer taxes, which you can do if you take your retirement funds as a lump sum. So make sure you think through the tax implications if you have a choice of how to receive the benefit. Also, though you have been promised a defined benefit when you retire, if you leave that job or retire before the set retirement date, your benefits will be redefined. The bottom line is that the company is responsible for funding the plan, and it is responsible for giving the full benefit that has been defined. By law, it cannot fall short of that goal.

What is a target-benefit plan?

This qualified retirement plan works somewhat like a defined-benefit plan except that the employees all have separate accounts. In this plan the benefit is defined as a target to be met at the time of retirement. So while a defined-benefit plan guarantees a specific retirement benefit, the target-benefit just estimates and hopes to come close to the target. When the plan is opened up, the employer sets a benefit goal and estimates (with the help of actuaries) how much money will need to be invested each year to reach it. Once this formula has been set, it is frozen. If the investment performance of this formula falls short, then you lose—you won't get the target benefit. If the account performs beyond expectations, however, any increase in benefit must also be passed on to the employees.

What is a defined-contribution plan?

Examples of defined-contribution plans include 401(k) plans, 403(b) plans, employee stock ownership plans, and profit-sharing plans. They are qualified retirement plans in which a certain amount or percentage of money is set aside every year for the employee's benefit. Simply put, the contribution is defined, but the benefit isn't; there is no way to know how much money the employee will get at retirement. The contributions in this plan may come from the employees, the employer, or both. In contrast to defined-benefit accounts, the funds of a defined-contribution plan are held in the employee's name. Sometimes the amount set aside is a set percentage of your annual salary. These contributions are generally invested on your behalf, and you will ultimately receive the balance—the contributions plus or minus any investment gains or losses. That means that the value of your retirement account will fluctuate with the value of your investments. There are restrictions on withdrawing these funds before retirement age.

What is a profit-sharing plan?

This is a retirement plan that usually, but not always, does just what the name suggests. In a profit-sharing plan, a company uses its profits to fund a qualified retirement plan for its em-
ployees. But the company has a lot of leeway. From year to year, it does not have to contribute to the plan, even when there are profits to share. On the other hand, it may decide to contribute to the plan even if there are no profits that year. Yes, you heard right—in a profit-sharing plan, the employer has the discretion to contribute or not, regardless of profitability. When the employer does contribute, the contribution formula is based on your compensation. As of the year 2010 (the latest available as of this writing), the contribution could be no more than 25 percent of your pay, up to a maximum eligible income of $245,000. The maximum dollar amount that could be contributed as of 2010 was $49,000. Percentages and maximum amounts may increase in years to come.

What is a money-purchase pension plan?

This is a qualified retirement plan that is similar to a profit-sharing plan, but because the frequency and amount of the employer's contributions are predetermined, I like this plan much better. In a money-purchase plan, the employer promises to contribute a fixed percentage of your annual salary, including any bonuses, each year, and that cannot change. Until 2002, another benefit of a money-purchase plan was that the contribution limits were higher than in a profit-sharing plan, but now the limits are the same: In 2010, the contribution could not be more than 25 percent of your pay, up to a maximum eligible income of $245,000 and a maximum dollar amount of $49,000. Percentages and maximum amounts may increase in years to come.

What is a stock bonus plan?

This qualified retirement plan works very much like a profit-sharing plan. The only difference is that the employer makes its contributions in the form of company stock instead of cash.

INDIVIDUAL RETIREMENT ACCOUNTS (IRAS)

The following section is devoted to traditional IRAs; it is followed by a section on Roth IRAs. Many of the features of a traditional IRA and a Roth IRA are the same. Where features are identical, you will see the designation T/R, for Traditional/Roth. Please be sure to look at both sections.

What is a traditional IRA?

A traditional Individual Retirement Account allows you to establish your own tax-deferred savings-and-investment account outside the auspices of an employer. In 2010, you can contribute up to $5,000 to your IRA and, if you are married, you can contribute up to $5,000 more for a nonworking spouse. This assumes the working spouse had at least $10,000 in earned income during the year. People aged 50 and over can contribute an additional $1,000 a year.

If you meet certain guidelines, you can deduct your annual IRA contribution from your income, thereby reducing the taxes that you owe that year. Once it is deposited in an IRA account, the money will grow tax-deferred until you withdraw it, at which time you will pay ordinary income tax on it.

What are the features and advantages of a traditional IRA?

A traditional IRA allows you to take a current-year tax deduction for your contribution, provided you meet the tax-law qualifications set forth by the IRS. If you are also covered by an employer-sponsored retirement plan like a 401(k), you might not be able to even partially deduct your contribution. If you do qualify for the deduction, you can subtract the amount of your contribution from your taxable income. Let's say you earn $28,000 a year and you qualify for the deduction. In 2010, you can contribute $5,000 to a traditional IRA and pay taxes on only $23,000 of your income. In addition to that terrific tax break, the money in the IRA—both your contributions and any income they earn—grows tax-deferred until you actually withdraw it. Also, when you withdraw money from an IRA you do not have to withhold 20 percent of the amount for taxes, which is required when you take money out of a 401(k) plan.

If I do not work, can I open and contribute to a traditional IRA?

If you are married you can open a Spousal IRA and fund it based on your spouse's income. Otherwise, only those people who have *earned* income or alimony can contribute to an IRA. Earned income is defined as wages, commissions, bonuses, tips, self-employment income, and fees for professional services. You *cannot* count Social Security, pension or annuity payments, interest or dividend income, income from real estate, or deferred compensation. If *all* of your income is derived from one or more of those nonearned sources, you won't be able to put any money in an IRA, unless your spouse has earned income.

Can someone give me the money to open a T/R IRA?

Yes, as long as you are otherwise earning at least the same amount of money as wages or other taxable compensation. In other words, if you make $5,000 in wages in the year 2010 and your parents want to give you up to $5,000 to contribute to an IRA, that's okay. But if you were not employed or did not earn at least $5,000, you couldn't put the full $5,000 gift into an IRA.

When I do take money out of my traditional IRA, what do I need to know?

When you withdraw money from your IRA, it will be taxed as ordinary income in the year of the withdrawal. Generally, you cannot make a withdrawal from a traditional IRA until you are 59½ without paying a 10 percent federal penalty on the amount you withdraw. On the other hand, you *must* start taking withdrawals from your IRA on April 1 after the year in which you turn 70½. If you don't begin withdrawing money by then, you will have to pay a 50 percent annual penalty on the amount of money that was supposed to be withdrawn!

Are there any exceptions to the 10 percent early-withdrawal penalty for a T/R IRA besides being 59½ years of age or older?

Yes, there are exceptions. But be aware that even if you avoid paying a 10 percent penalty for early withdrawal, you will still have to pay income taxes on that money (or, in the case of a

Roth, on the earnings portion of that money). You will not have to pay the penalty if:

1. *You suffered a disability.* For you to avoid the 10 percent penalty under this exception, you must prove that you cannot do any activity that would allow you to earn a living. A doctor is going to have to verify that you are seriously disabled and are expected to stay that way for a long time—possibly indefinitely—for this exception to fly.

2. *You have died.* When your beneficiaries inherit your IRA and start to take out the money, regardless of their age, they will not have to pay a penalty. However, they will have to pay taxes.

3. *You have incurred great medical expenses.* If you have medical bills that will not be covered or reimbursed by your insurance company, and those expenses exceed 7.5 percent of your adjusted gross income, you may qualify for this exception.

4. *You are a first-time homebuyer.* If you are planning to build, rebuild, or buy a house as a primary residence, you might be able to withdraw a maximum of $10,000 from your IRA without incurring a 10 percent penalty. This money can be used for a home for anyone in your family—you, your parents, your grandparents, your children, or your grandchildren. This includes your spouse's side of the family as well. There is a time frame on this withdrawal that you need to be aware of. You must use the money for a viable expense within 120 days of withdrawing it from your account. The money has to be spent on what the IRS considers valid expenses of buying or

building a home, such as closing costs, etc. Even though you are exempt from paying the early-withdrawal penalty, you will still have to pay income taxes on this money. "First-time homebuyer," by the way, does not mean first time ever. It simply means that you have not owned a home in the previous two years. So if you owned a home, sold it, and now, two years later, you want to buy another home, you can qualify for this exception.

5. *You need money to pay for college.* You or anyone in your family can use any of the money in your IRA to help pay for secondary, undergraduate, or graduate education. The money can be used for a variety of education expenses, including room and board (for students attending school at least half-time), books, supplies, tuition, equipment needed for classes. Again, please note: You will avoid the early-withdrawal penalty here but you will still owe taxes.

6. *You need to pay for health insurance.* If you need money to pay for medical insurance premiums for you, your spouse, or your dependents, and you meet *all* of the following criteria, you can take money out of your IRA and not have to pay the early withdrawal penalty.

- You are not employed because you lost your job.
- You have received unemployment compensation for at least 12 consecutive weeks.
- The money will be withdrawn from your IRA in the same calendar year you received unemployment.

If you do get another job, the money must be withdrawn from the IRA within 60 days of the date you were hired.

7. *You are using a technique known as substantially equal period payments, or SEPP.* If you are younger than 59½ and you need to get money out of a retirement account, such as a traditional IRA, and you want to avoid the 10 percent early-withdrawal penalty, you might consider making substantially equal periodic payments. Essentially, this means making regular withdrawals from your IRA until you are of retirement age (59½) or for at least five years, whichever is longer.

If I decide to use the SEPP method, how do I figure out how much my payments would be each year?

The three methods of calculation you (and the IRS) can use to determine the amount of your substantially equal periodic payments are based on life expectancy, amortization, and annuity. How much you must withdraw each month depends on the method you use; each method applies a different formula to several factors, including your life expectancy and the estimated rate of return on your investment. In most cases, people use the amortization method, because it's easier, but often the annuity method will give them the most income. Make this decision carefully—I recommend getting help from a CPA or professional financial adviser well versed in SEPP—because once you choose your method and start receiving SEPP payments, you cannot change it. Make sure the firm that calculates your SEPP states on company letterhead (not just the adviser's personal letterhead) that the company will be responsible for calculating your substantially equal periodic payments, and that it will be responsible for any mistakes and penalties.

What are the pitfalls of withdrawing money using substantially equal periodic payments?

There are a couple tricky things to keep in mind when withdrawing money this way. First, under the amortization method, you have to take out the same amount of money every month, or if you prefer annual withdrawals, they must be identical from year to year. If you aren't careful, and if you don't take the correct amount of money, which is set according to IRS rules, you could be vulnerable to penalties later. Please note: Some investments, such as annuities, meet the rules of SEPP even though the first year's distribution will vary from that of other years.

Does it matter how my retirement account is invested during the time I am taking SEPP?

Because the way in which your money is invested is significant under SEPP, whether or not you will need to make changes depends on how you are invested. As a general rule, when investing for SEPP, invest at least 80 percent of your funds for income instead of growth. Over the five years or more that you are taking SEPP withdrawals, you don't want to risk the stock market—and your income—dropping, potentially forcing you to make withdrawals from your principal. When the SEPP period is over, you can again invest for growth.

How do I figure out if I can contribute to a traditional IRA and deduct the amount of my contribution from my income for tax purposes?

Whether or not you can deduct your contribution to a traditional IRA depends on whether you are covered by a qualifying employer-sponsored retirement plan such as a 401(k) plan and what your filing status and income are in the taxable year. If you are covered by a retirement plan at work, you still may be able to deduct all or part of your IRA contribution.

What are the income limits on deducting contributions to a traditional IRA?

Please note: The full deductibility of the yearly contribution limit in an IRA is phased out from 100 percent deductible to zero percent after you have reached the income limitations. The phaseout income ranges rise each year; in 2010, the phaseout range is $56,000 to $66,000 for single taxpayers and $89,000 to $109,000 for married taxpayers filing jointly. If you are married and you make more than the yearly limit, you may still contribute to a traditional IRA, but you won't be able to take the deduction.

The chart below is a list of income ranges for use in determining the amount of an IRA contribution that can be deducted. See page 328 to learn how to calculate modified adjusted gross income.

If you earn too much to take the deduction, you may still qualify for a Roth IRA, which we will discuss in detail later in the chapter.

My income falls in the middle of the phaseout range. How do I figure out what portion of my traditional IRA contribution is tax-deductible?

You use a simple formula based on your income level and marital status. Essentially, you subtract

INCOME LIMITS TO DEDUCT YOUR IRA CONTRIBUTIONS	
SINGLE	
Year	**Modified Adjusted Gross Income Phaseout Range**
2009 and 2010	$55,000–$65,000
2011 onward	$56,000–$66,000
MARRIED, FILING JOINTLY	
Year	**Modified Adjusted Gross Income Phaseout Range**
2009 and 2010	$89,000–$109,000
2011 onward	Indexed to inflation

There is no income phase-out when neither spouse is active in an employer's retirement plan and when a single filer is not active in an employer's retirement plan.

your modified adjusted gross income from the largest figure for the relevant tax year, then multiply the difference by 0.20; that is how much money you will be able to deduct. Here's an example: Let's say that you are single and have a modified adjusted gross income of $60,000 in the year 2009. The maximum figure for your phaseout range in 2010 is $66,000. So you subtract $60,000 from $66,000 and get $6,000. Now you multiply $6,000 by 0.20 and you'll see that you can deduct $1,200 of your $5,000 IRA contribution that year.

I am covered by a pension plan but my spouse doesn't work. Can we deduct her contribution if we are within the income limits?

In that case, if you are covered by a pension plan and have a spouse who is not, the income limits for the non-covered spouse's IRA deductibility rise. If your modified adjusted gross income as a married couple filing jointly is less than $167,000, you can take a full deduction on a traditional IRA contribution for a nonworking spouse during that year. If your income is more than $177,000, you cannot deduct a traditional IRA contribution for your nonworking spouse at all. Of course, if you are not an active participant in an employer's retirement plan, you can always deduct a traditional IRA contribution from your taxes. Still, you might be better off with a Roth IRA if you qualify.

I have a 401(k) plan, so I don't qualify for a tax deduction for an IRA. Does that disqualify my spouse as well?

Keep in mind that one spouse is not considered to be covered by a pension plan just because the other spouse is. A spouse without a qualified pension plan can make a fully deductible IRA contribution as long as the couple's modified adjusted gross income does not exceed $167,000.

Where can I open up a T/R IRA account?

You can open an IRA account at many

institutions: a full-service or discount brokerage firm, a mutual fund company, an insurance company, a bank, or a credit union.

What can I invest in within my T/R IRA?

Once you open your account, you can invest it in a variety of ways—you can put your money in stocks and mutual funds, exchange-traded funds (ETFs), certificates of deposit (CDs), high-interest savings accounts, annuities, bonds, etc. Your selection will depend on what the firm you opened your IRA with offers, which, depending on the company, can restrict your options in ways you hadn't planned. For this reason, I always suggest opening an IRA at a company that offers you a variety of investments at a good cost, such as discount brokerage firms like TD Ameritrade.

What is the deadline for opening a T/R IRA for a specific tax year?

The deadline for opening an IRA for a given tax year is April 15 of the following calendar year. In other words, you can open up an IRA on April 15, 2010, and it will apply to the tax year 2009. Many people are aware of this deadline and don't open their IRA until April of the year *after* they could have done so. This is a mistake. For the tax year 2009, for example, you have the right to put $5,000 in your IRA on January 1, 2009. But most people wait until April 2010 to do so, thereby losing more than a year's worth of tax-deferred or tax-free compounding earnings.

Does it make a difference when I invest my T/R IRA contribution?

Waiting to invest almost always costs you. If you wait until the following tax year to make a con-tribution, you may be losing money. Remember the power of compounding gains. If you possibly can, put that money away at the beginning of the year rather than at the tax deadline. If you invest $5,000 in January of 2009, for example, and that money sits in your IRA earning an 8 percent return, by the time April 15 of the 2010 tax year comes along, you would have an extra $540 in the account.

Now look at the big picture. If you put away the maximum contribution allowed each year for the next 25 years, and this money earns an 8 percent average annual return, after 25 years of putting this contribution in every January like clockwork, you would have approximately $395,000 in your IRA. If instead you waited until April of the following year to make this contribution, you'd have about $340,000, a potential "opportunity loss" of $55,000.

If you don't have the money at the beginning of the year or can't make the investment all at once, put whatever you can each month into your IRA. You will still come out better than if you wait to do it in one lump sum.

If I have a 401(k) plan at work, can I also have a T/R IRA?

Yes, you can put money into both a 401(k) and an IRA but, depending on your income level and your tax filing status, you may not be able to take the full tax deduction of the traditional IRA. If you qualify for a Roth, that's a better investment.

If I am putting as much money into my 401(k) plan as my employer allows, should I bother getting a T/R IRA?

Yes, and the reason is very straightforward: If you give up a little bit of money now, you will have a lot more to live on after you retire. Every extra dollar that you save, whether taxed, tax-deferred, or tax-free, and invest today instead of spending will grow exponentially over time. However, if you can qualify for a Roth IRA, you would be better off opening up a Roth than a traditional IRA.

Can I have more than one T/R IRA?

Absolutely. You can invest in as many IRAs as you want, but you can't contribute more than the current annual maximum each year to all your IRAs. This means that if you have five IRAs in the year 2009, you can divvy up the $5,000 among the accounts any way you like.

Is there an advantage to having more than one T/R IRA account?

In most cases there is actually a disadvantage to having more than one. You see, most IRAs charge a yearly fee. That fee can run anywhere from $25 to $50, or higher. That may not seem like a lot of money, but it is when you look at it in terms of percentages. If you are paying $30 a year for an IRA, and all you have in the account is $300, you are paying 10 percent of the account value just for the custodial fee. This means that even if your investment went up 10 percent that year, all you did was break even. However, if you had all your 2009 contribution of $5,000 in just one account and the fee was $30, well, that's not so bad—less than 1 percent of the account value. So if your investment within the IRA went up 10 percent, after the custodial fee (assuming it is deducted from the IRA account

itself) you still would have made more than 9 percent on your money that year.

Does every brokerage firm charge a fee?

No, some do not.

Are the custodial fees you pay for a T/R IRA tax-deductible?

Theoretically, yes. If you pay these fees with funds outside your IRA, if you itemize deductions on your return, and if the fees and other miscellaneous itemized deductions total more than 2 percent of your adjusted gross income, the fees are tax-deductible. In practice, most people have custodial fees deducted right from the IRA account, in which case, they are not tax-deductible.

Once I've opened a T/R IRA, am I obligated to contribute the maximum amount allowed each year?

No. You can open an IRA and invest the maximum allowed in the year you open it and then never contribute another penny to it. You also may contribute less than the maximum to it in any given year. But I think you should make funding your IRA to the maximum each year a priority, particularly if you are not covered by another type of retirement plan.

What is the difference in monetary terms between a 401(k) plan and a T/R IRA?

In 2010, the difference amounts to about $11,500 a year—and more if you're age 50 or older. The maximum amount you can put into an IRA in 2010 is $5,000—not much to hope to retire on. In a 401(k), qualified employees are allowed to contribute up to $16,500 a year or $22,000 if they are age 50 or older. That difference should be a big incentive to push your employer to sponsor a retirement plan.

One important similarity is that IRAs, like 401(k)s, are protected in bankruptcy.

When I go to take money out of my IRA, can I take it out in stock? Or do I have to sell my stock and take it out in cash?

You can take it out in stock if you want to. Say you want to withdraw $15,000. You can withdraw it in cash, or in $15,000 of stock. If you do this, you will pay ordinary income taxes on the value of the stock on the day it was withdrawn (plus a 10 percent penalty if you are not at least 59½). If you later sell the stock at an increased value, you will owe taxes on that gain as well.

ROTH IRAS

Roth IRAs were created by an act of Congress in 1996. With a Roth IRA, you may not deduct your contribution, but your contributions can grow income tax–free. When you withdraw money from a Roth IRA at retirement, you will not owe any taxes on that money, no matter how much the money has grown in value, provided you have followed IRS guidelines. What few people seem to realize is that in a contributory, or non-tax-deferred, Roth IRA, you can withdraw your own contributions at any time without penalties or taxes, regardless of your age and how long the money has been in

the Roth. Any gains your contributions earn, however, must stay in the Roth IRA until you have turned 59½ *and* you've held your account for more than five years before you can withdraw them without taxes or penalties. Earnings from Roth IRA contributions *can* be withdrawn penalty-free if you become disabled or die.

What are the Roth's income limitations?

Single taxpayers whose modified adjusted gross income (MAGI) is less than $105,000 per year and married couples who have a combined annual MAGI of less than $167,000 in 2010 can contribute up to $5,000 each (or $6,000 if they are 50 or over). Your eligibility to contribute the full $5,000 (or $6,000 if you are over 50) is phased out between $105,000 and $120,000 for single taxpayers and between $167,000 and $177,000 for married taxpayers filing jointly. After those amounts you are not eligible for a Roth IRA.

What exactly is modified adjusted gross income?

Modified adjusted gross income, or MAGI, is determined by taking your adjusted gross income (AGI) and adding back a variety of items. Adjusted gross income is defined as your total taxable income minus certain expenses, such as qualified plan contributions, IRA contributions, and alimony payments. To figure out your MAGI, take your AGI and add back:

- Income from U.S. savings bonds used for higher education expenses;
- Any expenses your employer paid you to adopt a child;

- Foreign earned income and payments received for foreign housing;
- Any deductions claimed on regular IRA contributions;
- Any deductions taken for interest on an education loan.

What are the advantages of a Roth IRA over a traditional IRA?

There are several. First, the Roth potentially allows you to amass a lot over the long term in exchange for not taking a tax deduction now. If, from ages 21 to 30, you invested $5,000 in a Roth IRA averaging a yearly return of about 8 percent and never added another penny, you would have $758,000 at age 59½, income tax–free. That's a huge difference from a traditional IRA, on which you or your beneficiaries would eventually have to pay income taxes on that same sum. To have tax-free access to that Roth money, you simply give up the tax deduction that a traditional IRA offers you on your contributions—at a time when you may be in a pretty low income-tax bracket anyway.

Second, if you have a traditional IRA and you die, your spouse is the only person allowed to take over the IRA as a retirement account. Assuming that you haven't already started to withdraw the money, your surviving spouse can use the tax-deferral strategies of the traditional IRA until he or she really needs the money or turns 70½. But if you are not married, the named beneficiary on a traditional IRA will be required to start making withdrawals in the year after you die and will have to continue making them through his or her life—or until the account is cleaned out, which usually comes first. This presents a significant tax burden to the beneficiary. With a Roth IRA, a beneficiary will inherit the money free and clear of income taxes (as long as distribution started more than five years after the opening of the account). Estate taxes, if any, still apply.

Another major advantage of the Roth IRA is that you do not have to begin taking withdrawals at age 70½, as you do with a traditional IRA. If you don't really need the money but are forced to begin withdrawing money from a traditional IRA anyway, it will only increase your adjusted gross income—and thus your income taxes.

But the two main reasons Roth IRAs are so popular is that the earnings are tax-free instead of tax-deferred, and you can take out your original contributions any time you want, regardless of your age, without taxes or penalties.

Can I have a Roth IRA if I already have a 401(k)?

Yes, as long as you meet the income qualifications.

I already have a 401(k). Are there drawbacks to having a traditional IRA versus a Roth IRA?

There may be. Because you already have a 401(k), you can't take any tax deductions on traditional IRA contributions if you earn more than the IRA income limit (see the chart on page 325). Plus, you will still have to pay ordinary income tax on the growth of this money when you withdraw it. With a Roth IRA, you can't deduct your contributions either, but your withdrawals after the age of 59½ will be income tax–free.

If I qualify for both a Roth IRA and my company's 401(k), which should I invest in first?

Which you invest in first depends on four factors: (1) whether your employer matches your contributions to your 401(k); (2) the investment options your 401(k) plan offers; (3) your current tax bracket; and (4) whether you foresee needing the money in your retirement plan before turning 59½. If your company matches your 401(k) contribution, you cannot—and I stress—you *cannot* pass that up. So fund your 401(k) at least up to the limit of your employer's matching contribution. After getting the maximum match on your 401(k), I would suggest funding a Roth IRA, and then, if there's anything left, contributing whatever more you can to your 401(k). If your tax bracket is high and/or you may need to withdraw money before 59½, please see a tax professional.

Can I have a Roth IRA and a traditional IRA at the same time?

Sure. Remember, though, that you can contribute only the maximum amount allowed in total each year to your IRAs, no matter how many you have or what kinds they are.

I'm already contributing the maximum allowable amount to my pension plan at work. I make too much money to qualify for a traditional IRA or a Roth IRA. Is there any other type of retirement account I can look into?

You can open a nondeductible IRA, which is just like a traditional IRA except that you can't deduct your contributions. Go ahead and do this. Even though you won't be able to deduct your contributions, your money will still grow tax-deferred.

If I have a few separate Roth IRAs and I want to withdraw some of my money but am not yet 59½, does it matter which Roth I tap into?

For tax purposes, the IRS aggregates all your Roth IRAs and considers them one account. Also, once you begin to withdraw money from these accounts, your contributions are considered to be the first withdrawals that you make. So if you have contributed, say, $5,000 into each of two different Roth IRAs and one has grown to $10,000 and the other to $7,700, you do not have to withdraw $5,000 from each account. You can close out the $10,000 account.

Is there anyone who shouldn't have a Roth IRA?

In my opinion, there is only one situation in which it might make sense to have a traditional IRA rather than a Roth IRA. If you are in a high tax bracket during the years you will be making your contributions, really need the tax write-off that the traditional IRA will give you, *and* know, without a shadow of a doubt, that you will be in a very low tax bracket when you take this money out—then, yes, a traditional IRA might be better than a Roth. But it's tricky to predict the tax bracket you'll be in at retirement. In most cases, I would opt for the Roth IRA.

Why do you so strongly prefer Roth IRAs to traditional IRAs?

The Roth IRA protects you from some future uncertainties. For example, say an unforeseen expense comes up and you need money before you turn 59½. A Roth IRA allows you to access your contributions without taxes or penalties, no matter what your age or how long your money has been in the account. It's also hard to be sure what tax bracket you will be in when you make your withdrawals. With the Roth IRA, your money is protected from future taxes— you paid them at the time of deposit and won't have to pay them at withdrawal. You may not know, in many cases, if you will even need to use the money in your Roth IRA. If you don't, you can leave the Roth IRA to your beneficiaries income tax–free as well. This makes a big difference. Say you have $300,000 in a traditional IRA when you retire. You will owe taxes on that money at whatever tax rates are in effect at the time you go to withdraw it. Who can say how much of that $300,000 you will be able to keep? With a Roth IRA, that is not a problem— income taxes do not affect you if all requirements are met.

The bottom line: With a Roth IRA, you know exactly how much money you will have when you retire. Income taxes will not deplete your account.

ROTH CONVERSIONS

What is a Roth conversion?
Starting in the late 90s, people who had traditional IRAs were allowed to convert them into Roth IRAs. The process came to be known as a Roth conversion. Conversions are not subject to early-withdrawal penalties, but are subject to ordinary income tax.

Can anyone transfer or convert money from a traditional IRA to a Roth IRA?

Beginning in 2010 anyone, regardless of income, is eligible to convert a traditional IRA into a Roth IRA.

Can I convert my traditional IRA to a Roth anytime I want?
The traditional IRA money must be withdrawn by December 31 of the year in which you are converting and deposited to the Roth IRA within 60 days. All withdrawals and transfers should be done from trustee to trustee; you should not handle the money yourself.

Can you convert just some of a traditional IRA, or do you have to convert the whole thing?
It's common for people to think that they have to convert all the funds in a traditional IRA, but that's not the case. You can convert any amount of money.

Can I convert a 401(k) account to a Roth IRA?
Yes. Since 2008, direct rollovers from a 401(k) to a Roth IRA are allowed. You may owe income tax at the time of the rollover and conversion.

What are the tax consequences of converting from a traditional IRA to a Roth IRA?
No matter what your age, you will have to pay ordinary income taxes on the money you are transferring in the year that you make the conversion. If you are 70½ or older in the year that you want to convert, be especially aware of IRS rules that prohibit converting any mandatory distributions.

Is a Roth IRA started with conversion money the same as a contributory Roth IRA?

The rules that govern contributory and converted Roth IRAs are identical, with one exception. After you have converted a traditional IRA to a Roth IRA, you'll need to keep the money that was originally converted in the Roth IRA for at least five years or until you are 59½—whichever comes first—before you can withdraw the amount you originally converted. If you withdraw any of the money that was converted from the traditional IRA earlier than that, you will have to pay a penalty on the amount you withdraw. That would, of course, subvert the whole idea of converting to the Roth. Please note that, regardless of the amount you originally converted, the earnings on the money you converted will have to stay in the account until you turn 59½ to be withdrawn without penalty. To take the earnings out without penalties *or* taxes, you must be 59½ *and* the account must be more than five years old.

How do I know whether I should convert my traditional IRA to a Roth IRA?

Before you make a move, you need to make sure that you will be able to pay for the taxes out of your income or from assets other than your IRA. Keep in mind that you don't have to convert the whole IRA—converting only part of it could minimize your current tax liability. For 2010 only: The tax bill you owe for conversions made in 2010 can be paid over two years, 2010 and 2011. In this situation, I'd advise you to consult a professional. Try a certified public accountant or an enrolled agent (someone legally permitted to do tax returns) who does not make commissions by managing money.

How can I judge if I'm a good candidate to convert my traditional IRA to a Roth IRA?

Here are some general guidelines to help you make your decision:

- Make sure that you have some means of paying the tax bill aside from using your IRA funds. If you don't, converting is not a good idea.
- If the money that you are planning to use to pay the taxes is going to come from the sale of some other investment, will that sale cause you to incur capital gains or ordinary income taxes? How much future growth will you lose by paying the tax on the conversion? Make sure you factor this information into your calculations to see if converting still makes sense.
- Will the additional income from your IRA conversion make your (otherwise nontaxable) Social Security benefits taxable or reduce the amount of itemized deductions, personal exemptions, or rental losses during the year of your conversion? Can you afford that? If so, you may want to convert.
- Are you in a relatively low tax bracket right now? Do you expect to be in a higher one by the time that you retire? If both are true, you are a good candidate for conversion.
- Are you close to retirement and are you planning to use your IRA to live on? If so, it probably doesn't make sense to convert.
- Are you close to retirement but *not* planning

to use your IRA money for the foreseeable future? If so, you should consider converting.

- Is your goal to pass your IRA down to your beneficiaries income tax-free? If so, and if you have the money to pay the tax bill now, converting probably makes sense for you.

- Are you concerned that your beneficiaries are going to have to pay really high income taxes? If so, converting may make sense. Converting can eliminate future income taxation for you and your beneficiaries. Remember, though, that Roth IRAs are included in your gross estate for estate tax calculations, so your heirs may still need to pay estate tax on your Roth IRA.

- Have you named a charity or some other type of nonprofit organization as the beneficiary of your IRA? Since these types of beneficiaries won't have to pay taxes on the bequest anyway, it may not make sense for you to convert. Check with a professional.

- Do you have a nondeductible IRA that hasn't been earning great returns? In this case, converting may make sense, because you have already paid taxes on your contributions and the income from the conversion will only include your earnings, not your contributions. If your nondeductible IRA has been performing well, though, you'll have to run the numbers to see if converting makes sense.

Is there a website than can help me figure out if I should convert to a Roth IRA?

There are actually many websites that can help you do the calculations to answer this question. Just keep in mind that they may have been set up by companies hoping to wind up with your

IRA money. I recommend *www.rothira.com,* a site with very good conversion calculators.

Once I have decided to convert from a traditional IRA to a Roth, what is the best way to do it?

The easiest way to convert is to open a Roth IRA account with the same company that has your traditional IRA, assuming they have been doing a satisfactory job for you so far. They can convert the account for you.

RECHARACTERIZATION AND RECONVERTING OF A ROTH

What is a Roth recharacterization?

Recharacterization simply means moving money that was converted to a Roth IRA out of that converted Roth IRA and back into a traditional IRA.

What does reconverting mean?

If you have recharacterized your Roth into a traditional IRA and you want to convert the money back into a Roth again, this transfer is known as a reconversion.

Is there any reason that I might want to recharacterize my Roth IRA and then later reconvert?

Yes. You might want to recharacterize as a tax strategy. Let's say you convert your traditional IRA to a Roth IRA at the beginning of the year 2009. Over the course of the year, the account loses a significant amount of value. To make matters worse, you are going to be stuck paying taxes on the value of the traditional IRA at the time you converted. If you recharacterize your Roth back to a traditional IRA, you would avoid paying taxes on the amount that you originally converted.

Isn't it worth it to just pay the taxes on the higher value so I can have my money in a converted Roth?

It depends. If you expect to meet the income requirements for a Roth in the next year, it's most likely worth your while to recharacterize and then reconvert back to a Roth.

For example, say you converted a traditional IRA worth $100,000 into a converted Roth IRA in April 2009, and by October it was worth only $50,000. If you leave things as they are, you will owe taxes on that $100,000 conversion. But if you recharacterize your Roth IRA within the allowable time, you will not have to pay taxes for the year 2009 on $100,000. So, let's say it is November 2009 and your account is worth only $50,000. If you recharacterize on November 1, 2009, you will avoid paying taxes on that conversion. Now, let's say that you really want that money in a converted Roth, and as of January 2010, the account is still worth only $50,000. If you now reconvert back to a Roth, you will only be taxed on $50,000, and those taxes won't be due until April 2011. By recharacterizing and then reconverting you have saved paying tax on $50,000—a lot of money by anyone's standards. Make sure that the company holding your converted IRA gives you the option of recharacterizing and reconverting.

How long do I have to recharacterize my Roth?

According to IRS publication 590, you have until October 15 of the tax year following the year of your original conversion, as long as you file your tax returns in a timely manner.

Last year I recharacterized my Roth IRA, and now I want to reconvert it from a traditional IRA back to a Roth. Are there any time restrictions I need to be aware of?

An IRA owner who converts a traditional IRA to a Roth IRA and then recharacterizes it (that is, changes it back to a traditional IRA) may not reconvert the traditional IRA (change it to a Roth again) before the beginning of the next tax year or until the end of a 30-day period from the day the Roth IRA was recharacterized, whichever is later.

That sounds complicated, but it's not. An example with dates should clear it up. Let's say that you converted your funds from a traditional IRA to a Roth in the year 2009. You then found out in 2010 that your account lost half its value in the last months of 2009. You had until October 15, 2010, to do a recharacterization (move the money back into a traditional IRA). On April 15, 2010, you recharacterized your Roth. You cannot reconvert your traditional IRA back to a Roth IRA until May 16, 2010. The IRS stipulates that you must wait until the calendar year after the year of the orginal conversion, or more than 30 days after the date of the recharacterization, whichever date is later, to reconvert—in this case, more than 30 days. However, had you recharacterized on December 20, 2009, you would not be able to reconvert until 30 days after that date, or until about January 19.

IRA ROLLOVER

What is an IRA rollover?

An IRA rollover allows you to transfer (or roll over) assets from your tax-deferred 401(k) to another tax-deferred investment vehicle. Because both investments are tax-deferred, there is no tax consequence when you make the transfer. If you invested in a traditional 401(k) and do a rollover into a traditional IRA, when you ultimately withdraw the funds, usually at age 59½ or older, the money will be taxed as ordinary income in the year of withdrawal. Money rolled over from a Roth 401(k) to a Roth IRA will not be subject to tax when you make withdrawals. You also have the option of converting a traditional 401(k) into a Roth IRA at the time of your rollover. You will owe tax at the time of the conversion, but in retirement you will then be able to make tax-free withdrawals from your Roth IRA account.

How long do I have to transfer my money from a 401(k) plan to an IRA rollover?

If you take possession of your 401(k) funds yourself, you have 60 days from the date of receipt to get them into your rollover account. If you miss the deadline, you will be taxed on the entire withdrawal, and if you are not at least 59½, you also will be hit with a 10 percent penalty.

But the transfer of such funds is usually done from custodian to custodian in what is called a direct rollover. You open up an IRA rollover account at a discount brokerage firm (my preference), a bank, an insurance company, or a mutual fund company, and it arranges the transfer from your 401(k) into the new account. This is the best way to do a rollover, since the custodian of your 401(k) plan will not be required to withhold 20 percent of the money for possible taxes.

What are the advantages of an IRA rollover?

One advantage is that most IRA rollovers give you an unlimited choice of mutual funds, exchange-traded funds (ETFs), stocks, and bonds in which to invest your money, and you can usually trade as often and as many times as you want to. You can usually place orders to buy or sell by phone, and your transactions are usually confirmed immediately. You also may have access to a professional financial adviser.

Are there any disadvantages to an IRA rollover?

If you use a full-service broker, you may be charged annual fees and commissions. If you are younger than 59½, you can withdraw your IRA money only through substantially equal periodic payments or annuitization to avoid the 10 percent early-withdrawal penalty—unless you meet one of the exceptions for medical expenses, etc. But for most people in the majority of scenarios, an IRA rollover is a very smart move.

If I'm younger than 55 in the year I retire, is an IRA rollover the way to go?

Possibly. The flexibility and greater number of

investment options could make this a better choice than a company plan. If you have a really large amount of money in your plan and you are going to seek professional financial advice, you might want to consider dividing your rollover between two advisers to see which one performs better.

If I'm older than 55, which makes more sense?

If you are between the ages of 55 and 59½ in the year you retire, leave at least some of your money in the company plan (as long as you are allowed to). That way, you can take advantage of the investment flexibility of an IRA and you'll also have access to the money in your 401(k) without that 10 percent penalty limitation of an IRA.

If you are over age 59½ in the year you retire, the decision is up to you. If you want to expand your investment opportunities, an IRA rollover gives you the opportunity to do so.

I've been told that when I retire I have to take all my money out of my 401(k) and roll it over into a single IRA account. Is that correct?

Absolutely not! Many people think that they have to roll over their entire retirement account into one place, but they are mistaken. Here are just a few options:

- If your company allows you to do so, you can leave your money in your 401(k). As long as your account value is at least $5,000 you should be allowed to leave the money in the 401(k).
- You can roll over all the money into one IRA.
- You can do an unlimited number of rollovers into as many IRAs as you want.

- You can leave some of your money in the company plan (assuming that the company allows you to do this) and roll the rest of it over into one or more IRAs.
- If you are 55 or older in the year you retire, you can take distributions of all or part of your retirement account without penalty. You will still have to pay ordinary income tax on those distributions assuming your money was in a traditional 401(k).

RETIREMENT PLANS FOR THE SELF-EMPLOYED

If you're self-employed and are not an incorporated entity, you too have excellent options for funding your (and your employees') retirement. You can open what is known as a simplified employee pension (SEP) plan, a Keogh, or a SIMPLE. All three of these are tax-deferred pension plans, and great ways to save for retirement. In order to qualify for these accounts, your earnings must be reported on Form 1099-MISC, or earned as fees for services you've provided. If people work for you, you'll have to fund SEP, Keogh, or SIMPLE plans for them as well. Most retirement accounts for the self-employed are governed by the same restrictions as IRA and 401(k) plans. You should consult a professional for exact guidelines in your situation, but, in general, the same 10 percent penalty for withdrawing money before the age of 59½ applies; all money withdrawn will be taxed as ordinary income in the year of withdrawal, unless you and your plan qualify for 10-

year averaging; and in most cases you have to start taking money out by April 1 of the year you turn 70½.

What is a SEP-IRA?

SEP stands for simplified employee pension plan. It's essentially an extended IRA for self-employed people and their employees. But whereas in an IRA you can contribute a maximum in 2009 of only $5,000 a year (increasing in following years; please see page 369), in a SEP-IRA you can contribute up to $49,000 to your own account in 2010, or 25 percent of your adjusted earned income, as income is defined for these purposes by IRS, whichever is less; and up to $49,000 per year per employee, or 25 percent of his or her salary, whichever is less.

Where can I set up a SEP-IRA?

SEP-IRAs can be established virtually anywhere you would like to invest—at a bank, a mutual fund company, or a brokerage firm.

For an employer, what is the downside of a SEP-IRA?

If you fund a SEP for yourself and have employees who have worked for you for three of the past five years, you are also required to fund their SEPs. The money in these accounts vests immediately, and if your employees leave tomorrow, they will be able to take that money with them. With a SEP-IRA, employees are 100 percent vested at all times.

Can I have a SEP-IRA and a Roth IRA?

Yes. You can have both a Roth IRA and a SEP if you meet the income requirements.

Is it possible to convert a SEP-IRA to a Roth IRA?

Yes. This particular conversion can make a lot of sense, because it allows you to invest more than the maximum allowed per year in a Roth. Let's say that your income would allow you to contribute $12,400 a year to a SEP-IRA. You can make that deposit and then you can convert that SEP-IRA to a Roth. Essentially, you will have managed to put a great deal more than the annual limit into a Roth. You will have to pay taxes on the $12,400 after you convert, but you can deduct that same $12,400 from your income as a SEP-IRA deduction. If you are self-employed, consult a tax specialist to see how much you could contribute to a SEP-IRA, and consider making this conversion.

What is a Keogh plan?

A Keogh is a somewhat more complicated plan than a SEP-IRA, but it may allow you to save more money. The added benefit carries with it more immediate responsibility to your employees. If you fund a Keogh for yourself, you must also fund a Keogh for any employee who has worked for you for more than one year (two years if there is full vesting required in no more than two years).

There are three types of Keogh plans. The two most common types are a money-purchase plan and a profit-sharing plan. In both, you can put aside up to 25 percent of your qualified net income, as defined by the IRS (up to a maximum of $49,000 in 2010, the latest year available as of this writing), and invest the money in any way you choose. But be careful: In a money-purchase plan, when you open the account, you establish the percentage of your own (and of any employees') net earnings that you must continue to contribute each year from that time on, and that percentage cannot be changed. It doesn't matter whether you have a great year financially or a terrible one, you must still contribute the same percentage of your own (and of any employees') income to the money-purchase Keogh. Profit-sharing Keoghs are more flexible, in that you have discretion as to how much or how little to contribute each year, up to the maximum amounts allowed by the IRS.

The third type of plan, a defined-benefit plan, may allow much larger contributions for you and your employees. However, contributions are required every year, whether or not there are profits, in the amount determined by an actuary to be necessary to reach a defined benefit.

It is possible to create a combination of Keogh plans to give you the maximum opportunity to save while maintaining some flexibility. Consult your tax adviser.

SIMPLE IRA

What is a SIMPLE IRA?

A Savings Incentive Match Plan for Employees (SIMPLE) is an IRA set up by a small employer for the company's employees. Employees may contribute a percentage of their salary, up to $11,500 (or $14,000 if you are 50 or older) in the year 2010, to their SIMPLE IRA and will receive some level of a matching percentage from their employer. (The maximum contribution in subsequent years will be indexed to infla-

tion.) The employer must match contributions according to a certain formula. The employer and the employee together may contribute up to $16,400 in the year 2010 to the participant's account.

Do I have to set up a SIMPLE plan for all my employees?

No. Only employees who made at least $5,000 in any two prior years and are projected to earn at least $5,000 during the current year are eligible for a SIMPLE IRA.

How much of my employees' contributions am I required to match?

As a self-employed person with eligible employees, you either will have to follow a matching-contribution formula or a 2 percent contribution formula. If you choose the matching formula, you must match the dollar amount each employee contributes to the plan, up to a range of from 1 to 3 percent of his or her salary. (You can choose a 1 percent match for up to two of any five years.) Under the 2 percent contribution formula, you, the employer, agree to contribute 2 percent of the employee's salary up to a maximum of $4,900 per year (for the year 2010) for each employee, regardless of whether the employee makes any contribution that year. All these contributions, by the way, are vested the moment they are made, which means that any contributing employee can withdraw them if he or she leaves your company. Between your contribution for your employee and what he deposits for himself, in the year 2010 an employee may have up to $16,400 a year invested in a SIMPLE.

Can I have a SIMPLE IRA and a Roth IRA?

Yes, as long as you meet the income qualifications of a Roth.

I work for myself. What retirement plan do I want: a SEP, a Keogh, or a SIMPLE?

If paperwork makes you crazy, you should know that there's more paperwork involved with a Keogh than with a SEP or a SIMPLE (the paperwork requirements for which are almost nil). Once you have more than $100,000 in a Keogh account, and only you and your spouse or you and your business partners and spouses are covered, you'll have to file a 5500EZ form—it's not all that bad, but it's still paperwork, and paperwork is not required with a SEP or a SIMPLE. If the maximum contribution to a SEP or a SIMPLE meets your needs, you're better off staying away from the Keogh. If your income warrants it and you can use that extra tax break, then a Keogh is the way to go.

If you're self-employed, you should definitely take advantage of one of these options. Just don't forget that employees are 100 percent vested at all times with a SIMPLE IRA or a SEP-IRA. With a Keogh, there is a vesting schedule. Check with a professional.

If I take money out of a SIMPLE the year after I open it, will I have to pay a 10 percent early-withdrawal penalty if I'm younger than 59½?

It's worse than that—if you take money out of your SIMPLE plan within the first two years of opening it, your early-withdrawal penalty won't be 10 percent—it will be 25 percent. After the first two years, the penalty drops to 10 percent.

RETIREMENT TAX CREDIT

What is the retirement tax credit?

As of 2010, single filers with income under $27,750, joint filers with income below $55,500, and head-of-household filers with income below $41,625 can get a credit of as much as 50 percent of the amount invested in a retirement account, up to a $1,000 credit on a $5,000 contribution. That's $1,000 off your tax bill. It's like the IRS paid for 20 percent of your retirement contribution.

Put $5,000 in an IRA. If you're in the 27 percent bracket, that saves you $1,350. You also get the $1,000 credit. That means that you're only out of pocket $2,650 on a $5,000 investment.

This credit is available for elective contributions to a Section 401(k) plan, Section 403(b) annuity, SIMPLE, or SEP. It also covers contributions to a traditional or Roth IRA and voluntary after-tax employee qualified plans. You must also be at least

Joint Filers	Head of Household	Single	Credit Rate
$0–$33,500	$0–$25,125	$0–$16,750	50%
$33,501–$36,000	$25,126–$27,000	$16,751–$18,000	20%
$36,001–$55,000	$27,001–$41,625	$18,001–$27,750	10%
Over $55,000	Over $41,625	Over $27,750	0%

age 18, not a full-time student, and not claimed as a dependent on another person's return.

The credit is based on adjusted gross income as seen on page 339.

TAXATION OF RETIREMENT PLAN WITHDRAWALS

How are the funds I withdraw from my retirement account taxed?

Apart from withdrawals from a Roth 401(k) or Roth IRA (which, if done correctly, are tax-free), most withdrawals from retirement plans are taxed as ordinary income. There is one exception. If you meet certain restrictions, money withdrawn from a qualified retirement plan using the technique known as ten-year averaging is taxed differently.

TEN-YEAR AVERAGING

What is ten-year averaging? Who is eligible for it?

If you were born before January 1, 1936, you may be able to take advantage of a favorable tax treatment known as 10-year averaging. Here's how it works: First, you are required to withdraw your retirement plan money in one lump sum. You figure out how much you owe in taxes by dividing the total value of your account by ten, then adding $2,480 to that figure. Look up the 1986 single taxpayer rate for that amount, then take that number and multiply it by 10: That is how much you would owe on the total withdrawal. For an amount under $400,000,

10-year averaging could save you a considerable sum.

But there are restrictions. To be eligible to use ten-year averaging:

- You must have been born before January 1, 1936.
- You must withdraw all the money in your qualified retirement in a lump sum.
- You cannot roll over some of your money and apply ten-year averaging to the rest.
- You must have participated in your retirement plan for at least five years.

Please note: You can apply ten-year averaging only once in a lifetime.

If I qualify for ten-year averaging, should I do it?

It depends on how much your retirement plan's distributions would be, and also whether you need the money from your account right away or can afford to let it sit for a while, either in the plan or in an IRA rollover. If you have a few hundred thousand dollars in your plan, for example, it is not worth it to give up the use of the money that you will use to pay the taxes when it could be accumulating value for many years.

Besides ten-year averaging, is there any other way to get money out of a qualified retirement plan and not have to pay ordinary income taxes?

Tax law provides a special benefit if your company retirement plan includes stock of your company and that stock has appreciated in value within the plan. If you take a lump-sum withdrawal of the assets in your company plan, you will be taxed on your company stock in the plan based upon the cost to the plan of the stock rather than on its value at the time of distribution. Then, if you hold that stock for longer than a year, when you sell it you will get long-term capital-gains treatment for the difference between the cost of the stock to the plan and the stock's value at the time of the distribution. This difference is known as the net unrealized appreciation.

MANDATORY WITHDRAWAL FROM A RETIREMENT ACCOUNT

When do I have to start taking money out of my retirement account(s)?

You are required to begin withdrawing money from a traditional IRA and a traditional 401(k) (or a Keogh, SEP, or SIMPLE) by April 1 of the year after you turn 70½. With respect to a 401(k)—but not a traditional IRA—if you are still working at age 70½ for the company that holds your plan, this mandatory withdrawal rule does not apply, provided you do not own more than 5 percent of the company you work for. In that case, you will not have to begin making withdrawals until April 1 of the year after the year you retire. Please note that with a Roth IRA, these mandatory withdrawal rules do not apply; you can leave your money in a Roth IRA for as long as you like, even until your death.

Once I turn 70½ and I need to start making

IRA withdrawals, how do I know how much I should take?

The custodian of your IRA should help you determine the exact figure. The custodian's calculations are based on how much money you have in all of your IRAs and on the new Uniform Distribution Table. (Every taxpayer now uses this table, regardless of the named beneficiary—unless the sole beneficiary is the spouse *and* the spouse is more than ten years younger than the account holder. In that case, taxpayers will use the table for the actual joint life expectancy of the taxpayer and spouse, which will result in a lower required distribution than the Uniform Distribution Table.)

To determine how much you should withdraw, simply take the total value of your account and divide it by the appropriate figure on the table—that is how much you will be expected to withdraw in the first year after you turn 70½. People with IRAs often find it difficult to understand what decisions have to be made when they reach age 70½. One of the most helpful publications on this topic is *Barry Picker's Guide to Retirement Distribution Planning*, which can be ordered online at *www.BPickerCPA.com* or by calling (800) 809-0015. I recommend it highly.

Please note: in 2009 the RMD requirement was temporarily suspended. You can check at *www.irs.gov* whether the RMD has been reinstated for subsequent years.

Can I change my beneficiary after I have started taking withdrawals from my IRA?

Yes, you can. This is one of the great advantages of the new regulations. You can now change your beneficiary at any time, and the change will not affect your lifetime distributions.

Is it smart to postpone taking money out of my IRA until April 1 of the year after I turn 70½?

It depends on your tax bracket. In most cases, it's not wise to postpone your first withdrawal, since you'll have to take two distributions in the same year—one distribution for the year that you were 70½, and the other for the present year. By postponing your IRA withdrawal that first year, you could find yourself in a higher tax bracket the second year as a result of taking two years' worth of withdrawals in one tax year.

BENEFICIARY WITHDRAWALS

The rules for beneficiary withdrawals after the death of the account holder are pretty much the same for all retirement accounts, including IRAs, 401(k)s, 403(b)s, etc. Please note that the following answers apply to both contributory Roth IRAs and Roth IRA conversions.

What happens to the money in my retirement plan when I die?

When you die, your money goes to the beneficiaries you named on your retirement plan application forms. (Even if your will or trust dictates that all your money is to go to your brother, your primary beneficiary on your application is the person who will get the money in your retirement account[s].) What your beneficiary can do with the money depends on whether he or she is your surviving spouse and what is in your retirement plan document. The laws on what happens to a retirement account(s) when a surviving spouse is the beneficiary are very different from those on what happens when the beneficiary is not the spouse.

If I survive my spouse and I am the beneficiary, what can I do with the retirement account?

As the surviving spouse, your options depend on whether or not your spouse had started taking the minimum required distributions.

What are my options if my deceased spouse had already started withdrawing money?

If your spouse had already started taking the minimum required distribution before he or she died, you can do one of three things, provided the plan permits them:

1. Continue taking the distributions, which will now be based upon your life expectancy, recalculated each year. If you die before emptying the account, the remaining balance at your death will be distributed to your heirs over the remaining years in your life expectancy. Your remaining life expectancy will not be recalculated.
2. Accelerate the distributions; that is, take them more frequently.
3. Stop the distributions and transfer the account to a retirement account in your own name. Then start taking the distributions by either April 1 of the year after you turn 70½, or December 31 of the year after the year of your spouse's death, whichever comes later.

What should I do if my deceased spouse hadn't started to take distributions?

If your spouse had not started taking the minimum required distributions, you have many more choices:

1. You can roll the account over into your own retirement account and treat it as if it were your money—which is exactly what it now is. This means you can continue to make contributions to the IRA or roll other money that you may have from a company retirement plan into it. In my opinion, this is usually the best option, especially if your late spouse was older than you. If not, please see No. 5 in this list.

2. In the case of an IRA and other retirement accounts that permit it, you can keep the account just as it is, in your deceased spouse's name. However, if you do this, you must start taking money out of the IRA either by December 31 of the year your spouse would have turned 70½, or December 31 of the year after your spouse died, whichever is later. I would be hard-pressed to think of a reason to do this with the money, unless your situation falls into that described in No. 5.

3. You can withdraw the money in a lump sum. I don't endorse this option; the taxes could be substantial.

4. If you keep a retirement account in your deceased spouse's name, you can make withdrawals from it over the next five years, or make periodic withdrawals over your life expectancy. If you want to use the "five-year rule," you would need to inform the IRS of your intention to do so. But I can't think of any way that you would benefit from this.

5. If you keep a retirement account in your deceased spouse's name, you do not have to take any money until the end of the year when your deceased spouse would have turned 70½. You might do this if your deceased spouse was much younger than you, and you want to continue to defer income taxes on the money for as long as possible. You might also want to do this if you are younger than 59½ and need to make more withdrawals. If you roll the IRA into your own name and withdraw money before you're 59½, you may be subject to the 10 percent early-withdrawal penalty.

Most people roll their late spouse's accounts over into an IRA in their own name; it gives them the greatest number of options.

What are my choices if someone other than my spouse leaves me a retirement plan account?

If someone other than your spouse leaves you a retirement account, you should be able to take minimum distributions based upon your own life expectancy, provided the plan permits it. You can always just take the money out in a lump sum, but you might have quite a tax bill on your hands.

If the owner of the account had not started taking minimum distributions, then you have two choices, with one variation:

- By December 31 of the fifth year after the IRA owner's death, the entire account must be emptied. You must withdraw all the money from the account by that date. I can't think of any reason why you would do this.

- You can take out a minimum amount of money each year, calculated on your life expectancy. This is clearly the better option, and this option is now the default under new IRS regulations.

Of course, you can always take out more anytime you want. The above choices are simply the best options available if you want to take the least amount out.

After I die, will beneficiaries other than my spouse owe income tax on the assets I leave to them in my Roth IRA?

Not as long as the five-year holding period has passed. If the five-year period is up, your beneficiaries can withdraw all the money from a Roth immediately, with no income-tax implications whatsoever. If five years have not yet passed, your beneficiaries need to be cautious. If they withdraw more than the amount you originally contributed or converted to a Roth, they will owe ordinary income taxes on the earnings.

What if the five-year holding period has not passed?

If your beneficiaries take distributions over their own life expectancy, starting no later than December 31 of the year following the year in which you die, then they probably will not be withdrawing earnings until the five-year period has passed.

If my beneficiary is not 59½, will he or she have to pay the 10 percent penalty upon withdrawal?

No. The 10 percent early-withdrawal penalty never applies to beneficiaries' withdrawals of money in a Roth IRA, regardless of age or how long the money has been in the account.

If my beneficiary is my wife and I leave my Roth IRA to her, when does she have to take the money out of the account?

Your wife does not have to do anything with that money. She can treat the Roth IRA as her own. She can let it grow, withdraw it gradually, or take a lump-sum payment—the choice is hers.

STOCK OPTIONS AND STOCK PURCHASE PLANS

What kinds of employee stock options are available as part of a retirement package?

There are two kinds of stock-option plans available to employees: nonqualified stock-option plans (NQSOs) and incentive stock-option plans (ISOs). Both types of plans give employees of a particular company the opportunity (or option) to purchase a particular amount of the company's stock for a fixed price within a specified period. Acting on this opportunity is known as exercising the option, and the fixed price is known as the exercise price.

What are the main differences between nonqualified stock-option plans and incentive stock-option plans?

The two main differences between nonqualified stock-option plans and incentive stock-option plans are how they are taxed and who is eligible to receive the options.

With an NQSO, you are subject to ordinary income taxes and withholding for Social Security and Medicare as soon as you exercise those options.

With an ISO, you are not subject to these taxes when you exercise your option. However, when you exercise an ISO, you are subject to the alternative minimum tax (AMT), an income tax calculated by a different set of rules than those used to calculate regular income tax.

You cannot be given an ISO if you are not an employee of the company that is offering the options; outside consultants, for instance, cannot receive ISOs. An NQSO can be granted to consultants, as well as to employees of a corporation.

How do nonqualified stock-option plans work?

Let's say your employer offers you a nonqualified stock option to purchase up to 200 shares of the company stock during the next 10 years, and the exercise price for that stock is $10 per share. That means that you can exercise your option, or purchase up to 200 shares of stock at $10 per share, at any time over the next 10 years, regardless of the value of that stock. Say you waited to purchase your stock, and the price of the stock shot up to $100 per share. It is your right to exercise your stock options at $10 a share. But when you do this, you will be taxed on the difference between your exercise price of $10 and the value of the stock at the time you exercised the option ($100). In this example, you would owe ordinary income taxes on $90 per share for every share that you exercised. The $90 per share is called the bargain element, or spread.

When I exercise an NQSO, do I owe capital gains tax at the rate of 15 percent? Or do I have to pay ordinary income tax on the spread?

Because you didn't actually own the stock until you exercised the option, this money isn't considered capital gains. You will pay ordinary income tax.

When is the tax due?

You will be subject to income tax, Social Security, and Medicare withholding taxes right away, even if you only exercise the option and do not sell the underlying stock. Make sure you have the money to pay for the taxes as well as the money for the exercise price at the time you exercise.

I exercised some options but was not allowed to sell the stock right away. I was also told that I didn't owe taxes yet. Why?

You probably were in what is known as a "blackout period." During a blackout period, the Securities and Exchange Commission prohibits anyone from selling the underlying stock. The SEC imposes blackout periods to prevent people who hold too many stock options from diluting the market for that stock or profiting too soon from stock movements. Blackout periods also affect your taxes. Federal taxes are not due until the blackout period is over. If you exercise your options during a blackout period, you must make a tax decision that cannot be reversed: You must choose whether to report to the IRS the price of the stock at the date of exercise or the price when the blackout period ends.

When the blackout period is over, will I still owe taxes only on the difference between the exercise price and the share price on the day I exercised the options?

It depends. You can elect to recognize that taxable income on the date that you exercise your options, or you can postpone the income taxes until the blackout period is over. If you postpone, you will owe ordinary income taxes on the difference between the exercise price and the price of the stock on the day that the blackout period ends, not on the day you exercised your options. If you choose to pay the taxes on the day you exercise the option even though you are in a blackout period, you can file an election under IRC section 83(b). Remember that you have only 30 days from the time the stock is transferred to you to file this election. Please check with your tax adviser to see if it makes sense for you to postpone the taxes in this situation or to pay them up front.

EXERCISE TIME

I plan to exercise my NQSOs and hold onto my stock for more than a year. That way, when I sell the stock, all I have to pay on my gains is long-term capital-gains tax. Is this wise?
Exercising your options early might seem to be a good tax strategy, but in almost all circumstances you are actually better off if you don't. For you to benefit from exercising early, the stock must go up in value considerably after you've exercised your options. How far up? The rule of thumb is at least 16 percent. If the stock price does not go up by at least that much, exercising early really isn't worth it. Remember, when you exercise an NQSO, you not only have to come up with the money to exercise the option, you also have to come up with the money to pay the taxes due (please see the previous question). In most cases, exercising your options and holding onto the stock doesn't enhance your return, regardless of the tax benefits.

Can exercising my options early work against me?
Yes. Let's say you decide to exercise 5,000 shares of NQSOs, and the exercise price is $5 a share. To buy the stock, you will have to come up with $25,000 (5,000 shares × $5) in cash. Let's say the stock is trading on the market for $100 a share. You're happy—you now have $500,000 worth of stock. But the downside is that you owe income taxes on $475,000—the difference between your exercise price and the market price of the stock. After you exercise your options, if you hold the stock for at least 12 months and a day before selling it, you will owe only capital gains tax on the difference between the $100 a share and whatever it is worth when you sell it. In this scenario, if the stock is trading at $150 a share when you finally sell it, you will owe capital gains tax on $250,000 (5,000 shares × $50), but don't forget that you have already paid ordinary income tax on that first $95 per share. Plus you will have lost the use of $25,000 the year you exercised the options, not to mention the income tax on that $475,000, which would be about $166,000. All this just so you could pay a lower tax rate on the increase of the stock price a year down the road. That's a big gamble. What if the price of the stock goes down? Too bad. You still will have to pay the tax due when you exercise the options.

This also holds true for ISOs, especially if your marginal income-tax bracket is 28 percent or lower. If you are in a higher tax bracket, check with your tax adviser to see if exercising your options early makes sense for you. Please remember, the more volatile your stock (how much and how frequently it fluctuates in relation to the market), the more risk you take in exercising and holding the stock. Most people are better off if they exercise and sell at the same time.

CASHLESS TRANSACTIONS

My company is offering a cashless transaction when I want to exercise my options. How does that work?

Many employees exercise their options when they need to make a down payment on a major purchase, such as a home or a new car. Let's say your underlying stock is selling at $150 a share, and you want to exercise 1,000 options at an exercise price of $50 a share. This means you have to come up with $50,000 in cash to exercise those options. What if you do not have that $50,000? It stands to reason that if somebody needs to sell stock to make a down payment, that employee probably doesn't have the cash needed to exercise the options in the first place. This is where the cashless transaction comes in (although "cashless" may be a misnomer, as it could cost you in the end). Your company has probably made an arrangement with a brokerage firm whereby, when you exercise your option, the brokerage firm will sell the underlying stock on the very same day. In essence, you have been able to exercise your options without having to come up with any cash. Three business days later, you will get the difference between your exercise price and the price for which the brokerage firm sold the stock, minus any fees the company takes for allowing you to do this.

If your company doesn't, pay your friendly banker a visit. Since you have the options, the bank may use them as collateral and make you a short-term loan for the amount you need to exercise the options. Once the stock is sold, you repay the bank the principal it loaned you plus setup fees and interest. These fees and interest will be far less than that 25 percent your company would charge you.

INCENTIVE STOCK OPTIONS

How are incentive stock options taxed when exercised?

When you exercise an ISO, you may be subject to the alternative minimum tax amount. When the options are exercised, the AMT is calculated on the difference between market value and the exercise price. Because the AMT is calculated differently than regular income tax, please consult a tax professional.

With incentive stock options, you pay income tax only when you sell the stock. How long you hold the stock will determine whether you pay ordinary income tax or capital-gains tax. After exercising your options, if you hold the stock for more than a year before selling it, you will pay capital-gains tax, assuming that was more than two years from the date the option was granted. If you hold your stock for a year or less, you will pay ordinary income tax.

What happens if I don't hold the stock for more than one year before selling it?

Such a sale is called a disqualified disposition and the option spread (the lesser of the value of the stock when you exercised the option less the option price or the sale price less the option price) is taxed at your ordinary income-tax rate, not at the capital-gains tax rate. Any gain beyond the option spread is taxed as a capital gain.

I am eligible to exercise ISOs worth about $125,000. Does the value of the options have any bearing on the tax treatment?

Yes. Any stock options worth more than $100,000 that first become eligible to be exercised in one calendar year are automatically converted to NQSOs.

Are there any time constraints on when I can exercise my ISOs?

Yes. Usually you must exercise your options within 10 years from the time they were granted to you. If you happen to own more than 10 percent of all the classes of stock of a corporation (or of corporations that are directly related to that stock), you must exercise your options within five years.

Do I have to exercise the options? What if the stock is selling at a lower price than the exercise price?

You don't have to exercise options if you don't want to. But if the specified time period passes and the options expire, your options will not be renewed.

Can I still exercise my stock options once I am retired?

This is a question many people forget to ask when they prepare to retire. Most ISOs can be exercised only while you are an employee of the corporation that granted the options—or within a specified time of leaving that corporation. It is not uncommon for a company either to terminate an employee's right to exercise stock options or to reduce the amount of time an employee has to purchase stock after retirement. So if you retire in year six of a ten-year stock option, you might not be able to carry that option with you for another four years. If you have options that you want to exercise, either purchase the stock before you retire or be certain that you have the option to do so after you leave the company.

I am leaving my place of employment because I sustained a disability. Do I have to exercise my ISOs within the three months of leaving?

Maybe not. If you are considered disabled according to the Internal Revenue Service's definition, you have an extended period, up to 12 months, in which to exercise your ISOs.

How do I make sure that I can exercise my stock options?

Read your stock-option agreement with care, paying particularly close attention to the exercise dates. If there is anything that you do not understand, consult both your company's human resources department and a financial planning professional immediately.

Can I transfer my ISO to someone else?

No. ISOs are not transferable, though they can be inherited.

If I should die, can my spouse or life partner exercise my options?

Read the option agreement that granted you the options to begin with. Don't be surprised if your options must be exercised within three months to a year after your death by the personal representative of the estate—in other words, by a court-appointed executor. The problem starts here, for it could take more than three months to get that person appointed by the court. What I suggest you do is establish a revocable living trust and in the powers section of that trust give the trustee the right to exercise your options after your death. That way, your heirs have a better chance of not needing to appoint a representative.

option, employees do not acquire the stock until they "exercise" the options and usually the employee sells the stock immediately to cash in on any rise in value above the price he or she paid for it. The potential loss of a stock option is limited to the price paid to acquire the option. When an option is not exercised, it expires. No shares change hands and the money spent to purchase the option is lost. A stock option is issued by independent parties, such as a member of the Chicago Board Options Exchange, while a stock warrant is issued and guaranteed by the corporation that issued the common stock. The lifetime of a warrant is often years, while the lifetime of an option is generally months.

STOCK WARRANT

Can you tell me the difference between stock options and stock warrants?

Both a stock warrant and a stock option grant the holders the ability to exercise the warrant/option before an expiration date, for a certain number of shares at a specified price. The stock warrant allows the holder to buy stock at a fixed price, with the ability to sell at a far higher price, and thus make a profit. If the price of the security rises above the warrant's exercise price, then the holder can buy the security at the warrant's exercise price and resell it for a profit. Otherwise, the warrant will simply expire or remain unused. Warrants are traded on option exchanges as securities whose price reflects the value of the underlying stock. With a stock

STOCK PURCHASE PLAN

My company offers a stock purchase plan as a retirement-planning strategy. What is this?

Typically, with a stock purchase plan, employees can designate an amount of money to be withheld from their regular paychecks and used to buy stock in the company, sometimes at rates discounted from the market price. The money then grows (or shrinks!) tax-deferred until the employee sells the stock, usually after an extended period. While it's fine to take advantage of a tax-deferred growth opportunity, it's important to remain diversified in your stock holdings—you are already very dependent on your employer for a paycheck, so you don't want to have all your retirement savings riding on the company's fortunes as well.

VESTED VERSUS NONVESTED STOCK

What is the difference between vested stock and nonvested stock?

Your stock is considered vested if, according to the agreement you made with your employer, you retain the full value of the stock no matter what happens. "No matter what happens" includes your quitting your job or getting fired. It also means that you have the right, if you wish, to transfer this stock to anyone you want. Any agreement other than this means that you have been given nonvested stock.

Does nonvested stock stay that way? Or can my stock become vested over time?

Your stock may become vested over time.

What are the tax rules of being given stock as compensation?

It depends on whether you were given vested or nonvested stock. If your stock is fully vested when you receive it, its value (minus the amount paid for it, if any) will be taxed as ordinary income. If the stock is not vested, it cannot be taxed until it vests. If you get nonvested stock, however, you have 30 days to make a section 83(b) election. Under this provision, the value of the stock is reported as income when you acquired it (and when its share price was likely lower), instead of the year it vests. The tax consequences are based on the fair market value of the stock.

Can the company force me to sell the stock back to them if I lose my job?

In many cases, it can. It all depends on the terms of your agreement. If you paid for this stock when you acquired it, you may have agreed to sell it back at the same amount you paid for it, or at its fair market value.

What is the fair market value of a stock? How does the IRS figure this out?

The classical definition of fair market value is this: the price at which the property would change hands between a willing buyer and a willing seller, neither being under any compulsion to buy or to sell, and both having reasonable knowledge of relevant facts.

PENSION PLANS: KNOWING YOUR RIGHTS

I've heard stories about companies mismanaging pension plans, leaving their employees with nothing, and that makes me nervous. How can I keep track of what my company does with my retirement plan?

The Employee Retirement Income Security Act of 1974 (ERISA) is a federal law that sets minimum standards for pension plans in private industry. ERISA requires retirement plan administrators—the people who run the plans—to provide you with written information explaining the most important facts about your pension plan. The plan administrator is required to keep you regularly informed. This includes a summary plan description (SPD), which you should get when you begin participating in the plan. The SPD is a comprehensive document that tells you exactly what the plan provides and how it operates. The SPD should show when you began to participate in the plan, how your service and benefits are calculated, when your benefit becomes vested, when and how you will receive payments, and how to file for your benefits when you need to. If there are any changes to the SPD, your plan administrator is required to give you a revised summary plan description or a separate document detailing the modifications. Both the original SPD and any changes to it must be given to you free, and you should read everything carefully.

In addition to the SPD, the plan administrator must give you a copy of the plan's summary annual report, a summary of the yearly financial report that most pension plans must file with the Department of Labor. Finally, you should also receive, free of charge every year, an individual benefit statement that describes your personal total accrued and vested benefits.

If this information does not answer the questions you have about your plan, there is more information available, but you must request it from your plan administrator.

I haven't been able to get the summary plan description, the summary annual report, or the annual report from my plan administrator. How do I figure out what is going on?
If no one else you know in your plan is receiving this information either, this is potentially a serious case of mismanagement. Because the annual report has to be filed with the government, you may be able to obtain a copy of it by writing to the Department of Labor, EBSA, Public Disclosure Room, Room N-5638, 200 Constitution Avenue NW, Washington, DC 20210; *www.dol.gov/ebsa*

or calling (866) 444-3272. When you make a request, try to provide as much information as possible about the plan. The Department of Labor will charge you a modest fee to cover copying costs.

Meanwhile, make sure that you have made your requests to your plan administrator in writing and have kept copies of the requests. If a plan administrator refuses to comply with your request for documents, and the reasons for the delay were within his or her control, a court could impose penalties on the administrator of up to $100 per day.

Is it possible for my retirement plan to be terminated? What would that mean for my retirement savings?
Pension plans are supposed to continue indefinitely, but employers are allowed to terminate plans. You do have some protection if your plan is canceled. If your plan is a qualified plan, your accrued benefit must become 100 percent vested when the plan terminates, to the extent that it is funded—meaning what has so far been contributed by you and your employer. This is also true if your employer partially terminates a qualified plan, for example, if one division of a company is closed and a substantial number of plan participants are affected. All affected employees' plans become 100 percent vested, to the extent they have been funded, effective as soon as the plan terminates.

When my sister's pension plan was terminated, the company she works for didn't have enough money to pay out all the benefits. How can I make sure this doesn't happen to me?

If you have a defined-benefit plan, ask your plan administrator if it is insured by the Pension Benefit Guaranty Corporation (PBGC). If it is, the PBGC guarantees that you will receive your vested pension benefits, up to certain limits. If additional benefits that exceed the PBGC's limits or that were not guaranteed are due to you, whether you receive them and how much you receive will depend on the plan's funding and how much the PBGC can recover from your employer. If you find yourself in this messy situation, contact the Pension Benefit Guaranty Corporation, Administrative Review and Technical Assistance Department, (800-400-7242); (202) 326-4000; *www.pbgc.gov*, for more information.

Rumors of a possible merger are flying around my office. Should I be worried about my pension plan?

If your employer merges with another company, the two companies may merge retirement plans as well. But if your company's plan is the one that gets terminated, you would most likely receive benefits under the new plan that are at least equal to the benefits you were entitled to before the plans merged. By all means, ask your plan administrator what's going on.

What if I lose my job but I am vested in my pension? Will I keep receiving information about my pension?

If you leave an employer with whom you have a vested pension benefit that you won't be eligible to receive until later in life, your plan administrator must report that information to you and to the IRS, which, in turn, will inform the Social Security Administration. You can check with the Social Security Administration to ensure that you were reported as having a deferred vested benefit. Call the Social Security Administration toll-free at (800) 772-1213. Even if you don't request this information, Social Security will automatically fill you in when you retire and apply for Social Security benefits. Still, I think it is a good idea to double-check after you leave your job. Stay in touch with the plan administrator, keeping him or her informed of any name or address changes to ensure that you will receive your full pension benefit.

I have read the literature about my pension and benefit accrual, but I don't really understand how it works. Can you explain it?

When you participate in a pension plan, you earn and accumulate—or accrue—pension benefits. Your accrued benefit is the amount that has been accumulated or allocated in your name under the plan as of a particular date. Plans can use any definition of service for the purpose of calculating your benefit accrual, as long as they use basically the same definition for all participants. Usually, a company calculates your years of service for purposes of benefit accrual from the date you became a plan participant, not necessarily from your date of hire.

If I work part-time, how are my years of service calculated?

Employees who work at least 1,000 hours per year but do not work full-time must be credited with a pro rata portion of the benefit that they would accrue if they were employed full-time. In other words, if your plan requires that employees work at least 2,000 hours of service per year for full benefit accrual but you work only 1,000 hours per year, you will be credited with 50 percent of the full benefit. Check your summary plan description to see exactly how your plan calculates service credit.

Can my plan reduce my future benefits?

Your employer may amend your plan to reduce the rate at which benefits accrue in the future. For example, a plan that pays $10 in monthly benefits at age 65 for each year of service up through 2005 can be amended to say that benefits for years of service beginning in 2010 will be credited at a rate of $8 each month. If you are participating in a defined benefit plan, you must receive written notice of any significant reduction in the rate of future benefit accruals after the plan amendment is adopted and at least 15 days before the effective date of the plan amendment. That notice is supposed to describe the plan amendment and the date it becomes effective.

I was employed by one company for 15 years before leaving for a job that I thought would be terrific but which turned out to be a disaster. I'm pretty sure I'll be able to get my old job back, but what will happen to my service credit?

If a break in your employment lasts long enough, it can have serious consequences for your pension if you were not fully vested when you left. However, your accrued benefits are normally protected if you have a short break, usually less than five years. If you are actually planning a leave of absence, you need to examine the rules of your plan carefully so that you do not lose pension benefits unnecessarily.

When can I count on beginning to receive benefits from my qualified retirement plan?

According to the Employee Retirement Income Security Act, you must begin to receive plan payments from a qualified plan no later than the 60th day after the close of the plan year in which the last of the following events occurs:

1. you turn 65 (or the normal retirement age specified by your plan);
2. you have participated in your plan for at least 10 years; or
3. you terminate your service with the employer.

"Normal retirement age" is defined as the earlier of:

1. the age specified in the plan as normal retirement age; or
2. age 65 *or* the fifth anniversary of the employee's participation in the plan, whichever is later.

Normal retirement age is also the point at which a participant must become 100 percent vested in the plan. So, for most people, being 100 percent vested in a qualified retirement plan is the factor that determines normal retirement age. These rules apply for both defined-contribution plans and defined-benefit plans.

Does the type of plan I have affect when or how I can start receiving benefits if I want to access them before I reach normal retirement age?

Yes. Again, check your summary plan description for the specific details of your plan, but generally, there are several conditions under which your plan might allow you to begin receiving payments "early." A defined benefit plan could permit earlier payments by, say, providing for early retirement benefits, which might have additional eligibility requirements. A defined-benefit plan might also allow benefits to be paid out when you terminate your employment, suffer a disability, or die. Often, 401(k) plans allow you to withdraw some or all of your vested accrued benefit when you leave your job, reach age 59½, become disabled, retire, die, or suffer some other hardship that may be defined in the summary plan description. Profit-sharing or stock bonus plans may allow you to receive your vested accrued benefit after you leave your job, reach a specific age, become disabled, die, or after a specific number of years have elapsed.

Can my plan force me to start receiving benefits?

If the total value of your vested accrued benefit is greater than a specified minimum, the plan cannot force you to start receiving benefits before you reach the normal retirement age. If your vested accrued benefit is below that minimum, though, you might be required to take this money as soon as possible, often when you leave your job. If your plan is qualified, you must generally begin taking benefit payments by April 1 of the calendar year following the calendar year in which you reach age 70½, whether you want to or not.

Do I have any choice about how my benefits are paid out?

Your plan will establish the forms in which you can receive your benefits, but it usually offers a variety of options. If you have a defined benefit plan and you are not married, by law, your benefit must be made available at least in the form of a life annuity—equal monthly payments for the rest of your life. If you are married, your benefit choices must include monthly income to your spouse after your death. Some defined-benefit plans may also allow you to take all your benefits in a single payment. Most likely, you will have the right to choose any of these options.

I think I should have begun receiving my benefits already, but I'm not getting them. What can I do?

First of all, examine your summary plan description. All plans are required by law to provide participants with written instructions describing how to make benefit claims and how to appeal when claims are denied. If you don't understand the plan description or it doesn't include a procedure, write a letter making your claim directly to the plan administrator. If you make a claim for your benefit and it is rejected, your plan is required to notify you in writing of the rejection, along with specific reasons for the denial. In the denial letter, your plan is also required by law to explain how you can appeal the decision.

*My plan administrator hasn't officially re-
jected my claim for benefits, but he keeps saying that my claim is still under review. How
long can this go on?*

Not for long, at least not legally. If your plan has
a legitimate reason for needing additional time
to examine your claim, they have to send you
written notification within 90 days explaining
why additional review time is necessary and giving you a date by which a decision is expected. If
the plan is trying to deny or is delaying your
claim because it needs information, they are required to inform you, in writing, of what information is needed. If you don't hear anything
from the plan within 90 days of making your
claim, legally you can appeal as though your
claim had been officially denied.

*Once my claim has been denied, how long do I
have to appeal?*

Again, check your summary plan description for
details. Your plan is required to give you at least
60 days to appeal a denial, and the administrator
is usually required to make a decision within 60
days of the appeal. If you find yourself in this
situation, you should be communicating with
the plan in writing and keeping copies of all correspondence. Just as in the initial review stage,
the plan has to give you its decision, along with
reasons for it, in writing.

*What if the plan denies my claim again, but I
know I'm entitled to my benefits?*

At this point, you need to consult a lawyer; you
may have to file a lawsuit. Now it is crucial that
you complete all necessary stages of administra-

tive appeal available before you turn to the
courts. This is another reason for you to make
sure you understand the rules in your specific
plan and to keep careful records of all your communications regarding your benefits.

*I worked for my company for many years
without any problems. Then, out of the blue, I
was fired. I suspect it was done so my employer
could avoid paying my pension. Can they really do this?*

No. It's illegal. Employers are absolutely not
allowed to discharge, fine, suspend, expel,
discipline, or discriminate against you or any of
your beneficiaries for the purpose of interfering
with any benefits that you are entitled to under
their retirement plan, and they can be fined for
doing so. If you think your employer is interfering with your benefits, consult a lawyer who has
expertise in labor law and the Employee Retirement Income Security Act.

*What will happen to my pension payments if I
retire and then decide to go back to work?*

What happens to your pension payments really
depends on your particular plan. If you go back
to work after you retire at a company other than
the one from which you retired, in most cases, it
will have no effect on the pension payments you
have been receiving from the job you retired
from.

*What if I go back to work for the same em-
ployer?*

It will depend on the arrangement you make at
that time. If, for whatever reason, it has been

agreed that your pension payments will stop when you go back to work for your original employer, the company must allow you to continue to accrue benefits until you meet the maximum total years of service that the plan will allow.

If you retired early and are receiving early retirement benefits and then return to work for your original employer before you reach normal retirement age, some plans will suspend payment of your retirement benefits while you are re-employed. If your plan would *not* have suspended your benefits if you had returned to work after reaching normal retirement age, and the plan pays an actuarially reduced early retirement benefit, then your plan has to recalculate your monthly payment when you retire again.

The bottom line is, if you are retired and are thinking about taking another job or returning to your old one, before you start working again, consult the rules of your plan to see if and how your pension benefits would be affected. Write to the plan administrator if you're not sure how your situation would be interpreted under the rules in your summary plan description.

EARLY RETIREMENT

In order to entice long-term, relatively well-paid employees to retire early, many companies offer them additional benefits such as an increased pension, the opportunity to receive the pension immediately, and health-care benefits.

Another common inducement is to offer a lump-sum severance payment. This section will help you decide whether to accept your company's early-retirement offer. Even if you do not have a choice, you should still read this section carefully—it contains vital information regarding what to do with the money in your retirement account as well as how to take your pension offer.

Once I decide to retire, how long do I have to decide what to do with the money in my retirement account?

Making a decision about retirement is stressful. Fortunately, you don't have to make all of your financial decisions at the same time. Most companies will allow you to leave your money in the company plan for at least a year after you retire, and many will allow you to leave your funds there until you turn 70½, at which time you must, by law, begin withdrawing the minimum required distribution. So don't feel pressured to make any decisions or move your money if you're not ready. Find out your company's deadlines. You probably have some time to think about what to do with your retirement account.

I've been told that when I retire I have to take all my money out of my 401(k) and roll it over into a single IRA account. Is that correct?

Absolutely not! Many people think that they have to roll over their entire retirement account into one place, but they are mistaken. Here are just a few options:

- If your company allows you to do so, you can leave your money in your 401(k).
- You can roll over all the money into one IRA.
- You can do an unlimited number of rollovers into as many IRAs as you want.
- You can leave some of your money in the company plan (assuming that the company allows you to do this) and roll the rest of it over into one or more IRAs.
- If you are 55 or older in the year you retire, you can take distributions of all or part of your retirement account without penalty. You will still have to pay ordinary income tax on those distributions.
- If you were born before January 1, 1936, you may be able to take advantage of a favorable tax treatment known as 10-year averaging, which I explained earlier in this chapter.

Essentially, your options are leaving your money in the company plan, rolling it over into one or more IRAs, or doing a combination of both.

Monthly Pension Versus Lump-Sum Payment

I'm about to leave the company that I've been working for, and I have been given two options. I can receive the money in my pension plan in one lump sum, or the company will give me a monthly pension check for as long as I live. Which option should I take?

Whether you receive the money from your pension plan in a lump-sum payment or as a monthly pension check depends on the following seven factors:

- How much you have in your pension account.
- The amount of the monthly payment the company will give you.
- The amount of the monthly payment the company will pay to your spouse or life partner after you have died.
- Your age.
- Your life expectancy and the life expectancy of your spouse.
- Whether you need this income to live on.
- Whether this income needs to support another person after you have died.

To decide between taking your pension as a lump sum or as monthly payments, start by looking at the actual return you would get if you took the monthly pension payments and compare that to what you could reasonably expect to get on your own if you took a lump sum and invested it.

Let's say you are 60 years old and you are being offered a choice of $250,000 in one lump sum or $1,300 a month every month for the rest of your life. When you die, your life partner or spouse would receive half of the monthly pension ($650 a month).

To figure out the rate of return we need to do some math. Take the monthly pension amount that your company is offering you and multiply it by 12. This is how much you will receive in pension payments annually ($1,300 × 12 = $15,600). Take that answer and divide it by the lump sum you are being offered ($15,600 ÷ $250,000 = .0624, or 6.24 percent). This answer is, in essence, the percentage return the company is giving you on your money.

Do these calculations again, this time using the amount that your surviving spouse or life partner will get ($650 × 12 = $7,800; $7,800 ÷ $250,000 = .0312, or 3.12 percent).

Now take your answers and fill them into the following paragraph:

Do you think that over your life expectancy you can earn _____ percent a year on your money without risk and that after you die your spouse or life partner could earn _____ percent?

Using the numbers in the example above, the paragraph would read like this:

Do you think that over your life expectancy you can earn 6.24 percent a year on your money without risk and that after you die your spouse or life partner could earn 3.12 percent?

If you can safely say that you could not, now or in the future, earn anywhere close to the interest rate the company is offering to pay you, you might be able to stop right here and take the monthly pension option. But if the numbers are close, and they probably will be, then it will pay for you to look at the other variables that go into this decision. Don't overlook the fact that with monthly pension payments, you no longer have the principal available for you or your beneficiaries.

What does age have to do with whether I take a pension or a lump-sum payment?

Age has a lot to do with your decision. If you choose a lump-sum payment, in order to delay having to pay income taxes on the money in your retirement account you will need to transfer this money into an IRA rollover, and IRA rollover accounts are governed by age restrictions. In most circumstances, you cannot easily touch these funds before age 59½. Also, by April 1 after the year you turn 70½ you have to start making mandatory withdrawals. Let's say you are only 56 years old, and you need the interest from this retirement money to live on. If you take the lump-sum payment and roll over the money, you will not be able to freely access these funds without penalty for another three and a half years, or until you reach age 59½. There are ways around this, such as SEPPs, or substantially equal periodic payments, but they are somewhat complicated. If this is the case, you may find that taking the monthly pension works better for you.

If you are older, your age still comes into play, because you have to start taking those mandatory distributions at age 70½. Let's say you are 65 years old and about to retire. You need all the income your retirement plan can generate. You opt for the lump-sum payment, put all the money into an IRA rollover, and buy a five-year Treasury note earning 6.5 percent. Your monthly income is $1,345, just about what they would give you as a monthly payment. You think you can't lose, since you will even have money left to leave your beneficiaries if you take the lump sum. But you must remember that when you hit age 70½, you have to start making mandatory withdrawals from that IRA account. This is because the government wants the tax money that you have deferred for so long on those funds. Over time, because of taxes, you may find that you do not have anywhere near that $250,000 you started with to generate interest for you. And if, when this happens, interest rates stagnate or decline, you may find yourself with significantly less income per month than if you had taken the monthly pension.

What if I choose to take a monthly pension, and then I go back to work and don't need the money? Do I still have to take the pension and pay taxes on it?

Yes. That is another reason you need to look at your situation very closely. If returning to work is at all a possibility for you, you are probably better off taking a lump-sum payment and rolling over the funds. If you end up not needing that money for income, you can invest it for growth. If you take the pension and then get another job, you are double-dipping—you are getting a salary and a pension at the same time. The problem is that you are getting money that you may not need, you must pay taxes on this money, and you are missing the opportunity to invest it for growth.

Will my pension increase over time?

Some monthly pensions are indexed for inflation, but most are not. So please find out if your pension payment is indexed. This is yet another factor that you need to consider. If you invest a lump-sum payment wisely and interest rates go up, you could keep up with inflation—or maybe even outpace it. You will not be stuck with the frozen dollar amount of your monthly pension payment for the rest of your life. Keep

in mind, however, that if interest rates go down and/or you have not invested your lump-sum payment wisely, you could see your income deteriorate.

Are there reasons other than how much I'm earning in interest on this money to take a lump-sum payment rather than the monthly pension?

Yes. Remember, when you take a monthly pension, depending on the payment option you choose, it may stop when you die. Even if it continues to be paid to your spouse or life partner after your death, upon his or her death it definitely stops. If you have children, this means they will get nothing. But if you took this money as a lump sum and invested it wisely, even with mandatory distributions starting at the age of 70½, you probably could still have money to pass on to your beneficiaries. If you are married or have a life partner and/or children, always look at all your options when it comes to joint and survivor benefits.

JOINT AND SURVIVOR BENEFITS

Can you explain joint and survivor benefits?

If you receive a basic pension when you retire, you usually have the option of reducing your monthly pension in exchange for your spouse or life partner's continuing to receive some portion of your pension after you die. This is called a joint and survivor option, and you can often choose among several levels of joint and survivor benefits, usually 100 percent, 75 percent, 50 percent, and 25 percent. The larger the percentage of your monthly pension you want your spouse or life partner to get, the more money will be deducted from your basic pension each month. Federal law requires written permission from your spouse if you opt to take less than a 50 percent joint and survivor benefit on a tax-qualified plan, and some states require the same for non-company plans, such as IRAs.

Are joint and survivor benefits only for married people?

Most people with access to joint and survivor benefits are married, but there are some companies that do allow joint and survivor benefits to unmarried and same-sex couples.

I plan to take the 50 percent option, since I don't think my wife will need as much money to live on after I am gone. Why not enjoy the money together while we can?

Most people do opt for the 50 percent joint and survivor benefit, thinking that their surviving spouse will need less to live on. I totally disagree with this logic. Most people are wrong about this, unfortunately, and their surviving spouses, in addition to being alone, are left struggling financially. Think about it. For married couples, when one spouse dies, the loss of one Social Security check can make a big financial difference. Also, if at the same time, the survivor's monthly pension check is cut by 50 percent, the financial results can be devastating. Remember, after your death, your spouse is all alone. Therefore, he or she may incur more expenses. If the deceased partner did a lot of repair and maintenance work around the house or on the car, the surviving spouse may find himself or herself needing to hire—and pay—professionals to do that work. Also think about simple loneliness. You and your spouse may spend a lot of time at home together. But when one partner dies, the other partner is going to want and need to spend more time with friends and family members, and otherwise keep him- or herself occupied—which can cause his or her expenses to increase, not decrease.

All those possible increases are definitely scary. But we were careful to pay off the house before I retired, so I know my wife could always sell it if she had to. Isn't that a source of security?

It is. But although this is a common strategy, it has many potential problems. What if your partner doesn't want to sell the house? What if it takes longer to sell the house than you anticipate or if it doesn't sell for as much as you expect? Then where will your spouse be? Where will your spouse live after the house is sold? In all likelihood, the house you are living in now is the least expensive living situation available. And there are so many other factors aside from the financial value attached to your home. You don't want to put your spouse or partner in a situation where he or she is forced to sell the home just to pay bills.

What does the joint and survivor benefit cost if I choose to take it?

Each company has its own pricing system, and not all of them make a joint and survivor option affordable. You have to figure out if the options available from your company are cost-effective for you.

How do I decide whether the joint and survivor benefit my company is offering is cost-effective?

Use the following formula:

Item	J&S Options	Employee	Partner Benefit	Benefit Cost
1	Basic pension	A	B	C
2	50% option	D	E	F
3	100% option	G	H	I

BASIC PENSION

Under Item 1A, put the full monthly amount of your basic pension. This is how much you would receive each month if you took no joint and survivor option, and upon your death, your spouse will not receive anything. Under B put a zero, because your partner's benefit is nothing if you pass away first. Under C put a zero, because this option does not cost you a thing. The company owes you the basic pension, and you are not paying for any additional benefit.

50% OPTION

Under Item 2D, put the dollar amount that appears in the 50 percent joint and survivor section on your benefit statement. Take the figure you entered under D and divide it by two; put this figure under F. This is the benefit that your partner will receive each month after your death. Now subtract D from A. Put this figure under F. This is how much less you will receive from the 50 percent joint and survivor benefit while you're alive.

100% OPTION

Under Item 3G, put the dollar amount that appears in the 100 percent joint and survivor section of your benefit statement. Put whatever figure you have put under G under H as well. After your death, your spouse should receive the same monthly benefit that you were paid. Now subtract G from A and write that figure under I. This is how much the 100 percent joint and survivor option will cost you each month.

Once you have filled in the chart, the cost and benefit to you during your lifetime of each option should be clear (though if there is a significant age difference between you and your spouse, there are other options to consider; we'll discuss that in just a bit). It may make sense to multiply the numbers by 12 to get the yearly cost and benefit to you for each option. Then the question becomes, is there any way to secure the same or better benefits for a surviving spouse or life partner for less money?

LIFE INSURANCE VERSUS JOINT AND SURVIVOR OPTION

Joint and survivor benefits seem kind of like a life insurance policy. Is that accurate?

In a way, yes. And it is a simple matter to compare the costs of various life insurance policies to what your company is charging for that 100 percent benefit. They may be significantly cheaper. If, for example, your basic pension amount would be decreased by at least half in order to have joint and survivor benefits, that's expensive and you should be sure to compare the cost with other life insurance alternatives.

What happens if I receive these joint and survivor benefits and my spouse dies before I do?

In many cases, you will be stuck with those lower benefits for the rest of your life (in the sense that your pension remains reduced) even though no one is alive to use them after you die. This is a potential downside of the joint and survivor benefit

option. Some companies offer something called a pop-up option (also known as a reinstatement of original benefits), which, for a small additional fee, allows you to have your basic pension amount reinstated if your spouse dies before you do. As a general rule, pop-up benefits are available only to married couples, even if the joint and survivor benefits are available to unmarried partners.

What should I look for in a life insurance policy as an alternative to joint and survivor benefits?

The most important thing to keep in mind about any insurance you buy as an alternative to joint and survivor benefits is to make sure that the policy will pay out a specific death benefit no matter how long the covered employee lives and regardless of any fluctuations in interest rates. Ask the insurance agent for an example of the guaranteed values of the policy. These should show you what the minimum death benefit would be no matter what happens with interest rates. That way you can see what could happen in the worst-case situation.

What are the advantages of purchasing a life insurance policy versus the joint and survivor benefit option?

A life insurance policy offers you a tax advantage, because after the insured partner dies, the death benefit passes as a lump sum to the beneficiary, income tax-free. With the joint and survivor option, the surviving spouse receives the income in smaller, taxable monthly payments, and may see more and more of that monthly benefit go to taxes if his or her tax bracket becomes higher. The lump-sum life insurance proceeds also could be invested in tax-free bonds, which would make any income generated by them tax-free, too. Another advantage of life insurance is that you can invest the proceeds to take advantage of changes in interest rates, a hedge against inflation that a pension won't provide (unless your pension has a cost-of-living increase). If your spouse dies first, the life insurance policy can be discontinued and you can withdraw the cash value. Finally, if you, the policyholder, die first, and your surviving spouse inherits the life insurance proceeds and invests wisely, when he or she dies those proceeds, or what remains of them, can be passed on to other beneficiaries, whereas the joint and survivor benefit would simply stop being paid.

Which joint and survivor option do you like best?

The 100 percent joint and survivor benefit is probably the most cost-effective and beneficial option, even if initially it seems expensive. But explore the alternatives with a professional adviser, because, depending on the particular details of your company's options and your individual financial situation, health, and age, there could be a better choice for you.

If I have decided to take the joint and survivor benefit, is there any time that it is OK to take less than the 100 percent option?

Yes, and here are the exceptions:

- You are absolutely guaranteed to receive a significant inheritance or windfall in the immediate future that will take care of your spouse or life partner's needs no matter what.
- Your nonworking partner is significantly older than you are, or has a serious or terminal illness. In either of these situations, it may seem

to make sense to take the basic pension, in which case your spouse will not receive anything, because you assume that your spouse will die first. I think this strategy can be risky, though. What if you were the victim of a freak car accident, and your much older or ill spouse survived you, only to live—maybe for years—with no income?

What is the best way for a married person to deal with this kind of situation, if taking the basic pension without the survivor benefit is never a safe option?

Remember the pop-up option that we discussed earlier? Well, if your company offers such an option, these are excellent circumstances in which to use it. You can take the 100 percent joint and survivor option, and if your partner or spouse dies first, as seems likely, you can return to the basic pension amount and not have to continue paying for a benefit that your partner will never use. This is optimal protection for both of you.

What if my company does not offer a pop-up option?

Depending on your age and your health, term life insurance (only in this particular scenario) may be a relatively inexpensive alternative. If you know that, without a shadow of a doubt, your partner has no chance of living beyond the term of the life insurance policy, you can consider this option seriously. This strategy has the added benefit of possibly resulting in some additional money to leave your children—for example, if you died unexpectedly and your partner died shortly thereafter. The main benefit, of course, is that your partner would be protected in the event of your death.

Why can't I just take my basic pension and invest part of it on my own to accumulate the money my spouse will need in 20 or 30 years? Isn't that really what the company is doing with my money anyway?

I understand how you feel, but let me tell you why I don't recommend this strategy. Investing responsibly on your own for 20 years or more might be an alternative if you could forecast the day you're going to die. But, of course, you don't know when that is going to happen, and it is very possible that you won't have enough time to accumulate the money that your partner will need. For your partner's sake, do not tempt fate.

CIVIL SERVICE RETIREMENT BENEFITS

What are civil service retirement benefits?
A large number of Americans have been or are currently employed by agencies and departments of the federal government. Jobs in the civil service often pay less than comparable jobs in the private sector, but they do have one great advantage, and that is a very comprehensive retirement system. In fact, there are two federal retirement systems, the Civil Service Retirement System (CSRS) and the Federal Employees Retirement System (FERS).

What is the difference between the Civil Service Retirement System and the Federal Employees Retirement System?

Until 1984, every federal government worker in this country was part of the Civil Service Retirement System. Unless they had also worked in the private sector, these workers were not covered by the U.S. Social Security system. Starting January 1, 1984, any worker hired by the federal government has been made a part of a different plan, the Federal Employees Retirement System. These workers are insured by Social Security.

What kinds of benefits are government employees hired before 1984 eligible for?
In 1984, federal employees were given the option of remaining in the old system, the Civil Service Retirement System, or changing over to the Federal Employees Retirement System. Both programs are administered by the U.S. government's Office of Personnel Management, known as the OPM, and both are funded by employees' payroll deductions, as well as by contributions from federal agencies. Both systems offer disability, retirement, and survivors benefits. But neither the CSRS nor the FERS offers dependents benefits. The benefits are based on the worker's highest average salary for any three consecutive years of employment.

How do I know if I am eligible for either the CSRS or the FERS?
You are considered eligible if you have worked for at least five years for the U.S. government as a civilian employee. This means that you can qualify for a government pension, also known as a retirement annuity. Also, if you have worked for at least five years as a federal civilian employee, you are eligible to get retirement credit

for any years after 1956 that you served in the military, provided you pay a premium based on the amount of your military pay.

What kind of retirement benefits are offered by the CSRS and the FERS?

There are two kinds of retirement annuities offered under the CSRS and the FERS. One is an immediate annuity, and the other is a deferred annuity. An annuity is a type of investment that an insurance company invests on your behalf (see Chapter 10).

What are my choices for taking my retirement benefits?

If you have worked for the federal government for at least five years, you are eligible to retire at age 62. At this point, you have a choice: You can immediately begin to receive an annuity paid out of your retirement account, to which you have contributed through payroll deductions. (Again, the five years that you worked for the federal government do not necessarily have to be consecutive, nor do you have to have served five years in the same department.) Alternatively, you may take all of the money from your retirement account at once.

If you stop working for the federal government before you have reached the age of retirement, you cannot begin to withdraw your annuity immediately. You can leave the money that has accumulated in your CSRS or FERS account, or you can withdraw it in a lump sum. If you leave it in the account, you are deferring your annuity payments until age 62—that's why it's called a deferred annuity. If you change your mind and decide to withdraw your money before retire-

ment, you can receive all of it in a lump sum anytime before you reach the age of 62.

Which option is preferable?

It will depend on how much monthly annuity income you are eligible for, compared with the income that your lump-sum withdrawal could generate if invested. If the monthly annuity sum is 2 or 3 percent above what the lump sum would generate, take the monthly annuity income. Otherwise, roll over the lump sum, invest the money on your own, and withdraw the income as needed.

My husband has worked for the federal government for 23 years. Is he entitled to any special benefits?

Because your spouse has worked at least 20 years in a federal job, he is eligible to claim his immediate annuity at the slightly younger age of 60. This is just the tip of the iceberg as far as duration of service in federal employment is concerned. A worker who has served in a federal government job for 30 years or more, and who is covered by the CSRS or the FERS, is eligible to retire with a pension at age 55. (As of 2002, however, this minimum retirement age began rising at the rate of two months per year for both CSRS and FERS.)

What happens if I am laid off from my federal government job before I become eligible for my pension?

The CSRS and the FERS both have rules in place that will permit some, though not all, long-term workers to take an immediate annuity even if they are laid off before retirement age. If an employee is covered under the CSRS and has been working for at least one year in the two years immediately preceding the date on which he or she was laid off, and is age 50 with 20 years of service (or any age with at least 25 years of service), that worker may be eligible to collect an immediate annuity.

One difference in eligibility requirements for a comparable worker covered by FERS is that he or she does not need to have been employed for one year before he or she was laid off. Another difference is that if the FERS employee claims his immediate annuity before he or she reaches age 55, the amount of annuity is not reduced for age. Under the CSRS, the annuity is reduced by ⅙ of 1 percent for each full month under the age of 55 at retirement.

My husband is an air traffic controller. Are the rules for his job different from those for other government workers?

Yes. The federal government, noting the high-stress nature of such jobs as air traffic controller and firefighter, as well as most law enforcement jobs, makes it easier for workers in these jobs to claim early retirement. The government also has lowered the minimum number of years that a worker in one of these fields has to serve in his or her job to receive a pension. If you are a police officer or a firefighter who is covered under CSRS, for example, you are permitted to claim your retirement benefits at age 50. If your husband, the air traffic controller, is covered by the CSRS and he has been at his job for 20 years or longer, he can retire at age 50. If he has been working 25 years at his job, then he is eligible for his retirement benefits at any time.

How do the CSRS and the FERS calculate my benefits?

Both systems use a variety of factors. The first is how long you have worked and how long you have been making contributions to the retirement fund. A second and equally important factor that both the CSRS and the FERS use to calculate the amount of your retirement annuity is what is known as a worker's high-three average salary.

What is a high-three average salary?

This represents an employee's average salary over the three consecutive years in which the worker received the highest amount of compensation. Both the CSRS and the FERS base the retirement annuity that they will pay a worker on this high-three average salary, but the way each calculates the benefit is different.

How does the CSRS perform its calculations?

The CSRS starts with your high-three average salary. To that number, say $40,666, it adds 1.5 percent of your high-three average pay and multiplies it by 5 (for your first five years of service). Then it adds 1.75 percent of your high-three average pay, times the number of years over five and up to ten that you have been employed as well as the number of years of total service. Finally, it adds 2 percent of your high-three average pay, multiplied by the number of years more than ten that you have been employed. The grand total is your retirement annuity.

How does the FERS calculate benefits?

The FERS calculates your retirement annuity by taking 1 percent of your high-three average and multiplying this number by the number of years you have spent in your job. You are also eligible to take early retirement under the FERS system (for a reduced benefit) if you have worked for 10 or more years at your federal government job.

SOCIAL SECURITY

W hen planning for your retirement, don't forget to take into account your Social Security benefits. If you have a history of working for wages, you're probably receiving by mail an annual estimate of the monthly amount of Social Security benefits you can expect to receive at retirement. If you haven't received such an estimate, please call the Social Security Administration (SSA) at (800) 772-1213 and request a Social Security statement. Or log on to the So-cial Security Administration Website at *www.ssa .gov* and view your statement online.

When can I expect to begin receiving my Social Security benefits?

Full retirement benefits have traditionally been payable at age 65 (with reduced benefits available as early as 62) to anyone with enough Social Security credits, which are based on your earnings over time. The age at which full benefits are paid depends on the year in which you were born, and it will rise in future years. For example, if you were born in or before 1937, the SSA considers your full retirement age to be 65. If you were born in 1960, then the SSA considers your retirement age to be 67. People who delay retirement beyond their official retirement age receive an increase in their benefits when they do retire. In most cases payments will begin the month after

YOUR SOCIAL SECURITY BENEFITS BASED ON YEAR OF BIRTH			
If you were born in	You will turn 62 in	The benefits at 62	Full retirement benefits at age
1937 or before	1999 or before	80%	65
1938	2000	79.2%	65,2 mo
1939	2001	78.3%	65,4 mo
1940	2002	77.5%	65,6 mo
1941	2003	76.7%	65,8 mo
1942	2004	75.8%	65,10 mo
1943–54	2005–2016	75%	66
1955	2017	75.2%	66,2 mo
1956	2018	73.3%	66,4 mo
1957	2019	72.5%	66,6 mo
1958	2020	71.7%	66,8 mo
1959	2021	70.8%	66,10 mo
1960 or later	2022–	70%	67

your birthday in whatever year you decide to start collecting.

If I choose to claim my benefits at age 62, by how much will my retirement benefits be reduced?

Again, that will depend on your year of birth. It used to be that we were able to claim full retirement benefits at 65 and early retirement at 62, with a 20 percent reduction in benefits. Now there is a sliding scale. Consult the chart on page 367 to find out where you stand.

Does Social Security adjust my benefits for inflation?

Yes. The SSA automatically adjusts for inflation on January 1 every year, based on the rise or fall in the previous year's consumer price index (an index of prices for everyday goods and services). Since the cost of living rarely goes down, count on a yearly increase in benefits.

For financial reasons, I'm planning to work after I start to receive my Social Security benefits. Will I be penalized for continuing to work?

You may be penalized for continuing to work while collecting Social Security, but less so than in the past. As of January 1, 2000, if you are at full retirement age or older, you can earn as much as you like and not have your benefits reduced. Here's the basic formula the Social Security Administration currently uses:

- If you are under your full retirement age when you start getting your Social Security payments, $1 in benefits will be deducted for each

$2 you earn above the annual limit. For 2009, that limit is $14,160.
- In the year you reach full retirement age, $1 in benefits will be deducted for each $3 you earn above $37,680 (limit for 2009), but only counting earnings before the month you reach the full benefit retirement age.
- Starting the month you reach full retirement age, you will get your benefits with no limit on your earnings.

Will my retirement pension from my job reduce the amount of my Social Security benefit?

If your pension derives from work in which you also paid Social Security taxes, it will not affect your Social Security benefits. However, if your pension derives from work that is not covered by Social Security (i.e., federal, civil service, and some state or local government jobs), then it may reduce the amount of your benefits.

I'm self-employed. Does this mean that when I reach retirement age, I won't be eligible for Social Security benefits?

Until 1951, the self-employed were not eligible for Social Security benefits. But don't worry, these days Social Security is looking out for you, too. For more information, check the SSA Website (www.ssa.gov).

My husband is a veteran. Does he receive any special consideration from the SSA?

Yes. If your husband served in active duty between September 1, 1940, and December 31,

1956, he is eligible for an earnings credit equivalent to an additional $160 a month. If he served in active duty from 1957 to 1977, he will receive an extra $300 worth of earnings credits per quarter, and if he served in active duty anytime after 1977, he will receive $100 worth of earnings credit for every $300 of military pay he received during that period, up to an annual maximum of $1,200. For more information, log on to *www.ssa.gov*.

7

Stocks

THE BIG LEAP

Many, many Americans lost money in the stock market in 2008—and many of us who *didn't* lose money of our own have read frightening stories about others who did. The result is that many of us are now permanently gun-shy about investing in stocks. How can we know the proper time to buy and sell, we wonder, and how can we be sure that the companies we invest in are on the up and up?

Well, there are no guarantees in the stock market, and if you are a person who lies awake at night worrying about whether every penny is safe and sound, then stocks may not be the best investment for you. (But that doesn't mean you shouldn't invest. Please do see the chapters on Bonds and Annuities.) For most of us, with a long time line—at least ten years until we need the money we're investing—stocks still offer by far the best potential for the growth of our money. I believe that you really *can* learn to invest in stocks and other investment vehicles yourself, and that if you learn and follow the few simple rules contained in this chapter, you can do so with a reasonable degree of safety. In the long run you may do better than many an expert would do for you. Remember, you will never achieve a sense of power over your life until you have power over your money. And that means taking control of how your money grows.

Below are questions and answers that, taken together, will tell you much of what you need to know to begin investing in stocks. Hopefully, in time many of you will feel knowledgeable and confident enough to chart your own financial course. Others may be more comfortable working with a financial adviser. There are many excellent ones out there, and you should feel free to seek their help. Ultimately, however, it is your money and your responsibility. So if you choose to work with a professional, remain an active participant. See him or her as a partner, not as a surrogate investor.

It has never been easier—or, believe it or not, safer—to invest your money in stocks. If you have a computer in your home, the information available to you on the World Wide Web is extensive, generally accurate, and at your fingertips 24 hours a day. I urge you to explore the financial resources on the Web: the most instructive sites, the newsletters of stock trackers and economists, company annual reports, and much more. On my own Website, *www.suzeorman.com*, you will find links to just about every major financial site. And if you don't own a computer, you have many other options. If you have cable TV, you can easily flip to the financial news channels or watch *The Suze Orman Show* on CNBC. And scores of new business books find their way into bookstores and libraries every year.

For now, the financial classroom is right here in your hand. With the aid of these questions and answers, you will gain a solid foundation for a basic, satisfying, and potentially very rewarding investing life.

A BRIEF ECONOMICS LESSON

Interest rates, economic growth, unemployment, inflation—these are terms we hear every day. While most of us have a rough working knowledge of their meanings, we'd be hard-pressed to explain the impact they have on our daily lives. But they do have an impact—especially if we are invested in the stock market. So before we get into the heart of this chapter on stocks, let's take a moment to walk through some basic principles of economics.

We'll begin with *interest rates*. Interest rates are an indication of how much it costs to borrow money. When interest rates are high, people are slower to borrow to buy big-ticket items, such as houses or cars. When interest rates are low, consumers are quicker to take on debt, because paying it off will be less expensive. And when people are out there spending money, the economy grows.

As the economy grows, jobs are created, which means unemployment goes down. When there are fewer people out of work, employers generally have to look harder for workers and pay them more. Sounds like a good thing, doesn't it? Not necessarily, because low unemployment and rising wages are factors that contribute to *inflation*. In a period of inflation, goods and services cost more, and money doesn't buy as much.

Inflation occurs at times of high employment because as more people make more money, prices go up. (This is partially because companies' costs go up when they have to pay higher wages, and partially because when people have more money, they want to buy more than the economy is able to produce, which triggers that most basic economic principle: the law of supply and demand.)

A side effect of inflation is an increase in interest rates. The government tends to raise interest rates when the economy shows signs of inflation, in order to slow people's buying and curb economic growth. But higher interest rates also make it more expensive for companies to raise capital by borrowing, and that cuts into their profitability—which is one of the chief things investors consider in valuing stocks. Also, when interest rates are high, yields go up on bonds, and bonds begin to look like better investments than stocks. So investors take money out of stocks and put them into bonds, and stock prices fall. So inflation, as you can see, is an enemy of the stock market.

It's fascinating, isn't it? What seems to be good for you as a worker—lots of jobs and higher wages—may be bad for you as an investor. And the inverse is also true. The markets tend to go up in reaction to "bad" economic news, like a moderate increase in unemployment or a slowdown in wage growth. (Note, however, that I said "moderate." If unemployment is high, growth stagnant, and consumer spending low, that's just as bad for stocks as high interest rates are.)

The long bull (up) market at the end of the 20th century was truly unprecedented. It can be attributed to an economy that was in a remarkable state of balance. Economic growth was steady, but for a long time not too fast; unemployment was low, but wage inflation stayed reasonable; and interest rates declined more or less gradually as price inflation subsided. But history indicates that bull markets are followed by bear (down) markets—which are in turn followed by bull markets. That's why it's wisest to go into the stock market knowing that you're in it for the long haul. It's best not to get too excited by short-term upswings and not to despair when the market dips.

With this in mind, let's take a closer look at some of the terms used to describe the economy and how it's measured.

What is the difference between a bear market and a bull market?

If you are an investor, a bull market can give you many happy days—and a bear market can cause you many sleepless nights. A bear market usually means that over a prolonged period of time the market has declined by at least 20 percent. A bull market means just the opposite—that over a prolonged period of time the market has gone up by at least 20 percent.

What is the consumer price index?

The consumer price index (CPI) measures changes in the prices of everyday consumer goods, such as housing, electricity, transportation, and clothing. The CPI is commonly known as the cost-of-living index. Financial analysts keep a close watch on the CPI, since any upturns can be signs of inflation.

What is the index of leading economic indicators?

This index is perhaps the most closely watched index of them all. It is made up of approximately a dozen different reports, such as stock prices and employment information—including, for example, how many claims for unemployment were made across the country in a given recent period.

Many analysts and economists believe that this index can essentially predict the future of the economy—thus the name "leading economic indicators."

What do people mean when they talk about the gross domestic product?

The gross domestic product (GDP) is the estimated total value of services and goods produced by corporations in this country. This is a hugely important measure, since it tells analysts and economists whether our country's economy is growing at a healthy rate.

What is the durable goods report?

The durable goods report is another important indicator. It tells analysts about goods such as TVs, ovens, refrigerators, and cars. If no one is buying these things, the economy tends to slow down.

What is the producer price index (PPI)?

The producer price index is actually a family of indexes that measures the average change over time in the prices domestic producers of goods and services receive for their wares. PPIs measure price changes from the perspective of the seller. This contrasts with other measures, such as the consumer price index (CPI), that measure price change from the consumer's point of view. Sellers' and consumers' prices may differ due to government subsidies, sales and excise taxes, and distribution costs.

More than 10,000 PPIs for individual products and groups of products are released each month. PPIs are available for the products of virtually every industry in the mining and manufacturing sectors of the U.S. economy. New PPIs are gradually being introduced for the products of the transportation, utilities, trade, finance, and service sectors of the economy.

How are PPIs used?

Producer price index figures are widely used by the business community as well as by the government. They are often used as an economic indicator, since PPIs capture price movements before goods and services hit the retail level. Therefore, PPIs may foreshadow later price changes for businesses and consumers. The president, Congress, and the Federal Reserve employ these figures in formulating fiscal and monetary policies.

How does the producer price index differ from the consumer price index?

While both the PPI and CPI measure price change over time for a fixed set of goods and services, they differ in two critical areas: (1) the composition of the set of goods and services included, and (2) the types of prices collected for the included goods and services.

The target set of goods and services included in the PPIs is the entire marketed output of U.S. producers. Imports are excluded. The target set

of items included in the CPI is the set of goods and services purchased for consumption by urban U.S. households. This set includes imports.

The price collected for an item included in the PPIs is the revenue received by its producer. Sales and excise taxes are not included in the price because they do not represent revenue for the producer. The price collected for an item included in the CPI is a consumer's out-of-pocket expenditure to purchase the item. Sales and excise taxes are included in that price because they are part of what the consumer pays to purchase the item.

What exactly is the Fed, and why is it so important?

The "Fed" is short for the Federal Reserve Bank, this country's central bank, with headquarters in Washington, D.C. The Fed not only oversees all the banks in this country, it has the power to dictate the rate of interest it charges smaller banks to borrow from it. Most banks borrow from the Fed at a so-called discount rate, and the Fed charges them interest. Another interest rate that the Fed influences is called the federal funds rate.

What is the federal funds rate?

The federal funds rate is the interest rate one bank charges another, when one bank lends another money.

What is the prime rate?

The prime rate is the interest rate banks charge their most significant customers. By significant, I'm talking about giant corporations and big businesses. This rate doesn't affect the ordinary investor, you are probably thinking, but think again. If you want to borrow money from a bank or other institution, the interest rate you will be charged is based on the going prime rate, plus a few percentage points. If IBM wanted to borrow money from a bank, it would be charged the prime rate. If you wanted to borrow money from the same bank—say, to finance a new house or a car—you would be charged the prime rate plus.

STOCK BASICS

I hear a lot of talk about stocks but I must admit I'm not even sure what a stock is.
When people talk about stocks, they are usually talking about common stocks. A common stock is a certificate that represents partial ownership in a corporation, whether it's a big national corporation like General Electric or a little corporation out in Minnesota that makes corkscrews. When you buy a share of a stock, you are effectively buying a part of that corporation, and therefore you have equity (i.e., you are part owner) in it. Stocks are securities that are also known as equity investments.

What are the advantages of investing in stocks?
Three advantages: growth, growth, and growth—provided you pick the right stocks. Compared with other investment vehicles such as CDs, bonds, gold, real estate, and Treasuries, stocks have provided investors with the best annual investment returns. To give you an example, over a period of almost 80 years, from 1926

through 2008, the average return of the stock market as a whole was 10 percent a year. Now please make sure you understand that this does not mean stocks are guaranteed to go up 10 percent every year. I imagine it may be abundantly clear after the bear market of 2008 but I just want to spell it out for you: the 10 percent is an average over many, many years. Some years the market goes up, some years it goes down (way down). But the overall long-term trend is that the ups and downs have worked out to an average annual gain of about 10 percent. Over time, the stock market truly does provide the best opportunity for your money to grow.

I've always thought that the stock market seemed like legalized gambling. Is it really a safe way to invest my money?
Safe is a relative term: How much safety do you need? Or, putting it another way, how much risk can you tolerate? Historically, you should know that stocks outperform bonds and cash over very long periods. By long-term I mean ten years or longer. If you don't have at least ten years to let your money remain invested, you could be taking a significant risk, depending on what is happening in the overall economy.

What if an emergency arises and I have to get my money out of my stocks? Can I do so easily?
Yes. You're asking about something called liquidity, and most American and many foreign stocks are highly liquid, meaning that you can easily sell them. In most cases, you can turn your shares of common stock into money in three business days. But that doesn't mean that you'll be able to sell them at a profit or even for as much as you

paid for them; that depends on which stocks you own and when you need to sell.

Tell me about the disadvantages of investing in stocks.

Nothing is certain in the stock market. Just because stocks, in my opinion, are the best investment vehicle for the growth of your money over time does not mean that you will make huge profits—or any profits at all, for that matter—*in any given period of time.*

The stock market seems so complicated! Can I invest in it on my own?

Yes, you can. The stock market *is* a complicated entity that many people have spent much of their lives studying. One reason it is complicated is that it is made up of people just like you and me, buying and selling, and no one will ever be able to figure out exactly why we buy and sell when we do. In general, however, the stock market is absolutely something you can learn enough about to make safe and wise investment decisions. You will need to be patient, you will need to know how to gather information, and you will need to know yourself pretty well so that you do not buy or sell on impulse or hang on to a stock long after you should have sold it because you love it. But all these things have been learned by millions of people.

Why does the price of a stock go up or down?

Supply and demand. Demand for a particular stock by investors such as you and me pushes the price of the stock up. If there is less demand for a stock, or if people who own it want to sell it at any price, the stock's price will go down.

What determines demand for a stock?

You do, you and millions of other investors. At bottom, the price of a stock is controlled by your perceptions, more or less well informed, of the company's future prospects. I'll talk more later about the many factors that go into the making of those perceptions. But the rule is pretty obvious: If the informed word is that this stock is going nowhere fast, then demand for the stock will fall and so will its price. (Also, when many investors unload their shares, increasing the supply, the stock's price can fall further.) If the company's earnings are better than anticipated, or an important financial analyst recommends that investors buy the stock, or the company has a new product that the public loves, or if a new and well-regarded CEO comes on board, demand for a stock will go up and so will the stock's price. There are often other factors involved, as I said, but this is essentially how demand works.

TYPES OF STOCK

What are income stocks?

Income stocks are stocks of stable companies that generally do not reinvest a big part of their profits back into the company each year. This means that those profits can be distributed to the shareholders in the form of dividends. If you want income via dividends and capital appreciation, these are the stocks to invest in. Many stocks raise or lower their dividends yearly, so your income can change.

What are growth stocks?

Growth stocks are typically stocks of companies whose primary objective is to grow. The dividend income from such a stock is usually small or nonexistent, since many of these companies are just starting out and/or plowing most of their earnings back into the company. In my opinion, investing in good-quality growth stocks is one of the very best ways to make a satisfactory investment return over the long haul; remember, the long-term average annual growth rate is more than 10 percent. People who buy growth stocks do so because they believe the company in which they own shares will increase its profits over the years, and that the growth in profits will be reflected in the stock price.

What are value stocks?

Value stocks are typically stocks that have gone down in price but remain a good buy. Value stocks are measured in relation to their company's underlying assets—cash, real estate, plants, and equipment, for example—more than in relation to its earnings potential. People buy a value stock based not on future growth of the company but on the fact that they are getting shares of a solid company at a good price and that in time the market will realize this. When this happens, up goes the stock's price.

What are speculative stocks?

Speculative stocks don't have much of a track record. They are the riskiest stocks out there, which means they can make you—or lose you—the most money. You have to ask yourself if the risk is worth it. Typically, speculative stocks are issued by companies that are brand new or that few established investors have heard of.

What are cyclical stocks?

Cyclical stocks are stocks of companies that are closely aligned with what is happening in the business cycle—that is, with whether the economy is in a growth phase or is slowing down. These stocks can include steel companies and original equipment manufacturers (OEMs) of such items as automobile chassis or airplane parts. If you trade in cyclical stocks, you must be fairly sophisticated financially, and you also have to keep your eyes open for the economic indicators. If the economy is growing at a decent clip and production is keeping pace with increased demand, the earnings and stock prices of cyclical stocks will probably rise. If the economy isn't doing so well and consumers are turning their backs on new cars, for example, the earnings and stock prices of these companies will likely fall.

What are small-cap, mid-cap, and large-cap stocks?

Everything with a "cap" in it refers to a company's market capitalization, meaning the total amount of capital the company has at its disposal from all the shares investors have bought. This in turn signifies its size. (Companies of different sizes have historically demonstrated different returns.) Although different financial institutions define these categories differently, the following are, according to Charles Schwab, what the designations mean:

- **Small-cap.** Small-cap funds invest in companies with market values of under $2 billion (80 percent of the top 5,000 publicly held companies—as well as companies not ranked in the top 5,000). Small-cap funds are subject to greater volatility than those in other asset categories.

- **Mid-cap.** Domestic mid-cap funds invest in companies with market values of $2 billion to $10 billion (about 15 percent of the top 5,000).
- **Large-cap.** Generally, large-cap companies have a market value (capitalization) of over $10 billion. They are typically well established, with solid histories of growth and dividend payments.

What are blue-chip stocks?

Blue-chip stocks are the biggest of the large-cap stocks. They are what we usually think of as the heavy hitters: Exxon, Merck, and Microsoft, for example. All blue-chip stocks are large-cap stocks, but not all large-cap stocks are blue-chip. Blue-chip stocks have enormous liquidity, earnings, staying power, and economic importance.

What are American Depository Receipts?

American Depository Receipts (ADRs) are stand-ins for shares of non-U.S. corporations that are primarily traded on non-U.S. exchanges. It is very hard for most investors to buy those stocks directly. ADRs make it possible because they are traded on the U.S. exchanges.

What is the difference between common and preferred stock?

Common stock is the class of stock that most people buy and own. But a company can also issue what is known as preferred stock. Like shares of common stock, shares of preferred stock represent partial ownership of a corporation. The difference is that if you own preferred stock, you have a legal "prior" claim on the company's earnings, including dividend payments. This means that in times of trouble you will be paid your dividend before the owners of common stock participate in any dividend or gain. Also, your dividend is fixed, unlike dividends on common stocks, which can vary. And if the company goes bankrupt, as an owner of preferred stock you will share in the company's remaining assets, if any, before the owners of common stock do. People usually buy preferred stock because they want income, and preferred stocks generally pay not only a fixed but a higher dividend than common stocks. The downside is that preferred stocks very seldom benefit from growth in the company—again, because the dividend is fixed. They perform similarly to bonds, and are considered a debt of obligation of the company. But unlike bonds, preferred stocks do not have a maturity date. People buy preferred stock because they like the fixed dividend and they know that they have first dibs on the money in case of a default.

What are convertible preferred stocks?

Convertible preferred stocks are shares of stock that start out as a preferred stock but can be changed into common stock. Because of this conversion feature, the price of convertible preferred stock reacts more to the growth of the company than does the price of straight preferred stock.

If I own preferred stock that issues me a dividend, is that dividend tax-free?

Many preferred stocks do not qualify because they are actually making an interest payment, not a dividend payout. And interest payments don't qualify for the great tax break. So be very, very careful.

INITIAL PUBLIC OFFERINGS (IPOs)

Recently I wanted to buy shares in a company in my hometown, but the company spokesman says they are not publicly traded. What does that mean?

Many companies do not trade publicly, which means that they are privately owned and the public cannot buy shares in them. These companies are known as privately held corporations. Typically, they are owned by a single family or by a consortium of investors, neither of which is obliged by law to declare to anybody (except the IRS) how much money the company is making year to year.

Why would a company want to go public?

Because it wants to raise money. It aims to grow bigger and better, and in order to expand and prosper, it requires or simply wants the capital that comes from offering shares for sale in the public market. If I owned a pharmaceutical firm, say, and I needed to raise a lot of money to fund research for a new drug that promises to cure baldness, I would offer shares of the ownership of my company—common stock— to the general public. This is known as going public. This money would come into my pharmaceutical firm through an initial public offering (IPO).

How does a company go public?

A company going public uses a lead underwriter, or a brokerage firm that takes the company to the public markets via a stock offering.

What are the "primary" and "secondary" markets I sometimes read about in connection with IPOs?

They are, respectively, the original buyers and the later buyers of the stock. When shares of a company are initially offered, they are sold in what is called the primary market at a specific price. Let's say my company has contracted with a particular brokerage firm to take my stock public. The brokerage offers all the shares that are being sold at a set price: $15 a share. This is the primary market for those shares. The opportunity to buy a stock in the primary market for the IPO price is usually reserved for the brokerage firm's best clients. The people who buy shares in the primary market then have the right to turn around and start selling those shares to the general public in the open market. This is the secondary market, or after-market. There, the price fluctuates. Most of us get to purchase securities or stocks in the secondary market.

THE MARKETS

How many stock markets are there in the United States?

There are many, many different stock markets in the United States, but the ones that you will hear most about are the New York Stock Exchange (NYSE), the American Stock Exchange (now called NYSE Amex Equities and often referred

382 S T O C K S

to as the AMEX), and the NASDAQ. Think of them as arenas, or forums, in which people and companies can trade securities. Let's look at them one by one.

What is the New York Stock Exchange?

The New York Stock Exchange, now known as the NYSE Euronext, traces its history back to the Buttonwood Agreement of 1792—a pact between brokers and Wall Street merchants that spelled out how they would barter securities. It is still located on Wall Street in New York City, but in 2007 the NYSE merged with Euronext in order to expand globally. The NYSE Euronext is the largest and best-known stock exchange in this country, as well as the one with the tightest requirements for companies to become listed and traded. A company will not make the grade with the NYSE unless it is financially strong and an industry leader. In exchange for the privilege of being listed on the NYSE, a company must pay an annual fee.

Brokerage companies, incidentally, describe themselves as members of the New York Stock Exchange. This means they have bought a "seat" on the Exchange, which in turn means that one of their employees carries out orders to buy or sell stock on the floor of the exchange. It is expensive to become a member of the NYSE, usually costing a one-time payment of well over $1 million.

In 2008, the NYSE Euronext acquired the American Stock Exchange. The AMEX was known as a major exchange for options (more about these later) as well as stocks. All securities traded by the American Stock Exchange now trade under the umbrella of the NYSE Euronext.

What is the NASDAQ?

The National Association of Securities Dealers Automated Quotations, or NASDAQ, is the youngest of these three markets. Although the NASDAQ lists stocks from just about every industry, it is best known for its listings of technology companies, including Cisco Systems and Intel. It is the second-largest stock market in the United States. Launched in 1971, the NASDAQ is the nation's first over-the-counter, or electronic, stock market, linking buyers and sellers via a computer network. Brokers and dealers make a market in individual stocks by maintaining an inventory in their own accounts. They buy or sell when they receive orders from investors. Start-up companies issuing stock in initial public offerings frequently list on the NASDAQ.

BUYING OR SELLING A STOCK

What do you think the markets are going to do in the future?

In order to tell you what I think about the future of the stock market, I first have to go back and tell you a little bit about the past of the stock market. In 1966 the Dow Jones Industrial Average was 874, and in 1982, 16 years later, it was 875. This is not a typo; the market was just one point higher in 1982, but in between there was plenty of up-and-down movement. During those 16 years we were in what was known as a secular long-term down market. Within every secular bear market there are what are known as short bull market cycles—maybe a few months, or a few years—where stocks regain 25 percent or so of their losses. Then they'll turn right around and head down again.

From 1982 to 2000 we entered what was known as a secular bull market, where the market went from 875 to approximately 11,700. However, within those 18 years the market experienced secular bear trends such as in 1987, when the market went down 22 percent in just one day.

In the year 2000 we started another secular bear market, which should last until approximately the year 2015, but please remember that in every secular bear market there are bull market cycles. And that is what I expect to happen to us right now. We will have periods when the market is up 10 percent, 20 percent, even 30 percent; it could happen in a six-month period or three years. Then it will go back down. We are in for a period of up and down, up and down. That is why it is very important that you watch your portfolios very, very carefully. Now, all of this is very fine and well if history repeats itself, but that, my friends, is a big *if*, because anything can happen to upset the historical action of the market, such as a terrorist attack or corporate scandals yet to be uncovered. So the above will only hold true if nothing unexpected happens.

Why do I always hear you say you need at least ten years or longer if you are going to invest in the stock market?

At the end of 2002, the NASDAQ index, which controls many of the big-name technology stocks, had declined approximately 74 percent from its high of 1999 and the first half of the year 2000. That tumble caused many investors to lose 50 percent or more in their retirement plans, stock portfolios, and mutual fund investments—similar to the losses many investors experienced in 2008. And you need to understand that to recoup a 74 percent loss takes a 275 percent increase. Amazing, but unfortunately true. So even if the markets were to go up 9 percent every single year, it would take 15 years just to break even. That's why I think it is so important to understand that stock investing only makes sense when you have a 10- or 20-year time frame; sometimes you will need all the time to make up for losses.

What do you mean by "all or nothing" investors?

What I have noticed is that people either invest all of their money at once or they invest nothing. Or they sell all of their stock at once or they keep it all. They either do everything or nothing. And this can be very dangerous. There is nothing wrong, if something goes wrong, in selling 20 percent. And if something continues to go wrong, you sell another 20 percent. Unfortunately, many of you hold on until your investment becomes worthless and it's too late to do anything.

When I buy stock in a company on the stock exchange, how is my ownership recorded?

Traditionally, by certificate, though today most of us never see certificates of the companies we buy stock in. We see our stock purchases noted on monthly brokerage firm statements, and we receive transaction slips that say we purchased them. When the stock we bought is kept at the brokerage firm through which we purchased it, the brokerage firm is said to be holding our stocks for us in street name, or as a book entry.

Can I get my stock certificates if I want them?
Absolutely. If you want your stock certificates, you can request them, and they will be sent to you. Incidentally, most people guard these certificates very carefully, usually locking them away in a safe-deposit box at their bank.

In your opinion, which is better—to take delivery of the stock certificates or to leave your stocks in street name?
I prefer to leave my stocks in street name with my brokerage firm for the following reasons. First of all, ease. If I want to sell stock, all I have to do is make a phone call or place a trade online, and my wishes are carried out. If I hold my own certificates, I have to physically transport them to the brokerage firm to be sold. Second, timing. Let's say you want to sell your shares quickly when you're on a business trip. If your certificates are in a vault somewhere, you won't be able to. Third, a reputable brokerage firm sends you a monthly statement and arranges for your dividends to be paid immediately into your account. These services keep you abreast of the market for your stock and save you time.

I've often seen TV shots of Wall Street in action, with all these people jumping up and down, screaming, waving bits of paper. What are they doing, for heaven's sake, and what does it have to do with my stock orders?
It has everything to do with your trading orders, and the next time you visit New York, I recommend that you go and see what actually happens at 11 Wall Street, because it is quite a spectacle. Let's say you place an order with your stockbroker (who can be anywhere in the world these days), telling him to buy 200 shares of IBM stock. The broker receives your order, then sends it, via computer, to the order department of his firm, which relays it, again via computer, to a clerk on the floor of the New York Stock Exchange, where IBM is traded. The clerk passes your order on to the floor trader who represents your brokerage firm. The floor trader, armed with your "buy" order, tries to find another floor trader who, for whatever reason, wants to sell those 200 shares of IBM. (The jumping up and down, etc., usually occurs on unusually good—or bad—days.) The two traders haggle for a moment, settle on a price, and execute the order. All this information is then reported back to your broker, who lets you know what price you ended up paying for your 200 shares of IBM. A couple of days later, you will receive confirmation of your trade.

What if no one on the NYSE Euronext wants to sell the stock I'm trying to buy?
On the New York Stock Exchange, you will always find a seller, and you will always find a buyer for the stock you want to sell. You just might not get the price you want! Every stock on this exchange has what is known as a specialist, or a market maker. If no one else wants to buy your stock, the specialist has to. This way, there is always a market in the stock you want to sell on the NYSE Euronext.

How do I place an order to buy or sell stock?
You do it by placing a "market order" with your broker. But to do that you need to know a little of the terminology. Bear with me: This is the language of the market.

What is a market order?

A market order is an instruction to your broker to buy or sell your stock at the best price the trader can get for you at a particular time. Let's imagine that you are trying to buy 500 shares of the Orman Corporation. The day before, the Orman Corporation closed at $27 a share—that was the last trade price. When you enter your market order with your broker, you are contracted to buy 500 shares at the best available price. Does this mean you will pay $27 a share for your 500 shares of the Orman Corporation? Not necessarily. The actual price you will pay might be higher or lower, depending on the current bid price when your order makes its way down to the trading floor, what the seller is asking for the stock (the ask price), and what is happening to that stock and in the market generally. Share prices sometimes change quickly.

What are bids and ask prices?

A bid is the highest price any prospective buyer of a stock is willing to pay for a share of that stock at a particular time. An ask price is the lowest price acceptable to a seller of a stock. Together, the bid and the ask price are a quotation. The difference between them is known as the spread. Bid and ask prices are the two numbers that the person who is taking your order to buy or sell stock will throw at you. He or she will say, for example, that your stock is trading at $27 bid and $27.25 ask. If you want to buy that stock right now, the best price on the floor is $27.25, so if you place a market order that is probably how much you will pay. If you want to sell your stock, the bid—the most someone is willing to pay—is $27 a share, so if you place a market order you

might get only that amount. When you know the bid and the ask prices you can use that information to decide at what price you might be willing to buy or sell a stock. Remember, with a market order there are no price guarantees. But you *can* set the price at which you are willing to buy or sell your stock. This is known as a limit order.

What is a limit order?

A limit order is an order to buy or sell a specific number of shares of stock, with one very important condition: You will buy or sell only if you can get the exact price that you want or a better price on those shares. In other words, you are limiting the amount of money you will pay to buy that stock or the amount you will accept to sell it. Say you are still trying to buy those shares of the Orman Corporation. In our earlier example, they were trading for $27 a share. But you don't want to pay that much. You call up your broker and tell him or her that you want to enter a limit order of $26. That means the broker's trader may buy shares only if and when the price reaches $26 or lower. Similarly, when you enter a limit order to sell Orman shares at $27, that means that you will accept only a price of $27 or above.

What is a stop loss order?

A stop loss order is a protective mechanism, used to lock in a profit or to keep you (hopefully) from losing more than a predetermined amount of money on a stock. It is an instruction to your broker to sell your stock once it has traded at a specified price known as the stop price.

This is how a stop loss order works. Imagine that three years ago you bought stock in the Orman Corporation at $9 a share, and now it is trading at $27. You've done pretty well! Indications are that the price of the Orman Corporation is going to continue to go up, but your instinct is to protect that nice profit that you've built up over the past three years. You don't want to sell the stock if it's going to keep rising, but you also don't want to see it go back down to $9 a share and watch your profits go out the window. Here is where a stop loss order comes in handy. You enter a stop loss order at $24 a share. If the price of the Orman Corporation begins to fall and drops down to $24, your stop loss order immediately becomes a market order, and you will get the best price a trader can sell your stock for at that moment. Remember, a stop loss order means that when your stock hits a particular price you want to sell. It does not say at what price you will actually sell the stock. For this, you need a stop sell limit order.

What is a stop sell limit order?

A stop sell limit order is an order that declares that you want to sell your stock at a specific price or not at all. So if the Orman Corporation is at $27 and you want to protect your profits, you could place a stop sell limit order of $24 a share. This means that if the stock goes to $24 you want to sell it, but only if you can get exactly $24 a share. The problem with this kind of order is that you may not get your price, and if you don't, then you may not sell your stock at all. Just because Orman Corporation stock traded at $24 a share does not mean that it was your shares that sold at that price. If the stock price is plummeting fast and goes past your stop sell limit order, you could still be holding the Orman Corporation when it falls to $23, $18, or

even $16 a share. This is why many people prefer to use a stop loss order. With a stop loss order, you will sell no matter what, for as soon as the stock hits your stop price (or goes lower than that price), your stock will be sold for the best price the trader can get. Hopefully, that price will be close to your stop price.

When I place an order to buy or sell stock, how long is it good for? Do I need to keep renewing it?

There are many ways to enter an order. The two that you will most likely be dealing with are known as a good-till-canceled order and a day order.

A good-till-canceled order, or GTC, states that you are willing to buy or sell a certain number of shares of stock when they reach a specific price. As the name suggests, the order will remain in effect until the stock reaches that price—in theory, whether that's next week, next year, or seven years from now. If the stock does not reach that price, then your trade simply won't take place. With a GTC order, you have to monitor the stock carefully, because if you change your mind and no longer want your order to be executed, you have to make sure that you cancel the order. Many brokerage firms actually do have a set amount of time for which they will let you keep a GTC order in effect without your having to renew it. If your firm doesn't have such a policy, watch out—you may end up buying or selling a stock when you no longer want to.

A *day order* is used only with limit orders, and is good only for the day that you place the order. If the stock does not hit your designated price on that day, and you still want to buy or sell it, you can place another order of any kind the next day.

Does the brokerage firm care how many shares of a particular stock I buy?

Years ago it did, but not now. Shares of stock are traded in what is known as round lots and odd lots. A *round-lot order* is an order to buy or sell 100 shares, or multiples of 100. If you were going to buy 500 shares, that would be five round lots. An *odd-lot order*, on the other hand, is an order for fewer than 100 shares, or for a number of shares that is not a multiple of 100.

BUYING ON MARGIN

What does it mean to buy stocks on margin?

Buying on margin essentially means that you are buying stocks with borrowed money. When you buy stocks outright—say, 100 shares at $50 a share—you fork over $5,000 in cash. That's it. Buying on margin is different. Suppose you want to buy those same 100 shares of that stock, but you don't have $5,000, or don't want to spend it right now. If you qualify, your brokerage firm will lend you up to half the $5,000. So all you have to do is hand over the remaining $2,500. You have just purchased stocks on margin.

What is the minimum amount of stocks or money one can have in a margin account?

About $2,000, but each brokerage firm sets its own minimum amount.

Why would the brokerage firm want to lend me money?

You know the answer to that one! The firm isn't going to lend you that money for free. You're going to pay interest. This interest is another source of income for the firm. Not only that, but they are going to hold the stock you purchase as collateral against this loan—so they have nothing to lose and everything to gain.

Why do people buy stocks on margin, even though it costs them to do so?

Think about it. You can control up to twice the number of shares that you actually have the money to buy. Many people think of buying on margin as taking out a mortgage on their stocks. They do it with the hope that their stock will go up in price and make them twice the amount of money they would have made if they had bought half as many shares with cash. As long as their additional profit exceeds the interest they have to pay to the brokerage firm, they are sitting pretty. Most day traders buy on margin.

What is the danger of buying on margin?

The danger for you, the investor, is huge. It comes into play when the stock you bought on margin goes down in price. By law, the brokerage firm cannot let the stock price fall below a certain percentage (usually 30 percent) of what it has lent you. If the stock does go below that, the firm issues what is known as a margin call, whereupon you could be in trouble.

Why? What is a margin call?

A margin call means that you, the investor, must come up with the amount of money needed to bring the brokerage firm's risk down to the required level. If you do not have the money to do this, the brokerage firm will sell your stock and take its money back. (Even if you do have the money, your margin agreement with the stockbroker may allow a sale of these shares or other shares you own without your permission.) If there is any money left, the brokerage firm will return it to you. With any investment, there is a tradeoff between risk and reward. Buying on margin can increase your reward, but it also seriously increases your risk. I personally would advise you to stay as far away from margins as possible, unless you consider yourself a sophisticated investor and are willing to take a big financial loss in pursuit of a possible greater return.

SECURITIES PROTECTION INSURANCE

What happens if the brokerage firm that holds my stocks goes under?

There is something that will protect your investments, up to a point, in the event that your brokerage firm goes belly up. The Securities Investor Protection Corporation (SIPC) is a nonprofit membership corporation established by Congress in 1970 that insures cash and securities in customer accounts for up to $500,000 (including up to $100,000 in cash) in the event that your brokerage firm files for bankruptcy. If your brokerage firm is a member of the National Association of Securities Dealers (NASD)—and you should deal only with a brokerage firm that

belongs to the NASD—then you will be covered by the SIPC.

What happens if I have three accounts at one firm? Does that $500,000 SIPC ceiling represent a total for all three of my accounts, or for each one separately?

The $500,000 is the amount of insurance offered for each and every account that you hold in a separate capacity, i.e., as a custodian, a joint tenant, or a sole owner. But if you are a customer who, in a single capacity, maintains several different accounts held with the same investment firm or brokerage, then you would be considered a single customer as far as the $500,000 ceiling is concerned.

I have more than $500,000 in an account. Does this mean my money is at risk?

Most major brokerage firms do carry additional private insurance above and beyond the $500,000 provided by SIPC. There are some brokerage firms that will cover you for any amount that you have in your account, and others that set a cap on the extra coverage they carry. So please make sure that you ask your firm to verify the amount and who provides the coverage. This is also one of the reasons why it is so important for you to establish that your firm is a reputable one, with significant protection behind it. But remember, the account insurance offered by the SIPC and any other insurance coverage your brokerage firm has in place does not protect against losses due to market fluctuations. Note, too, that no insurance will protect against securities that aren't registered with the Securities and Exchange Commission. Securities ineligible for SIPC protection include, but are not limited to: commodity futures contracts, currency contracts, and limited partnerships.

THE INDEXES

I keep hearing about stock market indexes. What are these?

All stock market indexes are indicators used to measure and report changes of value in representative groups of stocks. An index is simply a statistical indicator of how a particular group of stocks (or bonds) is performing. There are several key indexes that track changing values in the stock and bond markets. The most familiar stock index is the Dow Jones Industrial Average, which is an index based on 30 large-cap stocks. If these 30 stocks happen to go up in value overall, so does the Dow Jones index.

What is the Dow Jones Industrial Average?

The Dow Jones Industrial Average (DJIA) is by far the most widely known, widely quoted daily financial index in the world. But as an indicator of the overall stock market, it is also somewhat misleading, since it tracks only 30 large-cap blue-chip companies and because it's "price-weighted," which means that the highest-priced securities in the index exert a disproportionate influence on how the DJIA does in general.

What are the 30 stocks that the Dow Jones is made up of?

As of press time:

3M
Alcoa Inc.
American Express Co.
AT&T Inc.
Bank of America Corp.
Boeing Co.
Caterpillar Inc.
Chevron Corp.
Cisco Systems
Coca-Cola Co.
E. I. DuPont de Nemours & Co.
Exxon Mobil Corp.
General Electric Co.
Hewlett-Packard Co.
Home Depot Inc.
Intel Corp.
International Business Machines Corp.
Johnson & Johnson
JP Morgan Chase & Co.
Kraft Foods Inc.
McDonald's Corp.
Merck & Co. Inc.
Microsoft Corp.
Pfizer Inc.
Procter & Gamble Co.
Travelers Cos. Inc.
United Technologies Corp.
Verizon Communications Inc.
Wal-Mart Stores Inc.
Walt Disney Co.

The Dow Jones is made up of stocks that supposedly represent areas of public interest. Microsoft and Intel were the first two technology stocks to be added to the Dow, in 1999. In 2009, Cisco Systems and Travelers were added to the index, while General Motors and Citigroup were taken out.

Is there more than one Dow Jones average?

Yes. There are actually four Dow Jones averages: the Industrial Average, which is made up of the 30 stocks listed in the previous question; the Transportation Average, which is made up of 20 transportation stocks; the Utility Average, which is made up of 15 utility stocks; and the Composite Average, which is made up of the other three together. However, the most widely quoted and the one that you probably should be watching is the Dow Jones Industrial Average.

What is the S&P 500?

Many people believe that the 50-plus-year-old Standard and Poor's 500 (S&P 500) index gives a far more accurate picture of the general performance of the market than the DJIA, since it measures not just 30 but approximately 500 stocks of the largest American companies. The S&P 500 selects and tracks stocks on the basis of their trustworthiness, liquidity, and sector representation. Almost as widely quoted as the DJIA, the S&P 500 differs not only in the number of representative stocks it tracks, but also in its calculations, which, unlike the Dow's, are "market-weighted." This means that each stock's influence in the index mirrors its market value (the price of the stock multiplied by the number of outstanding shares).

What is the Dow Jones Wilshire 5000 Total Market Index?

The Wilshire 5000 Total Market Index represents the broadest index for the U.S. equity market, measuring the performance of all U.S. headquartered equity securities, with readily available price data. The index was named after the nearly 5,000 stocks it contained when it was originally created, but it has grown to include over 6,300 stocks.

What is the Dow Jones Wilshire 4500 Index?

Take the number of stocks on the Wilshire 5000 Total Market Index, subtract most of the companies that appear on the S&P 500 Index, and you will have the Wilshire 4500 Index. Medium and small capitalization managers use the Wilshire 4500 as a performance benchmark.

What is the Russell 3000 Index?

The Russell Index, which, like the S&P 500, is market-weighted, tracks the performance of some 3,000 large-cap U.S. companies.

What is the Russell 2000 Index?

This index takes the 2,000 smallest stocks on the Russell 3000 and gives them an index of their own. (Remember, "smallest" here is a relative term, given the size and stability of the securities tracked by the bigger Russell 3000.)

What is the Schwab 1000 Index?

This market-weighted index comprises the 1,000 biggest publicly traded securities in America, including General Electric, Microsoft, Intel, Exxon, and Wal-Mart stores.

What is the S&P MidCap 400 Index?

Like the S&P 500, the S&P MidCap 400 Index is market-weighted and made up of stable, liquid companies with strong industry representation. Unlike the S&P 500, this index comprises 400 mid-cap securities.

What is the S&P SmallCap 600 Index?

The market-weighted S&P SmallCap 600 Index is made up of 600 small-cap stocks, again selected for their stability, liquidity, and industry representation.

What is the Morgan Stanley Capital International Europe, Australia, Far East Index (MSCI EAFE)?

This index is made up of roughly 1,100 stocks traded on some 21 different exchanges from Europe to Asia-Pacific.

What is the NASDAQ index?

NASDAQ is not only an electronic stock market; it is also an index that tracks approximately 4,000 mostly technology-oriented stocks and that, like the S&P 500, is market-weighted, so that the largest stocks have more impact on the index level than smaller ones.

How do I know which of these various indexes is best for me?

To decide which index is the best benchmark for you to use (remember, it pays to measure your investments' performance against the value of an index), you must compare the stocks that make up various indexes to your holdings. Is your particular portfolio chock-a-block with large transportation securities, such as railroad and airplane stocks? Then it is worth your while to keep a close watch on the Dow Jones Transportation Average. If your portfolio is heavily weighted with utility securities, such as telephone, electricity, or natural gas stocks, then you should keep your eye on the Dow Jones Utility Average to get a good idea of how utility stocks are doing overall.

You can also use the indexes that match your holdings to find out how well, or how badly, your stocks performed during extreme economic times in our history, such as periods of inflation or recession, or even during the stock market crash of 1987.

What if the index that I'm following is doing well, but my stocks aren't keeping pace with it?

This is a sign that you need to do some serious investigation into why your stocks are underperforming. You might uncover some very valid reasons to consider selling some of your holdings and putting your money elsewhere.

Which index should I use to evaluate the overall health of the stock market?

I use all three of the biggies: the Dow Jones Industrial Average, the S&P 500, and the NASDAQ. And I use one that takes them all into consideration, the Wilshire 5000. If we are in a truly healthy market, then all will be doing well. But if one is doing well and the others are not, which is known as a divergence in the market, I take this as an early warning sign that the market might be weakening.

What if everything looks good for the stock I'm about to buy, but the overall market is doing very poorly? Would you advise me to buy that stock?

Another key indicator I consider before buying any stock is the overall direction of the market. If I feel that the market is about to turn bearish,

I have to tell you, I would be reluctant to buy any stock, regardless of what an individual company is doing, unless I used a very handy investing technique called dollar cost averaging, which I'll say more about later.

What if the indexes show that the overall market is positive and I want to buy a stock, but the stock I'm interested in is hitting new highs? Does this mean I should not buy it?

No, but do your homework. Is everything else in line for the stock to go up further? Are the quarterly and annual earnings per share healthy and growing, is the volume strong, and is the company a market and an industry leader, with small institutional ownership? Is management good? Are the company's products diverse and new or updated? If so, then the stock's hitting a new high may be a positive sign.

INDUSTRY LEADERS

I always see in the paper that certain stocks are industry leaders. What does this mean?

An industry leader is typically a large-cap company that has a dominant position in its industry and creates a dominant product for that particular market. In other words, it leads all the companies in that industry.

How important is it that the stock I'm thinking about buying be a market and an industry leader?

In my opinion, very important. This is another of the key factors I look for before I buy a stock. I want my stocks to be market and industry leaders, and so should you.

MEASURING A STOCK'S VALUE

I want to know whether to buy a stock, and I know the financial websites can help me. But what do all those numbers mean?

The numbers won't seem so complicated if we go through them one by one. "High" and "Low" are the highest and lowest prices paid for the stock in the past year. The figure under "Dividend" is typically an estimate of the dividend amount the stock will pay based on recent past performance. "100s" tells you the number of shares sold for the day in question, or the trading volume, expressed in hundreds. (If 4,000,000 shares of a particular stock were traded that day, then under "100s" you would see "40,000.") Next you will see "High" and "Low" again. This time they refer to the highest and lowest prices paid for the stock during the business day in question. "Last" refers to the closing price, or the last trade of the stock that day, and "Change" reflects the difference between the closing price of the stock at the end of the session and the closing price the day before. You will also see the letters P/E. Those letters stand for the price/earnings ratio of the stock, which I'll explain later in this chapter.

What is one of the biggest pitfalls for people who buy stocks?

The biggest pitfall of all is that we tend not to watch the important predictors of a stock's performance *after* we have purchased it. We often thoroughly research a stock before we buy it, but then we slack off from performing ongoing research as we hold that stock. It is almost as if we want to believe blindly that the stock will be a success from the moment we buy it. But things change within a company, and a good investor has to monitor the changes as they happen.

What are some of the predictors that need to be monitored?

Here's a partial list: company revenues, earnings per share, price-earnings ratio, book value, daily trading volume, dividends, yield, debt, and volatility. Please note: While most people continue to watch a company's earnings per share to see how the company is performing relative to other, similar companies, that may not be the best available valuation method. There are many subtle but achievable ways for a corporation to manipulate the information that makes up earnings. I would pay more attention to revenues.

REVENUES

What are revenues?

Revenues are simply the amount of money a corporation takes in from sales of its products and services from year to year. As you consider buying or holding a stock, keep an eye on whether the company's revenues are going up, remaining stable, or going down. That figure is very hard to manipulate.

P/E RATIO

What is a price/earnings ratio?

A price/earnings ratio (P/E ratio) is a basic and very useful measure of how well a corporation is performing. Here's an example of what it means: If the price of a stock is $40 a share and the company has earnings of $2 a share, the P/E ratio is 20 ($40 divided by $2, which equals 20).

The higher the P/E ratio, the riskier the stock is likely to be. Traditionally speaking, stocks with a low P/E ratio might be considered a good buy at their current market price. Why? Because if a stock currently has a low share price relative to its earnings and research shows that it is a good stock, then its price will probably eventually go up. (Remember the definition of a value stock?) Also, if a stock has a low P/E ratio and the market heads south, the price of that stock may not fall as much as the price of stocks with high P/E ratios.

I know the price of the stock I'm interested in. How can I find out the earnings per share to figure out what the P/E is?

If all you want to know is the P/E of a stock, check financial websites. But it's a very good idea to know the earnings per share for other reasons—including that they measure profitability. To compute earnings per share, you take the net profits of the corporation after it has paid taxes and subtract any dividends due to preferred stockholders. (Remember, owners of preferred stock have a fixed dividend that must be paid before the owners of common stock receive any profits.) Divide that number by the number of outstanding shares of common stock, which you can find in the company's annual report, the company Website, or a financial Website.

Here's an example. Say that, after taxes, the Orman Corporation earned a net profit of $3,400,000 last year. It's time for the Orman Corporation to pay dividends to preferred stockholders, which come to $400,000. The Orman Corporation has 3,000,000 shares of common stock outstanding. After subtracting the preferred stock dividends from the net profit ($3,400,000 minus $400,000 equals $3,000,000), you divide the remaining number by the number of outstanding common shares ($3,000,000 divided by 3,000,000). The answer—$1 per share—represents the earnings per share. In other words, for every share of stock Orman Corporation has issued, it earned about $1 last year.

What does a company do with its earnings per share? Will I get them as a dividend, the way preferred shareholders do?

Possibly, but in most cases no. The company will keep those earnings to reinvest in its core businesses, or to acquire other companies that will help the company to grow.

Then why are earnings per share important?

Because if a company doesn't earn money, it can't grow (unless it borrows), people won't invest in it, and its stock price won't go up. If a company can't earn money for itself, chances are it won't earn money for you, either.

How often are the earnings of a corporation calculated?

Quarterly. This means a corporation makes the above calculations every three months to show if the company is meeting its projections for growth.

What kind of earnings per share should I be looking for in a company whose stock I want to buy?

That is a hard question to answer, because each stock is really in competition with itself. A corporation's goal is for its quarterly earnings to beat its earnings for the same quarter in the previous year and for its total annual earnings to beat the annual earnings of the year before. Remember, over the long term, earnings are what count to the market and to investors. Increases in earnings are a good sign.

How do I know if the stock I'm interested in has beat its earnings from last year?

The previous year's earnings (or earnings for the same quarter in the previous year) will be posted along with the current year's (or quarter's) earnings as soon as the current earnings are announced. If yours is a well-traded stock, these figures will appear in all major financial publications and financial Websites.

When I see the earnings of a stock, how do I know if they are good or bad?

In my opinion, what you always want to see is that the stock's quarterly and annual earnings increased over the same quarter in the previous year.

When it comes to buying a stock, do only the current annual earnings per share matter?

Absolutely not! You also should be looking at past

and future annual earnings and projections. For instance, with the Orman Corporation, you would want to see that the company has had good earnings growth over the past five years, and also that its earnings projections show a continued growth pattern. If earnings grow, so, probably, will the price of a company's stock.

If a stock that I have purchased continues to go up steadily, will the P/E ratio go higher as well?

Not necessarily. Remember, the P/E ratio is the current price of the stock divided by the current earnings of the company. If the company's earnings increase as rapidly, or more rapidly, than the price of the stock, then the P/E ratio could stay the same, or even decrease. But chances are, if the price of a stock goes up quickly, the P/E ratio will increase faster than the earnings of that company.

Should all price/earnings ratios for all categories of stocks be judged in the same way?

No. Each industry or economic sector has its own average P/E ratio. For instance, bank stocks sell at an average P/E ratio of 15 or 16, while energy stocks historically sell for an average P/E ratio of 25 or slightly higher. So which stock you own and which category it falls into will make a big difference in how you assess its particular P/E ratio. A P/E that is average in one category could be high in another category.

How do I know what the average P/E ratio is for the kind of stock that I am interested in?

This information can be easily accessed over the Internet. For instance, Yahoo! Finance (*finance.yahoo.com*) will give you the average P/E ratios of all the different categories of stock.

Do stock markets themselves have average P/E ratios?

Yes. The S&P 500 has had an average P/E ratio of 15 since 1870. The higher the P/E ratio of the market, the more speculative the market as a whole becomes.

PRICE/EARNINGS TO GROWTH

What is Price/Earnings to Growth?

Price/Earnings to Growth (PEG) is an indicator that compares the price/earnings ratio of a stock to the earnings growth of the company. What you want to see is a company whose earnings growth rate at least matches the P/E of the stock. If the company's earnings are growing by 30 percent a year, for example, the stock's P/E should be no more than 30. The PEG is, historically, a good indicator of value.

VOLUME

Why is it important to know how many shares of a stock have traded on a given day?

The trading volume of a stock on a given day tells you something about the current supply and demand of that stock. Remember that if demand exceeds supply, this can push the price of the stock upward. If you happen to see a spike in volume, this could be an indicator that there is sudden interest in this stock—either to buy or to sell—from a large investor or from many, many smaller investors.

Are supply and demand key factors in buying a stock?

Yes. Besides the quarterly and annual earnings per share, I always look at the supply and demand of a stock before making a purchase. When there is great demand for a stock and very little of it available for sale, then its price will be pushed up faster than that of a stock that has lots of supply and very little demand.

What are you looking for when you look at the volume?

One of the things I like to see is an increase in volume as a stock starts to move upward in price. If a stock's price goes up on very little volume, one possible interpretation is that the move is not a solid one. But if the stock's price rises on strong volume, I would tend to take it as a sign that the move is a more solid one. An increase in volume on a rise in price says two things to me: Many people are interested in the stock (which is good) and/or institutions are starting to buy the stock in large blocks. A big movement on little volume suggests that a few people who think the stock is going to move were suckered into paying more for the stock than they probably had to.

What if the stock I'm interested in has very small volume—or on some days it does not trade at all?

This stock is what is known as an illiquid stock. It is most likely very speculative, and one that I would be very careful about buying. Illiquid stocks can be difficult to sell without taking a loss.

BOOK VALUE

Why do I need to know the book value of a stock?

The book value of a stock is a measure of the worth of the company's assets, including real estate, equipment, inventories, cash, etc., less the company's liabilities. It is also called equity or shareholders' equity. It is the supposed "true value" of that corporation on the books, based on the historical value of the company's assets and liabilities. It is also a rough approximation of the liquidation value of a corporation. The book value does not necessarily bear any relation to the stock price and, in most cases today, is not anywhere close to that number.

How do I find the book value of a stock?

Like the P/E ratio and all the other terms we're defining, book value is listed in newspapers and updated on every quoting service that you will find on the Web. Book value per share is calculated by dividing the total book value by the number of shares outstanding.

Is there a way of using book value in evaluating a stock?

Yes, there is—the price-to-book ratio. The price-to-book ratio is used to compare the price of one stock to that of another stock, or to the market as a whole, in terms of a company's underlying value. There are problems with this as a method of evaluation, which I'll get to in a moment, but you can calculate the price-to-book ratio by dividing the current per-share stock price by the book value per share. Investors searching for bargains try to buy stocks near, or below, their book value. Another technique is to search for stocks selling below the marketwide average book value.

Historically, price-to-book has been a key ratio for determining the value of a stock, and was often used in the stock selection process. It is still important when evaluating financial companies such as banks, brokerages, and credit card companies. In these industries, takeovers are priced based on a multiple of book value. It is also valuable for industrial companies that have significant capital assets. The value of these assets often places a floor under the stock price. You should know, however, that price-to-book may be less useful when valuing today's service and technology stocks. A software giant like Microsoft produces high-margin products without a significant investment in either real estate or capital equipment. As a result, Microsoft's book value is relatively low. Another problem with the price-to-book ratio concept is that one of the terms—book value—is so easily manipulated. Valuation of inventory and real estate are easily adjusted on the books. Stock buybacks and write-offs of exceptional items also deflate book value, making high-priced stocks seem overvalued.

DIVIDENDS

I know that dividends are distributions of a company's earnings to shareholders, but when are they paid out?

Every three months, companies report their earnings, but only some of them send out dividends, or quarterly cash payments, to their shareholders. Companies are not obligated to do this. If a company is experiencing a hard time, dividends are usually the first thing to go.

How are dividends taxed?

Dividends are now taxed at the same rate as capital gains: 15 percent for most taxpayers, only 5 percent for those in the two lowest income tax brackets, at least through the end of 2010, when the rate on dividends is due to revert to ordinary income tax rates. Since dividends used to be taxed as ordinary income, with a top rate of over 35 percent, they are more attractive to investors than they were just a few years ago. But remember the tax rate is due to revert after December 31, 2010.

I'm thinking about taking money out of my CDs and investing in dividend-paying stock so I can get a higher yield and pay less taxes. Do you think this is a good idea?

Well, you are doing exactly what the government would like you to do. When interest rates are fairly low, as they had become in the year 2007, we are all forced out of our safe hiding places, like CDs, into dividend-paying stocks that will give us more bang for the buck. I think dividend-paying stocks are a smart way to get more income, but you need to be careful. Unlike your bank CD or money market, stock values can go down. So if you use dividend-paying stocks to get a better income payment, promise me that you will watch your investment carefully to make sure the stock does not tank.

Is a dividend the only thing to which I may be legally entitled as a shareholder?

No. As an owner of common stock, you are entitled to vote on matters of corporate policy. Granted, small investors have practically no influence on who the next CEO of the company is going to be, but by law, companies have to involve you in the decision-making process, usually by allowing you to vote for members of their board of directors and on proposals that are before the board of directors (and shareholders can make proposals, too). Also, in the event that the company files for bankruptcy and must liquidate its assets, you as a shareholder have the right to share in the company's assets after its debts have been discharged.

YIELD

What is the yield of a stock?

Yield is your return, in the form of dividends, on the shares of stock that you own. It is expressed as a percentage. That percentage is based on what you paid for the stock when you bought it—not, please note, on its current trading price.

Where can I find the current yield of a stock?

In the newspaper or on the Web. You also can compute the current yield of a stock yourself by taking the current market price of a share—say, $25—and dividing it by the current annual dividend per share, say, $1.50. This stock would yield you around 6 percent a year.

When I look in the papers, it seems as if the yield of a stock changes every day. Why?

The yield is determined by the current market price of the stock and the annual dividend that particular stock pays. So even though the annual dividend, when there is one, tends to stay the same, the price of the stock changes on a daily basis, which causes the listed yield to change.

Does that mean that even after I buy a stock, my yield can change?

Yes, if the annual dividend changes. Once you have purchased a stock, you are locked in at your purchase price. No matter what the market price of the stock may be, your yield will be based on what you paid for the stock, so the only way your yield can change is if the dividend changes.

Why is it important to know what the yield is?

People who buy stocks for income rather than growth need to know what the return, or yield, on those stocks is or is going to be. For example, you may find two stocks you like, but one has a yield of 6.5 percent and the other has a yield of 2 percent. This difference is significant if you need the money to live on. Yield also may tell you if it's wise to keep your money in a particular stock or not.

Let's say that in your Roth IRA you hold 500 shares of a stock that you bought when the share price was $10. You made an investment of $5,000. At the time you invested, the current yield on this stock was 6 percent, or $0.60 a share. This means your yearly dividends would amount to $0.60 a share times 500 shares, or $300 a year; your dividend divided by your initial investment ($300 divided by $5,000) gives you your yield: 6 percent. Three years later, the stock has gone up to $50 a share. Your $5,000 investment is now worth $25,000. But your annual dividend (and, of course, your original purchase price and number of shares) has stayed the same, so you are still getting just $0.60 a share, or $300 a year. (Meanwhile, new investors would only be getting about a 1.2 percent yield on their money—an annual dividend of $0.60 divided by the share price of $50.) Given that your money has grown considerably and since income is your objective, you might decide to sell the stock, cash in on the profits, and reinvest this money in a higher-yielding investment. So you sell the stock for $25,000. (Because it was in your Roth IRA, you do not have to pay capital-gains taxes on this money.) You invest all $25,000 in a stock that is yielding you 6 percent. Because your capital investment is five times your original investment, your current income also increases by a factor of five: from $300 a year to $1,500. Big difference for you—more than $100 a month.

Please note: Even if you owned this stock outside of a retirement account and you had to pay capital-gains tax on the gain, it still might be worth it. For instance, in the scenario above, you would owe taxes on the $20,000 profit you made ($25,000 minus $5,000 equals $20,000) at the capital-gains rate of 15 percent. This means you would owe $3,000 in taxes. This would leave you with $22,000 to invest after taxes. If you invested this $22,000 in a new stock or bond that was yielding you 6 percent, this would still give you $1,320 a year of income. If current income is your goal, this is still much better than the $300 you were getting, in spite of the capital-gains tax you had to pay.

If I'm not that interested in getting current income, is there any other reason I would buy stocks that pay dividends?

It depends on what the markets are doing and how you feel about your money possibly just sitting there, doing nothing. Many people who do not need current income like having a stock that pays them a dividend for two reasons. One is that they like to reinvest that dividend in more shares of the same stock as a way of accumulating shares. Second, when a market is going down and you see your stock shrinking in value, sometimes it is not so painful when you know that at least you are getting a good yield on your money.

I have been told that there is an investment strategy that has to do with buying stocks based on yield that will give me good growth on my money. Can you tell me what that is?

This is a popular investment strategy named Dogs of the Dow—in other words, buying the stocks that are currently considered the dogs (the ones not performing) of the Dow Jones Industrial Average. "Dog" status is determined by a stock's yield. If you were to use this strategy, you would start by finding out which ten stocks of the Dow were currently offering the highest yield, and you would buy them in equal amounts. One year later, you would look at all 30 stocks of the Dow again, and again you would see which ten stocks were currently offering the highest yield. You would then adjust your portfolio accordingly. You do this every year, and in theory, over time these Dogs of the Dow will rise in price and outperform the market.

Do the Dogs of the Dow always outperform the market?

In recent years the dogs have actually underperformed the market, so many people are trying to tweak the strategy and make it work again. Some people are buying five stocks rather than ten.

VOLATILITY

The volatility of a stock—how rapidly and dramatically its price rises and falls relative to the overall stock market—is tracked with a measurement known as beta. A stock with a beta of 1 is projected to move in direct correlation to the overall stock market. So if the market goes up or down 10 percent, this stock should also move up or down 10 percent. Anything greater than 1, and you are looking at a stock that will experience more dramatic moves than the overall market. If a stock has a beta of 1.5, it should move up or down about 50 percent more than the overall market. So if the market is up 10 percent, this stock should be up 15 percent, and if the market is down 10 percent, this stock will be down 15 percent.

What if my stock has a beta less than 1?

If you have a beta of 0.5, then your stock will be 50 percent less volatile than the market. A negative beta (say, −1) means that a stock moves inversely to the overall market, so when the market rises, the stock goes down, and vice versa.

Why is it important to know the beta of a stock?

When you know the beta of a stock (along with other information you have gathered) you can determine if that particular stock is one that you will feel comfortable owning, given your risk tolerance. Let's say you think the market is going to go way up and you want to take full advantage of that movement, so you have decided to invest in aggressive growth stocks. With this in mind, you might feel comfortable owning stocks whose betas are greater than 1. Theoretically, if the market goes on a major upward tear, your stock will outperform the market. But please remember that the higher the beta, the more money the stock can potentially lose. The lower the beta, the less you will participate in an upward market, but the less risk you'll have if the market heads south.

DEBT-TO-EQUITY RATIO

It's important to check out how much debt a company carries, traditionally measured by the debt-to-equity ratio. Here, you are looking for a low figure, less than 1. If the ratio is greater than 2, this means the company has a lot of outstanding debt for its size and therefore a lot of interest to pay on its debt. If the company ever needs money, the interest will come out of the stockholders' equity. You don't want this to happen.

What should I know about the debts that a company carries?

You should be concerned about the kind as well as the amount of debt a company carries. Like people, corporations can carry both good and bad debt. Good debt is the kind you carry as an investment in the years to come. Bad debt is the kind that drags you down and keeps you from investing wholeheartedly in the future.

Has a company incurred debt in order to finance its growth? Or is it in so much debt that it cannot possibly sustain future growth? Debt is something to keep a watchful eye on when you buy or own shares in a company.

I bought a stock that was an industry leader, had great revenues, rising profits and sales, and a very low P/E ratio in comparison to the S&P index, which is the main reason I bought it. It was off 25 percent from its high for the year. Now it's falling. What did I miss?

This is known as the value trap. You think that something is well priced, but as the price continues to fall, you suspect that this was no bargain after all. Usually, what has happened is that the main indicator you are watching is the stock price. But you should never buy a stock based on price, or even on P/E, alone. You should always purchase a stock based on its revenues, earnings, projected future earnings, whether it's an industry and market leader, and where the economy is, among other things. And when considering the P/E ratio, remember: The key factor that is *not* measured in a P/E ratio is debt. And as you know debt is a very important part of the equation. You always want to look at the debt of a company as well as the P/E ratio before buying.

How do I use enterprise value?

This indicator is best used when comparing stocks within the same industry, to see if the stocks are fairly valued.

INSTITUTIONAL INVESTORS

An institutional investor is a major player—for example, a mutual fund company, an insurance company, or a government pension plan—with the resources to invest huge sums of money in the stock market as a whole or in any one particular stock at a given time. Institutional investors account for the majority of overall trading volume on most exchanges.

Why is it important for me to know what institutional investors are saying and doing about my stock?

Because what they say and do can have a major impact on the price of your stock and on the direction of the markets. In fact, when I'm interested in a stock, the number of institutional investors who own that stock is one of the key indicators I look for. But I don't always follow their lead. Sometimes I'm attracted by a stock that is not yet owned by many institutional investors, because if and when they discover the stock, their money can move its price upward significantly. The converse is also true: If there are a lot of institutional investors in a stock and if they turn sour on it and get out, that could leave you with a big loss.

Where do I find out if my stock is currently being bought or sold by institutional investors?

An easy way to find this information is to look at the accumulation/distribution rating of your stock in a newspaper called *The Investor's Business Daily* or to check the institutional investors section under your stock on one of the larger financial Websites.

What does accumulation/distribution rating mean?

This rating tells you if your stock is under selling pressure or if it is the new sweetheart on the street when it comes to institutional investors. Remember, the more investors who buy, or who want to buy, your stock, the more its price will tend to go up; the more people who sell, or who want to sell, your stock, the more its price will tend to go down. The accumulation/distribution rating is usually based on an evaluation of the stock's daily price and volume action over the past 13 weeks of trading.

The scale consists of letters A through E-minus. A means that institutions are buying or accumulating a particular stock very heavily, but not selling it. As the letters move toward E-minus, the proportion of buying to selling decreases. C is what I call the midpoint, for it represents an equal amount of buying and selling. When you reach E-minus, this means very heavy selling, or distribution, and very light buying.

ANNUAL REPORTS

I recently sent away for the annual report of a company I'm interested in investing in. What should I look for as I read?

Among the things I would want to know are: How old is the company? If it's a new, untested company, I would be extremely wary. I'd also want to know who's in charge of the company.

Who is the chief executive officer (CEO), and has he or she been on the job for a while or is he or she newly appointed? Is poor leadership reflected in the company's past performance? Is the company profitable, and if so, how quickly are its profits growing year to year? Is it expanding its customer base, or is that base shrinking? What new products or services does the company have in its pipeline? Are there special challenges or opportunities that lie ahead for the year to come?

How can I find out if a company is profitable or not?

Profits for the past year will be itemized in the corporate annual report. You can also request this information by calling or writing the company directly, or find the statistics you seek—including revenues, expenses, profits, and debts—on the company's Website. When looking at profitability, try to go back at least five years, ten if you can. You want to make sure that the company has shown a consistent level—or, better yet, growth—of profits over the years.

ANALYSIS

Many indicators and signals can be used to analyze a stock. The two most widely talked about forms of analysis are fundamental analysis and technical analysis.

What is fundamental analysis?

Fundamental analysis is simply a way of evaluating whether a company's stock is financially sound based on the following information: how long the company's management has been in place and its record, the company's chief competitors and the competitive environment, the chances of its scoring big with a new product, and whether it will have good earnings. Simply put, no matter how the stock of a company is trading, analysts are looking to see if the company is fundamentally sound—not only today but also for the future. The downside of this type of analysis? A lot of people believe it is based on information that most investors can get hold of, and so it is nothing special. Also, many financial experts believe that the kind of conclusions you can draw from this kind of analysis are soft—that is, not particularly objective, or provable.

What is technical analysis?

Technical analysis is more concerned with market patterns and trends than with the dollars-and-cents fundamentals of a company. For example, it uses historical stock-price charts to see how high a stock's price can rise, or how far it can fall, before the stock's movement meets what's called resistance—the point at which the stock price is likely to switch direction and start heading down, or up, again.

I have been monitoring a stock that the technical analysts on TV said was a good buy at 50. It went down to 25, and I thought that made it a great buy. I bought it, and it's now sitting in my portfolio at 10. What happened?

I'm sorry to say that many individual investors think just as you do. If a stock is a good investment at X, it must be twice as good when the price is ½X. Wrong, wrong, wrong.

We saw this phenomenon in spades during the dot-com gold rush of the 90s, and stock analysts are very much to blame, if you ask me. How many analysts changed the opinions they were offering on some of those stocks whose prices plummeted by 50 percent, 60 percent, 70 percent, and more? Not many. The lesson: You have to know when to buy or sell based on your own analysis and not rely on a group of people who far too often react to news long after it is too late. That said, keep your eyes on the fundamental and technical warning signs.

INVESTING TECHNIQUES FOR EVERYONE

THE BENEFITS OF DOLLAR COST AVERAGING

I am afraid that the market may go down after I start investing. Needless to say, I do not want to lose money. What can I do to limit my exposure?

Assuming that the investments in your account are good, sound, and just going up and down due to the volatility of the market, you can use a technique I love, called dollar cost averaging. Dollar cost averaging is an excellent way to guard against paying too much for stocks in a volatile market. Here's how it works. You invest exactly the same dollar amount at regular intervals (preferably every month) into a specific investment vehicle or vehicles. This method actually *averages out* the price you pay for your shares, and puts time, your money, and the market all on your side, regardless of what your stock or the market does over the short term.

Why should I spread my investment over time? Why don't I just wait until the market is at the bottom and put all my money in then?

What you are suggesting is called timing the market: buying low and selling high. It's a wonderful trick if you can pull it off. But most people can't. A lot of people have lost a lot of money trying to outfox the market.

Can you show me the dollars-and-cents advantages of dollar cost averaging?

Yes. Consider this comparison of buying stock all at once, with a lump sum of money, and buying the same stock gradually, over time:

Outright Purchase

Let's say you have $12,000 you want to invest, and you know which stock you want to buy. You have been watching your stock for some time, and you have seen it go as high as $15 a share. Recently, it has taken a tumble to $10. You think to yourself, now is the time to buy. You invest all $12,000 at once by making an outright purchase of 1,200 shares at $10 a share. For the first three weeks you are happy, since the share price is staying at about $10, but all of a sudden the market as a whole turns down, and you watch the price of your shares start to decline. You still think this stock is a great investment and don't want to sell, because when the market turns around your stock will come back, too. One year later, your stock is selling at $5 a share. You are down $5 a share, and you now

DOLLAR COST AVERAGING: AN EXAMPLE		
Month	Price	Shares Bought
1	$10	100
2	$9	111
3	$8	125
4	$7	143
5	$8	125
6	$9	111
7	$6	167
8	$8	125
9	$7	143
10	$6	167
11	$5	200
12	$5	200
TOTAL: $12,000 invested; 1,717 shares bought		

have a paper loss of $6,000 on your 1,200 shares.

Dollar Cost Averaging

If you had taken that same $12,000 and invested it using dollar cost averaging, you would have divided up your lump sum and invested the same percentage of it, or the same sum of money, month in, month out, regardless of what the market was doing—in this example, $1,000 per month. And here is how you would have come out in the same scenario. (See the chart page 404.)

As you can see, by using dollar cost averaging, you are able to buy *more shares* of stock when the price is low, and therefore more shares overall. After one year, instead of having 1,200 shares you have 1,717 shares, and even though the price per share is still down, at $5 per share your holdings are worth $8,585 instead of $6,000 and your loss on paper is only $3,415, or about $2,585 less than if you had purchased the stock outright.

Comparison:
$3,415 loss with dollar cost averaging
$6,000 loss with outright purchase

But there is continuing good news when you use dollar cost averaging instead of making an outright purchase.

Let's say that after a year, you decide you don't want to invest any more money in your stock but just want to wait and see what happens to it. So you leave your $12,000 invested and become an observer.

Eighteen months later, the market starts to go back up, and slowly but surely the price of the stock you purchased inches back up to $10 a share. With an outright purchase, you bought 1,200 shares, so when the price returns to $10 you've broken even—your investment is now worth what you originally paid for it, $12,000. But using dollar cost averaging, you will have accumulated 1,717 shares, or 517 more than with an outright purchase. In this scenario, when your per-share price goes back up to $10, your 1,717 shares will be worth $17,170. This is $5,170 more than your original $12,000 investment, or about a 43 percent return on your money. With dollar cost averaging, you limit your loss in a down market, and when the price per share rises again, you also make more. Again, the key to this technique is that you are always buying additional shares of your investment at a lower price, as the chart shows.

I can see now that in a down market I can limit my losses with dollar cost averaging. But what if we are just coming out of a bear market and the bull is starting to make its run? Wouldn't I be better off investing everything I have at once?

If you are sure that this is the investment scenario, then of course you would be better off investing everything at once. The problem for most of us is that we do not know whether the bull is about to gallop, or merely take a few steps and graze or backtrack. If you feel you can judge this, then go for it. Otherwise, over the long run you will be better off using dollar cost averaging.

DRIPs

I hear people talking about DRIPs. What are they?

DRIP stands for dividend reinvestment program. The DRIP program started in the 1950s as a way for employees of corporations to accumulate stock in the companies they were working for. If the employee chose, every time the company paid a dividend, that dividend could be reinvested back into the employee's account to buy more shares of stock. This was usually done with very low—or no—commissions or fees, which made these programs quite cost-efficient. As time went on, many corporations decided to open up their DRIP programs to all their investors. Today, DRIP programs are offered by about 1,300 U.S. and foreign companies, and are open to almost anyone (employees or otherwise) who wants to buy the stock.

How do DRIPs work?

After you have purchased at least one share of stock of a company that offers a DRIP program, you can continue to buy shares or partial shares of stock in that company by instructing the company to reinvest your dividends and/or by sending the company money, in some cases in amounts as small as $10, $20, or $25. Money that you send in is known as an optional cash payment, or an OCP. Currently, about 100 DRIP companies will also offer you a discount on their stock, anywhere from 3 percent to 5 percent off the stock's current market price.

If I can find a stock in the DRIP program that gives me a 3 to 5 percent discount on my purchase, isn't this a good way to go?

Yes, if you like the stock. But please note that not many plans offer this discount. If you find one that does, please ask whether the plan offers that discount on any optional cash payments you may make. Many companies give you a discount only on shares purchased with reinvested dividends.

I've heard that in order to send in optional cash payments, I have to reinvest my dividends in the DRIP program. Is this true?

Many companies permit optional cash payments only if the shareholder participates in the DRIP (reinvests), but some companies do allow shareholders to receive all dividend payments and still participate in the optional payment feature of the plan.

Does it matter when I send in my OCPs?

It could. You should make it a point to find out when the corporation actually invests the money you send. For example, some DRIPs invest your money only every three months, or quarterly, but most DRIPs specify a monthly date when they make investments using your money. If that date is the 20th of every month, and you send in an OCP on the 2nd of every month, your money will just be sitting there for 18 days, doing no work and earning no interest for you.

Do all DRIP programs allow me to send in any amount of money I want whenever I want?

No. Each DRIP program has its own set of rules. Many DRIPs require an initial minimum investment from $250 to $1,000 or require you to buy a minimum number of shares. Be aware, too, that the program may charge fees to maintain the account.

Are the fees and expenses the same among all DRIP programs?

No. Fees, especially fees associated with selling the stock you have purchased, differ. DRIPs are becoming so popular that many companies are charging new and higher fees to maintain these programs. You can be charged an enrollment fee and a transaction fee, plus a fee every time you buy shares. On the other hand, there are still a number of companies that charge minimal or no fees.

Can you name a few of the companies that do not charge fees or require high minimum investments?

As of the writing of this book, the following companies charge no fees and require only a purchase of one share to get started:

3M Company
Black & Decker
Hasbro
Johnson & Johnson
Kellogg's
U.S. Steel Corporation

Are there other good companies in addition to the ones listed above that offer DRIPs?

Yes. The program is offered by many of the best companies in the world. In fact, almost all of the Dow Jones Industrial Average stocks offer dividend reinvestment programs. There is no shortage of quality stocks for DRIP investors. A fairly comprehensive list of DRIPs can be found at *www.stocks-drips.com.*

Are DRIPs a good way to dollar cost average?

Yes. Whether you invest with OCPs or through dividend reinvestment, or both, you are making good use of the dollar cost averaging technique.

How do I get started with a DRIP?

In most cases, to get started with a DRIP you must own at least one share of stock. (There are independent companies through which you can buy a single share of stock in any company to begin DRIP investing.) From that point on, you can send money to make additional purchases. Contact the DRIP plan administrator or the investor relations department in the company you are interested in. He or she will send you an application, which you will fill out and send back. Later, if you want to sell your shares, contact the same plan administrator, who will send you additional forms on which you will note the number of shares you wish to sell and the exact day on which you wish the sale to take place.

Can you name some of the independent companies or organizations that will let me buy one share of stock to begin DRIP investing?

The National Association of Investors Corporation is one such organization, reachable toll-free at (877) 275-6242 or online at *www .betterinvesting.org.* Another company is Temper Enrollment Service, at (800) 388-9993 or *www .directinvesting.com.* There's also First Share, at (800) 683-0743 or *www.firstshare.com,* and One Share, at (888) 777-6919 or *www.oneshare.com.*

You can also buy a share of stock through an online brokerage firm.

If I decide to buy one share of stock through an online brokerage firm, how much should that cost?

Many online brokers today are willing to execute a trade for any amount of stock (that means one share—or more, if you want more) for about $5 to $15 per trade. At that cost it pays to go straight through an online company to buy or sell your stock.

Two of the best, as of the writing of this book, are Muriel Siebert, reachable at (800) 872-0444 or online at *www.siebertnet.com,* and TD Ameritrade, at (800) 934-4448 or *www .tdameritrade.com.* You do not need a minimum investment to open an account, which is important if all you are doing is buying a share or two of stock. The price to make an online trade here will be about $10 to $15.

Are there any books that can help me to learn more about DRIPs?

Yes. In my opinion, two of the best are *Buying Stocks Without a Broker* and *No-Load Stocks.*

Do DRIPs have a downside?

Overall, DRIPs are a great way for the small investor to get started. Not all companies offer DRIPs, which can limit the stocks you invest in, but you do have a choice of most of the blue-chip stocks. The main drawback of investing in DRIPs not purchased directly with a brokerage firm is that you may have to sell your stock through the mail, and this can take some time. When you own a stock in a brokerage firm ac-

count, you can sell it in seconds if you need to. Not only will you get your money faster, you can also time the market better.

ASSET ALLOCATION

What is asset allocation?

Asset allocation is a fancy way of saying diversification, and it's one of the very first things you should think about when you begin to invest your money. Asset allocation is expressed in percentages: What percentage of my assets do I want to put in growth stocks, what percentage do I want to put in value stocks, what percentage do I want to put in bonds and cash equivalents, real estate, gold, and so on. Many people simply divvy up their money between stocks and bonds, but you can get as specific as you want to—for example, in stocks alone you can invest in aggressive stocks, large-cap stocks, small-cap stocks, international stocks, emerging market stocks, and global stocks.

The types of investments you choose to diversify into are important, and so is the amount of money you put into each investment category. After you have figured out your investment objectives and the kind of instruments you want to place your money in, then you have to decide how much money you should put into each kind of investment. This is asset allocation. Not only is asset allocation a time-honored technique for spreading investment risk over many competing classes of investment, it is also an important method of safeguarding your assets as you get older and your investment objectives change.

How do I determine the appropriate allocation of my assets?

At this point, we return to a very basic question: How much risk are you willing to take? What happens if your portfolio takes a dive? Will you be able to resist the impulse to bail out? The amount of risk you are comfortable with is a fundamental factor in your decisions about how to allocate your money.

Another basic element in decision making is your age. One rule of thumb is that you subtract your age from 110 and the difference is the percentage of your assets that you should invest for growth. For instance, if you are 40 years old, subtract 40 from 110, which gives you 70; by this reasoning you should be putting 70 percent of your investment assets into growth-oriented investments while keeping 30 percent safe and sound (e.g., in bonds). Your age is important because it determines your investment horizon. But many other factors also come into play: your comfort with risk, your employment outlook, your family situation, and your current goals, e.g., whether you want to buy a home and will need money for a down payment.

I'm 25 years old and I'm saving to buy a home in the next two years. All of my money is in a money-market fund to be used for a down payment. I was recently told that I am too young to keep that money where it is and that I need to allocate better. Do you agree?

No. The amount of time you have before you need your investment money is crucial. Is it ten years? If so, you can invest in the market. But if you will need your money in one, two, or five years, then a money-market fund is the right place to have it. This is why asset-allocation models based on age do not always work. You know the specifics of your situation, so do what is best for you.

NOT FOR EVERYONE: SELLING SHORT

I've been hearing about "selling short" all my life. What does it mean?

Selling short is a stock market technique that is applied by the most sophisticated investors. It is used when an investor thinks a certain stock is about to go down and wants to profit from the downward movement of that stock. Now, when people want to profit from a market they think is going up, they try to buy shares of a stock low and sell high. But when people want to profit from a market going down, they do the reverse. They sell high first, and then hope to buy back lower. In other words, they are selling something before they have bought it, so they are said to be shorting the stock. It is one of the riskiest ways to make money in the stock market, and unless you're a very savvy investor, I would stay away from it.

WHEN TO SELL A STOCK

What are some indicators that tell me when it is time to sell?

The first thing that I always look at is the overall market. If the stock market is not on your side, that's one indicator that you might consider selling out of your stock position—after taking into consideration any tax ramifications. It's worth noting again, however, that if you're in the market for the long term and own a great stock but are not sure what to do, it's probably best to wait out a downturn.

How can I tell if the market downturn will be short- or long-term?

There are four major factors that direct the movement of the stock market: inflation, interest rates, the stability and profitability of key companies, and political affairs. The short answer is that there is no sure way to predict the market.

If the market is strong but my stock is going down, when should I call it quits and sell?

My own rule is that if a stock I own goes down 7 to 10 percent or more from the price I paid for it while the overall market is going up and other, similar stocks are either staying stable or going up, I am out of that stock.

What if I sell when the stock is down 8 percent, and then it turns around and goes back up?

Stick to your rules. If you don't, there will come a time, as we all saw in 2001–2002, and again in 2008 when the stock goes from $200 to $50. Contemplate the following fact, and remember it: When a stock goes down 50 percent, it has to go back up 100 percent for you to break even.

What do you mean, if a stock goes down 50 percent it has to go up 100 percent for me to break even?

This is what I mean. If you buy a stock for $20 a share and it goes down to $10 a share, that is a 50 percent decline. For that stock to go from $10 back to $20 is a 100 percent increase. It is harder for a stock to go up than to go down.

What are some other signs that I should take into consideration when thinking about selling my stock?

There are many, but here are three easy ones for you to watch for:

1. Volume. Watch the daily volume of shares that trade in your stock. When you see the volume increasing dramatically at the same time that the price of the stock is falling, take that as a danger sign.
2. Future earnings. If the projected quarterly earnings/revenues are threatening a slowdown, this is a bad sign.
3. Splits. When a company distributes more stock to holders of existing stock, that is called a stock split. For example, a 2-for-1 stock split means that for every share you held before the split, you now hold two, and each share will be worth half of its pre-split value. I feel wary when a stock splits too many times too quickly. If a stock splits two or three times in less than a year, I take this as a warning sign.

Is there a technical indicator that I can use to help me make an emotional decision on when to sell a stock or not buy it at all?

Yes. One of my favorite indicators is the 200-day moving average. This is simply an average of the closing price of a particular stock each day, recorded over a period of 200 days. If you chart those closing prices, you will get a line that, in my opinion, can serve as a key indicator of when to sell a stock. If a stock you own breaks below its own 200-day moving average, this can be a key signal to sell the stock. Many major financial Websites let you view the 200-day moving averages for the stocks you own or in which you are interested.

Why is it that I always sell too soon?

Probably because of your fear that you will lose the profits that you see on paper. And we never like to lose.

But why do many of us feel we have to sell all or none of our shares of a stock? If you have made a tidy profit and you believe your stock may continue to rise, sell 25 percent of what you own. Or take out the dollar equivalent of your original investment plus maybe 10 percent of your profit, and then let your additional profits ride and see what happens. The same is true on the downside. If a stock starts to go down beyond your comfort level but you still have faith in the company and the stock, sell some of it. If it keeps going down, sell some more. Don't let your fear of loss keep you from a gain.

If I sell my stock because it has gone down 8 percent, do I go back in the market or do I stay out?

It depends on the overall direction of the market. If we are in a down market, it makes absolutely no sense to buy a stock, watch it go down 8 percent, sell it, and then buy another

stock and watch it slide 8 percent. For when the direction of the market is down, it usually takes everything with it. So if you have an 8 percent loss and the overall market is going down, I would sell and stay on the sidelines with your cash. But if you've got an 8 percent loss on your stock and the overall market trend is up, then take your proceeds and reinvest the money in the rising market.

Why do you say I should sell a stock at an 8 percent loss? I have heard that a great way to invest is dollar cost averaging. I'm confused.

Dollar cost averaging is a fabulous technique when you have additional sums of money to invest month in and month out for a long period of time. Sometimes, however, you may have a lump sum of money, let's say $25,000, and you decide to invest it all at once in one stock. In that instance I think it makes sense to sell if the investment falls 8 percent.

So are you saying that if I am investing every month in my 401(k) plan and I still have at least 20 or 30 years until I need this money, that I should continue to invest as the market goes down?

That's exactly what I'm saying. As long as time is on your side, and you are in good quality investments such as diversified mutual funds within your 401(k) plan, you should just keep dollar cost averaging. Remember the more the market goes down, the more the shares of your mutual funds decline in price and the more shares your contributions will buy. The more shares you own, the more money you make when it goes back up.

I understand how dollar cost averaging works when a market is going down, but is there a different technique if the market is going up?
Yes, it's a technique known as pyramiding. It is the strategy of adding to your initial stock purchase in smaller quantities, up to 5 percent, as the price of your stock increases. This is how it works: Once you determine the amount of money you can invest in a stock—let's use $10,000 as an example—use half ($5,000) to purchase one stock as your initial buy. If the stock goes down in price, don't buy any more. If the stock goes down 8 percent from the initial buy price, cut your losses and sell all of the stock as soon as possible.

If the stock increases 2 percent or 3 percent in price from your initial buy, and if you like how the stock is performing, consider buying $3,250 more. You would then have $8,250 of the $10,000 you are interested in investing in the one stock. If the stock increases 2 percent or 3 percent more, you can invest the remaining $1,750.

Now stop buying that stock and give the stock some time to grow. My recommendation is to buy and monitor: Monitor every stock or fund you own, and keep it only if it is still a good investment. Stocks and funds are just like relationships. You get into them because they are good, and when they are no longer good, you leave. You don't stay in a relationship because it *was* good, you stay in it because it *is* good. So constantly ask yourself if this is a stock or fund

that you want to stay in a committed relationship with. A simple test is to ask yourself if you would buy it today. Never add money unless your prior buys seem to be working.

I'm holding stocks and mutual funds that have gone down 50 percent in value and I don't have a clue if I should sell them or keep them. Can you help me? I don't want to sell them, because I don't want to take the loss. What is your opinion: Should I sell or hold on to them?
If I were you, I would make a list of every investment that I currently own and write down the value that investment is worth today. I would then ask myself the question: If I did not currently own that investment but I had that money in cash, would I take that exact same amount of money and buy the investment that I am currently holding? If the answer to that question is no, sell that investment. If the answer is yes, then hold it. And if the answer is I don't know, sell half. It is really that simple.

GAINS

What do investors mean when they talk about realized gains and unrealized gains?
A realized gain is your profit on the capital you've invested, which you take by selling a security that has gone up in value since you purchased it. It is taxable. An unrealized gain means that your stock has gone up in value but you have not sold it. Therefore, you have not actually

cashed in on, or realized, the gain. Unrealized gains are not taxed.

What is the difference in tax rates between ordinary income and capital gains?

Capital-gains tax is what you pay on your profits when you have bought a stock (or other "capital asset") and have held it for at least 12 months and one day before selling it; this is referred to as the long-term capital gains tax. If you do not hold your stock for at least 12 months and one day before selling it, you will owe ordinary income taxes on your gain; this is referred to as a short-term capital-gains tax.

In the two lowest income-tax brackets, the long-term capital gains rate is zero in 2010. For everyone else, it is 15 percent. The tax rate on stock dividends is also 15 percent or 0 percent. (Both of these rates are due to expire at the end of 2010.) You owe ordinary income taxes on interest payments you receive. The top tax rate for ordinary income is now 35 percent.

How do I figure my annual rate of return?

The rate of return is a percentage measure of the profit on your stock from the time you bought it to the time you sold it, or until the present if you have not sold it. The annual rate of return is the percentage increase of profit for a 12-month period.

Let's say you put $25,000 into a stock. One year later, this stock is valued at $30,000. That's a $5,000 gain. Add to this figure any dividends paid to you by the stock company during that year—let's say $750. Your total gain is $5,750. Now divide that number by the amount of your original investment ($5,750 divided by $25,000). The result is 23 percent, and that is your rate of return. For an annual rate of return, follow the same process, beginning with the dollar value of your stock at the beginning of the year.

What rate of return should I expect from my stocks?

You want at least to be keeping pace with the overall return of the stock market. If you are not keeping pace, you might be better off in an index fund or with SPDRs.

FINANCIAL ADVISERS

You haven't said much about financial advisers. What's wrong with handing my money over to one of them?

Nothing, as long as you pick one who's reputable. But employing a financial adviser doesn't let you off the hook. *You* are responsible for your money.

What should I tell my financial adviser?

If you have a financial adviser, I want you to begin by telling him or her very little about how much money you have to invest and a great deal about your overall financial goals and situation, including the amount of credit card debt you have. After all, if you are going to hire someone to look after your money, invest it for you, and make sure it remains safe, that person should know everything about your financial picture, including your outstanding debts and your hopes and goals for the future.

What kinds of questions should a financial adviser be asking me?

A financial adviser should try to find out all your financial particulars in as much detail as possible. If I were your adviser, I would ask: Do you have credit card debt? Do you own a home? If not, do you want to buy a home? Do you need to buy any large-ticket items, like a car? What are your total current sources of income? What are your expenses? Do you have a retirement plan? Will you be receiving a pension? And here are two important questions: If you want to invest, how long can you let your money work for you, without touching it? What are your investment goals and dreams?

A financial adviser should also ask you about your family. Will you inherit money from older relatives someday? If an accident or illness struck a member of your family, would you be financially responsible? Next, what about your children, if you have any? Will you be paying for their college educations?

And all this is just for starters. Only after many more questions should an adviser ask how much you have to invest. If the adviser asks that question first, find the door.

Are there different kinds of financial advisers?

Yes. There are many titles and certifications for advisers. Some financial advisers are far more qualified than others. Some advisers will just provide you with a financial plan and send you home to carry it out. Others will advise you for as long as you want, taking care of your money over the long term.

What sort of education, or degrees, should a financial adviser have?

If your adviser is simply a money manager, he or she could be a financial adviser at a brokerage firm or a registered investment adviser. If you need an overall financial plan, however, your adviser should, in my opinion, be a certified financial planner professional. A certified financial planner professional has had to pass a series of exams that test his or her knowledge of every aspect of finance, including risk management, retirement planning, taxes, and estate planning. It usually takes two years to study for and pass these exams. Those who do pass are required to stay up to date by taking continuing education courses and to abide by the standards of the Certified Financial Planner Board of Standards/CFP Board.

How should I prepare for the interview? Should my partner come with me?

If you are married, or living with someone with whom you are financially bound, you should go to see the adviser together. But before you go into the office of a financial adviser, you and your partner should do your homework. Discuss what you want to accomplish with the adviser. Find out whether you agree on your financial goals and investment strategies. Talk out all your hopes and fears about money. Make sure you both have a solid understanding of where you stand financially right now. And remember, after you've chosen an adviser, you and your spouse or partner must make all decisions as a team, and must both keep up to date with what the adviser is doing.

Once I've retained a financial adviser, what should I expect of him or her?

Insist, first and foremost, that the adviser contact you every single time he or she makes a change in your account. Not only that, but your adviser should also explain to you in clear, simple language the reason for every transaction. I would insist that you be informed about the tax implications of a sale. Each and every commission should be explained. After each transaction, your adviser should send you a transaction slip from the brokerage firm that holds your money, telling you what has been bought or sold—and that slip should always match transactions for which you gave permission.

Will I get a monthly statement in the mail?

Yes. On that statement, you should expect to see a detailed summary of the month's transactions, including deposits, withdrawals, and current positions held. This statement must come directly from the brokerage firm that is holding your money, not from your adviser's office. Along these same lines, your financial adviser must prepare for you both quarterly reports and an annual report.

What is inside a quarterly or an annual report of my account?

In both your quarterly and your annual reports, you should find the exact return your financial adviser is getting on your money, as well as all fees and commissions he or she has charged you. (The figure on his or her report must match the report that is generated directly by the brokerage firm.) These reports should also show you all realized gains or losses (all the money you actually made or lost from selling investments) and all unrealized gains and losses (gains and losses on investments you own but have not yet sold). If mutual funds are involved, these reports should include returns of the overall index, so you know whether you're doing better or worse than the index in question.

How much of a return on my money can I rightfully expect?

The return your financial adviser makes for you after all commissions and fees should be equal to or better than the return on the Standard & Poor's 500 Index.

What should I be careful of when dealing with a financial adviser?

A bona fide financial adviser will never, ever ask you to write a check made out to him or her personally. All the money that you hand over must be placed in an institution (such as Schwab, Merrill Lynch, or Fidelity, for example), and every check you write should therefore be made payable to that institution. This is absolutely essential. More than one "adviser" has flown the coop with the money of dozens of clients. And you should never allow your financial adviser to pressure you into doing something that runs counter to what your inner voice is telling you.

FEE-BASED ADVISERS

How do financial advisers charge for their services?

There are a few different ways. For example, some financial advisers will offer you a free consultation—a kind of meet-and-greet. An adviser who sees you for free is trying to convince you to allow him or her to invest your money for you, so that he or she can reap the commissions.

I went for a free consultation and wrote a check to buy a mutual fund. Did that include a commission for the financial adviser as well?

You betcha. If you go to see an adviser for free, so to speak, and hand over $40,000 to him or her to invest in a loaded mutual fund (a mutual fund with sales charges), then in fact you will have just paid about five percent, or $2,000, for that so-called "free" session. The moment you sit down in that office and tell a commission-based adviser how much money you have to invest, he or she knows exactly what it means for him or her. If you come in with $100,000, your adviser can make about $5,000—not bad for an hour or two of work!

What is a fee-based financial adviser?

A fee-based adviser is one who charges you an hourly fee to tell you what to do with your money. He or she does not actually invest the money for you. You leave the office in possession of what you have to assume is good advice, and then you make the various transactions yourself.

What about a fees-plus-commissions arrangement?

Here, you pay the financial adviser in two tiers: You pay him or her a fee to tell you what to do and, for that fee, the adviser will create a master plan for you. If you decide you want him or her to do the actual investing for you—which many people do—the adviser will receive commissions on the transactions.

REGISTERED INVESTMENT ADVISERS

What is a registered investment adviser?

A registered investment adviser (RIA) is a person who manages your money for you by buying and selling most types of investments on your behalf. Such an adviser makes all the decisions about your investment account. RIAs usually require a fairly large minimum initial investment, ranging from $50,000 to $5 million. The average minimum is between $150,000 and $250,000.

How do RIAs make their money?

An RIA manages your money on an ongoing basis, for a fee that is usually a percentage of the money under management. This percentage can range from 0.25 to 3 percent a year, but I believe you should not pay more than 1.5 percent, including all commissions.

Think about this fee structure for a moment. The amount you pay your RIA is a percentage of the money he or she is managing: Isn't this a terrific incentive for him or her to make your money grow? Suppose you gave your RIA $100,000 to invest and agreed to pay a 1 percent management fee. The RIA knows that if the account stays at $100,000 over the next year, he or she will make $1,000 in management fees. If the account doubles, he or she will make $2,000. But if the account is worth only $50,000 at the end of the year, your RIA will make only $500. If you make money, your RIA makes money. If you lose money, so does your RIA.

You seem to think highly of RIAs.

In many situations, I do, because an RIA is on your team, in downtimes and uptimes.

But isn't it dangerous to give someone else so much control over my money?

Good question. If you hire an RIA, please make sure that your assets are held in a reputable institution, such as Charles Schwab or Fidelity, and that all the RIA has the right to do is buy or sell on your behalf—not to withdraw money, except for any predetermined fees he or she is owed. And even though you are granting your RIA permission to trade your account without notifying you each and every time, it is still your responsibility to keep yourself informed about what securities and assets you own and what they are earning. And make sure you can terminate your agreement at any time if you don't like the performance of your RIA (whether or not there are fees for doing so).

BROKERAGE FIRMS: FULL SERVICE OR DISCOUNT?

What is the difference between a full-service broker and a discount broker?

Basically, the difference is the amount of money you pay the broker to hold your hand and your money. A full-service brokerage firm offers its customers just about every financial service you can think of—research reports, professional advice, and even tax preparation. But in return for all these services (and the overhead, which can be fairly high), you must pay high commissions. A discount brokerage firm eliminates all the extras in exchange for a significant reduction in fees. In my opinion, with the evolution of the Internet and all the resources that are now available to you, you can have access to all the vital information you need and still take advantage of the low costs of a discount broker.

Is there any way I can get a discount on the commission I pay my full-service broker?

If you do a lot of trading, it doesn't hurt to try. If your account is a good one, your broker may be glad to adjust the scale of his or her commissions. After all, this is a competitive profession, and your broker knows that there are discount brokerages out there that could do what he or she does for a lot less.

I have just inherited a lot of money and feel as if I want to use a full-service broker, but everyone is telling me that's an old-fashioned idea. What do you think?

I think that you are not alone. It seems to me that the more money people have, the more they tend to use a full-service broker. There's nothing wrong with this, per se. The real question is which full-service broker you should choose, for they are not created equal.

If you go the full-service route, be sure all your needs are going to be met, since you'll be paying for it. You also may want to check out an RIA.

When considering a full-service brokerage firm, what questions should I ask?

Here are the areas of importance to investigate:

1. How much does the broker charge to invest your money—for wrap accounts, commissions, and fee-based accounts attached to asset size?

2. Does the brokerage firm have a solid research department with a good track record in the stocks it recommends?

3. Does the brokerage firm monitor its brokers? Ask to see the conduct record of its brokers to see whether they tend to get into trouble or are honest.

4. Does the brokerage firm provide the services that you want in person and online?

5. Are the brokerage firm's statements easy to understand? Ask to see a sample statement. If you cannot understand it, chances are it will be hard for you to tell whether your adviser is doing a good job or not.

Which full-service brokers are rated most highly?

A 2009 *Smart Money* magazine survey ranked the top seven full-service brokerage firms. Raymond James was the overall winner. Next was Edward Jones, and in third place was UBS. The firms at the bottom of the list were Morgan Stanley, Merrill Lynch and Wachovia. But check each firm thoroughly; these things keep changing.

Smart Money's survey also ranked the brokerages by categories. For customer satisfaction, Raymond James and UBS ranked high.

For stock picking, Edward Jones and Wachovia were highly ranked.

Additionally, for statements, Merrill Lynch was a leading broker.

All these factors should be considered when choosing a broker, because it is not enough to get full service—you also want good service.

When I hear the term "discount brokerage," I think it sounds unsafe. Am I right?

Not at all. Paying less money doesn't necessarily mean you get less quality. The word "discount" here refers to the huge savings you can reap simply because discount brokerage firms do not perform the full array of services that full-service brokerage firms do. You can save up to 90 percent on commissions if you trade through a discount brokerage firm!

What don't discount brokerage firms provide me?

Typically, they will not give you any investment advice, such as when to buy or sell a particular stock. Good advice is one of those things that brokerage firms overprice, and that takes a giant bite out of your wallet. Knowing about stocks and what you want from them is up to you. I would recommend using a discount broker only when you feel confident enough to make your own decisions regarding stocks.

Can I get research reports from a discount brokerage firm?

In most cases, yes, though sometimes for a fee. At some firms, such as Fidelity and Schwab, these research reports will contain recommendations and opinions from experienced analysts. But once you're finished reading these reports, it's up to you to make the decision to invest or not.

Do discount brokers keep regular nine-to-five hours?

You can contact most discount brokerage firms 24 hours a day, every day, because these companies offer automated service lines. These days, a lot of discount brokerage firms also allow customers to monitor their investments online, via the firm's Internet Web page.

Do you recommend using a discount broker?

Again, I recommend using a discount broker when you are sure that you know the ropes of investing. Why pay a full commission if you don't have to? Once you have the know-how and the experience to manage your investments without the advice of a professional, I think discount brokerage firms are the way to go.

What about using a broker at my bank?

I would strongly advise against using a broker at your bank. Most of these people have very little true brokerage experience, and they seldom stay in the position of broker for very long. They usually can sell you only loaded mutual funds.

INVESTING ONLINE

I have a friend who says he makes all his trades online. Do you recommend it?

As with using a discount broker, it's important to make absolutely sure that you thoroughly understand how to invest, the risks involved, and what kind of an investor you are before you invest online. Your goals should be clear-cut, and the amount of time you have to let your money grow should also be well defined. You should have called the companies you are interested in investing in and requested as much information from them as they were willing to send you. In short, if you have done your homework and if you are reasonably confident about the decisions you're making, then investing online is the way to go.

Is giving out information about myself online, including the securities I'm investing in, safe?

In the past, I've been very wary of providing information such as credit card numbers over the World Wide Web, but much has been made of the high-security developments in encryption software used by most reputable online vendors. Many analysts involved in online brokerage firms swear that there is next to no risk in providing the firm with certain sensitive information, including how much money you have to invest and which securities you're investing in. Online firms generally offer top-notch security, though you might want to make sure that the online brokerage you choose offers SSL encryption services, which disguise the data you provide them with a sophisticated code. Still, I would advise you to give out only the minimum information required by the brokerage firm. Skip any listings with the word "optional" after them.

How do online brokerage firms charge for their services?

Many online brokerages charge different amounts for different kinds of trades. As always, read the fine print. Do you want to make a market order? This will cost you, say, $8. What about a limit order? This could cost you $12. And just as with an offline brokerage firm, there may be other hidden fees that you should know about before you commit to anything.

Do Internet brokerage firms' chat rooms—or any Internet chat rooms—have valuable information that I should be aware of?

Chat rooms are just that—chat rooms, forums in which people like you from across the country, and sometimes around the world, offer their opinions. Take whatever you hear in Web chat rooms with a grain of salt—even what you hear in chat rooms that are connected to an online brokerage firm's home page.

If I open an account with an online brokerage firm, will I be able to access my account whenever I want?

You can access most online—and even traditional—brokerage accounts 24 hours a day, though there may be some restrictions. Check with the firm you are considering for its particular rules.

What if I need to talk to a living, breathing human being and not a computer screen?

Again, an investor's access to a customer service representative varies from firm to firm. Check with the online firm in question.

Is it possible to get advice from an actual broker within an online brokerage firm?

In many cases, it is, though you will often have to pay for this service. Some online brokerage firms offer financial advice, portfolio tips, and even the results of their research to investors, but you should find out first how much, if anything, this will cost you.

How do I go about choosing an online brokerage firm?

First of all, ask yourself what you want out of it. Are you a fanatic buyer and seller? In that case, you would need constant access to the firm for those middle-of-the-night trades. Are you looking for a firm that trades not just in stocks and

bonds but also in mutual funds, and that can even arrange to pay your bills every month? Then you would probably be in search of an online brokerage firm that offers its customers a full menu of services.

What other questions should I ask an online brokerage firm?

After you've found out what products the online brokerage firm offers—mutual funds? money-market accounts? company analysis?—you should find out the firm's hours of operation. Are customer service representatives on call throughout the day? From nine to five? Or not at all? Is the firm registered with the Securities and Exchange Commission? (You can access the SEC's Website at *www.sec.gov* to find out if a firm is registered and also whether any complaints have been lodged against the firm. The firm you choose should be registered with the SEC.)

Here are some more questions to ask:

1) What is the fee schedule?
2) How much money does it take to open an account? (Most online brokerage firms require an initial investment of at least $2,000.)
3) If your balance falls below a certain amount, are any penalties assessed?
4) Does the firm offer stock quotes? Are they quoted in real time, or an hour behind? If the firm offers real-time quotes, is this service free or will they charge you a little extra for the privilege of watching your stock prices fluctuate?
5) Ask to see a sample statement. Can you understand it easily?

6) What does the online firm charge to trade on margin?

7) Is the firm responsive to your calls?

8) Does the firm's Website go down very often? (If everyone is trying to trade at once and the site goes down, you could lose a lot of money. This happens more often than you may think.)

9) Finally, I'd ask myself, is the site easily accessible? And is it easy to navigate?

Should I choose an online broker on the basis of how much it charges to make a trade?

No. Please choose an online broker based on its ability to get you the best execution, or per-share price, at the time you make a trade. With slow or sloppy execution, you could lose a lot more money than you can save with bargain-priced trading charges. For example, let's say you buy 1,000 shares of a stock selling at $35. With slow execution, you might pay $35.25 for the stock instead of $35. At that price your shares would cost you a total of $35,250 instead of $35,000. I'd rather pay a $25 trading charge than an $8 charge plus $250 in a higher per share price.

8

Mutual Funds

THE GOOD, THE BAD, AND THE UGLY

When you put money into a mutual fund instead of buying shares of individual stocks, you are essentially hiring a trained professional to pick your stocks for you. In good, active funds, the fund manager is trained to locate the best-performing stocks of the kind that you want to invest in. There are more than 8,000 mutual funds. There are mutual funds for people interested in investing in small companies, large companies, sectors of the economy such as technology or health services, specific foreign regions or countries, environmentally sensitive companies, and the broadest array of companies under the umbrella of one big diversified fund. There are also mutual funds that charge you too much in sales charges and annual fees, don't perform as well as they should, and generally slow you down on the road to financial freedom. This chapter will show you how to stay away from those. It's impossible to cover every type of mutual fund available. But it's not hard to grasp the fundamentals of mutual funds—their basic terms and operating principles. The most important things to look for are good management, a long history of good performance, and very low fees and charges. And once you understand the general idea, you open your investment options wide. The questions and answers in this chapter will provide you with a working knowledge of the fundamentals of this often excellent investment option.

MUTUAL FUND BASICS

What is a mutual fund?

A mutual fund is an investment vehicle that can be compared to a basket filled with stocks. You and many other investors pool your money to buy a portion of everything that's in the basket, which has been assembled with an eye toward meeting certain investment goals. What those goals are depends on the particular mutual fund. For example, one mutual fund might aim toward growth in the value of the stocks in the fund, and another might try to generate income from dividends. Every mutual fund has a clearly defined investment objective, as well as guidelines that determine how the objective may be achieved.

Who decides how to invest all this money?

Each mutual fund is run by a portfolio manager (or a team of managers) who chooses the stocks in the fund and makes other investment decisions. The fund manager decides which stocks to buy and when, and also decides if and when those stocks should be sold. The fund manager assembles a portfolio of stocks that he or she thinks will outperform the market—that is, will generate more growth or income than other, similar groups of stocks—with an eye toward giving investors the best return on their investment. A fund manager can make or break a fund, since he or she makes all the critical investment decisions regarding it.

What exactly am I buying when I buy a mutual fund?

You are buying actual shares in that particular fund. A share represents a unit of ownership in the mutual fund, just as a share of stock in a publicly traded company represents partial ownership of that company. The share price of a mutual fund is sometimes referred to as net asset value.

What does net asset value mean?

The net asset value, or NAV, is the share price of the fund. At the end of each day, the entire value of the portfolio of stocks and/or bonds, less any expenses and/or liabilities, is added up. That total is divided by the number of shares outstanding. This is the net asset value.

Why would I buy a mutual fund instead of buying individual stocks?

Mutual funds allow you to diversify your investments quickly and with minimal risk. Let's say you have $1,000 to invest. When you put it in a mutual fund, you are buying a small slice of a very big pie that can contain hundreds of different stocks. Let's imagine that one company whose stocks are held within the mutual fund goes belly-up. As a result, the price of your mutual fund shares may temporarily drop in value slightly, but this wouldn't be a financial crisis for the mutual fund or for you. If, on the other hand, you had invested $1,000 in shares of that individual stock, you would lose all your money. Intelligent diversification—that is, spreading your money out among a variety of investments—is the key to being a smart investor. With small amounts of money, a mutual fund is a great way to achieve diversification.

Are you saying that only people with small sums of money are candidates for buying mutual funds?

Certainly not! People with large sums of money buy shares of mutual funds, too, because they like the fact that a trained portfolio manager is making the decisions about what and when to buy and sell. For fund investors, the only decision to make is which mutual fund to buy. Once you have purchased a mutual fund, the only *other* decision you will have to make is when to sell your shares. From the time you buy until the time you sell, your money is in the hands of the portfolio manager. Of course, choosing a mutual fund is not easy. I'll have much more to say about this later.

What if there is an enormous drop in the stock market and practically everything loses value? Will diversification still protect me?

If the market as a whole drops in value, your mutual fund—despite its diversification among a number of stocks—will probably drop in value, too. When, in a bear market, the majority of stocks fall, diversifying probably won't keep you from participating in the losses everyone experiences, but it may prevent your losses from becoming greater than the average loss. Bad times require commitment. If you are willing to weather a bear market, history has shown that the market will likely rise again.

Are there mutual funds that make money in a bear market?

Yes. There are all kinds of mutual funds, including those—known as "bear market" or "foul weather" funds—that actually perform best in bear markets.

How long does a bear market last?

Well, there is no way to know for sure, but in the past, bear markets typically have lasted between six months and two years, with the norm being between six and eighteen months.

Are all managed mutual funds diversified among hundreds of stocks?

No. Some mutual funds own hundreds of stocks and others own only 20 or 30 stocks. According to Securities and Exchange Commission (SEC) rules, a so-called "diversified" mutual fund is required to invest in at least 16 companies. (A mutual fund is also prohibited from owning more than 25 percent of any one company.) Even with these regulations, mutual funds have plenty of discretion.

Is there an ideal number of stocks a mutual fund should have?

The best actively managed funds may have between 25 and 100 stocks in their portfolios. Very large funds—those with billions of dollars to invest—often have to overdiversify into hundreds of stocks in an effort to allocate all the money people have invested in them. Alternatively, some funds have too few holdings (this is much rarer than too many), which exposes investors to the extra risk of inadequate diversification.

Once I buy a mutual fund, am I ever allowed to take some of the money back out?

Of course. It's your money. You can sell all or any portion of your shares at any time through your mutual fund company, a broker or discount broker, or even an online broker. (Most mutual fund companies and brokerage firms offer an 800 number that investors can call to liquidate shares or you can place a trade online.) However, if your fund share price has gone down, you might not get what you paid for your shares.

What is the minimum initial amount I must invest in a mutual fund?

Most funds require an initial investment of $500 to $1,000 if the investment is made as part of an individual retirement account (IRA), and $2,500 to $3,000 outside of a retirement account. Vanguard, for example, requires a minimum $3,000 initial investment to open a fund account. But if you open an IRA using Vanguard's STAR mutual fund, the minimum falls to $1,000. Most mutual fund companies, or families, work in more or less the same way, although a few good ones will let you invest with minimums as low as $50 to $250. These include T. Rowe Price (800) 638-5660; Managers Funds (800) 548-4539; and TIAA (800) 223-1200. Many mutual funds waive the minimum investment if you sign up for automatic monthly withdrawals, in which the fund takes $50 to $100 a month from a checking account and invests it.

What are mutual fund families?

"Fund family" is the cozy name given to a group of mutual funds that are managed by one company, such as Fidelity, T. Rowe Price, or Vanguard. The fund family's individual funds are under the same umbrella, but tend to have different investment objectives. Within some fund families, you can move your money from one fund to another without hassle or expense.

Some of the great fund families are:

Fidelity Investments   (800) 544-9797
T. Rowe Price   (800) 638-5660
Vanguard   (800) 662-2739

TYPES OF MUTUAL FUNDS

It's crucial to know a mutual fund's investment objective (*and* its performance record, but more about that later) in order to know whether that fund is right *for you*. By "right," I mean suited to an investor of your age, your income, your tax status, and your short- and long-term financial goals, including goals for your children (for example, college tuition, graduate school, or wedding expenses), and your retirement plans. Whatever your financial profile, there is probably a mutual fund that will help you to achieve your dreams.

How many kinds of mutual funds are there?
There are hundreds of kinds of funds, each with a slightly different objective, but in general, mutual funds are divided into four large groups: growth funds; balanced funds; income, or bond, funds; and money-market funds. (In this chapter, we'll cover stock funds, such as growth and balanced funds. For more information on bond funds and money-market funds, please see Chapter 9.) Each of the four groups can be, and is, divided into many subgroups, including mu-

tual funds that are variously described as managed funds, index funds, exchange-traded funds, load and no-load funds, open-end and closed-end funds, and on and on.

GROWTH FUNDS

What is a growth fund?
Growth funds emphasize adding to your investment capital by choosing investments that will increase in market value over time. Growth funds invest in companies that are likely to increase their annual earnings and/or their market share. Such funds do not invest primarily in stocks of companies that pay a dividend—meaning money that is paid to shareholders out of earnings, which growth companies tend to reinvest in their business. If you are able to let your money remain invested for ten years or more, do not need income from your investments now, and if growth of your investment capital is your objective, good growth funds can be an excellent choice.

There are many kinds of growth funds, including aggressive growth funds, value funds, blended funds, international stock funds, global funds, emerging-market funds, sector funds, socially responsible funds, large-capitalization funds, mid-capitalization funds, and small-capitalization funds.

What is an aggressive growth fund?
Many growth funds are made up of stocks of large, well-established companies whose earnings are growing rapidly. An aggressive growth fund is made up of stocks that the portfolio manager believes have greater-than-ordinary po-

tential for growth and that, as a result, tend to be somewhat more speculative and move up and down in price faster than the overall market. An aggressive growth fund may bypass conventional blue-chip stocks, concentrating instead on less-well-known securities in an attempt to make larger profits if and when the stocks take off. The usual trade-off applies, of course: The higher the rate of return you seek, the higher the risk. This is *not* the best kind of fund for people whose objective is to keep their money safe in the short term.

What is a value fund?

Value funds tend to invest in companies whose stock prices are below those of average similar companies in relation to such factors as earnings and book value—in other words, whose stocks offer value for the price. These stocks tend to pay above-average dividends.

What is a blended fund?

Blended funds invest in both growth and value stocks.

What is an international fund?

International funds invest in foreign stocks and bonds. Some international funds invest in specific geographic regions, such as the Pacific Rim; others put all their investments into a single country, for example, Chile.

What is the difference between an international fund and a global fund?

International funds invest only abroad; global funds invest in securities in both the United States and abroad.

Given the volatile state of the world today, international funds sound risky. Are they?

Well, the world is a pretty big place. It's not volatile everywhere, not by a long shot. Some countries (and investments) are riskier than others—and what you might call risky, another investor might call a walk around the block. Besides, if your mutual fund invests in several countries, the risk to you, the shareholder, is reduced. For example, when the market in Europe falls, the market in Asia may rise—sometimes in reaction to that falling European market. If your fund invests in only one country, the chances for a huge loss—or, for that matter, an enormous gain—are greater. However, for most of us, diversification, whether we are investing here in the United States, abroad, or both, is alwaysimportant.

What is an emerging-market fund?

An emerging-market fund invests in developing regions of the world, such as Latin America or Eastern Europe. ("Developing," incidentally, is a duffel bag of a word, containing every kind of society that's not destitute or affluent.) They can be extremely volatile. Remember the meltdown in Southeast Asian markets and Brazil's financial woes? Volatility is one of the potential hazards for the investor in an emerging-market fund. Still, there are some extraordinary opportunities in these funds, too.

What is a sector fund?

A sector fund is also known as a specialty fund. These are mutual funds that invest in the stocks of one industry—such as telecommunications, utilities, chemicals, precious metals, or pharmaceuticals. Some specialty funds are riskier than others, but the risk depends on a particular fund's investments.

What is a socially responsible fund?

Socially responsible funds typically avoid investing in companies that may cause harm to people, animals, or the environment. There's such a vast number of securities out there, some investors reason, that surely it's possible to make money without damaging the planet or the creatures on it. So most socially responsible mutual funds do not invest in tobacco, nuclear energy, or armaments companies. Nor do they buy shares of companies that have a history of discriminating against women or minorities, mistreating their employees, or polluting the environment. You can find a comprehensive listing of socially responsible funds on the Internet, at *www.socialinvest.org*. My favorite is the Domini Social Equity Fund.

What is the difference between large-cap, mid-cap, and small-cap mutual funds?

These designations refer to companies of a certain size, "cap" being shorthand for capitalization. Broadly speaking, small-cap refers to a corporation whose capitalization (or market value) falls below $2 billion. Mid-cap refers to companies whose capitalization runs between $2 billion and $10 billion. Large-cap companies have capitalization of $10 billion or more. A large-cap mutual fund invests in companies with large capitalization; a mid-cap fund buys stock in mid-cap companies; and so on.

What is the difference between a large-cap growth fund, a large-cap value fund, and a large-cap blend fund?

A large-cap growth fund concentrates its investments in well-known, well-managed companies with proven track records of growth in share price and a history of outperforming the markets. They pay out relatively small dividends, if any; they invest for long-term growth. A large-cap value fund, on the other hand, generally focuses its investments on large companies that the fund manager believes are undervalued and that the rest of the investing world will someday recognize as winners. A large-cap blend fund combines these two financial strategies, investing in both growth stocks and value stocks.

Mid-cap and small-cap companies also use these classifications. A small-cap growth mutual fund will invest in new or smaller companies that are growing rapidly and that are typically focused on some up-to-the-minute industry, such as biotechnology. In general, fund managers purchase shares early in the game and hold them for a long time. A small-cap value fund will concentrate its investments on better-established though under-recognized small companies. A mid-cap or small-cap blend fund combines these two investment styles.

INCOME FUNDS

The objective of income funds is, of course, to provide regular current income to investors. Income funds commonly invest in bonds or high dividend paying stocks, and accordingly, they are not as likely as growth funds to make you a lot of money. Income funds pay the investor dividends and/or interest, typically on a monthly basis.

Bond or income funds are popular with retirees who have seen their money grow during their working years and now want a monthly income that they can count on. To investors in bond or income funds, regular income is more important than the growth or possible loss of principal. For a more thorough discussion of bond funds, Treasury bill funds, CDs, money-market funds, and other income funds, please see Chapter 9.

BALANCED FUNDS

What is a balanced fund?

A balanced fund is a marriage of a mutual fund that deals exclusively in stocks and one that deals exclusively with bonds, mixing the two, usually fifty-fifty. Balanced funds are less risky than stock funds, but in a bear market they can be a little more precarious than bond funds.

There are two basic types of balanced mutual funds:

- Traditional balanced funds invest in a fairly stable mix of stocks, bonds, and money-market instruments in an effort to provide growth, income, and conservation of capital. They are considered to be a relatively conservative investment option. Their net asset values will fluctuate along with the movements of the financial markets, but they tend to experience fewer price swings than a portfolio made up entirely of stocks.
- Asset-allocation funds also invest in a mix of stocks, bonds, and money-market instruments. However, as market conditions change,

these funds switch the percentage of their holdings in each asset class according to the performance (or expected performance) of that class. As a result, asset-allocation funds tend to be more volatile than traditional balanced funds.

OPEN- AND CLOSED-END FUNDS

What is an open-end fund?

Most mutual funds are open-end. This means that there is no limit to the number of shares that the fund can issue and sell—so the growth of the fund, in terms of investment dollars, is open-ended. An open-end fund's price is referred to as a net asset value (NAV) rather than a price per share (even though price per share is essentially what a NAV is).

So there is no limit to the amount of money investors can put into an open-end mutual fund?

Correct. But a fund manager may sometimes close the fund to new investors once the fund has taken in as much money as is manageable. (Investors who are already part of the fund can usually continue to invest money in it.)

What's a closed-end fund?

In a closed-end mutual fund, the number of shares available for sale to the public is established at the outset. After those shares have been sold, the fund is closed and new investors can buy into the fund only if someone who owns shares wants to sell them. A closed-end fund is priced and traded just like a stock. Shares are usually sold on the NYSE AMEX Equities, formerly known as the American Stock Exchange.

Closed-end funds are far less common than open-end funds. When people talk generally about mutual funds, such as those that are commonly offered in 401(k) and 403(b) retirement plans, they're talking about open-end funds.

MANAGED MUTUAL FUNDS VERSUS INDEXED MUTUAL FUNDS

Most mutual funds are managed funds—managed, that is, by an individual (or team) who decides what to buy and sell with the money the investors have deposited into the fund. Index funds, sometimes called passive funds, have managers too, but they simply buy the entire index that the fund is duplicating, such as the Standard & Poor's 500 Index.

MANAGED MUTUAL FUNDS

What do managed-fund managers look for in the companies they invest in?

Successfully picking a stock involves intuition and knowledge informed by research. Fund managers usually track the market in a number of ways that include, for example, scrutinizing price trends. Has the company in question shown a decent upward price trend? What about the in-dustry involved? Is the U.S. economy in a recession, or have interest rates declined? Either situation can influence which kinds of stock the fund manager elects to invest in.

Most fund managers do hands-on research, too, and analysts within their companies typically advise them. They want to understand and monitor the goals of the companies in which they are thinking of buying stock. They try to determine a company's commitment to research and development. Does the company have a product in the pipeline that can't lose? Has the company been profitable for a number of years? What factors contributed to its winning streak?

Does the mutual fund manager have to inform me whenever he buys or sells something? And do I have to pay a commission when he does?

If you had a financial adviser at a full-service brokerage firm like Merrill Lynch, he or she usually would have to consult you before making any transactions, and you would probably have to pay a commission whenever you authorized him or her to buy or sell anything. This is not the case in a mutual fund, where the manager has free rein over the money in the fund and you're not charged an *individual* commission when transactions are made. (Transactions do cost you, however, both in terms of yearly return and in end-of-the-year taxes, but more about that later). Before you purchase shares of your fund, you will receive a prospectus and reports outlining the mutual fund's activities, but you're not notified of day-to-day changes. By buying shares in the fund, you have placed your trust in the fund manager. (Once you buy shares, you'll receive regular statements of your account's activity and quarterly reports for the fund.)

Before you buy into a managed mutual fund, it's wise to check how long the manager has been in charge. Is the current manager responsible for a fund's terrific track record? Or has that person moved on, leaving someone new and relatively untested at the helm? It's the *manager's* track record you want to know, not the fund's. Ultimately, the fund manager is responsible for the fund's success.

INDEXED MUTUAL FUNDS

Why do so many people buy index funds?
Over many years, index funds have outperformed almost 85 percent of all managed mutual funds. In the late 90s, when the whole stock market was rising, many people made the greatest returns through investing in the S&P index funds, and an index fund is an easy way to invest. An index fund simply buys all the stocks in the relevant index, for example, the Standard & Poor's 500, and no one has to worry about the fund's manager leaving. In fact, one key to the better-than-average return on index funds is they cost so little to operate.

EXCHANGE-TRADED FUNDS

Exchange-traded funds (ETFs) are relatively recent investment vehicles, and they are def-initely worth looking into when you're thinking about investing in mutual funds. They even have some advantages over index funds.

What are exchange-traded funds (ETFs)?
Exchange-traded funds (ETFs) combine the features of a mutual fund with those of a stock. Like mutual funds, ETFs track either an index of the broad stock market or bond market, stock industry sector, or international stock. ETFs move up or down as the stocks or bonds on the index they are tracking move. Yet ETFs trade like stocks that you can buy and sell throughout the trading day, which you cannot do with mutual funds.

What exactly am I buying when I buy an ETF? Am I buying a stock or a mutual fund?
When you buy an ETF, you are not buying shares of a stock or shares of a mutual fund. You are buying units of ownership in a trust that holds shares of the stocks or bonds tracked by a particular index, such as the S&P 500, in almost exact proportion to the weighting of the stocks on that index. In this way, an ETF is like an index fund, since you are buying the composition of the entire index. Because of this, an ETF offers a level of diversification that would be difficult for you to achieve on your own or through outright ownership of individual stocks, yet it trades and behaves like an individual stock. So you can buy and sell your shares during regular market hours; and there is no minimum investment amount as there is in many mutual funds.

What are the main differences between an ETF and a mutual fund?

In an ETF you can buy and sell the ETF while the markets are trading. In a mutual fund you can only get the closing price of that fund for that day regardless what time you put your sell order in. So if something happens during the day and you want to sell your ETF immediately you can do so—that is not true with a mutual fund. Also ETFs usually do not have end-of-the-year capital gains distributions like mutual funds do. So if you are investing outside of a retirement account this is important for you to take into consideration. Also ETFs can be bought share by share at a time and there is no minimum investment as there can be with many mutual funds. Bottom line: ETFs can be thought of as the modern-day mutual fund that brings you the best of both—stocks that allow you to buy or sell at any time and the diversification and low costs of many mutual funds.

What are the risks of investing in ETFs?

It depends on the type of ETF that you purchase. Equity-based exchange traded funds have risks similar to stocks and/or equity mutual funds, so they will have market risk, while fixed income-based ETFs have risks similar to a bond fund.

What are fixed-income ETFs?

Fixed income ETFs track bond market indexes. Fixed income ETFs tend to be more stable than equity ETFs because the bond markets are often less volatile than the stock markets. Please note that although I said *tend to be* for there are times that the bond market can be very volatile as was the case in a seven-week period in the year 2003 where we saw a 150 basis point swing during that time.

Do ETFs have a maturity date like a bond?

Technically, yes, although that date is more than 100 years in the future and so probably won't affect you.

Do equity ETFs pay dividends?

The units provide quarterly cash dividend distributions based on the accumulated dividends paid by the stocks held in the ETF trust minus an annual expense ratio and management fees ranging from .10 percent to more than 1 percent of principal to cover trust expenses. Please note, however, that the dividend is very, very low, so you can't count on them for income. This investment is usually for growth and growth alone.

Do fixed-income ETFs pay dividends?

Yes. Dividends for fixed-income ETFs are distributed on a monthly basis, similar to bond mutual funds.

How can I buy an ETF?

ETFs are traded on the NYSE AMEX Equities, the New York Stock Exchange, and the NASDAQ. They can be bought or sold through a broker or online throughout the trading day in the same manner as common stocks. The shares trade in minimum increments and, as with common stocks, there is a typical spread between the bid (what buyers are willing to pay) and asked price (what the sellers are asking for).

Am I better off buying an ETF or a managed mutual fund?

That depends on which managed mutual fund you want to buy. In general, ETFs have very low management fees and minimal stock turnover; in essence, they are just an index mutual fund sold as a stock, and in the past they, like index funds, have outperformed the vast majority of actively managed funds.

Am I better off buying an ETF or an index fund?

The answer will depend on how much money you have to invest and if you are investing inside or outside a retirement account, as well as how often you expect to invest. Many of the good index funds require a high initial deposit ($1,000–$3,000) to open an account. This is not true of ETFs. If you like, you can buy one share of an ETF, which could cost you as little as $25. Also, outside a retirement account, ETFs have an advantage, taxwise, over both managed funds and index funds. With ETFs, there usually is not an end-of-the-year capital-gains tax distribution, as there is with mutual funds. Please note: Even index funds, which don't buy and sell the stocks they hold as often as do managed funds, can have an end-of-the-year capital-gains distribution.

If you plan to dollar cost average into your chosen investment, adding a small sum of money to it every month, you would probably be better off in a no-load index fund; in many such funds, when you invest regularly and directly, the minimum initial deposit is reduced and there are no transaction costs. If you were to buy ETFs every month, the commission costs, even at just $10 per trade online, would seriously cut into your ability to profit. On the other hand, the annual expenses for ETFs are somewhat less than the expenses of many index funds.

Are ETFs easier to buy and sell than index funds?

Overall, they are. ETFs are traded in the same manner as stocks, so you can get price quotes and make trades any time during the day. You can also designate the exact price that you are willing to pay (using a limit order). You can't do this with a mutual fund; because a fund's net asset value (the equivalent of share price) is calculated only once a day, you always get the closing price on the day your order for shares is placed. The ability to buy or sell ETFs at any time during the market day and to use limit orders gives you a wide range of opportunities to reduce your transaction costs and/or to implement market-timing strategies. This characteristic can be particularly important during a large one-day decline in the stock market, since ETFs enable you to liquidate your position during the course of the day, when you first see that prices are falling, rather than at the close of trading.

If I want to be able to make money in a bear market or time the market, which is better to have, an index fund or an ETF?

ETFs can be more useful than index funds for timing the market. An investor who practices market timing can employ certain stock market strategies that can't be used with index funds, such as a technique known as selling short. (I explain this in Chapter 7.) Short selling is a very risky strategy, suitable only for sophisticated investors, and won't be of concern to the vast majority of investors.

I have heard about gold ETFs. Can you tell me more about these?

There are two gold bullion ETFs currently listed in the U.S.: the U.S. SPDR Gold Trust Shares (ticker: GLD) and the iShares Comex Gold Trust (ticker: IAU). These Gold ETFs allow investors to buy gold bullion without having to actually hold the metal itself. Each share represents one-tenth of one ounce of gold. In July 2009 each gold ETF had share prices of about $93. Each share is one-tenth of one ounce of physical gold, deposited with a bank. But please be aware purchasing a gold bullion ETF comes with a higher capital gains tax than other ETFs. The tax law legislation that reduced maximum capital gain to 15 percent excluded collectibles, which includes gold, silver, and platinum. So a Gold ETF held for more than one year is taxed at a maximum rate of 28 percent.

Can I build a diversified portfolio just from ETFs?

Absolutely. As of 2009 there were more than 700 ETFs you could choose from. In addition to ETFs that track the S&P 500, there are now ETFs that mirror just about every slice of the investment pie. For an even broader mix of U.S. stocks than the S&P 500, the Vanguard Total Stock Market Index (ticker symbol: VTI) tracks a benchmark of thousands of U.S. large-cap, mid-cap and small-cap indexes. If you want to invest in high-growth stocks, the PowerShares QQQ ETF (ticker: QQQQ) tracks the Nasdaq 100 index. There are also ETFs that invest in international indexes. The iShares MSCI EAFE ETF (ticker: EFA) tracks a popular index of stocks from developed economies. For exposure to international emerging markets, there are many choices, including the Vanguard Emerging Markets Stock ETF (ticker: VWO). If you want to target a specific market sector, such as gold or energy, there are now sector and commodity-based ETFs that fit the bill. With hundreds of different ETFs available, it is easy to build a cost-efficient diversified portfolio that relies solely on ETFs. You can learn more about ETFs and get a complete list of current ETFs at *www .morningstar.com*. Click on the ETF link at the top of the page.

FUNDS OF FUNDS

There are so many mutual funds out there. Is there a fund that buys other funds?
Yes, this is what is known as a fund of funds (or fofunds). A fofunds is a mutual fund that owns other mutual funds. The great advantage of a fofunds is that you get broad diversification in just one fund. A fund of funds does what you would do by assembling your own portfolio of mutual funds.

Are there disadvantages to funds of funds?
There can be, depending on the fund. You will have to pay the managing and operating fees of not only the fund you purchase but also of each fund within the fund. This can get to be very, very expensive. Also, you don't pick the funds that the fund manager buys, so you'd better like the portfolio manager of the fund you are buying into.

Are there fofunds that do not layer all those commissions?
Funds that buy funds from their own family gen-

erally don't layer expenses. TIAA-CREF Managed Allocation TIMAX has no expense ratio, for instance. Nor do funds of funds from the Vanguard Group or T. Rowe Price. Fidelity's Freedom funds' expense ratios range from .51 percent to .79 percent, but their portfolios do evolve over time. The Vanguard Group is always a great family in which to look for funds with low expenses.

Are there any funds of funds that buy multiple iShares or ETFs?

Yes. There are now many companies offering target retirement funds (funds with a portfolio mix tailored to a specific retirement date) that invest in assets with a variety of underlying ETFs. Standard & Poors and Barclays Global Investors' iShares each offer a family of target date ETFs.

WHAT TO LOOK FOR WHEN PICKING A MUTUAL FUND

How do I decide which mutual fund is right for me?

First of all, you need to know your investment objective. What do you want to accomplish with the money you are about to invest? Do you want growth over five years, ten years, or longer? Do you want income starting now? A combination of both? After you've figured that out, you should be able to identify dozens of funds that fit your objectives, especially by using a good fund screener, such as the one at *morningstar .com*. Make up a preliminary list. Then you need to examine the nuts and bolts of each of the

funds and compare performance, expense ratios, turnover ratios, sales charges, and policies on cash reserves.

What is an expense ratio?

The manager of a mutual fund is paid by the fund's investors; his or her salary is a percentage of the invested capital per year. In addition to paying this management fee, the investors also pay the fund's operating costs. Together, all these fees add up to what's called the *expense ratio* of the fund. Whatever the expense ratio is, it will definitely affect your rate of return.

I would never buy a fund with an expense ratio higher than 1 percent. Here's why: Let's say that during the course of one year, your mutual fund makes a return of 10 percent. Do you get that 10 percent? Of course not. Before you get your money, the fund subtracts the expense ratio. If the expense ratio is 2 percent, your return will be 8 percent. Calculate the effect this high expense ratio has on the growth of your money over time, and you will be amazed.

One of my favorite index funds, Vanguard Total Stock Market Fund, has a total expense ratio of 0.18 percent, and it does really well. Why in the world would you pay someone to manage your money if that person couldn't consistently outperform the index that his or her fund is comparing its performance to? You wouldn't.

What is the turnover rate?

The turnover rate of a mutual fund refers to the cumulative dollar amount of securities that the fund manager buys or sells in a given year. A mutual fund with a 100 percent turnover rate has "turned over" the entire dollar amount of its portfolio.

What is the significance of a 100 percent turnover rate?

The higher the turnover rate, the more likely it is that you have a very aggressive fund manager; the lower the rate, the more conservative the manager. Personally, I prefer portfolio turnover rates of 20 percent to 50 percent—especially if the money is outside of a retirement account. This is because the higher the turnover rate, the more capital-gains taxes you may have to pay at year's end, and the more commissions the fund has to pay to cover all the trades.

Is a 300 percent turnover rate a bad sign, then?

No, not necessarily. But I still would feel better about a lower turnover rate—not more than 50 percent. Again, a portfolio with a high turnover rate may generate lots of year-end taxes, and if your mutual fund is not part of a retirement account, this could mean tax trouble.

Do index funds have a turnover rate?

Yes, but usually only about 5 percent per year. This is because the portfolio manager does not buy and sell stocks based on an active investment strategy. He does so only to match the index he is tracking.

What is the cash reserve of a fund?

A fund's cash reserve is the amount of actual cash kept by a fund to buy stocks or bonds. A fund's cash reserve is an indicator of how the portfolio manager feels about the overall stock market. If there's a large cash reserve, the fund is not fully invested, probably because its manager fears the market will go down and he or she doesn't want to risk exposure or wants to have available cash to buy stocks at a reduced price. On the other hand, if the cash reserve is low, then the fund is more fully invested, suggesting that the fund's manager feels confident that the market is the best place to realize high returns.

In a bull market, I like funds that need to be totally, completely invested all the time, as index funds are. If a mutual fund keeps a large percentage of its money in cash during a period of rising stock prices, then the overall return will most likely not be as high.

What is the "beta" of a mutual fund?

There are several ways to determine your mutual fund's volatility—how much the share price, or NAV, goes up and down within any given period of time. One is to look at the fund's "beta"—a measure of the volatility of your mutual fund in comparison to the overall market. A mutual fund with a beta of 1 is projected to move in direct correlation to the stock market. If the market goes up 10 percent, the share price or NAV of this fund should also move up 10 percent. If the mutual fund you are considering has a beta greater than 1, then the fund will probably move faster—both up and down—than the overall market. The higher the beta, the more aggressive, and therefore riskier, the fund.

What if my mutual fund has a beta of less than 1?

Your mutual fund will be *less* volatile than the market. In downtimes, it may not dip as low as the market, but in boon times, it probably won't match sharp market gains, either.

Are moving averages a reliable way to make decisions about investing?

Moving averages are useful, but a moving average should be only a part of the decision to buy or sell shares of a mutual fund.

Should I buy a fund based on its past performance?

A fund's performance history can't predict what will happen after you buy the fund. A fund's great performance may be the temporary result of special circumstances like investing in a hot sector—think of Internet stocks in the late 90s—and not from impressive overall strategy and management. On the other hand, a fund's past performance provides useful information—specifically, whether the fund is stable or not. Has it stayed in line with what the market did? Or did it wander? Has its share price, or NAV, increased steadily over three, five, and ten years? If you are buying a managed mutual fund, in particular, look for a stable fund that outperforms the most comparable market index.

What is the yield of a fund? How is it determined?

The yield is what a fund pays to investors in dividends over the course of a year, either in cash payments or by reinvesting in additional shares of the mutual fund. Yield is the ratio of dividends to the NAV. So, for example, if the NAV of your mutual fund is $12, and your mutual fund pays $0.72 a year in dividends, then the yield is 6 percent ($0.72 divided by $12).

What does the total return of a fund tell me?

The total return is a measure of all realized and unrealized appreciation or depreciation of the fund's investments for a stated period, plus any dividends the fund pays. The total return is a particularly salient statistic when it comes to bond funds. In a bond fund, you can get a yield of 5 or 6 percent, but, at the same time, the NAV of the bond fund may have declined. The total return of the fund, then, taking into consideration the yield and the decline of the NAV, could be a negative figure. Total return is the only figure that counts when analyzing a mutual fund's performance.

How much money can I expect to make in a mutual fund?

Historically, mutual funds that buy and sell common stocks have a return of about 10 percent annually. But keep in mind that this figure is a historical average. You could lose 15 percent one year and make 25 percent the next—which means your average yearly return would be 3.08 percent (because you'll earn the 25 percent on a smaller amount after you've lost 15 percent). However, over time and with patience, you should make money.

EVALUATING RISK

I'm ready to buy a mutual fund, I think. Would you caution me against anything in particular?

Yes—impatience. Remember that mutual funds are long-term investments. It takes time and effort to find the right one. Don't chase after the flavor-of-the-moment fund or the fund that somebody in a chat room gave you a tip about. Don't invest to make a quick killing either, because more often than not, you'll be disappointed.

Are you telling me not to take any risks?

No. Much of the *emotional* benefit of managing your money responsibly comes from discovering how you feel about risk—and learning to accommodate and respect what you discover. If you are an inexperienced investor, I would advise against taking great risks. But I would also advise against playing it too safe—say, with all your money in a money-market account or CDs. And all investors should guard against potential losses on higher-risk investments by balancing them with low-risk investments. Consider investing in two or three mutual funds. That way, if one of your funds outperforms the market and another underperforms or even loses value, you stand a good chance of coming out even, if not ahead, and you'll learn what works for you.

I'm young—can't I afford to take risks?

Yes, you can afford to take more risk because, statistically, the risk evens out with time, and time is on your side. For young investors, as well as those who are unmarried and childless, I would recommend investing some portion of your investment dollars in aggressive growth funds. The older you are and the more financial responsibilities you assume, the more I recommend that you concentrate on balancing your growth (which can be risky) with keeping your capital safe and sound in a mixture of growth funds, balanced funds, and income funds.

RATING MUTUAL FUNDS

When I read financial magazines, they each name a different mutual fund as the best of the year. How is that possible?

Good question. It is strange, isn't it? The answer is that each magazine uses a different formula and factors to calculate the funds' returns. They compare funds to different indexes, and they each have their own methods of analyzing the risks that the funds take.

What factors should I use to rank the mutual funds I'm interested in?

Consider its three-, five-, and ten-year performance history. Find out whether the fund has had the same manager for the last few years. But remember, just because a fund's manager did well in the past is not a guarantee that he or his fund will continue to perform well.

I would also go over the following checklist for every fund you consider:

- How has the fund performed compared to other funds that invest similarly? Not all funds, even though they may be the same *kind* of fund, are alike.
- How risky is the fund? If the fund has had a great performance but the risk it had to take to get it was extremely high, then this fund may not be right for you.

- How efficient is the fund? Get the prospectus and annual report of every mutual fund that interests you, and compare the funds' management, expenses, loads, fees, charges, distributions, tax implications, and services.
- How do professionals rank the fund? Use online services that rank the funds for you. The rating service Morningstar *(www.morningstar.com)* is my favorite.

I am afraid that the market may go down after I invest in it, and I'll lose a lot of money. What can I do to limit my exposure?
You can use a technique I love—dollar cost averaging. Please see page 403 for complete instructions.

I still don't feel that I have what it takes to pick my funds myself. Is there an unbiased resource that can help me?
One of my favorite resources is a newsletter called the *Bob Brinker Marketimer* (to order, call [303] 660-8686 or visit *www.bobbrinker.com*). Brinker is also on ABC radio for three hours every Saturday and Sunday. He's had his show for more than a decade and gives terrific advice on which funds to buy and sell.

HOW TO BUY A MUTUAL FUND

When I'm ready to buy a mutual fund, should I contact the company?
Yes, if only to talk to customer service and request a prospectus.

What is a prospectus?
A prospectus is a legal document that describes, usually in some detail, a mutual fund's investment goals, performance, and expenses. It also tells you who manages the fund. Anyone can request a prospectus; in fact, federal law requires that you receive a prospectus when you invest in any mutual fund.

If you're unsure of a fund's name but are interested in, say, aggressive-growth funds, a fund company will be able to send you information on various funds that meet your investment objectives.

What exactly is included in a prospectus?
A mutual fund's prospectus includes an explanation of the objectives of the fund. It has tables that compare the fund's performance over the past several years with that of various indexes, such as the S&P 500; a brief analysis of the risks of investing in the fund; and a schedule of any fees that may be charged to investors. You can find out from the prospectus whether the mutual fund is a growth or an income fund. The prospectus will also tell you who manages the fund. Typically, you will not find a current listing of the securities that the mutual fund owns, mostly because they may change from one month to the next.

I've got my prospectus in hand, and it's pretty intimidating. What should I look for?
Look for the important facts: the sales charges, the objective of the fund, the fees and expenses, and the manager. Then, if you haven't already done so, use your rating tools to compare it to other funds with similar objectives.

The prospectus in front of me says that the mutual fund is interested in "capital appreciation." What kind of mutual fund is this?

It's a growth fund. "Capital appreciation" means growth.

A section in the prospectus explains the fund's fees. What should I be on the lookout for?

When you examine the fund's management fees, you want to see no more than 0.25 percent to 1 percent for annual fund expenses. You will also find a list of fees for services—things such as electronic transfers. Also, check to see if the fund charges you for reinvesting dividends. And read the fine print for other minor operational expenses. But most important, you want to see if the fund is a load fund or a no-load fund.

Basically, load funds cost you money to buy or sell, and no-load funds are free. In my opinion, no-load funds are the way to go. The next section explains why.

SALES CHARGES

Over the years, mutual funds have become immensely popular, so it is important to understand how they really work. When mutual funds first came on the scene, you could buy them only through a broker or financial adviser. They were all what is known as "loaded funds," which means that there's a sales charge on the initial purchase and on every subsequent transaction. Then, slowly but surely, a new breed of mutual funds emerged—"no-load" funds that do not charge commissions. Investors soon recog-

nized the value of no-load funds and started investing heavily in them. This put a big dent in the profits of brokerage firms that sold only loaded funds, so they came up with another kind of fund—in my opinion, a way to make you think you can buy a no-load fund when you're not buying one. Thus was born the back-end-load fund.

The three most common are front-end-load funds, no-load funds, and back-end-load funds. The front-end load funds charge you a commission fee upfront for buying the fund. No-load funds carry no commission fee, although, like all funds, they have some maintenance fees. With back-end funds, you may pay when you take your money out of the fund.

What are front-end-load funds?

Front-end-load funds are identified as A-share mutual funds. If the name of a mutual fund contains "A" or "A shares," it's a front-end-load fund. Front-end-load funds charge a fee, or a load, up front. This is the commission that the broker or the financial planner takes before your money gets invested. The commission can be anywhere from 2 percent to 8.5 percent; the average commission is about 5 percent—out of your pocket! Think of this load as an unnecessary tax on your money.

What are no-load funds?

No-load funds are mutual funds that don't cost you a penny to buy or to sell. In other words, they don't have a load (commission). I believe no-load mutual funds are the only kind to buy. Look at it this way: If you were to invest $10,000 in a no-load mutual fund and you decided, two days later, that you wanted to withdraw your money, you'd get all $10,000 back, assuming the market hadn't moved. If you invested $10,000 in a loaded fund and wanted your money back, you would get back only about $9,500. Think about that—a loaded fund has to go up approximately 5 percent for you just to break even. That means you are starting out with a 5 percent disadvantage in a loaded fund.

What are back-end-load funds, also known as 12(b)1 funds or B shares?

In my opinion, B shares are the worst kind. B shares are back-end-loaded shares that lock you in to a period of time—usually five to seven years—during which you cannot sell the fund without being hit with a "surrender" charge, or load. This load usually starts at 5 percent if you sell during the first year, and drops to 4 percent the second, 3 percent the third, 2 percent the fourth, and 1 percent the fifth. You pay nothing if you sell thereafter.

My broker told me a back-end-load fund wouldn't cost me anything if I just stayed in it for 10 years. What's so bad about that?

I can't tell you how angry this makes me. What your broker failed to tell you is that you *are* paying to be in that fund. You see, the broker who sold you the fund probably received a 5 percent commission, paid by either the firm he works for or the fund itself, up front and in full when you made the purchase. The brokerage firm or mutual fund company gets its money back by charging you what is known as a 12(b)1 fee of anywhere from 0.75 to 1 percent yearly. This fee, which the SEC allows for

"marketing" costs, is used to pay the cost of the broker and is taken out of the fund's returns. So if your fund earns 10 percent, and your 12(b)1 fee is 1 percent, your return is only 9 percent, because the brokerage firm is taking that 1 percent to pay itself back for the broker's commission. That is why your surrender fee goes down by 1 percent each year. Suppose your fund paid a broker 5 percent up front and they take 1 percent a year from your return. If you were to sell after one year, your surrender charge would be 4 percent. Add that to the 1 percent they already took, and they've recouped the money they paid the broker. Pretty sneaky, don't you think?

Some B shares automatically convert to A shares after the surrender period, but some do not, and you continue to pay that 12(b)1 fee every year for as long as you own the fund—even though the broker has already been paid! Again, in my opinion, B shares came about simply because brokerage firms needed to find a way to keep your business by luring you into a load fund in the guise of a no-load fund.

Can you illustrate the effect of 12(b)1 fees?

I sure can. On the following page are the actual returns of a growth fund from a major brokerage firm that has both A and B shares. Note the difference between the returns of the two. Remember that these are shares of the *same fund,* managed by the same portfolio manager. The only difference is that one set of returns is on the A shares and the other is on the B shares.

Take a good look and you will see the return on the A shares is more than 1 percent higher than the return on the B shares. Why? Because of that 12(b)1 fee that you are paying out of your own pocket! If you look at the trailing return percentage, which is your average return if your money was in the mutual fund for all of one or three years, you will see that the 12(b)1 fee again makes more than a percent difference in your return. And this is the same fund with the same holdings and the same manager. But B shareholders realize a lower return—because they are paying the fund out of their return!

Is the 12(b)1 charge in lieu of any other charges in my mutual fund?

Hardly. The 12(b)1 fee is in *addition* to all the other fees. You still have to pay the management fees and other expenses of the fund, just as you do with a no-load fund or an A-share fund. The 12(b)1 fees exist only to pay the broker's or financial adviser's commission.

Why would my financial adviser try to sell me these B shares of a fund?

Because that's how he makes a living. Choose your financial adviser carefully—good financial advice informs you, the client, how to get the most from your money, even if it means the adviser won't make a lot of money from the transaction. Advisers are there to help you get rich, not to get rich off you. It's the adviser's responsibility to tell you if there's a less expensive way for you to make money—and to give you the choice of what you want to do.

Does a loaded fund perform better than a no-load fund?

The sales commission has absolutely nothing to do with the performance of a mutual fund; performance as based on the performance of an index (for index funds) and the talent of a manager (for managed funds). From that performance, you deduct expenses—including sales commissions—so in fact for a load fund to outperform, it must overcome its expenses.

So what you're saying is that if I am going to use a financial adviser to buy a fund, I'm better off buying A shares than B shares?

Yes. If, for whatever reason, you still want to use a financial adviser to buy a loaded mutual fund, you are better off buying A shares than B shares. If you do buy A shares, make sure you ask your broker about the breakpoint for the load on the fund you are thinking about buying.

What is a breakpoint?

The breakpoint is the amount of money you have to invest in a fund in order to pay a reduced commission. The amount varies from fund to fund but, in general, the more money you invest, the lower the sales load will be. The first breakpoint level for many mutual funds is $25,000. Keep in mind that breakpoints apply only to loaded mutual funds. In a no-load fund, obviously, there's no load that you need a break from.

I have heard that investors can qualify for a breakpoint if they sign a letter of intent. What is this?

A letter of intent (LOI) tells the mutual fund that eventually you will invest an amount of money equal to one of the fund's breakpoint lev-

COMPARISON OF A- AND B-SHARE RETURNS OVER TIME		
Annual Return Percentage	**Year A**	**Year B**
A Shares	28.70	33.49
B Shares	27.19	32.05
Difference	1.51	1.44
Trailing Return Percentage	**One-Year Average**	**Three-Year Average**
A Shares	19.88	27.86
B Shares	18.54	26.45
Difference	1.34	1.41

els. (It's not uncommon for mutual funds to have more than one breakpoint level.) If you write a letter of intent, then you will not be charged the higher sales load.

How long do I have before I must actually invest this money?

Typically, you have 13 months.

What if 13 months passes and I haven't invested the entire amount?

An LOI isn't legally binding. However, if you have not reached the investment level you stipulated in the LOI, you will be penalized by the fund for the difference between the lower load that you paid and the regular sales commission.

What is a right of accumulation?

For the investor who doesn't qualify for a breakpoint, a right of accumulation provides a lower commission if the investor manages to reach a certain investment threshold over several years'

time. Although the lower load is not retroactive, the new, reduced load applies to all future purchases, as well as to the purchase that catapulted the investor over the breakpoint limit.

What is a redemption fee?

A redemption fee is a percentage the fund charges you to withdraw your money from that fund. This is different from a back load or a surrender fee, which usually goes away after a period of time. A redemption fee is in place for the life of the fund, and it usually runs about 1.5 percent. It is important that you know whether or not your fund has a redemption fee.

Do no-load funds have redemption fees?

It's not very common, but some no-load funds have them.

My broker tells me that all mutual funds have loads. Is this true?

Well, it is true that all mutual funds have

expense ratios, and some are higher than others. This expense ratio, a percentage of the total investment in the fund, pays the salary of the portfolio manager who is buying and selling the stocks and/or bonds, as well as expenses incurred in actually running the fund.

However, the actual sales load, or broker commission, which is what we are referring to here, is an entirely separate issue. Not all funds have sales loads, and those that do, in my opinion, are a waste of your money.

So are you telling me that a no-load mutual fund is the only way to go?

That is exactly what I am saying. There are some 2,500 mutual funds out there that charge no commission whatsoever to invest with them. What's more, no-load funds can be purchased without the help of an adviser—no middleman, no commissions, no hidden costs, just smooth sailing to what might be greater and greater wealth over time.

How can I find a listing of all the no-load funds that are out there?

Once again, I prefer the Website *morningstar.com*. It has one of the most complete sets of listings anywhere—although even this excellent site may not list every single one of the hundreds of no-load funds in existence. After you log on, choose Morningstar's Mutual Fund Screener, in the Funds section, then select No-Load Funds. You can refine your search in any way you choose. Morningstar also has a broad database of Exchange Traded Funds (ETFs); ETFs can be a great low-cost way to invest lump sums, assuming you make your purchases through a discount

broker that charges a low commission fee. Remember, ETFs trade like stocks, so you will pay a commission to buy and sell shares.

I want to buy a no-load fund from a discount brokerage firm, but it charges a fee. Is this a load?

No. This is known as a *transaction fee*. If you don't want to pay it, just buy the fund directly through the fund family itself. And there are discount brokers who don't charge a transaction fee. It's worth your while to check around.

WHEN TO BUY AND WHEN TO SELL

A mutual fund is a long-term investment, so before you buy one, be sure to track its progress for a few months. What exactly should you be looking for? Look for answers to the following four questions: How rapidly has your fund been growing or shrinking in size—that is, attracting or losing assets? How risky has your fund been? How has your fund performed in relation to other, similar funds? And how long has your fund had the same manager? Once you've bought your mutual fund, keep asking these questions; when the answers are no longer satisfactory to you, you'll know that it's time to consider selling.

How do I decide whether to buy or sell a mutual fund?

The decision to buy or sell a mutual fund should begin with performance, and the best way to evaluate the performance of any mutual fund is to compare it to an appropriate benchmark. A fund that consistently performs below its benchmark is a strong candidate for sale.

BENCHMARKS

What is a benchmark?

Benchmarks—or something to measure your fund's performance against—come in many different varieties, but an index or index mutual fund is the preferred benchmark for most professional money managers. For example, the Standard & Poor's 500 stock index or the Vanguard 500 Index mutual fund can be good benchmarks for evaluating the performance of a mutual fund that invests in large-cap U.S. stocks.

How should I use a benchmark to evaluate funds I own or am considering buying?

You will probably want to use a benchmark whose composition is reasonably close to that of the fund you are evaluating. For example, if you are investing in a growth fund, you'll want to measure your fund against a benchmark for growth; if your fund is a large-cap fund, you'll want to compare it with a large-cap index. I'll list some good benchmarks for use with different kinds of funds later in the next question.

As a general rule, I suggest that you avoid performance comparisons over very short or very long periods (for example, one month or ten years). If I had to recommend a single performance *period*, I would suggest that you compare the performance of a mutual fund to its benchmark for the past three years. Even better, I think, is to compare a fund's performance to its benchmark over several periods—ideally 12 months, 36 months (three years), and 60 months (five years). When you examine multiple periods, you get more depth and perspective on the performance of your fund.

How do I choose a good benchmark fund?

In addition to the index itself, the following mutual funds offer good comparison.

- If you have a *balanced fund,* Vanguard Balanced Index Fund (symbol VBINX) is a good benchmark to use. This is a mutual fund that invests about 60 percent of its assets in large stocks and about 40 percent in high-quality bonds. The stock portfolio attempts to match the performance and risk characteristics of the Dow Jones Wilshire 5000 Composite Index. The bond portfolio attempts to match the performance and risk characteristics of the Lehman Aggregate Bond Index.

- If you have a *large-cap fund,* try using Vanguard 500 Index Fund (symbol VFINX), a mutual fund that attempts to match the performance and risk characteristics of Standard & Poor's 500 Stock Index.

- If you have a *domestic mid-cap fund,* a good benchmark might be Dreyfus MidCap Index Fund (symbol PESPX), a mutual fund that seeks to match the performance of the Standard & Poor's Mid-Cap 400 Index.

- If you have a *small-cap fund,* you can compare your fund to Vanguard Small-Cap Index Fund (symbol NAESX), a mutual fund that seeks to match the performance and risk characteristics of the MSCI U.S. Small Cap 1750 Index.

- If you have an *international fund,* you can use Schwab International Index Fund (symbol SWINX), a mutual fund that seeks broad international equity diversification.

DECIDING TO SELL A FUND

Benchmarking is an excellent way to measure the performance of a mutual fund relative to its peers and is a pivotal first step in the process of deciding to sell a mutual fund you own. Before you sell, however, there are a few other things to consider.

What if my mutual fund didn't outperform the S&P 500? Is that a sign that I should get rid of it?

No, not necessarily. In fact, in recent years it's been surprisingly difficult for a managed fund to outperform an index. And even index funds will show lower returns than the index they track, simply because some fees must be deducted. Often, a better way to measure the performance of your mutual fund is by watching the benchmark funds that are most relevant to it.

How does the riskiness of a fund enter into the decision to sell it?

If you want to start a lively discussion among financial professionals, ask each of them to say a few words about "risk" in relation to a mutual fund.

Cutting through the debate, I think that most investors perceive mutual-fund risk as the chance of having a "down" year, as well as the magnitude of the potential slide. But mutual-fund risk must be viewed in context. For example, imagine that you own Fund A and you are comparing it to a benchmark index fund (Fund B). Fund A is considered to be slightly more aggressive, and slightly riskier, than Fund B. However, Fund A has historically outperformed Fund B, so you might want to keep Fund A even if there is a good chance that next year it will have a worse year than Fund B. Now let's assume that Fund A has historically performed worse than Fund B. If it is likely that Fund A is going to have a worse year than Fund B, would you continue to hold Fund A? Probably not. In both cases, Fund A is "riskier" than Fund B, but in the first case the greater risk of Fund A has often been rewarded with greater return. In the second case, both risk and return are working against Fund A, and Fund A is a compelling candidate for sale.

What other factors enter into the decision to sell a mutual fund?

The two most important factors to consider are *manager turnover* and *change in fund assets.*

Why is manager turnover important?

By itself, a change in portfolio managers is not a reason to sell a mutual fund. But it is valuable information when you want to evaluate a fund's performance. A change in fund management can explain a pattern of deteriorating performance and reinforce a decision to sell that is based on performance information. In other cases, a recent change in fund management may encourage you to hold on to a fund that has performed poorly.

If your fund has underperformed its benchmark for the past twelve months/three years/five years, and the tenure of your fund manager is five years or greater, you know that the current manager is responsible for the poor performance. This is a strong signal to sell your fund—you've given a manager five years to beat the benchmark, and that manager has failed to do the job.

Now, say your fund has performed poorly for the past twelve months/three years/five years, but the manager is relatively new. Clearly, you can't hold the current manager entirely accountable for the fund's poor performance, but that doesn't mean you should continue to hold on to the fund. If the new fund manager had a good record at a similar fund, you might want to hold. If the new manager has never managed a fund before or has a relatively poor record managing another fund, you should probably sell.

How do you find out about a fund manager's history?

You can usually get that information directly from your fund. Call the 800 number and request the manager's professional biography.

Will the performance information for the fund always tell me how well the manager is doing?

It isn't easy to correlate performance information to a fund manager. Cause and effect are often hidden. For example, consider a large-cap fund with a manager who has been in charge for two years. The fund has the following performance information relative to the Vanguard 500 Index:

5 Years	−4.5
3 Years	−3.0
12 Months	2.0

In this case, it's reasonable to credit the recent good year to the new manager and to attribute the poor longer-term performance to the previous manager. But is 12 months enough time to form a valid opinion of the new manager? Probably not. The new manager might not have changed the fund's holdings, but the strategy that's been in place just happened to finally work. You might continue to hold this fund, keeping a close eye on the new manager's performance.

Why should I be concerned about a change in the assets of my mutual fund?

Some mutual fund managers are better at managing relatively small sums of money, and their performance may suffer as their asset base grows. Though it may sound counterintuitive, rapid growth of assets under management can help explain a mutual fund's poor recent performance.

For example, consider ABC Small Cap Fund, a hypothetical fund that grew from $50 million to $1 billion of assets under management. Let's assume that, at any given time, the manager of ABC Fund has 50 good investment ideas—in other words, a maximum of 50 stocks on his A list. When ABC Fund had $50 million in assets, the fund manager could take an average position of $1 million in each of the 50 stocks on his A list. Now that the fund has to invest $1 billion, the average position must grow to $20 million. The ABC Fund manager is faced with several choices, none of them particularly desirable from the standpoint of the fund's shareholders:

- The portfolio manager can take $20 million (or larger) positions in several of his best choices. However, since many small companies have total market capitalization of only $200 million or so, ABC Fund would probably end up owning 10 percent or more of the stock in several companies. Large positions like this prevent a fund from being liquid. There are also legal restrictions on how concentrated a mutual fund may become in any given company.
- The ABC Fund manager can expand his stock list beyond 50, considering less attractive investment opportunities—moving, in effect, to his B list.
- The manager can raise the median capitalization of his holdings—that is, buy the securities of larger companies—even though he is really only expert in selecting small-cap stocks.

No matter what the ABC manager does, fund performance is likely to suffer.

How will a change in assets affect my decision to sell my mutual fund?

When evaluating information on a change in assets, keep your fund's market capitalization objectives in mind. Generally, small-cap and specialty funds have the hardest time handling large increases or decreases in assets. Large-cap funds can handle asset swings of 10 percent, 20 percent, or more (though this doesn't happen very often). If you own a small-cap or specialty

fund with a changing asset base *and* deteriorating performance, you should be concerned. For more information, see the Website *fundalarm.com*.

WHEN THINGS CHANGE

Three years ago, I bought a mutual fund that started off great. Lately, it's in a slump. What's going on?

Your mutual fund could be disappointing you for a number of reasons.

If you invested in a growth fund, the market may be in a cycle where the securities typically chosen for growth are temporarily out of favor.

Your fund manager may have made decisions or judgments based on speculation that never paid off. (Remember, it is terribly difficult, if not impossible, to outwit the market.) Your manager might have bet that the stock market was poised for a fall and put a lot of the fund's assets in cash (a hedge against a massive drop in stock prices); but instead, the market, against all odds, kept going up.

Your fund could be doing poorly because of instability at home or abroad. Is there a war going on, or the threat of war in the wind? How are the foreign markets doing? Closer to home, what are interest rates doing? What is the unemployment rate? Did your fund manager buy small-cap stocks that may not have moved? There are many reasons why a fund does not perform.

My mutual fund just merged with another fund. This fund has a track record that is iffy

at best. Should I get out now, before it's too late?

This is a good question. The decision to sell a mutual fund is not based entirely on market performance or financial indicators. If, for any reason, you feel uncomfortable with the fund—for example, your investment objectives have changed, or you're skeptical about the fund's direction—then by all means, sell it (as long as you have considered the tax ramifications, of course).

Why would my investment objectives change?

Investors' financial objectives change regularly. The classic example is when investors retire and begin to want more income from their funds. Unexpected events can change your objectives, too. For example, what if you or your spouse were to suddenly fall ill? With the threat of ballooning medical expenses, you might not want your money in a growth-oriented mutual fund. Suddenly, a money-market fund might suit you better.

As you get older, you should reexamine your investment objectives from time to time. If your fund's objectives are no longer in sync with yours, it is time to sell your fund.

Is there a relationship between the strength of the economy and the performance of a mutual fund?

The answer is usually yes, but it depends on what kind of mutual fund you're talking about. Let's use sector funds as an example. With a sector fund, you are investing in a particular industry—such as chemicals, pharmaceuticals, or medical supplies. What happens when the economy starts to take off? The securities of industries involved in manufacturing, such as heavy metals and chemicals, tend to swing upward, anticipating work and demand. What happens when the economy starts to slow down? The general emphasis of buyers is on slower and steadier industries, such as health-care and consumer goods.

What economic signs are important in determining the market's long-term movement, which obviously will affect growth mutual funds?

The financial signs that have the biggest impact on the stock market in general are the following:

- Economic growth
- Interest rates
- Inflation
- Strength of the dollar

What am I looking for as I watch these different indicators?

Well, the stock market is like a pot of soup. For good results, all the ingredients have to be just so. In my opinion, for a truly strong market you need:

- Slow economic growth
- Low interest rates
- Reduced inflationary expectations
- A strong dollar overseas

Are all four factors equally important?

Yes, because they all work off one another. If you have a weak dollar abroad, interest rates tend to rise here in the United States. However, with rising interest rates come fear of inflation, the stock market's biggest enemy. Understanding how the economy works will help you make informed decisions about whether and when you should sell, buy, or just shift the balance of what you already have.

Is there a good time to buy and sell growth funds?

Whether we're talking about mutual funds or stocks, it's always easier to know when to buy than when to sell. Knowing when to sell is the hardest thing to master. The following guidelines are not set in stone, but they might help you decide.

A good time to buy:

- You won't need the money for at least ten years.
- Your research indicates the fund's assets are undervalued.
- You are looking for diversification and professional management in your investments.

A bad time to buy:

- You need your money within two years.
- You want to keep your money 100 percent safe and sound.
- The fund is about to distribute capital gains to shareholders *and* it's unlikely that the fund's value will increase more than the net tax amount of that distribution. (This only applies to funds outside retirement accounts.)

A good time to sell:

- There has been a fundamental change in the fund's investment style, which affects your portfolio strategy.
- Your fund has underperformed its competitors for the past couple of years.
- An important portfolio manager leaves.

A bad time to sell:

- Your mutual fund has a big back-end load (or deferred sales charge), and you haven't given the fund a chance to perform.

TAXES, TAXES, TAXES

The following applies only to mutual funds held outside of retirement accounts.

With mutual funds, what will I owe taxes on?

When you sell any shares of your mutual fund held outside a retirement account, you will have to pay taxes on whatever profit you make. If your mutual fund itself makes a profit, meaning the *fund* sells shares of stock at a gain, you will also have to pay capital-gains taxes on that profit, even though you didn't sell any of your shares in the fund. (This is known as a capital-gains distribution.) In either case, the amount of taxes will be different, depending on whether the profits from your mutual fund are considered short-term or long-term (see the next question). You also will owe taxes on dividends that the fund distributes to you or reinvests for you. (You do not have to pay any taxes on income that you earned from tax-free money funds or tax-free municipal bond funds.)

What is the difference between short-term and long-term profits?

Short-term profits are net profits from the sale of a stock or mutual fund that was held 12 months or less. Long-term profits are net profits from the sale of a stock or mutual fund that was held for longer than 12 months. If you have made long-term profits, the most you will be taxed is 15 percent. (This rate is set to revert to 20 percent in 2011.) Short-term profits are taxed at your ordinary income-tax rate, whatever that may be (presently up to 35 percent, but the current individual tax rates are also set to expire in 2011).

What is a capital-gains distribution?

At the end of every year, all mutual funds that have made gains distribute that money among their investors, who can take the cash or reinvest it in the fund. In both cases, this is an end-of-the-year capital-gains distribution, and it will be taxed.

Why does a fund have to make an end-of-the-year capital-gains distribution?

Mutual funds are not allowed to keep the profits made from the sale of stocks that they own. Profits must be distributed among shareholders.

Am I entitled to this distribution even if I just bought into the fund?

Yes, but this is not necessarily a benefit. You get money, but you also must pay taxes on it. In addition, the fund lowers the price of its shares (or NAV) by the amount of the distribution. Unfortunately, between taxes and a lower share price, an end-of-the-year distribution could end up costing you money.

I still don't understand why such an end-of-the-year gain would be bad.

Let's say that you just bought into a mutual fund at $45 a share at the beginning of December. The NAV of the fund has stayed at about $45 for the whole month. At the end of December, the fund pays out $3 per share in short-term capital-gains distributions. To reflect this distribution, the fund lowers the price of the shares to $42. You now will owe taxes on that $3. Let's say you are in the 30 percent combined federal and state tax bracket. You will now owe $0.90 of that $3 to the government in taxes. That leaves you with $2.10. Add that to the price of the mutual fund, and you now have a total of $44.10. Of course, you bought the shares at $45 apiece. Because of the capital-gains distribution, you now have a paper loss of $0.90 a share. Worse, if you owned a lot of shares of that mutual-fund company, the distribution of short-term gains could be large enough to bump you into a higher tax bracket, costing you even more money.

If I reinvest my capital-gains distribution, do I still have to pay taxes on it?

If you're investing outside of a retirement account, yes. Taxes are always owed, regardless of whether you keep or reinvest your end-of-year distribution.

So is the lesson to avoid investing in a mutual fund in the month of December?

Not necessarily. If the fund went up in value between the time you bought it and the year's end—and it went up by more than the amount of the taxes you will owe on the capital-gains distribution—you would benefit. For example, let's say that a fund is going to hand out 5 percent in capital-gains distributions at the end of the year. You will have to pay tax on that 5 percent distribution. Assuming that you are in a 30 percent tax bracket, 1.5 percent of that gain will be lost to taxes. So your decision comes down to this: Do you think the fund will appreciate by more than 1.5 percent before the end of the year? How clear is your crystal ball?

It's impossible to say that it's *always* better to wait until the beginning of the next year to invest simply to avoid capital-gains taxes. Sometimes it is and sometimes it isn't.

Please remember two things: First, end-of-the-year capital gains are a potential problem only if you own funds outside of a retirement account. In a retirement account, capital-gains distributions do not matter, since you do not pay taxes currently on that money anyway. Second, not every mutual fund makes significant capital-gains distributions.

Are there funds that don't make capital-gains distributions?

Yes. Index funds, for example. Since index funds buy all the companies in a given index, they do not generally distribute large capital gains. Why? Because they need to buy and sell only when one of the stocks of the index is removed and replaced. This happens rarely, so trades occur with nothing

like the frequency they do in a managed fund. If the thought of paying taxes on unexpected capital gains worries you, buy into an index fund. There are also mutual funds that are known as tax-efficient funds. Managers of tax-efficient funds aim to keep a low turnover ratio in their portfolios.

Can I avoid capital-gains distributions with a low-turnover-ratio fund?

Unfortunately, no. If you buy an index fund, turnover ratio will not be a problem. However, even if a fund has a low turnover ratio, that does not mean it won't have a large capital gain one day. By the late 1990s, for example, many managed funds had in their portfolios stocks that they had held for years. Even funds that don't buy and sell stocks at a high frequency have so-called embedded capital gains, which come from long-held stocks. Embedded capital gains are earnings that a fund has in its stock portfolio that it has not yet cashed in or realized.

How do embedded capital gains work?

Here's an example: Suppose Fund A has a low turnover ratio and has owned a certain technology stock for two years. This stock accounts for nearly 20 percent of the fund's portfolio. For one reason or another, the fund manager decides that he now wants to liquidate the entire holding of this stock, which, let's say, is currently trading at $350 a share. The original purchase price of the stock—or its "cost basis"—was $50. With a profit of $300 per share, you can imagine the capital-gains tax you will owe, even at the new reduced rate of 15 percent for long-term gains. If you really want to avoid unexpected capital-gains taxes, ETFs are the way to go.

I received a dividend from my mutual fund this January, but on my statement it said that it was declared in December of the previous year. Do I owe taxes on this money for last year?

You sure do. Often a mutual fund will declare a dividend at the end of the calendar year but not pay it until January of the following year. Nevertheless, you are considered to have received the dividend in the year in which it was declared. The maximum tax you will pay will be only 15 percent as of this writing. (In 2011, though, the dividend tax rate may rise again, reverting to your ordinary income tax rate.)

If I sell a mutual fund I have lost money in, can I write off the loss?

Yes—but *only* if you sold the fund and have a realized loss, not just a paper loss. Be advised that there is a maximum deduction for capital losses during a single year—currently $3,000—unless you have capital gains to offset them. If you have gains, you can offset an equal amount of losses against them.

If I sell my mutual fund, how will I know what gains (if any) to report on my income taxes?

Your mutual fund company will send you a Form 1099-DIV, which informs you what you must report on your tax return.

I have read that capital-gains distributions must be added to the original share price of mutual funds. Does this apply if the capital gains were not reinvested in the mutual fund?

No. If the gains were not reinvested, nothing changes in regard to your holdings. However, if you reinvest your gains into the fund, where they are used to buy additional shares of the fund, they become part of your original share price (or cost basis).

I have accumulated a lot of shares in a mutual fund over the last few years, and now I want to start selling just a few of them off. What is the best way to do that, tax-wise?

I would sell off the shares that have the highest cost basis first. This will lessen your immediate tax burden. However, not many people keep track of the dates that they purchased shares of a mutual fund and what their cost basis, or purchase price, was at the time. Most mutual fund companies provide only an *average cost basis,* which is the average price for all the shares that you have purchased. You can use this figure to calculate your capital-gains taxes.

SYSTEMATIC WITHDRAWAL

I want to stay invested in the stock market, but I need money to live on. Is there a way to get money out of my growth fund on a monthly basis?

Yes. Systematic withdrawal is an ideal option for people who want to leave money in a fund for growth, yet need money to live on. In this arrangement, your mutual fund company redeems a certain amount of your shares every month and sends you the full sale-price amount. The stock market historically has grown at a rate of close to 10 percent a year, averaged over time, and most people can afford to take a share of that, say 4 or 5 percent, out of their mutual funds every year without depleting the principal.

What if there's a bear market?

Then you can call your mutual-fund company and arrange to take less in your systematic withdrawal. If there's a raging bull market, you can arrange for more. It's your money, and it's up to you.

Will I have to pay taxes on the amount that the mutual fund sends me every month?

It will depend on whether you have realized a gain over your purchase price. If you do, you will. If you don't, you won't.

Does systematic withdrawal work with all types of mutual funds, or just certain kinds?

This is a crucial question, and the answer is that systematic withdrawal works best, naturally, with a high-performing fund. That means either a growth fund, or a growth-and-income fund. Since these funds typically invest in blue-chip stocks, the chances of these funds faltering are significantly lower. I would not use the systematic withdrawal system to take money out of a bond fund. These funds typically don't grow very quickly, so you may be unintentionally gnawing away at your principal. In fact, regardless of the kind of fund you're in, you may be chipping away at your principal. If you need income and you cannot risk losing any of the principal that is generating this income, then individual bonds would be a far better investment option.

BEWARE OF FALSE DIVERSIFICATION

Over the years, many of you will accumulate a number of mutual funds. And you may believe that you have a nicely diversified portfolio. But this may not be true. Although you own several funds, it is possible that the top ten holdings of each of these funds may be identical stocks. In the 90s many investors had money in five or six growth mutual funds. The top ten holdings in those funds were all almost surely tech stocks, and most likely the same tech stocks: Cisco, Intel, Microsoft, etc. Things were going great in the late 90s, but these investors probably saw their profits and even some of their principal go down the drain in the year 2000. To be truly diversified, it's important that the holdings in your many mutual funds are not all the same.

Where can I look to find out what my mutual funds' holdings are?

Simply go to *www.morningstar.com* or *www .smartmoney.com* and compare the top ten holdings of each of your mutual funds.

Besides the holdings of the stocks within a mutual fund, how else should I be diversified when buying a mutual fund? How many funds should a person own?

If you can invest your money for growth for at least ten years, the ideal scenario is to own ten mutual funds, two in each of the following areas:

Large-growth stocks
Large-value stocks
Small-growth stocks
Small-value stocks
International stocks

But with today's ETFs and index funds, most of your needs can be covered with just one or two funds. Consider an index fund or ETF that buys the Wilshire 5000 index, as well as a fund that buys an international index.

Is there a Website that will compare my mutual funds for me to show me how well I am diversified?
If you go to *www.morningstar.com*, you will really be able to find almost anything and everything that you need to help you evaluate the funds that you currently have.

9

Bonds and
Bond Funds

In Your Interest

Bonds fall into the category of debt investments, and most people buy them for the income they produce. They are issued by a corporation, a municipality, the U.S. government, or an agency of the government that is in need of money and is willing to go into debt and borrow that money to meet its needs. When you buy a bond, you are the lender, and the issuer of the bond is the debtor.

Every long-term investor comes to the bond market eventually, but to many people bonds are even less familiar than stocks. Bonds don't usually make headlines; they're not exciting, but the fact that they're unexciting, of course, is precisely the point. So read on.

Bond Basics

What is a bond?

A bond is a debt security, or IOU, issued by a corporation or government agency in exchange for the money you lend it. In most instances, bond issuers agree to repay their loans by a specific date—and to make regular interest payments to you until that date. The interest rate, called a "coupon," does not change. That's why bonds are often referred to as "fixed-income" investments. The end date that the issuer has to pay you your principal is called the maturity date.

How far into the future can a maturity date go?

Anywhere from one to 100 years, but the usual repayment period of a long-term bond is not more than 30 years.

Why do you call the interest rate of a bond a "coupon"?

Before securities were traded electronically, buyers actually received engraved bonds from the issuer. You kept them as if they were cash, in the bank or some other safe place, because they were as good as cash. Your name as the owner was not printed on them. In order to get your interest payments, you had to physically clip one of the coupons attached to the bond and give it to the bank, which would hand you the money. Ditto for when you wanted your investment money back at maturity. This system was a blessing for crooks, but everyone else found it a nuisance, and by the early 1980s the technology was in place to toss the so-called "coupon clippers" into history's wastebasket. We're still left with "coupon," though, as a synonym for the interest figure that was printed on the bond.

When do I get my interest payments?

Most bonds pay interest semiannually, calculated backward from the month on which the bond is due to mature. So if you bought a $10,000 bond with a maturity date of June

2014 and an interest rate, or coupon, of 6 percent, your interest payments would total $600 a year. You would get $300 in June and $300 in December.

When do I get my original investment back?

With most bonds, the issuer must give you your investment money back, at face value, on the maturity date of the bond—June 2014, in our example.

What does a bond cost to buy, and what is the face value of a bond?

What a bond costs depends on when you buy it and from whom you buy it. Did you buy it from the issuer—that is, in the primary market? Or did you buy it secondhand, so to speak? Most "new" bonds are issued at what's called "par." For corporate bonds, par value is normally $1,000; for government bonds it can be much higher. If you buy a bond when it is issued, you usually pay par for it. Then, when the bond matures, you get back the par price, or face value, of the bond. The secondary market becomes important when you want to sell a bond before its maturity date, but in that market you may get par, more than par, or less than par for your bond, depending on the demand among other investors.

OK, but why would anyone want to sell a "fixed income" bond before its maturity date?

There's a market for everything, as you know, and there's one for "used" bonds. Investors might want to sell bonds before their maturity date because they need the money, or because the price other investors are willing to pay for

the bond has gone up, or perhaps because the price has gone down and they want to sell the bond at a loss and deduct the loss from their taxes.

This leads to an important point: Although you pay regular income taxes on the interest payments from many bonds, you can also generate capital gains (taxed at a rate lower than ordinary income) by selling your bond at a profit on the secondary market, if you've owned it for at least a year. Conversely, if you sell a bond for less than you paid for it, you may incur a capital loss that you can deduct from your income taxes.

What makes a bond's price go up and down? I thought a bond was a fixed income investment, meaning nothing about it changes.

Even though a bond's interest rate and maturity date are fixed, the price at which you can sell a bond on the secondary market, before its maturity date, is not fixed. That's because the economic environment in which bonds are bought and sold is never fixed. In particular, as the Federal Reserve Bank tries to dampen inflation or spur growth by changing federal interest rates, the demand for bonds—and their selling price—goes up or down.

Imagine, for example, that you bought $10,000 worth of a ten-year bond that pays a 6 percent coupon. Now, suddenly, the Fed raises interest rates to 8 percent. Understandably, you might want to sell your bond and buy one with the higher interest rate. Trouble is, who in their right mind would want to buy your bond at the price you paid for it—par, or $10,000?—when the coupon is only 6 percent? No one, since anyone who wants a bond can go out and buy a new one and get an 8 percent coupon. So, in order to sell your bond, you would have to lower the price. Think about it. If the selling price for your bond were lowered to about $8,000 and the person who bought your bond would be getting $600 a year (6 percent of the $10,000 face value of the bond), then, at the $8,000 price, the bond's *yield* would rise to 7.5 percent. Someone might think about buying it at that price—especially because, when the bond matures, it will pay him or her the face value, or $10,000. So not only would the buyer be getting a good *current yield*, but his *yield to maturity* would be so good that it would make this bond competitive with the new bonds paying higher interest rates.

So I can sell a bond at any time from the moment I purchase it from the issuer to the moment of its maturity?

That's right. Depending on what is happening in the Fed-controlled interest-rate environment, the price of a bond on the secondary market may go above or below par. The dynamic is quite simple once you get the hang of it. When general interest rates go up, the current price of bonds goes down. And when general interest rates go down, the current price of bonds goes up. If you pay above par, you've bought at what's called a *premium*. If you pay below par, you've bought at a *discount*.

What does the term "current yield" mean?

It's a very important concept! The current yield is the real interest rate of a bond, based on what you paid for it. Let's go back to that 6 percent $10,000 bond that you bought from the issuer.

At the moment you bought it, your current yield was just what the coupon said—6 percent, or $600 a year. Since then, however, the interest-rate environment has changed, downward this time, with the result that your bond is now selling on the secondary market for more than you paid for it—say, about $11,000. You decide to sell. But the would-be buyer, if he's experienced, must now calculate his current yield before going on to purchase the bond for $11,000. The bond will always have a fixed coupon of 6 percent, or $600 a year, but since the buyer will be paying $11,000 for that yield, his *current* yield is really only 5.45 percent. Current yield is what a bond purchased on the secondary market will really yield, right now, once the price paid on the secondary market is taken into account. Never buy a bond from anyone other than the issuer without first calculating the current yield. Then, still before you buy, calculate the yield to maturity.

What is "yield to maturity"?

Yield to maturity is the actual percentage return you will make on your money at the end of the bond's life. It includes not only the coupon yield—in our example, $600 a year—and the $10,000 par value you get back at maturity, but also the discount or premium you paid for the bond on the secondary market. If you bought the bond from the issuer and you kept it to maturity, your current yield and the yield to maturity would both be 6 percent. But if you bought a ten-year bond, for example, two years after it was issued and paid $11,000 for it, then you would have to figure in an overpayment of $1,000 when calculating your yield to maturity.

Why? Because when the bond matures you will get $10,000, and that is a loss of $1,000, given what you paid for the bond. The current yield in this case would be 5.45 percent, but the yield to maturity, including that $1,000 loss, would be 4.5 percent. Basically, with yield to maturity, you have to spread your $1,000 loss over eight years of collecting interest on the bond. On the other hand, if you bought the bond two years after it was issued for $8,000 and it matured eight years later at $10,000, your current yield would be 7.5 percent, but your yield to maturity would be 9.7 percent. In this case, you are spreading out a $2,000 gain. That is, unless your bond has a *call feature*.

What is a "call feature"?

Most issuers of bonds protect themselves with a call feature against paying more interest than the current market demands. A call feature allows the issuer to give you your money back before the maturity date of the bond or, in the language of bonds, to "call in" the bond. The call feature tells you at what point the bond can be called in, as well as how much the issuer has to pay you if it does call in the bond.

Under what circumstance would an issuer call in a bond before its maturity date?

An issuer might call in a bond if interest rates come down after the bond has been issued. The issuer can then pay off all the investors and issue a new bond at a lower interest rate. But the call feature is not such a good thing for the investor. Let's say you bought a $1,000 30-year bond that was issued in 1989 with a coupon of 9 percent. And let's say that this bond had a call feature

specifying that after the year 2000 the bond could be called in at a price of $1,020 a bond. Remember that you paid par, or $1,000, for the bond when you bought it. The issuer could take the bond back by paying you a mere $20 premium. Now that may not seem like such a bad deal, but what if current interest rates are only at 7 percent when this happens? If you still need income, you will only be able to invest this money at 7 percent, instead of the 9 percent you were getting.

Beware of call features when you buy a bond. You do not want to have to give up a good interest rate without your consent. Corporate and municipal bonds can have a call feature; Treasuries seldom do. (The exceptions are Treasuries issued before 1985.) Government agency bonds (such as Ginnie Maes and Freddie Macs) are all callable.

PURCHASING BONDS

How can I buy a bond?

The most common way to buy bonds is to open an account with a broker and place your order. You can use either a full-service broker or a discount broker to execute your trades. EE, I Bonds, and Treasury securities can also be purchased directly from the U.S. Treasury Department. For more information visit the TreasuryDirect Website at *www.treasurydirect.gov*.

How much do brokers charge in commissions?

Watch out! Bond brokers are tricky when it comes to their commissions. They usually build them into the price of the bond. Moreover, commissions vary widely from brokerage firm to brokerage firm. Thus, the same bond can give you a different return on your investment, depending on where you buy it. Be sure to shop around.

Do all bonds trade on the secondary bond market as easily as stocks trade on the stock market?

Like some stocks, some bonds aren't readily sold, or "liquid." Others, like Treasuries, sell in huge numbers all the time. Make sure the bonds that you are considering are quality bonds that can be easily sold. (I'll say more about this later.)

How are bond prices listed?

The price of a bond is always quoted in hundreds—not in thousands—of its par value. In the newspaper and on your monthly statement, a bond will be valued at $100, for instance, which seems puzzling. But just add a zero to the number, and you will get the true figure—$1,000.

BOND RATINGS

What's the best way to gauge the quality of a bond?

The best way is by consulting the rating on your bond by the two major independent rating services, Standard & Poor's and Moody's. The agencies rate bonds for safety—that is, the trustworthiness of the issuer to deliver on his IOU. Here's how each agency rates bonds, from the highest quality to the lowest:

- Standard & Poor's: AAA, AA+, AA, AA-, A+, A, A-, BBB+, BBB, BBB-, BB+, BB, BB-, B+, B, B-, CCC, and D.
- Moody's: Aaa, Aa1, Aa2, Aa3, A1, A2, A3, Baa1, Baa2, Baa3, Ba1, Ba2, Ba3, B1, B2, B3, Caa, Ca, and C.

For safety, you should consider only bonds that have a rating in the A categories; otherwise, even though you might find a higher interest rate, you could be risking your principal.

INTEREST RATES AND BONDS

Why do different bonds offer different interest rates?

The interest rate offered by a company or government agency on its bonds depends on several things: the interest rate environment at the time of issue, the issuer's reputation for safety (the interest rate must be higher if there's any risk that the issuer won't pay you back), and the length of maturity of the bond. The bottom line here is that issuers are competing to borrow your money. They know that lenders—that's you—want to get the highest interest rate available, or one that's at least competitive with other comparable rates on offer. If you could get 7 percent on a safe bond with one issuer, why on earth would you buy a bond from an identically safe issuer at 6 percent?

How does the maturity date affect the interest rate?

Theoretically, the longer an issuer asks you to tie up your money, the more the issuer should be willing to pay. After all, the issuer is asking you to take the risk that interest rates may rise between the time you buy the bond and the time it reaches maturity, and so you may potentially lose out on higher rates. However, this is not always the way things work. If a bond is issued at a time when interest rates are higher and are projected to go down, the issuer may offer higher rates for shorter maturities than for longer maturities. Therefore, it's very important to check the coupon of bonds offered at different maturities, for it may not pay you to commit your money for longer periods of time. For instance, if a ten-year bond is paying 5 percent and a 30-year bond is paying 5.1 percent, it's probably not worth tying up your money for 30 years unless you really believe that interest rates are going to be considerably lower than 5 percent in ten years.

Can you go back over how the overall interest rate environment affects bonds?

Just remember the cardinal rule of investing in bonds. As interest rates go up, bond prices go down on the secondary market, and as interest rates go down, bond prices go up on the secondary market. It's as simple as that.

Reality, of course, sometimes puts a wrench into the works. A bond's price does vary with changes in overall interest rates. But a bond's price on the secondary market is also influenced by the quality of the bond, the coupon, and the years remaining until it matures. The further away the maturity date and the lower the quality of the bond, the more volatile the price of a bond will be—in other words, the more it will move up or down as interest rates change. The closer the maturity date and the higher the qual-

ity of the bond, the less movement in price there will be as interest rates change.

THE RISKS OF BOND OWNERSHIP

I was told that owning a bond was safe, safe, safe, but surely there are risks?

Yes, there are no fewer than six kinds of risk—risks people usually do not think of when buying a bond. They are interest-rate risk, call risk, credit risk, inflation risk, event risk, and reinvestment risk.

What is interest-rate risk?

Interest-rate risk takes into account the fact that the market value of your bonds could fall due to rising interest rates. In general, as we've seen, bond prices decline when interest rates rise—and rise when interest rates fall.

What is call risk?

Call risk is the risk that the issuer of your bond could call, or prepay, it. During periods of declining interest rates, corporate and municipal bond issuers prefer to prepay their loans before maturity and reissue the loans at a lower interest rate. You, as lender, then must reinvest your principal earlier than you had expected—and probably also at a lower interest rate.

What is credit risk?

Credit risk is a gamble on the creditworthiness of the issuer. If a bond issuer defaults—that is, fails to make timely payments of principal and interest—or if a bond's credit rating is reduced, thereby reducing its resale value, you could lose money.

What is inflation risk?

Inflation, a rise in the price of the goods and services we all consume, is a general risk of financial life. It can erode the value of your paycheck, of your stocks, and especially of your bonds. Before buying a bond, please take into account any signs of increasing inflation. Among other things, inflation can make your fixed interest rate less valuable and can mean a rise in overall interest rates above the rates on the bond you're considering buying.

What is event risk?

Event risk refers to the possibility that the company or agency that issued your bond will undergo a change and that the credit quality or market value of your bonds could suffer in response to an event such as a merger, a leveraged buyout, or other corporate restructuring.

What is reinvestment risk?

That's just another name for the risks you run from changes in the economic environment that cut into the yield of any new investment you are forced to make.

LADDERING BONDS

I can see that time is a huge factor in the bond market, so it might make sense to buy bonds with different maturity dates. Is that right?

That is exactly right. Buying bonds with different maturity dates is a time-tested technique called "laddering." Here's why it's a good idea. Let's say you have $100,000 to invest in bonds and you want to generate income. Instead of taking the entire $100,000 and buying bonds that mature at the same time—for example, in five years—you might put $20,000 each into bonds that mature in one, two, three, four, and five years. This way, you would have $20,000 coming due to you every year for the next five years. If interest rates went up, you would simply replace the maturing bond with another bond at a higher interest rate. If interest rates remained the same, you would have lost nothing. If interest rates went down, well, you would still have some of your money invested for the next few years in bonds at the higher rate.

But suppose bonds are selling with high interest rates at the time I buy?

When interest rates are high and are expected to fall (as in the early 1980s), it is best to buy bonds with long maturities (10 to 30 years) and not to ladder them. If you had bought 30-year Treasury bonds in the 1980s, you could still be getting 15 percent a year today.

TYPES OF BONDS

The bonds that you will most commonly come into contact with on the road to wealth are government-issued bonds such as Treasury bonds, savings bonds, and municipal bonds; U.S. mortgage-backed securities such as Ginnie Maes, Fannie Maes, and Freddie Macs; corporate bonds and convertible bonds; and zero coupon bonds.

TREASURIES

What is a Treasury bond?

A Treasury bond is a bond issued by the U.S. government. Income from Treasuries is exempt from taxes at the state and local level. This is important to keep in mind, because a Treasury paying 6 percent will give you more income after taxes than a CD paying 6 percent if you live in a state and/or city that imposes income taxes. Income from Treasuries *is* taxed by the federal government, however.

What is the yield on Treasury bonds?

The yield on Treasuries is usually the lowest of all bonds with comparable maturities. That's the price you pay for Treasuries' unequaled safety. Treasuries are 100 percent guaranteed by the U.S. government. Only a government can make that guarantee, of course, because only a government can print more money or raise taxes, or both, in the event that it has trouble meeting its obligations. But for this kind of security, you get a slightly lower coupon.

Do all Treasuries have the same maturity?

No. In fact, Treasuries of different maturities are known by different names:

A Treasury bill (T-bill) is usually 90 days to 12 months to maturity.

A Treasury note is usually 1 to 10 years to maturity.

A Treasury bond is usually 10 to 30 years to maturity.

Do Treasury bills pay interest?

Strictly speaking, no. Because they have such short maturities (one year and under), Treasury bills do not make interest payments before maturity. Instead, they are priced at a discount and mature at par. The difference between what you pay for the bill and what you get for it at maturity (par)—or what you get for it if you sell it prior to maturity—is the interest earned on the bill. For example, when you buy a Treasury bill, it might cost you $4,800; when it matures nine months later, you might get back $5,000. That extra $200 is your interest.

I suppose I owe federal taxes on that interest, but when do I pay it, in the year I bought the T-bill or in the year in which it matures?

With a T-bill, the year in which you receive back your investment plus interest is the year for which you owe taxes on any earnings. If you buy a T-bill in 2010 and it matures in 2011, you won't owe taxes on your interest until 2011. When people buy large numbers of Treasury bills, they should take tax vulnerability at the time of maturity into account.

What are TIPS?

TIPS are Treasury Inflation-Indexed Securities also sometimes referred to as Treasury Inflation-Protected Securities. TIPS are considered to be the safest type of investment because their ultimate value cannot be diminished by inflation.

Since the principal value of these securities is adjusted to the Consumer Price Index, TIPS are protected against inflation. TIPS are similar to other notes and bonds in that you receive interest payments every six months and a payment of principal when the security matures. *But* with TIPS the interest and redemption payments are tied to inflation. Unlike other marketable Treasury securities, TIPS can't be reinvested. Similar to other Treasury notes and bonds, TIPS are exempt from state and local income taxes, and subject to federal income tax. In regards to federal taxes, there is one issue to be aware of: In any year when the principal of your TIPS increases, that gain is reportable income for that year even though you won't receive your inflation-adjusted principal until the security matures.

Do Treasury notes and bonds pay interest?

Yes. Every six months you will receive your interest payments. Federal taxes will be due when you file that year's tax return.

Where is the best place to buy Treasuries?

The best way to buy a Treasury that's just been issued by the government is through what's known as a TreasuryDirect account, which you can set up directly with the U.S. Treasury Department. You can also buy a Treasury through a broker, but the broker—unlike TreasuryDirect—will charge you a fee.

Will a TreasuryDirect account do anything else besides provide me access to commission-free Treasuries?

Yes. A TreasuryDirect account will hold your TIPS, T-bills, T-notes, and T-bonds, and any interest you earn on these can be electronically deposited in the account. You will receive a statement when your Treasuries are issued, reinvested, or redeemed, or when any other changes are made to your account. Or, if you have a brokerage or money-market account, automatic payments of interest and principal can be made electronically to that account. Contact TreasuryDirect on the World Wide Web at *www .treasurydirect.gov*, or call (800) 722-2678.

SAVINGS BONDS

What is a savings bond?

A savings bond is another type of bond issued by the U.S. government. You can buy savings bonds in face values ranging from $50 to $10,000. One great advantage of these bonds is that they come in so many denominations. (Another advantage is that, like all federal bonds, they pay interest that is exempt from state and local taxes, though not from federal taxes.) Many people have received savings bonds as gifts from parents or grandparents, have bought them as savings vehicles for themselves, or have given them to children. The problem is that there's a tendency to put them away and never look at them again. This is a big mistake. After their maturity and an extension period (please see below), savings bonds, like other bonds, stop earning interest. Over a longer period of time, even a low rate of inflation can seriously erode their face value. If you buy or own savings bonds, please remember to redeem them when they have reached their full maturity and/or after you've reached the end of your extensions. There are two kinds of savings bonds currently being issued, known as series EE/E and I bonds. (Series E bonds, the predecessor to EE bonds, are no longer issued by the U.S. Treasury, nor are Series HH/H bonds, though many people still hold them.)

What is a series EE/E savings bond?

A series EE/E bond is a savings bond that you purchase at a 50 percent discount from face value when you purchase the paper bonds. When you buy a $100 EE/E bond, for example, you pay only 50 percent of that amount, or $50. However, electronic bonds purchased via TreasuryDirect are sold at face value—please see *www.treasurydirect.gov* for more details. As with Treasury bills, the interest on the bond is not paid out to you; it goes back into the bond until (or, sometimes, even after) the bond has reached its face value, in this case $100. At that point, the bond has matured. An EE/E bond these days pays a fixed rate of interest.

How is interest calculated on a series EE/E bond?

That depends on the date of the bond. If you had bought your bond before 1995, you would have been guaranteed a minimum rate of interest—for example, 4 percent—or a variable, or market, rate, whichever was greater. If you bought your bond after May 1995 through April 2005, your bond earns a variable, or market, rate based on market yields of U.S. Treasury securities. With a variable rate, the amount of time it takes to reach face value varies, too—it may happen quickly or slowly, depending on how high or low market interest rates are during the period you hold your bond. You can find details on how

interest is calculated for bonds issued in these years at *www.treasurydirect.gov*. Bonds purchased after April 2005 pay a fixed rate of interest. If you decide to redeem an EE/E bond before it reaches face value, please call the Treasury department to find out the current yield—that is, what dollar amount you'll get if you redeem the bond right now. If you redeem EE/E bonds in the first five years, you'll forfeit the three most recent months' interest. After five years, there is no penalty.

The interest on an EE/E series bond compounds twice a year (when new rates are announced, on May 1 and November 1 of every year), but interest is "paid" only when the bond is redeemed. As you have seen, you can redeem your bond at any time before maturity, at maturity, or even after maturity (during one or more extension periods that prolong your interest payments after the bond has reached face value). If you hold your bond long enough, its redemption value will eventually exceed its face value.

How do I find out when my EE/E bonds mature?

First, let me explain a little more about how EE/E bonds "mature." "Original maturity" is the term used for the date when an EE/E bond achieves its face value. Bond owners often mistakenly assume that EE/E bonds stop earning interest when they reach their face value, but they don't. They go on earning interest until what's called "final maturity."

Basically, with an EE/E bond, face value isn't crucial. Final maturity is what's really important. This is the point at which your extension periods run out and *beyond* which your bond will no longer earn any interest and not increase in face value. The final maturity on all EE/E savings bonds issued after 1965 is 30 years from the date of original issue. Check your savings bond inventory from time to time and promptly cash in or exchange all bonds that are no longer earning interest. If you don't redeem bonds that have reached their final maturity, you will be lending the U.S. government money free of charge.

Find the issue date on your series EE/E bond and match it to the issue date in the table on the next page, and you'll find your bond's original maturity and its final maturity.

What happens after a bond reaches its "original" maturity date?

It sounds complicated, but it really isn't. The original maturity date is simply the date when the bond achieves its face value. At this point, without your doing anything at all, the bond will enter what is known as an extension period. The extension period can last as long as the difference between your original issue date and 30 years from that issue date. During the extension period, your bond will continue to earn interest; in other words, it will keep accumulating value—but not forever.

After 30 years is when the trouble can begin. At *final* maturity, bonds stop earning interest, though you can still redeem them. So if you or your parents have some bonds hidden away, please go find them and check their final maturities.

What if the bonds I have in my desk drawer haven't reached final maturity?

They'll still be earning interest. During their extension, Series EE/E or savings bonds issued at the dates below earn these guaranteed minimum yield rates:

11/82–10/86	7.5 percent
11/86–2/93	6 percent
03/93–4/95	4 percent
05/95–present	There is no guaranteed minimum yield for bonds entering an extension during this period.

How can I calculate my interest?

The Savings Bond Earnings Report—online at *www.treasurydirect.gov/indiv/tools/tools_earnings reports.htm*—will tell you what your bond is currently earning and will give you the current value of $100 EE and E bonds. If you don't happen to have $100 bonds, you can calculate the value of your bonds by multiplying or dividing by the appropriate number. For example, if you have a $50 bond, just divide the current value of the $100 bond by 2. If you have a $500 bond, multiply the value of the $100 bond by 5.

How and when do I redeem my EE/E savings bonds?

You can redeem your bonds at any time, but be prepared for a significant tax hit if you have not been reporting your interest payments on your tax returns. The bonds are exempt from state and local taxes, but not federal taxes. Before 2004 you could spread out the tax bite by exchanging your matured bonds for HH/H bonds—whose interest must be reported annually—but that option is no longer available.

Is a series EE/E bond a good vehicle for saving for college?

THE FINAL MATURITY OF SAVINGS BONDS, BASED ON ISSUE DATE		
Original Issue EE/E Bond	Final Maturity, in Years	Final Maturity Date
1965 or earlier	40	2005 or earlier
01/80–10/80	30	01/2010–10/2010
11/80–04/81	30	11/2010–04/2011
05/81–10/82	30	05/2011–10/2012
11/82–10/86	30	11/2012–10/2016
11/86–02/93	30	11/2016–02/2023
03/93–04/95	30	03/2023–04/2025
05/95–present	30	05/2025–

Yes, it can be. If you redeem an EE/E bond to pay for a child's qualified education expenses, you may not owe any federal taxes on the interest—that is, if your income is not too high for you to qualify. (In 2009, the income limits on using tax-advantaged EE/E bonds to pay for your child's education were as follows: For single taxpayers, the tax exclusion began to be reduced with a $69,950 modified adjusted gross income and was eliminated for adjusted gross incomes of $84,950 and above *in the year the educational expenses were paid*. For married taxpayers filing jointly, the tax exclusion began to be reduced with a $104,900 modified adjusted gross income and was eliminated for adjusted gross incomes of $134,900 and above *in the year the educational expenses were paid*.) Consult a tax preparer to discuss your situation.

In what denominations are series EE/E savings bonds available?

The paper bonds are available in denominations of $50, $75, $100, $200, $500, $1,000, $5,000, and $10,000, while electronic bonds can be purchased for $25 or more. The maximum allowed purchase per calendar year in series EE/E bonds is $5,000 in TreasuryDirect electronic bonds and $5,000 in paper bonds ($10,000 face value). Before 2008, the maximum had been higher at $30,000. (There is no maximum on the HH/H series. See below.)

Tax considerations apart, do series HH/H bonds work the same way as EE/E bonds?

No. Series HH/H bonds are known as current-income securities. The HH/H bond doesn't accumulate value the way the EE/E series does. When an HH/H bond was issued, you paid the full face value ($500, $1,000, $5,000, or $10,000) and then you receive interest every six months—"current income," so it's taxed on an annual basis. The interest payments on HH/H bonds can be deposited directly into any account you designate. How much interest will you earn? You learned that on the day you bought the bond, because the rate is fixed. Bonds issued January 1, 2003, through August 2004 earn 1.5 percent for their initial 10-year maturity period. Though the U.S. Treasury no longer issues HH/H bonds, the HH bonds you already own are secure; you can find out more details about rates and terms at *http://www.treasurydirect.gov/indiv/products/prod_hhbonds_glance.htm.*

Here's a schedule for when HH/H bonds reach final maturity:

Series H

Original Issue Date	Final Maturity, in years
June 1952–January 1957	29 years, 8 months
February 1957–December 1979	30 years
Series HH (January 1980–August 2004)	20 years

What is a series I bond?

If you are looking for a place to park non-retirement account money that you want to keep safe and sound, don't need current income from, and will not need to withdraw for at least five years, you might want to look into purchasing a relatively new kind of federal savings bond called a series I bond.

Series I bonds are issued by the federal government as a protection against inflation. They have a variable interest rate, but differ from series EE/E bonds in that the I bond's interest rate changes according to rises or—theoretically—decreases in the consumer price index (a measure of inflation) rather than a change in market interest rates. If inflation goes up, so does the interest rate on these bonds. Series I bonds are available in a minimum denomination of $50 for paper bond certificates and a minimum denomination of $25 for I bonds purchased electronically. Paper I bonds can be purchased in denominations of $50, $75, $100, $200, $500, $1,000 and $5,000 while electronic I bonds can be purchased in amounts of $25 or more, to the penny. They are issued at face value, so a $500 I bond will cost you $500. You can buy a maximum of $5,000 in TreasuryDirect electronic bonds and $5,000 in paper bonds per calendar year. All I bonds mature in 30 years. They are exempt from state and local taxes, and you won't owe federal taxes until the bonds are redeemed.

How do series I bonds work?

The bond's inflation-adjusted interest rates are calculated twice a year by adding a fixed rate of return to a multiple of the current inflation rate. An I bond issued after May 2009 earns a 0.10 percent fixed rate of return over and above the rate of inflation. In May 2009, the market saw the rare case of deflation. The annualized rate of inflation as measured by the consumer price index was 2.78 percent. In other words, bonds bought from May 1, 2009, through October 31, 2009, earn 0.00 percent because the inflation rate of 2.78 percent fell by more than the fixed rate of the I bond. The I bond rate will never go below zero. Had the consumer price index instead gained 2.78 percent, a "composite," or compound, earnings rate of 5.66 percent would have been achieved. The 0.10 percent portion of the rate is fixed for the life of this bond, even though the consumer price index—and your inflation adjustment—will change. New inflation adjustments are announced on May 1 and

November 1 of every year. Your interest compounds semiannually and is paid when the bond is redeemed. Information on the current calculation of the I bond rate can be found at *www.treasurydirect.gov.*

Why shouldn't you invest in I bonds if you need current income? Because interest on I bonds is not paid out until the bond matures or until you cash it in. Why should you use only money that you won't need for at least the next five years? Because if you come out of an I bond before five years are up, you will be charged a three-month interest penalty. If you cash in anytime after five years have passed, you can come out without any penalty at all. (However, all I bonds must be kept for a minimum of twelve months.) Finally, why are I bonds not suitable for retirement accounts? Because the interest on I bonds is tax-deferred until you withdraw the money, and at that time only federal income taxes will be owed. It makes no sense to invest retirement money in a tax-deferred account, because all retirement accounts are tax-deferred anyway. All I bonds are exempt from state income tax. I Bonds can also qualify for tax-free withdrawals for certain higher education expenses if you qualify.

How do I purchase series EE and/or series I savings bonds?

Series EE and/or series I savings bonds can be purchased through most local banks or through a payroll savings plan offered by many employers. The bank takes payment and applications for bonds and forwards them to a federal reserve bank, where the actual bonds are issued and mailed to the owner. The bond issue date is the date of the application so no interest is lost. Bonds are delivered within 15 business days. You can also buy bonds online from the U.S. Treasury at *www.treasurydirect.gov.*

What is the difference between savings bonds and Treasury bonds?

Treasury bills, notes, and bonds are transferable, so that the owner of a Treasury bond can sell the bond prior to maturity, but a savings bond cannot be transferred. Savings bonds are a paper security, unlike Treasury bills, notes, and bonds, which are electronic. The minimum required to purchase Treasury bills, notes, and bonds is $1,000 (and additional amounts must be in multiples of $1,000), versus a savings bond, which you can purchase for as little as $25. Both savings bonds and Treasury bonds are issued by the Department of the Treasury.

MUNICIPAL BONDS

What is a municipal bond?

A municipal bond is a bond issued by a municipal, county, or state government agency. Generally, all municipal bonds are free of federal income taxes. If you want to avoid state income tax as well, you must purchase a municipal bond from the state in which you are currently living. Because of the tax advantage, the interest rate paid on municipal bonds is typically lower than that on other kinds of bonds. Also because of the tax advantage, they are typically held outside of retirement accounts.

How do I know if it is better for me to buy a

tax-free bond, such as a municipal bond, or a taxable bond?

To figure out whether it's better for you to buy a tax-free bond or a taxable bond, divide the tax-free yield by the difference between your tax bracket and 100 percent. That will give you the equivalent taxable yield. For instance, if your tax bracket is 28 percent, and you are thinking about buying a municipal bond with a coupon, or interest rate, of 4 percent, first subtract 0.28 from 1.00, which gives you 0.72. Then divide the interest rate of the bond that you are considering, 4, by 0.72, and that will give you the equivalent taxable yield: 4 divided by 0.72 equals about 5.5 percent. If you can get a taxable bond that gives you a yield higher than the 5.5 percent you would, in effect, be getting on a municipal bond, then you should buy the taxable bond, subject to safety concerns, of course.

When do municipal bonds usually mature?

The maturity of municipal bonds ranges from five to 30 years.

Are there different kinds of municipal bonds?

Yes, there are two kinds, revenue bonds and general obligation bonds. Revenue bonds are used to finance municipal projects that generate revenue (a toll road, for example). The revenue generated by the project is then used to make interest and principal payments to the bondholders. The danger here is that if the revenues do not come in, the bondholders are at risk of losing money.

General obligation bonds are my favorite. The best ones are those backed by the "full faith and credit" of the state or local government issuing the bond and repaid out of general tax assessments by that government. If the government is solvent, this makes them safe.

How do I know if municipal bonds are right for me?

They may be right for you if you are in a high tax bracket and the yield on a municipal bond is greater than the after-tax yield on a taxable bond. If so, it makes total sense for you to consider municipals.

U.S. MORTGAGE–BACKED BONDS

You mentioned Ginnie Maes, Fannie Maes, and Freddie Macs. How do they work?

They are bonds issued by quasi-governmental agencies, with some backing by the U.S. government. They are considered safe bonds. Ginnie Mae, for example, is an acronym for the Government National Mortgage Association. Ginnie Maes are issued to assure that there's enough money in the banking system for homeowners, especially those applying for mortgages through the Federal Housing Authority or the Veterans Administration, to tap into for mortgages. Fannie Maes are bonds issued by the Federal National Mortgage Association, and Freddie Macs are bonds of the Federal Home Loan Mortgage Corporation.

How do I know if these bonds are right for me?

Unlike Treasury bonds and notes, which make interest payments every six months, Ginnie

Maes pay interest once a month. If you are looking for monthly income, Ginnie Maes may not be a bad place to start—but learn the facts first, so you won't be surprised. Ginnie Maes typically pay 0.5 to 1 percent above the rate a regular Treasury pays, and they usually have maturities of 15 to 30 years. However, payment schedules show that 80 to 90 percent of Ginnie Maes are "called"—that is, paid off—by the 12th year.

What are the drawbacks of Ginnie Maes?

The reason Ginnie Maes pay monthly is that mortgage borrowers pay monthly, and those mortgage payments are passed right on to the investor. When interest rates go down and homeowners refinance their mortgages, or pay off their loans ahead of time, then Ginnie Mae has to pass those reductions on to you. Thus, at the very time when you want to be locked into the high interest rate of your original investment, you may be getting all your money back.

Another thing to consider: Mortgage payments comprise both interest and principal. Here's how this could affect you. Let's say you bought a Ginnie Mae bond for $25,000, with a coupon of 6 percent. The next month, you would get a payment of $125 in interest—but you might also get a $75 payment of principal. Because you got a principal payment, you no longer have a full $25,000 that's earning interest in the bond; you have only $24,925. This return of principal might (or might not) continue with every payment, so that by the end of the year (depending on how quickly people are paying off their mortgages), you could have only $23,500 earning 6 percent. The next year, that amount could dwindle to $21,000, and so on.

Your interest rate is staying the same, but the amount of money on which you are earning interest is declining.

People who invest in Ginnie Maes, Fannie Maes, and Freddie Macs tend to forget that these agencies are mortgage holders and that, as such, investors will be getting back some principal every month. Often, they spend the principal along with the interest, instead of reinvesting it. When the bond finally matures (or is paid back), these folks may have very little principal remaining in the bond, and that can be a rude shock.

Even so, U.S. mortgage–backed bonds are great bonds to look into, especially when interest rates are low and you would like a slightly higher interest rate. The minimum investment for an individual Ginnie Mae bond is $25,000; minimum investments in Fannie Maes and Freddie Macs vary according to the particular security, but tend to start lower. You also can invest in a Ginnie Mae fund, in which your minimum investment will be much lower. Make sure, however, that it is a no-load fund with low expense ratios.

CORPORATE BONDS

What are corporate bonds?

Corporate bonds (also called corporates) are debt obligations, or IOUs, issued by private and publicly traded corporations. They are typically issued in multiples of $1,000 or $5,000. Companies use the funds they raise from selling bonds for a variety of purposes, from building offices and factories and purchasing equipment to buying other companies.

When you buy a corporate bond, you are

lending money to the corporation that issued it, which promises to return your money, or principal, at a specified maturity date. Until that time, the company also pays you a stated rate of interest, usually twice a year. The interest payments you receive from corporate bonds are taxable. Unlike stocks, bonds do not give you an ownership interest in the issuing corporation.

Is it easy to buy and sell corporate bonds?

Yes. The corporate bond market is large and liquid, with daily trading volume estimated at $12.8 billion. Bonds are bought and sold on two separate markets: the New York Stock Exchange (NYSE), where major corporations' debt issues are quoted and traded every day, and the over-the-counter (OTC) market, which is made up of bond dealers and brokers around the country. The OTC market is much bigger than the exchange market; most bond transactions, even those involving listed issues, take place in this market.

What are the benefits of investing in corporate bonds?

The benefits include yields that are usually higher than comparable-maturity government bonds or CDs; relative safety (based on credit rating); and marketability. If you must sell a bond before maturity, you can usually do so easily and quickly because of the size and liquidity of the market.

Who issues corporate bonds?

There are five main categories of issuers, representing various sectors of the economy. These include public utilities; transportation companies; industrial companies; financial services compa-

nies; and conglomerates. Issuers may be U.S. companies or foreign companies. Foreign governments are also frequent issuers in the U.S. market.

I've heard of a sinking-fund provision—what's that?

A sinking fund is money taken from a corporation's earnings that is used to redeem bonds periodically, before maturity. If a bond issue has a sinking-fund provision, a certain portion of the issue must be retired each year. It's like a call feature, except that the bonds retired are usually selected by lottery.

One investor benefit of a sinking fund is that it lowers the risk of default by reducing the amount of the corporation's outstanding debt over time. Another is that it provides price support for the bond in the secondary market, particularly in a period of rising interest rates. However, investors may also lose a source of income if their bond is called in. In a period of falling rates, they may have to reinvest their money at a lower rate.

What happens if the company whose bond I hold goes bankrupt?

If the company defaults on its debt or goes out of business, you, as a creditor, will have priority for repayment over stockholders. But you may not have priority over other creditors. The order of repayment depends on the specific terms of the bond, among other things. So-called "secured bonds" are usually the ones to look for if you want safety in case of a default.

What is a secured bond? And what does unsecured mean?

If a bond is secured, the issuer has pledged specific assets (known as collateral) that can be sold, if necessary, to pay the bondholders. If you buy a secured bond, you will "pay" for the extra safety in the form of a lower interest rate than you would have received on a comparable unsecured bond, which is simply an obligation to pay backed by the issuer's general credit, with no collateral pledged.

Give me a rundown of the different types of corporate bonds.

Sure. It goes like this:

- *Debenture bonds.* Most corporate bonds are debentures—that is, unsecured debt obligations repaid out of the corporation's earnings on its products or services. However, even unsecured bonds have additional security in the event that the company subsequently pledges its assets as collateral on other debt obligations.
- *Mortgage bonds.* These are bonds for which real estate or other physical property worth more than the bonds has been pledged as collateral. They are mostly issued by public utilities. Sometimes the same assets are also being pledged to a separate group of creditors, so whenever you invest in mortgage bonds, find out how much of the issuer's other debt is secured by the same collateral.
- *Collateral trust bonds.* A company can deposit stocks and other securities with a trustee as collateral for its bonds. The collateral must have a market value at least equal to the value of the bonds being secured.

- *Equipment trust certificates.* Typically, railroads and airlines issue these bonds as a way to pay for new equipment. A trustee holds the ownership of the equipment until the loan is paid off, and the investors who buy the certificates usually have a first claim on the equipment.
- *Subordinated debentures.* Subordinated debentures are debt that is subordinated, or junior, and so has a lower repayment priority than that of other debt (but a higher priority than stocks). Only after secured bonds and debentures are paid off can holders of subordinated debentures be paid. In exchange for this lower level of security, investors earn a higher rate of interest.
- *Guaranteed bonds.* Guaranteed bonds are actually guaranteed by another corporation—that is, a corporation different from the one that issued the debt. For example, bonds issued by an incorporated subsidiary of a company might be guaranteed by its parent corporation.

How do I pay taxes on corporate bonds?

Interest payments from corporate bonds are subject to federal and state income taxes at your ordinary income tax rate. (If you own shares in bond mutual funds, your interest will come to you in the form of "dividends," but these are fully taxable, too.)

What is the minimum investment in a corporate bond?

Bonds are issued and sold in $1,000 denominations. For OTC bonds, the minimum investment is usually $5,000.

How much is the commission on a corporate bond?

Brokers often sell bonds from their firms' inventory, in which case investors do not pay an outright commission. Rather, they pay a markup that is built into the price quoted for the bond. If a broker has to go out into the market to find a particular bond for a customer, a commission may be charged. Each firm establishes its own markups and commissions, which may vary depending on the size of the transaction and the type of bond you are buying. Please shop around.

CONVERTIBLE BONDS

I've heard that you can buy bonds that can later be converted to stocks. Is that right?

Yes, it is. *Convertible* bonds are issued by corporations as debt with the option to convert the bond into stock, or ownership, in that company at a predetermined price.

How do I know if convertible bonds are right for me?

If you want the possibility of some growth in the value of your investment along with income, convertible bonds are well worth looking into. But be aware that when you buy a convertible bond, you may trade some income for growth, so these may not be for you if pure income is your goal. Also, the conversion feature and the quality of the corporation issuing the bonds is key here. Make sure that you understand these features before investing. These bonds tend to be far less liquid than others, so, again, be careful.

HIGH-YIELD ("JUNK") BONDS

What are high-yield bonds, and why are they called "junk" bonds?

A high-yield bond is simply any bond rated below BBB by a major rating agency, meaning that it is not "investment grade." Such bonds are typically issued by young companies without much of a credit history, by foreign companies, and by larger, older companies in some degree of trouble. Their rating—perhaps unfairly called a "junk" rating—reflects a negative view of the bond issuer's creditworthiness. The weaker a company's financial condition, the higher the interest rate it must pay to borrow money. Hence these bonds are called "high-yield" or "junk."

Are all junk bonds dangerous?

Some are more dangerous than others. Quality differences among junk bond issues are huge. To be on the safer side, look for bonds rated BB and Ba or higher.

Do high-yield bonds trade just like other bonds?

High-yield bonds often trade more like stocks than like high-quality bonds, such as Treasuries. They can be dangerous in recessions. Whereas high-quality bonds usually provide strong returns during recessions because their prices rise as interest rates fall, high-yield bonds, like stocks, may decline as company earnings (so important for repayment) fall off. In a recovery, high-yield bonds can outperform high-quality bonds, because the rise in corporate earnings is more important than the threat of rising interest rates—at least for a while.

Can you give me an idea of what the total return on high-yield bonds has been over the past few years?

Yes. Total return of junk bonds for each of the 15 years through 2005, based on the Credit Suisse High-Yield Index, are as follows:

Year	Total Return
2000	−5.21%
2001	5.80%
2002	3.10%
2003	27.94%
2004	11.95%
2005	2.26%
2006	11.92%
2007	2.66%
2008	−25.89%

Source: Credit Suisse First Boston

If I do not have much money to invest, is it better to buy individual junk bonds or a junk-bond fund?

As you will see in the Buyer Beware section later in this chapter, I am not a great fan of bond funds. As for individual high-yield bonds, they are not for the conservative investor, especially one with a small amount of money.

What should I keep in mind when investing in high-yield bonds?

Just remember the old saying, "There is no such thing as a free lunch." Junk bonds are not easy money. The price of receiving above-average income is above-average risk—the risk of potential price declines if you try to sell your bond on the secondary market. That market is not as active—as liquid—as the market for stocks or high-grade bonds, and even though returns on high-yield bonds have historically rewarded the investor for the additional risk, there is no guarantee that this will be true in the future.

ZERO COUPON BONDS

What is a zero coupon bond?

A "zero coupon bond," also known as a strip, is a bond that can be issued by a corporation, government, or government agency. Like other bonds, it has a coupon, or interest rate, of a certain percentage. However, unlike most other bonds (but like EE/E bonds and Treasury bills), the income that a zero coupon generates is not paid out to you; it stays in the bond, earning interest at the original rate. This can be a great advantage in a high–interest rate environment.

Is there anything I should be careful of with zero coupon bonds?

Yes. One characteristic of a zero coupon bond is that, even though your interest is reinvested rather than paid out to you, you are expected to pay income taxes on that money. To get around this, you can purchase zero coupon bonds in your IRA, or else buy a municipal zero coupon bond that is federally tax-free. Also, the market value of these bonds tends to be more volatile than that of conventional bonds with respect to price movements and interest rates. Be careful if you think that interest rates are heading up and you think you might have to sell your bond before its maturity date—you could take quite a hit when you sell.

How much do I pay for a zero coupon bond?

When you buy a zero coupon bond, you ordinarily do so at a discount. For example, if in the year 2002 you bought a zero coupon bond with a face value of $50,000 maturing in the year 2010 with a coupon of 5 percent, it might cost you around $30,500 up front. When the bond matures, if you haven't sold it, you would get $50,000 back.

Is there only one kind of zero coupon bond, or are there several?

Zero coupon bonds come in many variations—such as zero coupon Treasuries, municipals, and occasionally corporates. Regardless of the issuer, it is essential that you get one with insurance. Since the interest is not being paid to you, nothing could be worse than if the bond defaulted and you got nothing at all from it, not even the interest income.

What would you say is the best thing about zero coupon bonds?

The upside of zero coupon bonds is that in a high-interest-rate environment when rates are expected to come down, zero coupon bonds let you reinvest your interest at your original higher rate. In fact, any decline in the rate environment could make this investment well worth your while, since the price of zero coupon bonds tends to go up in response to falling rates faster than that of conventional bonds. But the opposite is also true—when interest rates go up, zero coupons decrease in market value more rapidly than conventional bonds. This type of bond is volatile.

Still, zero coupon bonds are very useful for keeping the money in your retirement account safe, sound, and growing. Or consider this scenario: You may know without a doubt how much money you are going to need by a certain date, for example, to pay for college. Very few investments other than certain Treasuries and a zero coupon bond can assure you of a certain return on a certain date. That is because no other investment can lock in the rate of return for the reinvestment of your interest.

BASICS OF BOND FUNDS

What is a bond fund?

A bond fund is simply a mutual fund that is made up entirely of bonds. Bond funds come in all shapes and sizes, just as bonds do, but the interest rate on a bond fund is not fixed, as it most often is on a single bond. It will fluctuate along with interest rates in the economy. Bond funds pay income every month, however, and investors like knowing they can rely on that check. Another difference: Bond funds do not have a maturity date. In other words, there is never a fixed date on which you will get back your principal investment. You have to sell your shares in the bond fund in order to get your money back, and those shares will rise or fall in value according to whether interest rates are rising or falling. In spite of the fact that the fund does not mature, however, the bonds within the fund do mature.

Why does the interest rate for a bond fund fluctuate?

The interest rate moves in tandem with interest rates in the economy, as the rates on individual bonds do, but the fund rate will lag behind them a bit.

What's the significance of the fact that bond funds don't have maturity dates?

Because bond funds don't have maturity dates, you can't be sure how much of your original investment you will get back when you sell your shares. You might get more than you paid, or less. Let's say that you decide to sell your bond fund shares at a time when interest rates have risen since you originally purchased them. Because your fund has a lower interest rate than newer funds do, your shares won't be in much demand and you will most likely get back less than the full amount you invested in the fund. But the reverse is also true. If interest rates have fallen since your original purchase, you will probably get back more than you invested when you sell your shares. This uncertainty about how much of your original investment you'll be able to recoup is a big difference between bond funds and individual bonds.

What determines whether the price of the bond fund goes up or down?

Primarily, it's the old seesaw of general interest rates that determines whether bond-fund shares gain or decrease in value: If interest rates go up, the price of the shares of the bond fund will tend to fall. If they go down, the price of the shares of the bond fund will tend to rise.

Is that price movement guaranteed to be predictable?

No, which is another disadvantage of bond funds. If the fund is poorly managed, the price of the fund could go down and you could lose money even if interest rates fall.

Why would I want to invest in a bond fund?

Bond funds are useful as parking places for your money while you ponder a decision about what else to do with it—before making a big consumer purchase, say, or undertaking a makeover of your investment portfolio. Money-market funds and CDs (certificates of deposit) are technically bond funds, and are particularly suitable for parking.

KINDS OF BOND FUNDS

Now that you know the different characteristics of bond funds, you need to know the different categories. Remember that each one of these bond funds can be made up of long- or short-term maturities. Categories include U.S. Treasury bond funds, municipal bond funds, mortgage-backed security funds held by U.S. agencies, corporate bond funds, and international bond funds. Let's take a look at them in order.

What is a U.S. Treasury bond fund?

A Treasury bond fund invests exclusively in U.S. Treasury bills, bonds, and notes. Most people who invest in Treasury bond funds are looking for absolute safety in terms of the quality of the bonds in the portfolio. But remember, even with Treasury bonds the price per share of your fund can fluctuate according to interest rate movements.

What is a municipal bond fund?

A municipal bond fund invests in various municipal bonds whose interest is paid by cities, counties, and/or states. If you are considering investing in one of these, please check to be sure the fund manager insures the bonds in the fund.

I assume that whether or not a municipal bond fund is insured affects its yield—am I right?

Yes. Insured municipal bond funds have to pay for their insurance, and what they pay comes out of the shareholders' take.

Do all municipal bond funds escape taxation?

Partly, but not wholly. The same tax rules that apply to individual municipal bonds apply here. In order to avoid state taxes, you must buy a municipal bond fund that invests only in bonds from the state in which you are a resident.

How do I know if a municipal bond fund has my state's bonds in it?

The name of the bond fund will include your state's name, as in the Vanguard California Tax-Free Fund.

If my state does not have a state income tax, should I still buy a municipal bond fund that invests only in bonds issued by my state?

No. Buy the municipal bond or bond fund that will give you the highest yield regardless of the state, keeping in mind your tolerance for risk, of course.

What is a mortgage-backed security fund?

Let's take Ginnie Mae bond funds as an example. Investments in individual Ginnie Mae bonds are used to finance home mortgages across the country. Ginnie Mae bond funds are made up of Ginnie Mae bonds. The funds pay a little more than most Treasury bond funds do and, as with individual Ginnie Maes, there is a federal guarantee behind them. However, the funds have some of the same disadvantages as the bonds do. For one thing, your income is derived from monthly mortgage payments, so you have to be on the lookout for declining interest rates; in a period of declining rates, many homeowners decide to refinance, paying off their entire original mortgage at once. This means that your bond fund, which holds those mortgages, will get back a large chunk of its principal sooner than expected. The fund will then transfer that principal to you. This means that you will have to reinvest the principal.

What should I know about corporate bond funds?

Such funds are made up of bonds issued by corporations. By definition, they are less safe than government bond funds, but they pay you a higher yield. In my opinion, however, individual corporate bonds are a better way to go than corporate bond funds.

How can I get the highest yield from a corporate bond fund?

The highest-yielding bond funds are also the riskiest. Many high-yield, or junk, bond funds offer very attractive interest rates, and investors light up like pinball machines when they hear they can get a 2 percent higher yield per year than they could get with most other bond funds. But there are risks—almost as many with the funds as with the individual bonds. If the companies that issue these bonds default, investors in individual bonds may get little or nothing back—no interest and little or no principal. Investing in a high-yield bond fund means you do not risk the loss of all your principal and interest, but if even one company in the fund defaults, it can cause the fund's share price to drop dramatically. Always remember that the longer the average maturity of the bonds in your fund, the higher its yield and the greater the risk. Add junk bonds to this mix, and you will find yourself the owner of a very high-risk, potentially high-yielding bond fund. You can buy funds containing high-yield bonds of almost any kind, including municipal bonds. Most of the issuers are cities or companies that have low credit ratings. Do you really want to take this chance with your money? You might or might not, depending on the interest rate and the specific cities or companies involved.

Last, what about international bond funds?
These are funds that invest in bonds of foreign countries, but please note that they are not for the first-time bond-fund investor. The least risky international bond funds invest in bonds issued by foreign governments, or by stable foreign companies that focus on a number of industries, not just one. The riskiest international bond funds are those that invest in so-called emerging market countries, i.e., countries in Latin America, Asia, or Eastern Europe. The fund's prospectus will tell you exactly where the bond fund intends to put its money. The tricky part of investing in these funds is that whenever you invest abroad, your money (and thus your yield) is subject to the fluctuations of the currency markets as well as of interest rates. Your international bond fund will lose money if the value of the U.S. dollar increases against foreign currencies. Also, the interest rates of other countries cannot be predicted in the same way as those in the United States. I know of many people who have done well with the higher yields offered by international bond funds, but I also know people who have had some unpleasant surprises because of currency devaluation.

THE MATURITY FACTOR IN A BOND FUND

You mentioned that bond funds had no maturity dates. What about the maturity dates of individual bonds within the fund? Do they make a difference?
Yes, they do. Although your bond fund has no maturity date, the maturity dates of the individual bonds in your fund will have a big influence on your total returns. The longer the average maturity of the bonds in your fund, the greater the risk to you—or, rather, to the price of your shares—when interest rates fluctuate. The quality of the bonds in the portfolio also makes a big difference in regard to risk. The lower the quality of the bonds, the higher their yield, but the higher the risk as well. Because bond funds come in all sizes and shapes, you can have different

kinds of funds that are sold under the name of a specific category of fund. For example, you can have a Treasury bond fund with bonds that have short-term maturities and one with bonds that have long-term maturities—each is a Treasury bond fund, but their share prices react very differently to a change in interest rates. You can see it is important to know not only what type of fund you might want to invest in, but also the characteristics of the specific fund as well.

What is a short-term bond fund?

Short-term in this context means that the bond fund typically owns bonds with average maturity dates of anywhere from one to five, and sometimes fewer, years. This doesn't necessarily mean that this bond fund only buys short-term bonds; it's simply an overall investing philosophy. In my opinion, short-term bond funds could be a good temporary shelter for your money, since it is unlikely that they will rise and fall dramatically with interest-rate fluctuations. Of course, since they are less risky than other kinds of investments, their yield will be lower. Still, they will generally outearn a CD or a money-market fund.

What is an intermediate-term bond fund?

It's a fund holding bonds whose average maturity date is from five to ten years. These funds can be quite a bit more volatile than short-term funds, though they are still generally considered less risky than long-term bond funds.

What is a long-term bond fund?

Its bonds have a typical maturity date of anywhere from 10 to 20 years or longer. Such bond funds usually pay the highest interest rates, but they can be extremely risky as well. Often, intermediate-term bond funds can provide investors with approximately the same total returns, with a lot less risk attached. I would not recommend long-term bond funds unless interest rates are extremely high and projected to come down. Even if this were the case, you would still be far better off, in my opinion, in long-term individual bonds.

How can I determine which of these terms is right for me?

As is often the case with bonds, the answer totally depends on what is happening with overall interest rates. If interest rates are about to go up and you are sure you want to buy a bond fund, then I suggest looking for one with very short-term maturities. If interest rates are relatively stable, an intermediate-term fund would be okay. And if interest rates are about to come down after a period of being very high, long-term funds might be the best choice. Remember, the longer the average maturity of the bonds within a bond fund, the more volatile the per-share price and the greater price fluctuations will be. Share prices will move farther downward when interest rates go up, and vice versa. Again, individual bonds of the same duration would probably accomplish your goals better than funds.

How can I find out the length of the maturities of the individual bonds in a bond fund?

Morningstar, a mutual fund–rating service (www.morningstar.com), lists the maturities of individual bonds in bond funds.

BUYER BEWARE

What do you think of bond funds?

As you have probably gathered, I am not a fan of bond funds. If your aims are fixed income and the stability of your principal, bond funds are not the best way to go, especially if you have $10,000 or more to invest. I believe the best bets are individual bonds or stocks of stable companies that pay generous dividends.

Many investment advisers will disagree with me about bond funds. They will argue that you need a bond fund, especially if you do not have a lot of money, because individual bonds always carry a risk of defaulting. You need to protect yourself, they say, by diversifying among a lot of bonds, which you can't do if you don't have a lot of money. So they will tell you to buy a bond fund. I understand their point of view, but I'm not persuaded.

So I should never buy into a bond fund?

Well, bond funds have their uses. For example, if you have less than $10,000 to invest, you need the highest current yield you can get, and if yield is more important to you than knowing that you will get your principal back in full, then you might look into purchasing a bond fund instead of individual bonds. Some people who need a monthly income prefer bond funds to individual bonds because the funds offer monthly instead of semiannual income. Also, if for some reason you need cash in a hurry, you can write checks against the amount of your principal in a bond fund. I would advise against doing this, however, since whenever you do, you are selling off shares, and you will have to pay capital-gains taxes on any profits.

Safety through diversification, which they say is easy to come by with a fund, still sounds good to me.

In theory, it seems wise to want to diversify. However, while it is true that some individual bonds carry a risk of defaulting, not all bonds do. Treasuries, for instance, are the safest investment you can make. If you have a small sum of money that you want to invest in bonds, your investment does not have to be diversified as long as your money is absolutely safe. You could put every penny you have into a Treasury, regardless of your age, and your money would be secure from default. This may not be the wisest thing to do with respect to inflation risk, but it demonstrates that the reasoning that tells us the only way to be safe is to diversify by using a bond fund simply does not hold water.

What if I don't want to buy a Treasury? I am in the 28 percent tax bracket, and I would prefer to buy municipal bonds because I do not want to pay taxes on the interest.

We need to look at your financial situation more closely. The taxes on an investment of $10,000 or less in a taxable bond are not going to be that great. If you're in the 28 percent tax bracket, and you put $10,000 in a Treasury that earns 5 percent, then of the $500 you will earn in interest, $140 will go to the IRS in taxes, leaving you $360. If you were to put that same $10,000 in a municipal bond fund—let's say it paid you 3.5 percent—you would get $350 after taxes, less than the after-tax yield of the Treasury. With a

Treasury, you know you will get back all $10,000 on the maturity date. With a bond fund, you do not have that assurance, because bond funds do not have a maturity date. Furthermore, if interest rates go up after you purchase the fund, you will not get back as much as you invested when you sell your shares. The bottom line is, what you earn in interest after taxes is essentially the same between the Treasury and the municipal bond fund ($360 versus $350). The difference is that one guarantees your investment principal and the other guarantees nothing.

I have a lot more money than $10,000 to invest, and I do not want any more taxable income—so, in my case, wouldn't it make sense to buy a municipal bond fund?

The answer is still no. First of all, if you have a lot more money to invest, you can diversify by buying individual municipal bonds. Second, if your main desire is to avoid paying taxes, you have an even stronger reason to stay away from bond funds: There's one tax you may have to pay anyway. Most funds have an end-of-the-year capital-gains distribution. So even if you go into a municipal bond fund with the sole intention of never having to pay taxes while you own it, you may very well find you are paying taxes at the end of the year.

If I purchase a bond fund, will I have to pay capital-gains taxes at the end of the year, as I do with stock mutual funds?

All bond funds distribute capital gains, just as stock mutual funds do. In addition, bond funds reduce their share price by the amount of their distributions, just as stock funds do.

I bought my bond fund when interest rates were high. Why is my income going down with interest rates?

Because as new money comes into the fund, the portfolio manager buys bonds with this money. If interest rates have dropped since you invested your money, the bonds the fund manager is buying with the new money will have a lower yield. This will affect the overall yield of the bond portfolio, which in turn affects every shareholder's yield, including yours.

Can you summarize why you like individual bonds over bond funds?

Sure. Even though bond fund prices are supposed to go up when interest rates go down, and vice versa, it doesn't always happen that way. This makes bond funds unpredictable in spite of the fact that bonds are typically very predictable investments. In addition, when interest rates go down, the interest rate that you are earning in a bond fund will also fall. If you are on a fixed income, this could be disastrous. Not only will you be getting less money monthly, but the offering price—that is, the price you could get for your shares—might stagnate or, worse, decline. Then you could really be in trouble. Also note that when you buy into a bond fund, you pay the current offering price of the fund on the day you place your order. You can tell your broker how much you want to spend, but you will not know for sure how many shares you will actually own until the fund closes for that day.

Imagine you've bought into a bond fund that is yielding 7.8 percent at a time when you could have bought an individual bond with a coupon, or interest rate of 7 percent. Let's say that you are retired and living on a fixed income. Although you could have locked in that 7 percent for the next ten years, when you bought your fund, you were told not to worry: If interest rates go down, your fund's value will increase. So you buy. Interest rates start to come down. You notice that your income is going down and the price per share of your bond fund is also declining. What is going on?

Well, it's the story I told just a moment ago. New investors are entering your mutual fund all the time, even as rates go down. The portfolio manager has to keep buying new bonds— at lower yields. This affects the rate of return for everyone who is in the fund. Also, as the fund prices start to go down, investors may start to pull their money out of the fund. If the manager does not have the cash to give them, he or she may have to liquidate bonds to raise cash. Depending on how the portfolio is invested, losses within the fund may have to be taken and you will see the share price go down as well.

Meanwhile, if you had bought an individual bond when the interest rates were high, you would be reaping the rewards, since your yield is fixed and you would have seen the price of your bond increase. Why? You are not subject to new money being invested and you do not have to worry about others liquidating, as you do in a fund. Furthermore, since bond funds do not have a maturity date, you are never guaranteed to get back your original investment. Individual bonds do have a maturity date, and in Treasuries you are always guaranteed to get back your principal investment.

Can you summarize all the advantages of buying individual bonds over bond funds?

Yes. Here they are. With an individual bond:

- You know precisely the amount of money that you will get back at maturity date.
- You will never have to pay end-of-the-year capital-gains taxes.
- You will not have to worry about the portfolio manager leaving. Nor will you have to worry about inside fees and expenses of the fund. If interest rates go down or up, you will most likely see an honest movement to the upside or downside.
- You will know your exact coupon rate and it will never change, even if interest rates go down.
- You will know the exact price that you are paying per bond and the yield that you will be getting.

But if individual bonds are better for all these reasons, why do people buy into bond funds?

Because there are exceptions to everything—and that holds true for bond funds. As I've said, sometimes bond funds can be a good place to put money in the short term or even the intermediate term. However, for the long haul, when you are looking for a stable income and want control over your money, I would go with individual bonds. Make sure they have a safe rating, or stick with Treasuries.

If I happen to think I should still get a bond fund, do you have any tips on what to look out for?

The first thing I would look at is the load, or the

sale commission. The way loads work on bond funds is identical to how they work on mutual funds. The only kind of bond fund I would want to see you buy would be a no-load fund. Again, no-load means no commission. You can buy or sell shares anytime you want, and it will not cost you a penny.

If I do buy a bond fund, does the expense ratio make a difference?

Yes, it makes a huge difference. Annual expense ratios come right off the total return of this fund. The higher the expense ratio, the lower your return. Be careful here and check.

If I decide to buy a bond fund, how much should I pay in management fees and expense ratios?

In a good fund, the management fee—that is, the fee paid to the person or team buying and selling the bonds in the fund—should be half a percent, give or take a fraction. If it's more than this, you've got a greedy manager. Please note: Every fund has charges in addition to the manager's fees. The expense ratio comprises all the fees the fund charges its investors. The expense ratio for a good bond fund should not be greater than 0.6 percent. The higher the expense ratio, the lower your yield.

MONEY-MARKET FUNDS

A money-market fund is simply a mutual fund that invests in liquid debt instruments, such as short-term Treasuries or short-term cor-

porate debt. Money-market funds offer investors access to their money along with higher interest rates than are available from passbook or checking accounts—and, in many cases, at a cost that's far less than the monthly expense of a checking account.

My bank offers money-market deposit accounts. What are they, and should I consider one?

It's important not to mix up money-market funds with money-market deposit accounts, MMDAs, which are offered by banks and credit unions are insured up to $250,000, assuming the bank or credit union participates in the federal insurance program. (You can find out by going to *myfdicinsurance.gov* for banks and *ncua.gov* for credit unions.) Money Market Mutual Funds offered through a fund company or brokerage do not offer any insurance. As of this writing, bank MMDAs offer better yields than bank savings accounts or money market mutual funds, around 1.20 percent.

You say "funds." I didn't realize that there were different types of money-market funds.

There are four main types of such funds, and they deal in the debt obligations of the same four kinds of issuers that we've been talking about from the beginning of this chapter. They are:

- *U.S. Treasury Funds.* These funds invest primarily in direct U.S. Treasury obligations whose principal and interest payments are backed by the full faith and credit of the U.S. government.
- *U.S. Government Funds.* These funds invest in high-quality obligations of agencies of the

U.S. government as well as the U.S. Treasury. The full faith and credit of the U.S. government does not back agency securities.

- *General Purpose Corporate Funds.* These funds invest in the short-term debt of large, high-quality corporations and banks.
- *Tax-Free Money-Market Funds.* These funds invest in municipal bonds. You pay no federal taxes on your return on these investments, and no state tax, either, if you reside in the state in which the obligations are issued.

What is the best use of a money-market fund?

Use it as a parking place for money that you want to keep safe and/or for money that you know you will need within the next two years.

What questions should I ask myself before I open a money-market fund?

Here are a few: Have you got a sum of money that you want to keep safe and have easily available for spending? Do you want that money to be earning more interest than you can get from a savings account or a checking account? Do you want to stop paying $10 a month for check-writing privileges? If your answers are yes, start checking out money-market funds.

Why are money-market accounts so low-risk?

Because they typically invest in very short-term instruments of debt. By this I mean certificates of deposit (CDs), government notes, and T-bills with very short maturities—usually of 90 days. The best thing about money-market funds is their near guarantee that whatever money you put in, you will be able to get back out at any time, without penalty.

Uh-oh. What do you mean by "near guarantee"?

When you invest in a money-market fund, you buy shares—$1 for one share. The equation is supposed to remain constant, and until 2008 it almost always had. These funds are not FDIC insured and there are rare cases where investors did not receive their full investment back after bad investments by the fund. This is extremely rare. If you are concerned you have a few options; invest your money in a Treasury money market fund; your investment is safe because Treasuries are backed by the full faith and credit of the U.S. government. The Reserve Fund money market fund that dropped its NAV below $1 per share in 2008 ran into trouble because one of its investments was a Lehman Brothers security. When Lehman went bankrupt the value of that security plummeted, causing the overall NAV of the Reserve Fund to drop below $1 a share. I want to repeat, that is extremely rare. But if you want to be very safe you can either keep your savings in a federally insured bank or credit union money market deposit account (MMDA) or keep your money market mutual fund (MMMF) investment in a Treasury-only MMMF.

What are some other advantages of investing in a money-market fund?

Again, since money-market funds invest primarily in short-term debt instruments, any risk due to changing interest rates is significantly lowered. Plus, the rules for diversifying money-market funds are far more rigorous than the rules governing diversified mutual funds that invest in stocks. No more than 25 percent of a regular mutual fund's assets can be put in a single investment.

With money-market funds, the rule is no more than 5 percent. This ensures that if one or another investment starts to do poorly, the rest of the fund will not be seriously affected. Also, if a money-market fund invests in commercial paper—that is, corporate debt—a very high percentage of that debt instrument (almost 95 percent) has to be rated A1 by Standard & Poor's or Moody's, and if a money-market fund has invested in a debt instrument that carries a variable rate, the fund manager must ensure that the initial rate is solid enough so that if it wobbles it won't affect the overall value of the fund. As you can see, money-market funds are designed to minimize risk and to provide you with protection from jiggly markets.

How do I start looking for a good money-market fund in which to invest?

I am glad that you said, "invest," since it is important to remember that you are investing your money, not just putting it into a savings account at the bank. As with any kind of mutual fund, I would first read the fund's prospectus and any annual or quarterly reports you can get your hands on. Some of these can be downloaded right off the Internet. Second, I would check to see what kinds of debt instruments the money-market fund invests in. The least risk (and probably the lowest yields) would be in a fund invested in Treasury securities. You could probably find a higher yield (and a slightly higher risk) with a money-market fund that invested in Eurodollars or commercial paper, i.e., corporate debt. To find the money-market funds paying the best interest rates, check a financial magazine such as *Kiplinger's, Money,* or *SmartMoney,* or the Website *www.bankrate.com.* They list the best-performing money-market funds in the United States, along with their telephone numbers.

Is there anything else I should look out for?

As always, read the fine print. Find out if there is a minimum amount on your check-writing privilege, in case you need your money in a hurry. Does the fund offer wire or electronic transfers so you can get your money sooner rather than later? Is there a charge for writing a check or for withdrawing some of your money? Keep these things in mind.

How much cash do I need to open a money-market fund account?

You can usually open one with as little as $500 to $1,000.

Do I always get check-writing privileges with my money-market fund?

Not always, but usually.

Then why shouldn't I just transfer all the money in my checking account into my money-market account? That way I can earn higher interest but still have check-writing privileges!

Good question, but be careful. Most money-market accounts will permit you to write checks against your account balance, but many institutions set a limit on the number of checks you can write every month, or stipulate that the checks you write have to be in amounts of $300 or greater. Ask about this before setting up your account.

How else is a money-market fund account different from my regular bank account?

Bank accounts are insured by the FDIC;

money-market funds are not. However, money-market funds generally pay higher interest rates and cost you far less in fees.

My bank offers a money-market fund to its depositors. If I take them up on the offer, will my money not be insured?

Here's an exception to what I said above. Banks have begun to offer money-market funds in order to compete with the mutual-fund companies. These accounts are insured by the FDIC, but their yields tend to be a lot lower, because of the high cost of the banks' overhead.

I have a money-market fund with about $30,000 in it. Is there any danger in this?

Not with regard to the safety of your money. But there's another sort of risk—that the bank will start pestering you with offers you can't refuse, but should. If you have more than $5,000 or $10,000 in a money-market account, it is possible—probable, in fact—that someone representing the bank or brokerage firm where the money is kept will call you, offering to help you invest this money for a better rate of return. (Many banks now have in-house brokerage services to help their clients invest.) Obviously, the bank or brokerage firm will make more money in the long run if you invest this money in certain ways rather than others. So these companies keep an eye on accounts with a consistent stash of cash, in the hope that if they call you, you will be open to listening to their ideas. Please be careful if this happens. Don't do anything you don't want to do. It's your money. Just keep in mind, and tell them, that your goal with these funds is to keep them safe and sound and available in case of an emergency.

CERTIFICATES OF DEPOSIT (CDs)

Certificates of deposit, or CDs, are a type of savings instrument issued by a bank or a credit union (or even a broker). Like individual bonds, they pay you a specified rate of interest over a specified period of time, and pay back your principal at maturity.

Are CDs insured?

CDs are insured up to $250,000 through December 31, 2013, by banks and credit unions that are part of the federal insurance program. That $250,000 is a general per person per bank limit. It includes the aggregate value of your accounts at that bank. (You can indeed qualify for more than $250,000 in insurance coverage based on the types of accounts you have at a bank or credit union. Your bank or credit union has information on how you can broaden your coverage beyond $250,000.) Granted, banks don't make a habit of going belly-up, but as we saw in 2008 and 2009 it does happen during hard economic times. That's why you always want to make sure your bank or credit union participates in the federal insurance program. Banks will display an FDIC logo on their door and in all correspondence with you; credit unions will crow that they are backed by the NCUA insurance program. You can confirm your institution is federally insured by going to *www.myfdicinsurance.gov* for banks and *www .ncua.gov* for credit unions.

Why should one invest in a CD?

Like money-market funds, CDs are a very safe, very conservative part of an investment portfolio. I think CDs are a very good place to park savings you might be holding for an expense you anticipate in the near term, or until you decide what you are going to do with them on a long-term basis. However, I would not recommend keeping the lion's share of your money in CDs, unless it is the only place where you feel your money is safe and sound and you need current income.

Should I buy a CD from the bank where I keep my checking and savings accounts, or is it worth my while to shop around?

I would certainly inquire at your bank whether or not the fact that you are already a customer affects the rate of the CD (and also whether opening a CD may lower your banking fees). Sometimes banks favor their long-term customers and customers with larger combined balances. If the answer is no, then I would shop around for the best rate.

What is the most important thing for me to keep in mind as I shop for a CD?

The first thing I would want to know is what the CD's maturity is. The next thing to find out is the current interest rate. For a list of current CDs, their maturities and rates, log on to *www .bankrate.com.*

Will I be penalized if I take my money out of a CD before the maturity date?

Yes. You will usually be charged an early-withdrawal penalty (EWP). Check with the bank that's offering the CD to find out how much this penalty is, as it varies. Typically you do not lose any principal; the penalty is often a forfeiture of interest earned.

Do all banks penalize customers if they withdraw their money early from a CD?

The majority of them do, but I've noticed that more and more banks are now waiving the EWP. This waiver has a price, however: lower interest rates. So you have to ask yourself whether or not it's worth it. Better yet, decide beforehand, to the best of your knowledge, if you might need this money before the maturity date. None of us can predict the future or those times when life will throw us a curveball, but you can certainly prepare for uncertainty—for example, by buying CDs in smaller denominations and/or staggering their maturity dates. If you invested $80,000 in a CD and for some reason you decided to take your money out early because you needed just $10,000, the bank would charge you an EWP on all $80,000. Wouldn't it have been just as easy—and in the end, cheaper—to have bought eight certificates of deposit at $10,000 apiece? This way, if you need emergency money and want to cash out one of your CDs, the bank will levy an EWP on a CD of only $10,000.

What other questions should I ask?

I would ask about variable-rate CDs. Depending on the interest-rate climate, these may offer higher or lower returns than a fixed-rate CD. If you think that interest rates are bound to rise in the near future, then you should definitely think about putting your money in a variable-rate CD. It allows you to take advantage of rising rates and protects you, by its withdrawal features, in case rates fall or you need access to your funds.

I've already mentioned the advantages of staggering your maturity dates. This means that you have one CD that comes to maturity in six months, another that comes to maturity in a year, etc. This acts as a partial protection against interest rate fluctuations.

Most important, find out about the rate of return (the annual percentage yield, or APY). Interest rates are dependent on the maturity of the CD, and they also vary from bank to bank.

Finally, you should also ask how often interest is paid or credited to your CD. Is it daily? Monthly? Quarterly? The more often it is credited to your account, the better for you.

Are brokers useful here?

Actually, I recommend buying CDs through a broker. Yes, you read that right! Some CDs that are bought through your broker have one big advantage that CDs bought from a bank do not have: They can be sold (and bought) on the secondary market. Let's say you bought a five-year CD, and six months into it you need your money. Rather than taking an automatic interest rate hit or an EWP, you can instruct your broker to sell your CD for you on the secondary market. If interest rates have fallen since you purchased your CD, you could get back more than you invested. (This is because another investor may be willing to pay a premium for the higher interest rate attached to your CD.) If they have stayed the same, you could get back what you put in; if they have risen, you could get back less. In any case, you will probably come out better than you would at the bank. And a brokerage firm can shop the whole country for you to find you the best rate or a buyer, if necessary. So check it out, for this may be one time a broker is worth consulting.

What is an "odd-term" CD?

An odd-term CD has an unconventional time period until maturity—for example, 5 months or 17 months—as opposed to the standard 6-month maturity.

What is a "step-up" CD?

A step-up CD allows you to lock in the current interest rate and take advantage of rising rates during the term of the CD—usually between one and five years—by converting to the higher yield without penalty. Most banks will allow you to step up to a higher rate once during the term of the CD, but you must notify the bank to initiate the step-up process; it does not automatically occur once rates change.

Do you think buying a Treasury note is better than buying a CD?

There are plusses and minuses to both CDs and Treasury notes. Treasury notes pay you interest that's not taxed at the local or state level. Any interest that you make on your CD is taxable at the local and state levels, as well as at the federal level. So the bottom line depends on your tax bracket and the interest-rate difference. Overall, I prefer Treasuries to CDs because of the tax advantages and government guarantees. Also, you can invest far more than $100,000 in a Treasury note and still have your money safe and sound.

10

Annuities

BUYER BEWARE

Annuities are controversial investments, even within the financial community. It's important to understand what annuities are and how they work, for without a doubt—and probably sooner rather than later—a broker or insurance agent will try to sell you one. Although there are circumstances in which buying an annuity may make sense, in a majority of cases I believe that annuities cause more harm than good.

All annuities are contracts with an insurance company for a specified period of time. But annuities are not really life-insurance policies; for one thing, they do not include an extra death benefit payable to heirs. They are *investment* contracts, and as such must be compared to other investment vehicles, such as bank CDs and mutual funds. Annuities have one advantage over other investment vehicles outside a retirement plan, however, and this is what makes them so popular and such an easy sell: The money they earn for you, whether in interest or in increased value, is tax-deferred until you withdraw it. In this respect, annuities behave very much like nondeductible IRAs or even like 401(k)s, and so they also have to be compared with retirement-savings vehicles. They are complicated. In most cases, you are penalized for withdrawing your money from an annuity until the surrender period expires *and* until you're 59½ or older; but you can always choose what's known as an "annuitization" option that lets you start taking a lifetime income—at a price. Most annuities also carry an ongoing price in the form of special annual charges and fees that come straight out of your annuity account—and therefore out of any profit.

Frankly, I take a dim view of annuities. Yet in a few cases, they make excellent financial sense. In the following sections, I've made clear what those cases are and also the major drawbacks in most other cases—perhaps even yours. If you already own an annuity, this chapter will give you the tools to evaluate it and—should you decide you want to extricate yourself—to avoid mistakes when disposing of it.

ANNUITY BASICS

What is an annuity?

An annuity is an investment contract or policy between you, the policyholder, and an insurance company. There are many kinds of annuities. Some are tailored for income, some for growth, some as savings vehicles. All offer tax-deferred growth of your earnings within the policy or account. None, however, offer an additional death benefit, and this makes them very different from a life insurance policy. Also unlike an insurance policy, an annuity is purchased with a single lump-sum payment; the minimum investment in a typical annuity is about $5,000. Depending on what kind of annuity you buy, in return for your investment the insurance company will provide you with certain contractual guarantees—for example, it will guarantee a minimum rate of return over the life of the contract and/or a guaranteed interest rate for any given year. Such guarantees are one of the reasons annuities are popular and are widely believed to be safe investments.

Can you remind me what tax deferral means?

It means that you put off paying taxes—in this case, taxes on the interest or other earnings in your account—until you start making withdrawals at age 59½ or older (or, in the event of your death, until your beneficiaries withdraw the investment and the earnings). The advantage of tax deferral is that money you would otherwise pay in taxes every year is allowed to remain in your account, earning additional interest or creating further gains. In the arena of tax deferral, annuities function very much like some IRAs. In essence, they act as a tax shelter, and this is one of their big draws.

When an annuity is part of a qualified retirement plan, it is referred to as a "qualified" annuity and has one added tax benefit: Your initial investment, or premium, is also tax-deferred. But most annuities are "nonqualified" annuities and offer tax deferral only on the interest and other earnings that accrue in your account.

Can you elaborate on the difference between a qualified and a nonqualified annuity?

If you are investing with money on which you have already paid taxes, you are buying a nonqualified annuity. If you're investing with pretax money within a qualified retirement account, such as a 401(k), or as a rollover from a qualified retirement account, then you are buying a qualified annuity. Typically, you buy a qualified annuity within a retirement plan at work or as a transfer of money from a 401(k) or 403(b) plan.

Is it a good idea to own an annuity within my retirement plan?

I'm glad you asked this question. The answer is, usually not. Although brokers often try to sell annuities as investments within retirement plans, for the most part I see this as a bad idea. What sense does it make to hold a tax-sheltered product, such as an annuity, in an already tax-sheltered account, such as a 401(k) or an IRA? Not a lot.

Are there exceptions to this rule? Yes. Apart from being offered a particular type of annuity called a tax-sheltered annuity as part of your retirement plan at work, in my opinion the *only* two reasons to purchase an annuity in a retirement plan are the following:

- You are under the age of 59½, need to get access to the funds in your traditional IRA, and want to avoid paying the 10 percent early-withdrawal penalty tax levied by the IRS on withdrawals made before age 59½. By purchasing what's called an immediate, or income, annuity within your traditional IRA, you can receive monthly income right away *and* avoid the 10 percent IRS penalty tax.
- You are approaching retirement age and you want to invest in the stock market but are afraid of losing your principal. You are willing

to take a smaller potential profit in exchange for a guarantee against any losses. In this case, you might consider an index annuity, which lets you participate in stock-market gains on a limited basis while completely protecting you against losses. This strategy can make sense either inside or outside an IRA.

Again, my general advice is to steer clear of investing in annuities in a retirement plan.

Can I cancel an annuity, or take my money out, any time I want to?

No. Once you buy an annuity contract, you're pretty much locked in. For one thing, if you take your money out of an annuity before you turn 59½, the IRS will impose its 10 percent early-withdrawal penalty tax. (In exchange for the privilege of tax deferral on the earnings in an annuity, the IRS limits your access to that money until you reach what the agency considers to be retirement age.) This penalty tax will come on top of the ordinary income taxes you will owe on any earnings in the account.

Second, the majority of annuity contracts contain what is known as a surrender period. This is a specified period of time—usually 5 to 10 years—during which you must keep the greater part of your money in the account, even if you're already 59½ and are off the hook as far as the IRS is concerned. If you don't honor the surrender period, the insurance company will levy surrender charges. Those charges typically start at about 5 to 7 percent of the amount of the withdrawal and drop to zero by the time the surrender period is over. Most contracts *will* allow you to withdraw about 10 percent of the ac-

cumulated value of the account each year (after you are 59½) without a surrender charge, even during the surrender period. But if you withdraw more than 10 percent a year, you will pay a surrender charge on the amount that you withdraw in excess of 10 percent.

Let me give you an example. Let's say you are 60 years old and have put $50,000 into an annuity. Say the annuity is paying you a guaranteed annual interest rate of 5 percent a year for the five-year duration of the contract. At the end of the third year, your annuity is worth $57,881. Suddenly you find you need $7,000. You can withdraw 10 percent of the $57,881, or $5,788, without any penalty whatever. Withdrawing the additional $1,212, however, will cost you approximately $60, based on a surrender charge of 5 percent. And since the IRS has funny rules about annuities, for tax purposes the entire amount of your early withdrawal will be considered to have come from the earnings portion of the account. So you will also owe ordinary income tax on the whole $7,000.

Please note: If you were 40 rather than 60 years old and needed $7,000, you would owe the IRS a 10 percent early-withdrawal penalty tax—or $700—plus ordinary income taxes.

Do all annuities have a surrender charge?

Most do, but not all. No-load annuities, such as those offered by the Vanguard Group, do not carry brokers' commissions or sales charges, and Vanguard's variable deferred annuity has no surrender charges, either.

Are annuities federally insured, as bank CDs are?

No, annuities are not federally insured. If for some reason the insurance company from which you've purchased an annuity flounders or goes belly-up, your annuity account can be frozen and/or reduced in value.

What if I want to change the insurance company I hold my annuity with? Can I switch?

Yes. In most cases, the IRS allows what is known as a 1035 exchange between insurance companies (the exception is an immediate, or income, annuity). A 1035 exchange lets you switch companies while continuing to defer taxes. You can either fill out exchange paperwork with your original insurance company or create a new contract with a new insurance company and let the new company take care of the transfer. Don't switch before the end of the surrender period, however, if you can help it; if you do, you may have to pay the surrender charge. The surrender charge will probably be deducted before the money is transferred, reducing the amount you have available for reinvestment.

Can you tell me about the annuity contract?

Yes. For every annuity contract, there is an *owner,* an *annuitant,* and a *beneficiary.* This is a little complicated, so bear with me.

The *owner* of the contract is the person who purchases the contract or policy. The owner owns the policy, and is entitled to make changes in the beneficiary designation on the policy at any time. The owner can also "annuitize" the policy, which basically means choosing to take a monthly income for life instead of leaving the annuity to beneficiaries or taking a lump sum payment at age 59½ or older. (I'll say more about this later, but annuitizing is not always a good deal.) When two or more people own a policy together, they are known as co-owners. The owner or co-owners can also name a successor owner, someone they designate to step in as owner in the event of the owners' death or, in some cases, incapacity.

The *annuitant* is the insured party—which may seem odd in an investment contract that has no additional death benefit. But in order for an annuity to qualify as a legitimate insurance contract, which is what makes possible its tax advantages, someone has to be insured. Usually the insured person is also the owner; if the annuitant is *not* the owner, he or she has no power over the money in the account.

The annuitant becomes important if and when you choose to annuitize your contract. In that case, the monthly income you receive will be determined not by your own age but by the annuitant's age and life expectancy. For example, if I bought an annuity and named my mother the annuitant, she would qualify for much more money each month than I would if I were the annuitant. The older the annuitant is and the shorter his or her life expectancy, the larger the monthly payments; this makes sense if you consider that the insurance company is predicting that it will have to make fewer payments to an older person.

The *beneficiary* is the person (or people) whom you, as owner, designate to inherit whatever is left in the annuity when the annuitant (who may be you) dies. Remember, every annuity must have a named beneficiary (even though, in some cases, if you choose to "annuitize" an annuity, your beneficiary won't inherit anything; most annuitization payments end with the annuitant's death). The owner decides how much to leave each beneficiary. The beneficiary and the annuitant cannot be the same person, but when the owner and annuitant are separate, the owner and the beneficiary can be the same person. So, for example, if I buy an annuity insuring my mother, I could be named the beneficiary on her death. Usually, however, the owner and the annuitant are the same person, and often a spouse or a child is the beneficiary.

PURCHASING AN ANNUITY

How do I buy an annuity?
Typically, you buy an annuity directly from an insurance company. You can also buy an annuity through a brokerage firm or discount brokerage firm or, in some cases, through a bank or mutual fund company.

Are there commission charges when I buy an annuity?
Typically, yes. Except for annuities offered by no-load mutual fund companies such as Vanguard Group, most annuities carry a load, or commission percentage, of about 5 or 6 percent.

How do I choose an insurance company from which to purchase an annuity?
Start by looking at how the insurance companies you have in mind are rated for financial strength by the following insurance-rating services. The only acceptable ratings are:
AM Best—A or better
Moody's—A or better
Standard & Poor's—AA or better
Ask each insurance company to give you written notification of its ratings when it sends you its prospective materials, or call the ratings companies directly.

If I like the company's ratings, what else should I look for in an insurance company?
Here are a few more things to bear in mind when shopping for an annuity. Take a look at the quality of the investments held by the insurance company, because the company's investments can affect the return you get on your investment. If more than 10 percent of your insurance company's total invested holdings are junk bonds, meaning bonds that have a rating of BB or lower, be wary.

How can I get all this information? Presumably, the insurance companies themselves won't volunteer it.
Actually, insurance companies will provide this information if you ask. Many publish their ratings and holdings in a brochure or in a corporate annual report.

Besides checking into the safety of the issuing insurance company, how do I know if an annuity is a good deal or not?
Whether an annuity is a good deal for you will depend on your financial goals, your tax bracket, and the type of annuity you are considering.

KINDS OF ANNUITIES

Today, for all practical purposes, there are six major kinds of annuities available for purchase: a single-premium deferred annuity; a variable annuity; an index annuity; a split annuity; an immediate, or income, annuity; and a tax-sheltered annuity. When the time comes to withdraw your investment from an annuity, most of these let you either take a lump sum or convert your investment into a monthly income payment for life—an option known as "annuitization." Here's what you need to know about the basic kinds of annuities and how to withdraw your money from them.

SINGLE-PREMIUM DEFERRED ANNUITIES

What is a single-premium deferred annuity?
A single-premium deferred annuity, or SPDA, is a fixed annuity that you buy with a single premium. You get a guaranteed interest rate for a specified period of time, and the taxes on the interest you earn are deferred until you make a withdrawal.

Who would want to buy an SPDA?
Anyone who wants to let his or her money grow risk-free while deferring income taxes on the earnings portion of his or her account, with the goal of creating income later in life, may choose an SPDA. Many people enjoy the idea of a fixed interest rate that will remain in effect for a specified period of time, typically from one to seven years. In most cases, the longer the guarantee, the lower the interest rate. This type of annuity is most easily compared to a certificate of deposit at a bank. In both cases, you get a guaranteed rate for a prescribed period. In an annuity, you incur surrender charges if you take your money out, and in a CD you are faced with a three- to six-month early-withdrawal penalty. The difference, however, is that with a certificate of deposit, you will be paying taxes each year on the interest you earn, even if you don't withdraw it. With the SPDA, you will not pay taxes until you make a withdrawal.

Are you in favor of SPDAs, or should I steer clear of them?
I do like SPDAs for some people. You might consider an SPDA if:

- Your goal is to invest money with minimal risk and you are attracted to vehicles such as CDs and Treasuries; and
- You know you are not going to need any of the money you're investing until after age 59½ and
- You do not need current income but will need income sometime after age 59½ and will be in an equal or lower tax bracket; or
- You are already 59½ or older, you need current income, and the SPDA you are considering offers a guaranteed five-year interest rate that is higher than the interest on five-year CDs and Treasuries.

In summary, there is one set of circumstances in which I would definitely advise you to consider an SPDA. If your goal is to have income during your retirement years, but you don't want to take any market risk with your capital, *and* you want to avoid paying taxes now but are not in a high enough tax bracket for municipal bonds to make sense, *and* you believe that you will be in a lower tax bracket when you retire, then an SPDA may be a great investment, regardless of your age.

I also recommend an SPDA when someone is under age 59½ and needs to take SEPPs, substantially equal periodic payments, for income (payments you can take without paying a 10 percent IRS penalty tax).

What should I watch out for when shopping for an SPDA?

The first step you should take is to check to be sure the insurance company issuing the annuity is safe. Next, and this is very important, ask about the interest rate being offered, the period of time during which the interest rate will be guaranteed, and the surrender period stipulated by the contract. Ideally, the interest rate should be a good one, and the period for which the rate is guaranteed should be at least as long as the surrender period. (In other words, if the interest rate is 7 percent and the contract has a five-year surrender period, the company should pay you 7 percent for all five years.) If you are offered an attractive interest rate for a guaranteed one-year period but the surrender period goes on for seven years, please be wary. Even if the first-year rate is *outstanding*, in the absence of a longer guarantee you are taking a big risk as to what the interest rate will be for the second year, the third year, and so on. Many companies sucker you in with a good first-year rate and then lower it consider-

ably in the remaining years. Finally, ask how the company sets its renewal interest rate, if applicable, or do some checking on your own. That way you know exactly what you are getting.

How can I check on a company's renewal rates?

Ask to see the history of renewal rates for older SPDA policies that the company has in force. If the company tends to lower the interest rates on policies as they get older, chances are good it will reduce yours, too. Make sure you compare the company's renewal rates in previous years to the rate on Treasuries and CDs for the same years. That way, you'll know whether it makes sense for you to purchase a particular SPDA.

I know that the IRS will allow me to switch my annuity from one insurance company to another. Is it ever worthwhile to transfer money to an SPDA at a new company if you are still in the surrender period?

Yes, if the new interest rate in the new company makes up for what you paid in surrender charges in the first year or two, then it may be worthwhile.

When my surrender period is up, I don't have to change my SPDA, do I?

No, although some insurance agents will make it sound as though you do—because if you switch, the agent earns a new commission. In general, if you are pleased with your current interest rate, stay where you are. Be careful: When you sign a new annuity contract, you start a new surrender period. And be sure to check on the new company's renewal rate history.

Can I annuitize my SPDA?

Yes, although it might not be wise to do so. Insurance companies that offer annuities tend to use different annuitization factors when annuitizing—that is, when calculating how much to pay you on a monthly basis over your life span. If you're looking for income from an annuity, it would be best to find out which companies are offering the best annuitization rates and/or to buy outright an immediate, or income, annuity. Typically, the annuitization rates offered by SPDA contracts are not as advantageous as those offered by immediate annuity contracts, and even immediate annuity rates vary from company to company.

VARIABLE ANNUITIES

With billions of investors' dollars pouring into traditional mutual funds, insurance companies are offering a competing product called a variable annuity, which combines elements of an annuity with elements of mutual-fund investing. For many reasons, including high fees and benefits that, in my opinion, are routinely overstated by salespeople, variable annuities are an investment I often warn against. If you are considering buying one, please read this section thoroughly. If you are still tempted, please do your homework and shop around for a no-load variable annuity.

What is a variable annuity?

Like other annuities, a variable annuity is a contract with an insurance company for a specific period of time. However, unlike some other an-

nuities, a variable annuity does not offer a guaranteed rate of interest or earnings. In some ways, it is more like a 401(k) or an IRA; for example, when you buy a variable annuity, you are asked to choose from a menu of mutual funds within the insurance contract in which to invest your money. A variable annuity may offer a broad selection of funds or just a few to choose from, depending on which insurance company you go through. You can buy, sell, and switch funds at any time without incurring taxes until you begin to withdraw your original investment and income after age 59½. At that time, your gains are taxed as ordinary income.

How is a variable annuity different from an IRA?

Unlike many IRAs, a typical variable annuity cannot be funded with pretax dollars. It is a nonqualified annuity. In other words, you make your initial investment with money on which you've already paid ordinary income taxes. A variable annuity and an IRA *are* the same in that the earnings that accrue to your original investment over the years are tax-deferred until you withdraw them after age 59½. But this tax-deferral feature is typically less valuable in a variable annuity than in an IRA. I'll explain this later.

How is a variable annuity different from a single-premium deferred annuity?

When you buy an SPDA, your premium is deposited in the insurance company's general account. This account represents the assets of the company, and the company's financial experts decide how to invest the money and offer you a guaranteed rate of return. When you buy a variable annuity, your money is placed in what is known as a "separate account." Within limits, you decide where to invest. The insurance company gives you a menu of investment options, in the form of different mutual funds; you choose which funds to invest in and what percentage of your money will go in each of the funds you choose. As a result, your return is not guaranteed and you are subject to a certain amount of investment risk.

What if I can't figure out which funds to choose?

Many people share your dilemma, so insurance companies typically offer something called an asset-allocation fund. This is a mutual fund that decreases investment risk (and also decreases potential rewards) by allocating your money in a range of investments, or assets, including stocks, bonds, Treasury bills, and more. This provides a relatively stable, though not entirely risk-free, choice.

Are there any very safe places to park my money in a variable annuity?

Yes. Many variable annuities have a fixed, or interest-bearing, fund as one of their investment offerings, so you can simply choose (or switch into) that one.

What are the advantages of variable annuities over regular mutual funds?

One of the big attractions of all annuities, including variable annuities, is that you enjoy tax deferral on your earnings. Even if you switch— that is, buy and sell—the mutual funds you hold

within a variable annuity every day, you won't have to pay taxes on your realized gains until you actually withdraw money from the annuity. This is a great benefit, especially when compared with the tax policy on regular mutual funds you may be holding outside a variable annuity or other tax-deferred account. When you have large gains in an ordinary investment account, you may hesitate to sell the fund because you'd immediately owe capital-gains taxes on your earnings. If you invested in the same mutual fund within a variable annuity, you could sell it and not pay taxes until you withdrew money. When you do make a withdrawal, however, your gains will be taxed not at the low capital-gains rate, but as ordinary income.

Second, at the end of the year many mutual funds have what is known as an end-of-the-year capital-gains distribution. With a variable annuity, you will not have to pay taxes on your end-of-the-year distributions at that time.

Finally, an advantage of most variable annuities is that they guarantee that the owner or beneficiaries of the annuity will get back *at least* the amount of the initial investment when the annuitant in the contract (the insured party) dies. In other words, no matter what happens to the particular mutual funds in which you choose to invest your premium, when the annuitant in your contract dies, you (the owner) or your heirs will not receive less than the amount you originally invested *or* the current value of the account, whichever is greater. In a regular mutual fund, there is no such guarantee. But hold your horses! In most cases, this so-called benefit is less valuable than you might think, and it is not without cost. Soon we'll discuss the downside of variable annuities, which you should keep in mind as you consider buying one.

Does this mean that a variable annuity is a good way to invest in the market without having to worry about losses or taxes?

No. While it's true that there is some security in the guarantee described above and an attractive short-term benefit in tax deferral on earnings, in my opinion, a variable annuity that *is* profitable will not save you much in taxes over the long run—which, for most people who buy a variable annuity, is the point of owning one.

Are there fees that I have to pay with a variable annuity that I wouldn't have to pay with mutual funds held outside of an annuity?

Yes. Remember that an annuity shelters the growth of your money from immediate taxation because it is considered an insurance product. For it to qualify as such, there has to be someone who is insured—the annuitant. Most variable annuities carry what is called a mortality fee, which is associated with the risks attached to the death of the annuitant. This fee is not charged by mutual funds outside a variable annuity. Many variable annuities also charge application fees and additional expenses that do not exist in a regular mutual fund. Finally, you also have to pay the expense ratio (typically, from 1 percent to 2 percent a year) that mutual funds levy, whether they are within a variable annuity or not.

How big is the mortality fee?

A mortality fee will typically cost you 1.3 percent of your investment a year, or $13 a year for every $1,000 that you invest. Insurance companies justify the fee by claiming it is necessary to cover the cost of the guarantee they give you against losing any of your money when the annuitant, or insured party in your contract, dies. (Remember, one attraction of variable annuities is that the owner and/or the named beneficiaries are guaranteed to get back the full amount of the original investment *or* the account value at the time of the annuitant's death, whichever is greater; this is what this fee covers.) But here's the fallacy: In most cases, the owner and the annuitant are one and the same person—you. If this is the case, you don't benefit at all from the guarantee, and you lose out by paying the mortality fee. Here's why: Say you need your money—you want to withdraw it all and close the account—while you are alive. If your balance happens to be less than you originally deposited, you are out of luck. You will have lost money. The guarantee only applies in the case of the annuitant's death. If you are the annuitant, a lot of good this guarantee—for which you have been paying dearly—does you. However, if you *don't* need your money before you die, the guarantee may benefit your family after you are gone.

Tell me about the tax disadvantages of a variable annuity.

One serious disadvantage of variable annuities is relative: that is, the tax *advantages* they promise are not always everything they're cracked up to be. Most variable annuities are sold with the promise that you'll not only get a long-term tax deferral on your gains, but you will also save a lot of money in taxes on (1) end-of-the-year mutual fund distributions and (2) gains on which you would otherwise be taxed every time you buy and sell a mutual fund. But you don't need a variable annuity to avoid paying taxes on end-of-the-year distributions; you can accomplish the same end outside an annuity with a good tax-efficient mutual fund, such as an index fund, or with an exchange-traded mutual fund, or ETF. As to item (2), most people don't regularly buy and sell mutual funds, especially index funds; they hold on to them for years. So if you have a tax-efficient mutual fund that you do not sell, then the truth is that you do not have a tax problem.

What about the long-term tax deferral that a variable annuity offers? Well, that's not so hot, either. Remember, when you withdraw your money after age 59½ you will have to pay taxes on the earnings portion of your annuity account. However, the earnings on your annuity, which constitute the tax-deferred part, are subject to ordinary income taxes rather than to the lower capital-gains taxes that you would owe if you owned an ordinary mutual fund outside an annuity account. If you hold your money in the same mutual fund outside an annuity for longer than 12 months, you will only have to pay taxes at the lower capital-gains rate (up to 15 percent through 2010) rather than at the ordinary income rate (up to 35 percent as of 2009).

OK, you say, no big deal about the tax rate. You plan to leave the annuity to your children. But such a strategy merely shifts the tax burden to your kids—and at a steep price. When they withdraw money, they, too, will owe income taxes on the growth of your funds (which could be considerable) at ordinary income-tax rates, plus they will have to pay a state premium tax, if applicable, of about 2 percent of your original deposit. If you had simply purchased mutual funds directly and left them to your children via a will or trust, they would get what is called a step-up in cost basis on the value of those funds, based on the funds' worth on the day you died. If they then sold those funds before there was a further increase in the funds' value, they would not owe a penny in taxes.

Another disadvantage: If you lose money in a variable annuity account in any given year, you can't deduct any of your losses from your taxes, but you can deduct any losses you take or any distributed losses if you have the money in a mutual fund outside of an annuity or in a retirement account.

If I have a loss in my variable annuity, can I take it off my taxes?
If the variable annuity is part of a payout in a qualified plan, then the loss can be taken off your taxes, subject to a 2 percent threshold rule.

Can you give me an example of how placing regular mutual funds in a trust might be better for my heirs than buying an annuity would be?
Yes. Imagine that you have invested $25,000 in a variable annuity and that by the time you die your investment has grown to be worth $125,000. Your children inherit the annuity and withdraw the money. They will owe ordinary income taxes on $100,000 in capital gains, along with state premium taxes, if applicable. Depending on their income-tax bracket, they might owe as much as 35 percent of the gain in your annuity in federal tax, and possibly more if they live in a state that levies its own income tax.

Let's imagine that you put that same $25,000 into a few really good, tax-efficient mutual funds. When you die, your kids inherit the funds. If the funds were worth $125,000 on the day of your death, then $125,000 is your children's new cost basis for tax purposes. If on the following day they were to liquidate the funds and withdraw all $125,000 from the account, they would not owe a single penny in income taxes, since the funds have not increased in value since your death. If the funds did increase in value—say, to $127,000—they would owe taxes on a mere $2,000. This step-up in cost basis applies to inherited investments such as mutual funds, real estate, and stocks—but not to annuities, traditional IRAs, and retirement plans.

Can you give me an example of how I might be better off investing in a mutual fund outside an annuity account?

Yes. Let's look at the end-result difference between investing $100,000 in a variable annuity and investing $100,000 in a mutual fund outside an annuity.

Say you put $100,000 in a variable annuity. You have chosen an index fund within the annuity, and you have left your money in the fund for the 25 years without ever having touched one penny. You have averaged a 12 percent annual return, not taking into account the annual fees charged by the insurance company.

Let's see how you would fare in the variable annuity after all the insurance company fees are taken out.

Your $100,000 at 12 percent a year over 25 years, minus a 1.3 percent mortality fee per year and a 0.2 percent expense fee per year, equals $1,213,547.

Now let's say you die and leave your entire account balance to your kids. You all live in the state of California where the top income tax rate is 10.3 percent. Your kids will have to pay state and federal income taxes on about $1,113,547 in earnings as though it were ordinary income.

Let's say your children take the money out in one lump sum. Between federal and state taxes, they would owe about $500,000 in taxes. So when it is all said and done, your children would end up receiving about $610,000.

Okay, now let's see what would happen if you had purchased the same index fund in a regular account instead of an annuity. This is how it would look to your kids.

First of all, your children would inherit close to $1.7 million instead of $1.2 million, simply because you would not have had to pay the annual 1.3 percent mortality fee or the extra annual or 0.2 percent expense fee attached to the annuity. Believe it or not, after 25 years, that 1.5 percent per year subtracts about $500,000 from your annuity account.

Now you die and the kids receive all $1.7 million. Since they inherited your index fund instead of cash they will get a step-up in cost basis to the $1.7 million mark. If they cash the fund out at that valuation, they will not owe one penny in taxes, so they will possess $1.7 million to use as they choose.

With a variable annuity, they would have $700,000. Without a variable annuity, they would have $1,700,000. You decide.

Do you think it's better to buy mutual funds outside a variable annuity and give up the advantage of tax deferral?

Yes—*if* you invest in tax-efficient mutual funds that help you to avoid a big annual tax bite *and* hold your mutual funds for longer than a year, so that your earnings qualify for the lower long-term capital-gains tax rate. This way, your tax bill won't be substantially higher, and you'll be able to gain access to your money anytime, at any age, without worrying about a 10 percent IRS early-withdrawal penalty tax or an insurance company surrender charge.

Is there any way to take money out of a variable annuity and still take advantage of its no-loss guarantee via the mortality charge that I have been paying for?

Yes. If you need to withdraw money from a variable annuity at a time when it's worth less than the amount you deposited, what you can do is this: Leave the account open, but withdraw most of your money. This way, when you die, your beneficiaries will receive the difference between what you have withdrawn and the guaranteed amount.

Let me give you an example. Say you deposit $25,000 into a variable annuity. You are the owner and the annuitant. Sometime later, you need money. When you go to cash out, the account is worth only $19,000. You withdraw $18,000, leaving $1,000 in the annuity. Years later, you die. Your beneficiaries will get $7,000. Remember, you have continued to pay the mortality fee of 1.3 percent of your original deposit amount each year to guarantee that on your death your beneficiaries will get back 100 percent of the original deposit, or the current worth of the account, whichever is greater. In this case, your original deposit of $25,000 is greater. Since you withdrew $18,000

before dying, the insurance company will owe your beneficiaries an additional $7,000.

Did the guarantee help you while you were alive? No. Were you able to take the loss in your account off your taxes, or use it to offset a gain? No. And what if you hadn't died in a few years? How long would the remaining money have had to sit in your account, losing value? For a long time, perhaps, even as the annual mortality fee and other charges continued to accrue.

Do I think that paying the mortality fee to protect your deposit is worth it? No, I do not.

Are there special disadvantages to a variable annuity in a bear market?

Yes. Even if you decide to hedge any stock-market losses by investing in or switching to a money-market fund within your variable annuity, the fees and charges you will pay on your annuity account diminish your return. Therefore, your return will not be as great as it would be in a money-market fund outside a variable annuity.

I'm considering buying a variable annuity to hold in my retirement account. Is this a good idea?

No! As a rule, buying any annuity to hold in a retirement account is a bad idea, and a variable annuity is no exception. The problem, in a nutshell, is this: You are buying a tax-deferred investment product to hold within a tax-deferred investment *account,* and so you are paying for the benefit of an extra layer of tax protection that you don't need. The price you pay for that extra tax deferral is about 1.5 to 2 percent of your annuity balance every year in fees and charges.

TRADITIONAL IRA VS. VARIABLE ANNUITY WITHIN AN IRA: WHICH IS BETTER?		
	Traditional IRA	Variable Annuity Within an IRA
tax deferral	yes	yes
pre-59½ tax penalty	yes	yes
70½ mandatory withdrawal	yes	yes
surrender charges (before about seven years)	no	yes
state premium tax	no	yes
mortality charges	no	yes

Above is a quick comparison of the advantages you get with a traditional IRA and a variable annuity.

As you can see, you gain nothing extra with an annuity, besides fees and charges. (This comparison is not applicable to annuities held in Roth IRAs.)

Can you remind me what the fees and charges you mentioned are?

Yes. In addition to a possible surrender charge if you cash out early, your annuity insurance company will charge you an annual mortality fee and expense fees, and that's all on top of any fees associated with the mutual funds you choose. Now, whether paying these fees makes sense, even outside of a retirement account, is something you'll have to decide yourself; but *within* a retirement account, I believe that they are much too hefty a price to pay for a privilege that is already inherent in your retirement account.

Let's look at an example. Say you have two IRAs, each with a $25,000 balance. One is invested in a variable annuity. In this account, you have divided your money equally among five mutual funds. The second account is an IRA but *not* invested in a variable annuity. Here, too, you have $25,000 invested in equal proportions in the same five mutual funds. Let's say that during the next 15 years together those mutual funds average an 8.5 percent annual return. How much will you have in each IRA?

In the first IRA, invested through the variable annuity, you will have $68,976. In the second IRA, invested directly in the mutual funds, you will have $84,994. Why the $16,018 difference? That's the damage the 1.5 percent in annuity-specific fees can do to the growth of your money. And remember, these fees aren't buying you a tax advantage, either, because all your money has been in tax-advantaged retirement accounts.

Finally, don't forget that a variable annuity carries its own early-withdrawal surrender charges on top of the 10 percent IRS penalty tax that applies to both annuities and IRAs.

My financial adviser is recommending that I buy a variable annuity within my retirement account. What should I do?

Get yourself another financial adviser, pronto.

What if I already own a variable annuity in my retirement account?

Unless the variable annuity is an unbelievably great performer, I would advise you to cash it in as soon as the surrender period expires. Take your money and buy into some solid, well-rated, no-load mutual funds within your IRA. If your annuity returns have been horrible, on the other hand, you might want to consider cashing out even if the surrender charge is still in force. Or you could simply withdraw the 10 percent a year you are allowed to take without incurring the surrender penalty and transfer those funds into a good no-load mutual fund; you can do this every year until the surrender period is up. Since the money is already sheltered within a retirement plan, you will not have to worry about the tax implications.

What should I do if my variable annuity is not sheltered within a retirement account?

Everything I noted in the previous answer applies to you, too. But if you're considering cashing out of your annuity altogether, you must also take into account penalties for withdrawals prior to age 59½ *and* ordinary taxation on the money when withdrawn, plus a possible state premium tax. Because of all these pesky factors—the reasons I do not like variable annuities to begin with—I would advise you to see a good, honest fee-based financial planner. Give him or her an exact, detailed description of your financial situation—including your age, your family situation, your financial goals, your assets and liabilities, your tax bracket, the terms of the annuity you purchased, and how long you have owned it. He or she will take these particulars into account and advise you on how to proceed with your contract.

How do I know if a variable annuity is right for me?

In my opinion, it *may* be an advantageous investment only if you like to trade—that is, buy and sell—mutual funds often, won't need your money for years to come, and are in a very high tax bracket now but plan to be in a much lower tax bracket at retirement.

INDEX ANNUITIES

In its effort to keep up with mutual funds, the insurance industry introduced yet another kind of annuity in the mid-1990s—the index annuity. It was created to compete with very popular index funds, mutual funds that track a stock-market index. I have to admit I like the concept—for the right investors.

How does an index annuity work?

Like all annuities, an index annuity is a contract with an insurance company for a specific period of time. An index annuity tracks a particular stock-market index, such as the Standard & Poor's 500. Your rate of return will usually be a set percentage of the increase in that index in the corresponding index year, up to a maximum of a given percent. There is also a guarantee against losses. The surrender period on an index annuity is typically longer than other surrender periods—about seven to ten years.

Can you give me an example of how the set percentages work?

Yes. Let's say that your index annuity promises to give you 50 percent of what the S&P 500 index returns, up to a maximum return of 10 percent per year. You invest $20,000 on March 15. By March 15 of the following year, the S&P 500 index has increased 30 percent. According to the terms of your annuity, the insurance company has to give you 50 percent of that increase, up to a maximum of 10 percent. Since 50 percent of 30 percent is 15 percent, which is 5 percent higher than the preset yearly maximum of 10 percent, you will be credited with a 10 percent gain on your original deposit, in this case $2,000. If the S&P 500 index had gone up only 15 percent for the year, you would be entitled only to a 7.5 percent gain on your investment.

You say there is a guarantee on the downside. What if the S&P 500 goes down 30 percent?

Yes, there is a guarantee on the downside, which is why investors in index annuities accept a ceiling of 10 percent a year on their gains. In fact, for those who do not want to take any downside risk, the index annuity can be a good option. Unlike regular index funds, where you claim 100 percent of the gains but also suffer 100 percent of the decreases, in an index annuity your money can only go up; it cannot go down. If you invest $20,000 in an index annuity on March 15 and by the following March 15 the index has fallen by 30 percent, you will still end up with $20,000 at the end of that year. The next year, when the market rises by 20 percent, you will be credited with 50 percent of that increase up to a maximum of 10 percent or, in this case, 10 percent, or $2,000. So instead of having a total of $18,000 after two years (you would have lost $5,000 in the first year and gained back only $3,000 in the second year), as you would in a

typical mutual-fund account, you will have $22,000. This kind of annuity limits your upside but effectively protects you from a downturn.

Please note: This safety feature is not included in all index annuities, so be sure to ask your insurance company whether it applies to the annuity you're considering.

Are there any other safety features attached to index annuities?

Yes. Index annuities typically come with a guarantee as to your total return over the life of the annuity. No matter which available index you choose to track, in the long run you can't lose. Why? Because once your surrender period is over, the insurance company typically guarantees that you will get back at least 110 percent of what you originally invested *or* the balance of your account, whichever is greater. If you invest $20,000, the worst-case scenario will leave you, after seven years, with $22,000, or about a 1.4 percent minimum guaranteed annual return on your investment. Again, if you are willing to give up some upside potential, an index annuity can help you protect yourself against downside risk, both in the short term and the long term.

Are index annuities better in bear or bull markets?

Because of the protections they offer in exchange for limiting upside potential, I like index annuities best in markets that are going down. In a down market, the company has to pay you something even if the indexes plummet. If the indexes go up one year, you can lock in gains for that year. Either way, you avoid taking the hits in the down years.

What would you look out for with an index annuity?

Be sure you know exactly what percentage you'll earn on any increases in the index you choose, as well as the annual and the total maximum and minimum gains. Ask whether the insurance company has the right to change any of these percentages during the contract period. If so, be wary. Finally, be sure you know the length of the surrender period and the size of all fees and sales loads you'll be charged.

How do I know if an index annuity is right for me?

If you do not want to take any risks but still want to play the stock market, a good index annuity may be right for you.

SPLIT ANNUITIES

My financial adviser has put me into a split annuity that gives me monthly income, but he says I will also get all my money back in five years. What is a split annuity, and how is it different from an immediate annuity that is held outside of a retirement account?

A split annuity is a tax-efficient annuity tailored to give you a regular income *plus* growth. In a split annuity, the insurance company simply divides the money you give it into two accounts. One account repays you a designated sum of money each and every month over a specific period of time. The other account is left in place to grow, either through stock-market investments or through accumulated interest payments fixed by the company. The goal is that, by the time the first half of the money is totally depleted through payments to you, the second half will have grown to be worth at least the amount of the original deposit.

The reason people split annuities is this: During the first years, when you are withdrawing money from one half, since you are mainly getting back your principal, you do not have to pay taxes on the majority of the money you are receiving. At the end of the contract, the other half of your annuity is still intact, and you can do it all again. If interest rates are higher or the economy is better than it was during the first contract period, you may do even better the second time around. That is why people like split annuities better than an immediate annuity, where you lock in your income forever at the start.

Are there drawbacks to a split annuity?

It will depend on your goals and on whether the money that you deposit into a split annuity is in a retirement account or not. Outside of a retirement account, in my opinion, in most cases they make no sense whatsoever. This is because you are converting money that you have already paid taxes on slowly but surely to taxable dollars again.

Let's say you deposited $100,000 with money you have already paid taxes on into a split annuity. The annuity company splits that money into two accounts, each with $50,000 in them. You start to receive monthly income from one of those accounts, which makes you very happy—not only are you receiving a higher monthly check than what the interest on the $100,000 could have generated for you, but you also have to pay less taxes on those checks because they are made up mainly of your own money coming back to you.

All this while the $50,000 on the other side is left to grow back into your original $100,000 by the time the monthly stream of income runs out. And, sure enough, this is exactly what happens. But here is the problem. The $100,000 now in your account is made up of $50,000 of money you paid taxes on, and $50,000 that you have *never* paid taxes on. So if you go to take out that $100,000, you will pay ordinary income tax on $50,000 of it. What if you are in a higher income-tax bracket at that time?

What usually happens, however, is that you do not need the money and you start the process all over again. This time around, you are paying more in taxes on your monthly income, because more of the payment is from money you have never paid taxes on. At the end of the second cycle, *all* $100,000 is taxable if you take it out. What if you then die? Your beneficiaries now owe income tax on all that money. Or what if you need a large sum because you are ill or you want to buy a retirement home or you need to pay to stay in a nursing home? Now you are in trouble. A split annuity can make sense in some cases, such as in a retirement account, where all the money is pretax anyway, but I would check carefully before I signed up for one.

IMMEDIATE, OR INCOME, ANNUITY (SPIA)

What is an immediate, or income, annuity?
An immediate, or income, annuity guarantees the annuitant a fixed income that begins to be paid as soon as the investment is made. This income continues for the rest of his or her life.

Also known as an SPIA (single-premium immediate annuity), this is the only type of annuity where you don't incur a 10 percent IRS penalty tax when you take withdrawals before age 59½. In some cases, beneficiaries receive the income from an immediate annuity for a certain period after the death of the annuitant. For the promise of lifelong income, however, you must sign over all the money in the annuity to the insurance company with full knowledge that you will never be able to touch it again.

Are there tax advantages to an immediate annuity?
Yes. If you hold an immediate annuity outside a retirement account, part of each monthly payment is considered a return of principal on which you've already paid taxes, so that portion of the income is not taxed. The return of some of your principal along with the interest your funds are generating creates a higher monthly payment than you could probably get elsewhere on a guaranteed basis. Understand, however, that the higher monthly payment *includes* your principal; with other fixed-return investments, such as CDs or bonds, your principal remains intact.

If you hold an immediate annuity within a retirement account, you have probably purchased the annuity with pretax dollars and so will have to pay income taxes on the entire amount you receive each month.

What determines the amount of monthly income from an SPIA?
The interest portion of the payment is based on the size of your investment, your age, the current interest rates, and the maximum amount of

time you have chosen for the company to pay out the stream of income, even if you were to die. The income options range from the highest monthly amounts, for life only, to lower amounts, known as life-plus-five or life-plus-ten years certain.

How do I know if an SPIA is right for me?

Are you looking for a guaranteed monthly income with some tax benefits? Are you someone who immediately needs a higher income than a straight interest-bearing investment can provide? Can you afford to give up access to the principal paid for the annuity? Do you want to take advantage of a high-interest-rate environment? Are you without any beneficiaries? Then an SPIA may make sense for you. The perfect time to have purchased an immediate annuity, for example, with respect to interest rates, would have been in the 1980s, when interest rates were high.

Do you recommend SPIAs?

In most cases, no, because you are giving up all claim to your principal investment. Purchasing an SPIA in a low-interest-rate environment is something I would be especially wary of. If interest rates go up, you are stuck at the lower rate for the rest of your life. In fact, unless interest rates are very high, the rate guarantee tends to work in favor of the insurance company, not you.

TAX-SHELTERED ANNUITIES (TSAs)

Last but not least is the tax-sheltered annuity, or TSA, which many schoolteachers and hospital workers are offered in their retirement plans. The TSA really falls into the category of a retirement plan, since money is invested monthly in a TSA, unlike other annuities that are bought with a lump sum. All the money you invest in a TSA is qualified, or pretax, money—money on which you haven't yet paid taxes. In most cases, the TSA is an excellent investment vehicle. If you have a TSA in your retirement account, just make sure that the funds are performing in a satisfactory way.

ANNUITIZING YOUR INVESTMENT

When you "annuitize" your investment in an annuity, you agree to receive a fixed monthly income from the insurance company, typically for life. In return, you give up any claim to a lump-sum payment at the end of your original contract with the insurance company—in effect, you hand over all the money in your annuity account to the insurance company forever. Immediate, or income, annuities are set up this way from the beginning; all other kinds of annuities can be converted to this arrangement any time the owner chooses. The amount of your monthly income is typically based on your age, the amount of your original investment, the current level of interest rates, and the annuitization policy that was part of your original contract.

In some rare cases, annuitization makes sense. But there *are* alternatives. You do not have to annuitize (or even buy an immediate annuity or a split annuity) in order to get monthly income from your annuity. You can simply withdraw money every month from, for example, a single-premium deferred annuity. This way, you are not locked into a fixed interest rate; you have access to your money or you can leave it to your beneficiaries. But for those who want a guaranteed rate of return and a stable income, here is what you need to know.

I need income from my annuity. How do I decide whether to annuitize or simply take withdrawals?

Unless you want to lock in interest rates that are extremely high and bound to come down *and* the interest rate factors the insurance company uses to figure out your annuity payments are favorable, I would never annuitize. If you need income, just take monthly withdrawals.

LIFE-ONLY OPTION

The most basic annuitization option is called "life only." When you choose this option, the insurance company pays you a designated amount every month, starting immediately, for the rest of your life. The monthly payments tend to be the highest of any of the annuitization options and continue for as long as you live, even if you live a hundred years.

If, on the other hand, you opt for the life-only option and die a month after you start to receive your income, well, too bad—the payments stop, and your heirs get nothing. The reason this option gives you the highest monthly income is that the insurance company knows that once you die, it's off the hook.

How does the insurance company decide how much the monthly payments will be?

Your monthly payout—known as your "income per thousand"—is determined by a number of factors, including your age, your medical history, the size of your investment, and the current interest rate environment. An insurance company can project your life expectancy with pretty fair accuracy. Still, different companies offer different rates, so it's a good idea to do some research.

I don't understand the term "income per thousand." Can you elaborate?

Yes. Let me use an example. Let's say that you are a 70-year-old man and you enter into a life-only annuity. Based on the insurance company's experience and its trusty actuarial tables, it will assign you a specific monthly income per each $1,000 that you have invested in the annuity. Let's say that you have purchased an annuity worth $100,000 with a single premium. And let's say that the insurance company has agreed to pay you the grand sum of $9.42 per thousand dollars, for the rest of your life. This means that every month the insurance company will pay you $942.00.

Can you give me an idea of what the current life expectancies are?

Sure. According to the American Council of Life Insurance statistical tables, if you are a 60-year-old man, you are expected to live another 24.6 years. If you are a 60-year-old woman, you are expected to live another 27.4 years. If you are a 65-year-old man, you are expected to live another 20.4 years; a 65-year-old woman is expected to live another 23 years. At age 70, a man's life expectancy is 16.6 years, and a woman's is 18.8 years. If you are a man who has made it to age 75, you are expected to live another 13.2 years. At age 75, a woman is expected to live another 14.9 years.

What happens if the insurance company is wrong and I die sooner than the company expects?

In that case, the insurance company wins, big time. If you live longer than expected, the insurance company loses. But companies spread their risk over many annuity holders, so it's hardly a financial calamity when some of them outlive the predictions.

What if I fool the insurance company, take good care of myself, and live to be 100 years old?

Then you will get the last laugh. Using the above figures, in which the insurance company is paying you $942 a month, or $11,304 every year, on a $100,000 annuity you bought when you were 70, you would receive $339,120.

So are you saying that I should consider a life-only annuity option only if I can be pretty sure that I will outlive the company's life expectancy tables?

No, I am not. There is no way to know how long you will live. Your decision should be based on other considerations. If you have a spouse, children, or other people you'd like to take care of after your death, I would avoid this type of annuity like the plague.

LIFE-PLUS-FIVE-YEARS CERTAIN OR LIFE-PLUS-TEN-YEARS CERTAIN OPTIONS

What is a life-plus-five or life-plus-ten-years certain option?

With these annuitization options, the insurance company will pay you a designated amount every month for as long as you live, with one big difference: If you die soon after the payments begin, the annuity will continue monthly payments to your beneficiaries for five or ten years (your choice) from the date of the annuitization contract. In other words, this kind of annuity guarantees income for at least five or ten years *or* for as long as you live, whichever is longer.

What happens if I die the day after I sign up for a life-plus-ten annuity?

Your beneficiaries would get the income you were scheduled to get for the next ten years. If you were to die three years after you started receiving your monthly income, the company would pay your beneficiaries the same monthly amount for seven more years.

Is there any way to renegotiate during the course of my life how much income I will be getting?

No. Once you have chosen an option and started receiving your income, the amount remains the same for the rest of your life and/or for the rest of the time your beneficiaries receive the income. Even if interest rates skyrocket, your fixed income remains the same—fixed. This annuity contract is one that can most easily be compared to a monthly pension from a corporation.

TAXATION OF ANNUITIES

When I take my money out of an annuity, how will I be taxed?

Whether your annuity is qualified or nonqualified, when you withdraw your money from it at age 59½ or older, you will pay ordinary income taxes on any interest or earnings you have received above and beyond your original contribution. If, for example, you purchased a $5,000 annuity, the interest or gains you earned on that $5,000 would be taxable as ordinary income in the year you make your withdrawal. If your annuity is a qualified annuity—that is, if you have purchased it with pretax money—you will also pay ordinary income taxes on the original investment portion of your withdrawal.

The manner in which you are taxed on your withdrawals can vary, depending on whether you have a qualified or a nonqualified annuity.

What is the taxation policy on a nonqualified annuity?

Nonqualified annuities that have been purchased after August 13, 1982, are taxed on a Last In, First Out (LIFO) method. Any interest or gains the annuity has earned are considered to have accrued to your account last and therefore the earnings must come out first—and are treated as taxable income. Once you have withdrawn all your earnings, you can withdraw your original investment without incurring any additional taxes. If you happen to die with money remaining in a nonqualified annuity, your beneficiaries will have to pay income taxes on the earnings when they withdraw the funds.

What is the taxation policy on a qualified annuity?

Since you have never paid taxes on your original investment in a qualified annuity, the original investment and the earnings are both taxable when you (or your beneficiaries) take money out.

Do I pay annual income tax on undistributed earnings on annuities?

No. This is one of the good things about annuities—in fact, it's one of their main selling points. You don't pay taxes on earnings until you withdraw them. As a result, your initial investment tends to grow more quickly than it otherwise would, since not only your principal but also your tax money earns interest or gains. Still, remember: If you withdraw money before age 59½, you will be assessed a 10 percent early-withdrawal fee by the IRS, added to which there may be an insurance company surrender charge.

Besides income tax, is there any other tax I will pay if I take money out of my annuity?

Again, if you're younger than 59½, you may have to pay a 10 percent IRS penalty tax on any earnings you withdraw. There are exceptions; no penalty tax will be in force if you own an immediate annuity or if you take substantially equal periodic payments from the annuity that you have.

I have been told that if I close out the annuity totally, I will owe a state premium tax. What is that?

Very few people know about the state premium tax, but it can certainly take a bite out of your annuity. In some states, when you close an annuity account (even if you are simply transferring the balance to another company), you will owe a tax in the state in which you originally purchased the annuity. The state tax ranges from about 0.5 percent of your original deposit on a qualified annuity to about 2.5 percent on a non-qualified annuity. In many states, this is the price the state exacts for letting your money grow tax-deferred all these years. Please make sure you ask about a premium tax before buying an annuity in any given state.

What happens if I take my money out of the annuity and then put it directly into a new contract with a different annuity company?

Please don't do this. If you do, you will probably owe ordinary income taxes on anything above your original after-tax contribution, a state penalty tax, and, if you are not at least 59½ years old, a 10 percent IRS penalty tax on your earnings.

What if I leave my annuity to my spouse or children? What taxes will they owe, if any?

If you have purchased a nonqualified annuity (i.e., using after-tax dollars), they will owe ordinary income taxes on any interest or earnings on the account above your original contribution. Say you deposited $25,000 of after-tax money in an annuity, and the annuity is now worth $100,000. If they withdraw all $100,000 at once after your death they will owe taxes on $75,000, the difference between your original after-tax deposit ($25,000) and how much is in the account when they close it out ($100,000). If you purchased a qualified annuity (i.e., using money you had not yet paid income taxes on), they would owe ordinary income taxes on the entire $100,000.

Do annuities have to go through probate for my beneficiaries to get my money?

No. If you name a beneficiary who survives you, your annuity will avoid probate. If, however, you name your estate as beneficiary, the annuity will probably have to go through probate.

11

Wills and Trusts

FOREVER MORE

If you've ever had someone close to you die, you know there are no words to describe the pain and loss that follow. And the long period of adjustment after a loved one's death is often complicated by issues concerning money. Sometimes the person who has died has failed to plan ahead. Sometimes those left behind do not understand how to go forward financially.

Everyone will leave loved ones behind when he or she dies. If you want to behave lovingly toward those you leave behind, please take the time now to plan so that, in the event of your death, your family and heirs will not become financially unstable at the precise moment they are most emotionally vulnerable. I urge you to discuss your estate with your spouse or partner, with your children, and with anyone else who will be financially affected by your death. Also, if you are married or hold joint assets with someone else, please take time now to learn everything you can about your joint finances, so that if you are the one left behind you will not have to cope with financial confusion on top of your grief.

Thinking about your own death or the death of a family member is no easy assignment. Neither is contemplating serious illness or incapacity. But planning for the future does not have to make you feel morbid; it can, and probably will, provide you a sense of control over your own life. It's freeing to know that you've protected those you care most about in this life.

This chapter addresses questions people commonly have about how to care for themselves and those they love in case of illness, incapacity, or death. Estate planning is actually a fascinating process, for it involves examining your goals, your values, and your financial priorities. If you plan carefully, you and your family can save thousands or even hundreds of thousands of dollars in probate fees, estate taxes, and attorneys' fees as well as the nuisance of going through an unnecessarily complicated and lengthy probate process. In my experience, once you begin to take steps to protect the future of the people you care about, you will have started down the path toward securing your own financial freedom.

WILLS: DEFINING THE TERMS

What is an estate?

The term "estate" can have more than one meaning. Your *taxable* estate is the sum total of all your financial interests, both money and property. Basically, your taxable estate is made up of everything you own at the time of your death, including life insurance, retirement plans, and IRAs, less your outstanding debts. Your *probate* estate includes only those assets covered by your will.

What is a will?

A will is a legal document that designates how you want your money and property (your estate) to be distributed after your death. It also specifies your wishes regarding funeral and burial arrangements, and, if you have children who are minors, it states whom you request the court to appoint as their guardian.

Who is the testator?

If you are a man and you have created a will, you are called the testator of your will. A woman who has created a will used to be called the testatrix; however, in most legal arenas today the term testator is used without regard to gender.

What is a beneficiary?

A beneficiary is a person or organization designated to receive some or all of your assets upon your death. You can name as many beneficiaries as you like.

What is an executor?

An executor is the person you appoint in your will to settle your estate. This person will have the administrative responsibility of paying your bills and taxes (including estate taxes), supervising the process of locating and safekeeping your assets, and making sure that the wishes expressed in your will are carried out. In essence, an executor is in charge of the estate. A personal representative of an estate may be known as an administrator, executor, or fiduciary, depending on the type of document signed or not signed by you.

What is probate?

Probate is a court procedure by which assets pass from a deceased person to the proper beneficiaries. A judge has the authority to validate a will and then order that the assets subject to the will be distributed. A court order signed by the judge transfers ownership to the beneficiaries—without a court order, the beneficiaries cannot take ownership (with some exceptions), even if they are named in the will. We'll discuss the probate process in greater depth later in this chapter.

THE IMPORTANCE OF HAVING A WILL

How do I know if I need a will?

If you want to decide who should receive your assets upon your death—even if all you have is a car—you need a will. If you want to name a person who will be responsible for the care of your young child or children, you need a will. If you want to decide who will take care of your taxes, debts, and financial affairs when you die, you need a will.

What happens if I don't have a will?

You *do* have a will, so to speak, whether you know it or not. Even if you haven't personally drawn up a will, the state you live in has something called intestate succession rules. These intestate rules determine exactly who receives any assets held in your name when you die. Usually, your spouse and children receive your property first; if you aren't survived by a spouse or children, your grandchildren might be next in line, followed by your parents, siblings, nieces, nephews, and cousins. If you die without any relatives, or without relatives that anyone can find, your assets will pass to the state.

If you care about the things you have worked hard for in your lifetime and what will become of them, you need a will. In most cases, you also need a living trust.

What if I am estranged from most of my relatives and don't want them to inherit my assets?

All the more reason to have a will! Most people leave the bulk of their estate to their relatives, and most states assume that this is what you would have wanted, too. If you don't want your relatives to inherit your assets, you have to take the time to create a will and name your beneficiaries.

If I have been living with my life partner for 20 years and she dies without a will, do I have any legal right to the assets we share?

It depends. If you and your life partner own any property or accounts in joint tenancy with right of survivorship, you will be entitled to that property or money. But assuming that you don't have property or accounts held in joint tenancy and your partner does not have a will or a trust, the state will not recognize your relationship for the purpose of distributing your life partner's assets. In that case, your partner's blood relatives, or even the state itself, will receive your partner's assets before you do.

Is jointly held property the only type of asset that will not be disposed of by the state if I die without a will?

No. If you have designated a beneficiary on a retirement account, annuity, or an insurance pol-

icy or a pay-on-death account, for example, the beneficiaries who survive you will receive the money in those accounts whether or not you have a will. These assets will not have to go through the probate procedure, either.

I am so deep in credit card debt at this point that I wouldn't have an estate to leave to anyone. Shouldn't I deal with my debt first, before I spend money to draw up a will?

While it is very important that you map out a strategy for eliminating your debts, planning for the future of the people you love is the most important, most responsible thing you can do—for them *and* for yourself. In my experience, once you do so, you will gain peace of mind that will help clear a way to financial security. Even if you don't have many assets, a will can help your family with the costs of a funeral or burial. (State law may also allow you to specify burial/cremation directions in a separate letter that's drafted and signed. You may want to sign such a letter and keep a copy outside your safe-deposit box, with the original given to your executor.) When your grieving family goes to see a funeral director, they may not know that you didn't want them to pay thousands of dollars for embalming or an open casket ceremony. Similarly, if someone does not have the clear authority to take care of your personal property—your car, your clothes, or your furniture—your landlord (if you are a renter) may be very confused and not know what to do with them. A will enables you to specify how you would like your personal property and your funeral to be handled.

Another thing to bear in mind is that your estate may be worth more than you think, particularly if you have equity in your home or a life insurance policy through your job. The bottom line is that planning ahead is important no matter how much or how little money you have.

My neighbor and her husband have a joint will, which they said saved them some attorneys' fees. Do you think joint wills are a good idea?

I have to say that I don't. A joint will is a single will shared by two people, usually spouses. It typically contains the same provisions for each person—a husband leaves all his property to his wife, say, and vice versa, and after the death of both spouses the property typically goes to the children. The problem is that, in many states, as soon as one of the signatories dies, the joint will goes into probate. This means that the terms of the will are frozen for the surviving spouse. Though right now it may be hard to imagine ever wanting to alter your will, you should always preserve the right to change your mind. If you should remarry years after the death of your partner and want to will your assets to your new spouse rather than your children, you might be prevented from doing so by an old joint will.

Is a joint will the same as a mutual will?

No. A joint will is a single will shared by two people. Mutual wills are, typically, two separate wills that are identical in most ways, each person's will benefiting the other party. If you and your spouse each sign a will that has mirror or identical provisions, specifying that you leave everything to your partner and he or she leaves everything to you, these are considered mutual wills. You are not bound by promises made together, as you are in a joint will, so either of you can change your mutual will at any time.

I have a house in Maine where I spend my summers, but I spend most of the year in Virginia. Do I need a will for both states?

No. A single will is all you need, and you should have it drawn up in the state where you have your domicile (permanent residence). Get legal advice on establishing your domicile and on any special provisions that need to be included for your property in another state. And with all that property, please seriously consider a revocable living trust. (If you have only a will and not a revocable living trust, your beneficiaries may be required to go through two probates—one in Virginia, and an ancillary probate in Maine.)

My neighbor has a videotaped will. Is that a good idea?

Since most states do not recognize videotaped wills as legally binding, what I assume you mean is that your neighbor has a written will but also had someone videotape her talking about its contents. I sometimes recommend this as a precautionary measure to people who are concerned that someone will challenge the terms of their will or trust. Videotaping may not be necessary for you, but if you decide to do it, it should not cost you very much. Most videographers charge by the hour, and an experienced attorney will usually be able to refer you to someone who can provide this service.

THE KEY PLAYERS

EXECUTORS

What do I have to do if I am named an executor?

First, you must locate the will or trust and all the assets owned by the deceased person (bank and retirement accounts, stocks and bonds, insurance policies, real estate holdings, etc.). Once you have found the will, you must submit it to the probate court for authentication, usually with the assistance of an attorney. Once the will has been validated ("proved"), the court will officially appoint you as the executor of the will and give you a set of documents called letters testamentary. Some states call these letters of authority or letters of appointment. These legally empower you to do things in the estate's name, such as take charge of a bank account. (You will not have the authority to act on the estate's behalf without these letters.) You should get multiple copies of the letters testamentary—at least seven.

As executor, you are responsible for protecting the estate, which means, first and foremost, that you cannot give the beneficiaries any of the assets left to them until the probate court has approved the distribution (unless the laws of the state you're in allow some distributions without court approval). In some states, you are required to identify creditors and debts of the estate to the probate court.

You will need to monitor and record all the expenses and income that the estate pays out and receives while it is in probate.

You should obtain at least 15 certified copies of the death certificate. You may need these to transfer title to real estate or investment holdings, or even to a car. You may also need them to settle any life insurance claims or to close bank or brokerage accounts, if necessary.

You must notify all insurance companies, banks, brokerage firms, retirement plans and administrators, the Veterans Administration, or any other institution that had financial dealings with the deceased person. This includes any institution where the deceased person had joint accounts.

You must pay all bills still owed by the deceased out of a special checking account that you will have to establish in the name of the estate.

Sometimes the deceased's individual bank accounts will be changed into your name, as executor on behalf of the state, so that you can access funds to pay bills for the estate. Any accounts, money, or property held as a joint tenancy with right of survivorship (JTWROS) will go directly to the surviving person whose name appears on the title of that asset.

Before you close any bank accounts, make sure that the surviving spouse's (if relevant) financial needs will continue to be met until the estate is settled. You should also double-check with an estate attorney before closing any accounts.

If there is a safe-deposit box, make a complete inventory of its contents.

Look for the past three years of state and federal income tax returns. Besides providing information about the deceased's holdings, they should be held because the deceased can still be audited for three years after death. You will also be responsible for paying any taxes owed by the deceased to the government.

What kinds of bills still have to be paid after death?

Typically, all of them. Until an estate is settled, regular payments, such as mortgage payments and utility bills, need to be paid each month, as do any credit card bills or loans. Also, any expenses that result from the death or the illness preceding it, such as medical bills, funeral expenses, taxes, and executor, court, and probate fees must be paid. All of these obligations will have to be paid before the estate can be finally distributed.

What if there isn't enough cash in the estate to pay all the expenses due?

The executor will have to start selling off (liquidating) assets from the estate, such as a house or car, in order to cover these bills, even if payments cut into specific bequests for the beneficiaries. Some debts (such as attorney fees) are given priority over other debts, so that no other debt can be paid until these priority debts are settled.

Whom should I choose to be my executor?

Your executor should be someone you trust completely. He or she will sign for everything, manage the selling of your assets if you have debts to settle, and exercise control over your estate. As you can imagine, it is crucial that your executor be a responsible person. It is common to name a spouse or life partner as your executor. When you think about whom to choose, think about whom you would want to be the first one to arrive at your house after your death and become the keeper of the keys thereafter until everything is settled.

Can an executor get paid?

Yes. The fee varies depending on the state you live in. It is often calculated as a small percentage of the total value of your estate, usually between 2 and 5 percent. An executor's fee can easily be higher, particularly if your executor has to do anything out of the ordinary, in which case he or she may charge the estate additional fees.

Your executor has the power to choose not to be paid, and you can request, but not require, that he or she do this. For most people, serving as an executor can be very demanding, as he or she may be asked to perform many tasks. The amount of time it takes to settle an estate depends on factors beyond the executor's control, including how contentious the heirs are!

Why would an executor choose not to be paid?

It may make financial sense to decline to be paid if the executor is also the main beneficiary (which, again, is common if you have a surviving spouse or partner). Executor's fees are subject to income tax, but inherited property generally is not (the exceptions include retirement plans and traditional IRAs). If you find yourself in this situation and the estate is large enough to be subject to federal estate taxes, ask an attorney or an accountant to help you determine which option will afford you the best tax result. (Executor's fees are deductible for the estate on an estate tax or income tax return.)

Who will act as the executor of my estate if I die without a will?

If you die without a will, there will not be an executor. Instead, the court will appoint an administrator, who will perform most of the same tasks an executor would have performed, in terms of collecting and paying your debts and distributing your property. The laws of your state determine who serves as the administrator; usually a spouse is chosen first. But the person must petition the court to be appointed, so there is no guarantee about who will actually end up serving.

I am the executor of my father's estate and I've learned that funerals and burials are incredibly expensive! How do I know if I'm paying too much?

People often make very poor decisions when they are arranging funerals and burials, and that's understandable—you are tired, upset, stressed out, and probably don't know much about what you are buying. As a general rule, if a funeral home wants you to purchase something that will cost more than $10,000, you should probably go elsewhere or demand another type of service. A simple, dignified service that you can afford can be just as loving as a lavish one.

Your dad may have burial benefits through his life insurance policy, from the Veterans Administration (if he was in the service), through his job or a union, or from Social Security. Even if these benefits are modest, there's no reason not to use them if he has them.

Many people are concerned about the high cost of dying. If you are among them, I urge you to read Jessica Mitford's informative and surprisingly funny book, *The American Way of Death Revisited.*

Can an executor be sued?

Yes. As an executor, you are liable for any action you take on behalf of the estate, so you can be sued by the beneficiaries if the estate is managed carelessly. You also can be sued by someone you've contracted with on the estate's behalf. Let's say you hire a gardener to take care of the property surrounding the house of the deceased person until you sell the house, but then the estate doesn't have enough money to pay the gardener. If you, as the executor, entered into a contract with the gardener, you could be personally liable for any damages.

My aunt has just died and in her will she named me the executor of her estate. This is very unexpected, and I'm not sure that I can take on the responsibility right now. Do I have to?

No, you always have the right to refuse to serve as an executor. You don't have to give a reason. This raises an important point: People need to make their wishes known to each other while they are still alive. If your aunt had discussed her choice with you beforehand, you could have told her that you had reservations and she could have made other arrangements. It's not a good idea to surprise anyone with this responsibility. It's also a good idea to designate possible alternate executors in your will.

If you refuse the role of executor and no

alternate executors are named in the will, state law sets forth a preferred order for appointment among the options of spouse, child, parent, etc., but anyone can request or refuse appointment.

In addition to the financial aspects of planning my estate, is there anything else I should do to assist my executor or my loved ones after I die?

Although written instructions do not take the place of a will and may not be legally binding, it's not a bad idea to write out a list of instructions about the execution of your will and leave it in an accessible place. This list can state where to find your will and trust instruments (if you have them), bank and brokerage accounts, checkbooks, deeds, insurance policies (if you have them), and safe-deposit or post-office boxes. Alternatively, if you don't feel comfortable having all this information in one place, the list might simply mention the names and phone numbers of your attorney, financial adviser, and primary doctor. Finally, the list might contain other practical information, such as any specific wishes you have regarding your funeral and burial or any unusual maintenance needed for your house or your pet. If you do not have a friend or family member who is very knowledgeable about the details of your daily life, instructions such as these can be particularly helpful. There is no need to repeat anything you've already included in your will.

Generally, if most of your property is held in a revocable living trust, and your will has been properly organized and you have left clear instructions behind, you will greatly simplify your executor's job.

BENEFICIARIES

What happens if my beneficiaries die before I do?

You should designate alternate beneficiaries to receive your assets. In other words, you would state that you want your wife to receive all of your assets, but if she were to predecease you, then your assets should go to your daughter; your daughter becomes the alternate beneficiary to your wife. If the will is properly drafted, your attorney will have asked you to make decisions that cover every possibility.

My will talks about my beneficiaries receiving my residual estate. What does that mean?

A well-written will designates someone to receive your residual estate, which is whatever is left of your assets after beneficiaries have received their specific bequests. If you said, for example, that you wanted your local public library to receive anything left in your residual estate and one of your beneficiaries predeceased you, the portion of your estate that the deceased person would have received will pass to the library (if no alternate is named or called for under your state's law).

Some states will protect certain types of bequests from lapsing in this way. The most common example would be if you left something to your child but your child predeceased you. In some states, that bequest is automatically passed down to your child's children if you have not designated otherwise.

Can I have more than one residual beneficiary?

Sure. You can say that you want all your surviving children to share your residual estate equally (this is very common), or you can name several people and have them divide your residual estate, either equally or according to some other set of percentages specified in your will.

What if my beneficiary is a minor?

States do not usually allow children under the age of 18 to hold property valued at more than $2,500 to $5,000 as individuals. In your will you can designate a guardian to manage the property until your child reaches a certain age, but many states have complicated requirements for regular court supervision of property held for children. If, under a living trust and possibly under a will, you establish a trust and name a trustee to manage your child's property, you can save your child the often substantial costs of dealing with the courts. You will also give the trustee greater flexibility in managing the assets in the trust, as you can set the terms you want for the age(s) at which the children can gain access to the money, and what it can or can't be used for. For example, you can allow the trustee to hold back distributions if the child is going through a difficult time with alcohol or other substance abuse, or a divorce.

If my mother's will said that she wanted to leave everything to me, but she had an old life insurance policy that named her sister as the beneficiary, do I have any right to that life insurance money?

No, you don't. Retirement accounts, insurance policies, and other assets that require or have a beneficiary designation are entirely separate from, and are not controlled by, a will.

What happens if I have made specific monetary bequests in my will and I die without sufficient funds to cover gifts to my beneficiaries?

You can't give what you don't have. If your estate doesn't contain enough money to cover all your bequests, then all your bequests will be proportionally reduced. The system by which the court prioritizes those reductions is called an abatement. If, on the other hand, you have left a specific bequest—say, your car—to your daughter, but in the intervening years, you stopped driving and sold that car, then your daughter would not be entitled to any adjustment to make up for it.

I lived with my partner for ten years before he died, unexpectedly and without a will. I know he wanted me to inherit everything. How do I prove that?

I'm sorry to say that, generally, if your partner did not make provisions for you with a will or a revocable living trust or if you don't have jointly owned property, you have no inheritance rights at all. That is why it is so important that you do not assume things will take care of themselves after you're gone.

What if something terrible happens, like a car accident or a plane crash, and my husband and I die at the same time?

In most cases, the state will assume that each of you predeceased the other, which means that each of your estates will be distributed as if the other person had died first. You can request a different assumption in your will or living trust, with certain limitations that you should discuss with your attorney.

My wife, who is my main beneficiary, can use my life insurance proceeds to pay for my funeral expenses, right?

Not necessarily. Your life insurance company may not release the death benefit for many months, particularly if the cause of death seems unclear or suspicious. This is why it is important to anticipate any immediate financial needs. For example, how much money will your wife need to live each month? In the best-case scenario, you would create an emergency fund that would cover at least six months of living expenses and any death-related costs, and you would keep the fund in an account with a joint tenant with right of survivorship designation. Then, in the event that there is a delay in the release of your insurance proceeds, financial hardship will not be added to your wife's grief.

When my mother died, she left everything to me as the sole beneficiary. To help me out, the funeral director offered to process her life insurance and Social Security claims for an additional fee. Do you think this is a good idea?

The reason a funeral director would offer to perform these services for you is to make sure that the funeral costs will be paid as quickly and efficiently as possible—in other words, the funeral director is attending to his interests, not yours. Now, that doesn't necessarily mean the funeral director is dishonest, but I think the better way to handle this is to have the executor (or whoever is handling your deceased mother's affairs) make the life insurance and Social Security claims. The process will be better coordinated if one person handles all the claims.

I have a beloved dog who is like a member of my family. Can I leave her money after I die, so that I know she will be taken care of in the best possible way?

Most states consider pets your property, which means that they cannot receive property themselves or be the beneficiaries of a trust. Nevertheless, there are many passionate dog and cat owners who share your concern. Many states now allow you to create a trust for the care of a pet, within certain limitations—including that the trust must terminate when your pet dies and that a court can reduce the amount of money in the trust if it feels you have set an excessive amount aside. Check with a local attorney to see if your state allows such a trust and whether it is appropriate for you. If there's someone you love and rely on and who will be taking your pet after you die, you may just want to leave this person the money outright, with the understanding that he or she will use it to care for your dog.

As a beneficiary, if I inherit a house that still has a mortgage on it, will I get the house and mortgage as a package deal?

Probably. A will should be carefully drafted to avoid confusion about whether the person who is leaving you the house intends to pass the house on free and clear or subject to the mortgage. The promissory note and deed of trust held by the bank may require the mortgage be paid in full on the death of the mortgage holder. Be sure you know what the terms of the mortgage are before you take any action. And remember that even if the monies and the home are tied up in probate, any mortgage payments will still be due.

My father won't have much money when he dies, but he does own the house I grew up in free and clear. I know that it gives him a lot of comfort to know that, as his only beneficiary, I will be able to live in the house. Is a will adequate for him?

No, it is not! Let's think about what could happen to that house if your father passes it on to you through a will. You will have to pay probate fees. If your father has no other money that he is leaving you, you will have to pay those fees out of your own pocket immediately, before you can take ownership of the house. You might have to take out a loan in order to pay those fees. What if you do not qualify for a loan, and the only way you can pay the fees is to sell the house? These are choices you don't want to have to face, especially at a time when you are emotionally least equipped to do so. I'm sure this is not what your father would want for you. A revocable living trust, which I discuss later in this chapter, can eliminate probate fees. But please note: If there are estate taxes due on the house, you'll need to pay them whether your father had a will or a living trust.

GETTING A WILL

How do I make a will?

You can see an attorney to have a will drawn up, or you can write it yourself, if you are careful to fulfill certain requirements. You can also buy will forms from many bookstores and stationery stores (these are preprinted, with blank spaces where you write in the names of your beneficiar-

ies and otherwise personalize the will), or you can buy computer software that will help you write a will. Many states now have a statutory will form that the state legislature has approved for use. This is the best choice if you are buying a form. You will see that preparing a will is relatively simple; it's after you die that the complications tend to arise. Still, keep in mind that any do-it-yourself will really needs to be reviewed by an attorney to make sure it is right for you. It probably won't include provisions to save on estate taxes or handle special situations—such as two families connected by a second marriage. And you'll need advice on title and beneficiary designations.

Can't I just write a will expressing my wishes on a regular piece of paper?

Yes. This is called a holographic will, and many states recognize it. If you decide to do this, you must write everything out in your own handwriting, date and sign the document, and then make sure that there is no other handwriting on the document—any marks in another person's handwriting will render your will invalid. If you make a mistake while you are writing a holographic will or change your mind after you have completed it, don't cross anything out, because that will also invalidate the will. Instead, tear it up and start over again. Be aware that a holographic will may ultimately turn out to be very expensive for your beneficiaries, since it is not unusual for special court hearings to be held to interpret what the will really says and to remedy omissions from the will. Contesting of the will may also be more common with a holographic will.

How much does a will cost?

If a lawyer draws up your will, it could cost between $100 and $3,000, depending on the complexity of your financial and personal situation and how much tax planning and drafting you require. A computer program costs about $50, and if you buy a will form at a stationery store it should cost less than $10.

Does a will have to be notarized?

No, but it needs to be witnessed when you sign it. Witnesses must be present to verify that you were of sound mind and weren't subject to undue influence or duress.

How many witnesses are required?

Most states require two, but some require three.

Can anyone witness my will?

Witnesses must be competent adults who are not named as a beneficiary or executor in the will. Remember, they simply need to be mature people who, if need be, could testify under oath that they watched you sign and that you did so by your own free will.

Do witnesses usually have to testify in court after someone dies?

Rarely, if ever. In fact, most states now have rules that allow witnesses to sign a brief affidavit at the time of witnessing declaring, essentially, that various signing formalities and requirements were followed. This means that, after you die, the will is "self-proving."

Do I have to reveal what's in my will to the witnesses?

No. All they are witnessing is that you are signing the will. As you sign, you tell them that what you are signing is your will, but they do not have to read it or be told anything about its contents.

WHERE TO KEEP THE WILL

I keep my will in my safe-deposit box. My sisters say that's a bad idea. Are they right?

Probably not. Although it's true that banks are capable of "sealing" a safe-deposit box after you die, this is not as common as it used to be. There are potential drawbacks, however. If your spouse or partner's name is not also on the box, and if no one has a key, it can be difficult for your loved ones to get access to your will after you die. Naming your children and spouse as joint tenants on the box or registering it in the name of your trust will make it easier for your successor, trustee, or loved ones to gain access to the box. The important thing is to keep your will in a place that you feel is safe. It can be your safe-deposit box, a home fire box, or the top drawer of your desk.

What if I have a safe-deposit box held in joint tenancy?

In this case, either joint tenant can open the box at any time, although in some states the box will be sealed after the death of one of the joint tenants, which means that the survivor will need a waiver or a government-approved inventory before gaining access to the box.

CHANGING YOUR WILL

Can I change my will whenever I feel like it?
Yes, you can change your will at any time, for any reason. Call your attorney and ask him or her to draft a codicil, a separate document that incorporates your changes. My attorney prefers to rewrite the will, since it is easier to read a single document than to compare two separate documents and figure out which covers what topics. To avoid confusion later on, you should destroy any wills you have that are no longer valid. This is a good reason why you and you alone should hold all your original documents and not have them held for you by a lawyer (who may die, become disabled, retire, or move away).

Are there times when you can't change a will?
No, not unless you are mentally incapacitated or have signed another agreement that controls the contents of your will. The most typical examples of this might be a divorce decree or a prenuptial agreement, if you and your spouse (or maybe your ex-spouse on behalf of your children) have negotiated a specific bequest or other arrangement.

Instead of changing my will from time to time, couldn't I just leave everything to my estate?
Please do not do that, for remember, your estate will be distributed according to the last will that you had drawn up. If your will says your husband is to get everything and you have since divorced him and no longer want him to inherit your assets, he may still get everything upon your death if you don't change your will. If you do not have a will and you just leave everything to your estate, your assets will pass according to the intestate rules.

CONTESTS OF YOUR WILL

Can just anybody contest my will?
Relatives and others—creditors, significant others, those who gave you care—who think that they are entitled to a part of your estate can ask the court to award a share to them. The judge ultimately may not award the contestors anything, but your beneficiaries will have to wait during the probate until the claim is resolved, and they will need to spend some of your money fighting the claim.

Are there any circumstances in which my will is more likely to be contested?
The accepted grounds for contesting your will are that you were incompetent when you signed it and did not understand what you were doing, you were being pressured by someone to create a will that read a certain way and that he or she exerted undue influence on you, or there was some mistake made in the paperwork. It is not easy to win on any of these grounds. A will is most likely to be contested on the grounds of undue influence when one child is given considerably more or less than your other children or, if you are in a second marriage, your current wife or children from that marriage are given considerably more than you leave for the children from your first marriage. If you leave an unexpected

bequest, such as to a lover or other individual whom your family does not know, there may be contests.

How can I discourage people from contesting my will?

Some attorneys advise that if you know someone may be hostile to your distribution plan, you leave him or her more than a token amount of money (not too large and not too small) as a bequest in the will and then include a "no contest" clause in the will. This means that a person contesting the will will receive nothing. The hope is that the person will be afraid of losing the bequest and so won't challenge the will. Such a bequest will probably cost your estate less than a court battle would, even if your intended beneficiaries won. Think of this bequest as an anti-contest insurance policy to protect your beneficiaries.

If you unintentionally omit a child or spouse from your will, however, the spouse or child can claim a share of your estate even if there is a no-contest clause. The law assumes that you would not intentionally exclude a spouse or child and will correct your "oversight" if it is challenged. This assumption covers even children born out of wedlock who you may not have known were yours! If you think there is even a remote possibility that you could have a child that you have not mentioned in your will, your attorney should include a special clause in the will called a pretermitted heir provision, which will make your intentions clear. However, state law may give your spouse or child a right to a portion of your estate no matter what.

A recent news item illustrates this seemingly farfetched point: A billionaire left his estate to his three known children. After he died, eight people from around the Pacific Rim made claims against the estate, saying that they were also his children and therefore rightful heirs. Their claims were initially denied in court. However, the man had had a biopsy done on a mole some years before he died and the doctor still had the sample. DNA from the sample was tested and, sure enough, all eight children were found to be his! Since the will had no pretermitted heir provision, they all were able to take shares equal to those of the other three children. The estate was divided into eleven shares.

Is there any way to completely prevent having my wishes contested?

No. You cannot prevent someone from going to court. However, if most of your property is transferred via a trust, you probably can minimize the possibility of having your wishes contested. Also, making an effort to clarify your wishes and decisions with your family, particularly if you are not leaving your children equal shares of your property, may abate potential confusion and resentment that could lead to a challenge. This could be as simple as a statement in your will or to your heirs reading, "I am leaving Jane half as much as I am leaving Cindy because Jane's income as an attorney is significantly higher than Cindy's as a nursery school teacher," or "John's bequest is larger than what I am leaving the rest of my children because he is disabled and has special expenses." The danger of putting in such explanations is what may happen in the event that Jane's earnings go down somewhat, or she stops working to be a stay-at-home mom, or she becomes disabled.

WILLS AND RELATIONSHIPS

Does a divorce automatically void a will that leaves property to a former spouse?

It depends on the state. In California, for example, this is true but is not automatically true in all states. Please don't make a mistake about this matter. The wishes you want to express in your will can be affected by a marriage, separation, or divorce, or even the birth of a child. When you experience a major life change of any kind, remember to review your will to be sure it still reflects your priorities and desires.

Another instance in which people often forget to review their wills or trusts is after a spouse or partner dies. In most cases, the deceased partner was designated to receive the bulk of the estate, so it's important to change your will or trust in this situation. While you're at it, don't forget to change the beneficiary on your IRA, 401(k), annuities, bonds, and life insurance policy, too.

What if I remarry and I die before changing my will to include my new wife?

Most states will award your new wife a share of your property, unless you have left her enough money via some other vehicle, such as a life insurance policy, or in a joint bank account, so that she is already receiving an amount equal to that to which a spouse is entitled under the intestate succession laws in your state. But don't rely on state laws. Take the time to revise and update your estate plan after this significant life change.

I'm in a second marriage, but I want to make sure that my children from my first marriage inherit my whole estate. How can I arrange this?

The first thing to do is to make sure that you have a will or a trust that expresses your wishes, because if you die without one, the rules of intestate succession will probably automatically entitle your current spouse to a specified portion of your estate. This is one area where you should definitely see an attorney. You will probably need a marital agreement with your second spouse specifying who owns income earned during the marriage. Also, be sure to avoid commingling of assets and to take title to your personal assets, keeping your goals in mind.

My wife and I drew up a will after our daughter was born, leaving everything to her after we're both gone. About ten years have passed, and we just realized that we've had two sons since then who aren't mentioned in our will! We're going to update it, of course, but what would happen if we died without doing so?

Your sons would probably be able to make a claim on your estate, but the probate court would control how much they could receive, and it would be a time-consuming and costly process for everyone involved, including the estate. They would also receive their entire share, probably at age 18, in one lump sum. This is another good reason to review and update your estate-planning documents regularly.

My son borrowed $30,000 from me for the down payment on his first house. He has been paying me back gradually but still owes me a lot. Are there any tax consequences if I forgive this debt in my will?

Yes, there are. Whether or not the loan was agreed to in writing, you are free to release your son from the obligation to pay you back. If you forgive the debt, however, you should know that the outstanding amount on the loan will be considered part of your estate for estate tax purposes. Also, the loan must be made at customary rates of interest. If you have charged only 2 percent interest when the standard rate is 8 percent, the IRS will say that you made a gift of the 6 percent difference. There are exceptions to this under so-called "gift loans." Get tax advice before forgiving debts in your will.

PROBATE

What is the point of probate, anyway?

Probate is an ancient process. It dates back to the feudal period in Europe. The reason for its existence today is essentially to make sure that an estate is distributed properly, according to the wishes of the deceased person. While this may be preferable to having no oversight process at all, the process involves expense, delays, and drawbacks. There are good alternative ways of controlling the distribution of your assets, mainly with a revocable living trust (more about trusts later).

How long does the probate period last?

The probate process can last anywhere from six months to two years or more.

I understand that my property won't formally be transferred while my estate is in probate. That's just a formality, right?

Wrong! It's not a formality to have your bank accounts under the jurisdiction of the probate court. While a spouse and minor children may be able to receive a family allowance during the probate process, allowances must generally be approved by a court. In the meantime, if your assets are not properly managed, or if the estate has to pay substantial fees while it is being managed, it could decrease significantly in value. Waiting too long to control what is rightfully yours is hardly a formality.

I recently saw a book in my local bookstore that was a collection of the last wills and testaments of famous people. Can just anyone learn the contents of any will?

This is something about probate that surprises a lot of people: Everything in your will becomes a matter of public record after the will has been probated. This means that anybody who can do a little research can discover the value of your estate. Even Jacqueline Kennedy Onassis, who was so protective of her privacy when she was alive, was not exempt from this—her will is available as a $4.95 paperback book! Unfortunately, it is not only the wills of the famous that are of interest: Some unscrupulous people regularly monitor all such records, because they are on the lookout for a person who's just inherited a chunk of money and might be vulnerable and gullible enough to invest in some scheme.

Do all states have probate?

Yes.

If I live in California but die while I am on vacation in Nevada, where will the probate take place?

Probate will take place in California, your primary state of residence—in legalese, the state of your domicile.

I am a single parent. Does the probate of my will concern only my financial affairs or could it affect my guardianship decision, too?

There are two types of guardianship: that of a person and that of an estate. The guardian of your child will control where the child lives and goes to school, give consent for medical treatment, and decide what religion the child will practice. The guardian of the estate will control the money. These guardians need not be the same person.

While the will is in probate, the court will establish a probate guardianship of the person. Typically, it will choose the guardian you selected, but it could, in certain circumstances, find that he or she is not in your child's best interest. It could also exercise control over any money your children are due to inherit until they turn 18. Trusts under a will or living trust can extend the payment date.

Keep in mind that the court will almost always appoint the surviving natural parent of a child as guardian, even if you had a terrible divorce and were granted sole custody of the child. If you are in this situation, you definitely want your child's money to be managed in a trust to prevent your former spouse from handling the child's money as the guardian of the estate.

THE COSTS OF PROBATE

How much does probate cost?

A lot! Your beneficiaries may have to pay court fees, attorneys' fees, and possibly even executor's fees. The total cost can range from about 3 percent of the total gross value of a large estate to more than 8 percent of a smaller estate, including the executor's fee. (The executor's fee may be waived, especially if the executor is the sole or main beneficiary.) Just as an example, in California, here are the fees you could expect to pay:

Estate Size	Combined Basic Fees for Executor and Attorney
$100,000	$8,000
$200,000	$14,000
$300,000	$18,000
$400,000	$22,000
$500,000	$26,000
$600,000	$30,000
$1,000,000	$46,000

In states where there is no schedule of fees set forth by law, attorneys are free to charge whatever they like, subject to any agreement they make with you. If there is a small estate that takes a long time to settle due to unexpected details (and there are always unexpected details), the attorney can wind up charging a lot of money. In New Jersey, for example, a $70,000 estate left to your children could cost them $20,000 to probate! Keep in mind that these fees have to be paid before the remaining assets are distributed.

My mom and I live together in her home in California. A few years ago she took out a big *mortgage to help with our expenses. Her house is worth $200,000, but she still owes about $190,000 on the mortgage. I plan to continue to live in it after she dies. How much will I owe in probate fees?*

All states base probate on the fair market value of an asset, not on the equity in the asset. Because California law will calculate the value of the home without taking into account any loans taken against it, your mom's house would be valued at $200,000 for probate fee purposes. The same would hold true for cars or other assets your mother might still owe payments on. In this case, if all your mother owned was her house, the probate fees on it would be $10,000—more than the equity she has in the house.

What if I want to keep the house that was left to me, but I don't have the money to pay the probate fees?

Unless you can get a loan on the house, the house will be sold to pay the fees and you will be out of luck. Remember, when you go through probate, in most cases, the attorneys' fees are the first to be paid out of the estate. You avoid this with a trust.

My mother has Alzheimer's disease. Is it too late for her to get a living trust, or are we stuck with her will and going through probate?

It depends. State law may allow a judge to authorize establishment of a living trust as part of a court conservatorship or guardianship.

Can I save money by having my attorney serve as my executor?

In some states an attorney cannot take a fee for serving as the executor as well as the attorney for a probate estate. He or she must choose to be paid as one or the other. Although having a single person perform both jobs would, in theory, save you money, as a practical matter you won't find many attorneys willing to do both jobs. Some states see the double role as a conflict of interest and have laws that allow beneficiaries to prevent the attorney who wrote the will from acting as executor. Since some states go to such lengths to discourage this type of arrangement, it's generally not a good idea, unless the attorney is a relative or a close personal friend whom the beneficiaries are unlikely to find objectionable.

If an estate is going through probate, is there any way to reduce attorney fees?

You may be able to negotiate a lower fee. You can ask for a written agreement from the attorney stating that he or she will not charge extraordinary fees (which are in addition to the state-set statutory fees), or that such fees will not exceed a certain dollar amount.

Does the court charge a fee?

Courts charge a filing fee in order to accept a probate case. Most states require you to pay to have a notification of the death published in a newspaper for a period of several weeks. There are also recording fees, certification fees, and a fee for a court-appointed appraiser, who places a value on the estate. These various charges, which will differ depending on what state the deceased lived in and how much the estate is worth, can easily add up to several thousand dollars.

I've heard that I need to have my death published in a newspaper. Why would I need to do that?

Because it is required by law. The law exists to prevent fraud and to allow legitimate claims to be made against an estate. The small but significant possibility exists that an estranged relative or former business associate with whom you were on poor terms could read such a notice and decide to contest your will and seek a part of your estate or file a creditor's claim for money owed to him.

If it takes two years for my executor to probate my estate, will the estate have to pay income taxes on the money earned by the estate while it is still in probate?

Yes. This is something that many people overlook. An estate is like a person in that it must file an annual income tax return. It is the executor's responsibility to make sure the estate pays its taxes, and the executor is personally liable for the payment of the tax if the taxes aren't paid with estate funds. However, the executor is not liable if the estate had insufficient funds to pay the tax when the executor took over.

PROBATE ALTERNATIVES

Some states have begun to simplify their probate rules and procedures in certain circumstances (if, for example, you have a very small estate), allowing property to be transferred after someone dies by either an affidavit or a summary probate. If you're interested in pursuing this further, I'd recommend you check out *8 Ways to Avoid Probate*, published by Nolo Press.

What is a probate affidavit?

This is a legal form that certifies that your assets that would otherwise be subject to probate are worth less than a certain designated dollar amount. Your beneficiaries present this affidavit to the institutions that hold your assets, to show that they are legally entitled to them without a probate or court order.

How does the affidavit process work?

It simply requires whoever is going to own the deceased person's property to file an affidavit to transfer the title. Not all states will allow people to transfer real estate holdings in this way.

What is summary probate?

If the estate doesn't meet the requirements of a probate affidavit, some states might allow a summary probate, which means that the beneficiary petitions the court for immediate title to the estate's assets without the more formal probate process. An accounting is still required because, as with an affidavit, the estate has to be worth less than a value specified by the state to qualify for this special summary procedure. Owning real estate, though, does not generally disqualify you from a summary probate.

So you can't actually avoid the probate court with these procedures?

Not with summary probate—that always involves the court, albeit usually in a limited way and for a shorter time period. A probate affidavit avoids the court altogether.

If a person dies without a will, can you still use one of these less formal procedures?

If your state allows these alternative procedures, the state typically won't require that the deceased person have a will in order to implement them. There are, however, a few states that permit less formal procedures but require the deceased person to have authorized in his or her will the heir's use of them. A few others require all the beneficiaries of the will to consent to this procedure. A simplified probate procedure is available in all states. Check with a local attorney specializing in trusts and estates about how the system works in your state.

How do you figure out whether an estate qualifies for this procedure?

The rules vary from state to state. Most states set a dollar figure, and generally the estate has to be quite small, sometimes smaller than $10,000 or $20,000. This usually means that you cannot use this type of probate alternative if you own any real estate other than raw land. As noted above, some states do not allow you to use these procedures if you own any real estate, no matter what it is worth.

Can you give me an example of an estate that would qualify for a probate alternative?

A typical example would be a person who either does not own a home or owns one jointly, whose bank account is under the statutory limit for a probate alternative or is held jointly, and who has beneficiary designations in place for retirement accounts.

How does the transfer of assets work through use of an affidavit?

If you are the beneficiary, you will simply give a certified copy of the affidavit, plus a copy of the death certificate and a copy of the will, if there is one, to, say, the Department of Motor Vehicles, if you are transferring title on a car, or to a bank, if you are transferring title to a bank account. There is usually a waiting period, such as 40 days from the date of death, to use these procedures.

TRUSTS

What is a trust?

A trust is a written agreement that sets forth who will manage the assets placed in it during your lifetime, in the event of your incapacity, and upon your death. It allows you to transfer the legal title of your assets to a trustee—either another person or yourself—and is often a more cost-effective alternative to a will.

What is a revocable living trust?

The most popular kind of trust is called a revocable living trust—"revocable" because you can change it at any time; "living" because you create and fund it while you are alive; and a "trust" because you entrust it with the title to your property.

The use of the term "living" to describe trusts has caused a lot of confusion among non-lawyers, so I'll try to offer a clear explanation on this point. Every trust is created while you're living. (The only exception is something called a testamentary trust, which is established after your death under the terms of your will.) The most significant fact about a trust is not whether it's "living" or not but whether it is revocable or irrevocable. Some trusts created during your lifetime can be changed, and others cannot.

Think of your revocable living trust as a suitcase into which you can put the title of your house, stocks, and other non–retirement plan investments. You carry that trust with you while you are alive, with the ability to put new things in or take things out of it whenever you want. Everything in this suitcase is yours to own and enjoy the benefits from while you live. When you die, the suitcase is handed directly to your beneficiaries without passing through probate or any court. It's wonderfully uncomplicated, isn't it?

Another important aspect of a trust is that it provides for estate management in the event of incapacity. As of 2010, there are approximately 79,000 people alive in the U.S. who are 100 years of age or older. By the year 2050, this number is projected to be 600,000! When people reach their 80s or 90s, they can be quite vulnerable and aren't always capable of making decisions in their own best interest. The ability to choose who will manage your money if you are unable to do so, as well as who will decide when you should no longer be managing it for yourself, is a tremendous benefit of having a living trust.

How is a revocable living trust different from a will?

Revocable living trusts are an increasingly popular alternative to wills. With a revocable living trust, you transfer title to your assets from your name as an individual to your name as trustee of your trust. (Married couples, especially with separate property, have special issues.) Since all your property is in the name of the trust, when you die, your successor trustee has the immediate legal authority

to sign over the assets held in the trust directly to the people you want to have them. Because your beneficiaries don't need to go to probate court in order to get your assets transferred to them, there won't be probate fees, and there will be no delays in transfer (except for the payment of death taxes and creditors); further, there may be no need for a public notice of death. Remember, the wishes expressed in your will can only be carried out with an order from the probate court. A revocable living trust will avoid this complicated and expensive process, although there are usually at least some attorneys' and accountants' fees to be paid.

Why would my property not be subject to probate just because it's in a trust?

The end result of probate is a court order signed by a judge that transfers the ownership of the assets from the deceased to the beneficiaries. With a living trust, you transfer title from your individual name into the name of the trust while you're alive, and you designate the beneficiaries who will receive the assets of the trust once you die. If you do this while you are alive, there is no need for the court to be involved in the transfer. No court, no probate. It really is that simple.

Think about it this way. Let's say my mother wants to leave me her home when she dies, and the deed to her home is in her name. She states in her will her wish that I inherit her house. Now, when she dies, I have a problem. Even though her will says the house is to go to me, how is it going to get into my name? She is no longer alive to sign the deed over to me. That's where the probate court comes in. A judge must approve the transfer. If my mother had left me the house in a living trust and had taken the step while she was alive to sign the deed of the house over to the name of the trust, then probate on the house would be avoided. If, however, she signed the trust but didn't sign a deed to put the house into the living trust, it would take a probate process to get the house into the living trust.

How does my revocable trust work when I die?

When you die, the successor trustee will take your death certificate and the trust documents to the bank, the brokerage house, the insurance company—any and all custodial institutions with assets held by the trust—and these institutions will change the title to the successor trustee's name. Subject to delays for appraisals, payment of debts, and the payment of estate taxes, the trustee will then sign the assets over to whomever they are designated to go by the trust documents—or, in some cases, will hold them in a new trust for the benefit of a minor child or for tax-planning purposes. If you hold real estate in a trust, a title company or lawyer will charge roughly $150 to prepare and record an affidavit of death of trustee and a new deed giving ownership to the beneficiaries. If the real estate is to be sold, an attorney, real estate broker, escrow company, or title company will do all the paperwork needed to transfer title as part of the sale.

If I have a revocable living trust, do I still need a will?

Yes. When you have a trust it is also essential that you have what is called a pour-over, or backup, will. Any assets not in your trust are "poured over" by your will. A pour-over will covers anything you might have left out of your

trust by mistake. Basically, if your will states something like, "I leave the residue of my estate to the trustees of the Joe Smith Trust created by me on January 1, 1999," any assets not held in the trust are poured over into the trust by the will. The will also states any preference for a guardian, and expresses wishes about your memorial service and the disposition of your remains.

DEFINING THE TERMS

What is a trustor?

This is the legal term for the person who creates a trust and owns the property that has been put into the trust—namely, you. Sometimes a trustor is also referred to as the grantor or the settlor. When you create a trust, you may want to clearly claim certain rights that only you, as the trustor/grantor/settlor, have, such as the right to make changes in the trust.

What is a trustee?

This is the person or group of persons (or an entity such as a bank or a trust company, though I'd discourage you from using one of those) who controls the assets in the trust. Before you die, this person can be you. The trustee signs for and approves all the financial transactions of the trust. The trustee writes checks and makes investment choices for the trust, subject to the guidelines and provisions in the trust, and generally controls the trust's assets. If, after your death, your estate is distributed through a trust, the trustee that you named will distribute and sign over the assets according to what you have set up in the trust.

Is it advisable for me to be my own trustee?

Absolutely. The trustor, while he or she is alive, is usually the trustee. That's the great thing about a trust. You can continue to control everything as long as you are alive, and appoint a successor trustee to take over when you become incapacitated or die.

What is a successor trustee?

This is the person or entity who will succeed the original trustee when the trustee can no longer function in the capacity of the trustee, or no longer wants to. The conditions under which the successor trustee will step in should be spelled out in the trust document.

Does a trustee get paid?

Unless the trust agreement specifies otherwise, the trustee or successor trustee is entitled to compensation, based on how much in assets he or she is managing or in an amount that a court decides is "reasonable." If you have more than one trustee, there may be a separate fee for each trustee. Trustee compensation is one reason you want an attorney to look over your trust, to make sure that you have either arranged for an appropriate fee or have included a provision for your trustee(s) to waive it. Be wary of banks and financial institutions serving as trustees. They frequently charge between 1 and 2 percent of the asset value of the trust every year, or an even higher amount, as a minimum fee. In addition, they may charge transaction fees for selling and buying assets and then reinvest those assets in their own investment vehicles, making another commission. They are also more likely to seek court approval for routine trust matters that could be handled outside the court, thereby further increasing the administrative costs of the trust. Consider whether you want to require your trustee to obtain court approval for being paid in light of the expense incurred in such proceedings. In other words, select a trustee who has your and your beneficiaries' best interests at heart.

How much should my trustee be paid?

A trustee should be paid enough on an hourly basis so that the time spent administering the trust isn't a hardship. On the other hand, your trustee should not be profiting from the trust. Beware of the percentage fee.

If I am my own trustee, how should I choose a successor trustee?

A successor trustee must do three things. First, if you are disabled during your lifetime and unable to look after your own financial affairs, this person will manage them for you. Second, when you die, this person will locate your assets, pay your debts, file your taxes, and sign over the assets in the trust to the beneficiaries of your trust. Third, if there are beneficiaries who are minors, or others for whom you have continuing trusts as adults, the successor trustee will follow the trust's provisions on how to manage and invest the assets and make distributions for them until they are entitled to receive all the funds. In choosing a successor trustee, please consider all three functions. Remember, too, that the job of the trustee is not to act as a moneymaking machine. It is to be honest, to have your and your beneficiaries' best interests at heart, to be cognizant of your goals, and to be willing to seek help with things he or she doesn't understand. Someone who handles his or her own money in a responsible way is the best choice. On the other hand, be aware that people with demonstrated financial savvy will sometimes take greater risks than you would. The job of the successor trustee is, in essence, to carry out your intentions in the truest and most responsible way possible.

What is the principal?

The principal consists of the trust assets. Let's say you put 100 shares of General Electric stock in your trust. The shares of stock are the principal. When the stock pays a dividend, the dividend is considered income. Trusts often make distinctions between how the principal and the income can be spent. In tax-planning trusts, there may be significant tax consequences based on how the trust describes the distribution of the income and principal. Make sure to ask your attorney if any limitations on spending are created by the language used in your trust.

What is a beneficiary?

A beneficiary is any person who benefits from the assets held in the name of the trust.

Can I be my own beneficiary?

Absolutely. You will almost certainly want to be the one who benefits from the assets in your trust while you are alive. In this case, you are the current beneficiary and whomever you designate to receive your property after you die will be the final beneficiary or beneficiaries.

WHO NEEDS A TRUST?

How do I know if I need a living trust?

Whether you need a living trust depends on the state in which you live, the size of your probate estate, and which assets you are leaving to your beneficiaries.

For smaller estates, there are three ways to avoid probate: probate affidavits and simplified court procedures, as well as POD, or payable-on-death, accounts, which I'll explain later. But if the assets you want to leave are larger than allowed for above, you should seriously consider a living trust. If you have a financial interest in a business, if you have children, if you are in a second or third marriage, if you are on bad terms with one or more of your heirs, if one of your family members is physically or mentally ill, developmentally disabled, in need of creditor protection, or just bad at managing money—you should seriously consider establishing a trust.

I always thought of trusts as primarily for rich people. Is that not true?

Sure, there are certain kinds of trusts expressly designed for people with a lot of assets, but revocable living trusts are very useful even if— *especially* if—your assets are more modest, because the less you have, the less you can afford to pay in probate fees.

Is it more important to have a trust if I have young children?

Yes. If you have young children for whom you want to provide asset management in the event of your death, you should seriously consider a living trust.

My sister says that she is leaving money for her young children to a custodian via a will. How is this different from a guardian? And would a living trust be better?

Some states allow you to make gifts or leave an inheritance to a minor by giving the gift or inheritance to a custodian who will hold, invest, and manage the property for the minor's benefit until he or she is old enough to care for it. (The state may require the child to take title of the property when he or she turns 18, 21, or 25.) Basically, a trust will allow you to do everything for your minor children that you could do by appointing a custodian, and will also let you retain greater flexibility and control. However, in some cases custodianships can provide a less expensive way to protect your children.

I am single and sold my house a few years ago and now my assets are in a couple of savings and retirement accounts. If I have more money than is allowed to qualify for a probate affidavit, do I need a revocable living trust?

Maybe not, since there is yet another way to avoid probate. Any account that has a designated beneficiary will not have to go through probate; it passes directly to the named beneficiary. One way to designate a beneficiary on your accounts is to ask your bank or brokerage firm to make your accounts payable on death (POD), which means that when you die the account balances will pass immediately to whomever you have identified as a beneficiary. Retirement accounts, such as IRAs, and insurance policies require you to designate a beneficiary on the application form, and those accounts will automatically avoid probate if you designate a beneficiary other than your estate. If you name your estate, however, your beneficiaries will have to go through probate. (That's because your estate is governed by your will, and wills typically have to go through probate.) To avoid probate, always name a person, not your estate, as beneficiary.

That said, I still think the best way to avoid probate is by setting up a trust. Let me explain. Let's say you have ten retirement accounts at ten different banks and brokerage firms. You want to change the primary beneficiary on each of these accounts. To do so, you must contact all ten institutions and fill out the required paperwork for each account, submitting a new form and providing necessary information about the person to whom you now want to leave your money. This is a lot of work. Alternatively, let's say the person you named as a primary beneficiary dies and you have not designated a contingent beneficiary. If you do not change the original beneficiary and you die, whether you wished it or not, your assets will go to the heirs of the deceased beneficiary. On the other hand, if you name your trust as the primary beneficiary and want to make a change, the process is easy. All you have to do is change one designation—that of the primary beneficiary of your trust.

One caveat, however, for married couples: Each of you should always name your spouse as the primary beneficiary of your retirement accounts, and your trust as contingent beneficiary. For you, naming a trust as a primary beneficiary of IRAs or other retirement accounts may cause tax problems.

Remember, the main point of the revocable living trust is to avoid probate fees, save time, and designate a way to manage your assets in case of an incapacity.

If I spend part of the year in one state and part of the year in another, do I need a separate trust for each state?

No. Your trust should make clear which state law applies to the validity of the trust. This allows you to move, hold assets in different states, and not have to review or revise the trust based on a change of residence. Get legal advice as to whether a change of domicile requires changes to your plan if you are married or have children. If the trust is not clear on this point, then it will be governed by the law of the state of your domicile (your permanent state of residence). There are tests under the law to determine one's domicile.

If my spouse is not a U.S. citizen, do I need a trust?

While there is an unlimited marital deduction on estate taxes when one spouse inherits money from another spouse, if your spouse is not a U.S. citizen, the law sets a limit on the amount that can be inherited tax-free unless a special trust known as a QDOT is part of your will or living trust. In 2009, for example, the most a spouse who is not a U.S. citizen can inherit tax-free is $3,500,000 without a special trust. Consult an attorney, because the laws are complex.

If I have an interest in a business, is a living trust a good idea?

Yes. A living trust can be an excellent thing for you, especially if you want to protect the privacy of your business by keeping it out of probate. Your interest in the business can be transferred to the living trust without the court ever having to get involved. If you have business partners, you will probably need their permission in order to transfer title into the living trust, and you'll want to encourage them to set up their own trusts.

I've heard that a revocable living trust not only benefits my beneficiaries but also can help me during my lifetime. How so?

If you became incapacitated for any reason, your trust could make things much smoother for you, personally and financially. If you have an incapacity clause in your trust stating who can determine whether you should no longer be acting as trustee, the successor trustee can take over and protect you from yourself or others. This is one of the most important benefits of the trust.

Let me try to illustrate this with a worst-case scenario. Let's say you have a stroke and cannot sign your name. Without a living trust, in order for anyone, including you, to access your money (even to provide care for you), you would have to be declared incompetent in a court and have a conservator appointed for you. Each year, the conservator would have to prepare a statement accounting for every disbursement of your funds, as well as an assets-and-liability statement, and submit them to the court for approval. The conservator might also need to gain approval to buy or sell certain assets. A judge would then oversee all financial decisions made on your behalf.

If you already have a partner, friend, or relative whom you would trust to make these decisions, do you really want that person to have to go through this? The bottom line, in this scenario, is that you would have to pay unnecessary attorney and court fees to establish and continue the conservatorship and permit a judge whom you don't know to control your finances. If you have an incapacity clause in your revocable living trust, you maintain some control in this situation, because your wishes are likely to be followed, without going through the court.

Can I name someone in my will to take over my financial affairs if I become incapacitated, or can I only do this with a trust?

A will expresses your wishes to the court only after you die. If you have not made arrangements in case you became incapacitated (through a living trust or a durable power of attorney for asset management, which we'll discuss later), your loved ones would have to go to court to establish a conservatorship. That means they would have to prove your incompetency in order to gain control over your financial affairs. This is a time-consuming, unpleasant, and expensive process.

The importance of making provisions in such circumstances simply cannot be emphasized enough. After age 65, almost half of the population will spend two years and nine months of their lives unable to care for themselves due to a physical or mental incapacity. It is a sobering statistic, without a doubt, and what it suggests is enormously unpleasant for us personally, though no less important if we choose to ignore it.

Let's say that you are in your 80s and starting to have a bad time with numbers, and you have made some poor investment decisions. Your spouse and children can see that something is wrong, but you are not "incompetent," as that term is defined by the law: You can still get dressed by yourself, care for your basic needs, and tell people what you want. In this case, you would be found not to be in need of a conservator. Meanwhile, you could lose all your money and leave your spouse penniless. However, if you had a trust or a power of attorney, then your successor trustee or agent could manage your funds for you. With a trust, you could grant those closest to you financial control and keep the courts out of it.

I have personally seen this very situation unfold several times. One of the first signs of Alzheimer's disease is difficulty remembering numbers, which can affect your investment decisions. Often, however, it is weeks or months before an authoritative diagnosis is made, even though your loved ones already know that something is wrong because they know you. A trust allows action to be taken when it's necessary to take action, and before it is too late.

The living trust sounds good, but it sounds like something I don't need to think about until I have had a chance to accumulate some assets. Right?

Wrong as can be. Even if you haven't had a chance to accumulate significant assets, you should still think about creating a living trust. Also, you may have more assets than you think: For example, if you have young children and have purchased a term life insurance policy to protect them, a living trust can best help you preserve as much of that money for them as possible by deciding who will oversee those funds for them, avoiding probate, as well as reports and accountings to a court.

Is there anyone who should not have a trust?

If you own only raw land as your real estate, your state might have a procedure called informal administration or a probate affidavit, which allows you (depending on the size of your estate) to pass assets on without going through the formal court probate process. Also, if you are in the process of applying for Medicaid, or think you will do so within five years, you should probably not be setting up a trust. If you are in this position, you need to consult a good attorney with some expertise in elder care and Medicaid eligibility in your state.

This all sounds fine, except that I don't want to have a penny left when I die. If I'm trying to spend it all while I'm alive, I don't need to worry about trusts, do I?

That might be true, but what if you die unexpectedly in a car accident before you've spent all your money? Or if you're seriously injured and don't die immediately? In cases such as these, you would still need to take responsibility for decisions about your health care and your financial affairs.

SETTING UP A REVOCABLE LIVING TRUST

How do I set up a revocable living trust?

A certain amount of paperwork is required in order to set up and fund a trust. As with a will, you can have an attorney draw up the trust document for you or you can use a book or computer program to write one yourself. I recommend that you have an attorney draft it. If you do write it yourself, have an attorney look it over and make sure you have done it correctly. Once you've created the document and signed it, you need to transfer the ownership (the legal title) of almost all your assets (get legal advice on what *not* to transfer) into the name of the trust to avoid probate and to allow a successor trustee to act on your behalf in case of incapacity. This last step is known as funding the trust. You must fund the trust after it is created for the trust to take effect.

How much will it cost to set up a trust?

You'll want to ask your attorney about this up front, and you should not accept a vague answer. Any experienced attorney who knows the size of your estate, the assets you own, and the type of planning required should be able to give you a written agreement on the cost of setting up the trust. I prefer that you have someone bill you on a project basis, which means that he or she will charge you a flat fee for the cost of drawing up your trust and funding it for you, rather than bill you on an hourly basis. That way, if setting up your trusts takes the attorney longer than anticipated, this misjudgment will not cost you money.

In California, a simple revocable trust for an individual—for example, one that takes into account a piece of property and a few basic bank accounts, calls for outright distributions for beneficiaries (not complicated trust arrangements), and does not include any tax planning—should cost between about $1,500 and $2,000. Be wary of anyone who charges you only a few hundred dollars, or anything significantly below market rates. He or she probably will not be able to spend an adequate amount of time researching your situation or explaining it to you, and may charge extra for services that should be included, such as funding the trust.

How do I decide what assets to leave to whom?

Everyone's family is different, and so is everyone's idea of what is fair. In light of this, your first step is to decide what your own objectives are. If you are currently helping to support an elderly parent, for example, then you won't want to forget that parent in your trust; you'll want to continue to provide for him or her in case you die before he or she does. If, on the other hand, leaving assets to your parents will only increase their estate and create estate tax problems, you should bypass their estate. (There *are* ways to benefit your parents through carefully designed trusts that will not be taxed in their estates. An estates attorney can help you find one that's right for you.) There are many ways to benefit a spouse through a trust, but a lot of them have tax implications and should be discussed with an attorney. You may also want to discuss trusts for your children. Don't forget to consider what you would want to have happen if one or more of your children predeceased you, or if your children died before you did and left no grandchildren. At this point, there might be a charity or friends that you would rather name as your beneficiaries than distant relatives.

The most difficult issues in naming beneficiaries seem to arise when there are children from different marriages. If you have two children,

for example, and your husband has one, don't be surprised if he feels unhappy when you suggest that everything be split in three equal shares. He may believe that one half of your shared assets is his and should go to his child and the other half is yours and should go to your two children. Without a doubt, stepparent relationships can pose challenges. You'll need to make some indication in your trust about these matters to avoid confusion. Be ready to compromise if need be. Also, beware of making children too financially independent—the pitfalls of such arrangements should be obvious to you.

How important is it to review my beneficiary designations once I create a trust?

It's very important. Many years ago, a woman I knew got divorced from her husband of 30 years. Recently, she died. Because she never reviewed the trust she had set up while she was married, she left everything to her ex-husband. Since many people hold significant assets within a trust, it is crucial to review the beneficiary designations as your life situation changes.

How often should I review my trust to update it?

If your revocable living trust is simple, with no estate-tax planning, you may never have to make any changes in it unless there is a major change in your circumstances or relationships. Even if circumstances do change, your trust may last a lifetime if it has been properly written and you have been guided through all the contingencies by your attorney. For example, if one of your beneficiaries dies before you, there should be a provision in the trust to meet that contingency.

I set up a trust a number of years ago when I lived in Colorado. Do I have to change it now that I have moved to Arizona?

Most likely you won't have to change your trust just because you have moved to a new state, though your trust documents should say which state's laws govern it. You should consult an attorney in your new state to see whether your trust will need to be revised.

I thought you couldn't make changes to a trust. Am I wrong?

Whether or not you can change a trust depends on whether the trust is revocable or irrevocable. Remember, revocable means that you can make changes whenever you want to. In fact, it can be easier to make changes to a revocable living trust than to a will, because you don't need two witnesses to authenticate your signature (although you usually want your signature notarized to avoid disputes as to whether you were the one who signed the document). An irrevocable trust, usually used for advance tax-planning purposes or after you become incapacitated or die, cannot (except under special circumstances) be changed once it's created.

How is a trust terminated?

Your trust agreement will have a provision that states how or when your trust can be terminated. For example, a grantor can create a trust to last for 20 years, or until his or her youngest beneficiary turns 35 or dies, whichever comes first. A beneficiary usually may not terminate a trust on his own, unless it's specifically permitted by the trust agreement. If you are concerned about someone terminating the trust too soon, make sure that you express your intentions clearly in the trust agreement. A court will try to honor your intentions if it knows what they are.

FINDING A GOOD LAWYER

How can I find a reliable trusts and estates attorney?

The best method of finding an attorney is by word of mouth. If your friends or relatives have found an attorney they like who is a specialist with trusts and estates, check that person out. Otherwise, ask your state bar association for a list of knowledgeable trusts and estate attorneys in your area.

How do I know if my lawyer is up to par? What should he or she do for me in exchange for the fee I'm paying?

It's important that the attorney you are going to rely on to help you organize the financial future of your family have at least ten years of experience with wills, trusts, and estate planning. He or she should ideally have drafted at least 200 wills and trusts before drafting yours. And you and your family should be comfortable with him or her.

Since the attorney probably already has a boilerplate trust agreement that he or she will fill in with your particulars, preparing the document should not account for the bulk of the fees. Ask whether the attorney will be drafting the documents himself, but don't worry if an associate will be doing the paperwork, as long as that person is properly supervised. (The cost to you may be less if an associate does the work.) You do want to know exactly what you will be paying for. To that end, get an agreement in writing stating what services you will receive and how much the attorney will charge for them, including any charges for calling him with questions. (If your questions do not exceed the time limit spelled out in your agreement with him, you shouldn't be charged.)

What you are really paying for is the time your attorney will take to review your situation and explain everything about your documents and how your trust will work. Among the things he or she should do for you are: review your deeds and title documents to look for past mistakes; ask you questions about estate planning issues that you may not have considered; and create a plan for your individual situation, encompassing your financial goals. He or she should also review your beneficiary designation forms on your IRAs, Keoghs, annuities, and life insurance policies and bring them up to date.

While creating your trust, your attorney should be thinking about your overall interests and asking you questions about estate planning issues, including long-term care insurance, health care, durable living powers of attorney, gifting programs, and/or any charitable preferences you have. After all, what's the point of drawing up a trust to protect your assets if someday you have to use them to pay long-term care costs?

Once the trust is set up, your attorney should fund it for you, changing the title of the appropriate assets from your individual name to the name of your trust and adding your beneficiary designations. This is crucial. Without the funding component, you have wasted the money you spent to create the trust.

Finally, for the single project fee, I would like

to see your attorney draft a backup will and a durable power of attorney for your health care.

Why does my lawyer think that I don't need a revocable living trust?

Do you remember those probate fees I mentioned earlier? Well, they get paid to your executor and to your attorney. So, in most states, attorneys stand to profit from your having only a will and not a revocable living trust. This may explain why your attorney has told you that you don't need one.

Also keep in mind that your attorney may not be an estate specialist and may not be familiar with all the benefits of trusts. Ask him how many trusts he has written in the last three months and how many allocation agreements for A-B trusts he has prepared. If he looks at you as if you're speaking Greek, politely get up and leave.

To prove the point, I want you to ask your attorney to estimate for you, in writing and on his or her letterhead, the following:

1) How much it would cost you to have a will drawn up, if you don't already have one;
2) How much it would cost your beneficiaries to probate your entire estate (including court costs and attorney and executor fees) if you and your spouse died today with wills alone;
3) How much it would cost to create and fund a revocable living trust; and
4) How much it would cost your beneficiaries to settle your estate if you and your spouse died today with that revocable living trust.

Add the cost of drawing up each document to the respective cost to your beneficiaries after your death and compare the two totals. The option that costs less is the one your attorney should recommend. If the calculations suggest that you would be better off with a trust, and you've been told it's unnecessary, you may need to get a new attorney.

If the calculations suggest that you do not need a trust and your attorney can clearly explain this to you, be sure to review your financial status and the relevant laws every few years to be sure that having only a will still makes sense for you.

FUNDING THE TRUST

How do you fund a revocable living trust?
Funding a trust means transferring ownership of certain assets into the trust while you are still alive. The process can be as simple as changing title to an asset like a bank account, or it can involve preparing a new deed and recording it, depending on the types of assets you will be holding in the trust.

Do I have to fund (transfer assets into) my revocable living trust?
If you don't fund the trust, your trust will be nothing more than a document stating who gets what. In other words, it is "empty." If you die with an "empty" trust, your beneficiaries will have to go through probate with your will in order to get your assets into the trust.

Which assets belong in my trust?
Real estate, bank accounts, stocks, bonds, investment accounts, partnership interests, the stock in your family corporation, and credit union accounts.

Be careful how you record any deeds for real estate, because correcting mistakes once a deed has been recorded may be very difficult. Have your attorney or a title company prepare and record your deeds. Be careful, too, of including assets that are tax shelters. If you move those assets to the trust, such a transfer may be considered a change of ownership, which means you lose the tax advantage. Finally, accounts that designate a beneficiary—such as life insurance, annuities, employee benefits, incentive stock options, IRAs, Keoghs, and other pension plans—will continue to be owned by you rather than by the trust, but the trust can be named the primary or contingent beneficiary, depending on the asset. Get tax advice before making any transfers or changing any beneficiary designations.

Except for life insurance, incentive stock options, retirement plans, and the like, should I put everything I own into a revocable living trust?
Yes. I recommend putting in everything as outlined above, including personal property. Personal property includes household items, jewelry, cars, tools, computers, clothing, and anything else without legal title.

After the trust is funded, will my name still be on the titles to my property?
Yes. If you originally owned your house as Mary Smith and you have created a revocable living trust, the title will have been transferred so that the house now belongs to "Mary Smith, trustee for the Mary Smith Revocable Living Trust."

And when a new deed for any real estate you own is prepared and recorded, it might say, for example, that Mary Smith grants all her interest in the property to Mary Smith as trustee of the Mary Smith Trust, dated 1-1-01. The naming process will apply to bank accounts, brokerage accounts, mutual funds, partnership and business interests, stocks, and more.

After the trust is funded, will I be giving up control of any of my assets by changing the titles in this way?

Not at all. You can retain complete control and management over all your assets for as long as you are alive, willing, and able to handle your own financial affairs. That means that nothing can be done without your signature. If you resign as trustee, become incapacitated, or die, the successor trustee you have named will become the new signer for the trust.

After I fund my trust is there any difference between owning my bank accounts as an individual and owning them within the trust?

The only possible difference concerns the $250,000 FDIC protection on savings accounts. If you and your spouse each have $250,000 in savings, normally you would each be protected for that amount. If your assets are combined in a trust, however, some banks will only insure the trust for up to $250,000. Check with your bank. (Please note the $250,000 insurance limit is in place through 2013.)

What about my house—should I be aware of any differences once I put it in the trust?

Some banks may not be willing to refinance your house while it is in a trust, for the simple reason that they don't want to pay an attorney to read the trust. If you encounter this, it is a simple matter to transfer the title to your house out of the trust and into your name as an individual, and then to transfer the title back to the trust after the refinancing is completed. A title company and/or your attorney can assist you with this for a modest fee.

TRUSTS AND DEBTS

How will the trust work if I die and still have debts to be paid off?

In all cases, debts are paid according to a priority list designated by your state—for example, funeral expenses and taxes, then the cost of administration of the estate, family allowance, etc., until finally all legitimate debts are paid off.

Will a trust protect my assets from creditors?

This is a common question. A revocable trust is considered a "transparent" trust, which means that creditors can reach it, as long as the creator of the trust is also a beneficiary of the trust. The simple answer is that, in most cases, the assets are not protected.

TRUSTS AND RETIREMENT ACCOUNTS

Should I make my revocable living trust the beneficiary of my retirement accounts?

This depends on whether you are married or single and on the proper tax advice for your situation. If you are not legally married, you may want to name the trust as the primary beneficiary. If you are married, you should name your spouse as the primary beneficiary, and you may want to name the trust or a subtrust as the contingent beneficiary. The reason for this is that spouses have specific rights regarding retirement proceeds that are highly beneficial tax-wise, and you don't want to lose those tax advantages. The reason you may want to name your trust as the contingent beneficiary is so that, if you make a change in the trust, you won't have to change all your contingent beneficiary designations; they are keyed to the trust. A change in the trust automatically changes all the beneficiary designations.

TRUSTS AND RELATIONSHIPS

Should I have the same person act as the guardian for my children, the executor of my estate, and the trustee of my revocable living trust?

Most people appoint their spouse or partner to all three positions. (You should also think about what would happen if both you and your partner were to die.) Generally, it will simplify things greatly if one person has control over everything, as you do now. But you will have to decide whether the person you want to raise your children is also the best person to make financial decisions for them. If there are different people in your life who would bring different skills to

benefit your children, you may want to appoint different individuals to each position. Just make sure that the people you appoint will be able to work comfortably with one another for as long as your children will need them.

I have been told that if my children are still young it is a good idea to appoint a professional trustee. Is this true?

No. I wouldn't recommend a professional trustee unless there is absolutely no one else who can serve in that role. Professional trustees are expensive and may not necessarily manage assets well. It is critical that the person you choose to act as your trustee be honest, trustworthy, and able to communicate with your beneficiaries, because he or she will have a great deal of discretion in the management of your affairs. If I were you, I would look to a friend or relative who is capable of filling the role.

One of my children has a substance abuse problem. I don't want to disinherit her, but I'm worried about her ability to manage money responsibly. What's the best option for me?

This is the perfect example of how a discretionary trust under a will or living trust can be beneficial. With a trust under a will or living trust, you can arrange for your daughter to receive a small but consistent amount of income over time rather than a lump-sum inheritance.

Is it possible to disinherit your spouse or your children?

It depends on state law. If you're married, a prenuptial agreement may control the result.

Can I put a condition on my bequests, such as that I want to give my daughter money only if she marries?

Theoretically, yes, in which case you would be making what's called a "conditional gift." The state you live in may refuse to enforce your condition if it would cause your daughter to do something illegal or against public policy. An example of this would be if you said you would give your daughter a gift only if she converted from her current religion. Such a condition is against public policy, so your daughter would be entitled to the gift anyway. Before you are tempted to complicate your bequests in this way, please think carefully about why you are trying to control your daughter from the grave and whether your wishes are truly in her best interest.

TRUSTS AND INCOME TAX

Is having a revocable living trust going to complicate my tax returns?

Not at all. You need not file an income tax return for a revocable trust of which you are the trustee. You simply file a regular tax return as you always do. There are no special income-tax-reporting consequences during your lifetime.

Are there any income tax benefits to establishing a revocable living trust?

No. The main purpose of having a living revocable trust is to avoid probate after your death and to help with the management of your affairs in case of incapacity.

If I sell my house after I have transferred it to my revocable living trust, can I still take advantage of tax benefits I would have received if I had sold it as an individual?

Absolutely. The sale will take place in the same way that it would without the trust, and you will be able to claim the income tax benefits as the grantor of the trust. (The tax result may be different if you're married, the house is sold after one of you dies, and some or all of the house is held in certain trusts.)

If I am still working when I die, would I owe income taxes for that year?

Yes, you would. Your executor or trustee will be responsible for filing an individual income tax return for you, a separate tax form for your estate, and, if the estate is large enough, a federal estate tax return.

The executor or trustee may not file the final tax return until the year following the death. Since the return will be marked "deceased," this is an invitation for the IRS to review the previous three years of tax returns; they know they won't get another chance. (The IRS has three years from the date of a filing to challenge it.) Because the executor or trustee can be personally liable for the payment of taxes, you want to be sure that the trust holds in reserve an amount sufficient to pay any back and/or current taxes. The IRS reviews every estate tax return that is filed, and it audits approximately one out of every ten. The IRS will send you a letter, usually within a year of the filing, saying it has received the return and has no current plans to challenge it. However, until the three-year period has passed, the agency may initiate an audit at any time.

ESTATE TAXES

For many people, one of the most important things to know when considering estate-tax planning is that married spouses can leave each other as much money and property as they like without the surviving spouse owing any estate tax. This is called the unlimited marital deduction and is a significant benefit of being married. But for single people, unmarried partners, and married people concerned about leaving assets to children and others, serious planning may be in order.

What is estate tax?

Although recent legislation has passed eliminating the federal estate tax as of 2010, at the time of this writing estate taxes are federal taxes that are owed nine months after death on the net value of a taxable estate if it is worth more than a specified amount. The net value of an estate is determined by adding up the gross value of your stocks, bonds, bank and investment accounts, real estate or other jointly held property, life insurance proceeds, retirement accounts (IRAs, pension funds, or Keoghs), personal property, and any other assets you leave behind, and subtracting from that amount the costs of your funeral, your debts, any administrative expenses, and any assets that you leave to your spouse or a qualified charity (in a manner approved by the IRS). What's left is subject to estate taxes, if the amount exceeds that allowed for the year in which you die.

Please note that estate tax has always been distinct from probate fees and state inheritance taxes, both of which vary by state. It is also distinct from income tax, which you pay on personal income every year.

How much can you pass on to beneficiaries before they owe estate tax?

Right now, depending on the year in which you die, your taxable estate is subject to federal estate tax if it exceeds:

2009	$3,500,000
2010	No estate tax
2011	$1,000,000, unless Congress extends repeal

These limits may be changed by Congress in the future. Go to *www.irs.gov* for up-to-date estate tax limits.

These exempt amounts can be reduced by lifetime gifts above the annual federal gift-tax exclusion.

Are these figures a kind of tax deduction?

That is a common question. These figures are called "unified credits" and they actually do function as a deduction of sorts, by zeroing out the tax up to the amount shown for a given year. This means that the value of your estate will be calculated in full, but you will already have a credit for the amount of estate tax that would have been "owed," for example, on the first $3,500,000 if you died in 2009.

What are the rates of estate taxes?

As of 2009, basically anything over the exemption amount will be taxed at 45 percent. (The highest estate tax rates have changed. See below.)

There are other special estate tax rules and even another type of federal estate tax, the generation-skipping transfer tax. With such substantial tax owed on estates over the exemption amount—and since estate tax is due within nine months of your death—you can imagine the potential problems for your heirs: They could be forced to sell off some of your assets at less than their optimal value in order to meet tax obligations.

Are there ways to reduce my estate tax?

You reduce your estate taxes whenever you reduce the value of your taxable estate. There are a number of ways to do this. You can give gifts of $13,000 (as of 2010) to as many people as you like each year without incurring a gift tax. You also can pay another person's college tuition in any amount each year and it will not be subject to gift tax, even if it's more than $13,000. But if you do this, you must be sure that the check is made out directly to the school and not to the student. You may also pay medical expenses for another person in any amount if you pay them directly to the medical provider, and the money will not be subject to gift tax. If you own a home, you may gift that home in a qualified residence trust and receive a substantial discount in the way the home is valued for estate tax purposes. (Please note, there are many complications and risks with this type of trust.)

How does the IRS determine how much the estate is worth, since some of my assets may change in value over time?

Generally, the value of your estate is established according to its fair market value on the day you die. Alternatively, your executor can choose a date exactly six months from the day of your death, if doing so will result in a lowering of your estate tax. These are the only two dates that can be used.

Is estate tax due before my will is probated or after my beneficiaries receive their assets?

Federal estate tax is due nine months from the date of death, regardless of whether the estate is in probate or its assets have been distributed to heirs. Sometimes it is possible to arrange to make a series of smaller payments—if, for

Calendar year	Estate and GST tax deathtime transfer exemption	Highest estate and gift tax rates
2006	$2 million	46%
2007	$2 million	45%
2008	$2 million	45%
2009	$3.5 million	45%
2010	N/A (taxes repealed unless Congress changes law)	top individual rate under the bill (gift tax only)
2011	$1 million (unless Congress extends repeal)	55%
Source: Joint Committee on Taxation		

example, you have a family-owned business that would incur great hardship if it had to pay an estate tax in one lump sum. But please note that, in most cases, this money is due and payable in full within nine months.

What happens if the executor doesn't file a federal estate tax return within the mandated time period?

It could get expensive. If the executor doesn't have a good reason for having failed to file the return, the estate could owe a fine of 5 percent of whatever tax is due for each month that the tax return is late, up to a maximum of 25 percent of the tax bill. This is yet another reason to choose a responsible executor.

You mentioned earlier that federal estate tax is separate from state inheritance tax. Which states charge separate inheritance taxes?

Indiana, Iowa, Kentucky, Maryland, Nebraska (county inheritance tax only), New Jersey, Pennsylvania, and Tennessee all charge inheritance taxes. Sometimes these are called death taxes.

How do the state inheritance taxes work?

Every state is different, but, as of 2009, here's the general idea: Until recently, most states did not impose their own estate tax. Instead, they had what is known as a "pickup tax" that let them take a share of the federal estate tax paid by large estates. But with the phaseout of federal estate taxes, states don't get a share of federal estate tax anymore. To recoup part of that loss, some states are collecting tax from estates that are not big enough to owe any federal tax. (Surviving spouses still get a break; property left to them is exempt

from state estate tax, just as it is exempt from federal estate tax.)

Some states have additional inheritance taxes—again, as of 2009. Unlike estate taxes, which depend on how large your taxable estate is, inheritance taxes are calculated on what each beneficiary receives. Inheritance tax rates will depend on the closeness of the relationship of the beneficiary to the decedent. Distant relatives or unrelated persons pay more than spouses or children. In most cases, you will not pay more in state taxes than what you are assessed in federal taxes.

Are things that don't go through probate, such as a life insurance policy, subject to estate taxes?

Generally, yes. Remember, retirement accounts, life insurance, property held as joint tenants with right of survivorship, and retirement benefits will all avoid the delays and fees of probate but still will most likely count toward calculating your taxable estate. However, you can set up a life insurance trust or make other arrangements that could keep the life insurance proceeds out of your taxable estate.

If my life insurance proceeds go to my designated beneficiary, why does that amount count toward the assets of my estate for tax purposes?

I'm glad you asked this question, because insurance agents love to say that life insurance is tax-free, and this is a misleading statement. While it is true that your heirs won't have to pay income tax on these benefits, if you are the owner of the policy and you control the right to designate its beneficiary, the proceeds will be considered an asset to be included in your estate, and taxed accordingly, when you die. As mentioned earlier, there are ways to exclude life insurance from estate tax.

So my retirement account is subject to income taxes and estate taxes?

Yes, if you have a traditional IRA or employer-sponsored retirement plan, you will owe income tax on the value of the account and it also may be subject to estate taxes after you die. If it is subject to estate tax, you may get an income tax deduction. Roth IRAs are subject to estate tax, but not to income tax if all the requirements are met.

Can I avoid estate taxes altogether?

Here is where married people have a big advantage: You will not owe estate taxes on property that you leave to your spouse, as long as your spouse is a U.S. citizen. (Your spouse's beneficiaries, however, may end up owing estate tax on these assets after your spouse's death.) Another option to consider is to create an A-B trust, which I'll explain a little later.

GENERATION-SKIPPING TAX

Is estate tax the same as the generation-skipping tax?

No. The generation-skipping tax is an additional tax, on top of any estate tax, that applies to any portion of your taxable estate more than $3,500,000 (for 2009) that you transfer to a grandchild or grandchildren while your own child is still living, or to anyone else who is two or more generations younger than you are (as of 2001). The generation-skipping tax is not a per-beneficiary exemption. It's a per transfer exemption of up to $3,500,000 (for 2009—for other years see the chart below). For 2009, anything above that left to grandchildren is taxed at a flat rate of a whopping 45 percent. The generation-skipping tax is meant to keep affluent families from passing on assets without having to pay taxes. It is scheduled to disappear in 2010, but will revert to $1.06 million in 2011, if Congress does not act to extend the current exemption amount. You can get up-to-date information at *www.irs.gov*.

GENERATION-SKIPPING TRANSFER TAX RATE

Year	Rate	Taxed on amount that exceeds
2008	45%	$2,000,000
2009	45%	$3,500,000
2010	N/A	N/A
2011	55%	$1,060,000 (Plus increases for inflation)

Does this mean that if I left money to my granddaughter, she would owe this tax, but if I left it to my daughter, she wouldn't?

Yes, if the gift is very large and if you leave it before the year 2010. This is the point: If your daughter were to receive money from you and then left that money to her own daughter, the government would theoretically be entitled to tax the money twice, once upon your death and once upon your daughter's death. If your granddaughter receives the bequest directly, the money is subjected to estate tax *and* the generation-skipping tax because you have "skipped" her mother. So, in effect, the transfer is still being taxed twice. You shouldn't be too concerned about this tax, since the first $3,500,000 (for 2009) that you transfer directly to your granddaughter is exempt from it, though not, of course, from estate tax. (Married couples can exempt up to a combined $7,000,000 [for 2009].) If you intend to pass on more than that amount of money or property to your grandchildren, you should consult an attorney. There are other types of exemptions and trust plans that are designed to preserve as much of your estate as possible.

My daughter has predeceased me, and her sons are my beneficiaries. It doesn't seem fair that my grandsons will have to pay the generation-skipping tax on what I leave them, when I couldn't leave anything to my daughter.

Don't worry. There are a number of exceptions to the generation-skipping tax, and this is one of them. In this case, the law allows you to leave assets to the children of your deceased child as if they were your own children.

What about the $13,000-per-year gift rule—does that count toward the exemption on the generation-skipping tax?

No. If you give your granddaughter $13,000 each year, the accumulated funds will not be subject to the gift tax or the generation-skipping tax, and you do not need to apply that gift to the exemption for the generation-skipping tax.

A-B TRUSTS

An A-B trust (also known as a tax-planning trust, a credit shelter trust, a marital trust, or a bypass trust) is a single trust made while both spouses are alive. When one spouse dies, the trust is normally split into two shares, an A share and a B share. (Sometimes there are three shares: A, B, and C.) One share remains a revocable trust, and the other becomes an irrevocable trust. You can create an A-B trust through a revocable living trust or through a will.

A-B trusts should be considered if you are married and have assets in excess of the nontaxable exemptions amounts ($3,500,000 in 2009). An A-B trust, established while you and your spouse are alive, essentially allows you to double the money you can leave to your beneficiaries without incurring estate taxes, depending on how you hold title to your assets and how much each of you owns.

What is the difference between an A-B trust and a revocable living trust?

Revocable living trusts are primarily meant to avoid probate fees, to transfer the legal titles to your assets as quickly as possible to beneficiaries, and to protect you if you become incapacitated. A-B trusts can save your beneficiaries significant estate taxes if you are married and expect to have an estate valued at more than the allowable nontaxable amounts.

How does an A-B trust work?

Let's say you have real estate and other income and assets worth about $7,000,000, owned equally by each of you. If you create an A-B trust, if you die in 2009 your "half share" of the estate, in this case $3,500,000, will pass into either the A or B portion of the trust rather than directly to your spouse. (You will decide with your attorney if you will select the A or B portion.) For this example, we will determine that your portion will pass into the A part of the trust at your death. Your spouse can be the trustee of the trust and can receive any income it produces or, at the discretion of the trustee subject to an ascertainable standard, access the principal of the A trust for as much as is needed for his or her health, support, maintenance, and education. For the surviving spouse, all of this basically operates practically as if the money weren't in a trust.

But here is the difference: When the second spouse dies, both the A and B portions of the trust are passed on to the beneficiaries, but because the A portion went directly into an estate tax–saving trust, it never became a part of the surviving spouse's estate. This means that the beneficiaries can receive the A part of the trust with your spouse's estate tax exemption applied to it and the B part of the trust with your estate tax exemption applied to it at your death. If the estate is valued at $7,000,000, that means that the beneficiaries will not owe any estate taxes, because they will technically be receiving $3,500,000 from each partner rather than $7,000,000 from one partner. If the first to die has assets above the exemption amount ($3,500,000 in the year 2009), then the excess needs to go to the surviving spouse, either outright or in the right kind of trust to defer taxes on the first death.

If you want to give your spouse the right to receive income from your assets during his or her lifetime but no say as to who inherits your portion of the trust after your spouse's death, you may also want to consider a variation on an A-B trust. This type of arrangement may involve a QTIP trust as one of the trusts. If you and/or your spouse have children from previous relationships, this is something to think about.

That sounds great, but there is no way that my estate is going to be worth $7,000,000. So I don't have to think about an A-B trust, right?
Seven million dollars is not the magic number. If you and your spouse together have property valued above the exempt amount ($3,500,000 in the year 2009), an A-B trust may benefit you. If you own your home outright, for example, control any business interests, or have any interest in a retirement plan, pension, or other investments, you may be surprised at how quickly the value of your estate adds up. If you have owned your home for a long time, it is likely that its value has increased substantially and, given the performance of the stock market over the longer term, the same may be true of investments you've held for many years. Make sure that you are counting everything you will leave behind, including your life insurance policy, any retirement plans with death benefits, art, and antiques, before you make any trusts decisions based on the value of your estate.

Is there a limit to the amount of assets a husband and wife together can shelter in an A-B trust?
Yes. Here are the maximum amounts for estate

credits for current and future years. The credit limit may be changed by Congress; please check with your estate attorney for current information:

For those dying in:	Maximum estate credit is:
2009	$7,000,000
2010	Unlimited
2011 and beyond	$2,000,000

Are A-B trusts only for married couples?

Yes, if they involve the unlimited marital deduction. (Remember, married couples can leave each other as much as they want, and the surviving spouse will pay no estate tax.) But unmarried couples, same-sex couples, or any two people can set up A-B trusts that will remain in place until both partners have died. The tax benefits will be experienced by those who receive the assets after both partners have died. But there is no comparable tax deferral for unmarried couples like the unlimited marital deduction between spouses.

What is a bypass trust?

Also called a life-estate trust, a bypass trust lets unmarried partners each create a trust that, in the event of the first partner's death, pays income to the surviving partner for life. At the second death, the remaining assets in each trust go to their respective beneficiaries.

I am a widow. Is it too late for me to create an A-B trust?

I'm afraid so. Both spouses must be alive at the time you set up an A-B trust. However, if less than nine months have passed since your husband's death and you have not accepted the benefits of an asset, you may be able to arrange to "disclaim" your interest in part of his estate and achieve the same result. Without a formal disclaimer trust (a variation on an A-B trust that also must be set up before either spouse's death), however, your disclaimer will keep your husband's assets out of your estate but won't let you benefit from them. The assets will pass as if you were deceased. You must see a trust lawyer to disclaim your interest in your inheritance, but it may well be worth your while.

Who will really benefit from an A-B trust?

Your beneficiaries, who are usually your children, will enjoy the tax savings from this trust. With or without an A-B trust, a deceased husband or wife can pass assets to the other spouse with the unlimited marital deduction, which means without any estate tax at all at the first death, but a potentially gigantic estate tax at the second death.

What happens if both partners die at the same time? In that case, will an A-B trust still benefit the beneficiaries?

Yes, the trust should have a simultaneous death provision, which says that if it is impossible to establish the order of death, then for the sake of funding the A-B trust the less wealthy spouse survived the wealthier spouse. This helps protect the benefit.

How much will it cost to set up an A-B trust and have it funded?

Your A-B trust could cost between $2,000 and

$3,000 to set up, depending on how many assets need to move into it. The more real estate and other title transfers you have, the more it will cost you to establish the trust.

OTHER KINDS OF TRUSTS

SPECIAL-NEEDS TRUSTS

A special-needs trust is designed to permit funds to be held in trust for the benefit of a developmentally disabled person throughout his or her lifetime without making him or her ineligible to receive public benefits such as Supplemental Security Income (SSI) and Medicaid. The purpose of this type of trust is to supplement government aid without causing a loss of that aid. As a result, the terms of the trust need to be very restrictive.

The trustee of a special needs trust must be aware of the rules regarding distributions for SSI purposes. Currently, if you give an SSI recipient food, cash, clothing, or shelter paid for with funds from the trust, these gifts are supposed to be reported to the SSI representative. The following month's SSI check will be reduced by the value of the gift. For example, if I give a disabled person $100 from the trust, he will receive $100 less from SSI the next month. The trustee can, however, pay for dental work, utilities, phone bills, a car, car insurance, vacations, and basically anything else that does not come under the heading of food, money, clothes, or shelter— which SSI money is supposed to provide—

without reducing the SSI recipient's monthly SSI income. It is difficult to find out the rules about such distributions, and they vary from state to state, but this should not stop you from creating such a trust for someone who truly needs it. It can be a great boon to the long-term care and happiness of your loved one.

I have two daughters, one of whom is disabled. Although I am concerned about the welfare of my child, a special-needs trust seems very complicated. Couldn't I just leave everything to my healthy daughter, with the understanding that she will take care of her less fortunate sister?
I really discourage this, for the same reason that I discourage people from just gifting to their children to avoid probate fees. What if the daughter to whom you leave all your assets gets divorced and your ex-son-in-law makes a claim on half the money? What if your daughter gets into serious financial difficulty and a creditor or a court tries to attach her money? My point is that anything can happen, and your disabled daughter will not necessarily be protected.

TESTAMENTARY TRUSTS

A testamentary trust is a trust that is created via your will, after you have died. At that time, your assets are put in a testamentary trust by the order of a probate court judge.

Are testamentary trusts a good idea?
Since a testamentary trust is created through your will, it will have to go through probate. It's my

belief that one should avoid probate wherever possible, so I don't recommend testamentary trusts.

INTER VIVOS TRUSTS

Inter vivos trust is simply another name for a revocable living trust, which you establish while you are alive, as opposed to a testamentary trust, which is established in your will and doesn't become effective until after you die.

TOTTEN TRUSTS

Totten trust is a term for a bank account that you set up with documentation stating you are the owner of the account and instructions that upon your death, the account is to be paid to your designated payee. If the payee is alive at the time of your death and an adult, he can receive the funds simply by producing your death certificate at the bank and proving his identity.

QPRT TRUSTS

A qualified personal residence trust (QPRT) is a kind of grantor-retained interest trust that can be used to pass a house out of an estate at a discounted value even if the trustor is still living in it. The purpose of this trust is to save on estate tax. Here's how it works: You choose a term of ownership of the house. At the end of this term, the house is distributed to someone you have designated in the trust agreement. (He or she may or may not let you live in it.) Once you put the house in the trust you can't take it back; it is considered a gift to the person, who will receive the house after your term of ownership is up. But since you retain an interest in the house for a number of years, the gift is not worth as much to the recipient as if you had given it to him outright. So, for example, you can pass a house worth $1,000,000 to your children for an estate-tax value of $500,000 if you put it in a QPRT with a 7.5-year term. As of 2009, if you are in the 45 percent estate-tax bracket, this could mean a savings of $225,000 in estate taxes. (If you die before the term expires, your children don't get the savings.) Once the house has been given to your children, if you continue to live in it you will need to pay them market-value rent (and if your child rents it to you and he or she dies, you may be dealing with a daughter-or son-in-law). The ability to move this money from your estate to your children as rent can be a further benefit of a QPRT trust. Note that with a QPRT your children's income tax basis may be lower than with an inheritance.

QTIP MARITAL DEDUCTIONS

QTIP stands for qualified terminable interest property, and here's what it means: The spouse to die first can leave assets (above the estate tax-exempt amount) in trust for the surviving spouse and have those excess assets taxed upon the death of the second spouse. The spouse who dies first may retain control of who inherits the estate upon the death of the spouse who dies second. So, effectively, there is no estate tax due on the first death. Among the requirements for this type of trust is that the surviving spouse must be entitled to all the income of the trust at least once per year. The surviving spouse may not assign this right to anyone else.

CHARITABLE REMAINDER TRUSTS

There are different forms of this type of trust, but, basically, if a charitable remainder trust is established, it means that you have given your assets in trust to benefit a tax-qualified charity (which gives you an income-tax deduction) but that you can receive income based on the value of the assets you have given away for as long as you are alive. This type of trust is very good for people who have assets that have gone up in value significantly since they bought them. If they need income and don't want to lose dollars to capital-gains tax when they sell their assets, this trust allows the assets to be sold income tax–free, so that every dollar is available to earn income for the beneficiary. However, at death, the entire principal of the trust is paid to the charity (and not to other beneficiaries, such as your children). In the year you set up such a trust, you will receive an income tax deduction, which can be spread out over five years. So, for example, if you make a gift of $100,000 in this way, you will receive tax benefits that will give you back as much as $50,000 of the gift. Every university and charity with a planned giving department can run the figures for you for free.

Does it make more sense to give money to charity or to let my children inherit it?
That depends on your financial situation and your desires. But if your children or other beneficiaries are going to be paying estate tax and income tax on what they inherit, it may make more sense to give some assets away and get a tax deduction now, or to leave some of your assets to charity upon your death. For instance, if you name a tax-exempt organization such as a church, school, or animal shelter as the beneficiary of any tax-deferred plans (for example, IRAs or Keoghs), the organization—unlike individual beneficiaries—will not have to pay income tax on the distribution. One hundred percent of the money will go to the charity because charitable organizations are not subject to estate tax. Let's say you are in the 55 percent estate-tax bracket—that's the highest rate that will be levied in 2011—and that your beneficiaries will have to pay 28 percent federal and 7 percent state tax on the proceeds of your retirement account. It is possible that as much as 90 percent of your IRA will go to the government! This would be a good time to think of the great work that private charitable organizations do. Private charities and social programs flourish in the United States because our tax laws encourage generous giving. See the upcoming section on gifting for more information on this option.

LIFE INSURANCE TRUSTS

I hope that by the time you die you will no longer have or need life insurance (please see Chapter 4), but if you do still have it, a life insurance trust is a type of trust that protects life insurance proceeds from estate taxes. A life insurance trust makes the trust, rather than you as an individual, the owner of the policy. Consult an attorney before you buy life insurance if you think you might want to do this, as it is best to create the trust before you buy the insurance.

Do I need a life insurance trust?

Young families frequently carry high amounts of term insurance in order to protect their children in the event of the premature death of a parent. Since the proceeds of these policies are included when calculating the value of an estate, a lot of that protection may be lost to estate taxes. If you take out $500,000 or more of coverage, you may want to discuss this option with a trust attorney.

GRANTOR-RETAINED ANNUITY TRUSTS

A grantor-retained annuity trust (GRAT) can be used to reduce taxes on your estate by sheltering shares of company stock. You can reserve the right to receive payments each year from the shares held within the trust for a designated period of time. When the period of time that you designate is over, those assets will be gifted to whomever you have chosen to receive them. The gift to your beneficiaries is based on the size of the gift less the amount of income you receive from the trust. In other words, if your stocks were worth $150,000 at the time of your gift and you received $35,000 in income from the trust, the gift will be valued at $115,000 (less than the $150,000 that would otherwise be taxable in your estate)—a pretty good savings.

A note of caution: Choose the length of time

you wish to receive income from the trust carefully. If you die before the transfer goes into effect, the trust will dissolve and the stocks will be considered part of your estate.

TITLING ASSETS

Titles to assets affect your will, living trust, estate tax, income tax, and possibly property tax.

JOINT TENANCY WITH RIGHT OF SURVIVORSHIP (JTWROS)

Joint tenancy with right of survivorship allows two or more people to hold the title to an asset. If one person dies, the title immediately transfers into the name of the other joint tenants without having to go through probate.

A potential problem with joint tenancy with right of survivorship, though, is that it will override any provisions in your will or living trust. There are many good reasons for you to hold something in joint tenancy, but trying to use it as a substitute for a will (or a trust) is not one of them.

Do all states have joint tenancy laws?

No, not all, but most states do. A few states have specific limitations about what can be held in joint tenancy, such as only real estate, or who can hold this type of title, such as only spouses. You should check with an attorney who specializes in estate planning and knows the laws of your state.

Is my house the only thing I can hold in joint tenancy?

No. Real estate is the most common thing held in joint tenancy, but bank accounts and other assets with titles can also be held this way.

What about holding a bank account in joint tenancy? How does that work?

Many people hold their checking or savings accounts, or their certificates of deposit, in JTWROS, which requires only that all the joint "tenants" sign as such when the account is opened. When one joint tenant dies, the surviving joint tenant (or tenants) may continue to use the account without having to go through probate, and automatically inherit the deceased tenant's share of the account.

My husband and I own everything in joint tenancy with right of survivorship (JTWROS) and I am the sole beneficiary of his life insurance policy and IRA. How will the estate be settled when he dies?

You have done a pretty good job of minimizing the paperwork and time that will be involved in settling your husband's estate, unless you are in a community-property state, in which case you might be missing the step up in cost basis for your real estate. Otherwise, once the appropriate institutions have received a certified copy of your husband's death certificate (and any other documentation they may require), everything will simply switch over into your name. But this sim-plicity may come with a big cost down the road—increased estate taxes for your children because you didn't utilize a death tax–saving trust.

What if my husband and I hold our house as joint tenants with right of survivorship but then we both die at the same time?

This is one of the drawbacks of using joint tenancy as an alternative to a will—there is no provision for an alternate beneficiary. If you have no other will or trust providing for the disposition of your house, the house would pass as if you had died intestate, with one part going to each of your blood relatives, in an order established by your state.

I've heard that once I hold something in JTWROS, I can't get a reverse mortgage if I want it. Is that true?

It's possible. A reverse mortgage is a kind of loan available to senior citizens who need extra income and own their homes outright, in which the homeowner receives monthly payments during his or her lifetime. The loan is repaid, plus interest and finance charges, after the death of the homeowner, by the beneficiaries. Since the age of the applicant for a reverse mortgage is relevant, if someone under age 62 (your child, for example) is a joint tenant on your house, you might not be eligible for a reverse mortgage.

My sister is in serious credit card debt, and we own property in joint tenancy. Can her creditors come after my share of the property?

The general rule is that your sister's creditors can only come after her half of the property, but this is a tricky area of the law, so be careful.

My daughter and I hold the title to our house in JTWROS. Now she and her husband are getting a divorce, and I want to move to my daughter's state in order to be closer to her and my grandchildren during this difficult time. The problem is that my son-in-law's lawyer says that I will need my son-in-law's signature in order to sell my house, because he is still legally married to my daughter and therefore entitled to an interest in her half of my house! Can this be true?

Unfortunately, it is true. You will have to wait to sell your property until your son-in-law signs those papers or until his divorce from your daughter is finalized, even though his name is not on the title. Title companies do not like to take any chances. They will want to make sure her husband does not make a claim. A title company can require more of you than the law does. So, while a transfer of ownership may be legal, the title company can still refuse to insure the title to a new buyer if you don't meet their requirements.

My neighbor held her house in joint tenancy with her oldest son, with the understanding that when she died, he would sell it and share the proceeds with her other two sons. She thought this would be a good way to avoid probate fees. But then her oldest son died a month after she did, before he had changed his will or done anything with his mother's house. His wife has inherited the house, and now she is refusing to share anything with the two surviving sons, who will have to go to court to try to get the house back. Isn't this unfair?

Yes, it is. But even if your neighbor's oldest son had changed his will to leave that house to his two brothers, in some states his wife would have still been entitled to as much as half the house, if she decided to challenge the will. If only your neighbor had set up a trust or held a title in all three sons' names, this terrible situation could have been avoided.

It seems like a will doesn't matter if you hold your property in joint tenancy. Is that true?

I'm afraid it is. If you own property as a joint tenant and you die first, that property passes immediately to your joint owner, even if you leave a will that says it's to go to someone else. Assets held in joint tenancy are not subject to a will, and will always be awarded to the surviving joint tenant.

Once I hold property in joint tenancy, can I ever take it back and hold it separately again?

When you terminate joint tenancy, it turns into tenants-in-common or co-tenancy, in which each party owns his or her share of the property outright. You won't get the whole property back even if you were the one who put the name(s) on the title, unless the other tenant agrees to sign it over to you or let you buy his or her share.

How is the estate tax figured on a piece of jointly held property?

For joint tenants other than spouses, the estate tax will be based on the amount of money you invested when you created or bought the property. In other words, if you paid for the entire property when it was first purchased, then the full value of the property should be allocated to your estate for tax purposes.

If joint tenants are not married, the IRS assumes that the joint tenant who dies first is the one who made the entire investment. Unless you can offer proof that the surviving tenant did so as well, the property will be taxed 100 percent to the estate of the first to die. There are special rules for married couples, depending on when an asset was purchased.

If I make my son a joint tenant with right of survivorship in my home, can he then take control of at least some of my affairs if I become incapacitated?

Actually, this sort of joint tenancy is a potential problem, particularly if one of the parties becomes incapacitated. Everyone on a joint tenancy title of a house needs to be able to sign the necessary documents in order to do anything with the house. Say you were incapacitated and in need of long-term care, and your son decided he needed to sell or refinance your house in order to pay for your medical expenses. As a joint tenant, your son will still need your signature on any documents, which, since you are incapacitated, you may be unable to provide. Your son will have to go to court and have the court appoint a conservator for your interests, and the court will be the one signing off on your son's decisions.

In this situation you are better off setting up a trust and making your son a successor trustee. If you are incapacitated, this will let him act independently on legal matters without having to get court approval.

My wife and I hold our property in joint tenancy, but we are separating. I'm moving to another state, and my wife is going to stay in our house and keep up the payments until we ***sell it, when she'll receive a bigger share of the proceeds in exchange for taking care of it now. Does this seem like a reasonable plan?***

I'm sorry to say that this plan leaves you extremely vulnerable. What happens if your wife fails to keep up with the mortgage payments or taxes on your house? What if something happens to your wife and she dies before the house is sold? Change the title to equal tenants-in-common right away.

My brother and his wife held their house in a joint tenancy, but after she died my brother was told that he had to file papers with his county clerk, who required a tax clearance from the probate court in order to file the forms! Wasn't avoiding probate the whole point of holding something in joint tenancy?

Some states or local governments require people who own property in joint tenancy to file papers with a local clerk in order to formally transfer ownership after one tenant dies. And some county clerks won't record the necessary forms without proof of a tax clearance—which, of course, sends you right back to a probate court. Again, if your state or local government requires this, you can avoid probate by holding that property in a revocable living trust. This is another reason to check the laws of your particular state before assigning title to assets.

TENANCY BY THE ENTIRETY

About 30 states allow you and your spouse to hold real estate in tenancy by the entirety, which means that neither one of you can transfer the property while you are both alive without the other's permission. This is because each of you owns the entire property as opposed to an equal share of it. Only real estate can be held in this type of tenancy, and only legally married couples can have this type of tenancy.

TENANCY-IN-COMMON (TIC)

When a property is held as tenants-in-common, it is owned by multiple individuals who each hold an undivided proportionate interest in the property. Each person can own a different percentage. Anything you own as a tenant-in-common will be subject to probate. Or you can transfer your shares in the property into a living trust and avoid probate.

My sisters and I are joint tenants with right of survivorship in a summer home. We all want our children to inherit our individual parts of the house after we die. We have designated that in our wills—will that accomplish what we want?
If you and your sisters own a house as joint tenants with right of survivorship, upon your death, your surviving sisters, not your children, will automatically inherit your portion of the home. If you and your sisters were to change how you hold title to tenants-in-common, on the other hand, you could leave your share in the house to your children, but remember, your share would have to go through probate unless it was also held in a living trust. It's best to put your share in a trust and ask your sisters to do the same. That way, everyone is protected.

COMMUNITY PROPERTY

Nine states (Arizona, California, Idaho, Louisiana, Nevada, New Mexico, Texas, Washington, and Wisconsin) have community-property laws, which define a particular form of co-ownership for married couples. Additionally, in Alaska married couples can opt in to community property. While the particular laws in each state are different, as a general rule, community-property states hold that the income and property acquired by a married couple should be divided equally in the event of a divorce unless both spouses agree in writing to an alternate arrangement. Thus, all marital property in such a state is owned by you and your spouse equally; this includes all property acquired during the course of the marriage other than by gift or inheritance. As long as residents of community-property states keep their gifts and/or inheritances in their own individual names (John Doe, a married man, as his separate property) or a separate trust, and do not commingle them by depositing them in joint accounts with their spouse, the gifts and/or inheritance will retain their separate property character.

Agreements changing the character of property from separate to community or vice versa must be in writing to be fully enforceable.

Please note: The following community-property states—Alaska, Arizona, California, Nevada, Texas, and Wisconsin—let couples add the right of survivorship to community property, permitting you to bypass probate and transfer title automatically at death. The only drawback: If both partners die simultaneously, the property goes to probate.

Does this mean that in a community-property state I would have no claim to my husband's half of our property?

The answer is yes. Generally, you are entitled to half of anything acquired during your marriage while you were living in a community-property state, but your spouse has the right to dispose of his half of the property as he wishes.

If I live in a community-property state, what is the best way to take title of property?

It depends. The best way to take title for assets that go up in value after the date of purchase in a community-property state is in community property, not joint tenancy with right of survivorship.

I'll illustrate this with an example. Let's say that you and your spouse bought $10,000 worth of a certain stock many years ago and you have been holding it in joint tenancy. The IRS will consider that $10,000 to be the cost basis of the stock for tax purposes, which means that you will owe capital gains taxes on the profit you will make when you sell the stock, assuming it has gone up in price. By holding the stock in joint tenancy with your spouse, you are each entitled to half the cost basis—in this case, $5,000.

Now, we'll say that the stock is worth $100,000 when your spouse dies. Because you held the stock in joint tenancy, you will receive a step up in tax basis of your deceased spouse's half of the stock equal to fair market value at the time of his death. In this case, that half would increase to a tax basis of $50,000 while the tax basis of your half of the stock would remain at $5,000. Since you own the stock by yourself now, the new tax basis on that same $100,000

worth of stock is $55,000 ($50,000 plus $5,000). If you sold it today you would only have to pay capital-gains tax on $45,000, or the amount of your gain ($100,000 minus $55,000).

Next, let's look at what would happen to this scenario if you lived in a community-property state and held the stocks in title as community property. Just as in joint tenancy, you each will have an original cost basis of $5,000. However, when your spouse dies, each half will receive a step up in tax basis—both your spouse's half and your own. Both halves will step up to $50,000, for a total tax basis of $100,000. Therefore, if you sold the stock for $100,000, you wouldn't have to pay any capital-gains tax at all. That's a huge savings! However, if the stock goes down in value, both halves with community property will get a step down in tax basis.

If I live in a community-property state, can I hold assets in joint tenancy with someone other than my spouse?

If the asset is separate property, sure. But if the asset is community property, then your spouse would have a claim against you and the other joint tenant for the interest he or she would be entitled to under community-property law.

What if I own property from the time before I got married?

The property itself will usually be considered separate, as long as you are careful not to mix your individual property with community property that you have acquired during your marriage. If you make income on that property during your marriage, however, the income may be considered community property. Because the laws are changing fast in this area, it really would be best to spell this out in a prenuptial agreement.

I live in a community-property state. Is my wife automatically entitled to half of my life insurance, too, even if I name someone else as a beneficiary?

If you paid the insurance premiums with community-property dollars, then, yes, unless you and your spouse have an agreement to the contrary.

GIFTING

Gifting can be a great way to minimize the size of your estate and, subsequently, your estate taxes, but be careful, for there are more pitfalls in this part of the law than many people are aware of. Gifting and estate limits are closely intertwined. Read on.

How much money can I give away each year without having to file a gift tax return?

You can give $13,000 each year (as of 2010) to as many individuals as you want without paying a gift tax and without filing a gift tax return. This limit is rising and will be indexed for inflation. However, the increase is very modest.

Can my husband and I each give away $13,000 per year to the same person, or must only one of us give?

You each can give $13,000 per year to as many people as you'd like, even if you have recipients in common.

My daughter really needs money. What would happen if I gave her more than $13,000 in one year?

You will need to file a gift tax return. In the year 2009, for example, in addition to the $13,000 per year, per person gift exemption, you are also limited to a total of $1,000,000 in gifts over the course of your lifetime. What this means is that if you have not exceeded the annual per year, per person limit, there would be no gift or estate tax owed on the first $1,000,000 of your estate. Whatever amount over $13,000 you have given away in any one year to the same person will be subtracted from this lifetime gift exemption.

In other words, you and your husband can each give your daughter $13,000 per year, for a total of $26,000 each year, without any tax consequences. If, in one year, each of you gave her, say, $25,000, you would each need to file a gift tax return for $12,000, which is the amount by which your gift exceeds the annual limit. That $12,000 would be subtracted from your lifetime maximum gift figure. So if you and your husband died in 2009 and left everything outright to each other and wasted one of your tax exemptions, your heirs would owe taxes after the first $987,000 ($1,000,000 minus the $13,000 gift above the $13,000 annual exclusion).

Is the gift tax a federal or state tax?

There are two levels of taxation—federal *and* state. The federal tax is due to the IRS and is computed by looking at the total of all gifts made during your life and what you leave at death.

The state gift tax is paid to the state of residence and due only on gifts made during life. Connecticut and Tennessee are the states that impose a state gift tax. Puerto Rico also has its own gift tax. Louisiana abolished its gift tax in 2008, and North Carolina abolished it in 2009.

Can't I avoid all this hassle and just put my kids' names on my accounts as co-owners?

You could, and if everything goes smoothly, they will avoid probate but not necessarily gift or estate taxes. But this makes you vulnerable to other difficulties.

If your children are sued for any reason (say they cause a car accident or someone injures himself on their property) and there is a judgment against them, any assets you have put their name on could be used to pay that judgment. Similarly, if your children get into trouble with the IRS, your shared assets are now in danger, because they belong, at least on paper, to your child as well as to you.

Co-owning assets may also create unintended gift tax consequences for your children. If you add your children's names to the title of your house, for example, it may be construed by the IRS as a gift, since your children did not contribute to the purchase price of your home. Once you put them on the title, you can't take them off without their signatures. And once you record any document, it becomes a part of the public record, and you can't act as if it never happened.

What if I just give my children my assets?

Well, if your estate is not going to be worth more than the lifetime gift/estate maximum ($3,500,000 in 2009), then you don't really need to put things in your children's names for estate tax purposes, since there won't be any estate taxes to pay. If your estate is going to be worth more than this, you should consult a lawyer with some expertise in estate planning before you simply give any of your assets away. By making a gift, you may cost your children income tax by them losing the step up in cost basis inherited assets may receive.

My mom gave me her home and all her stocks before she went into a nursing home. She has since died. Do I now owe estate and income tax on what she left me?

The amount you owe for estate taxes depends on the unified credit exemption for the year in which your mother died. The unified credit exemption is the amount your beneficiaries can inherit from you without having to pay federal estate taxes. If your mom died in 2009, you will pay federal estate taxes up to 45 percent on every dollar over $3,500,000. If your mom died in 2010, you will not owe any federal estate taxes as the tax was repealed for 2010 only. (As of early 2010 Congress was considering reinstating the exemption.)

UNIFIED CREDIT EXEMPTION

For Deaths Occurring In	Highest Estate Exemption	Highest Estate & Gift Tax Rate
2009	$3,500,000	45%
2010	N/A	top individual rate
2011	$1,000,000	55%

Please check with your estate attorney or *www.irs.gov* for the most current information regarding the Unified Credit Exemption. The entire topic of federal estate taxation remains a hot topic in Washington, and Congress may act before 2011 when many limits are scheduled to revert to 2001 levels.

Income tax works differently. Stocks and real estate that you inherit will not be taxed until you sell them, and the amount of tax you will owe will depend on your tax basis (see the answer to the next question). Also, if your mom received any type of Medicaid assistance prior to her death, the state may attempt to recover the costs of such assistance through these assets.

What difference does it make whether my mom gave me her stock while she was alive or if I inherited it after her death?

Actually, it makes a big difference. If your mom left you her assets after she died, you'd have inherited them. When you inherit something, you get a step up (or down) in tax basis on that asset. That means that if your mom bought stock in a company for $10,000 20 years ago, $10,000 is the cost basis—the original price—for that stock. If she left the stock to you in her will or revocable living trust, your tax basis will be the value of the stock at the time she died. This gives you a terrific benefit. If that stock was worth $200,000 at her death, then *your* tax basis for tax purposes is going to be $200,000. When you go to sell the stock, you will only owe capital-gains tax on anything worth more than $200,000. Your cost basis went from $10,000 to $200,000.

Now, if your mom gave you the same stock while she was still alive, you'd have received it as a gift. Along with the title to that gift, you also receive your mom's original cost basis on the asset, which was $10,000. You're not entitled to a step up in tax basis with a gift. So if you sell the stock, now worth $200,000, you will owe taxes on $190,000. You will pay 15 percent of $190,000 to Uncle Sam, plus whatever your state charges for capital gains. Therefore, if your mom has assets such as stock or real estate that have increased in value since she bought them, her beneficiaries will save a great deal of income tax if they receive these assets after she dies.

I own my own business. Is it a good idea to give my children stock in my business before I die?

If your business is doing well and the value of that stock is increasing steadily, then giving away some of your stock now will allow them to keep its appreciated value since it's been transferred out of your estate. But, remember, if their names are on the stock and if you want to sell the company later in life, you will need your children's agreement. (And they may leave stock to a spouse or others if they die before you.) Again, the stock is also subject to capital-gains tax, and your children will not receive a step up in cost basis as they would have if they'd inherited the stock after your death.

What if my parents make me a joint tenant but just don't file the paperwork? Can we avoid these taxes that way?

Many people do this, either because they think they can avoid taxes or they don't know that they need to file paperwork beyond adding a new name to the title of their property. But when your parents die, you will need to file an estate tax return for them if the value of the assets is above the exempt amount, and on the return is a section that will ask you to list all the property that your parents held in joint tenancy. You will want to answer this honestly, because the IRS can ask you to prove that you either purchased the property or filed a gift tax return for the gift. If your parents did not file a gift tax return, you could be subject to penalties on top of the gift tax. The maximum penalty for failure to report is the tax you owe plus a 75 percent penalty and interest calculated from the date that the tax would have been due.

My parents have given me their home as an outright gift (although they still live there) because it seemed to make sense to them at the time. What steps should I now take to make sure that if I were to die before them, they wouldn't have to go through probate and pay taxes on their house?

The best way to protect anything they have already given to you is to put it all in a revocable living trust and designate whether the property should go outright or in trust to your parents, if they are still alive at the time of your death.

Is there ever any circumstance in which my mother could give me something in joint tenancy and we would not owe gift taxes?

There are a few such cases, for example, if your mom buys U.S. savings bonds in joint tenancy or if she creates a joint convenience bank account (to which she contributes all the money).

Are the gifts I leave to a charity upon my death subject to estate tax?

No. Gifts to charity are free from taxation and are not considered a part of an estate for estate tax purposes.

Can I give as much money to charity as I want?

In many states there are limitations on how much you can give to a charity if you have a surviving spouse or children. If you are not married and are childless, then there are no limits to what you can donate.

At what point does gifting to a charity become a true estate-planning tool for me to consider?

If you are a married couple and have an A-B trust in the year 2009 with combined assets exceeding $7,000,000, or you are an individual with an estate that will be worth more than $3,500,000, you may want to consider charitable gifting. Your decision depends on your age, whether you have long-term health-care insurance, the financial situation of your children, and many other factors. Be sure to consult an attorney if you are in this category, as your state's tax rules for gifting also must be considered. Discuss your goals for gifting fully before making a decision. Ask yourself (and your financial adviser) the following questions:

- What is the purpose of my gift?
- Does it make sense in the context of my personal situation?
- If gifting seems appropriate, which assets should be gifted?

POWER OF ATTORNEY

A power of attorney is a document that authorizes another person to act for you as if they were you. This person is called your "agent" or your " attorney-in-fact." You can have a very broad power of attorney, which allows someone else to do things that usually only you can do, such as write checks from your bank accounts, pay your bills, or sign documents on your behalf. Alternatively, you can have a very limited power of attorney, which may authorize someone to do just one particular thing for you.

In my opinion, the best power of attorney is one that is authorized by a specific state law (also known as a statutory power of attorney); is a general power of attorney; and survives the incapacity of the maker. These three factors will give you the greatest ease in getting people and institutions to cooperate with you when you transact business through a power of attorney. However, a general power of attorney has been called a license to steal, since it's like signing a blank check.

Bear in mind that certain institutions may refuse to honor your power of attorney if it is not in the form the institution itself prints, even if it is a statutory form. The IRS requires you to use only their form for power of attorney, for example. Also, if you try to limit the scope of the power of attorney or make it too specific, brokerage houses may not want to accept it because they feel it does not cover all the types of actions they deem necessary. Finally, your power of attorney needs to be "durable"—to remain in effect if you become incapacitated—as this is the main reason for any power of attorney.

What is the difference between a power of attorney and a durable power of attorney?

A power of attorney authorizes someone to make legal and financial decisions on your behalf while you are alive. But, generally, if you become incapacitated, the power of attorney becomes void. A durable power of attorney stays in effect even after you are incapacitated, which is when you really need someone you trust making decisions for you. Keep in mind, though, that all powers of attorney die with the maker. So once the person who gave you the authority dies, you no longer can legally sign for anything as the person's agent. Such an act constitutes an ethical breach that could be used against you if there were any future disputes with heirs or creditors or the IRS.

What is the difference between a durable power of attorney for financial matters and a durable power of attorney for health care?

A durable power of attorney for financial matters deals only with financial matters. The durable power of attorney for health care (also called, depending on your state, a medical power of attorney, health-care proxy, or medical proxy) is a document you create to give your agent the authority to make health-care decisions for you as if he or she were you. This may include the authority to take you off life support.

If you don't give someone this power, it will be almost impossible for your loved ones to take you off life support, if it comes to that, even if they know that this is what you would have wanted. Remember, you have a right to die, but you cannot exercise that right unless you put your wishes in writing.

What is an agent?

This is the person empowered to make decisions for you under the durable power of attorney.

I already have a living will. Do I still need the durable power of attorney for health care?

Yes, because the two documents have different purposes. The durable power of attorney for health care lets you designate a person who can take you off life support (and to dictate under what circumstances) and to make less drastic medical decisions, too. A living will gives guidance to a doctor as to what types of medications you would want, but it does not authorize anyone to make decisions for you. Also, living wills cannot be changed significantly if your needs should change. I strongly recommend a durable power of attorney for health care as the most efficient and effective way to deal with your medical needs should you become incapacitated.

Some lawyers don't use anything but the power of attorney for health care since only this document gives someone other than your doctor decision-making power. The durable power of attorney for health care shifts the decision-making power from the doctor to your agent as soon as your doctor determines that you are no longer able to make decisions for yourself. This happens when you are unconscious or delirious, for example. You can tell your agent your preferences for treatment, but if there are unexpected circumstances, the agent will not be locked into what was written in a directive years before. The one thing I advise you to write out is that the management of pain is of primary importance to you.

If there aren't any circumstances under which

I would want to be taken off life support, then I don't need to bother with the durable power of attorney, right?

Quite the contrary. You can state in your durable power of attorney for health care that you want heroic measures taken to save your life, no matter what kind of prognosis you might have for recovery. That is the point of the durable health power of attorney—that there will be a document that lets your family and your doctors know definitively what your wishes are if and when you can't communicate them.

Here are the three basic options that people generally choose from:

1. You want to prolong your life as long as possible, without regard to your condition, chance of recovery, or the cost of treatment.
2. You want life-sustaining treatment to be provided unless you are in a coma or ongoing vegetative state, which two doctors, one of whom is your attending physician, will determine in their best judgment.
3. You do not want your life to be unnaturally prolonged, unless there is some hope that both your physical and mental health might be restored.

Now, please keep in mind that this is an emerging area of the law. The U.S. Supreme Court just granted us the right to die in the past decade. This landmark case said that if you have expressed your wishes in writing about the manner of your death in a clear and convincing fashion, doctors must honor it. Each state has come up with its own definition of what qualifies as "clear and convincing." This does not mean that every doctor will abide by them. A recent study indicated that in as many as 50 percent of cases, doctors do not follow the known wishes of the person. One reason may be that the doctors did not know about the existence of the patient's document. So be sure to send copies to your physicians and ask them to make the copies a permanent part of your medical records. Be sure your relatives have copies, too.

Most major hospitals now have ethics committees to help with difficult situations, so if you feel a situation merits some intervention, ask if you can speak to someone from the hospital ethics committee.

Should I choose the same person to be my attorney-in-fact for my durable power of attorney and my durable power of attorney for health care?
That is entirely up to you. Remember that, particularly in terms of your durable power of attorney for health care, whomever you select as your agent must be strong enough to act in accordance with your wishes, even if your loved ones strongly disagree. You should choose someone in whom you have confidence, who lives no more than a day's travel away, and with whom you have discussed your preferences for health care. Also consider whether your agent has too much of a conflict of interest (if, say, the person who can authorize pulling the plug also inherits a lot of money from you). If they have any hesitation about acting in that role, you should ap-

point someone else. If possible, it's also good to choose several alternate agents as well.

Can I make both of my daughters co-agents on my durable power of attorney for health care?
You can, if your state allows it, but I don't generally recommend it. Here's why: Even if you are very specific about your wishes, your agents will most likely have a lot of discretion to determine whether your medical circumstances meet the qualifications for carrying out your instructions. If your co-agents were to disagree with each other about anything, it is likely that no action would be taken, thus making all your planning worthless. In most cases, your child will consult with his or her siblings anyway, and you can express ahead of time your preference that he or she do so.

Another possibility is to make your other children backup agents. That means that you would have a second or third alternate agent if your first agent were unavailable for some reason.

A friend of mine had a durable power of attorney and appointed her daughter as her agent. But when the worst happened, her son went to court to try to stop her daughter from carrying out her wishes, saying that his mother had been incompetent when she signed the papers. Is there any way that situation could have been avoided?
Maybe not, but I would suggest doing two things. First, you want to talk to your family about your wishes beforehand so that they understand and respect them. Don't let anyone tell you this is too difficult or grim to talk about, be-

cause it is too important a matter not to discuss. If, after talking with your family, you get the feeling that certain family members might have difficulty carrying out your wishes, have the following sentence inserted into your durable power of attorney for health care: "I want the wishes of my agent to be respected regardless of the contrary wishes or intentions of other members of my family."

My mother had a durable power of attorney drawn up and made her brother attorney-in-fact. She is now in a nursing home, and my uncle is spending all her money on himself. What can we do?

This is why you really need to trust the person you name as your attorney-in-fact. You need to be sure that he or she will act in accordance with your wishes, in the best interests of you and the people who will be affected by your incapacity. While you can have a power of attorney revoked, it can take time and cost money. It depends on the state you live in, among other factors.

In some states, all that needs to happen is for the person who created the durable power of attorney to declare, preferably in the presence of witnesses, that he or she no longer wants the attorney-in-fact to keep acting in that capacity. The problem is that if the attorney-in-fact refuses to stop acting and still has copies of the original durable power of attorney, it may be difficult to prevent him or her from continuing to draw money out of accounts. How would banks know that the durable power of attorney has been revoked? You will probably need to see an attorney specializing in probate and trust litigation or elder-law litigation to resolve such a situation.

If your durable power of attorney has been recorded—that is, if it was taken to a county recorder's office and entered—you'll need to record a revocation, too.

This situation is yet another good example of why I believe so strongly in trusts. If you do have a rebel agent, it can be very tough to bring him or her in line: It may take a civil lawsuit, and that's expensive. If a trustee needs to be called to task, you usually have faster access to the probate court—a much better way to deal with the problem. If you are incapacitated, you can still be protected by the remainder beneficiaries of your trust, and, if the assets are moved, it will be easier to find them since they are in the name of the trust and not an individual agent.

Can I have a durable power of attorney in which the attorneys-in-fact are two people who must act jointly before they can do anything?

Yes, and although this will offer some protection in terms of making sure that one person doesn't violate your wishes, it can also slow things down. If you need a decision made immediately, requiring two people to sign off on everything might complicate matters.

Is it difficult to get a durable power of attorney for health care?

Not at all. Most states have a standard form for this, and many hospitals and public health services can provide it to you at no cost. You may want to speak with an attorney to help you fill it out, particularly if you have a special situation or particular illness that you want the form to cover. Choice in Dying has an excellent Website, *www.choices.org,* from which you can download the relevant forms for your state.

How much should a durable power of attorney for health care cost me?

If an attorney is setting up a trust for you, the preparation for a durable power of attorney for health care should be included in his fee. In any case, it shouldn't cost more than $75 to $150.

Where should I store my durable power of attorney for health care?

You should always keep the original. Give a copy of the form to the person you have chosen to act as your agent, and send copies to your doctor and your health insurance company, to be kept as part of your medical records. This can be helpful if something happens while you are away from home, particularly if you keep the name of your doctor or insurance company in your wallet.

Once I draw up my durable power of attorney for health care, is it good forever?

Yes, although make sure to amend it if you experience a major change in your relationship, or if the person whom you have appointed as your agent dies. You can, of course, always change your durable power of attorney for health care if you change your mind about what kind of medical treatment you would want in dire circumstances.

I have a durable power of attorney for my

mom, but the bank refuses to honor it. Does this happen often?

Because powers of attorney are so easily abused, many banks tend to be wary about accepting them. If your durable power of attorney is legitimate, a lawyer can help you get the bank to accept it, but this may take some time. If you have an incapacity clause in your revocable living trust, this situation can be avoided.

This is such a big problem that California created a statutory form for general power of attorney and passed a law that says if an institution refuses to honor the power of attorney in the statutory form, you can sue the institution and recover the costs of your suit, attorney fees, and damages. When they pass a law like that, you know it's been a problem!

If I live in a different state than my parents, and they want me to be their attorney-in-fact, do we need to set up the durable power of attorney in their home state?

The rules governing powers of attorney vary from state to state. I would recommend that you have the durable power of attorney drawn up by an attorney in the state in which your parents live.

What is a "springing" power of attorney?

This type of power of attorney, which is not legal in all states, becomes activated only when the person who draws it up becomes incapacitated. I don't recommend it—first, because it isn't accepted in all states, and, more important, because it isn't always clear what constitutes incapacity. Durable power of attorney is a much better choice.

Why don't more people have a durable power of attorney for health care?

I think it's simply because so many of us are afraid to confront our own mortality. Signing a paper like this makes death seem like an imminent reality, and that can provoke frightening and painful feelings. Another reason people don't sign such a power of attorney is they think they are too young to contemplate such things. But I promise you, no matter what your age, this is one of the most important things you can do to protect yourself and your finances.

INDEX

Suze Orman is undeniably America's most recognized expert on personal finance. She is a two-time Emmy Award–winning television host, *New York Times* mega bestselling author, magazine and online columnist, writer/producer, and one of the top motivational speakers in the world today.

Orman is a contributing editor to *O, The Oprah Magazine*, the *Costco Connection Magazine,* and for the last eight years host of the award-winning *Suze Orman Show*, which airs every Saturday night on CNBC. Not only is she the single most successful fund-raiser in the history of public television, but she has also garnered an unprecedented six Gracie awards, more than anyone in the thirty-four-year history of this prestigious award. The Gracie recognizes the nation's best radio, television, and cable programming for, by, and about women.

In May 2009 and May 2008 *Time* magazine named Orman as one of the TIME 100, The World's Most Influential People. In July 2009 *Forbes* named Orman eighteenth on its list of The Most Influential Women in Media. In May 2009 Orman was presented with an honorary degree Doctor of Humane Letters from the University of Illinois.

Orman, who grew up on the South Side of Chicago, earned a bachelor's degree in social work at the University of Illinois and at the age of thirty was a waitress making four hundred dollars a month.